Designing Interactions

Digital technology has changed the way we interact with everything from the games we play to the tools we use at work. Designers of digital technology products no longer regard their job as designing a physical object—beautiful or utilitarian—but as designing our interactions with it. In *Designing Interactions*, award-winning designer Bill Moggridge introduces us to more than forty influential designers who have shaped our interaction with technology. Moggridge, designer of the first laptop computer (the GRiD Compass, 1981) and a founder of the design firm IDEO, tells us these stories from an industry insider's viewpoint, tracing the evolution of ideas from inspiration to outcome. The innovators he interviews—including Will Wright, creator of The Sims, Larry Page and Sergey Brin, the founders of Google, and Doug Engelbart, Bill Atkinson, and others involved in the invention and development of the mouse and the desktop—have been instrumental in making a difference in the design of interactions. Their stories chart the history of entrepreneurial design development for technology.

Moggridge and his interviewees discuss such questions as why a personal computer has a window in a desktop, what made Palm's handheld organizers so successful, what turns a game into a hobby, why Google is the search engine of choice, and why 30 million people in Japan choose the *i-mode* service for their cell phones. And Moggridge tells the story of his own design process and explains the focus on people and prototypes that has been successful at IDEO—how the needs and desires of people can inspire innovative designs and how prototyping methods are evolving for the design of digital technology.

Designing Interactions is illustrated with more than 700 images, with color throughout. Accompanying the book is a DVD that contains segments from all the interviews intercut with examples of the interactions under discussion. (Please go to http://www.designinginteractions.com for information and downloads.)

Award-winning designer Bill Moggridge is a founder of IDEO, one of the most successful design firms in the world and one of the first to integrate the design of software and hardware into the practice of industrial design. He has been Visiting Professor in Interaction Design at the Royal College of Art in London, Lecturer in Design at the London Business School, member of the Steering Committee for the Interaction Design Institute in Ivrea, Italy, and is currently Consulting Associate Professor in the Joint Program in Design at Stanford University.

Designing Interactions

Designing Interactions

Bill Moggridge

The MIT Press
Cambridge, Massachusetts
London, England

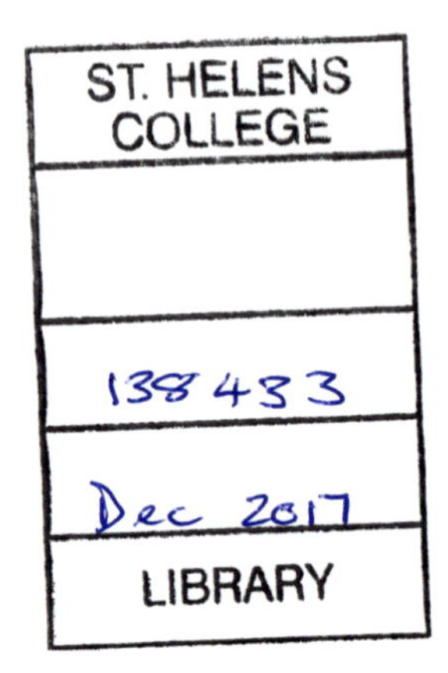

For information on quantity discounts, please email special_sales@mitpress.mit.edu.

Set in Officina Sans and Bembo by the author. Printed and bound in Spain.

Library of Congress Cataloging-in-Publication Data

Moggridge, Bill
Designing interactions / by Bill Moggridge
p. cm.
ISBN-13: 978-0-262-13474-3 (alk. paper)
ISBN-10: 0-262-13474-8 (alk. paper)
1. Human-computer interaction. I. Title.

QA76.9.H85M64 2006
004'.019—dc22

2006049446

10 9 8 7 6

Contents

Foreword

What Is Interaction Design?

by Gillian Crampton Smith

Photo Ivan Gasparini

Gillian Crampton Smith

Gillian Crampton Smith, the director of Interaction Design Institute Ivrea, is the foremost academic in the emerging discipline of interaction design. She studied philosophy and art history at Cambridge University, graduating in 1968. She spent the next decade as a designer, first in book publishing, and then on the *Sunday Times* and *Times Literary Supplement*. In 1981, at the leading edge of desktop publishing, she designed and implemented a page layout program to help her with magazine design. This experience convinced her that designers have an important role to play in creating information technologies. In 1983 she joined the faculty of London's St Martin's School of Art and established a graduate program in graphic design and computers for practicing designers. In 1989 she moved to the Royal College of Art, Britain's only purely graduate school of art and design, and set up the Computer Related Design Department with advice from Bill Moggridge, the external assessor for the program. Now called the Interaction Design Department, this was the first program in the world where graduate designers could learn to apply their skills to interactive products and systems. Under her guidance, the CRD Research Studio achieved an international reputation as a leading center for interaction design. In 2001 she moved to Ivrea—the Italian town in the foothills of the Alps famous as the home of Olivetti—to establish Interaction Design Institute Ivrea,[1] which offers the world's first post-experience interaction design program.

HIGH SCORE
340
70

In the same way that industrial designers have shaped our everyday life through objects that they design for our offices and for our homes, interaction design is shaping our life with interactive technologies—computers, telecommunications, mobile phones, and so on. If I were to sum up interaction design in a sentence, I would say that it's about shaping our everyday life through digital artifacts—for work, for play, and for entertainment.

Gillian Crampton Smith, interview of January 30, 2002[2]

Designing for Everyday Life

■ "Collabolla," a video game with Spacehopper balls as input devices. Interaction Design Institute Ivrea, Triennale di Milano, 2004.

Photo Ivan Gasparini

TWENTY YEARS AGO, when personal computers were first becoming popular, they were mostly used as professional tools, or games machines for teenagers. The situation has changed radically. Now everybody—kids, parents, grandparents—uses them every day, at work, at school, and at home. So today we need to design computer technology differently, to make it a graceful part of everyday life, like the other things we own: our clothes, the plates we eat off, the furniture we buy for our houses. We've come to a stage when computer technology needs to be designed as part of everyday culture, so that it's beautiful and intriguing, so that it has emotive as well as functional qualities.

This book traces how the design of the way people interact with computer technology developed: from the earliest days of Star, the first screen-based graphical user interface and the precursor of the Apple and Windows interfaces, to the plethora of mobile multimedia devices and systems we use now. It describes the challenges designers face in making this powerful technology fit easily into people's everyday lives, rather than forcing their lives to fit the dictates of technology.

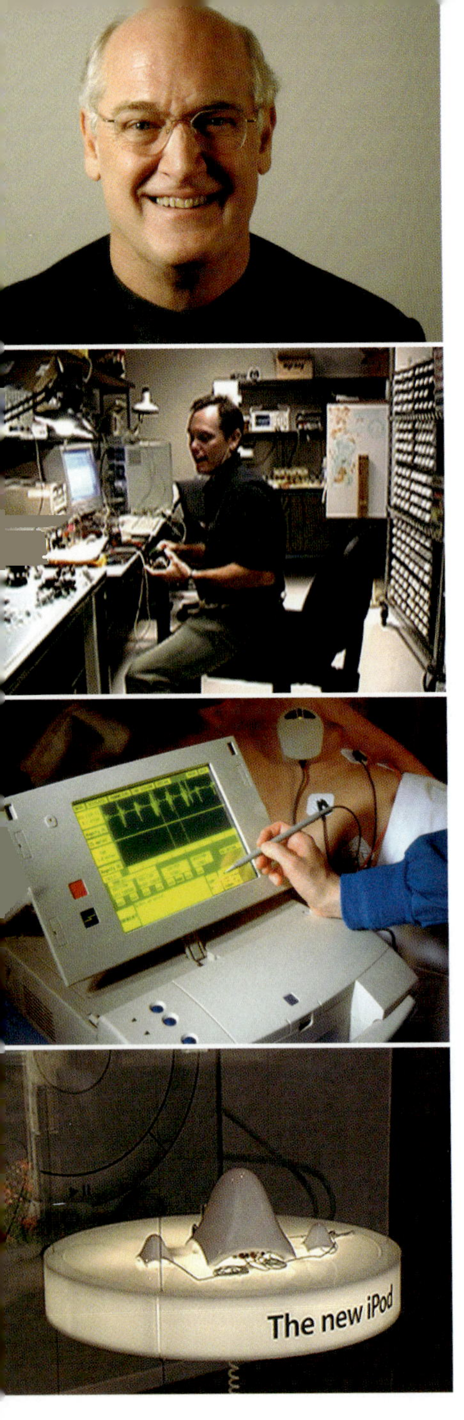

- David Liddle
- Stage 1: enthusiast—EE Lab at IDEO
- Stage 2: professional—medical equipment
- Stage 3: consumer—iPod at Apple Store

Three Stages of Technology Use

DAVID LIDDLE,[3] WHO led the team that designed the Star graphical user interface, has talked about three stages in the development of a technology—of photography, for instance, or computers—and how people interact with it. The first stage is the *enthusiast* stage. Enthusiasts don't care if the technology is easy or hard to use because they're so excited by the technology itself or by what it will do for them. They want it, however difficult it is to use.

The second stage is the *professional* stage, when those who use the technology are often not those who buy it. Office computers, for example, are usually chosen by a purchasing department, not by their users; the purchasers don't care about the difficulty because they don't experience it, and are anyway more interested in factors like price, performance specifications, or after-sales support. At this stage, indeed, some people even have a vested interest in the technology being difficult because they're selling their ability to use it; the harder it is, the more valuable their skills.

The third stage Liddle identifies is the *consumer* stage. People now are less interested in the technology in itself than in what it can do for them. They don't want to spend much time learning how to use it and hate being made to feel stupid. So if it's hard to use, they won't buy it. This is the current stage in the use of computer and telecommunications technology: it's no longer used only by professionals but by a wide range of nonexperts, who just want to use it to pursue their everyday lives.

In the past, those who built interactive systems tended to focus on the technology that makes them possible rather than on the interfaces that allow people to use them. But a system isn't complete without the people who use it. Like it or not, people—irritable, demanding, and often distracted people like ourselves—and their goals are the *point* of our systems, and we must design for them.

Designing for this new broad spectrum of humanity is more challenging than devising specialist tools for technical professionals. Our users are, justifiably, not prepared to spend time mastering tricky new systems. And they're not obliged to use our products: if they can't make them work, they take them back to the store.

From Usability to Sociability

Many advertisements now boast about computer technologies that are easy to use: *usability* has become a buzzword. But usability is only the first of the qualities we should expect from the systems we use; they also need to be *useful*. This sounds obvious, but too many systems don't really help people do what they want to do. Mitch Kapor, creator of the hugely successful spreadsheet Lotus 1-2-3, proposed an "architectural" model of software design, distinguishing design from engineering and building. His 1990 "Software Design Manifesto"[4] reminded us that we must start by thinking about designing things so that they're right for people, rather than by thinking first about how to build it. He admitted he was no software engineer, no ace at writing code. Rather, his role was to design what Lotus 1-2-3 should be and do, making sure that this was what people needed. Others more skilled in software engineering ensured that it worked. Lotus 1-2-3 wasn't the first spreadsheet, but it was the first that really did what people needed in a way that fitted how they worked. Thus its success.

That said, there's more to living than utilitarian needs and the functions which satisfy them. As computers begin to shape everyday life, we're interested not only in what this technology can do for us, but also in what owning it *means* for us. When we buy something for our home, a toaster for instance, we choose it because it toasts bread, certainly, but maybe also because of how it looks, feels, sounds. What does it *say* to us? Is it satisfying? Does it enrich, by however little, our just-crawled-from-bed state of mind?

And of course we choose the things we surround ourselves with not just because of what they mean to us, but also because of what they mean to other people. Most Italians have a mobile phone but many young Sicilians, for instance, can't afford the calls. They still buy the phones, though, because sporting one says, fairly explicitly, "I'm connected to a network of family and friends." The symbolic function is as important as the practical one, perhaps more.

The interactive systems we design have implicit as well as explicit meanings. A design may communicate its purpose clearly, so that it's obvious what it is and what we should do with it. But its *qualities*, its aesthetic qualities particularly, speak to people in a different way. Consciously or not, people read meanings into artifacts. A chapel speaks a different architectural language than a supermarket, and everybody can read the difference. In a drugstore we can usually distinguish a medicine bottle from a perfume bottle even if we can't read the label. Artists and designers are trained to use the language of implicit meanings to add a rich communicative element over and above direct functional communication. If we only design the function of something, not what it also communicates, we risk our design being misinterpreted. Worse, we waste an opportunity to enhance everyday life.

To designing for usability, utility, satisfaction, and communicative qualities, we should add a fifth imperative: designing for *sociability*. When IT systems fail to support the social aspect of work and leisure, when they dehumanize and de-civilize our relationship with each other, they impoverish the rich social web in which we live and operate, essential for both well-being and efficiency.

The technologies we design can erode or enhance this social web, so we must design for this explicitly, because technologically driven social changes can be creative. When young people are out socializing they are reluctant to make appointments. They say "Oh yeah, I'm around tomorrow. Don't know when. Give me a call, I'll see where I am."

The mobile phone has brought to hanging out—indeed, to time itself—an altogether more fluid and relaxed approach.

Good Interaction Design

An electromechanical object, a radio say, links its physical mechanical components to its electronic elements in a fairly direct way. When we turn the dial, our fingertips and muscles can almost "feel" the stations being scanned. With computers, however, the distance between, on one hand, keystrokes and screen image, and, on the other, what's happening inside the computer, is usually much less direct. Our physical world and the computer's virtual world seem miles apart.

In this (historically unprecedented) situation we need a *clear mental model* of what we're interacting with. HyperCard,[5] for instance, an early scripting system on the Apple, had a very clear mental model, a stack of cards: a precise analogy of what and how the program worked. It was obvious to its users that in effect they were flipping through a stack of cards: everything about the design reinforced this metaphor. Sadly, the same can't be said of many other applications.

A well-designed system has *reassuring feedback*, so that we know what we've done when we've done it. On a keyboard, for example, we can tell what we've just done because not only do characters appear on the screen but we can the feel the travel of the key itself and hear the little click it makes. Using an early word processor to do something repetitive, I often had to do a sequence of key commands that went "tetick, tick, tick-tick; tetick, tick, tick-tick." If it went "tick, tetick, tock," I'd know I'd made a mistake. The aural feedback let me go faster than if I'd relied just on my eyes.

Navigability is also essential, particularly with things that are primarily on screen. You need to know where you are in the system, what you can do there, where you can go next, and how to get back. The Star and Macintosh interfaces were very influential in this way. The menu at the top of the screen lays out all the possibilities; it's clear how you access them and what will happen when you do.

Equally crucial is *consistency*. A certain command in one part of the system should have the same effect in another part. An example, again from some time ago, was Appleworks, one of the

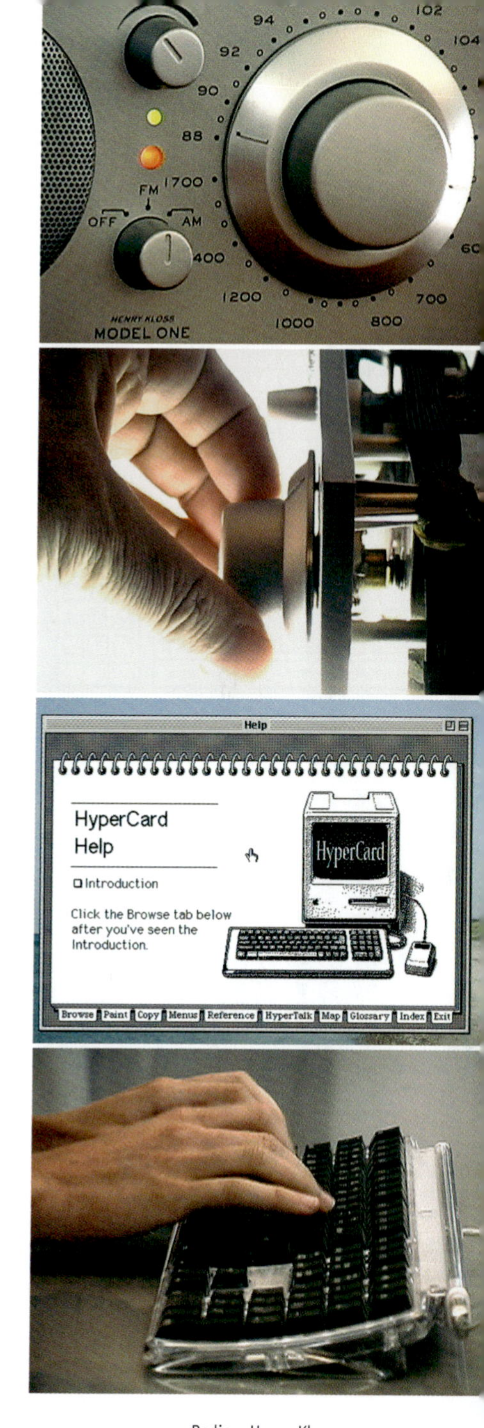

Radio—Henry Kloss ■
Radio dial mechanism ■
HyperCard ■
Keyboard ■

first integrated office programs on the Apple II. Those were the days of green "ransom-note" characters on a black screen, and very limited functionality. But Appleworks was beautifully, satisfyingly, consistent. You knew exactly what to do. A command in the database did exactly the same in the word processor; wherever you were, the escape key took you back up a level. You never got lost and rarely made a mistake. Compare that with modern "integrated" applications. Consistency, like all forms of satisfying simplicity, is very difficult to achieve.

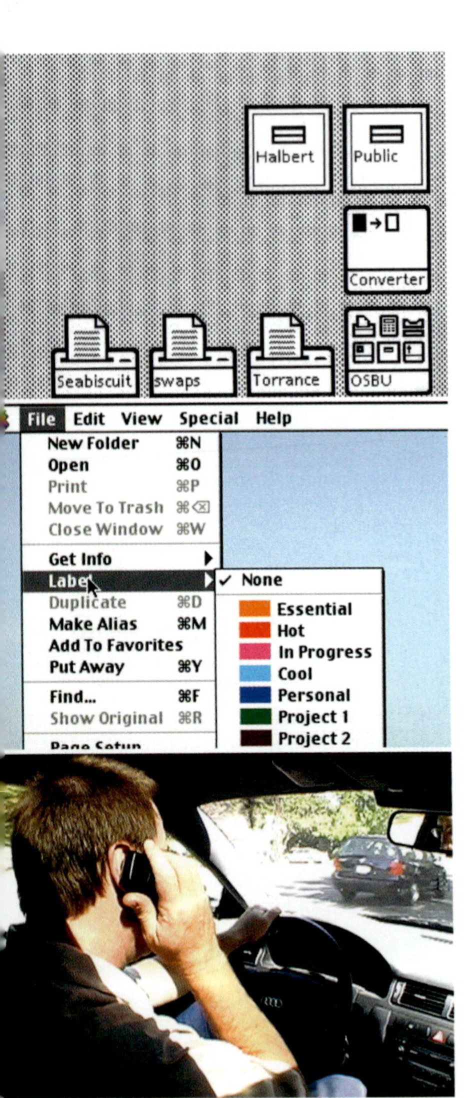

- Xerox Star interface
- Apple Macintosh menus
- Driving

When we interact with everyday artifacts, like a car, we don't spend too much time thinking about the interaction: we think about where we're heading and what we want to do. *Intuitive interaction* minimizes the burden of conscious thought needed to operate the system, leaving us to concentrate on our goals. A good example was Quark Express, which let you almost unconsciously zoom in on your image by holding down two keys and clicking on what you wanted to see better. It was like shifting your gaze: you didn't have to march off somewhere to find the right tool. But too many systems still keep demanding too much attention, like incompetent bosses, distracting us from getting on with the job.

When we design a computer-based system or device, we're designing not just what it looks like but how it *behaves*. We're designing the *quality* of how we and it interact. This is the skill of the interaction designer. It's partly responsiveness: when you move your mouse, for instance, does it feel sluggish, or nippy and sprightly? When you manipulate your iPod dial, the combination of sound and feel, as well as telling you what you're doing, is subtle and satisfying. We can design those qualities of interaction, relating what we see to what we hear or feel with the same refinement with which typographers adjust the spacing of type, or product designers the radius of a curve.

But the qualities of interaction must be appropriate to the context. An adventure game needs an interaction offering subtlety of atmosphere and intriguingly challenging navigation; central-heating control systems offering these qualities, however, would be as welcome as a fire alarm with a snooze button.

Languages of Interaction Design

When new technologies are born, we tend to think of the new in terms of the familiar. When cinema started, people thought of it as pointing a camera at a theater stage, and divided silent films with "chapter headings" as if they were books. New "languages" eventually emerged that were true to, and fully exploited, the unique qualities of cinema itself—Eisenstein's language of montage, for instance. But the old analogies never lose their validity: films continue to use the conventions of the theater and the novel. They are just augmented by the new languages.

I believe that interaction design is still in the equivalent of the early stages of cinema. As yet, we have no fully developed language unique to interactive technology. So we are still drawing on the language of previous creative modes. It may help to categorize these languages according to their "dimensions": 1-D, 2-D, 3-D, and 4-D.

1-D includes words and poetry. Are the words in a menu the most accurate encapsulations of the action they denote? Are they used consistently? And the "tone of voice" of the dialog boxes in your system: Are they too abrupt and imperious, or too cloyingly conversational?

The 2-D languages that interaction design can borrow from include painting, typography, diagrams, and icons. When we look at a painting, even if it's not representational, it's difficult not to interpret it as a perspectival space; we can use such compositional tropes to layer the screen in apparent depth or to foreground its currently most important element. We can use the familiar hierarchical conventions of typography to structure the screen, and our shared sensitivity to minute differences in letter forms to add distinctions of tone and meaning. We can also use the language of diagrams and information graphics to communicate a complexity which can't be intelligibly rendered in standard text, particularly on a small screen. Another specialist 2-D language, much used in

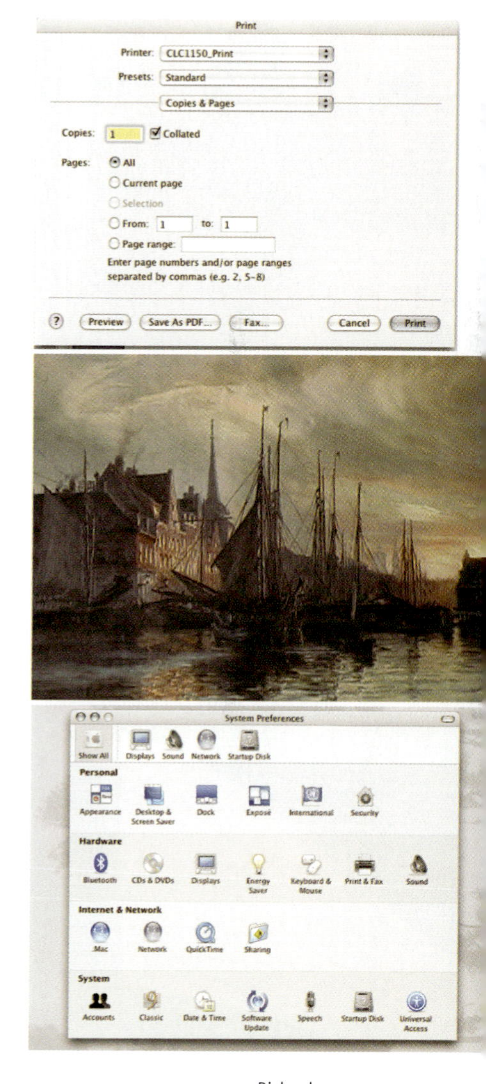

Dialog box ■
Painting ■
Icons ■

computer interfaces, is of course that of icons: tiny simplified images that stand for a larger idea or a thing.

3-D languages are those of physical, sculptural form. One movement in product design, "product semantics," explores how people understand what the different elements of a product represent. If something has a handle, for example, we know we are meant to grab it; if something has a base bigger than its apex, our experience of gravity suggests that we should keep the base downward. Designers use this language to make things clear, but sometimes also to play with expectations, inserting an element of surprise and wit in what otherwise might have been mundane.

The fourth dimension is time. The 4-D languages include sound, film, and animation. In the 1980s Bill Gaver[6] designed a beautiful sonic interface, the SonicFinder, an augmentation of the Apple Desktop: when you dropped a folder into another folder, it made a sound according to its size: an almost-empty folder went "pink," a fuller one "plonk." It gave good feedback, but the sounds were also poetic and appropriate for their purpose. Another important 4-D language is film: in twenty seconds a TV advertisement can tell a complex story understood by everyone. And animators have been developing their spare language for more than a century, so that with very limited means they can express plot, emotion, anticipation, and action.

We're designing for a public that understands the richness of all these different languages: dialog, graphics, typography, 3-D form, sound, film, and animation. This makes things difficult because nobody can be fluent in all these languages. We must collaborate with those who have other skills and experience. An interaction designer can never be a hermit.

However, after twenty years of drawing on existing expressive languages, we now need to develop an independent language of interaction with "smart systems and devices, a language true to the medium of computation, networks, and telecommunications. In terms of perceptual psychology, we're starting to understand the functional limits of interaction

- Fridge handle
- Bill Gaver
- Animation

between people and devices or systems: speed of response, say, or the communicative capacity of a small screen. But at the symbolic level of mood and meaning, of sociability and civility, we haven't quite achieved the breathtaking innovativeness, the subtlety and intuitive "rightness," of Eisenstein's language of montage.

By telling the stories of those who have been committed to making interactive products useful, meaningful and joyful, however, this important book nevertheless suggests that we are on our way.

Preface

Aim

The information revolution has changed the way we interact with everything, from the games that we play and the appliances in our homes, to the tools that we use at work. Some interactions are designed so that we don't notice them, as in the electronics that make a car easier to drive, safer, and more economical. Other interactions are designed so that we are very conscious of them, as in the personal computer or a TV remote control. The aim of this book is to give you a sense of the history of interaction design and to introduce you to many of the people who have been instrumental in making it happen and whose ideas will influence its future.

In the book, and on the accompanying DVD, you will meet forty people who are making a difference in the design of interactions, read the stories about what they have done and why they did it, and watch them tell you about their ideas, illustrated by examples. Interactions happen in time as well as physical dimensions, so I have combined this book with a time-based medium. You can tell stories and communicate ideas in words, and you can show what things look like with images on the page, but it is difficult to show the flow of a time-based interaction. I therefore decided to create the DVD, so you can see interactive examples in action and get a glimpse of what the people are like in the flesh and how they express themselves. The DVD only has room for a little over three minutes per person, so the contents are truncated compared to the interviews and stories in the book, but I hope it serves to bring the people and the examples alive.

Desktop publishing and video editing have made it possible for one person to assemble this combination of words, graphics, and video. I have enjoyed trying to write this book, design the layouts for the text and images, record the video, and edit it for the DVD. I have had help from The MIT Press and from friends and colleagues, but nothing of the scale of the traditional approach to these arts. The resources needed for a traditional film crew and book development team are expensive, so topics are limited to high-profile subjects that can command television broadcasting contracts and best-seller lists, rather than a first-time author tackling a new topic. I am disappointed in my limitations when it comes to the quality of execution for all these skills, but I hope my standards are high enough for you to enjoy the result.

I have chosen to tell true stories about designing interactions, rather than structuring the content around a more polemic point of view. This is because of the nature of design; when you go to a design conference, most of the presenters describe their process and show lots of examples. They tend to say, "We did this, and then I did that, and I liked it because it was good!" I know that this can be irritating to people with objective minds, if they are used to rigorous presentations from PhDs, but it is a pragmatic approach to describing design. I try to explain why design is like that, but to give a rich impression first. If you want the explanation straight away, jump to chapter 10, "People and Prototypes."

Acknowledgments

FIRST I WANT to thank all of the people who were willing to submit themselves to my lenses and microphones, giving of their wisdom and helping me with my follow-up questions and requests. These are the people I interviewed, in the order that they appear in the book; Doug Engelbart, Stu Card, Tim Mott, Larry Tesler, Bill Atkinson, Paul Bradley, Bill Verplank, Cordell Ratzlaff, John Ellenby, Jeff Hawkins, Bert Keely, Rob Haitani, Dennis Boyle, David Liddle, Mat Hunter, Rikako Sakai, David Kelley, Paul Mercer, Bing Gordon, Brendan Boyle, Brenda Laurel, Will Wright, Takeshi Natsuno, Chris Downs, Lavrans Løvlie, Ben Reason, Fran Samalionis, Terry Winograd, Larry Page, Sergey Brin, Steve Rogers, Mark Podlaseck, Hiroshi Ishii, Durrell Bishop, Joy Mountford, Bill Gaver, Tony Dunne, Fiona Raby, John Maeda, and Jun Rekimoto. Thank you all for most of the material that is here.

Gillian Crampton Smith has helped me learn about interaction design over our fifteen years of collaboration. I thank her for answering the question "What is interaction design?" in the foreword. She would have been a coauthor for the whole book if she had not been so busy founding and developing the interaction design program at IDII (Interaction Design Institute Ivrea). I also thank the other leaders and staff at the Institute for their inspiration and support, especially Franco Debenedetti, Barbara Ghella, Mauro Demarziani, and Marco Zanini.

For inspiration, I would like to thank Tracy Kidder for his delicate documentary style, Howard Rheingold for his forward vision, Mitchell Waldrop for his thorough and engaging history, and Studs Terkel for his radio interviews, which show the powerful connections to people that are possible in a recorded medium.

Many of my colleagues at IDEO have helped me enormously, six of whom are among the list of interviewees above. I am particularly grateful to Jane Fulton Suri and Duane Bray, who collaborated with me on the final chapter to the extent of an interview, without their contributions being presented in that way. Thanks also to Tim Brown, for helping me make time for the book; Naoto Fukasawa, for his lifetime of aesthetic inspiration; Scott Underwood, for his wisdom about words; Whitney Mortimer, for guidance about publishing; Stephanie Lee, Hunter Wimmer, and Katie Clark, for help with the graphic layout; Lynn Winter, for her sources of images; Gary Jones and Albert Chen, for technical support; and Craig Syverson, for advice and help with everything to do with video and DVDs.

My original inspiration for the graphic design of the book came from Lorraine Wild, and Erik Spiekermann crystallized the design for me. Yasuyo Iguchi at The MIT Press perfected the layouts. The MIT Press have been wonderfully supportive and generous throughout the process, particularly my editor, Doug Sery. Many thanks to Tom Kozachek and Matthew Abbate for editing the text, and to Jennifer Kuca for putting it all together. Special thanks to Stu Card and Tom Erickson, who reviewed the first draft and helped me improve the structure.

Many thanks to Hilary Arnold for introducing me to the world of publishing and pointing me toward Caroline Herter, who became my agent and steered this innocent first-time author in the right direction. It would never have happened without the endless support and encouragement from my wife, Karin, and thanks to my son Alex for all those hours transcribing videotapes. Many thanks also to my son Erik and his friend Guy Higby for composing, performing, and recording the music for the DVD.

Introduction

Two personal stories

no sleep at all

Here are two stories of personal experiences that led me to start working toward a new design discipline, eventually called "interaction design." The first, about buying a digital watch for my son, made me see that I needed to learn how to design controls for products that contain electronics. The second, about designing the first laptop, made me see that I needed to learn how to design user interfaces for computers. The next nine chapters contain thirty-seven interviews, both in the book and on the DVD, with people who have made interesting or important contributions to this field. In chapter 10, "People and Prototypes," I expand my personal point of view about designing interactions.

The Radio Watch

■ The author with his son, in front of the Southland Runabout trailer where many of the ideas for this book were formed

Photo Catherine Ledner, published in *Dwell* magazine

I WAS BROWSING in the duty-free store in Narita airport outside Tokyo while waiting for my flight back to San Francisco in 1983. When I was on business trips, I tried to find gifts to bring home for my two sons, aged thirteen and ten at the time. I already had a Yomiuri Giants hat for the baseball-crazed ten-year-old but still needed something for the teenager, who was starting to get interested in heavy metal music and realizing that dad was not necessarily always right about everything. He was saving the money from his paper route to buy his first electric guitar.

I drifted across to a large array of glass-topped cases and found in them a seemingly endless collection of watches. My designer soul was mesmerized. How could there be so many great looking watches in the world? As well as the international brands that I was used to, there was case after case of beautiful and innovative designs from Japanese manufacturers. Some were for running or swimming, some had interchangeable dials with alternative functions, and many were just elegant. Then I saw a digital watch

■ Yomiuri Giants hat
■ Interested in heavy metal

that had a radio in it. It was black rubber with a rectangular face blending smoothly into a ribbed strap; it included alarm functions and had a neat little tuning knob for the radio. It was not too expensive and amazingly small for all that functionality. What a perfect present for the teenager! I paid for it and purred with the gratification of my techno-lust until I fell asleep on the plane. He was already in bed when I gave it to him, and we were both excited as he unwrapped the package, took it out, and fastened the strap on his wrist. He tried the radio first. There was a tiny earpiece for listening, attached to the watch by a delicate cord. He tuned to his favorite station, but I could see the excitement in his face fade to disappointment as he heard it.

"The quality's not that good, Dad," he said, glancing at his boom box. I was flustered, but did my best to disguise my chagrin as I tried it myself and heard the crackly and distorted sound. That was the end of the radio!

I recovered by explaining the digital functions, and he brightened up as he suggested that he could use it as an alarm clock to get up at five o'clock every morning for his paper route. He asked me to set the alarm and adjust it to the local time. There were four buttons as well as the tuning knob. The instructions were on a tightly folded sheet, printed in seven languages, and it took me twenty minutes of concentrated effort to set everything up; following the instructions step by step and pushing the right combinations of buttons in the required sequence eventually prevailed. I kissed him goodnight and took the big old alarm clock with the bells on top with me as I turned out the light and closed the door to his room.

Everything went well for six weeks. He didn't seem to miss the radio, used the alarm every morning, and enjoyed the cool design. Then two things happened; daylight savings time ended, and he gave up his paper route. He left the watch on the chest of drawers in our bedroom, as he said, "Could you cancel the alarm and change the time, please, Dad?"

By that time of course the instructions were lost, so I tried to make the adjustments by pushing buttons in a vague and unstructured way, hoping that some automatic memory would make me get it right.

My wife is a lighter sleeper than I, so it was she who got out of bed to cancel the alarm when it went off at four o'clock in the morning, an hour earlier after the time change. I tried to reset it again the next night, but with the same result. She was starting to get irritated, so the following night I took the battery out, and assured her that an undisturbed night would follow. At four o'clock the next morning, there it was again, "Beep-be-be-be-beep," in an ascending volume and persistent shrill tone. That was too much! She woke me up, marched out of the bedroom and returned in a moment with a hammer. That was the end of the watch! It turned out that the battery that I had removed was for the radio; there was another one buried deep inside that powered the watch.

Kind to Chips but Cruel to People

THIS SAD STORY made me think about the design of the controls. I never had any trouble with a traditional analog watch. Pull out the knob and rotate back or forward to set the time. Pull out a second click to change the date. Why did the digital watch have four buttons, and a sequence of operations that was too complicated to remember?

I talked to some people who worked at watch companies and knew about the history of watch designs and came to the conclusion that the problem was caused by too much kindness to chips. The engineers who developed traditional mechanical watches and clocks were motivated by the ambition to create a machine that could keep accurate time, and the finest instruments were the most accurate and expensive. The controls had evolved from the analog clock mechanisms, and the design decisions that made them easy to use had happened long ago. Along came a computer chip that contained a time keeping circuit of impeccable accuracy, and offered the possibility of creating a watch that would not only keep perfect time, but could be manufactured to sell for as little as $25.

The natural first step was to make a watch that was built around the requirements of the chip, so the controls were designed to fit the electronic circuit as extensions of the logic diagram, causing the user to operate a sequence of simple push buttons. This was the simplest form of control for the chip, and the easiest solution for the hardware and software engineers, but it was so difficult for the people who wanted to use it that it amounted to cruelty. For a while, the digital watch was a novelty and sold well to enthusiasts, even with controls that were cruel to people; in the longer term it led to a backlash and a resurgence of analog watches, with successful designs like the Swatch series.

In my education as a designer of everyday things back in the sixties, the products that we learned to design usually had simple controls that were easy to understand, comparable to the mechanical watch. The demise of the radio watch made me realize that designers needed to face new challenges, as electronics started to replace mechanical control systems. In order to create products that are enjoyable, satisfying to use, and aesthetically pleasing in behavior as well as shape, designers would need to learn how to design hardware and software as well as physical objects. For me, this was the beginning of designing interactions between people and products that contain electronics.

Photo Don Fogg

GRiD Compass computer, 1981

The First Laptop[1]

THE NEXT CHALLENGE was to design the interactions between people and computers. The stimulus for me came from designing the first laptop computer and starting to use it myself in 1981. I had designed the physical enclosures for some computers in the seventies but had never used them myself, so the frustrations and pleasures of using the software were something that I had watched, rather than experienced.

My first design was for a mini computer in 1972, for an innovative British company called Computer Technology Limited (CTL), but it was not implemented. The first computer to be manufactured was in 1974 for ITT, in Spain. It was a data entry workstation, similar to an IBM product of the time. I observed people using the IBM product and worked out some improvements for the physical design, but the software task was only tedious numeric entry and was already defined by the IBM mainframe that used the data.

By 1978 my design practice was well established in London. I thought that a good way to keep expanding would be to start a second office, and the USA seemed to offer opportunities for a designer from Europe. I decided to mix business with adventure by taking a vacation in the USA and look around for possible locations for the office. We rented a Ford wagon with plenty of room for kids and camping gear and went from one national park to another. Whenever I had a contact in the vicinity, I would don my business suit, brush the dust off my shiny shoes, and head into town for a meeting or presentation to potential clients. We looped around the East Coast and Midwest, and I came to the conclusion that the Boston area seemed the most promising. There were plenty of companies along Route 128 full of eager young engineers creating high-tech products. Then I heard that Silicon Valley in northern California was a place with even more innovation than Boston.

I had an image in my head of Silicon Valley as an industrial wasteland in the desert, with enormous machines gouging raw material from burnt sandy rock. What a surprise to find that it was

1972—Minicomputer for CTL ■
1974—Data entry workstation for ITT ■
1978—Brochure from Design Practice ■
Ford Fairlane wagon ■

- Stanford University
- Freddie Laker
- John Ellenby in 1981

a gentle landscape of orchards and fields around San Francisco Bay, being gradually gobbled up by low office buildings and suburbs, with a well-established area around Stanford University and "Professorville" in Palo Alto.

The innovation was certainly there, with connections between Stanford and the industry that emerged from it, a rapidly expanding venture capital community, and startup companies all over the place. It was very exciting for me to discover that the valley was evolving from a place where electronic chips and printed circuit boards were invented to a product development community with the chips included in the products; this meant that they would find themselves needing good industrial designers.

Direct flights from London to San Francisco had recently started, and thanks to price wars between the major airlines and the Skytrain service from Freddy Laker, the cost of flying standby was only £40 more to the West Coast than to the east. What's more, the Pan Am–operated jumbo jets that I traveled in were usually only half full. I perfected the art of being the last passenger to board the plane, so that I could claim an unoccupied row of four center seats and settle down after takeoff to catch up on some sleep. I spent ten days a month for six months in the San Francisco, Palo Alto, and the Silicon Valley area, showing my portfolio to vice presidents of development and marketing, venture capitalists, and anyone who was interested in design. When I took the plunge and moved the family to Palo Alto, I already had a list of a dozen likely clients and another dozen "possibles." We rented an Eichler, a flat-roofed wooden house with lots of glass walls, and I converted the garage into a studio in the best Silicon Valley startup tradition. Work was slower to start than I had hoped and expected, but when it came it was worth the wait.

A few months before we moved to California, I noticed a stranger sitting on the front steps of our neighbor's house across the street in London, waiting for someone to come home. We started chatting and found that we had lots to talk about. John Ellenby[2] was visiting from Palo Alto. He had moved to Silicon Valley a few years before and worked at Xerox PARC (Palo Alto

Research Center) to try to improve the transition from research findings to real products. He was an ambitious engineer from Scotland, with a glint in his eye and an outrageous sense of humor. He told fascinating stories of life in the San Francisco Bay area, reveling in the excitement of innovation and technology, while complaining of the suburban lifestyle, synthetic-seeming bread, and weak coffee. He was immediately interested in my plans for a design office in the valley and came to see our office in London to find out more about our work. We became friends, and I got to know him better on my monthly trips to Palo Alto.

The airlines allowed two suitcases per person without a charge for excess baggage, so when we moved to California in the summer of 1979, the four of us had eight suitcases of the maximum size allowed. They were tightly packed with as many of our worldly possessions as we could fit into them. John's wife Gillian met us at the airport with a big welcoming smile and ushered us into her huge Dodge van. It swallowed all of us, and our suitcases, and still looked empty. There was a cooler by the seats, loaded with champagne and soft drinks. What a welcome to California. Thanks, Gillian! We settled into our Palo Alto house and enjoyed the California summer weather, spending weekends exploring San Francisco and the beautiful coastline and mountains. John was busy raising venture capital and putting his startup company, GRiD Systems, together. GRiD became my first major client.

Soon after we had settled in, John revealed his plans to me. He was raising venture capital to start a new company, and he was determined to develop a computer with an electronic display that would be small enough to carry around. There were a few precedents to build on; Alan Kay had developed the Dynabook concept model in 1968,[3] and there were several portable data terminals, such as the Silent 700 from Texas Instruments (1973);[4] there were also several luggable computers more the size of a sewing machine than a laptop, the best known of which was the Osborne, but that was designed in parallel with the GRiD Compass. John saw the components used in a computer steadily shrinking and had the vision to realize that there was a potential market for people who needed to move around for their work

Texas Instruments Silent 700, 1973
Osborne 1 computer, 1981

- First model for GRiD
- GRiD Compass computer: first sketch, 1980
- Compass computer side view

and would like to carry the information with them in their computers. He set out to create a computer that would fit in a briefcase and be usable away from the office.

He first asked me to visualize a design to help people understand what he imagined and to show to venture capitalists and potential employees. We felt that a three-dimensional model would communicate much more powerfully than drawings, so I designed and drew up a concept and sent it back to my office in London, where they made a completely realistic-looking model out of very unreal materials. The shape was like a fat dictionary, opening like a clamshell, to reveal a flat display on the top half and a keyboard on the bottom. John had identified a display technology with a set of characters that glowed bright green, and I made up a simulation of a keyboard with modern-looking keycaps on a pastel green field. The model did its job of convincing people that the concept had potential. John successfully raised money and put together an amazingly talented team of founders for GRiD Systems. The plan was to sell the products to large companies, so that individuals could gain access to company-wide information on the road. Potential applications included a salesperson confirming an order in real time, or an executive tracking the performance of the company. All this was very new at the time, as there was not yet even an IBM PC or an Apple Mac, let alone a pervasive Internet.

My responsibility was the physical design, and I had the experience of a lifetime developing a design that was innovative in so many ways. I developed the way that the screen was hinged to fold down over the keyboard for carrying. This geometry accounted for only one of the forty-three innovative features in the utility patent that we were awarded. Most of these innovations are taken for granted today, but they were new at the time: for example, the flat electroluminescent graphic display, the low-profile keyboard, bubble memory, and the enclosure in die-cast magnesium. The metal housing offered a combination of strength and lightness, creating an amazingly tough machine that was sent up in the space shuttle and dropped from military helicopters.

The epiphany for me occurred when I started trying to use the software. GRiD had developed a unique operating system

(OS) that was very advanced at the time; it was a graphical OS (but without a mouse) that had resizing fonts and many features that later took hold in the computer industry. The system also had a linked suite of applications, which allowed people to move data from program to program, for example between spreadsheet and word processor.

I had helped with information and graphic design for the summary of commands above the keyboard and the design of the typefaces for the screen, so I knew something about what to expect. I was surprised to find that I became absorbed in the interactions with the software almost immediately. I soon forgot all about the physical part of the design and found myself sucked down into the virtual world on the other side of the screen. All the work that I had done to make the object elegant to look at and to feel was forgotten, and I found myself immersed for hours at a time in the interactions that were dictated by the design of the software and electronic hardware. My frustrations and rewards were in this virtual space. As I gradually mastered my personal computer, almost all of the subjective qualities that mattered most to me were in the interactions with the software, but not with the physical design. At that point I realized that I had to learn a new sort of design, where I could apply as much skill and knowledge to designing satisfying and enjoyable experiences in the realm of software and electronic behaviors as I had with physical objects.

Interaction Design

LEARNING THIS NEW form of design was a gradual process. I discovered more about using software in the first half of the eighties, as I started to rely more and more on the GRiD Compass computer that I had designed, as I learned to use computer-aided design (CAD) systems, and then fell in love with the Mac. I found that there was a well-established community of human-computer interface (HCI) designers, busy creating the software that people were using on mainframes, minicomputers,

Apple Mac, 1984

and the emerging personal computers. There were people with computer science backgrounds who were writing code and had a technical and performance-based vision of the design requirements. There were also human factors specialists, who had backgrounds in psychology and had been educated to evaluate and test designs that were already prototyped. This approach tended to generate incremental improvements to the designs but did not encourage more radical innovation.

I felt that there was an opportunity to create a new design discipline, dedicated to creating imaginative and attractive solutions in a virtual world, where one could design behaviors, animations, and sounds as well as shapes. This would be the equivalent of industrial design but in software rather than three-dimensional objects. Like industrial design, the discipline would be concerned with subjective and qualitative values, would start from the needs and desires of the people who use a product or service, and strive to create designs that would give aesthetic pleasure as well as lasting satisfaction and enjoyment.

I gave my first conference presentation on the subject in 1984, and at that time I described it as "Soft-face," thinking of a combination between software and user-interface design. At that time a fashionable toy was called the Cabbage Patch Doll, a soft stuffed doll with chubby cheeks. A friend pointed out to me that "Soft-face" sounded like a description of one of these dolls, but not so much like a design discipline, so we went on thinking of possible names until I eventually settled on "interaction design" with the help of Bill Verplank.[5] I had started to assemble a team of interaction designers to work with our industrial designers in San Francisco, drawn from various backgrounds, as there was not yet any education in interaction design. One had been trained in information design, one in graphics, and another in industrial design. I was lucky to persuade Bill Verplank to join the team, as he brought with him a guru status in the subject and already knew how interaction design worked. By the end of the eighties we were starting to feel that we had momentum, and that we could declare ourselves to be interaction designers.

■ Bill Verplank

1

The Mouse and the Desktop

Interviews with Doug Engelbart, Stu Card, Tim Mott, and Larry Tesler

When you were interacting considerably with the screen, you needed some sort of device to select objects on the screen, to tell the computer that you wanted to do something with them.

Douglas C. Engelbart, 2003, referring to 1964

Why a Mouse?

■ Apple mouse
2002

Photo
Courtesy of Apple

WHO WOULD CHOOSE to point, steer, and draw with a blob of plastic as big and clumsy as a bar of soap? We spent all those years learning to write and draw with pencils, pens, and brushes. Sharpen the pencil to a fine point and you can create an image with the most delicate shapes and write in the tiniest letters; it's not so easy to do that with a mouse.

Doug Engelbart[1] tells the story of how he invented the mouse. When he was a student, he was measuring the area under some complex-shaped curves, using a device with wheels that would roll in one direction and slide sideways in the axis at ninety degrees. He was bored at a conference, and wrote in his notebook about putting two wheels at right angles to track movement on a plane. Years later, when he was searching for a device to select objects on a computer screen, he remembered those notes, and together with Bill English, he built the first mouse. We use the mouse not just because Doug Engelbart invented it, but because it turned out to be the pointing device that performed best for

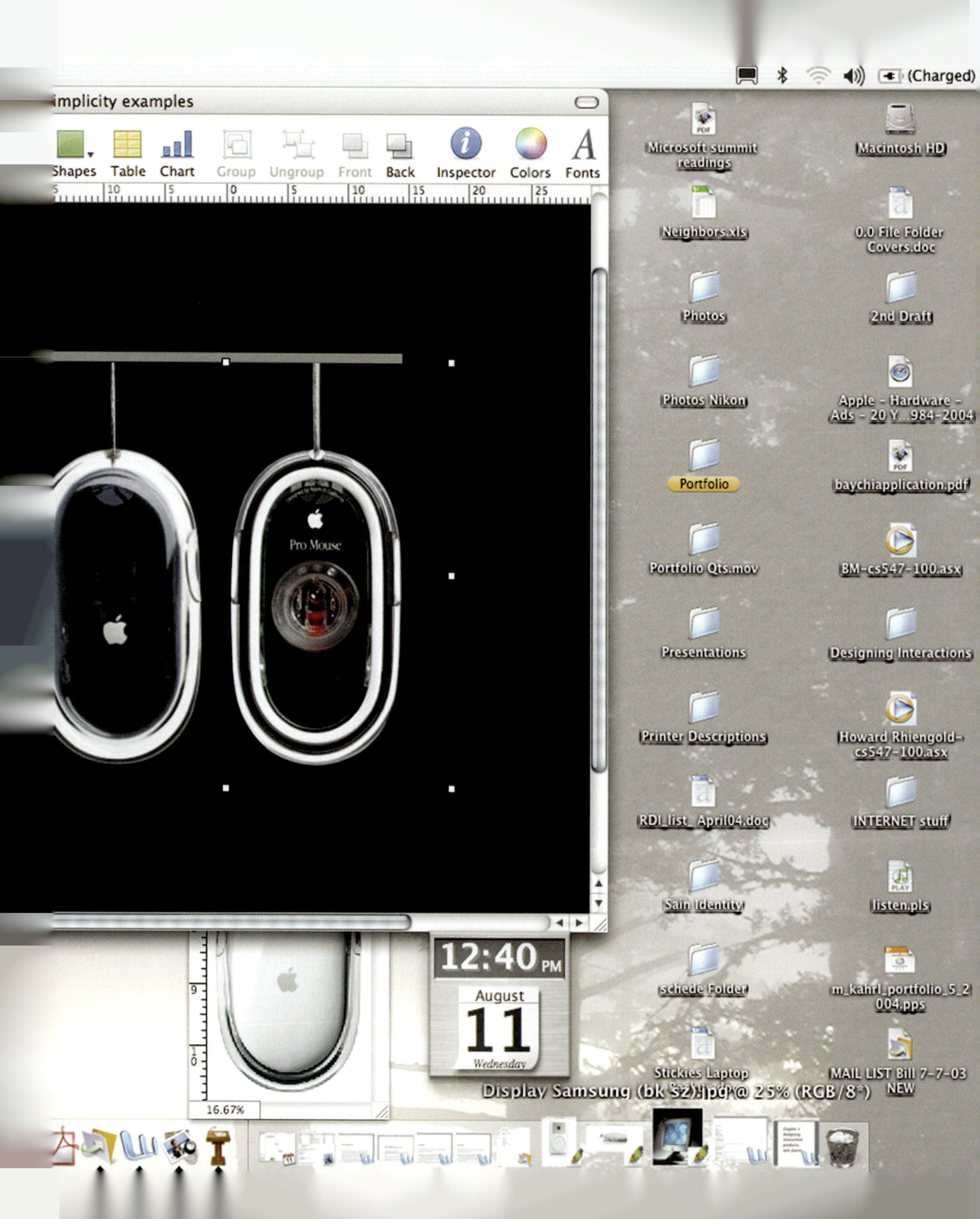
(Charged)
implicity examples
Shapes
Table
Chart
Group
Ungroup
Front
Back
Inspector
Colors
Fonts
Pro Mouse
16.67%
12:40 PM
August
11
Wednesday
Display Samsung (bk s2).jpg @ 25% (RGB/8*)
Microsoft summit readings
Macintosh HD
Neighbors.xls
0.0 File Folder Covers.doc
Photos
2nd Draft
Photos Nikon
Apple - Hardware - Ads - 20 Y...984-2004
Portfolio
baychiapplication.pdf
Portfolio Qts.mov
BM-cs547-100.asx
Presentations
Designing Interactions
Printer Descriptions
Howard Rhiengold-cs547-100.asx
RDI_list_April04.doc
INTERNET stuff
Sain Identity
listen.pls
schede Folder
m_kahrl_portfolio_5_2004.pps
Stickies Laptop
MAIL LIST Bill 7-7-03 NEW

pointing and clicking on a display, outperforming light pens, cursor keys, joysticks, trackballs, and everything else that was tried in early tests with users. The mouse won because it was the easiest to use.

We understand the reasons for the triumph of the mouse much more clearly from the story of developing the early designs told by Stu Card,[2] who joined Xerox Palo Alto Research Center (PARC) in 1974 and has spent much of his time there perfecting scientific methods to integrate with creative design. He has developed a process to predict the behavior of a proposed design, using task analysis, approximation, and calculation. His idea is to accelerate the movement through the design space by a partnership between designers and scientists, by providing a science that supports design. He tells the story of applying this science to the development of the mouse.

Why a Desktop?

- Apple Mac OSX desktop with images of Apple mouse

Photo
Author's screen capture

It seems surprising to find a "desktop" on the spherical surface of a glowing glass display, housed in a bulky plastic box that in itself takes up half your desk. Or is it on the cramped flat screen of your laptop? Who came up with that idea? What were they thinking about, and why did they choose to design a desktop rather than a floor, or a playing field, or a meadow, or a river? Why does this desktop have windows in it? You usually think of windows being on the wall, not all over the surface of your desk. Why does it have a trashcan on it? It would seem more natural to put the trashcan on the floor.

In 1974 Tim Mott[3] was an outsider at Xerox PARC, working for a Xerox subsidiary on the design of a publishing system. He describes how the idea of a desktop came to him as part of an "office schematic" that would allow people to manipulate entire documents, grabbing them with a mouse and moving them around a representation of an office on the screen. They could drop them into a file cabinet or trashcan, or onto a printer. One of the objects in the office was a desktop, with a calendar and clock on it, plus in- and out-baskets for electronic mail.

There were lots of other people at Xerox PARC at that time thinking about desktops and other metaphors for use in the design of graphical user interfaces (GUIs), but Tim was working most closely with Larry Tesler,[4] and the two of them worked out processes for understanding users by talking to them, using guided fantasies, participatory design, and usability testing. Larry describes how he developed these processes and how icons arrived on the desktop. Larry insisted on simplicity and designed interactions that were easy to learn as well as easy to use. He went on to Apple and formed another partnership in the development of the desktop, working with Bill Atkinson[5] to create the designs for Lisa, including the pull-down menus, dialog boxes, and the one-button mouse. These ideas stayed in place as the user's conceptual model for the Macintosh and all of the GUIs that followed, stretching the desktop metaphor almost beyond the breaking point.

NLS, Alto, and Star

When Doug Engelbart invented the mouse, he arrived at the dominant design for input devices in a single leap from the light pen, and the development of the mouse since has been more in the nature of evolution than revolution.[6] Engelbart also invented the point-and-click text editor for the NLS system (oNLine System) that he developed at the Stanford Research Institute (SRI), and that system migrated with members of his design team to the fledgling Xerox PARC and became the foundation of the Alto, the first computer with a GUI. In the versions of NLS that were built at PARC for the Alto, the text-editing demonstrations were impressively fast, with a clattering of keystrokes that sounded businesslike and productive. Direct manipulation made it so easy to pick things up and move them that people would often find an instance of a word they wanted in the text and move it into place, instead of typing it. For programmers, this was a wonderful interaction, but the patience needed to acquire the skills proved a fatal barrier for novice consumers when computers became accessible to ordinary people. It took the influence of Larry Tesler and Tim Mott to create a text editor and page layout design system that was really easy to use, and this was based on rigorous user testing and rapid iterative prototyping. They came close to the desktop metaphor that survives today.

One of the major innovations of the Alto was the bitmap display, making it easy to show graphics. You could make any dot be black or white, allowing you to put any image, whether a font or a picture, onto the whole screen. The memory to do that for a full-page display was exorbitantly expensive at the time, but it meant that you could translate the tradition of graphic and typographic design to the computer. Earlier computers had primitive and pixelated type fonts, but the bitmap display meant that what was on the display of the computer could look exactly like a book, except that it was only 72 pixels per inch instead of about three times as high a resolution for the printed page. A white background and dark text was used on the screen, so that the displayed image was like the printed result, and the screen size was chosen to be exactly the same as a page of text, enabling the concept of WYSIWYG (What You See Is What You Get).

The idea of the desktop was floating around Xerox PARC as part of the communal consciousness. David Canfield Smith had devised an office metaphor as part of his PhD thesis, "Pygmalion: A Creative Programming Environment," published in 1975. His icons looked like mathematical symbols and boxes that you could type into but defined the characteristics of the icons that have become commonplace. Here is his explanation:

> The entities with which one programs in Pygmalion are what I call "icons." An icon is a graphic entity that has meaning both as a visual image and as a machine object. Icons control the execution of computer programs, because they have code and data associated with them, as well as their images on the screen. This distinguishes icons from, say, lines and rectangles in a drawing program, which have no such semantics. Pygmalion is the origin of the concept of icons as it now appears in graphical user interfaces on personal computers. After completing my thesis, I joined Xerox's "Star" computer project. The

> first thing I did was recast the programmer-oriented icons of Pygmalion into office-oriented ones representing documents, folders, file cabinets, mailboxes, telephones, wastebaskets, etc. These icons have both data (e.g., document icons contain text) and behavior (e.g., when a document icon is dropped on a folder icon, the folder stores the document in the file system). This idea has subsequently been adopted by the entire personal computer and workstation industry.[7]

When Dave Smith had finished his PhD, he was hired to join PARC to work on the Star system. Alan Kay had always talked about the desktop metaphor and he came up with the idea of overlapping windows, from a metaphor of papers on a desktop. "You can have a lot more papers on a desk if they overlap each other, and you can see the corner of one, pull it out and put it on top."

Detailed accounts have been written[8] about how long it took to convince a copier company to commercialize the Alto, but Xerox did make a major effort to develop and market an "Office of the Future" machine. They did a thorough analysis of the business potential to find what the requirements of that machine should be, concluding that people would pay a lot for the Alto technology. Star was conceived in response to this; based on the combination of Smalltalk and Alto, it became a design that fit all of the requirements. Star was a very futuristic machine; when they were asked in the market research surveys, people responded that they would not give up that advanced interactive performance for a much inferior but less expensive machine. After it was launched, the IBM PC came out, and the people who said in the research that they would pay a lot for Star proved to be only willing to pay much less for an inferior interface.

Photo Author

Dr. Douglas C. Engelbart

Doug Engelbart is best known as the inventor of the mouse. At the time of writing, in 2004, at the age of seventy-eight, he is still going to work at his "Bootstrap Alliance," trying to persuade us of the value of his ideas about augmenting the human intellect, and evangelizing the virtues of his "Augment System." His office is located in the headquarters building of Logitech, the world's largest manufacturer of mice. Taking credit as the inventor of such an ubiquitous product is not enough for Doug; in fact, he is charmingly modest about that achievement, preferring to discuss other ideas that have not met with such spectacular success. He has always wanted to create designs that enhance human performance and is not interested in ease of use for the novice. He grew up in Oregon, and his electrical engineering studies were interrupted by service in World War II. During his stint in the Philippines as a naval radar technician, he came across an article by Vannevar Bush in the *Atlantic Monthly*[9] and was inspired to think of a career dedicated to connecting people to knowledge. This idealistic ambition led him to the Ames Laboratory (later NASA Ames Research Center) on the edge of the San Francisco Bay, where he worked on wind tunnel research, and then to the Stanford Research Institute, where he invented the mouse and built up the Augmentation Research Center (ARC) with funding from ARPA. In the early seventies he took several members of his team to Xerox PARC, where he helped put the mouse and the desktop together.

Doug Engelbart

Inventing the Mouse

Doug Engelbart conducting a workshop circa 1967–68

Photo Bootstrap Institute

In 1995 the International World Wide Web Conference committee presented the first SoftQuad Web Award to Dr. Douglas C. Engelbart, to commemorate a lifetime of imagination and achievement and to acknowledge his formative influence on the development of graphical computing, in particular for his invention of the mouse. This is the contribution for which Doug is universally acclaimed. In spite of this, he himself is inclined to give credit to the trackball:

> When I was a senior in electrical engineering, some of the experiments we had to do in the laboratory would end up resulting in funny shaped curves that curled back on themselves, and it was the area under the curve that we were experimenting with. They had an elbow shaped device there, a platform sort of thing that would set down on the table. You would run the pointer around that area, and there was a small wheel next to the pointer, resting on the tabletop, and the other side of the joint there was another one. I couldn't figure out how that would produce the area under the curve.
>
> "I'm not sure myself about the mathematics," said the professor, "but it is a fact that the little wheels will only roll in the axis of the rolling direction, and will slide sideways."

I began to understand that the wheel would roll only as far as you went in the one direction, irrespective of how many sideways movements you made.

I thought of that again one time during a conference on computer graphics, when I was feeling rebellious and bored, so I wrote in my notes about putting two wheels at right angles to each other, so that one would always be measuring how far you went north and south, and the other east and west. It would be easy to convert that into potentiometers and things so that the computer could pick up that signal. It was a very simple idea. At the time I was unaware that that same thing was sitting underneath the tracking ball, and that was how a tracking ball worked. Later on the manufacturers put the wheels against the table, which is exactly like an upside down tracking ball. There should be credit given to the tracking ball, except for my ignorance about it at the time.

It says a great deal about Engelbart's extraordinary modesty that he makes so light of his achievement. It also says a lot about his methodical persistence that he used his moments of boredom at that conference to fill a notebook with ideas and that he remembered what was in that notebook when he was looking for the best input device solutions many years later:

When you were interacting considerably with the screen, you needed some sort of device to select objects on the screen, to tell the computer that you wanted to do something with them. We got some funding in the early sixties, I think it was from NASA, and set up an experimental environment with several different kinds of devices; a tracking ball, a light pen, and things of that sort that were available at the time.

As we were setting up the experiments, I happened to remember some notes that I had made in a pocket notebook some years before, and sketched that out to Bill English, who was the engineer setting up the experiments, and he put one together, with the help of a few draftsmen and machinists. That one was put in the experiments, and happened to be winning all the tests. That became the pointing device for our user interface. Somebody, I can't remember who, attached the name "mouse" to it. You can picture why, because it was an object about this big, and had one button to use for selection, and had a wire running out the back.

Graficon experimental pointing device

"It looks like a one-eared mouse!" someone said. Soon all of us just started calling it a mouse.

Thinking of the possible relevance of those orthogonal wheels was the first step; working with Bill English to design an object to contain them was the second. The recognition that this idea might be important for interaction came from the tests that compared the mouse with other possible input devices; it was the people who used it in the tests who proved the point. The designers came up with as many alternatives as they could that seemed plausible, built prototypes and created tasks in the relevant context, and then ran the tests. Here's what Doug says about the testing process:

> We listened to everybody who had strong ideas, and it seem to us worth just testing everything that was available. The light pen had been used by radar operators for years and years, and that seemed to most people would be the most natural way to do it. I couldn't see that, but why argue with them; why not just test and measure? The time it takes to grope for it and lift it up to the screen seemed excessively large, so it didn't do well in the tests.
>
> For the test we had naive users coming in, and we explained everything that would happen so that they weren't surprised. We asked them to put their hands on the keyboard, and all of sudden an array of three-by-three objects would appear at an arbitrary place on the screen, sometimes small objects and sometimes large, and they had to hit a space bar, access the pointing device and go click on it. The computer measured time, overshoot, and any other characteristics we thought were valuable. The assessment just showed the mouse coming out ahead. It was many years later that I heard from Stuart Card, a friend at Xerox PARC, what the human factors explanation was.

There is an objectivity in this process of letting the user decide, the value of which is a recurring theme in this story of designing the desktop and the mouse. Come up with an idea, build a prototype, and try it on the intended users. That has proved, time and time again, to be the best way to create innovative solutions.

First mouse in hand, 1963–64 ■
First mouse ■
First production mouse ■

The Demo that Changed the World

There is a gentle modesty, even diffidence, in the way Doug Engelbart talks, but he holds your attention much more firmly than you would expect from his manner of speech. His passion for philosophy and ideas shines through, with an underlying intensity, almost fanaticism, that is charismatic. He remembers his early motivations:

> My initial framework for thinking about these questions got established in 1951. I had realized that I didn't have any great goals for my career. I was an electrical engineer with an interesting job, recently engaged to be married, but had no picture of the future, and I was embarrassed about this.
>
> "What would be an appropriate career goal for me?" I asked.
>
> "Why don't I design a career that can maximize its benefit to mankind?" I ended up saying.
>
> I was an idealistic country boy. Eventually I realized that the world is getting more complex at an ever more rapid rate, that complex problems have to be dealt with collectively, and that our collective ability for dealing with them is not improving nearly as fast as the complexity is increasing. The best thing I could think of doing was to try and help boost mankind's capability for dealing with complex problems.

By this time he had been working for a couple of years at the Ames Laboratory, in what is now the heart of Silicon Valley but was then still a pleasant agricultural countryside full of orchards. His job researching aerodynamics and wind tunnel testing was interesting and enjoyable, he was engaged to the girl of his dreams, and life might have been good enough; then that idealistic itch to change the world took over, and he started his lifelong search to develop electronic systems that would augment the human intellect. He remembered the "Memex" that Vannevar Bush had described as an "enlarged intimate supplement to a person's memory" that can be consulted with "exceeding speed and flexibility." He felt a kinship for the vision and optimism that Bush communicated and set out to find his own way of realizing an equivalent ambition.

When I was half way through college, I was drafted for World War II, and had the good fortune to get accepted in a training program that the navy was running for electronic technicians, because the advent of radar and sonar had changed the aspects of navy problems immensely. They had a year-long program which taught me a lot of practical things about electronics and exposed me to the fact that the electronics of radar could put interesting things on the screen, so I just knew that if a computer could punch cards or send information to a printer, then electronics could put anything you want on the screen. If a radar set could respond to operators pushing buttons or cranking cranks, certainly the computer could! There was no question in my mind that the engineering for that would be feasible, so you could interact with a computer and see things on a screen. That intuitive certainty made me change my career path totally to go after it, but I had an extremely difficult time conveying that conviction to anybody else successfully for sixteen years or more.

His first step in that sixteen-year path of dogged determination was to leave his job and go to the graduate school at the University of California at Berkeley, where one of the earliest computers was being constructed. His fixed idea that people should be able to interact with computers directly did not fit with the prevailing view, so he started to get a reputation as an eccentric. Once he had his PhD, he started to look around for a place that would be more accepting of his vision than the UC Berkeley community. He talked to Bill Hewlett and David Packard, but although they were enthusiastic about his ideas, they were determined to focus on laboratory instruments rather than computers.

He finally landed a job at SRI, whose leaders were interested in researching possible uses for computers in both military and civilian applications. He started there at the end of 1957, soon after Sputnik had been launched, and the space race was getting under way. After learning the ropes at SRI for a year and a half, he started to lobby for the opportunity to start his own lab to experiment with new ways of creating and sharing knowledge by combining man and machine. His wish was granted when the U.S. Air Force Office of Scientific Research provided a small grant, and he settled down to the task of articulating his views.

"I wrote a paper that was published in 1962 called 'Augmenting the Human Intellect: A Conceptual Framework'[10] that steered my life from that point forward." In his paper he defined four areas in which human capabilities could be augmented:

1. **Artifacts**—physical objects designed to provide for human comfort, the manipulation of things or materials, and the manipulation of symbols.

2. **Language**—the way in which the individual classifies the picture of his world into the concepts that his mind uses to model that world, and the symbols that he attaches to those concepts and uses in consciously manipulating the concepts ("thinking").

3. **Methodology**—the methods, procedures, and strategies with which an individual organizes his goal-centered (problem-solving) activity.

4. **Training**—the conditioning needed by the individual to bring his skills in using augmentation means 1, 2, and 3 to the point where they are operationally effective.

The system we wish to improve can thus be visualized as comprising a trained human being, together with his artifacts, language, and methodology. The explicit new system we contemplate will involve as artifacts computers and computer-controlled information storage, information handling, and information display devices. The aspects of the conceptual framework that are discussed here are primarily those relating to the individual's ability to make significant use of such equipment in an integrated system.

In this short quote one can see the seeds of triumph and tragedy. The triumph is Doug's powerful vision of a complete system, where people and computers are engaged in a symbiotic relationship for human benefit, working cohesively as an integrated system. From this came the mouse and the other elements of interactive computing that he pioneered. The tragedy is that training is a necessary component of the system. He developed concepts for experts, and the pursuit of the highest capability drove the design criteria; it was therefore inevitable that training would be needed to reach the level of proficiency that would let people benefit from this capability. That proved a barrier to acceptance by ordinary people, and as computers became less expensive and more accessible, the barrier got in the way more and more.

But we are getting ahead of ourselves in the story. Let's go back to 1964 when, to the surprise of the SRI management, the Defense Advanced Research Projects Agency (DARPA) offered to fund the Augmentation Research Center (ARC) to the tune of half a million dollars a year, as well as providing a new time-sharing computer system, worth another million. Engelbart's energetic lobbying for funding and his flow of papers describing the high-level potential of automation had not been ignored by everyone, so now he had the resources he needed to move from theory to practice. He put together a stellar team of engineers for both hardware and software and set about developing NLS. Bill English was a partner for Doug in much of the work they did, leading the hardware development as the team grew to seventeen people. He joined ARC in 1964 and was the perfect complementary talent, having the technical ability to implement many of the ideas that were expressed by his boss as high-level abstractions. After four years of development, Doug took a chance to show the computer science community what he had been doing:

> For the Fall Joint Computer Conference in 1968, I stuck my neck out and proposed giving a real-time demonstration, if they would give me a whole hour-and-a-half conference session. We had a timesharing computer supporting our laboratory, and small five-inch diagonal screens that were high resolution, but worked by moving the beam around (vector graphics). We put a TV camera in front of the screen and used a TV display for a larger size image. We rented microwave links (from the Menlo Park civic auditorium) up to San Francisco, and borrowed an enormous video projector, three feet by two feet by six feet, to project onto a twenty-foot screen for the audience to see, using a very novel way of converting the video sweep into modulated light.
>
> Bill English, the genius engineer that I worked with (on the mouse also) managed to make all this work. He built a backstage mixing booth, where he could select from four video feeds, one from

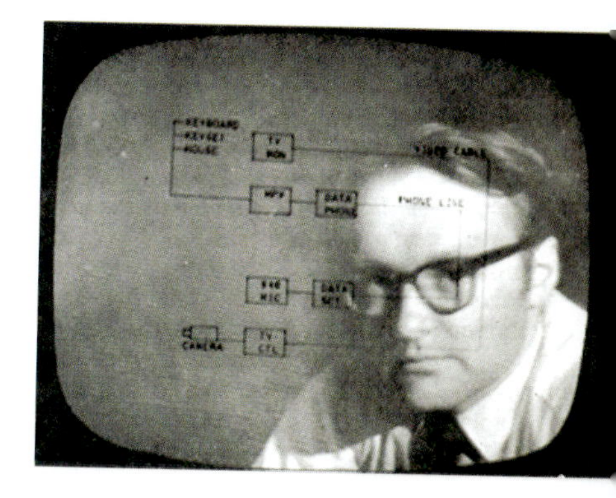

Bill English

each of the linked displays, one looking at me, and one overhead showing my hands working. He could select from the feeds so you could see a composite image in real time. He had experience doing the stage work for amateur plays, so he was the director. I had written a script for different people to come onto the stage, so he put a speaker in my ear to let me hear his cues: sometimes it was so distracting that I would fumble words.

We were able to show high-resolution links, graphics for schematic diagrams of what was going on, the faces of members of our team in the Menlo Park Laboratory, as well as the screens that they were looking at. We had cursors controlled by two people simultaneously interacting on the screen; one guy started buzzing at my cursor as if in a fight. The audience all stood up and applauded at the end of the demo.

This was the demo that changed the world. The computer science community moved from skepticism to standing ovation in an hour and a half, and the ideas of direct manipulation of a graphical user interface became lodged in the communal consciousness. This was not punched cards and Teletypes. It was something entirely different. Doug sat alone at a console in the middle of the stage, with the twenty-foot screen behind him showing the view from the video feeds. He was wearing a short-sleeved white shirt and a thin tie, with a microphone dangling on his chest, and a headset like an aircraft controller's. The overhead camera showed his right hand using a mouse, seen for the first time by most of the audience, to point and select with; a standard typewriter keyboard in the center and a five-key command pad under his left hand. In his calm but mesmerizing voice, he described and demonstrated an amazing array of functions on the NLS system. Words were manipulated with full-screen text editing, including automatic word wrap, corrections and insertions, formatting, and printing. Documents were planned and formatted using headings and subheadings. Links were demonstrated between one document and another, and collaboration between remote participants was demonstrated in real time:

One of the basic design principles that we started with was that you want to be able to talk about any other knowledge object out there.

> You want your links to point in high resolution, for example to a given word in another document, so you want a link addressing string that will let you get there. You also should be able to have optional alternative views.
>
> "I just want to see that one paragraph," I might say.
>
> "Okay! When I get there, I'd like to have certain terms highlighted."
>
> "Okay! I'd also like to know who else in my group has links to it, and what they say about it."
>
> I wrote in 1962 that we are all used to the idea that we can diagram sentences, based on the syntactical rules for a properly structured sentence. Now we might want to see a similar set of rules for the structure of an argument, so the computer has a graphic diagram of the argument with nodes connected to other arguments, expressions and statements, and meaningful links connecting them.

The demo was truly amazing, proving that interactive computing could be used for real-time manipulations of information in ways that very few people had imagined before. The assumption that high levels of training would always be acceptable did not get in the way until ordinary people tried to become users of NLS.

The demo also positioned Doug and his band at ARC to receive continuing funding for their research until 1975. His team grew to thirty-five people at one point. In 1969 they were connected to ARPAnet as one of the original nodes of the military research connected network, which eventually developed into the Internet. NLS grew in sophistication and content as time went on but remained essentially the same in concept. In 1971 a group of the best people at ARC, including Bill English, were tempted away from SRI by the opportunities at the new Xerox PARC, where so many exciting things seemed to be about to happen. This was the start of a slide for Doug Engelbart, during which his long-held dreams seemed to have less and less influence. You can feel the frustration behind his words as he describes the determined pursuit of his ideals and bemoans the success of the desktop:

> I've been pursuing for fifty years something that required higher and higher levels of capability. "How do you achieve capability," I was

Demo at Joint Computer Conference, 1968

> asking, "and when you achieve capability levels as high as you can get, then how do you reduce the learning costs in a reasonable way, but not try to set what I think of as an artificial level of learnability ease, and have to keep your capability enhancements within that level?"
>
> In the business world, I understand, that is awkward to try to do, because you are competing with other people for sales, and people will try computer interfaces that will strike customers as easy to use early on when they purchase them. I don't object to having a difference, but I feel that the world should recognize that there are really high levels of capability there to pursue that will be very important for society to have reached. That's been my pursuit.
>
> Many years ago it became clear to me that what you need to do is develop a basic software structure that will have file designs, capabilities, and properties that the very expert person could use. Then it is easy enough to support the beginner, or pedestrian user, by plugging a very simple user interface with simple operations on the front, but they can both work on the same materials.
>
> Yes, you can point with a GUI, I admit, but our system had an indefinite number of verbs and nouns that you could employ.
>
> There's no way that pointing and clicking at menus can compete with that. You wouldn't want to give someone directions by that limited means.

It is easy to understand the idea of going for the best, of catering to the expert user, and then providing a path to get there from a simple user interface designed for the beginner. In practice, however, this has proved to be the wrong way round, as it's not easy to get something right for the beginner when your design is already controlled by something that is difficult to learn. Look, for example, at the use of the five-key keypad for typing text. Like the stenographer's keyboard used for recording court proceedings, it enables impressive typing speeds when you have been trained long enough to become expert.

> Quite a few users adopted the chording key set that I built for myself. You could type any of the characters in the alphabet with one hand, and give commands with the three-button mouse in the other hand at the same time as pointing. This gave a much richer vocabulary and a much more compact way to evoke it than the GUI.

This is how the interactions were designed. On the mouse, one button was to click, another was called *command accept*, and the third was called *command delete*. If you wanted to delete a word, you would hit the middle button on the keypad, which was the letter *d*. It was *d* because it is the fourth letter in the alphabet, and this was a binary coding, 1, 2, 4, 8, 16. If it was the letter *f*, it was the sixth letter, so you'd hit the 2 and the 4 keys at the same time. Then you pointed at and clicked the beginning of the thing you wanted deleted, then you pointed at and clicked the end of the thing you wanted deleted, and if you hadn't made any mistakes, you would hit the *command accept* key on the mouse. It was *d*, point/click, point/click, *command accept*. If you made a mistake at any point, you would hit the *command delete* key to back you up one step.

That process was complicated to learn, and it took a long time for most people to memorize the binary-based, five-finger alphabet. Alternatively, they could invoke commands with keypad, or even the keyboard, the mouse for pointing, and a conventional keyboard in between for typing text. This would have been a very good solution for people with four hands, but is not as fast as the chorded keyboard and three-button mouse, as it takes longer to move your hands to and from the keyboard.

Doug Engelbart strives consistently toward a goal of the best possible performance, and his intuitions and insights have set the scene for the dominance of the mouse and the desktop. His influence has been limited by his decision to design for people as determined and proficient as he is himself, rather than for those who require an easy-to-use system.

Photo Author

Stu Card

At first meeting, Stu Card seems to be a serious person. He looks at you intensely from behind his glasses and speaks in bursts, often veering off on a new tangent of connected thought. You have to concentrate hard to keep pace with him, but when you do, the reward is immediate, as he has thought everything through and arrived at a beautifully balanced view of the whole picture. Occasionally his face breaks into an impish grin, and you see that there is a rich sense of humor under the seriousness. He joined Xerox PARC in 1974, with probably the first-ever degree in human-computer interaction. As a freshman in high school, Stu built his own telescope, grinding the mirror himself. His ambition to be an astronomer led him to study physics, but he was always very interested in computers. In the eighth grade he read navy circuit manuals about how to build flip-flops out of vacuum tubes. His first evening course in computing was to aim the college telescope in the direction defined by a computer program that he wrote. At graduate school at Carnegie Mellon University he had designed his own program, studying computer science, artificial intelligence, and cognitive psychology. After graduation he was offered three jobs; PARC was the most interesting, had the highest salary, and was in California, so it was an easy decision. Doug Engelbart and Bill English had brought the mouse to PARC from SRI, and Stu was assigned to help with the experiments that allowed them to understand the underlying science of the performance of input devices.

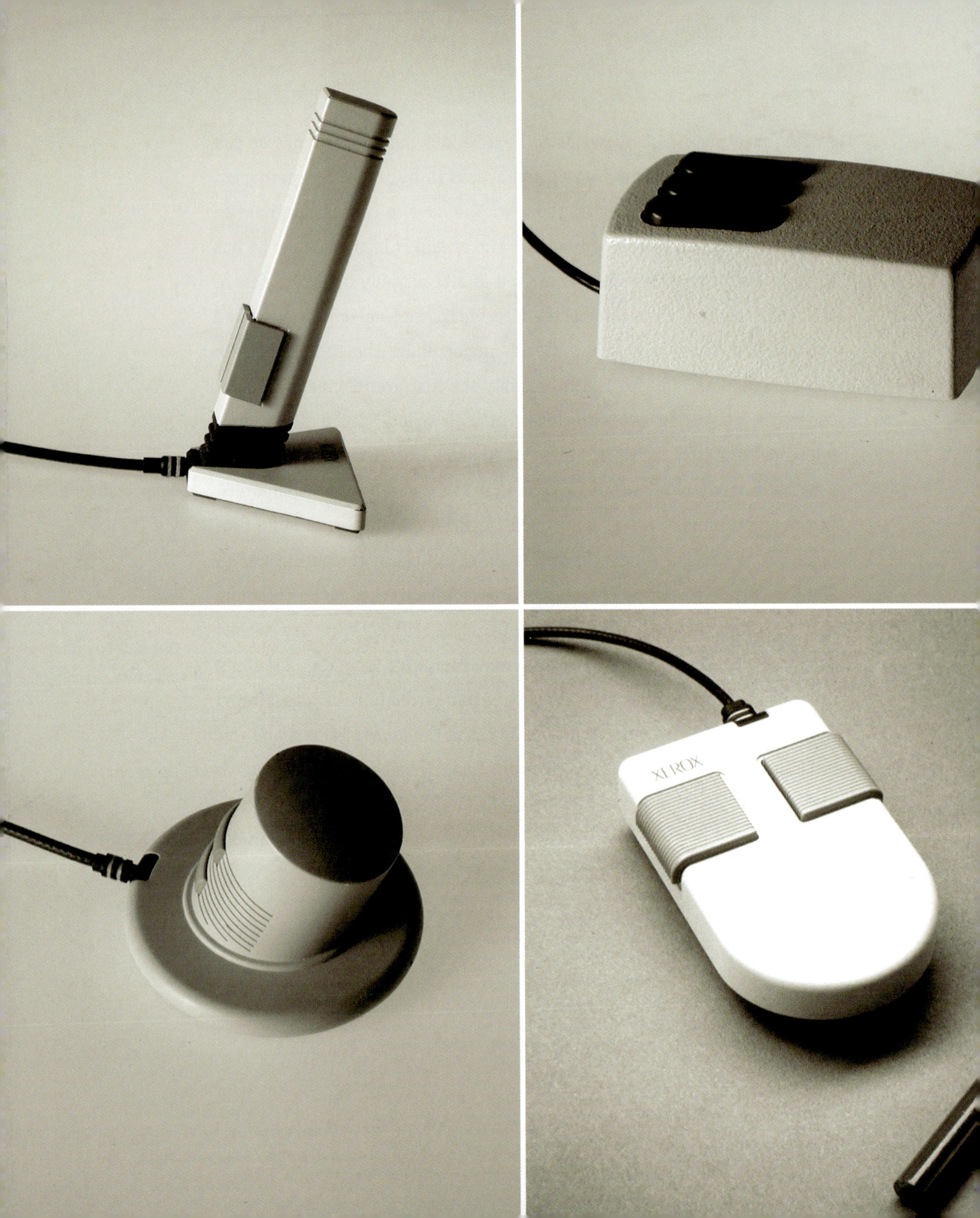
XEROX

Stu Card

A Supporting Science

■ Xerox mice; *clockwise from top right:* existing concept 1—flat concept 2—puck concept 3—pen

When Stu joined PARC in 1974, he set out to invent a supporting science for the design of human-computer interactions. This made his position somewhat different from the other researchers. There had been several attempts to develop similar sciences, for example human factors, but that focused too much on the evaluative side, waiting until the structure of the design was already complete and then measuring the result. Stu was more interested in contributing to the design process at the beginning, when the significant choices were still in flux and the science would be able to influence the outcome before much work was complete:

> Newell, who was a consultant at PARC at the time, wanted to try to do a kind of applied psychology. The idea was that computer science is a very asymmetrical discipline. If you take things like time-shared operating systems or programming languages, there is obviously a computer part to them, like how you parse them and do the compiling. There is also obviously a human part; what kind of languages can people program most easily, and what kind of errors do

they make, and how can you make them more efficient? All of the work that had been done in computer science was on the computer side and none on the applied psychology side. Information processing psychology showed real promise as a theory, but there were problems with psychology; it tends to be faddish and impractical and hard to build on.

The idea was that any science worth its salt should have practical applications, allowing you to test the theory in a more pragmatic context than a journal article. It would really have to work, as you were not immune to the hostile reactions of the people that you were trying to do this for. It would be difficult to do this in a university, because universities, especially psychology departments, would not tolerate applied work. In order to do basic research, you had to do it in a place like PARC.

"Design is where all of the action is!" was one of our slogans.

If this was going to work at all, you had to have something that could be used as you were designing. This did not mean that you could do all of design from science. You could have the equivalent role to that of structural engineering in relation to architecture. You could have a technical discipline that would support the design activity. In fact, we had a particularly concrete notion of what kind of supporting science this would be; task analysis, approximation, and calculation. The idea was that you would be able to look at a situation, make zero parameter computations about it, and then say things about what would happen in that situation without running full experiments to see, rather with just occasional experiments to spot check. The idea was that this would give you lots of insight that it would otherwise be hard to have gotten.

"Don't bug us for ten years," we said, "and at the end we'll deliver this to you."

The wonderful thing about PARC was that they said, "Sure." We had to make arguments up front, but once they were made, we got ten years to do this. I've always appreciated the freedom that I got to do this at PARC.

To think that design is where all the action is was very forward-looking at that time, when innovation was usually thought to come from genius or pure scientific research. The core skills of design are synthesis, understanding people, and iterative prototyping. Even now, the idea that these skills are central to innovation is not very widely accepted, but you will see evidence of their significance again and again throughout this book. The unique contribution that Stu Card made was to create a supporting science, connecting the theoretical underpinnings of research to the pragmatic synthesis of design.

Bill English was Stu's first boss at PARC. Bill and Doug Englebart had coinvented the mouse when they were at SRI, with Doug providing the idea and Bill the engineering development and prototyping. A large part of English's group had come over to PARC from SRI. They wanted to do more experiments on the mouse to determine whether it or some other device was really the better one. There were devices like rate-controlled isometric joysticks, almost identical to the one in the IBM ThinkPad keyboard today; there were various kinds of trackballs; and there were many versions of buttons and keys. Stu remembers the experiments:

> English was pretty busy, so I agreed to help him do the experiments. He set up the usual kind of A-versus-B experiments between devices, but the problem with them was that he did not really know why one was better than the other, as the results varied when you changed the context. Since we were trying to do the science of this stuff, I modeled each one of the devices so that I had the empirical differences between them, and I was trying to figure out how numerically to account for why those differences occurred. The most interesting model was the model of the mouse.
>
> Fitts's[11] law says that the time to point goes up as the log of the ratio between the distance and the size of the target. What's interesting about this law is that the slope of that curve is about ten bits per second, which is about what had been measured for just moving the hand alone without a device. What's interesting about that is that the limitation of the device is not then in the device itself, but in the eye-hand coordination system of the human. What that meant was that the device was nearly optimal. The hand was showing through the machine instead of operating the machine at a loss, and so if you were to introduce this onto the market, nobody would be likely to come up with another device to beat you. We could know this theoretically once we had this one empirical fact.

Stu went down to El Segundo to meet the Xerox engineers who were trying to invent a pointing device for the office system

- Xerox Alto
- Xerox Star
- Xerox Star mouse

that was planned. They resisted the idea of something outside the normal cabinet full of standard electronic racks that needed a work surface and a connection cable and would have to be packaged separately. Stu presented the results of his tests, with a lot of interruptions.

"Why didn't you run it this way?"

"Who were your subjects?"

"Why didn't you have eighty-year-old grandmothers try it?"

There was some flack and hostility, but when Stu gave his theoretical explanation of his supporting science, the room fell silent and he won the day. Xerox put a mouse on the market, and what Stu had predicted was true. It is still the most successful pointing device to this day.

In introducing the Star system, which was the next step after the Alto toward commercialization, there was a certain circuit in the machine, and Stu was asked whether the circuit would be fast enough to track the mouse. If they had to make it faster, they would have to rip out the existing circuit and put in a more expensive one. Stu discussed this over lunch one day with a colleague, and because he had a theory of the mouse he was able to whip out a napkin and make a calculation, which indicated that the circuit was going to be too slow. He went into the laboratory and took a little video of a mocked up task to check the theoretical curve, and that confirmed the problem, so they had to change to the more expensive circuit. It was possible to arrive at this definitive result four hours from the initial formulation of the problem because there was a theory. There was no need to run lots of user experiments and counterbalance them and do the analysis. In a design context you want to very rapidly say, "I believe it should be thus because of such a thing," and then do a little checking to be sure that you didn't leave something out.

Stu demonstrated that you could use the same theory to understand how to develop a better pointing device:

> Just as we showed the advantages of the mouse, you could use the same theory to show that you could beat the mouse. The mouse was optimum, but it was based on movements of the wrist. If you looked at Langoff's thesis, he had measured Fitts's law slopes for different

sets of muscles. In particular, when you put the fingers together you can maybe double the bandwidth.

"That's where you want to put your transducers!" I said.

If you see these maps of the motor cortex and how much of it is devoted to different sets of muscles, you want to put you transducer in an area that is covered by a large volume of motor cortex. You could probably do one with the tongue too, because there's a lot of space devoted to that. That's another example of how having some notion of the theory of this thing gives you some structuring of the design space.

In the mid eighties ID TWO[12] was engaged by Xerox to design the enclosures for a new workstation and wanted to push the design of the mouse farther. Stu Card was able to help the designers think about new concepts for pointing devices. He demonstrated one idea with a pencil stuck onto an eraser, to make it easier to grasp when you are only seeing it out of the corner of you eye. He believed that it had become feasible to build a mouse like this because of the purely optical mouse that had been developed at PARC by this time. The whole mouse was on a chip, so most of the case was empty, and that meant that you could shape the casework to be optimal to the shape of the hand, instead of needing to make it big enough to cover the mechanism.

As soon as Stu explained how to structure the design space from his theory, the designers were able to quickly create alternative designs for pointing devices. They produced three models, based on progressively more radical assumptions. One was a conventional mouse that was flatter and more elegant, the next was a puck shape, like a top hat of about an inch diameter, with a skirt at the base for the fingers to rest on. The most radical one was the penlike device with a weighted base, causing it to stand upright on the desk, giving form to Stu's idea of the pencil stuck into the eraser. At the end of the project Stu concluded:

> This was my ideal model of how the supporting science could work. It required good designers to actually do the design, but what we could do was help structure the design space so that the movement through that design space was much more rapid. The science didn't design the mouse, but it provided the constraints to do it.

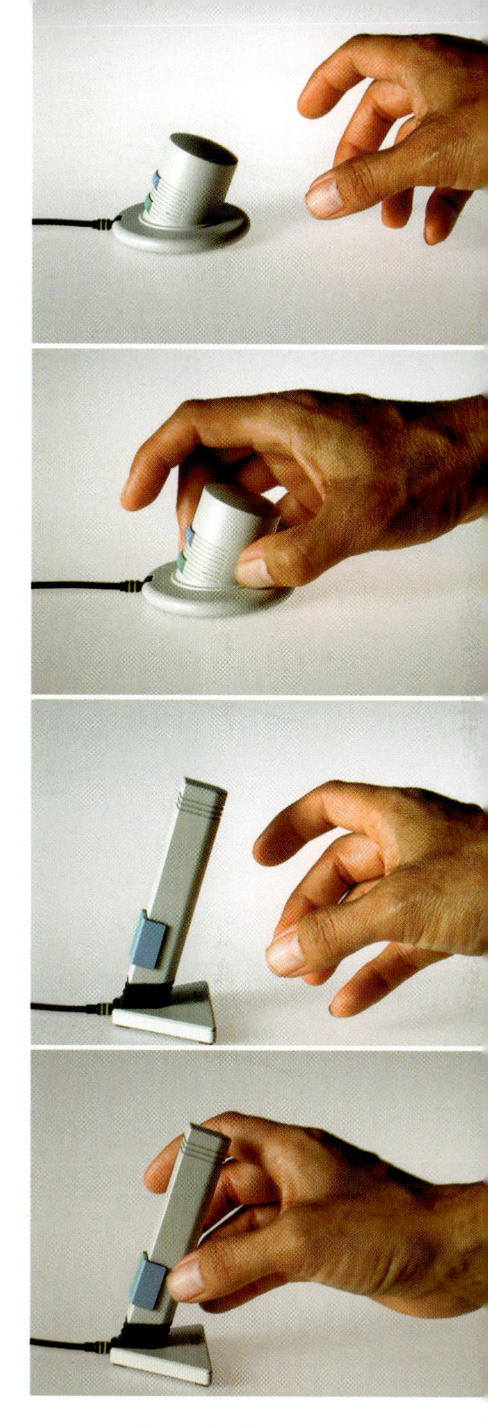

Xerox puck and pen mouse concept designs

Tim Mott

Tim Mott created the concept of "guided fantasies" to learn about user needs, and was one of the very first people to apply rigorous user testing to the design of user interfaces. He studied computer science at Manchester University in England in the sixties and found a job with a publishing company called Ginn, near Boston, that was owned by Xerox. This led him to work with the researchers at Xerox PARC, and he collaborated with Larry Tesler to design a publishing system that included a new desktop metaphor; together they invented a user-centered design process. In the late seventies he became more interested in designing processes for management and business and honed his management skills working for Versatec, another Xerox subsidiary that manufactured electrostatic printers and plotters. In 1982 he cofounded Electronic Arts (EA) and set about building a set of processes to enable the creation and production of really rich interactive entertainment experiences—as soon as the supporting hardware was available. From the very beginning, they built the company with people who were just crazy about games. Once EA was successful, Tim went on to run a small company called Macromind, whose founders had invented a user interface design tool called Director, leading the company to expand into multimedia and become Macromedia. He was a founding investor in Audible, setting the precedent for the MP3 players that came later, and moving from "Books on tape" to the spoken word Web site that supports public radio. He is a pilot, flying jets as well as the single-engine back-country plane that he loves to fly over wild mountain scenery.

Tim Mott

Tim put the editors in front of a display with a keyboard and a mouse. Nothing was on the display and no programs were running, but he asked them if they could walk him through the process, imagining what it would be like to use that hardware to edit. This was 1974, before word processors, so they were using typewriters, pencils, and erasers.

■ Tim Mott in 1974

Guided Fantasy

GINN WAS ONE of several companies in the publishing industry that Xerox acquired around 1970. They were based in Lexington, Massachusetts, in one of the first buildings equipped with office systems furniture from Herman Miller. When the Ginn management team found out how their contribution to Xerox corporate finance was being spent, they put in a request:

> We're taxed for your research center; every division of Xerox has to pay money to support Xerox PARC research, and we want something back! What are you going to do for us?

This challenge eventually reached Bill English, who assigned the task of developing a publishing system for them to Larry Tesler. Larry started working with Ginn and writing specifications for their system and suggested that they hire somebody; they could send the new person to PARC for a year or so to work on the design of the new product. As it moved from design to implementation, he could write some of the code and then return to Ginn to provide support. They found Tim Mott at Oberlin College, where he was working on the help desk for a mainframe. Larry remembers interviewing Tim:

> When we talked to him, we realized that this was the perfect guy; he writes good code, he's really fast, he understands about usability because he helps customers all the time, he loves doing support and he loves programming, and he thinks it's an interesting problem. We hired Tim Mott, and we got ten times more than we bargained for.

Tim spent a little time at Ginn, observed how they worked, started thinking about how to make it easier for the publishing team to get their job done, and then flew out to PARC. He remembers his first encounter with POLOS (PARC On Line Office System):

> When I got out there, what I found was that, in my judgment at any rate, the system was completely unusable by anyone other than the people who built it. Their background was in building editing systems and design systems for themselves and for other computer professionals, and at least in my judgment it just wasn't going to be usable by editors and graphic designers who worked in a publishing company, so a month after getting to Palo Alto, I wrote a letter of resignation to the executive editor back in Boston, saying, "This is not a project that you should be doing." That letter found its way to Bob Taylor, who was running the computer science lab at the time. I spent some time with Bob, and he said, "Why don't you figure out what it is that we should be doing then?"

That was a challenge that Tim couldn't resist, so he teamed up with Larry Tesler, and together they set about discovering what the people who worked at Ginn really needed. Tim went back to Lexington and put the editors in front of a display with a keyboard and a mouse. Nothing was on the display and no programs were running, but he asked them if they could walk him through the process, imagining what it would be like to use that hardware to edit. This was 1974, before word processors, so they were using typewriters, pencils, and erasers. He used the "guided fantasy" technique that Larry had told him about, explaining that the mouse could be used to position a pointer on the screen and that the text would be on the screen. The editors described the process that they used at that time with paper and pencil. Together they imagined typing in the text and creating a manuscript, and then editing that manuscript using the mouse and keyboard in the same way that they would use a pencil.

The Alto and the POLOS in 1974 both had mice on them based on the Engelbart mouse developed at SRI, and the Alto display was already a bitmap display, but the design of editing programs was still based on the prior generation of character displays; no one had really thought about how to use the characteristics of the bitmap display to create a more flexible editing environment.

None of the text editors that had been designed for computers up to that point had a space between characters. They were based on character matrix displays that didn't allow for an editing mark to be placed between the character cells. If you wanted to mark an insertion point in the text, you either selected the character before where you wanted to add the new text, and said *append*, or you selected the character afterwards and said *insert*. Tim explains the difficulty that this caused:

> That was one of the first things that I got from working with these editors. One of the concepts that they worked with was the space between characters, or the space between words.
>
> "I want to use the mouse and put this insertion point or this caret between these two characters, and then I just want to type in the new text," they said.
>
> When it came to deleting text, they talked about wanting to strike through it, just like they would with a pencil. They wanted to use the mouse to draw through the text. Up until that point, the way that a span of text had been selected was to mark the beginning point, and mark the end point and say "select." No one had actually used a mouse to draw through text.
>
> These techniques that we see in all the word processing programs today came directly from working with people who spent their entire lives editing text and asking them, "How do you want to do that?" Once Larry and I hit on this idea of having people talk about how they would want to do the work, the design itself became pretty simple. There was a new design methodology that came out of it. We talked about the design process as one that began with building a conceptual model that the user had today.

The Alto didn't have a user interface; rather, it came with a toolbox. You could build any kind of program you wanted, based on this very flexible architecture, and people started building applications on it. The Smalltalk system incorporated menus and editing techniques. There was a graphics program that William Newman built called Markup and a paint program that Bob Flegal created—applications started springing up.

Tim and Larry took the code base from Bravo,[13] a text editor that already existed at PARC, and put a completely different user interface on top of it. They called their design "Gypsy"; the implementation program was straightforward, but they worked hard. They shared one Alto between them, working fourteen-hour shifts so that they would overlap by an hour at both ends and could tell each other what they had done. In this way they could work on the same code around the clock and could protect their access to the computer, as there were only four Altos at PARC when they started.

Using "drag-through" selection for text was not the only innovation that came out of the work on Gypsy. The origin of the cut-and-paste metaphor is described by Larry in his interview, as is Tim's idea for double-clicking the mouse. There was also the first dialog box; this was a little bar with a place for typing commands such as *Find*. It was more like a noniconic toolbar of today, as in Apple's Safari browser.

Gypsy had a file directory system with versions and drafts, not just a list of files. You could have versions of the document and drafts of the version; it remembered them all and organized them all for you. It had bold, italic, and underline—used very much like they are today. You could select something by dragging through it or clicking the two ends, and do the equivalent of *Control b* for bold. They changed the name of the control key to *look* with a paper label, so you said *look b* for bold.

Larry had come up with the "guided fantasy" technique in 1973, and he and Tim developed other user-centered methods with frequent usability testing in the fall of 1974 and the spring of 1975; their work really caught the imagination of the people in the PARC community. In the spring of 1975 Tim took the text-

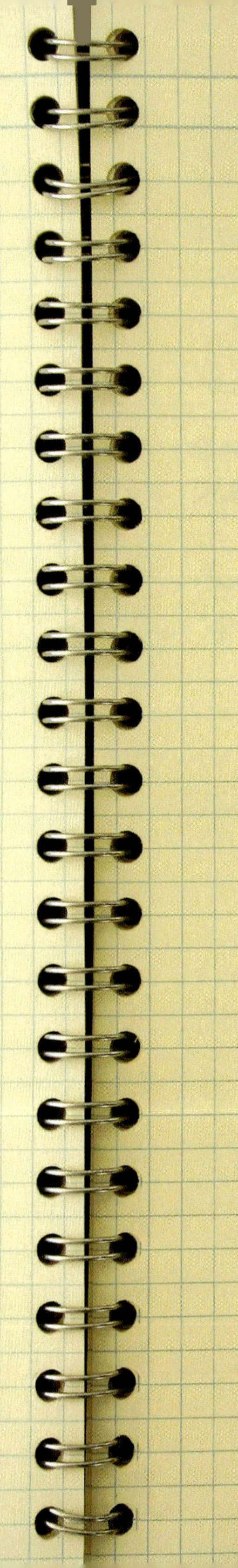

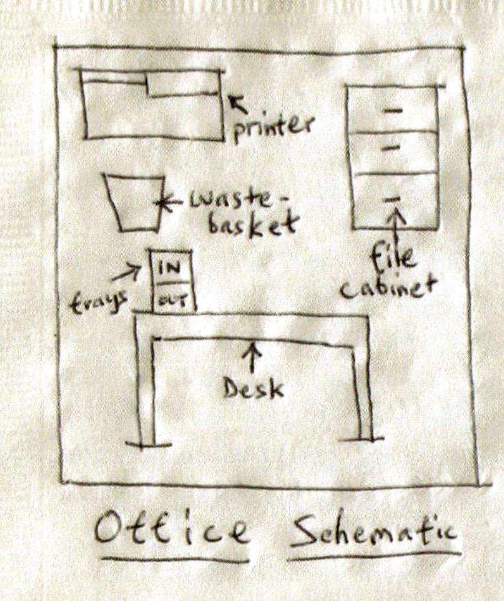

PRINT, FILE, DELETE, MAIL

↓

all are inter-doc actions

—‖—

INTRA-DOC we Cut & Paste
physical metaphor
whats analog for
INTER-DOC ??

↓

Grab & Move !!!

editing program back to Lexington to try it out with the people at Ginn. For the first test he picked the most senior editor, figuring that, since she was the most entrenched both in her work habits and the company, if he could win her over, it would be smooth sailing from then on. After the first day she said, "You know, I think the quality of my work will be better going forward, because it's just so much easier to edit with this than it is with a typewriter and a pencil!" The approach had proved itself!

The Desktop (Office) Metaphor

In parallel with completing the text editor, Tim and Larry were pretty far along in designing a page layout system for graphic designers. They were still struggling with the issue of how to think about the user interface for documents and files, and the actions that take place on an entire document, rather than on the pages or text within a document. Tim describes his moment of inspiration:

■ Tim Mott's reconstruction of his sketch on the bar napkin

Photo Author

> I was in a bar late one afternoon waiting for a friend, doodling on a bar napkin and thinking about this problem. I was just obsessed with this design at the time; I was just consumed by it. I was thinking about what happens in an office. Someone's got a document and they want to file it, so they walk over to the file cabinet and put it in the file cabinet; or if they want to make a copy of it, they walk over to the copier and they make a copy of it; or they want to throw it away, so they reach under their desk and throw it in the trash can.
>
> I'm sitting there thinking about this and I'm doodling. What ended up on the bar napkin was what Larry and I called the "Office Schematic." It was a set of icons for a file cabinet, and a copier, or a printer in this case, and a trash can. The metaphor was that entire documents could be grabbed by the mouse and moved around on the screen. We didn't think about it as a desktop, we thought about it as moving these documents around an office. They could be dropped into a file cabinet, or they could be dropped onto a printer, or they could be dropped into a trashcan.

> The desktop was part of the design, and on it there were those things that you might normally find on a desktop like a calendar, a clock, and baskets for incoming and outgoing mail; the notion was that we would be able to use that as the controlling mechanism for electronic mail.

When Larry heard about the idea and saw the bar napkin, he showed Tim the illustrations from "Pygmalion,"[14] Dave Canfield Smith's thesis. He said that people had tried to implement similar designs before, but they had always attempted to do very complex, three dimensional, true-to-life simulations, as opposed to just a simple two-dimensional iconic representation. The simplicity of the representation was the breakthrough! Somewhere in one of Tim's notebooks in Xerox there is a bar napkin covered in the doodle of his office metaphor, complete with a desktop and trash can.

Photo Author

Larry Tesler

When he was at Apple, Larry Tesler had a license plate saying "NO MODES," emphasizing his passion for designing software that would be simple and easy to use. He had been writing code since he was in high school and worked at the computer center at Stanford while studying there in the early '60s. He founded his own company to offer programming services while he was in his junior year and soon discovered that his customers had a different way of thinking from the software engineers in the Computer Science Department. He realized that the best way to design the software was with participation from the customer, and he developed techniques for watching how people did things and designing software that allowed people to use new technology in familiar ways. He learned to create prototypes rapidly and to test them with the intended users early and often. After working at the Stanford Artificial Intelligence Laboratory, he went to Xerox PARC in 1973 in time to be a key player in the development of the desktop and desktop publishing. In 1980 he moved to Apple, where he was core to the design of Lisa. He invented cut-and-paste and editable dialog boxes, and he designed the Smalltalk browser. He simplified the use of the mouse by reducing the controls to a single button. He insists on truth and accuracy and is willing to challenge anybody's assumptions about the best way to do things, always thinking from basic principles. After a three-year stint at Amazon, running the usability and market research groups, he is now helping Yahoo improve the design of their online interactions, as VP of user experience and design.

HOW DO I GET
MONTH
YEAR
NOMODES
OUT OF THIS MODE?

INSERT
FIND
FEB
CA 96
H 1920079
NOMODES
REPLACE
FILE NAME

Larry Tesler

"Iconic naming systems will be explored. A picture of a room full of cabinets with drawers and file folders is one approach to a spatial filing system."

From a white paper called OGDEN (Overly General Display Environment for Non-programmers), by Larry Tesler and Jeff Rulifson

Participatory Design

■ Larry Tesler's "No Modes" license plates, front and rear

Photo Author

LARRY WAS QUICK to realize the value of participatory design and usability testing. His first lesson occurred while he was still studying at Stanford, when he was asked to get involved with a project to organize the "card stunts" at football games and to automate the production of instruction cards. At halftime during the football game, when the students flipped up the cards, instead of hand-written instructions they would be computer-generated. Students from the Computer Science Department had already written a programming language on punch cards, with all numeric commands. An art student would draw polygons to represent the shapes and colors and describe an animation, and then a computer science student would code all the instructions to generate the instructions and print out the cards. Finally the cards would be torn along perforations and set out on the seats. Larry was persuaded to take over the coding role.

"The trouble is that the art students have a great deal of difficulty with this language, so you end up coding all the stunts," he was warned; "if you don't want to code all the stunts, you better find a way of making it easier to use!"

He started talking with the art students and trying to figure out what they wanted. It was a different world! Over the next three years, he reworked this language several times, until even the art students could use it.

In 1963, when he started a software consulting business in parallel with his studies, he developed a rapport with users and worked out how to ask them the right questions, so that he could make programs they could use. He did not have to run the software for them; they could do it themselves. One of the programs he wrote was a room-scheduling program for the Stanford Psychiatry Department. They were trying to arrange for patients who came in to get assigned to rooms with doctors. They had scheduling problems because appointments overlapped, and rooms had to be used at certain times during the week for other things.

■ Larry Tesler at Stanford, 1961

> One of the psychiatrists and I designed it together. That worked out really well, as they needed no help from me at all to use this. That's when I realized that the best way to design the software is with the customer, which is now called participatory design. With the art students and the card stunts, I would watch how they used it and see when they got confused. That was my first experience with what we call usability tests today, observing people and seeing what the problem was and then going and fixing it, and realizing that I could make something simpler. That was really the beginning of my interest in usability.

Since 1995, when he retired from General Magic, Bill Atkinson has been pursuing his passion for nature photography full-time. The basement of his home in the hills above Silicon Valley is full of sophisticated equipment for photography and color printing. He has published a book[4] of photographs of polished slices of rock that glow with the most amazingly vivid colors, in designs as rich as any Kandinsky. His love of perfection comes across in every detail of this work. He has researched and published color profiles for accurate printing; he has taught the art of printing to the most famous nature photographers in the world; and he has photographed the very best samples of rocks from the collections of gem and mineral specialists. In 1978 Bill was a graduate student in neuroscience at the University of Washington when he got a call from Apple, suggesting that he visit. Steve Jobs persuaded him to join, saying, "If you want to make a dent in the world, you have to come to the place where it's happening!" He was hired as the "Application Software Department," and went on to lead the development of the software for Lisa and Macintosh, and to design MacPaint and HyperCard. He was a leader and inspirational designer at Apple for twelve years, during which time Apple grew from thirty people to fifteen thousand. In 1990 he branched out with two friends to found General Magic, based on a notion called Telecards, "Little electronic postcards that would fly through the air and, like magic, land in a loved one's pocket." Bill Atkinson designed several of the interactions that define the desktop.

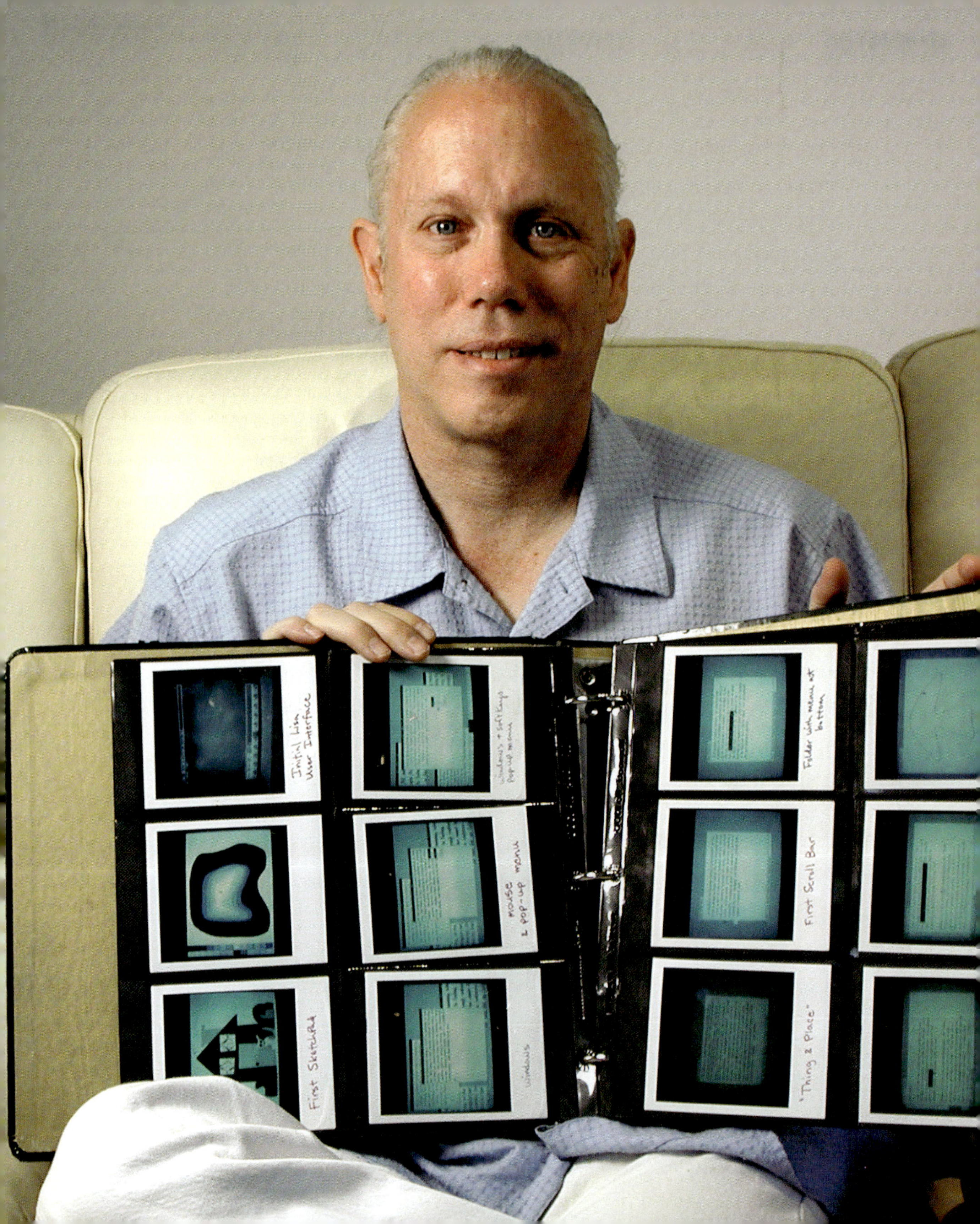
Initial Lisa User Interface
Windows + Soft Keys Pop-up menu
Folder with menu at bottom
mouse & pop-up menu
First Scroll Bar
First SketchPad
Windows
'Thing & Place'

Bill Atkinson

Apple Lisa

■ Bill Atkinson holding his file of Polaroid photographs, which he used to document the interaction design of the Apple Lisa

Photo Author

As a boy, Bill was fascinated by chemistry. He combined different ingredients to make homemade gunpowder and rigorously tested for the optimum mix to power his skyrockets. This passion for research and experiment pushed him toward a career in neurochemistry. As he studied the human brain, the other side of his own brain was always engaged with taking beautiful photographs and making exquisite prints. Perhaps that dichotomy was a sign of his design talent, as he was habituated to both problem solving and aesthetic values.

His undergraduate studies in chemistry were at UC San Diego, and that's where he met Jef Raskin, whose book *The Humane Interface*[5] makes you think hard about the underlying concepts behind today's user interfaces. Bill describes Jef:

> Jef Raskin was a very brilliant and very independent-thinking professor. I remember one time he got in trouble with the campus computing center because he used his computing budget to buy a minicomputer, terminals, and bean bags for his students. This was at

Apple II graphics for Pascal

"#$%&'()*+,-./0123456789:;<=>?
@ABCDEFGHIJKLMNOPQRSTUVWXYZ[\]^_
`abcdefghijklmnopqrstuvwxyz{|}~

First Characters on Lisa

LISA DISPLAY SYSTEM

SECOND DRAFT

OCTOBER 8, 1979

The LISA display screen is a bitmapped CRT display with 356 scan lines of 720 dots each. Each dot can be set or cleared to produce a white or black dot. Lines, characters, and solid areas can be displayed by setting and clearing the appropriate bits.

This straightforward bitmap approach allows considerably more flexibility than could be obtained with a hardware character generator. Regular, boldface, and italic characters of different styles and sizes can be placed anywhere on the screen, with fixed or proportional spacing. The bitmap representation allows lines, solid areas, and arbitrary designs and logos to be mixed with the text. Forms, charts, and graphs can take advantage of these display capabilities to simplify the human interface to application programs.

The LISA display system provides a core set of routines used by all programs which access the screen. These routines have two main purposes. First, they actually draw lines and characters, scroll and move blocks of memory. Secondly, the display routines organize the screen and other bitmap images into structured logical units called windows.

Hand-Built Font Proportional Spacing

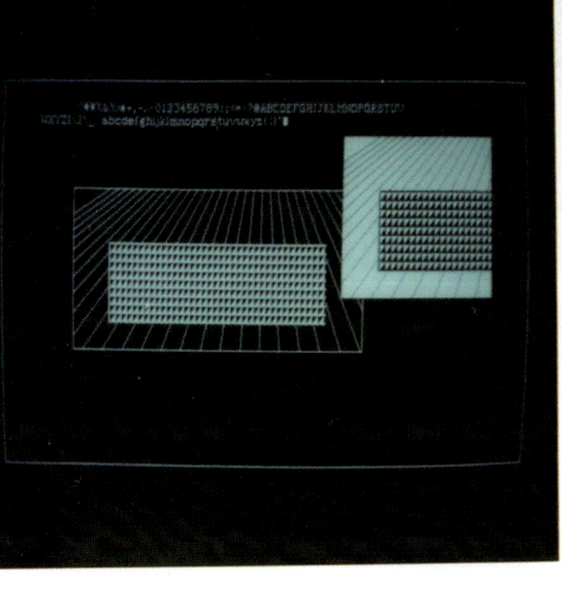

Text, Lines, Patterns

a time when computer science students had to punch cards, submit a deck to the mainframe operators, and come back the next day to find out what mistakes they'd made. Jef was always thinking in terms of user interface and making things more humane for people. I credit him as giving me my interest in how to make things more humane. Later he was the one who invited me to Apple Computer and got me started there.

Bill picked up programming and computer science as a peripheral aspect of his studies, but his habitual thoroughness pushed him to master both the science and the black arts of writing code for software. Jef Raskin saw the latent design talent in his young student and thought of him when Apple needed some help in designing application software; in those early days at Apple, software was thought of as a necessary evil to sell the hardware products. When Bill got there, at first he brought together and cleaned up user-contributed software—little basic programs for calculation, games, and so on. The first major project that he did for Apple was porting over the Pascal system from UC San Diego to the Apple II.

His big opportunity came when he was given responsibility for leading the design of the graphics and user interface for Lisa, writing the QuickDraw graphics routines that all the applications used and designing the user interface. He talks about his process:

■ Polaroids of Apple II graphics for Pascal and early Lisa development on dark background

Photos
Bill Atkinson

In the user interface design, a lot of it was by trial and error. We tried different things and found out what did and didn't work. A lot of it was empirically determined. I kept bringing new stuff in and saying, "What about this?" and Larry would set up tests so that different people could try it.

For example, if you have a scroll bar, which way should the arrows go, and where should they be? When you scroll toward the bottom of a document, the document moves up, so there's some reason to think of a down arrow, and some reason to think of an up arrow. A really good question to ask is, "What do people expect? When people see an arrow, which way do they think it will move?"

What I found mattered much more than whether the arrow went down or up was where the arrow was; if the arrow was at the top, they expected to see more of what was above, whereas if it was at the bottom, they expected to see more of what was below.

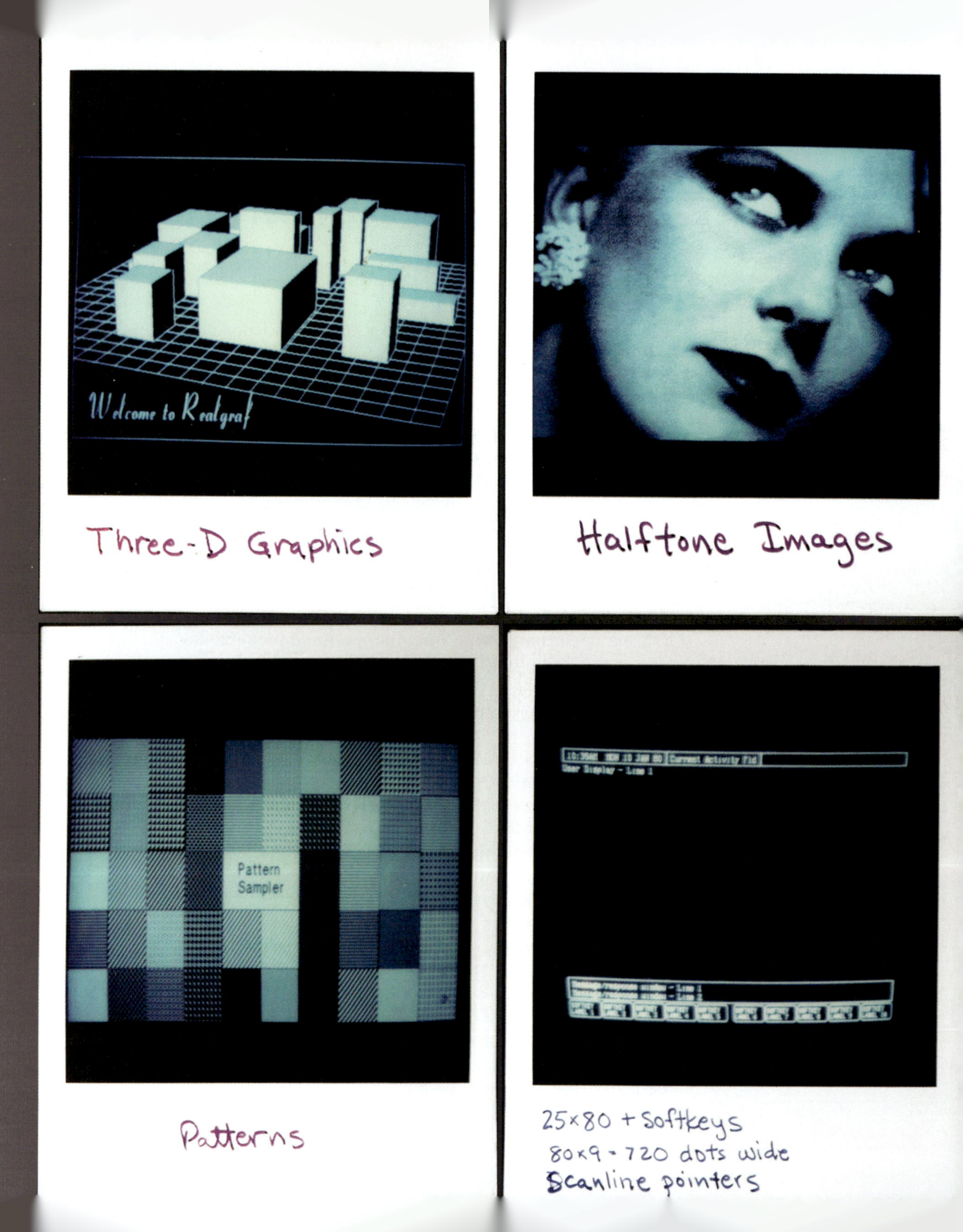

Welcome to Realgraf
Three-D Graphics
Halftone Images
Pattern
Sampler
Patterns
25×80 + Softkeys
80×9 = 720 dots wide
Scanline pointers

Bill also had to defend the value and importance of user interface issues against the pressures of cost and technology limitations. For example, the screen initially had a black background, with labels for soft-keys at the bottom of the screen. The black background was different from the printed version on white paper and could not obey the WYSIWYG (What You See Is What You Get) maxim, so Bill insisted in changing to a white background. The engineers complained like crazy, saying that it would draw more power and burn out the tube faster, but he said, "Get over it! Find a way around it."

Lisa was designed for an office worker, whereas the Mac was aimed at a fourteen-year-old boy. The investment that Xerox had made in Apple and the agreement to use the mouse fueled the legend of Apple stealing from PARC. Bill Atkinson is irritated by this:

> The people at Xerox had done some wonderful work on using a mouse and using windows, and that was work that presaged what we did at Apple. What we did was not just to replicate that, but to start anew with a fresh research project, asking the question, "What is the best user interface for this whole thing?" We tried a lot of things. We didn't just take what they had done; in fact, many of the things that we did they didn't have at all.
>
> I actually got to go to Xerox PARC for one and a half hours; that's the whole time I've ever been at Xerox PARC. There was a whole lot of original research done at Apple on the user interface design, and I was in the center of that. I wasn't the only person doing the design, but I was sort of lead, and I kept throwing up ideas and seeing which ones worked and which ones didn't. What we saw when we went there for that hour and a half was the Xerox Alto, their older system, and it was running Smalltalk. We didn't get to see their Star, which I think was later.

- Polaroids of early Lisa design concepts for graphics, soft-keys

Photos
Bill Atkinson

Larry Tesler is more sanguine, as he had actually come over from PARC:

> The people who had come from Xerox had a rule that we could not ever disclose what we had done at Xerox. When I got there, I asked them how this worked.

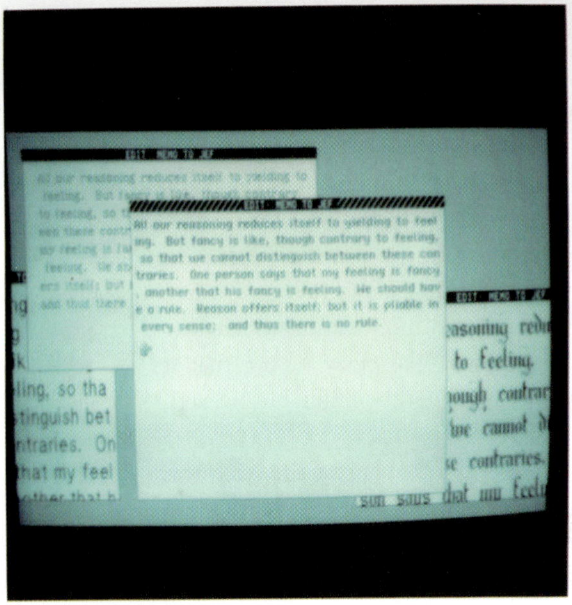

windows

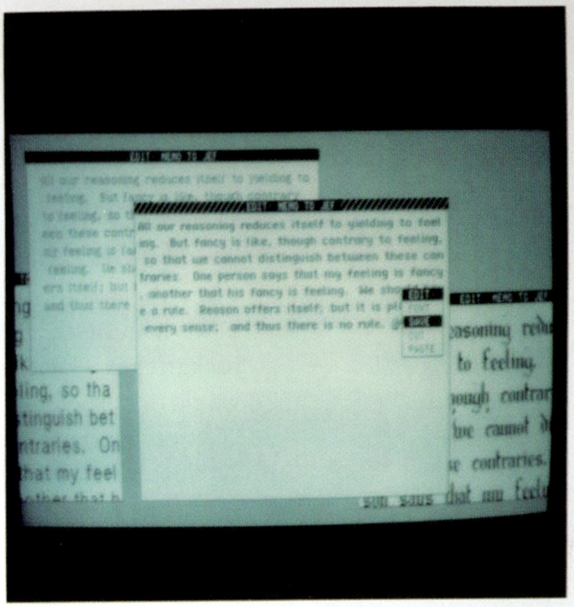

mouse
& pop-up menu

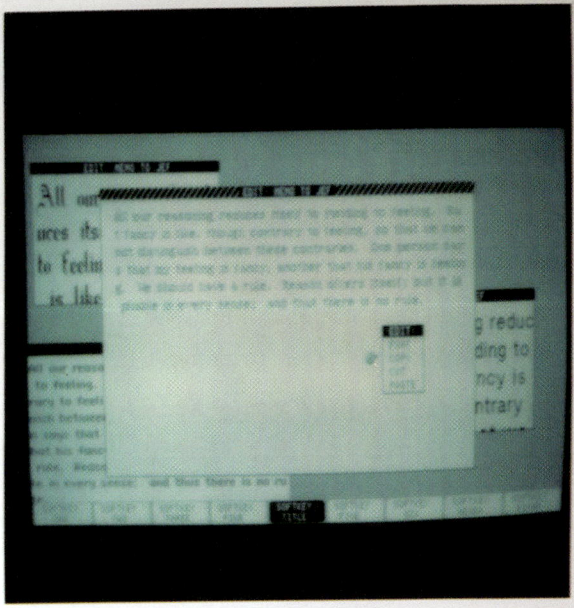

windows + soft Keys
Pop-up menu

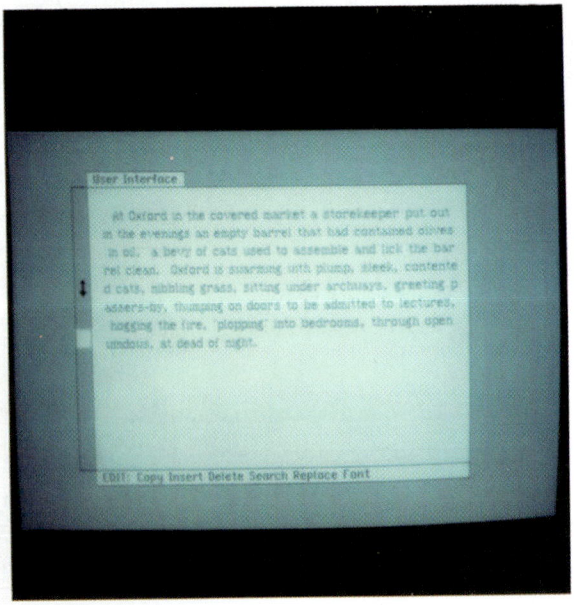

First Scroll Bar

"We never tell them anything that's in a Xerox product that is secret," they said, "but we just let the discussion go, and encourage certain directions, and discourage other directions. We just help them not to spend a lot of time on the dead ends, and encourage them to explore the good stuff. What's funny is that they usually come up with a totally different way to do it that's actually better."

That's why the Lisa looks quite different from the Xerox Star. Very few people working on Lisa had ever seen the Xerox Star. I was one that had, but we were intent on having it not be a Star, and not letting the Star things come into it. It looks a little more like Smalltalk, which they had seen and were allowed to see. Most of Lisa was made up by these people. It was like letting a designer see a concept car through smoked glass, so he couldn't quite see it, and then having a discussion with him, and letting him design his own car.

In some cases the PARC precedent spurred the Apple team to invent new designs that were not part of the Alto, as for example with the partly covered window. Bill Atkinson saw overlapping windows during his hour and a half at PARC, and he thought he saw text and graphics being refreshed in one of the windows that was partly covered, with only an L-shaped part of it visible. Because of this mistaken glimpse, Bill was convinced that it could be done, so when he was working on the QuickDraw graphics, he came up with a really innovative new way to solve the problem and developed a solution that was perhaps a hundred times faster than the previous state of the art. Later he was told by someone who used to work at Xerox:

■ Polaroids of development of overlapping window management, first scroll bar

Photos
Bill Atkinson

No, no! We didn't have a clever way of doing that; when you wanted to draw into a window with another one on top of it, you had to completely redraw the one that was behind, and then the other one on top.

Sometimes believing that something is possible is empowering! Bill thought he had seen it done, so he found his own way to achieve it.

pull down menus, grow icon next to title, separate horiz & vert scroll bars

rounded folder tabs, active folder hilited by bold. Double click on tab to open or close.

Menus moved to top. Grow icon in bottom right. Both scroll bars required

Pull-Down Menus

As THE FIRST user interface specification for Lisa was being formulated, Bill and Larry formed a close partnership and developed a round-the-clock working relationship, similar to the way that Larry had worked with Tim Mott on Gypsy. Bill would work nights and Larry would work days. During the night Bill would make prototypes of user interface concepts, written in a robust enough code to support some form of testing. Then Larry would run user tests during the day. It was easy to find subjects, as many of the new Apple employees had never used a computer before. Larry would give Bill a report at the end of the day and tell him what he had learned from the tests. Then they would brainstorm and decide what to try next, so that Bill could go off and spend the night programming. In the morning he would bring in a new version and then go home to bed. They used this method for several intense weeks, until the specification was solid.

After that it became much more methodical. The team was getting bigger, so different members would implement code, and Larry would run usability tests whenever something was ready to try. He would write up the results and make recommendations. The group would argue about what to do and what not to do. Larry was always seen as the guy who was delaying the project because he would want to make changes, but he would defend the need to develop a system that was easy to use. Lisa ended up taking over three years to develop, from 1979 to 1983: the marketing people thought it was a six-month project that took three years, but the engineering team felt that it was not that long to develop a new user interface, a new operating system, as well as five unprecedented applications.

■ Polaroids of development of designs for pull-down menus

Photos Bill Atkinson

It was during the intense early collaboration that Bill and Larry designed the arrangement of pull-down menus across the top of the screen that is so familiar today. Initially there were a lot of people from HP working on the Lisa team, and they had already made many decisions about the design of the hardware. They had a bitmap display; at the bottom of the display, imitating an HP machine, was a row of buttons as rectangles, and at the top

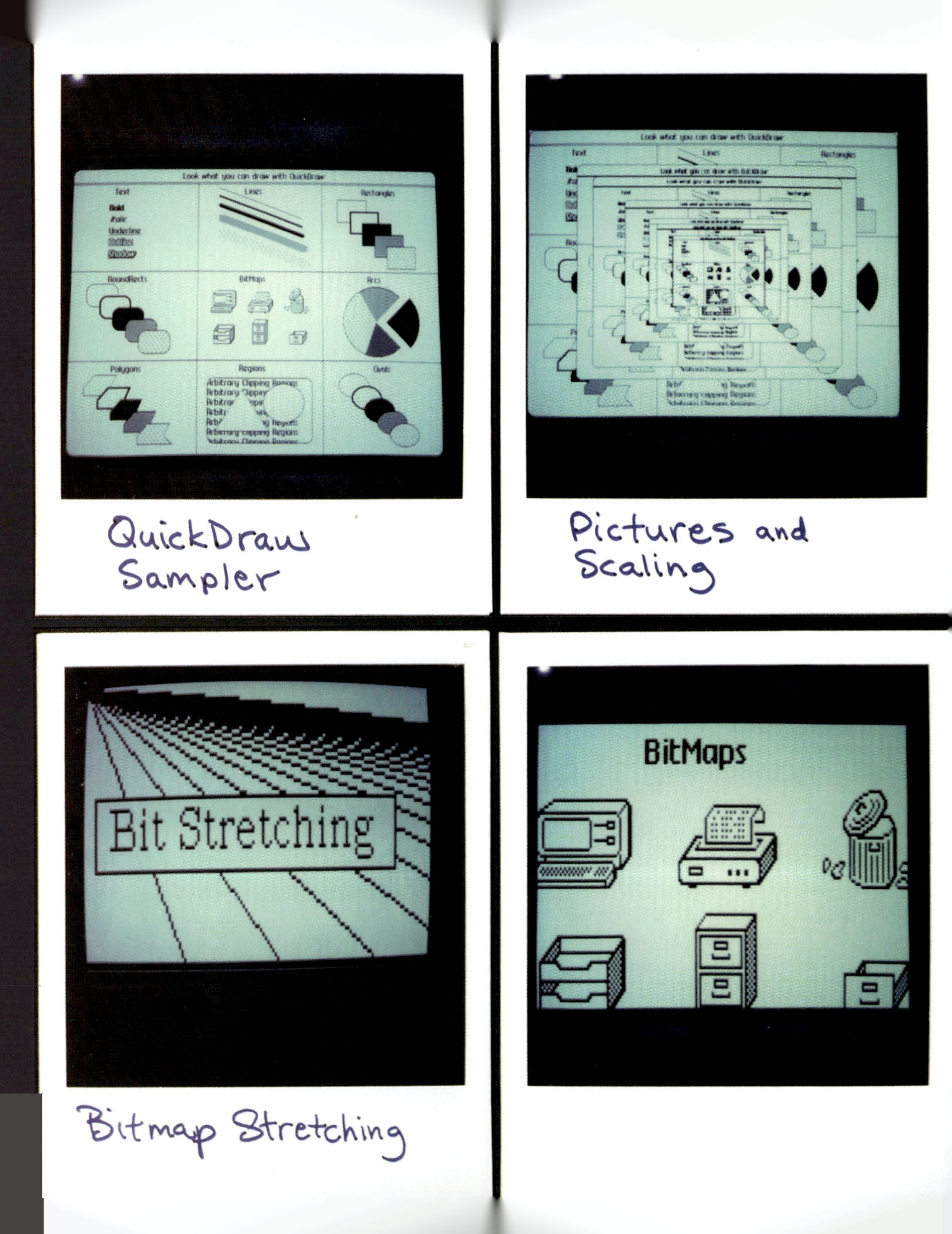

QuickDraw Sampler

Pictures and Scaling

Bitmap Stretching

of the keyboard there was a row of unlabeled physical soft-keys, with the labels on the screen above. If you pressed one of the keys, you had to look on the screen to see what the key meant at that moment. There was a hierarchy of menus: when you pressed the key, all the labels would refresh and change to the next level. Larry objected to this approach, as the only advantage it offered the user over the HP machine was the option to use the mouse to select, instead of using the soft-keys.

For the next iteration they tried putting a row of buttons along the bottom of every window, and a keyboard without the soft-keys, so you always had to use the mouse. Larry complained:

> No, guys! People can't keep all these menu hierarchies in their heads. Everything needs to be apparent. If you want to do something, there should be a key on the keyboard or a menu choice on the screen that you can see right now!

Bill agreed but was not sure what to do instead. Larry suggested making a menu appear when you clicked one of the buttons along the bottom of the window, but the problem with that idea was that if your window was near the bottom of the screen there was no room for the menu to drop down.

■ Polaroids of QuickDraw manipulations, bitmaps of icons

Photos Bill Atkinson

"Why don't we move it to the top of the window instead of the bottom?" Larry suggested.

Bill was willing to try anything, so he tried the top. Next they had a problem with narrow windows, where the menu titles would have to wrap around and have multiple rows of buttons, or go off to the side of the window, which looked really weird. The breakthrough came when they thought of putting the menus along the top of the screen, rather than in the windows. They both remember it as their own idea, that they suggested it to each other, and that they pushed it forward in spite of resistance from other members of the team. Larry describes the night when Bill converted the concept into a design:

> In one night he developed the entire pull-down menu system! Everything! He hadn't just moved it to the top of the screen; he had the idea that as you scanned your mouse across the top, each menu would pop down, and they would ruffle as you went back and forth,

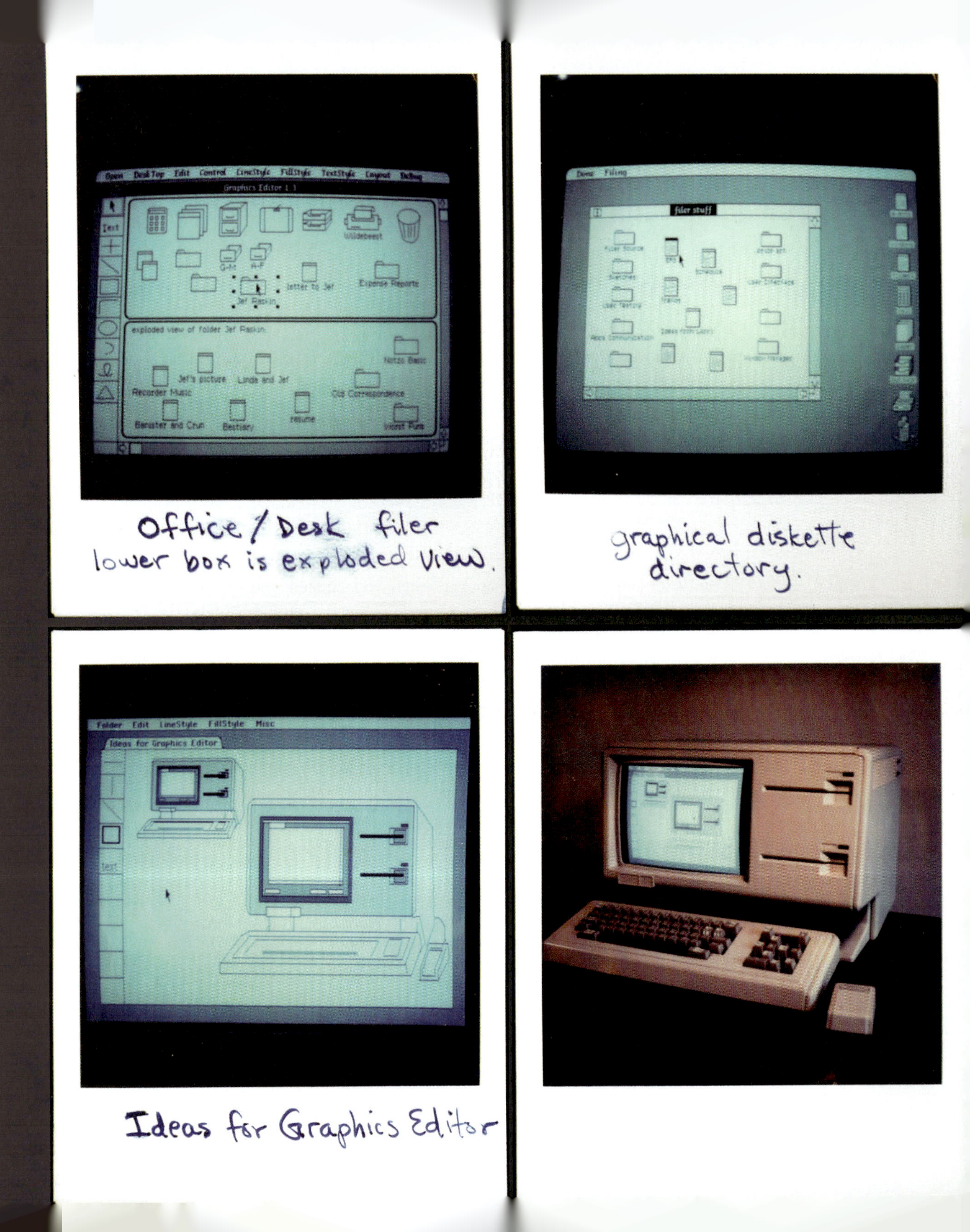

Open Desk Top Edit Control LineStyle FillStyle TextStyle Layout Debug
Text
Wildebeest
G-M
A-F
letter to Jef
Expense Reports
Jef Raskin
exploded view of folder Jef Raskin
Notzo Basic
Jef's picture
Linda and Jef
Recorder Music
Old Correspondence
Banister and Crun
Bestiary
resume
Worst Puns
Office / Desk filer
lower box is exploded view.
Done Filing
filer stuff
graphical diskette
directory.
Folder Edit LineStyle FillStyle Misc
Ideas for Graphics Editor
text
Ideas for Graphics Editor

and appear so that you could scan them all. When he came in the next day he went directly to Steve Jobs's office to show him first and then came to show us.

"Oh right!" I went, "This is what we want. We want everything to be apparent!"

He had come up with highlighting them as you moved you mouse down inside them, command shortcuts, and a way of showing which window was active and associated with the menu bar. He'd thought up the whole thing in one night! I can't imagine what happened that night.

One advantage of having the menus at the top is that you have the whole screen height to work with, and always the full width, regardless which window was using it. A kinesthetic feel of where that item can be found is soon learned subconsciously; you start reaching for it before you even think about it. Another advantage of the top edge of the screen is that the size of the target for the menu extends into an endless vertical column in virtual space; when you move your mouse upward, you need to be accurate in the side-to-side location, but you don't have to worry about the vertical position; it just has to be at the top or above the top of the screen. Surprisingly, the design of Microsoft Windows lost this advantage by putting an active header bar above the menus, forcing you to target the menus accurately in both planes.

■ Polaroids of designs for file management, and graphic editor showing an illustration of Lisa

Photos Bill Atkinson

Bill recorded his prototypes by taking Polaroid photos of the screens, annotating them, and storing them in binders. You can see the development of new ideas very clearly as you look through these Polaroids.[6] For a time there was some confusion between folders and windows. They had a tab that looked like a folder on every window, but then they realized that a folder is a container that contains documents, rather than being the document. Another new feature of Lisa was the dialog box, which came down as an extension of the menu and offered check boxes and radio buttons to choose the parameters of a command. This was different from Xerox Star, which had a "property" key on the keyboard, so that you could select something and then press the key to see and edit the properties.

building word processing software that used the two buttons, and all the documents for the user interface referred to functions for the left button as well as the right button. Larry kept trying to promote his theory about pointing with one hand and commanding with the other, but most of the engineers were strongly for the two-button approach. Bill Atkinson was neutral, but Jef Raskin was interested in the one-button idea.

Larry and Bill ran some experiments and proved that the single button was acceptable. Then they went through the whole interface and found alternatives to using the second button, the most controversial of which was using the shift key to find the other end of a large selection. Larry wrote a single-page memo called "One button mouse," advocating the approach, and Trip Hawkins, the head of product marketing, got really excited when he read the memo:

> This is what we need to do! We need to make this for the average person and this is the kind of simplification we need to have. We're going to go with the one-button mouse!

Larry remembers:

> Tom Malloy was very unhappy about it. We're good friends now, but we had many years of taunting each other about one- or two-button mice.
>
> "You know," he was always saying, "we should have put just one little tiny extra button on that mouse."
>
> I had to finally admit a few years ago that I now sometimes use a two-button mouse. My argument at the time was that our job was to take people who had never used a mouse before and convince them that it would be easy to use by going to the extreme of so easy that you couldn't make a mistake.
>
> "Once they get really good at it," I said, "then you can use a two-button mouse, but not now!"
>
> Apple still does that; they ship a one-button mouse with the new machines, but implement the software so that you can change to two buttons when you are expert.

The third item in the spec, "Will not require a special pad to roll on," caused the Hovey-Kelley team the most work. They

- Alternative designs for external shape
- Early working prototype
- Developed prototype
- Life test with record turntable

spent a lot of time researching and experimenting with materials and coatings for the mouse ball, in order to find a solution that would run smoothly on the normal surface materials of desks, and at the same time would operate the x and y encoders.

A reliable solution was a more complex requirement. They came up with a simple way of accessing the ball for cleaning and removing any dust on the rollers that operated the encoders. They devised a life-testing fixture for operating the ball and were not content until "after an effective three years of running in circles on Formica, the mouse has shown only a minor degradation in performance."[12]

Reliability of the switch for the single button was another challenge. Larry Tesler was responsible for the functional performance of the mouse in the context of the interactions, and he warned that the characteristics of the switch needed to be just right, as if it was hard to push down it would resist and tire your finger, and if it were too easy you would click it by mistake. After a few iterations they found a switch that seemed good. Larry recalls a conversation with Bill Lapson, the Apple project manager:

> "How many times will you be able to click it before it wears out?" I asked.
>
> "Oh, these are the best; a hundred thousand times," he replied.
>
> "A hundred thousand? That's not enough! It's got to be millions."
>
> Bill couldn't believe it; he thought that most of the time would be spent typing, and just once in a while you would need to point at something and click on it. Would that be once every five minutes, or once an hour?
>
> "No, no!" I said, "Constantly, click, click, click, all the time!"
>
> We grabbed a piece of paper and calculated the number of clicks, and it was two orders of magnitude more. The switch would have lasted two weeks. They had to find a better switch, which raised the cost, but it was essential.

The characteristics of the cord were also important for the interactions. If the cord were too stiff it would cause the mouse to move on its own, which was very disconcerting as the cursor would move across the screen; if it were too floppy, the mouse would trip over the cord. The Hovey-Kelley team collected samples of all the available cords, and Larry Tesler experimented with them, and with the length.

The Apple mouse set a precedent for the design of a pointing device that worked well at the right price for personal computers. Alps developed comparable products, and Logitech entered the market with a series of pointing devices, but the precedent that Apple had set continued to be the design to study until Microsoft decided to develop a mouse in 1987. Paul Bradley tells the story of designing the Microsoft mouse in the interview that follows.

Photo Author

Paul Bradley

"The Microsoft mouse was my personal favorite design. Designers enjoy doing something that is well regarded not just by the design community, but also by the people that use those products. I can still remember the early reviews that came out about the Microsoft mouse. It won design awards, but if you looked into the business press and the trade press, it was winning all the awards there too. There was a certain pride in designing something that had a legacy and was really well accepted by all the audiences that it was intended for." Paul Bradley discovered his vocation while he was studying architecture at Ohio State, changing to the industrial design program there when he found out about it. He joined Mike Nuttall at Matrix Product Design in 1984 and continued with the organization when it became IDEO. After only three years of experience, Paul had the chance to work on the design of the Microsoft mouse, and since then he has designed more than ten other input devices, including mice, trackballs, joysticks and new types of devices for Logitech. He was recently invited to Logitech to celebrate the production of their five hundred millionth mouse, with an acknowledgment that he had made a significant contribution to this success. Paul has designed many different technology and consumer products for companies such as Dell, Intel, Samsung, and Nike, and he helps the other designers at IDEO with his design philosophy, ideas, tools, and advice. The Microsoft mouse was unique in that he had an opportunity to search for and set a new standard for the design of mice.

Microsoft

Paul Bradley

Microsoft Mouse

Microsoft mouse with development models

Photo
Rick English

In 1987 Microsoft approached Matrix Product Design with a brief to design a mouse that was going to be better than anything that preceded it. What an exciting challenge for a group of designers! Matrix specialized in industrial design at the time, so they turned to their usual partners to form an interdisciplinary team, ID TWO for interaction design and human factors research, and David Kelley Design for mechanical engineering design and to support the manufacturing. This partnership worked well and formed a precedent for the three companies to come together to form IDEO a few years later.

Mike Cooper, the program manager from Microsoft, proposed a schedule that seemed impossibly ambitious at the time, wanting to bring a product to market within seven months. He managed to bring it off in spite of the fact that a typical development and tooling cycle at that time was over a year, but the vendors were so eager to work with Microsoft that he was able to jump to the head of the queue and get the fastest service that they could offer.

- Mike Cooper and team—Paul Bradley RH
- Handhold example
- Testing setup
- Test for mouse designs—tapping task

Paul Bradley describes the initial exploration of possible design concepts:

> The question was really, What could a mouse be? We were going out and talking to users about how they use the mouse, observing them, watching them. Looking at the nuances led us to certain beliefs, so we built prototypes to test the ideas. We thought that by building small mice that were symmetrical, a small round or square mouse, that you could capture the mouse in your fingertips like you capture a pen, and create a higher degree of accuracy. We were very surprised when we did testing with prototypes against other mice. Although these smaller mice felt better, they failed in 70 percent of the tests against the more traditional elongated mouse.
>
> We discovered that having the mouse fully encompassed in your hand gave more control, although the sense was that your fingertips would give you more control. It was the resting posture of your arm and hand on the table that allowed you to perform more accurately and quickly.

Tests

Bill Verplank,[13] who at that time was working with the author at ID TWO, devised tests. He worked out five tasks that would exercise the ways in which a mouse is used and wrote a program in HyperCard to compare time and errors for these tasks with different mouse designs. The tests were run on a Mac SE, with a range of experienced and naive users trying out the various prototypes and existing mice.

A tapping task measured the tradeoff between speed and accuracy for the most common mouse usage, that is, move and click, by asking the user to click twenty times back and forth on pairs of targets ranging in size.

Next they were asked to trace their way through a maze to reveal steering ability; this showed a dramatic advantage in moving the ball to the front of the mouse, so that it lay between thumb and finger, rather than in the conventional location further back.

A task to test precision asked the user to position the cursor exactly in the center of arrays of dots, and then to click; this revealed the importance of having the buttons on the top rather than on the side.

Writing the word "TAXABLES," with one character in each of eight boxes, required repeated short strokes with the button down and then up; for this task a mouse is much better than a trackball, where the buttons are hard to hold while rolling the ball.

The final task required typing, then pointing, then typing, then pointing, again and again; it measured homing time as you move from keyboard to pointing device, showing that the mouse did just as well as devices with fixed positions.

These human factors trials allowed quick evaluations of a wide range of design concepts. The combination of user testing and rapid prototyping was a key to the success of the project.

Industrial Design Development

Paul Bradley remembers the many hours he spent making models, and how the inspiration for the shape came to him during the process:

> We built about eighty foam models, quickly exploring different possibilities and directions. The core idea for the appearance of the final design actually came from a traditional rubber sanding block. We were in the shop, exploring shapes in foam models, working with this thing that requires a movement which is very similar to the movement of a mouse on the surface of a desk—the movement of sanding side to side or back and forth. That traditional rubber pad is a somewhat crude shape, but a very appropriate shape for what you're doing. The symmetrical curvature from the front to the back of the mouse was inspired by those sanding pads. By adding a curvature in the side to side direction, and details of the form in other places, we were able to improve on the traditional ergonomics in the sanding pad.

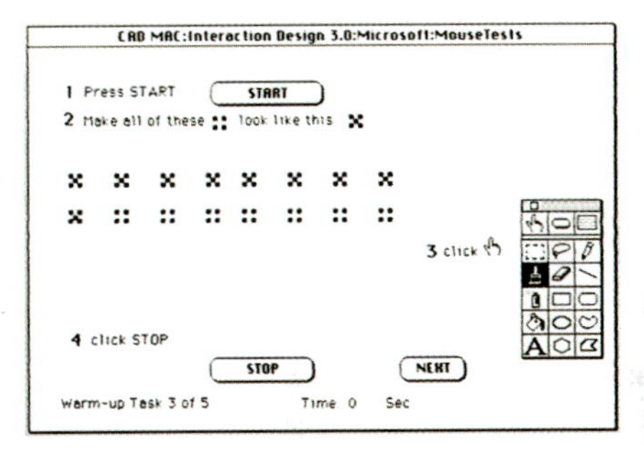

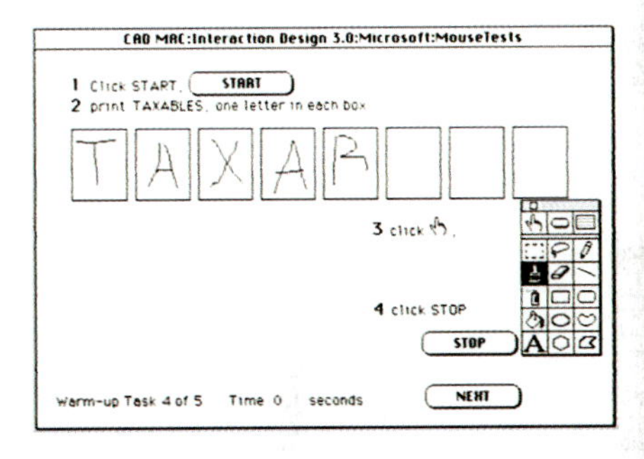

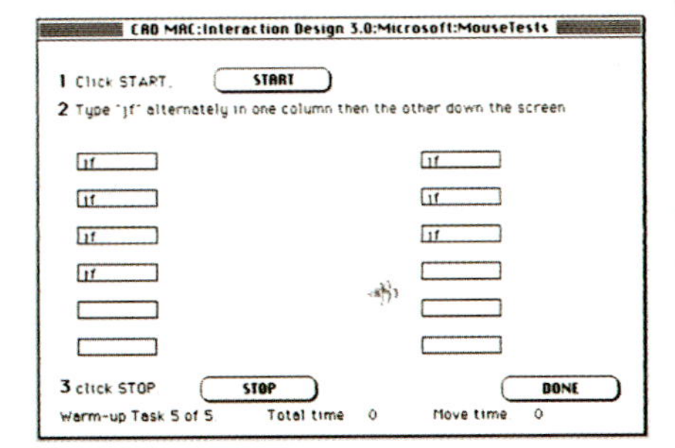

Test for mouse designs—maze task ■
Test for mouse designs—precision task ■
Test for mouse designs—writing task ■
Test for mouse designs—homing task ■

Earlier mice were designed as extensions of the computer, borrowing their visual design language from desktop computers, the early PCs, and Macs. They were rectilinear and architectural, having little to do with the human form and human touch.

"Does this look right next to our keyboard?" was the question, or "Does this look right next to our CRT?"

The Microsoft mouse took a different approach: "This is about your hand. This is about the human being. This is the contact point between people and product."

Paul was searching for a shape that looked like it belonged in the computer environment but was more connected to the person interacting with it. He developed a soft shape in pure white, and made it very shiny so it felt smooth to the touch, unlike the heavy textures that previous mice had used. He extended the buttons over the front and side edges, doubling their surface area, simplifying the appearance, and avoiding the risk of touching the surrounding frame by mistake.

Moving the ball forward caused the biggest single change to the internal geometry, as it was cheaper to have the ball in the back, leaving room in front of it for a PCB carrying the switches for the buttons. The observations of the motions of wrists and arms during the user testing, particularly for the maze task, made the designers think that positioning the ball between thumb and finger might offer better control. When they prototyped and tested the idea, the improvement was dramatic, and Microsoft was very excited; this was the kind of functional and usability improvement that they were looking for. They were happy to incur higher manufacturing costs to get something that would perform better. When they launched the product, they published the data from the tests, and soon all of the other manufacturers followed suit.

In most applications the left button is used 65 percent to 85 percent of the time. The testing process was recorded on videotape, and when the design team reviewed the tapes, they noticed that both right-handed and left-handed people tended to skew their grip asymmetrically to be centered over the left button. This made them decide to make the left button larger than

- Sanding block inspiration
- A softer shape to fit the hand
- Ball location moved forward

the right, but the people at Microsoft were worried that by designing an asymmetrical mouse, it would be more appropriate for a right handed person than a left handed person. Working prototypes were tested as soon as they were available, and the asymmetrical design won the day, but it was necessary to add a ridge between the buttons, so that people could feel the separation without looking down at the mouse.

The design was coming together, and it was time to commission manufacturing partners for the implementation. Paul Bradley describes the trips to Japan and long meetings in smoke-filled rooms:

> We talked to a shortlist of four or five possible manufacturing partners, but it came down to Alps and Mitsumi. A typical meeting would involve Mike Cooper, the program manager from Microsoft, his assistant, Jim Yurchenco from David Kelley Design, and myself. I would tell them our design vision and what we expected.
>
> "No, we can't do this," they would push back, and, "The schedule doesn't allow this!"
>
> Then Jim would explain to them how they could do these things. It turned out to be a good process because Jim was extremely knowledgeable in tooling and manufacturing processes, and he very quickly gained their respect. They realized that either they would have to come up with better reasons for staying with their existing ways of doing things, or they would have to meet our requests.
>
> Microsoft wanted a look and feel for this mouse that was different, so the idea of doing something white in a world of beige, and the idea of doing something high gloss in a world where everything was textured and matte was a way of differentiating themselves; in this case we demanded that we have a super high polish on every part, consistently across millions of parts.
>
> Microsoft had also seen a lot of mice that had a year or two of wear on them, when the pad printing or screen printing of the Logo began to peel around the edges, so the brand was made to look sloppy on the device. That was completely unacceptable to them.
>
> "We can't have Microsoft wearing off the surface of the mouse!," Mike Cooper said. "How can we avoid this?"
>
> "You can avoid it with a double-shot molding," we replied; "you take a second color of plastic for the Microsoft logo and inject it into the actual mold."

Paul Bradley enjoying karaoke ■

> He was very excited about that idea, but the manufacturer was not. After a week of negotiations, they came back.
>
> "We can do this, but it's going to take two more months on the schedule."
>
> Mike Cooper decided to build two sets of tooling, one just for the first two months of production. That was pad printed and coated with Urethane to give a high degree of durability. This actually turned out to be a problem on the white mice, because with exposure to sunlight the Urethane started to yellow. In parallel we built a more complex set of tools for the double-shot process, and when they were ready we replaced the initial tooling.

The feel of the mouse was just as crucial as the appearance in order to achieve a higher standard of interactivity. Central to the feel was the way the ball rolled as the mouse was moved across the work surface; it had to be smooth and delicate and connected to the movement of the cursor with consistent directness. The design team explored options for the surface and material of the ball, and discovered the performance improved with a heavier ball, so they went with a dense material that was heavier than steel. This gave the mouse itself a heft and weight, making it feel more accurate, and creating more traction on the surface of the table.

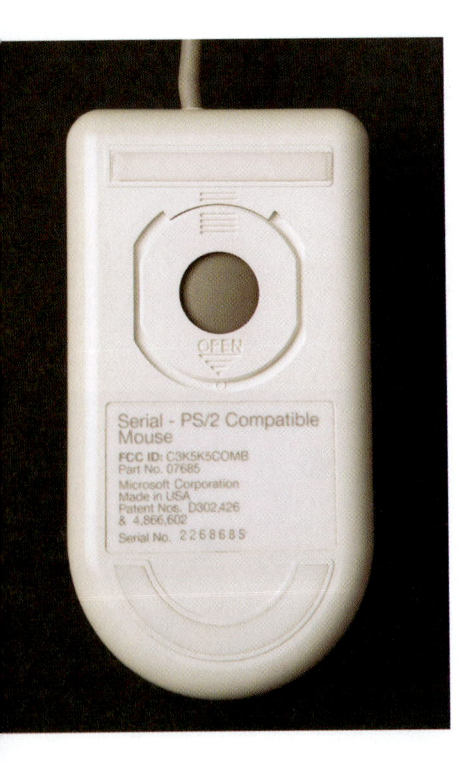

■ Underside of mouse

They also used Teflon pads on the underside. The whole lower shell was designed to be as clean as possible, so instead of four feet in the corners, Paul designed two wide pads that wrapped across the front and back. He used those Teflon feet to cover the screw holes as well as the label, so when you turned the device over it was clean and simple and had no mechanical details exposed.

The feel of the buttons was another challenging problem because of the larger surface area. With many of the mice at the time, when you pushed on the front edge of the button, there was a noticeable difference in the force needed to actuate it than if you pushed on the back edge. Paul tells how they worked hand-in-hand with the manufacturer to design a switch geometry that would bring the arm that attached the button as far back into the body as possible:

> The further that you bring it back, the longer the lever, and therefore the actuation force is more even over the length of the button. We

had a sixty to eighty gram spec, so that anywhere you pushed on the button it had to be within that bracket. When the parts started rolling off the tools, Jim Yurchenco came in with his little force meter and started pushing on the buttons. If it didn't meet that spec, Jim said that they must go back and make changes to the design until it was just perfect.

Microsoft made a big splash for the product launch. They sold more than a million in the first year, and eleven million before it was replaced by another model. Initially it was packaged with Windows, and later as an independent product, but it was always retained as an exclusively Microsoft design, as they wanted to use it to enhance their own brand rather than offer it to Dell or another PC manufacturer. They went on to form an internal group for the development of physical products and began to offer peripherals to support new software features that they were developing. The success of the first mouse blossomed into a much broader offering. Paul remembers being invited to go to New York for the launch:

Bill Gates rented a hall next to the Museum of Modern Art in New York, and brought all the press there. Then he got up, took the mouse in his hands, and said, "Microsoft has designed the best mouse in the world!" He took us all to Broadway shows, lobbied the Museum of Modern Art pretty hard to put it in the museum right then and there, and published comprehensive promotional documents that really talked about ergonomics. He not only wanted to put out a message about the look of this device, but also that the interactivity was really important, and how they'd improved it.

First credit for setting a new standard in the design of mice goes to Mike Cooper for his determination to drive the program forward and to create a leadership position for Microsoft. It was also a precedent-setting collaboration between the three companies that came together to form IDEO a few years later. Paul Bradley, from Matrix Product Design, brought his passion for designing beautiful physical forms for products. Jim Yurchenco, from David Kelley Design, built on his experience designing the first Apple mouse and enforced the highest standards of engineering and manufacturing quality. Bill Verplank, from the author's team at ID TWO, brought his knowledge of interaction design and human factors research. The partnership worked well.

Bill Verplank had joined ID TWO the year before, bringing with him a wealth of experience in designing interactions, both input devices and screen-based interfaces. Bill had already worked out how people think about computers and software, and he had developed a design process. In the interview that follows, he illustrates his ideas with drawings.

Photo Craig Syverson

Bill Verplank

Bill Verplank has an amazing ability to draw at the same time as he talks. If you meet him and ask him a question about interaction design, you can sit at the nearest table or desk and be mesmerized by the fluency of his answer. His words are easy to understand, and as he talks he builds a beautiful diagram that reinforces what he is saying. You can take the drawing with you as a reminder and summary of his ideas about interaction design, which have evolved over many years. His PhD from MIT was in man-machine systems, applying information and control theory to measuring human operator workload in manual control tasks. At Xerox from 1978 to 1986 he participated in testing and refining the Xerox Star graphical user interface. From 1986 to 1992, he worked as a design consultant with the author to bring graphical user interfaces into the product design world. At Interval Research from 1992 to 2000 he directed Research & Design for Collaboration. He has helped to establish the Interaction Design Institute Ivrea and is now a visiting scholar in haptics in the Music Department at Stanford University. He summarizes interaction design by answering three questions about how you act, how you feel, and how you understand. He explains the context of the history and future of interaction design with paradigms that serve as patterns for the way people think about the subject. He describes the process of designing interactions with a concise diagram, and gives an example to illustrate it. He created the drawings that follow as he talked about his ideas during his interview.

Bill Verplank

Bill says that the interaction designer has three questions to answer; they are all "How do you . . . ?" questions.

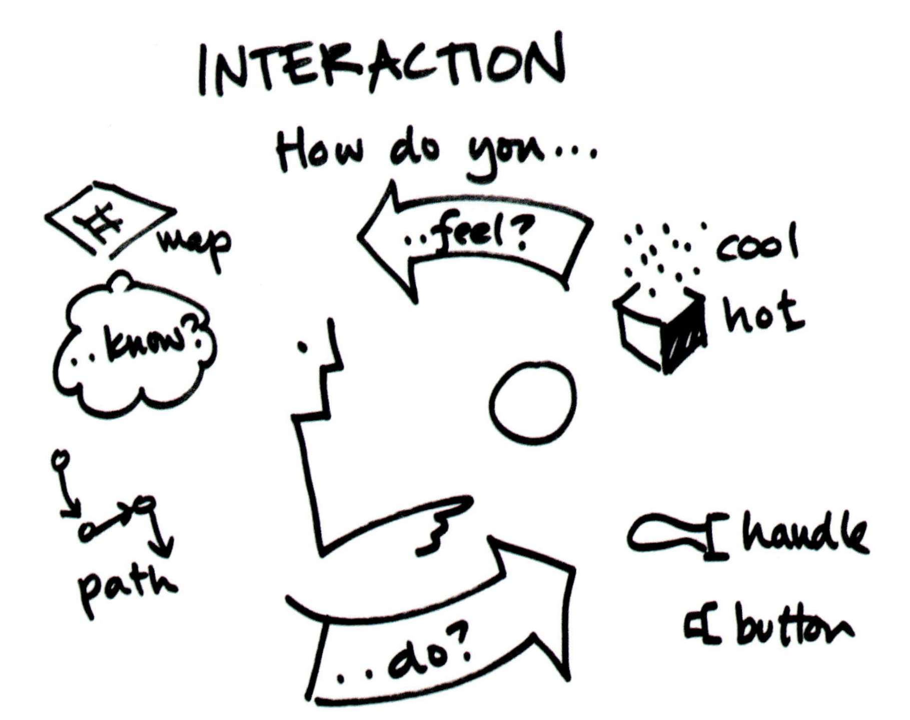

How Do You . . . ?

1. "How do you do?"

    How do you affect the world? A human, a person that we are designing for, does something, and we provide affordances. We either present handles that they can continuously control, or we give them buttons for discrete control, pressing the button and giving up control to the machine. When you are designing the way people act, there is a choice between handles and buttons. You can grab hold of a handle and manipulate it, keeping control as you do it. Alternatively you can push a button, or click on one, delegating control to the machine.

2. "How do you feel?"

    How do you get feedback? McLuhan made the distinction between what he called "fuzzy," or "cool," media, and "distinct," or "hot," media. Early TV was a cool medium, with its fuzzy images. Cool media draw you in. A book with careful printing or a gravestone with carved lettering is hot, or immutable—you cannot touch or change it. We design the way that the machine, or the system, gives feedback to the user, or the book looks to the user, or the sign communicates. That's where a lot of feelings come from; a lot of our emotions about the world come from the sensory qualities of those media that we present things with.

3. "How do you know?"

    As we design products with computers in them, it is very difficult for a user to know exactly what they are going to do. A map gives the knowledge that you may need if you are designing complex systems. A path offers the kind of understanding that is more about skill and doing the right thing at the right moment. It is the responsibility of the designer to help people understand what is happening by showing them a map or a path. The map shows the user an overview of how everything works, and the path shows them what to do, what they need to know moment by moment.

Interaction Design Paradigms

A PARADIGM IS an example that serves as a pattern for the way people think about something. It is the set of questions that a particular community has decided are important. For interaction design there is often some confusion about what paradigm you are working with. The basic question is, What is a computer?

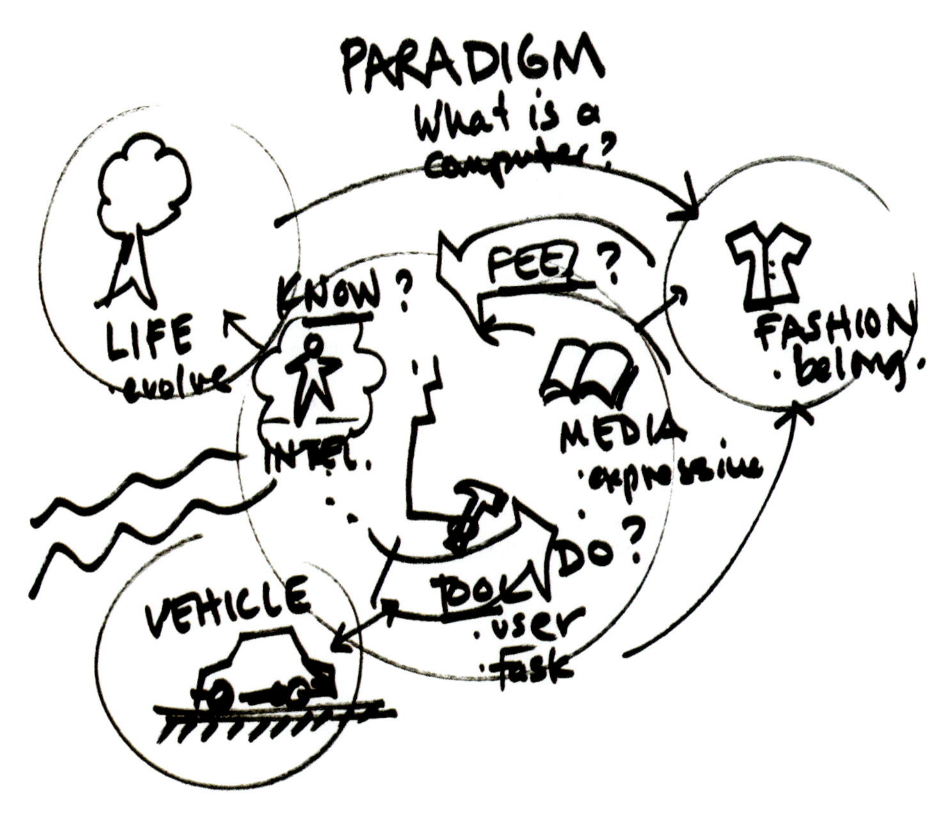

Intelligence

In the early days, designers thought of computers as people and tried to develop them to become smart, intelligent, and autonomous. The word "smart" is one that we associate with this paradigm, expecting the machine or product to be smart and to know how to do things for the person who uses it.

Tool

Doug Englebart, the inventor of the computer mouse, thought of the computer as a tool. Styles of interaction changed from dialogs, where we talk to a computer and a computer will talk back to us, to direct manipulation, where we grab the tool and use it directly. The ideas of efficiency and empowerment are related to this tool metaphor.

Media

In the nineties, designers thought of computers as media, raising a new set of questions. How expressive is the medium? How compelling is the medium? Here we are not thinking so much about a user interacting with or manipulating the computer, but more about them looking at and browsing in the medium.

Life

Starting in the mid nineties, people have been talking about computer viruses or computer evolution; they are thinking of artificial life. When the program has been written, it is capable of evolving over time—getting better and adapting. The programmer is in a way giving up responsibility, saying that the program is on its own.

Vehicle

Another metaphor is the computer as vehicle, and we have to agree on the rules of the road. There has to be some kind of infrastructure that underlies all computer systems. People spend their careers determining the standards that will define the infrastructures, and hence the limitations and opportunities for design.

Fashion

The media metaphor plays out to computers as fashion. A lot of products are fashion products. People want to be seen with the right computer on. They want to belong to the right in-crowd. Aesthetics can dominate in this world of fashion, as people move from one fashion to another, from one style of interaction to another style.

Interaction Design Process

Bill Verplank suggests a four-step process. First, the designers are motivated by an error or inspired by an idea and decide what the ideal goal for the design should be. Next they find a metaphor that connects the motivation to the end goal and develop scenarios to help them create meaning. Then they work out step-by-step what the tasks are and find a conceptual model that ties them all together and clarifies the modes. Finally they decide what kind of display is needed, what the control are, and how to arrange them.

1. Motivation—errors or ideas

Design ought to start from understanding the problems that people are having, and also from ideals. A lot of people are motivated by problems that they see, breakdowns of one sort or another, errors that they observe. Another place that design starts is with ideas. These are the brilliant concepts, the ideals that we have for making the world wonderful.

2. Meaning—metaphors and scenarios

If you can tell a good story about something, or spin a good metaphor, it makes sense to people. This is where the meaning of the design comes from. A clear metaphor is the strange idea that connects two things; for example the cloud and the bolt of lightning, saying—Ah hah! This isn't a computer, it's a desktop! Along with the metaphor, we also need a variety of scenarios, to understand the context of Who is using it, Where are they, and What are they trying to accomplish?

3. Modes—models and tasks

In order to create a conceptual model that users will understand, you have to have a clear picture of what they are thinking about. The mode that they are in depends on what the task is, and what they are trying to accomplish. How they can move from one mode or model to another, or from one environment to another, will then define the tasks. This is the conceptual cognitive science of understanding what the person doing the task needs to know

4. Mappings—displays and controls

Often, as an interaction designer, you design some kind of display and some controls. The display is the representation of things that you are manipulating. You need to be able to map the controls to the display. Those mappings can be really complicated with computers, as they can remap things in an instant, giving very strange powerful modes that can select everything or delete everything.

Process Example, "A Haptic Pager"

Bill Verplank uses a story of the development of a tactile pager to illustrate the interaction design process. The example was created by one of the students at Stanford University, where Bill teaches. It shows the progress of the concept, going from error and idea to display and control, and how metaphor, model, scenario, and task are the core of that process.

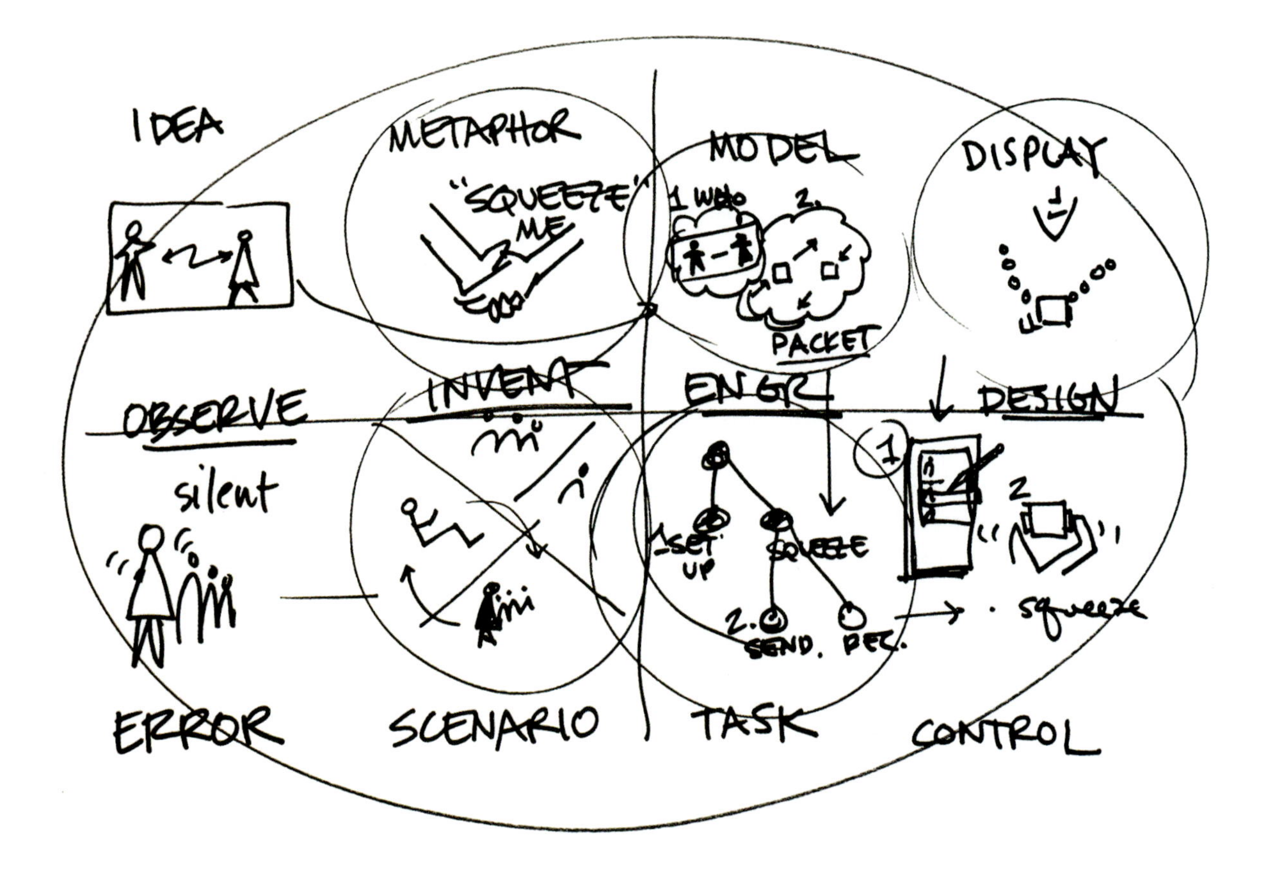

1. Error and idea

Celine was annoyed by pagers and cell phones going off when she was waiting for the checkout at a supermarket—and embarrassed when her own went off. The problem that she wanted to solve was how to make a silent pager that she could feel without having to listen to it. Her ideal was that she and her friend could be linked, and whenever they wanted they could give each other a squeeze.

2. Metaphor and scenario

The metaphor is that she really wants something that is more like holding hands, so that she can hold hands at a distance and give a squeeze. She is thinking about a scenario that Fred is at home, and she is taking longer shopping than she had expected. She wants to be able to communicate without interrupting whatever he is doing.

3. Model and task

One conceptual model is that she is connected to him and no one else, so that when she squeezes, it is him that is going to feel it. Another is that when she sends off the squeeze, it is a packet, so she is not squeezing him at that moment. One task is to set up the connections, and another is to trigger the squeeze, both for sending and receiving.

4. Display and control

The idea for the display is that she could wear some kind of necklace that could vibrate, like the vibrating mode in pagers and cell phones, to let her know that someone is calling. The sending could be controlled by a squeeze. It turns out that Celine works for a company that makes a handheld computer operated by a stylus, so she uses this to set up the connection.

BILL VERPLANK HAS made connections among people of diverse backgrounds who are trying to understand how to design interactions. He shows his expertise in computer science, grasp of human factors issues, and ability to engage an audience—both with words and drawings—as he explains a concept. Bill helped to move the desktop toward the PC when he worked on the design of Xerox Star graphical user interface, and has helped designers in many different situations since then.

Cordell Ratzlaff,[14] whose interview follows, has been responsible for pushing the design of the operating systems for personal computers to the limits of progress to date. He has taken the desktop from close to the place that Bill Atkinson and Larry Tesler left it to Mac OS X, so far the most advanced graphical user interface there is.

Cordell Ratzlaff

"The big difference with Mac OS X was that it was completely design driven, based on what we thought novice users would need in an operating system," says Cordell Ratzlaff, who managed the Human Interface Group for the design of Macintosh System Software at Apple for five years. He led the team that designed the versions of Mac OS from Mac OS 8 all the way through Mac OS X. Cordell graduated with a degree in psychology from the University of Nebraska. Passionate about the study of human behavior, he eventually became fascinated by technology; he moved into design to combine the two interests. After graduate studies at Ohio State University in industrial engineering, his first job was at the NASA Ames Research Center. Next he designed user interfaces for telecommunication systems at an aerospace company. He ended up at Apple in 1990, in the group that was designing networking and communication products for LAN-based networks. In 1994 he began work on system software at Apple and led the design of four major versions of the operating system, culminating in the innovative Mac OS X. When the design of the new interface was completed and just before it was shown publicly, he went to a startup called GetThere.com to head up the design and development of online travel reservation sites, staying with them until they were established as market leaders in corporate online travel, had gone public, and been acquired by a larger company. He is now creative director for the Digital Media Group at Frog Design, in San Francisco.

Stickies File Edit Note Color Window
About This Mac
Mac OS X
Version 10.2.8
Memory: 512 MB
Processors: Dual 1 GHz PowerPC G4
More Info...
™ & © Apple Computer, Inc.
Mac OS X
When Cordell
was a great place
were rolling. The c
re than IBM at 2
margins to sponsor
, and some good
exciting to be a desi
lot of freedom t
interference from ar
iPhoto
04 Paradigms
PARADIGM
What is a computer?
LIFE
KNOW?
FEEL?
FASHION
MEDIA
VEHICLE
DO?
00:04:39
Show All
Displays
Sound
Network
Personal
Desktop
Dock
General
Hardware
CDs & DVDs
ColorSync
Displays
Internet & Network
Internet
Network
QuickTime
System
Accounts
Classic
Date & Time
Back
video
Brenda Laurel
Compilations
Desktop Folder
Durrell Bishop
Excerpts Radio Watch
Excerpts reel intros
Final Cut Pro Documents
Connect to laptop: computer
name "Bill Moggridge",
Password "mogric"
or Karinmogg
1111aa
or alexmoggridge
tuna

Cordell Ratzlaff

Mac OS X

■ Mac OS X

Photo
Author's screen capture

WHEN CORDELL RATZLAFF arrived in 1990, Apple was a great place to work. The good times were rolling. The company had a bigger market share than IBM at 26 percent and large enough profit margins to sponsor generous development budgets—and some good-time extravagance. It was exciting to be a designer at Apple because you had a lot of freedom to explore ideas without much interference. The development organization was fractured into separate teams, with seven or eight different human interface groups.

This situation only lasted a few years before Apple seemed to lose its identity. They started playing catch-up with me-too products, while Windows was becoming more and more popular and other companies were exploiting the Internet. Apple was chasing after too many different things—Newton, digital cameras, printers, projection systems, and other products that never made it to the market. That was when Cordell moved into system software development and took responsibility for the Human Interface Group for Mac OS.

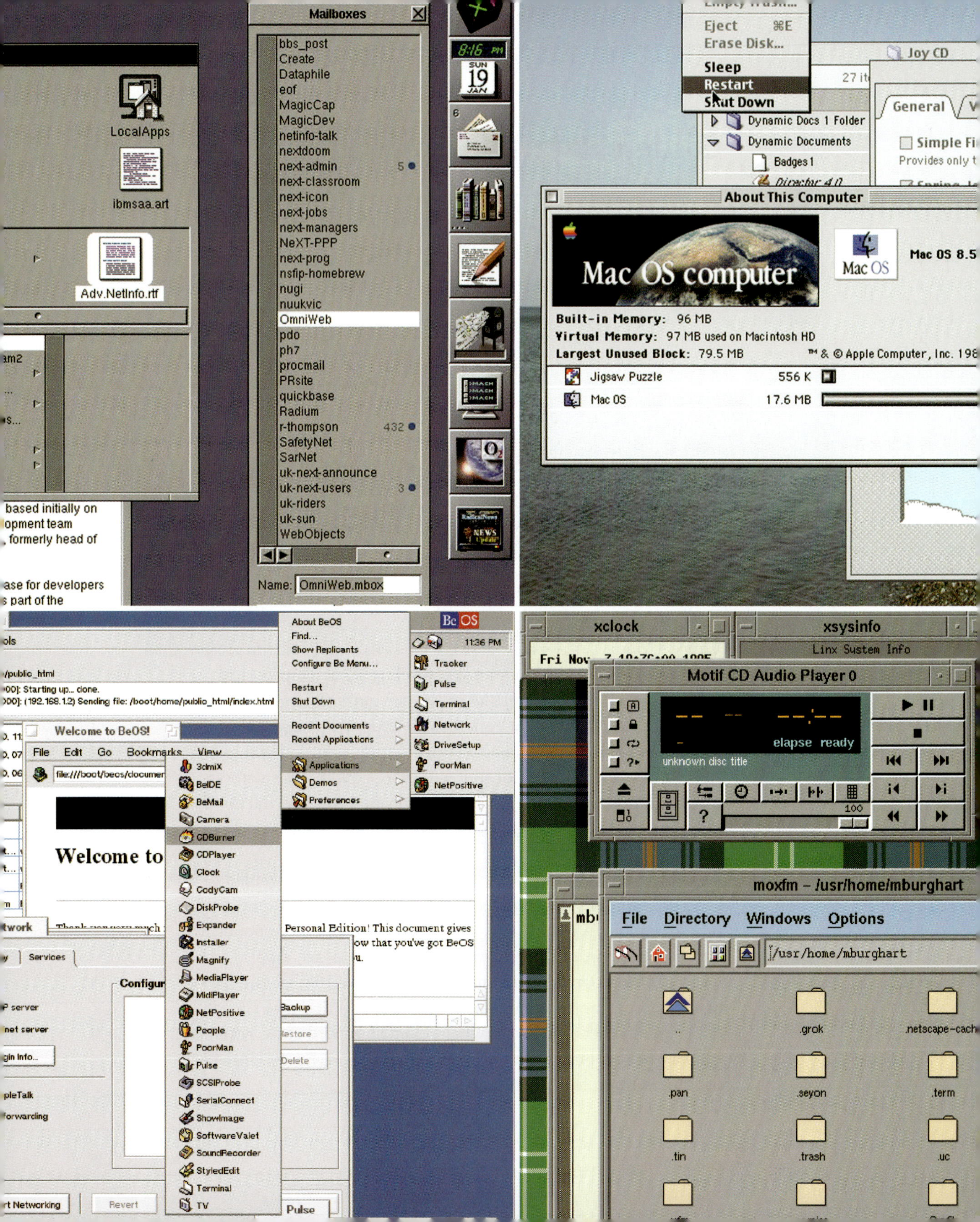
Mailboxes
bbs_post
Create
Dataphile
eof
MagicCap
MagicDev
netinfo-talk
nextdoom
next-admin
next-classroom
next-icon
next-jobs
next-managers
NeXT-PPP
next-prog
nsfip-homebrew
nugi
nuukvic
OmniWeb
pdo
ph7
procmail
PRsite
quickbase
Radium
r-thompson
SafetyNet
SarNet
uk-next-announce
uk-next-users
uk-riders
uk-sun
WebObjects
Name: OmniWeb.mbox
LocalApps
ibmsaa.art
Adv.NetInfo.rtf
8:15 PM
SUN 19 JAN
based initially on
opment team
formerly head of
ase for developers
s part of the
Eject ⌘E
Erase Disk...
Sleep
Restart
Shut Down
Joy CD
General
Simple Fi
Provides only t
Dynamic Docs 1 Folder
Dynamic Documents
Badges 1
About This Computer
Mac OS computer
Mac OS
Mac OS 8.5
Built-in Memory: 96 MB
Virtual Memory: 97 MB used on Macintosh HD
Largest Unused Block: 79.5 MB
™ & © Apple Computer, Inc. 198
Jigsaw Puzzle 556 K
Mac OS 17.6 MB
About BeOS
Find...
Show Replicants
Configure Be Menu...
Restart
Shut Down
Recent Documents
Recent Applications
Applications
Demos
Preferences
Be OS
11:36 PM
Tracker
Pulse
Terminal
Network
DriveSetup
PoorMan
NetPositive
3dmiX
BeIDE
BeMail
Camera
CDBurner
CDPlayer
Clock
CodyCam
DiskProbe
Expander
Installer
Magnify
MediaPlayer
MidiPlayer
NetPositive
People
PoorMan
Pulse
SCSIProbe
SerialConnect
ShowImage
SoftwareValet
SoundRecorder
StyledEdit
Terminal
TV
Welcome to BeOS!
File Edit Go Bookmarks View
file:///boot/beos/documen
Welcome to
Personal Edition! This document gives
ow that you've got BeOS
/public_html
00]: Starting up... done.
00]: (192.168.1.2) Sending file: /boot/home/public_html/index.html
Services
Configur
Backup
Restore
Delete
Revert
Pulse
xclock
xsysinfo
Linx System Info
Motif CD Audio Player 0
elapse ready
unknown disc title
moxfm – /usr/home/mburghart
File Directory Windows Options
/usr/home/mburghart
.grok
.netscape-cach
.pan
.seyon
.term
.tin
.trash
.uc

His first project was Mac OS 8, which allowed people to customize the interface more than system 7 and also had richer graphics with more color. For Mac OS 8.5 he took customization further by adding themes. People could choose from a number of prepackaged themes, but they could also change their desktop pattern, color scheme, and the way some of the controls worked.

For Mac OS 8.5 his team designed sounds to enhance the interface. Until that time, the attempts to integrate sound[15] had failed, because people just took sounds and attached them to actions or behaviors, rather than designing them as integral elements of the interactivity. Cordell brought in Earwax Productions,[16] a sound design company, and worked with them to study the events, objects in the interface, gestures, activities—everything that people were trying to do as they interacted with the user interface elements on the screen. They discovered that when people hear the same sound repeatedly, it soon gets annoying. They coordinated the tempo and duration of the sounds with the activity, while varying a number of different parameters, so that there was an element of randomness.

- Operating system user interfaces; *clockwise from top left:* NeXTSTEP, Mac OS 8.5, Motif, Be OS

In the mid nineties Apple had a project called Copeland, which went on for a number of years. It was meant to be the next-generation operating system for the Macintosh. Eventually everyone realized that Copeland was never going to come to fruition, so Apple started looking for an operating system to buy from outside the company. One candidate was NeXTSTEP, another was Be OS, and a third was Motif on X Windows. They even considered a Java operating system. They eventually decided on NeXTSTEP because it had been out for a number of years and had rock-solid reliability. That decision led to the purchase of NeXT, and Cordell and his team[17] set about integrating NeXTSTEP into Mac OS.

Initially the strategy was to keep the user interface unchanged. They were hoping to take the technology that came with NeXTSTEP and swap it out with Mac OS technology, with the user interface remaining the same so that nobody would ever know that there was different code running underneath. It soon became apparent that it would be impossible to exactly replicate the Macintosh human interface on top of the NeXTSTEP architecture. For individual applications, like a media player, you can separate the interface from the roots, but for operating systems a lot of the behaviors go right down through the layers to the core of the technology. Cordell remembers his dilemma:

> We discovered we could only get 95 percent of the way there, which was the worst possible situation. We were going to end up with something that was almost—but not quite—like the Mac OS, and we knew that was going to be a problem. On the other hand, we saw a lot of interesting capabilities in the NeXTSTEP technology that could be exploited to enhance the Mac OS user experience. I took a couple of designers, and we started exploring some of these ideas—for example, using NeXTSTEP's advanced graphics system to introduce translucency and real-time shadowing into the user interface.
>
> A few months into this exploration, we had a two-day off-site with the engineering managers from just about every group within Apple. We got together to discuss how we were going to pull off the NeXTSTEP integration—what resources we would need, what the interdependencies were between groups, and to work out how to actually achieve and ship Mac OS X. During the two days, each team was getting up and talking about their particular part of Mac OS X, what their challenges were, and what their needs were from other teams.
>
> I was asked to show some of the new user interface ideas we had, to demonstrate that we were looking beyond just the near-term engineering task that we had in front of us. I was the last person to present at the end of two days, and I got up and showed things like translucent menus, gel-like buttons, and composite shadowing. When I described what we wanted to do and started talking about the technical requirements and what we would need to make that happen, there was literally laughter in the room. We had just gone through two days of realizing how we had this huge mountain ahead of us that we would have to climb, and I was just adding to that. It didn't go over too well and I left that meeting very depressed.

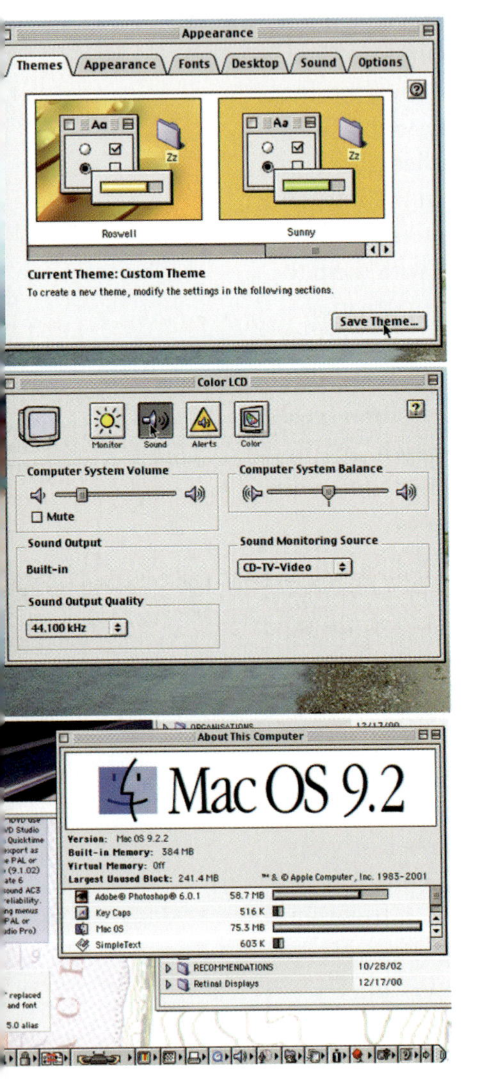

- Mac OS 8.5—themes
- Mac OS 8.5—sounds
- Mac OS 9.2

At that time Apple was a very engineering-driven company. A lot of the products were designed to fit easily into the technical possibilities, so they were easier to develop and to release on time, but they did not necessarily have to be easy or enjoyable to use.

Then Steve Jobs came back and applied a ruthless rationalization and a much-needed focus for the company. The "Think different" ad campaign communicated the change brilliantly; before it, Apple was scorned for being different from everybody else, but the campaign turned that completely around to say "Being different is good!" When your products are great, they are not for everybody: they are designed for people who are the best in the world. Still, Cordell was understandably nervous:

> A couple of weeks later I got a call from Steve Jobs's admin, saying, "Steve wants to talk to you. He hears you're heading up the Human Interface Group at Apple, and he has some things he wants to discuss with you."
>
> I thought, "Oh, great!" This was a time when Steve was reviewing everything that was going on at Apple, projects were getting cut, and people were leaving as a result. I took a couple of our designers, and we went to meet with Steve.
>
> We were sitting in his boardroom, and he comes in, late as usual, and the first words out of his mouth were, "You guys designed Mac OS, huh?"
>
> I said, "Yeah, we did that."
>
> "I've got to tell you, you're a bunch of amateurs!"
>
> For twenty minutes he just railed on about how bad the Macintosh human interface was and how we were idiots for designing it that way.
>
> Steve hadn't seen the new work that we had done, so we started talking about some of the ideas that we had come up with, and we were able to turn that conversation around into something more productive. We discussed what was broken in the current human interface and what we could do to fix it. About halfway through that meeting, I thought, "Well, he wouldn't be wasting his time talking to us about this if he was going to fire us, so I guess we still have our jobs!"
>
> We were able to actually have a pretty good meeting and listed a number of ideas that we wanted to look at some more. At the end Steve said, "Why don't you go work on these things? Come back in a couple of weeks, and let's see what you've got."
>
> The next few weeks we worked night and day, building prototypes and fleshing out design ideas. We spent an entire afternoon showing them to Steve, and he was blown away by what he saw. From that

Cordell Ratzlaff at Apple ■
Steve Jobs ■
Photo by Gary Parker, courtesy of Apple

point on there was never any debate that we were going to put a new human interface on top of Mac OS X.

The designers at Apple, for both physical products and software, find it rewarding to work with Steve Jobs. It may be much more chaotic and challenging, but his leadership encourages them to do their best work. He focuses intensely on design and on building products around his vision of what Apple customers want. He made big changes in the way the development community went about designing, developing, and releasing products:

> We did the design first. We focused on what we thought people would need and want, and how they would interact with their computer. We made sure we got that right, and then we went and figured out how to achieve it technically. In a lot of cases when we came up with a design that we knew really worked for people, we didn't know how we were going to build it. We had a design target, and we worked with engineering to reach it. We ended up doing a lot of things that we initially thought were impossible, or would take a long time to do. It was great because we were applying a lot of creativity and ingenuity on the design side and then pushing the engineers to use the same kind of creativity and innovation to make that happen.

Steve Jobs made a choice to focus on the consumer market, and that helped Cordell decide how to simplify the design. Apple has a fanatic fan-base of developers and power users, who hate to lose features that they have grown used to, so Mac OS X initially met with some very strong criticism and resistance. Interaction designers are often not able to stand up to that kind of pressure, and it took firm leadership from the top to allow Cordell and his team to focus on the new customers who did not have much computer experience.

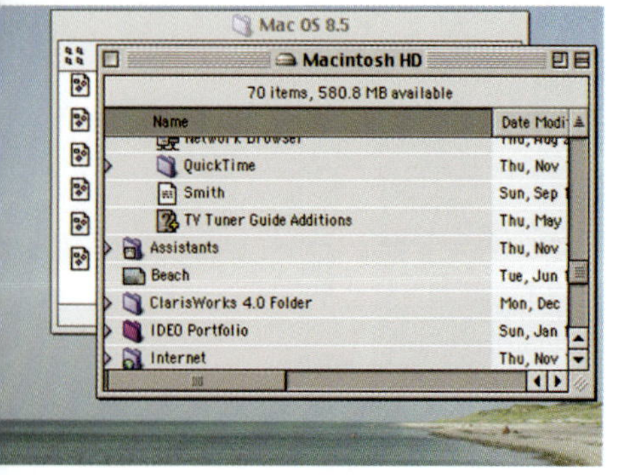

■ Mac OS 8.5 Windows

In Mac OS 8.5 there were no less than seven different ways to manage windows. For Mac OS X they created a simplified approach to window management. They eliminated window frames, replacing the heavy structure with a delicate shadow. In 1997 if you looked at operating systems from an aesthetic point of view, whether it was Mac OS 8.5, Windows 95, or

NeXTSTEP, their appearance was chiseled and beveled. Everything was rectilinear, with quasi-3D shading on the controls and windows. On the interaction side, a lot of the interface elements had crept up and taken over the experience, with thick window frames, big chunky beveled buttons, and big icons. It seemed that the interface elements and controls had become more important than what you really wanted to do with the computer, which was either to look at content, like the Web, or create content, like writing a note or an email.

Cordell saw a great opportunity to change to an appearance that was fresh and fun, in contrast to the existing state of the art. He decided to change from gloomy, square, and beveled, to light, fun, and colorful, with a very fluid expression. He asked, What's the opposite of a computer interface? He came up with things like candy, liquor, and liquids, to inspire a new visual design of the interface. The designers collected magazine ads for liquor, with delicious looking liquids in glasses with ice cubes, sparkling with reflections and highlights. Around this time Apple came out with the original iMac, and translucency was a big feature of the design, so they tried to design an interface that complemented the industrial design:

> We didn't want to use translucency gratuitously; we wanted to make sure that translucency added value to the experience. A good example of that was window layering. As windows move to the background they become translucent; in fact they become more translucent the farther back they are in the window stack. The translucency not only tied the interface into the industrial design of the product, but also showed off the graphics capabilities of Mac OS X, and provided a useful clue about window ordering.

When Cordell was designing Mac OS X, he was looking for some simple interactive features that were also powerful. He did not want to take away any of the capabilities or functionality of the OS, but to clean out a lot of the detritus that had accumulated over the years. One of these features was the addition of the "column view" in the Finder, which made it easier to manage access to folders and files. The view allows users to navigate deep into the hierarchical file system within a single window. It's much

Translucent iMacs
photo courtesy of Apple
Translucency used to show window ordering

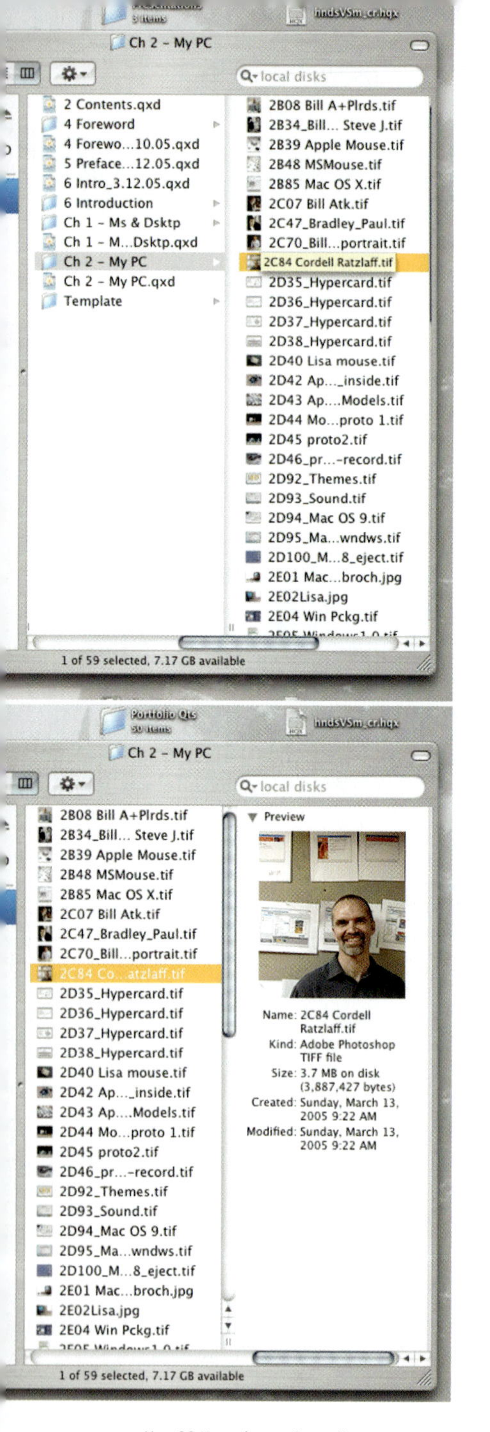

- Mac OS X—column view—list
- Mac OS X—column view—thumbnail

quicker, allows for easier backtracking, and doesn't leave the desktop cluttered with extraneous windows that the user needs to clean up later.

Mac OS X is an evolutionary step forward in the series of graphical user interfaces that originated with the desktop and windows metaphors, but it feels like a design for computer interaction, rather than a metaphorical connection to the familiar world of physical objects in offices. We still use words like window, desktop, and folder, but the appearance and behavior of the designs have evolved to a level where they communicate their own attributes rather than the characteristics of a throwback to a physical world.

Cordell believes that design should be driven first by user needs and desires:

> There is nothing that I would not consider changing; I think an interface really has to be appropriate for the people who are using it, and the task that they are performing. People don't use a computer to enjoy the operating system; they don't care about setting their system preferences, nor do they care about choosing what kind of scrollbars they want. They use a computer because they want to create something; they want to communicate with somebody; they want to express their own personality, everything from writing a novel to balancing their checkbook—some more fun than others, but it's all about accomplishing something that really doesn't have anything to do with using a computer. The computer is just a tool.
>
> As interaction designers, we need to remember that it is not about the interface, it's about what people want to do! To come up with great designs, you need to know who those people are and what they are really trying to accomplish.

The Time Dimension

The design team developed the concept of a time-based operating system, using not only the two dimensions that you have on the screen, but also the third dimension of time. For example, everybody's favorite complaint about the Macintosh human interface was that dragging a disk icon to the trash would eject it. That confused new users, because normally if you had a file that you wanted to delete, you would drag it to the trash and it would be gone; it seemed so wrong to make the same gesture eject a very valuable disk, full of information. In Mac OS X, depending on what you are doing at the time, different options are available to you. When you select an object that can be ejected, the trashcan changes to an eject icon, making sure that the action and what was showing on the screen are appropriate to the context. Similarly, when you select an empty CD or DVD disk, the trashcan changes to a "burn" icon.

In previous versions of Mac OS, when you selected an application, all of that application's windows came to the forefront. In Mac OS X, those windows appear in the order that you used them. If, for example, you are switching from Photoshop to an HTML editor, the Photoshop window is only one window behind; the system does not bring all of the other HTML editor windows to the front. This keeps the windows ordered in a way that people use them. As long as you can access the close button, even if it is behind several other windows, you can just click on it and it is gone.

The principle of the time-based interface was built on some of the work that had been done in the Apple Advanced Technology Group (ATG) many years before:

> There was a project in ATG called Rosebud that explored how the dimension of time could be used to help people find things. This was based on an insight that people sometimes associate information with chronological events or sequences. For example, people may not remember where they saved a particular document on their computer but know that the last time they modified it was two days ago. Or

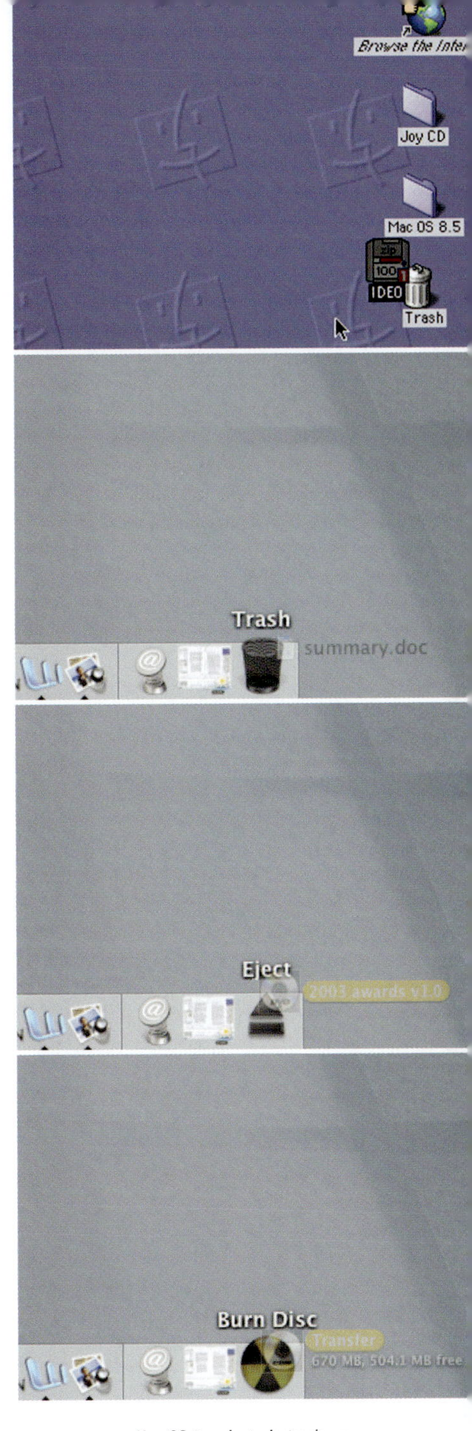

Mac OS 8—eject via trash ■
Mac OS X—trash ■
Mac OS X—eject ■
Mac OS X—burn ■

they may remember reading or creating information in relation to other events happening in their lives at that time.

What we found was that a lot of people thought about the content on their computer in terms of time, “When was the last time I read this? When was the last time I changed this? What else was I doing the last time I opened this document?”

Thinking about this, we came to the conclusion that time is a useful way for people to organize information on their computer. Seeing objects and information arranged chronologically could be just as helpful as hierarchical or spatial organization. Time is something we all flow through; there are people who associate objects with events that happen in time, so why not take advantage of that in the interface?

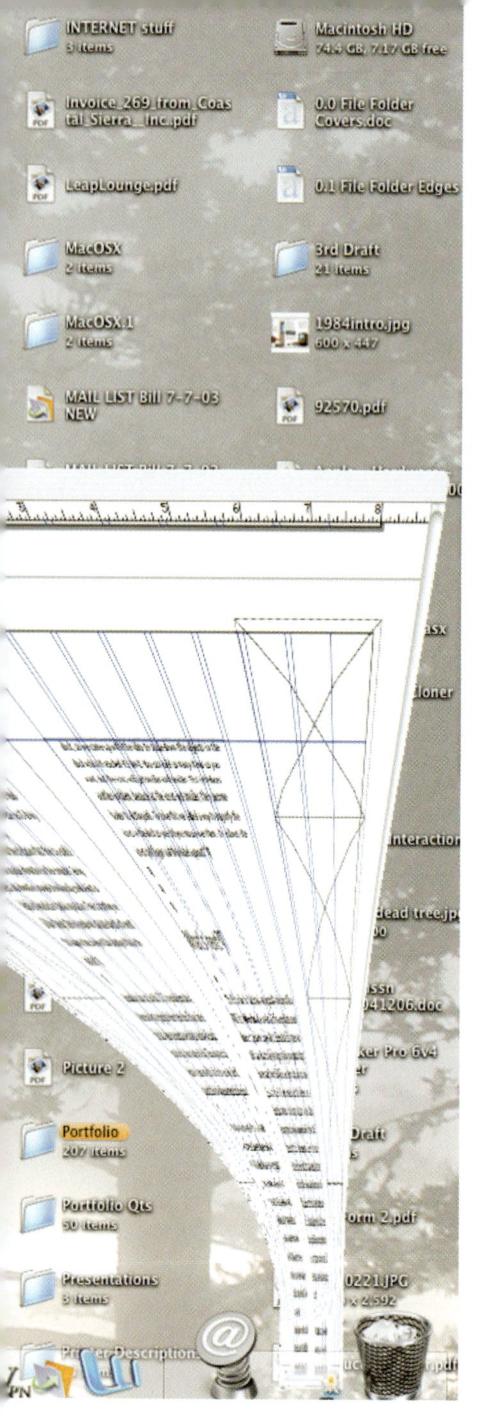

■ Mac OS X—animation to minimize a window

Animation is also used in Mac OS X to provide hints about where an object is going and where it came from. You see that in the dock, when you minimize a window, the window will morph into the place where it rests in the dock. When you restore that window it comes out of the dock in the same way. Cordell explains that the dock was the answer to more than one problem:

We worked on the dock for a long time. It was a way to consolidate a lot of the things that people were using in previous versions of Mac OS. We knew that people wanted an easy way to launch applications and documents. We knew people wanted an easy way to switch between applications. We knew people needed a way to manage their windows and minimize them, so that they could get back to them very quickly. There were several different components in previous versions of Mac OS that allowed people to do that, but they were scattered over various parts of the interface. We were looking for one consolidated, consistent way to combine and simplify them. The dock was a way to achieve that.

One of the biggest challenges we had with the dock was working with a finite screen size. You can keep adding things to the dock, but at some point you run out of space. That’s where animation comes in. As more and more things are added to the dock, it spreads out. What happens when the dock expands to the edge of the screen? You can’t add any more things; you’ve got to take something out!

We didn’t want to limit the number of items people could put in the dock, so we came up with the idea to scale down the objects in the dock when it reached its limit. You can add as many items as you want, but the icons will get smaller and smaller. This introduces another problem, because as the icons get smaller, they become harder to distinguish. To solve this we added a way to magnify the icons in the dock as you roll your mouse over them. On rollover, the icons get bigger and their label appears.

Mac OS X—dock icons magnifying ■

What's Next?

The Finder for the Macintosh was originally developed for a 400K disk with no hard drive, so that all of your applications and documents could live on one disk. A hierarchical file system was added later, when the disk got bigger, to help you organize things in a structured way. Hard drives are huge today, and you have access to your local area network and the Internet, so a hierarchical browser is no longer adequate. In the future, operating systems for personal computers are likely to have "find" functionality that is better integrated. Google[18] uses search techniques that work much better than hierarchical structures would, for the almost infinitely large information source of the Web, but similar methods could also be applied to information on a PC, or local network. Operating systems are likely to be more active in organizing themselves and presenting information to the users when they want it, in a way that suits them. Cordell believes that at some point the whole desktop metaphor is going to go away:

> We've got this metaphor that's based on real world objects—like documents, folders, and a trash can—which is good, but it's becoming obsolete. For example, my two daughters, ages eleven and seven, have been using a computer since they were one or two years old. Their first experience with a folder came to them from the computer, not a manila file folder that sits on a real desk. For them, the concept of a folder as a container didn't come from a real-world object; it came from something they saw on a computer. Similarly, the whole application/document model was developed for people who

were creating content; what most people do today with computers is consume content. If you look at the trend of more people wanting to access information rather than produce information, that could call for a completely different metaphor. I'm not sure what that is yet.

The metaphor of the desktop has already been replaced by the metaphor of the page for browsing the Web. Although you still start from your desktop when you use a PC, as soon as you open a Web browser, you are moving away from file folders toward sites made of pages, with pieces of information linked to each other by cross references; this feels different from documents stacked in folders, and folders collected in volumes. The desk is being invaded by loosely connected pages, which float and flutter in infinite free space, making it very hard to keep tidy!

Transactions are also leaving the desktop. If you go to Amazon.com to buy a book, you step through the interactions page by page. That is different from the desktop and also very different from the experience you have when you go to a physical bookstore. Cordell hopes that future interactive technologies will make the Web a much richer experience:

> Maybe it's an agent model, where you just tell your computer, "This is what I want, this is the price I'm willing to pay for it. Go off and do it, and come back to me when you've got it."
>
> You could think of your computer more as a personal assistant that helps you do things. You give it high-level directions, it goes off and does it and comes back to you with the results. Knowledge Navigator[19] was a great attempt to visualize the agent-based interface. I wish someone would build it. So far, all efforts to develop something like that have failed miserably. They come off as either an idiot-savant, who does some things brilliantly but flounders at others; a four-year-old child, who tries to help but only gets in the way; or an amnesiac, who completely forgets what you told it to do the last time.
>
> For agents like the Knowledge Navigator to really work, they've got to be right 99 percent of the time, because you're not going to put up with something that misreads your intentions or interrupts with inane questions. It's a level of trust: "Do I really trust this thing to do the right thing for me?" It doesn't take too many instances of

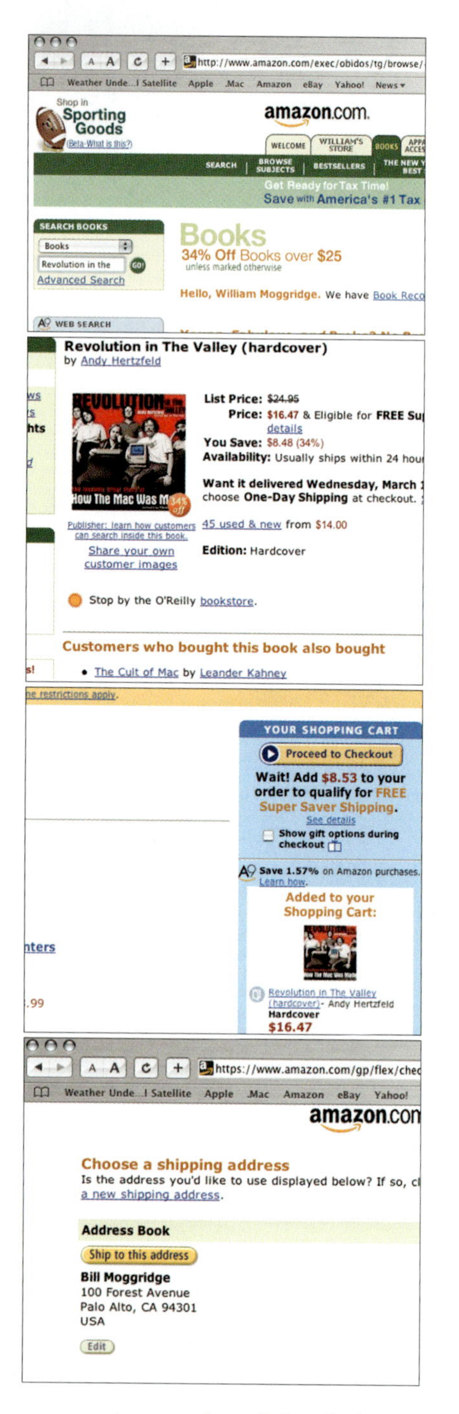

- Amazon purchase—finding a book
- Amazon purchase—seeing the details
- Amazon purchase—checkout
- Amazon purchase—shipping

an agent suggesting something completely out of context, or doing something that you really didn't want it to do, to make you lose confidence in its ability.

Maybe the fallacy of the Knowledge Navigator is having one agent that can do everything for you. Perhaps I need a book-buying agent that's great at going out and finding exactly the book I want, for the lowest price, and it can get it to me the fastest, and it can also recommend other books that might interest me. It just does one thing and it does it very well.

I don't think we are ever going to get computers to replicate the creativity, flexibility, and irrationality of humans. I think that's the great thing about being human!

3

From the Desk to the Palm

Interviews with John Ellenby, Jeff Hawkins, Bert Keely, Rob Haitani, and Dennis Boyle

In the 1990s there will be millions of personal computers. They will be the size of notebooks today, have high-resolution flat-screen reflexive displays, weigh less than ten pounds, have ten to twenty times the computing and storage capacity of an Alto. Let's call them Dynabooks.

Alan Kay, 1971[1]

■ Desktop workstation from Metaphor Computers, designed by Mike Nuttall of Matrix Product Design and Jim Yurchenco of David Kelley Design

Photo
Rick English

Designing the laptop and the palmtop was about shrinking the computer so that you could take it with you, first as a luggable suitcase, then in your briefcase, and eventually in your pocket. The transition from desktop machines to laptops was about designing the physical interface to be small enough to carry easily without changing the interactions on the display significantly because of the smaller size. And the same interface and applications had to work on both.

Alan Kay is well known for his summarizing the Xerox PARC credo as: "The best way to predict the future is to invent it!" His conceptual contributions helped in the formation of the Alto and the Dynabooks in parallel, so we look first at how his ideas about portability emerged, and how his group at PARC developed the first luggable computer, the NoteTaker. The next dramatic shrinking of the machine was the leap from luggable to laptop. The author's personal account of the story of designing the GRiD Compass, the first laptop computer, is included in the introduction, as it triggered his quest for interaction design. The rest of the story of how the Compass came into being is told in an interview with John Ellenby, the founder of GRiD Systems.

treo
handspring
powered by
News
Stock Quotes
Sports
Directions
Weather
Directory of Mobile
Google

Jeff Hawkins joined GRiD as an entrepreneurial young engineer and, after gaining some experience working for John Ellenby, was given responsibility for developing GRiDpad, the first tablet computer to reach the market. He describes how he went on to create the palmtop, leading the team that created the Palm operating system (OS) and developing the series of PalmPilots that were so successful. The Palm OS was developed in 1995 and was an immediate success. It is dramatically different from the operating systems that evolved for personal computers: there is no mouse or desktop. Rob Haitani was a key member of Jeff's team right from the beginning and was in charge of the interaction design for the Palm OS and its applications; he discusses the reasons behind the design of the operating system in his interview and recounts the details of the process.

Jeff Hawkins went on to found Handspring, extending the range of products using the Palm OS. He had worked with Dennis Boyle of IDEO to develop the Palm V, a design that was attractive enough to dramatically increase the popularity of electronic organizers, and continued to work with Dennis for a series of products at Handspring. Dennis tells how the Palm V was designed and how he and his team developed a camera to plug into the Handspring Springboard slot. The chapter concludes with the story of the development of the Handspring Treo, which combined the PDA organizer with an email communicator and a cell phone.

■ Handspring Treo

Photo Courtesy of Handspring

Alan Kay

Alan Kay argues that user interface design started when the people who were designing computers noticed that end users had functioning minds. He describes his own epiphany:

> For me it was the FLEX machine, an early desktop personal computer of the late sixties designed by Ed Cheadle and myself. Based on much previous work by others, it had a tablet as a pointing device, a high-resolution display for text and animated graphics, and multiple windows, and it directly executed a high-level object-oriented end-user simulation language. And of course it had a "user interface," but one that repelled end users instead of drawing them closer to the hearth.[2]

In 1968 he felt that he was "hit on the head" by several amazing innovations. At the University of Illinois there was the first little piece of glass with glowing text characters, giving a glimpse of the future potential for flat screen displays. He then read McLuhan's *Understanding Media* (1964),[3] and the concept that "the medium is the message" made him believe that it is in the nature of people to be reshaped by tools, that the invention of the printing press really did make us a scientific society, and hence living in the age of computers will reshape us again:

■ Alan Kay

Photo Courtesy of The National Academies

> The computer is a medium! I had always thought of the computer as a tool, perhaps a vehicle[4]—a much weaker conception. What McLuhan was saying is that if the personal computer is truly a new medium, then the very use of it will actually change the thought patterns of an entire civilization. He had certainly been right about the electronic stained-glass window that is television—a remedievalizing tribal influence at best.[5]

Shortly after reading McLuhan, Kay visited Seymour Papert at MIT's Artificial Intelligence Laboratory. Papert had spent five years working with Jean Piaget, a psychologist who studied the ways in which children learn, and had found that they could explore computer-simulated worlds as they explore the real world. Alan saw children writing computer programs that generated poetry, translated English into Pig Latin, and created arithmetic environments. Before that he had thought that people would need to be able to program a computer before they could feel that they owned it, but here was a demonstration, even with children, that as long as you can "read" a medium, you can make use of and enjoy material and tools that are made by other people, and if you can "write" in the medium, you can create material and tools for other people:

> If the computer is only a vehicle, perhaps you can wait until high school to give "driver's ed" on it—but if it's a medium, then it must be extended all the way into the world of the child. How to do it? Of course it has to be done on the intimate notebook-sized Dynabook! But how would anyone "read" the Dynabook, let alone "write" on it?

This was a moment of inspiration that changed Alan Kay's life. He became fascinated by the idea of developing computers for children and started on a quest in that direction that still engrosses him. It is disappointing that this decision has kept him an abstract contributor in the world of the laptop and palmtop, as the earliest products to be developed for manufacture and sale were inevitably high priced,[6] and therefore aimed at the people who could afford to pay the most, such as executives, spies, and soldiers, rather than children. The portable machines that Alan developed and inspired were laboratory prototypes and much less influential than Smalltalk and his other software contributions. In spite of this, he is recognized as the father of the laptop.

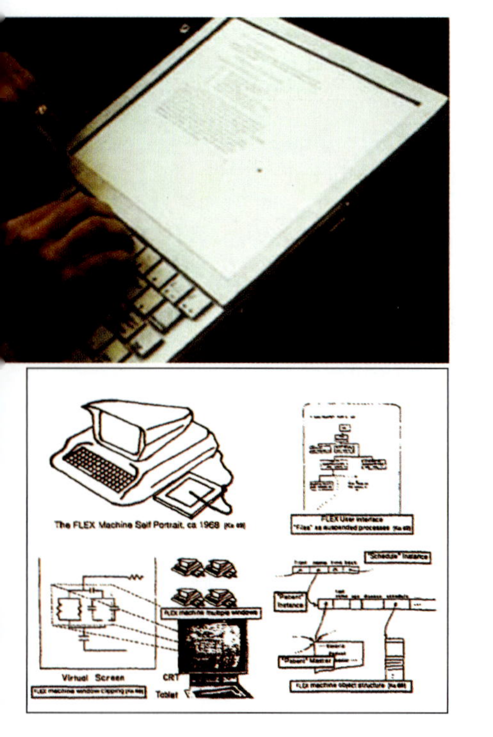

■ Dynabook concept
■ FLEX Machine

Learning

THE IDEA THAT learning involves more than one state of mind has emerged from Alan's thinking as a basic principle of interaction design, applying to adults as well as children. After the visit to MIT, he started to study child psychology and learning processes, and he discovered the work of Jerome Bruner.[7] Bruner described three distinct stages in the learning process, each of which has a different state of mind: "Enactive, iconic, and symbolic." This was illustrated by an experiment with two water glasses, one short and fat, and the other tall and thin. When children are shown the contents of the short glass being poured into the tall one, they will say that there is more water in the tall one, even though they saw the pouring. If you then hide both glasses, the children change their minds, reasoning that the water had nowhere else to go. This could be done several times; each time the children would repeat the assertion that there was more water in the tall thin glass whenever they could see it but deny it when it was not visible. The experiment illustrates the different mental states that underlie our learning process.

> Bruner convinced me that learning takes place best environmentally, and roughly in stage order—it is best to learn something kinesthetically, then iconically, and finally the intuitive knowledge will be in place that will allow the more powerful but less vivid symbolic processes to work at their strongest. . . .
>
> Now, if we agree with the evidence that the human cognitive facilities are made up of a doing mentality, an image mentality, and a symbolic mentality, then any user interface that we construct should at least cater to the mechanisms that seem to be there. But how? One approach is to realize that no single mentality offers a complete answer to the entire range of thinking and problem solving. User interface design should integrate them at least as well as Bruner did in his spiral curriculum of ideas.[8]

What I hear, I forget.

What I say, I remember.

What I do, I understand.

Lao Tse

Designers are used to the idea of learning by doing. They know that creative work is more likely to succeed when they experiment before they try to understand, moving from doing things to creating an image of a design intention and then iterating this process until they recognize the value of the resulting design. Only later, or perhaps never, do they understand the symbolic relationships of the solution that they have created. Understanding these three stages could help us design interactions that allow a similar learning process.

Luggables

Alan Kay inspired the researchers at PARC by promoting a long-term vision that he called "Dynabook." The Dynabook was to be a computer so portable and so connected that a pupil would carry it between home and school daily, instead of carrying printed textbooks and paper notebooks. Around 1970 Alan drew pictures of what, today, we would think of as small laptops, large PDAs and tablet computers. In 1976, having developed Smalltalk, he shifted his attention toward a new project called NoteTaker, another notebook-sized computer. The central idea was to take a percentage of the Alto's functionality and put it in a compact portable machine. The design was to include a custom-built display screen that was touch-sensitive—to eliminate the mouse—stereo audio speakers with a built-in microphone, a rechargeable battery, and an Ethernet port. However, the technology at the time was highly limited. The actual NoteTaker was a plump attaché case that looked like the first generation of the "luggable" computers that were created six years later. The lid flipped down with the screen and disk drive set in the body, which faced the user when the box was laid flat on a table. The lid held the keyboard, which was connected to the computer inside the body by a flexible cable. Larry Tesler was part of the team at that time. Here's his description of the process.

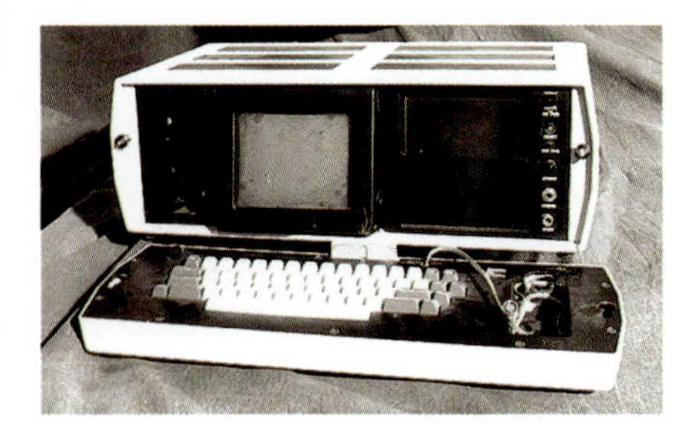

■ NoteTaker

> For the first time in my life, I got involved in a hardware project. With a little help, I designed the CPU board. I also figured out a way to squeeze an Ethernet controller on a single, small circuit board, something the hardware engineers thought was impossible at that time. The NoteTaker was an amazing machine. It contained three 8086 processors. (We got early samples of the 8086 from Intel in 1978.)
>
> It was heavy—35 pounds plus 10 pounds if you inserted the batteries—but it was the most powerful portable computer of its time, if not the only one in existence. After we got it running, and Smalltalk was ported to it, we vowed to convince the Xerox management to fund development and mass production. We scheduled trips to demo the system to various Xerox executives. Unlike the Alto, which had to be shipped as freight, we were able to carry the NoteTaker with us on the plane. Once, when nobody was around, we turned on this top-secret machine in an airport lounge and ran a Smalltalk program. This may have been the first time a portable computer was used in an airport by a business traveler.

Ten prototype machines were built, but that was not enough to convince the Xerox management to produce them. The director of service got excited about the idea of every technician who serviced copiers replacing a big stack of blueprints and manuals with a portable computer. His vision was that they could connect the NoteTaker to a modem and download the repair manuals for the copier that was being serviced or repaired. He was willing to back the production of the design but never got top management approval.

The most famous luggable computer was the Osborne, which was released in 1981. The tiny five-inch diagonal screen displayed white characters on a dark green background and was symmetrically flanked by two 5¼″ floppy drives. It weighed almost twenty-five pounds without the battery pack and when closed looked like a sewing machine case. The symmetry gave it a strangely facial expression when open, with the floppy drives like armored eye slits, and the cable that connected the keyboard like the tongue of a cheeky little boy. Priced at $1,795, the Osborne 1 was wildly successful at first, selling more than eleven

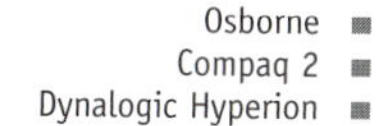
Osborne ■
Compaq 2 ■
Dynalogic Hyperion ■

thousand units in the first eight months. The boom was short lived, as the IBM PC was starting to dominate the market, and Osborne did not bring out an IBM-compatible machine in time to prevent bankruptcy in 1983.

The demand for "luggables" was filled by the Compaq Portable, running MS-DOS on an Intel 8088 processor, and with a nine-inch diagonal screen that could display twenty-five lines of eighty characters. Priced at $3,590, this design served Compaq well, and by 1986 they were on the Fortune 500 list, breaking a speed record in arriving there. The Dynalogic Hyperion was another MS-DOS machine, released three months earlier than the Compaq. The keyboard could be slid underneath the main unit and locked into place for carrying.[9] It lost the battle with Compaq because it was not fully PC-compatible and had some reliability problems with the disk drives. It vanished after two years.

These "luggable" machines were battling for market share in the same timeframe as the GRiD Compass computer, which was released in 1982 at a price of $8,150. The story of how that led the author toward the design of interactions is told in the introduction. Next, John Ellenby, the founder of GRiD Systems, gives his account of how it happened.[10]

Photo Author

John Ellenby holding the briefcase that determined the size of the first laptop

When John Ellenby arrived at Xerox PARC in 1974, he was surprised by the thing called a mouse; he was used to a solid-feeling trackball to manipulate the cursor on the big graphic displays at Ferranti in the UK, where he had spent the previous few years working on a multiprocessor system for communications and process control, while simultaneously holding a faculty position in the Computer Science Department at the University of Edinburgh. He was tenured as an assistant lecturer at the London School of Economics when he was still in his twenties, using computers as a research tool. Xerox invited him to PARC, hoping that his combination of academic background and experience in industry would help in the transition from research findings to real products. He was impressed by the research and the people and enthusiastically signed up to build the first twenty-five Altos. He went on to reengineer the Alto and to develop Dover, the first preproduction version of a laser printer. In 1977 he was given responsibility for "Futures Day,"[11] a demo to show off the achievements of the PARC researchers to the entire top management of Xerox. John teamed up with Tim Mott to make it spectacular. He hired talent from Hollywood to make sure the presentations were professional and arranged for the majority of the prototype equipment at PARC to be shipped to Boca Raton in Florida for the event. It was a huge success, but Xerox remained focused on the reproduction of documents, causing an exodus from PARC. It was then that John decided to found his own company to create a new kind of computer.

Quarterly Projections
7000
6000
5000
4000
3000
2000
1000
Group A
Group B
Group C
Compass Computer
GRiD

John Ellenby

Developing the First Laptop

■ GRiD Compass computer preproduction prototype, 1981

Photo Don Fogg

WHILE JOHN ELLENBY was at PARC he got to know Alan Kay and appreciated the promise of the Dynabook concepts. At the same time, he was worried by Alan Kay's goal of developing machines for children. John was pragmatic enough to know that the initial price point would be too high for normal kids for anything as innovative as Alan was describing. The starting point had to be the customer with the most money and the most demanding need. Here is his description of the conversation that inspired the laptop:

> I was meeting with a guy in the government. He was actually in the executive office of the White House. He said, "I really like the Alto, John. I really like the Dover laser printer. I really like this gateway to the ARPAnet. I really like that. It's really good. I get emails this way, and documents this way, and the documents fly backwards and forwards, and this is really terrific and I really love it!"
>
> And I said, "Well, do you have anything that you don't like?"
>
> "Well, I don't use it!"
>
> "What do you mean? You said you like it."

> "I learnt enough about it very quickly, it's very simple to use. I've got my secretary using it, and she's a bright person, and she's the one that uses it."
>
> "Is that how you think it's going to go forward?"
>
> "No. Let me tell you what I want. I want all this capability of your beautiful Alto, and I want it in half your briefcase."
>
> And he went and grabbed my briefcase, which I actually still have. It was a classic one for a Xerox executive—leather, with a solid wooden liner. I said, "This briefcase? That's hard!"
>
> He said, "I want it to go in half that briefcase, because I carry papers around."
>
> "Do you think you are typical of people?"
>
> "Yeah, let me tell you. My job as a senior member of this establishment is to go to where the problems are. It's not my job to hang around in the office. I have staff here. I call them on the phone, I get to them by fax, I send them telexes: do this, do that, and they do it. My job is to go to where the problems are, so I want a computer, a real computer (he actually referred to it as an RFC—you can guess what the F is for), I want a real something-or-other computer to carry around with me that has the communications, has all the capabilities of the Alto, but is downsized for me to carry."
>
> Boy, that was a real opening for me, because at Ferranti I'd been looking at the technology of flat panels and the technology of microprocessors, and nonvolatile storage, and I was projecting out when all of those would come together into something that you could carry. Because I had lots of people that wanted them for fire control and process control—somebody who wants to go out and look at the process and also look at the thing that's controlling it. So to be able to link, and ideally by wireless, with something tablet like.

It was the briefcase that did it. It had to fit in the briefcase; not just inside, but in half of it! That became the design brief for developing the GRiD Compass computer. It was a seemingly impossible challenge that appealed to John's imagination and set him going with boundless energy and determination. He had seen the components used in computers steadily shrinking, but if you piled them on a table they would still amount to a volume that was probably double that of the briefcase, not half. He would have to attack each individual component, either completely reconfiguring the item for a new shrunken configuration or thinking of a lateral solution that would allow him to use a completely different item.

First he had to start a company to do this, so he left Xerox in January 1980 and started structuring the dream team to make it possible. He gathered key Silicon Valley figures for his board, successfully raised money, and put together an amazingly talented team of founders for GRiD Systems. The company was structured in the best Silicon Valley tradition of attracting people of the highest caliber by offering an exciting challenge and founders' stock. They would then be motivated to dedicate their lives to the success of the company, working long hours and doing everything themselves to begin with, with the expectation of becoming the highest officers in the company when the product proved its value. There were key players in charge of R&D, manufacturing, marketing, and experts in electronic hardware, software, and physical engineering and design. John transformed himself as he got the company going. In three months he changed from a free-living and easygoing person to someone who was dedicating every second of his life to a single purpose.

One of the challenges was to find a way to hold the data and avoid the bulky disk drives that were being used for machines like the Alto. The Alto certainly sported a beautiful high-resolution display and mouse for interacting with the software, but the rest of the machine was huge and clumsy, too large to fit on top of a desk, let alone in a portable unit. John called it the "Gzunda."

> I called mine Gzunda, which no one understood. In Britain Gzunda is the potty you put under the bed. People said, "Why Gzunda?"
>
> I said, "Well, it goes unda the desk."
>
> It occupied the whole of the desk, so you had to sort of cramp your way in. You had to dedicate a large part of your office to this box. Much of it was taken up by a big Diablo disk drive that held almost nothing at all, but in those days, that was all we could get. The processor was big and chunky, and the screen and everything else needed a lot of work.

Alto

The answer was to use bubble memory, a nonvolatile storage component from Intel. This could then be combined with modem access to remote data, to be provided from servers at "GRiD Central," and each individual customer could have access to a larger file capacity than the 256K of bubble memory that was built into the laptop. The modem was also an essential part of the communications solution, but modems were big then too.

> We managed to get a modem built. We went and met with Racal Vadic. We said we wanted a 1,900-baud modem, and they said, "Oh yeah, we make those. We'll go get one."
>
> They brought this thing out that's twice the size of a shoebox. We said, "Yes, we want a 1,900-baud modem, and we want it to use only 55 watts, and we want it to be this size," showing them something the size of two packets of cigarettes.
>
> "No way! Absolutely no way."
>
> "Well, we've spec'd it out, we have to have a 1,900-baud modem, so either you're going to do the work for us, or someone else is gonna do it."
>
> "No, no, we can't do that!"
>
> Our hardware guy was sitting across the table from his counterpart in Racal Vadic, who gave him this wink, and we thought, "This guy had obviously figured out that, yes, with a monolithic, they know how to do it."
>
> So we engineered a sort of around-the-corner discussion with this guy, and sure enough, they could do it. It was a wonderful example of the Valley working.

The electronic components were starting to look somewhere close to feasible. They settled on the Intel 8086 processor. The details of the size tradeoffs would drive the physical design, with the most obvious questions being the size and weight. The first question for the component arrangement was which half of the briefcase to fill; a blockish volume could fill the left or right half, and a large flat arrangement would fit in the top or bottom half. The large flat alternative was advantageous for the keyboard and display—and an elegant proportion.

The first keyboard was too wide and too thick, so they developed a layout that still had the QWERTY arrangement but made do with fewer additional keys. They then found a vendor who was be willing to develop a thinner construction that still had good human factors of key travel and snap action for tactile feedback. The first display that they found was too small, using a limited number of characters on five lines, so that the amount of information that you could see was disappointing. They eventually found a prototype of a bright electroluminescent display of tiny golden yellow squares, developed by Sharp in their labs in Osaka, with individually addressable pixels rather than an array of characters. John describes the negotiations with Sharp:

> The small screen that we had for the launch was an amazing screen; it was done for us by Sharp. We found it through a wonderful Japanese guy called Glen Fukuda, who came in and said, "I don't know anything about electronics, but this is exciting, and I understand you need a screen, and where would you go? Obviously Japan. And where would you go in Japan? Well, let's go talk to these companies."
>
> He did a bit of research. It was wonderful to work with this guy. He convinced Sharp Corporation, who were working on electroluminescent panels in the lab, to come and meet with us. I think it was Mr. Okana, who was the head of all research at Sharp Corporation, who came out first. He came to my house in Palo Alto and had to walk under this enormous oak tree. It had been raining, and the rain was still dripping from the oak tree. Afterwards his translator told Glen Fukuda to give the message to Mr. Ellenby that Mr. Okana, "Visited, knew the future, and raindrops fell, even though it was not raining."
>
> I still get goose bumps when I think of that. This guy was head of Sharp's research. He had decided some time back to take the money that they would have used for a huge show of all the Japanese electronics companies and create this research laboratory for the EL panel and other advanced components. There was this wonderful moment when Sharp committed to build the electroluminescent panel for us. It was gorgeous, a wonderful, beautiful orange; I'd never seen anything like it.

The six-inch diagonal seems tiny now, but it was amazing to find such an excellent flat display at the time, which supported bitmap graphics as well as characters. Sharp built a factory

John Ellenby with the GRiD Compass computer at launch ■
IBM PC ■

especially to manufacture it for GRiD. All this was very new at the time, as there was not yet even an Osborne, an IBM PC, or an Apple Mac, let alone a pervasive Internet.

The power supply needed to deliver a whopping eighty watts, and was a huge brick at the beginning, so they worked on breaking it down and integrating it with the main printed circuit board to reduce the volume.

The first calculation for the weight was over eleven pounds, enough to stretch your arm if you carried it around for long in a briefcase that already had papers in it. The founders of the company were equipped with sets of weights, and asked to adjust the amount that they carried around in their briefcases so that it was starting to hurt, but without being completely intolerable. They came to a consensus that there was a dramatic cross over point at eight pounds, so that became the weight specification.

John wanted a repair service that would benefit from the overnight shipping offered by Federal Express, so that customers could send back a faulty machine and have it returned to them with a two-day turnaround. This set a standard for a drop test that was more demanding than the accidents that were likely if the machine fell off a table or was dropped by someone carrying it. They rented an impact recorder to find out how much rough handling the shipping would entail and sent it by Federal Express to Washington and back. When it returned, they unfurled the chart paper of the recorder in a long snake across the floor of the office. They saw the 20g impact (twenty times the force of gravity) when the recorder was collected from the office and tossed into the truck. They saw about the same impact when it was loaded on to the plane at the airport, but the big shock was at three in the morning when it was put through the automated sorting system at the central office of Federal Express in St. Louis. There it saw 60g, the equivalent of dropping it from three feet onto a concrete floor. This then became the specification for the robustness of the enclosure, a demanding mechanical engineering challenge. They chose to design the enclosure in die-cast magnesium, for the combination of strength and lightness, succeeding in meeting the specification and creating an amazingly tough machine. It was sent up in the space shuttle and used on Air Force One as a result.

The GRiD Compass computer was launched to the public at the Office Automation Conference in the spring of 1982 and was highly acclaimed. The price was double that of the luggable machines, so the market was limited to cases where high value was attached to small size, prestige, performance, and durability. The plan was to sell the products to large companies, so that the individuals could gain access to company-wide information on the road, connecting in to the "GRiD Central" server with the built-in modem. The most common users were expected to be sales and business executives. This audience did prove to be the mainstay for the company, but the business climate for computers was dramatically altered when IBM unveiled their personal computer in August 1981, and by the time the Compass was out, the world was moving fast toward MS-DOS and PC-compatibles. GRiD OS had a set of central common code that was very compact and supported a spreadsheet, a text processor, a terminal emulator, a message/email solution, and a draw program—all with a consistent user interface. They also had a universal file system structure so that a call from a program would go directly to the data, wherever it was. It could be in RAM, ROM, bubble memory or local disk, external local disk, out over wire at "GRiD Central," or over the GRiD server within a client company. These were strong advantages, but not enough to resist the surge of demand for IBM PC compatibility, so John decided that the next version of the Compass would have to run MS-DOS, and it would be needed fast.

> In order to do an MS-DOS machine, we had to do an IBM-compatible machine that ran MS-DOS. I remember going up to visit with Bill Gates; Charles Simonyi was up there at the time. Charles and I had worked at Xerox together. We showed them what we were doing, and Bill says, "This is great. Of course we'll do a special version of MS-DOS for you."
>
> I could have reached across the table and given this guy a kiss.

Pictures of GRiD Compass in space ■

GRiD GRiD
GRiD GRiD

The speed with which the GRiD team created the new version to run both GRiD OS and MS-DOS probably saved the company, which avoided the fate that had overtaken Osborne. The extraordinary toughness of the design also gave the unit an appeal for intelligence agents and soldiers, and soon GRiD was doing a thriving business in Washington. John talks about soldiers playing games:

> We were selling a lot of GRiD computers to the armed forces. We had this wonderful game called Flak Attack. These tanks shot at each other and at airplanes—a great game. You selected the device and fired the gun by hitting the spacebar. We had a lot of equipment with the ninth infantry division in Fort Lewis, Washington. They bought a whole lot of GRiDs because they were developing mobility concepts—how can you move fast, run around in ATVs—a pretty exciting outfit. They took them out to the Yakima firing range and used them out there, which is sort of high deser—very cold at night, very hot during the day, very dusty. They were charging around with their GRiDs, and several GRiDs came back. I thought that this was a problem. It turned out that all of them had broken space bars. We thought, "Have these guys been playing Flak Attack?"
>
> They were getting carried away. Whack! Whack! They'd actually been smashing the spacebar like proper infantry men should. You know, FIRE, FIRE, FIRE, FIRE! So that was a relief.
>
> Once I was in Fort Lewis, in the officers' mess. I was talking to one of the senior officers there, and he said, "The officers won't use this stuff. It's going to be used by the staff sergeants. We're kind of the executive level here."
>
> He was a bit full of himself. There was a guy from what I think was a special forces unit standing there. I asked him afterwards, "You think officers will be using it?"
>
> "Absolutely. They're going to be some of your biggest users. Let me show you."
>
> And he took me out into the rec room that was part of the officers' mess, and it had this row of video games. And there were all these young officers . . . "NNEEAAAOOO! CLICK CLICK CLICK!" There was Atari, all this stuff, all these fire, fire, bang, bang, bang games.

■ 1984 version of the GRiD laptop, with LCD display, floppy disk drive, and IBM compatibility

Photo Courtesy of IDEO

The basic design for the GRiD Compass computer stayed the same for more than ten years. There were many different components, with larger displays using plasma and LCD technology, floppy disk drives, and of course all of the electronics. The way in which the screen folded over the keyboard for carrying was one of the innovative features protected by patent, and it was this feature that generated income for GRiD, by licensing the design to other laptop manufacturers such as Toshiba and Sanyo. This geometry remained the dominant design for laptops until the components had shrunk enough to fit them around the keyboard and display, so that a clamshell arrangement became possible without a volume projecting out of the back behind the hinge.

The interaction design advances in this first laptop included the physical interaction of the shape and size, the folding geometry, and achieving a tolerable weight for carrying. The operating system was also very innovative, building on many of the concepts that had come out of Xerox PARC in the seventies. Jeff Hawkins, the founder of Palm and Handspring, worked at GRiD just before the launch of the Compass.

> The GRiD OS was far ahead of anything anyone had conceived of at the time. We had a graphical OS—although without a mouse, but it was a graphical OS—scalable fonts, and a lot of the other concepts that later took hold in the computer industry. It was a true multitasking operating system, it was small, it was fast; it just was leagues ahead of everything else. We had email running on it way before anyone in the business had even heard of email; it had servers; it really had all the technology.

The precedent was set for laptops to follow, but it was Jeff who created GRiDpad, the first tablet PC and the next step toward Palm.

Photo Author

Jeff Hawkins

Jeff Hawkins has two sides to his life: one is designing mobile computers, and the other is working on brain theory. The side that is focused on the design of mobile computers led him to develop the first tablet PC, the GRiDpad, and then to found Palm Computing. At Palm, he was responsible for a series of products from the PalmPilot up to Palm V. He then went on to found Handspring, continuing with the evolution of designs with the series of Visors, and culminating with the Treo platform. The other half of his persona, dedicated to understanding the science of the human brain, has led him to start Numenta, where he is developing a new type of computer memory system modeled after the human neocortex. This technology is based on the ideas in his book *On Intelligence*,[12] which expounds an overall theory of how the brain works, and its implications for the design of computers. He sums it up as, "What makes humans special first and foremost is that we can model the world and we can predict the future; we can imagine the future. How the brain does this is what I detail in the book." This double passion has helped Jeff to clarify his strategies for success as an entrepreneur and designer of handheld computers, while at the same time developing a point of view about neuroscience that has caught the attention of prominent scientists. Jeff went to Intel after studying electrical engineering at Cornell and was attracted to join GRiD Systems in 1982, working as part of the launch team for the Compass computer. He was there for ten years, except for a two-year break to study neuroscience at UC Berkeley.

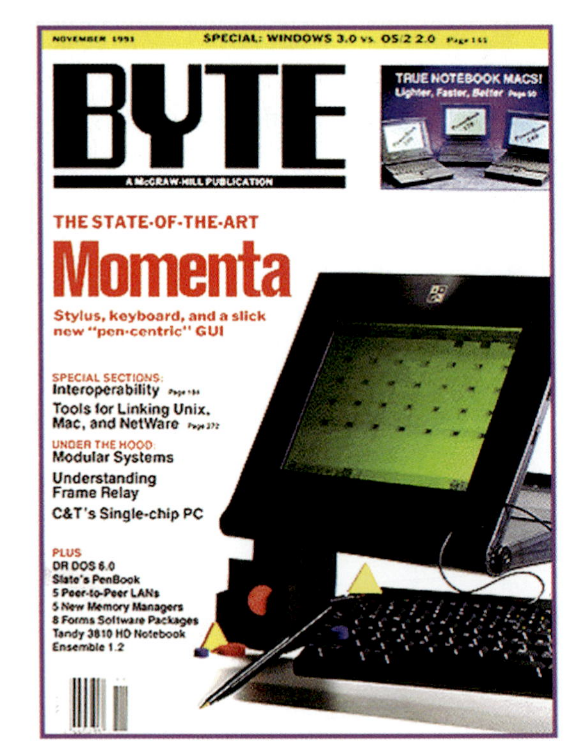
NOVEMBER 1991
SPECIAL: WINDOWS 3.0 vs. OS/2 2.0
BYTE
A McGRAW-HILL PUBLICATION
TRUE NOTEBOOK MACS!
Lighter, Faster, Better
THE STATE-OF-THE-ART
Momenta
Stylus, keyboard, and a slick new "pen-centric" GUI
SPECIAL SECTIONS:
Interoperability
Tools for Linking Unix, Mac, and NetWare
UNDER THE HOOD:
Modular Systems
Understanding Frame Relay
C&T's Single-chip PC
PLUS
DR DOS 6.0
Slate's PenBook
5 Peer-to-Peer LANs
5 New Memory Managers
8 Forms Software Packages
Tandy 3810 HD Notebook
Ensemble 1.2

Jeff Hawkins

While I was away at UC Berkeley, I conceived of the idea of doing a tablet computer. I was getting interested in pattern recognition, handwriting recognition. It's easy to put two and two together—a portable computer with stylus interface. It wasn't even my idea, but I saw the potential of it and said, "This is something we can do." I came back to GRiD in 1988 on the premise that I was going to develop the first tablet computer for them. I became the manager of the GRiDpad, the software suite and all the applications that came with it.

Jeff Hawkins, 2004

GRiD

Clockwise from top left

- GRiDpad
- Workslate
- Momenta
- GO

When Jeff Hawkins arrived at GRiD Systems in the spring of 1982, the Compass computer was designed but not yet launched, so he joined as part of the launch team, working on sales and marketing to put together training materials and write demo programs:

> It was very exciting because GRiD was a startup company, and they were inventing the first real laptop, a real innovation at the time. I became involved in figuring out how to sell the product, which was challenging. It was a beautiful machine, but it was very expensive. In 1982 dollars, it was $8,150. I will remember that price forever, as it was an incredible amount of money.
>
> We were trying to sell a laptop to business executives, when at the time no businessperson used a computer or knew how to type. This turned out to be one of the biggest problems we had. The keyboard was something that your assistant or your secretary used; it was associated with word processing. Business people were afraid to use anything with a keyboard: they didn't want to be seen using it;

they didn't want it in their office, because it made them look like their secretary. One of the largest obstacles, besides the price of the product, was just getting over people's expectations about what a business tool is and what a computer is and how business people use it. When you think back on it, it was amazing that it was difficult to get business people to use a laptop computer.

GRiDtask was a programming language that I developed as a marketing tool, to help people put together demos. I started making it more powerful to give it control of the computer, and to make it do anything you want. Soon our sales people were putting together applications for customers, using it as a sales tool. I was in marketing at the time I was doing this, so no one from engineering was looking over my shoulder. I had unfettered access to do whatever I wanted, and I created a very powerful tool. This became a language, which really became the heart and soul of much of what the company did from a software perspective going forward.

Jeff spent four years working hard with the marketing team at GRiD, struggling to sell the first laptop computer to customers who were not quite ready to pay so much for something that they thought their secretaries should use. The experience served to educate him about the nature of mobile computing, but at the same time he was hankering to learn more about neuroscience, and in 1986 he decided to leave GRiD to become a full-time graduate student in biophysics at UC Berkeley. He remembers the day he resigned:

John Ellenby was the founder of GRiD. I said, "John, I'm leaving, I'm going to go become an academic, I'm going to Berkeley."

And he was really smart. He said, "Well, maybe you should just take a leave of absence. You might come back. You never know."

I said, "I'm never going to come back, but fine, I'll take a leave of absence."

I left for a couple of years, but even when I was at Berkeley, I continued consulting for GRiD.

Jeff never really escaped the lure of developing mobile computers, or the excitement of working in Silicon Valley startup companies. It was during the two years that he was studying at

Berkeley that he came up with the idea of a tablet computer with a stylus interface.

> While I was away at UC Berkeley, I conceived of the idea of doing a tablet computer. I was getting interested in pattern recognition, handwriting recognition. It's easy to put two and two together: a portable computer with stylus interface. It wasn't even my idea, but I saw the potential of it and said, "This is something we can do." I came back to GRiD in 1988 on the premise that I was going to develop the first tablet computer for them. I became the manager of the GRiDpad, the software suite and all the applications that came with it.

Jeff was not the only individual with entrepreneurial visions of tablet computers. In fact, there was a flurry of new startup ventures at that time. As far back as 1983, Convergent Technologies had come out with a tablet computer called the Workslate[13] that was only 8½ x 11 x 1 inch, but it only had a small display and no stylus input and never found the right applications to make it successful.

By the time Jeff was ready to go back to work, there were several very interesting ventures under way in Silicon Valley. One option for Jeff was to join a startup company called Go:

> The whole tablet computer market was messy. We had the company Go, which took the high road. It had a whole new operating system, high-class hardware, high-class backers, and so on. I went and interviewed with them, because I didn't have to go back to GRiD, as I could have gone anywhere I wanted. I said, "Well, if there's a company formed to do this, I'll go check them out."
>
> I met with Go when there were five people there. I immediately sensed that they had too grandiose plans. They were going to change the world, do all this stuff. Startup companies struggle, and you have to be more focused.

The physical design for Go was elegant,[14] and they made a significant advance in the use of gestures for commands, so that the stylus could be used not just for handwriting and sketching, but also to trigger actions without relying on a pull-down menu structure. Jerry Kaplan chronicled the development of this attempt to start from scratch with a pen-based interface in his book *Startup: A Silicon Valley Adventure Story*,[15] including his loudly voiced challenge to Microsoft that he would dominate the future of computing. He had gone through $75 million in investment funding over a six-year period before he lost control of Go to AT&T.

Momenta was also a high profile startup company, funded by venture capital in the expectation that a general purpose market would emerge for tablet computers. They built a pen-based interface on top of a Windows PC but were unable to stay the pace of improvements in the underlying PC from competitors like Compaq, IBM, and Sony. The design was innovative in the use of the stylus for directional flicking as well as clicking and tapping. They introduced a command structure[16] based on a flying menu that appeared at the tip of the stylus when you tapped, and offered a menu of choices selected by flicking the stylus in one of eight directions.

Apple was another possible opportunity for Jeff, as by this time the research program that led to the Newton was well under way:

■ Apple Newton

> I had heard rumors that Apple was working on something like this; this was before the Newton came out. I talked to them, but at the time they didn't want to tell me what they were up to, so I had no idea that they were developing a completely new operating system. I thought the idea of porting the Mac OS onto a tablet was a more likely direction. In fact, when we were at GRiD, we approached Apple several times, trying to convince them to work with us on doing it, because we felt they had the best software platform for doing this. At that time, they weren't interested. I had an opportunity to pursue it further, but I had two solid options at GRiD and Go.
>
> I decided to go back to GRiD, as I knew that I would be in charge of the whole thing there, and that was more fun for me. GRiDpad was focused on simple form filling. GRiD was an existing company that was trying to survive; we were much more pragmatically focused. We were looking at vertical applications that we knew we could sell. I think GRiD had the most success of any of the new ventures. GRiDpad came out in the fall of '89, a little bit before the other tablet

computers. We built a business, I think its peak was around thirty million dollars a year, which was leagues ahead of what anyone else was doing in sales, but that's because we were very focused on vertical markets.

The shakeout in the pen computing and tablet computing area was not long in coming. It is typical in any emerging market that people get ahead of where the real business is. This was a situation where there was such confidence in the potential for pen computing to become the next wave of general-purpose machines that speculation fueled the investment in new ventures, and a lot of money was lost when sales turned out to be limited. It also got out of control because there was a big rivalry between Go and Microsoft, which stepped up the level of investment in both companies, but the business just wasn't there. Jeff believes that the problem was that these products were trying to replicate paper, putting them in competition with paper and books, a situation he has always tried to avoid:

I think paper is just this wonderful medium; it's been honed for a thousand years. It's really great! To try to do what you do with paper, with just drawing—line width, sketching, and so on—it's very hard to get a good experience. Where the tablet type of computer really shines is where you're not trying to capture the paperness of paper, but you're trying to get the electronic or the back end of it. Form filling is a great example, because actually forms are pretty hard to do on paper. You never have the right space, it's hard to know where to put things, there's not enough room for instructions. So, there's an example where an electronic version of a paper equivalent would be better. But in terms of the general idea that I'm going to sketch, draw and have a free-flowing paperlike experience—I'm skeptical about that.

Similarly with electronic books. Paper in books is just wonderful. It's a beautiful medium. It's superior in many ways to any sort of electronic form, especially if you're trying to create something in a similar form factor. Also for the readability of text. Paper is amazingly good for different light angles and brightness and so on. It's hard to get that on today's digital technology.

GRiD

"The essence of what I'm trying to bring to the personal computer, you should probably think of as a 'tablet mode,' that is, the easy option of using the computer with one hand, even when you're holding it with the other. While speech, touch, and buttons will all have a role, the pen is the most exciting tool with which to do that in the current generation of PCs."

When Bert Keely graduated from Stanford with an engineering degree, he went to a startup called Convergent Technologies, where he spent eight years developing desktop work stations. He first latched on to the concept of a handheld computer in 1988, when he joined John Ellenby to develop rugged devices for the police, fire service, and military markets at Agilis,[18] but the company was short-lived. Next he joined Silicon Graphics to develop work stations for design and scientific applications. It was there that he built an advanced prototype for a magazine page display with a powerful workstation behind it; the information, he thought, should be at the center of manual interactions. Silicon Graphics decided against taking this concept to market but gave Bert the opportunity to shop it around, leading him to a dialog with Bill Gates at Microsoft. He joined Microsoft in 1998, working first on software for electronic books, and then on a skunkworks tablet PC project, designed to help people take notes silently and intuitively in face-to-face meetings; this was launched as a service pack on top of Windows in 2002. Since then, Bert has been leading the efforts at Microsoft to improve the design of the tablet PC, earning the title of "architect of tablet PCs and mobility."

Windows Media Player 11
Share Your Library
Recycle Bin
AcerC200
Link to Desktop
Sticky Notes
Snipping Tool
How to Share Feedback
acer
TravelMate C200
IDEO
Alma
University

Bert Keely

The breakthrough will come when mainstream users find themselves thinking, "Oh, there are lots of situations in which I just use tablet mode, because of the physical freedom I get. I don't mind the fact that a keyboard can enter more words per minute than handwriting can, as I prefer tablet mode most of the time!" With the second service pack for Windows XP, some users are already there.

Bert Keely, October 2004

Displays

■ Acer TravelMate C200 Tablet PC

WHEN BERT KEELY arrived at Microsoft in 1998, he brought with him a wealth of knowledge and experience of displays and high-resolution graphics, so the first question he was asked to address was, "What can we do to improve the visual characteristics of on-screen reading, to make the display more like paper?"

He suggested a project to see if they could take advantage of all those little subpixels on the display and went on to develop ClearType, a program that takes advantage of the red, green, and blue subpixels, to smooth the fonts and create the best word shapes on screen. He explains how this works:

> Anti-aliasing is the process of saying, "Okay, I don't have an edge that directly represents the edge of the character, so what I'm going to do is kind of smear the edge I do have. I'm not going to have white on one side and black on the other side of that edge, I'm going to have grey on both sides of that edge." ClearType starts by using the edges within the pixel, the edge between the red and the green

stripe, and the edge between the green and the blue stripe, and adds anti-aliasing within the pixel.

As the eye has very different sensitivity to red, green, and blue, it turns out that it's not a simple matter of smearing; we had to adjust the luminance values. Then because the human eye is much more sensitive to luminance edges than it is to color edges, we were able to take advantage of the eye's willingness to accept some color error in order to create much sharper fonts.

A challenge for the design of displays for pen-based computers is to precisely align the sensed location of the pen with the actual location of the pen. The ideal would be to eliminate the displayed cursor and just have the pen tip represent itself, but this is hard to achieve.

More important than parallax, what you actually see on most tablet PCs is just a pure XY misalignment between the position of the pen tip and the coordinate the digitizer is reporting, either because of a lack of linearity or a lack of calibration. People commonly call this parallax, but it's not a depth issue, it's an XY error issue. Actual parallax, which means a perception of depth difference between where the tip of the pen is and the image plane, is not as big a factor. Notice when you're looking at an angle down into a swimming pool, the foreshortening of the image actually translates it nearer to your line of sight through the surface.

What you want is to have the digitizer be accurate enough to really sense the location of pen tip and then let the user just think in terms of positioning it. When they see an onscreen object, they should be able to point at it directly with the pen tip, the way they did when they were three or four years old, learning how to draw with a crayon. They shouldn't have to worry about positioning some direct but slightly indirect cursor.

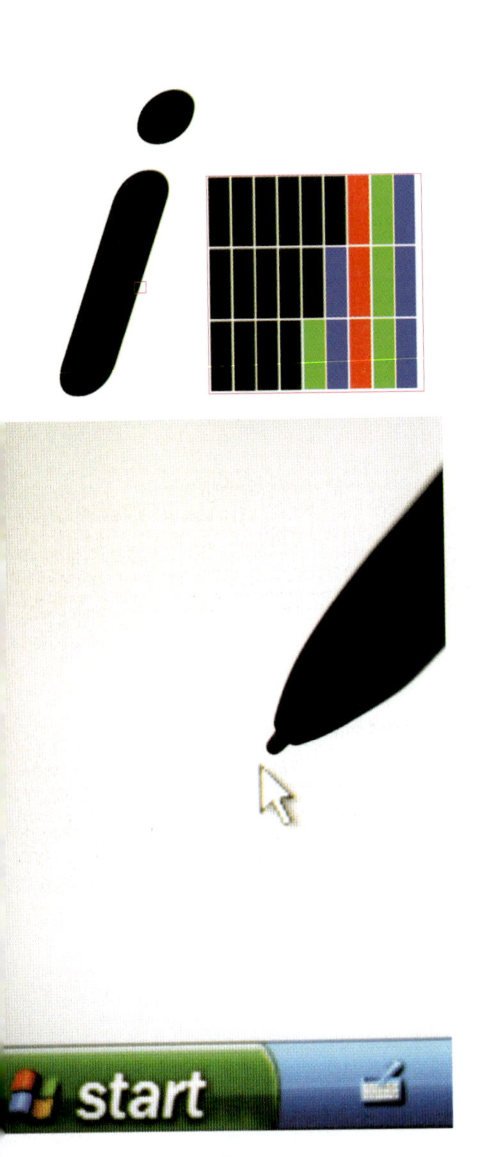

- Close-up of pixels
- XY error between pen tip and cursor

Portability

A STYLUS INPUT should be designed to let you interact with your computer with only one hand. This in turn promotes portability, as you can be holding the computer with the other hand while you stand or walk around, or you can be sitting at a table and have your hands on something else, like some food or some documents that you are looking at, and use the computer at the same time.

The cell phone is something you carry with you all the time—WYATT, as Bert says. The personal computer can become something that you want to have with you at least most of the time, because it carries your whole digital world. Bert sees PCs becoming the second device for each person in a family to carry with them, so that the phone and the PC become digital companions:

> Your family pictures, your music, your calendar, your contacts, your recent email threads, the documents that you're reading, other things that you might have looked at recently that you want to get back to, every Web site you've seen since you bought that computer, all of this stuff; having your whole digital world on hand is something that the PC lets you do, because it's fundamentally visual. You find yourself, when you go to dinner, a meeting, or an outing in a car, thinking, "Well, if I've got every street on the United States on that thing, and I'm comfortable with the user interface because I've figured out how to use it, that's going to be the handiest way to carry maps, and all my visual information.

Standing use ■

Pen and Paper

THE METAPHORS OF desktop and window were originally helpful to the novice users of PCs, because they made the behavior of objects in the abstract digital world relate to the familiar experience of the physical world. The personal computer has evolved a lot since then, and one can argue that the design has outgrown the metaphors. The actual behaviors of the electronic objects have more meaning to the user than the simulation of a physical world that now seems archaic; many children start playing with computers when they are two or three years old, probably before they have ever seen a file folder. Bert believes that the pen-based computer will grow up in a similar way, starting by trying to simulate pen and paper, and then evolving unique characteristics that have special advantages in the digital context.

The main uncertainty is whether it will take off in the first place, as there has to be an immediately recognizable value for people to make the leap from the laptop to the tablet. Jeff Hawkins is skeptical about this potential, in spite of the fact that he developed the first successful tablet, but he stayed clear of simulating paper by concentrating on form-filling applications. Bert Keely is much more ambitious and hopeful, and he bases his optimism on the unique value that pen-based computing offers. He sees the tablet supporting single-handed interaction, and hence operation when standing, or in social situations. He also believes that the ability to capture thoughts in a free-form fashion is unsurpassed with the pen. You can sketch and enter text with one hand with a fluency that you have been developing from childhood. It is impossible to do that with just a keyboard, or with voice input, and it is difficult to do it with a combination of keyboard and mouse.

Bert was experimenting with pen-based inputs when he was still working at Silicon Graphics:

> We were focusing on how to make the pen and the finger great pointing devices, and great devices for capturing thoughts. That was because essentially we wanted to work directly with the display, and

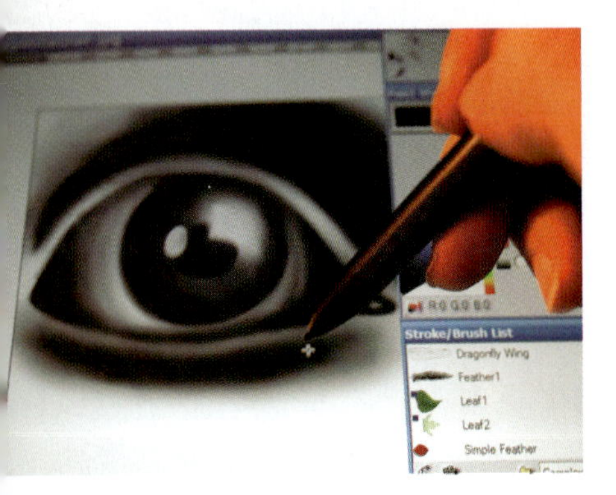

■ Drawing

we knew that we needed a pointing device. The graphical user interface had clearly proven itself. We knew that the pen was excellent for capturing thoughts, and the finger was probably the most natural and most convenient thing to use for just reaching out and touching some piece of information.

The classic thought with regard to the electronic pen is that you want to make it look and feel and behave as much like a pen on paper as you possibly can. Now, the reality is that there are many different types of pens that behave very differently on paper, and pencils of course, and there are also many different types of paper. So, there's quite a range of "pen on paper feels" that people can become accustomed to.

In the end, I think it's going to remain a user preference. Some people love the feel of a fountain pen, and they even like the sound that a fountain pen makes. The feel of a fountain pen is literally a piece of steel scratching across fiber; that's a very rough, very high-friction feel. The essence of a ballpoint pen is that you're rolling almost frictionless, but if you press hard, you get the tooth of the shaft that's actually trapping that ball, so you get a little bit of that scratch. The feeling of a pencil, of course, is one of graphite being deposited on the paper. One thing about a pencil is that the static friction is low, but there's lots of sliding friction, because you're actually pulling that pencil apart. So, what is the static friction? What's the sliding friction? What's the ratio between those two? What is the sound that the system makes? All of those are factors in "emulating" pen on paper.

Today we have a few coatings that can be placed on glass or on plastic that really do a good job of establishing the kind of "stiction" that makes a person feel comfortable tapping, and makes them feel more or less comfortable writing. We still have lots of experiments going on with regard to the kind of sliding friction that's best. Once a person becomes accustomed to less friction and to the efficiency of movement that the slipperiness brings, they tend to like it and find that going back to paper starts to feel a little more tedious.

With a pen-based user interface you have the opportunity to leverage motor skills, which go far beyond the motor skills of moving a bar of soap around, which is essentially what it's like to use a mouse. When we design for the pen and finger, we are trying to leverage the fundamentals of being able to do expressive things with your hands.

From keyboard to stylus ■

Successful handwriting recognition may be a basic requirement for the tablet PC market to really take off. Microsoft is making a huge investment in what they call "Ink Analysis," or the recognition of shapes within ink marks on paper or tablet. They are also studying the context in which particular strokes are being created, looking at the text to the left and the text to the right, and using those as part of the decision of what to elevate in the list of candidates. Analysis of the vocabulary of the individual user can also narrow the possibilities effectively, allowing the system to make better guesses about what each scrawl might represent.

Bert thinks that Microsoft is making good progress in handwriting recognition, but his optimism about the future of tablet computers is also based on the combinatorial advantages of using a stylus:

> Something that you only find out when you're using a pen as a text input device and also using it as a pointing device is that the interleaving of pointing and writing happens so fast that you really are able to compose as quickly with a pen as you can with a keyboard. This isn't a function of handwriting recognition being an equal number of words per minute. This is a function of handwriting recognition, plus pointing, plus correction, plus placing your cursor, selecting, dragging text around, reformatting, and undoing. You've got this combination of things you're trying to do, some of which is text input and some of which is pointing. When you can do that in a fraction of a second back and forth between the activities, it's really astounding.

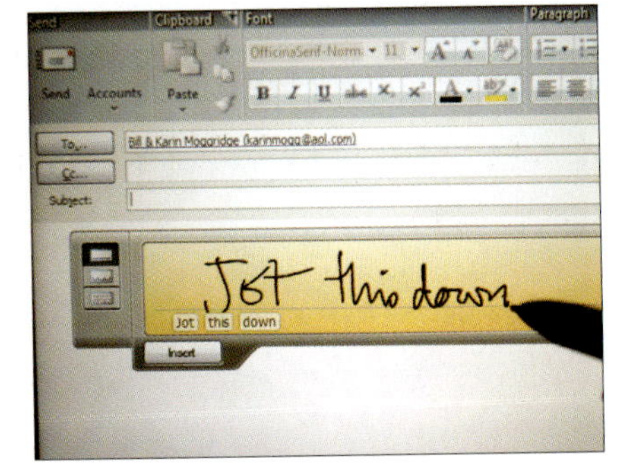

■ Handwriting recognition

Using handwriting or voice recognition software gets very frustrating if there is even a very small proportion of errors, as it is annoying to have the flow of your consciousness interrupted by the need to make corrections. Many people attribute the failure of the Apple Newton to the lack of reliability of their handwriting recognition. Artificial intelligence (AI) promised to solve these problems but failed badly in the twentieth century, leaving the keyboard, and hence the laptop, in a dominant position. Jeff Hawkins had been studying how the brain works in parallel with his work on tablets and he thinks that it was his knowledge of "consciousness" in a literal neuroscientific sense that led him to take a lateral approach to handwriting recognition. We now return to him, as he describes the development of the PalmPilot and Graffiti handwriting recognition software.

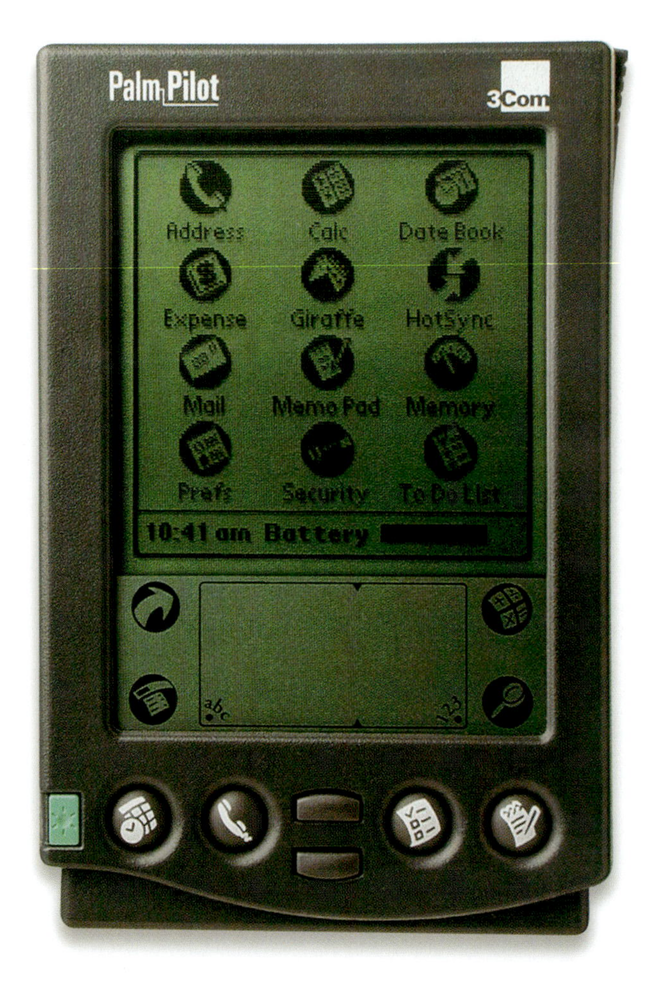

PalmPilot
3Com
Address
Calc
Date Book
Expense
Giraffe
HotSync
Mail
Memo Pad
Memory
Prefs
Security
To Do List
10:41 am Battery
abc
123

Palm Computing

■ 3Com PalmPilot

Photo Courtesy of 3Com

WHILE AT GRiD, Jeff Hawkins learned how to design the software and hardware of laptops and tablets and how to understand the business issues that limited the scope of the market. He began to yearn for the opportunity to reach more people than was possible in the vertical market segment where GRiD was operating—selling business applications to other businesses. His intuition told him that the future of portable computers was likely to be for smaller devices that appealed to consumers:

> When I was at GRiD, we made laptops and we made the GRiDpad. When we were still doing the GRiDpad, it struck me that a lot of people loved the product. I had numerous people come up to me who were using it for some vertical application who said, "You know, if you could only make this thing smaller and I could put my personal data on it, it would be really clever."
>
> I heard this a few times, and said, "Well, this must mean something."
>
> I realized that the idea that people wanted a small computer to carry around with them was very powerful. It struck me that, in the future, everyone would be carrying something in their pocket; Moore's law would just lead to that ability. I didn't know what it would look

like yet, but I concluded that this was inevitable. People will have small electronic devices in their pockets, or on their belts. They will have storage and will be little computers of some sort. I decided this was a great thing to work on—not just fun, but also important.

I started seeing desktop computers as clunky things. What a big monstrous machine on your desk! That can't last forever. And as soon as you have five of them, you have to have an IT professional to maintain them—this was impossible. I said, "This is not a computer for the world. This is not going to work in a world of billions of people. You can't have these big, complex, power-hungry boxes in everybody's life."

So, the idea that something portable would be the main interface for the world just struck me as an inevitable consequence of the evolution of technology.

Jeff realized that GRiD was not the right company to support the birth of a consumer electronics company, so he decided to leave and founded his own startup.

The idea of smaller computing devices was taking hold by this time, even if there had been no commercial successes so far. Back in 1987, Apple had created a vision of computing in a video called the "Knowledge Navigator"[19] that featured a professor being helped by a humanoid avatar with a much-more-than-feasible level of artificial intelligence. The video was created by a design team who let their imaginations run wild, but it was widely publicized and very influential, causing the name of PDA (personal digital assistant) to gain popularity as a generic label for the next generation of smaller and smarter machines.

Jeff was searching for a name that would fit within the overall context of the PDA but would be strongly differentiated from this connotation of artificial intelligence. He came up with the name Palm Computing, but at first it was controversial:

The "Palm" part was easily accepted, as it was a friendly word, it was international, and of course it could apply to your palm. The controversial thing in "Palm Computing" was that I called it "Computing" as opposed to "Palm Software." Software was hot when we were starting the company in late 1991. In the venture capital world, everyone was building software; no one would build hardware.

I was being pushed to call it "Palm Software," as we were initially a software company, but I felt that as we were trying to build the next generation of computing, none of us knew where that would take us. I consciously said, "I want to call it 'Computing,' because that incorporates anything we might want to do in this space." "Palm Software" would be more limiting. My colleagues and backers didn't like it; they were scared of the idea that sometime we might do something other than software.

Palm Computing started by writing software for the PDAs that were being developed by large companies with plenty of resources to invest in R&D, partnering first with Casio to develop the Zoomer, and then with a consortium of other companies, including Sharp. They found that they were being forced into compromises in the design of the software by first one partner and then another, so Jeff was getting increasingly frustrated. He remembers a particular day when he was bemoaning the situation to one his board members:

I said, "We don't have much money, and it doesn't look like anyone's going to build PDAs anymore," because so far everyone had failed with their PDAs.

So he asked me, "Do you know what product you should be building?"

I hadn't really sat down and thought exactly what I would do if I started from scratch, but I kind of lied and said, "Yeah, I know what we should be building! We have to do the whole thing. We have to do the hardware, the software, the operating system, everything. I have to do it from scratch."

He said, "Well, that's what you should do then!"

I said, "All right, great."

Within a day and a half, I had a design for what ultimately became the PalmPilot.

Casio Zoomer ■

Design Criteria for the PalmPilot

By this time in 1994, Jeff had learned a lot from working on Zoomer (Palm's failed product with Casio) and by examining Apple's Newton and the General Magic products, so he was ready to make some bold decisions. In that first day and a half, he came up with four design criteria to define his premise; size, price, synchronization, and speed.

Size

He went home after the defining conversation and made a wooden model that same evening, cutting it down until he felt that it would fit conveniently in the pocket of a shirt or jacket. He then wrapped the block of wood in paper and presented it to his design team.

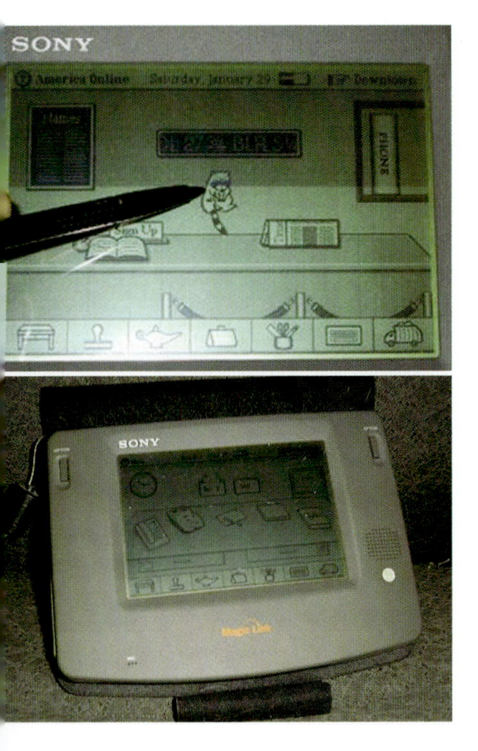

- Sony General Magic screen detail
- Sony General Magic product

Price

He picked a price point of $299, as he believed that was the most that people would pay for a consumer product with broad appeal. It seemed very hard to achieve at the time.

Synchronization

Another goal was to have synchronization with your desktop computer built into the design. Up to that time, everyone thought that synchronization should be optional, but Jeff realized that it was the most significant advantage that could be offered for a pocket-sized device:

> Synchronization wasn't an add-on—it was a core application! Credit goes to Walt Mossberg of the *Wall Street Journal* for that. He had written a critique of some of our earlier products, saying, "This is crazy! Why should you be selling this add-on that everyone needs? If everyone needs it, include it in the product. He was absolutely right, so we said we were going to design around synchronization.

Speed

The last attribute was that it had to be fast. Jeff realized that he was competing with paper, not computers, as he was trying to get people to replace their paper systems, not their digital systems. He used the metric that you had to be able to do things just as fast with the new design as if you were using a paper-based personal organizer. This was a difficult challenge as the price point meant that they could not put a fast processor in the first version of the product. Jeff talks about the implications:

> The software guys came back and said, "We can't do all that stuff you want to do in software with that slow a processor."
>
> I said, "Sure you can, because when we were at GRiD, we had a more sophisticated operating system which ran on a slower processor, and it was fast. So, if we could do it back then, we can do it now."
>
> Sure enough, they were able to do it. They made a product that was very fast. One of my design goals was that there would be no "wait cursors." I said, "Why should there be wait cursors? That's a mistake. We don't want those. That's a crutch for a bad design. Ban them!"
>
> I also insisted that we would have no error dialogues, especially the ones that ask a question of the user, where the user has no choice, like, "You have an error in the fla-fla-flop file, what do you want to do? Continue or abort?" Why ask the user a question like that? Just do something, don't even ask them.

Those four design criteria solved a lot of the problems that were prevalent on personal computers and PDAs at the time, and turned out to be a defining formula for success.

Graffiti

While Jeff was studying brains at UC Berkeley, he went to a conference about neural networks and came across a company that built handwriting recognition software. They were offering the package for sale for a million dollars, which made Jeff think it might be worth developing his own version of handwriting recognition software. Two days after the conference, he had a working prototype of an approach that looked promising, starting him down the path of designing traditional handwriting recognition.

When he returned to GRiD, he made his approach work well enough for forms, with numbers and some limited text entry, but it never worked well for anything sophisticated. When he started Palm Computing, there was a lot of pressure to produce handwriting recognition software for the early Palm products, like the Zoomer, but he resisted, saying, "I don't think it's going to work. What I want to do instead is focus on ink."

This led to work on capturing and resizing the shapes of handwriting and sketching, but without recognition. Ultimately he realized that the value of this was limited, and that he would have to come up with a way of entering text into a handheld computer with character recognition. In 1994 someone sent him an email with the title of a paper by David Goldberg and Cate Richardson from Xerox PARC, "Touch-Typing with a Stylus."[20] Jeff describes the epiphany:

> That was the spark that I needed. I didn't even read the paper. I just saw the title, which inspired me. It made me think of the analogy of the keyboard, which is hard to learn; to learn to type takes months, but everyone does it. The accepted paradigm at that time was that computers should adapt to the users, not the other way around, and I said, "Why is that? Well, people don't mind using a tool as long as it helps them perform the task. I think they like to learn. They pride themselves on learning how to use tools, as long as the tool is consistent, it's learnable, it has a good model, and it's reliable." So, the idea of Graffiti was to say, "Okay, throw away traditional handwriting recognition, and then do something which is reliable and works."

Letter	Strokes	Letter	Strokes
A	Λ	N	N
B	B B	O	O O
C	C	P	P P
D	D D	Q	Ơ
E	ε	R	R R
F	Γ Γ	S	S
G	G 6	T	¬
H	h	U	U
I	|	V	V V
J	J	W	W
K	ᒪ	X	X ∞
L	L	Y	y γ
M	m m	Z	Z
Space	—	Back Space	—
Carriage Return	/	Period	tap twice

■ Graffiti alphabet

It was easy for me to see this because up until this time, the old handwriting recognition software I had created always worked best with my handwriting, because I was the guy who created it. One of the industry analysts quipped, "If you write like Jeff, it works all the time!"

I tried to generalize and said, "What if we just told people to write a particular way?" What if we said, "Write your *e* this way and your *f* this way and your *g* this way!" It would reduce the problem significantly. That was the genesis of Graffiti. We just came up with a simplified system that was fast and reliable, based on the way I write an upper case character set; then we tweaked it from there.

I don't think I would have come up with this idea if I didn't understand some of the stuff about brains already. I knew that brains want a consistent model, and they want to be able to predict what's going to happen. The problem with traditional handwriting recognition was, when you wrote something and it didn't work, you had no way of knowing why. You wanted a system where you could say, "All right. If it fails, I know why; it was my mistake, I'll fix it. I can change my behavior." That gives you a predictable relationship between behavior of the machine and your own behavior.

When Jeff finally did read the PARC paper, he was impressed by the research, but he realized that the goal of the authors was to create fast text entry, whereas his goal was to create reliable text entry that would be easy to learn. He focused on trying to make the pen strokes as much like regular handwriting as possible, keeping the characters very close to standard letterforms. The PARC approach was designed to maximize speed, so they chose the simplest strokes for the most frequently used characters. The *e* was a dot, because that was the most common letter, and the *s* and the *t* were single strokes, with more complex strokes reserved for the least common characters.

The combination of Graffiti and Jeff's four design criteria for the PalmPilot were the keys to a good product, but the dramatic success that they enjoyed was also due to the unique interaction design. For this, Jeff relied on Rob Haitani, who had worked with him from the very first days of Palm Computing.

Photo Author

Rob Haitani

Rob Haitani was responsible for designing the user interface of the operating system for Palm, as well as all the original applications. He is modest about his abilities, claiming to be an "applied practitioner," as he has no formal training in interaction design. One morning the president of Palm, Donna Dubinsky,[21] asked him if he had ever done this before. He wondered if she meant whether he had designed a user interface, but as he had never even managed a software project before coming to Palm he said, "Uh, no." Before joining Palm he worked at Sony in Japan for several years, in the camcorder group. There he was surrounded by people who were dedicated to miniaturization, which proved to be useful experience for Palm. After Sony he worked on digital video cards for Macintoshes, and when he joined Palm, he was asked to work on a project to answer the question, "What can we do about making an organizer work better?" It was something he knew nothing about from the product side, but from the customer side he could very easily pick up one of those products and realize that there was something wrong. Rob insists on putting people first and brings a combination of common sense and ruthless analysis to any problem that he is confronted with, never forgetting the end user. He stayed with the team when they spun out of Palm to start Handspring and went on to lead the interaction design team for all of the Handspring products. In 2004 Handspring and Palm came together again to form PalmOne, with PalmSource as a separate company for the Palm OS operating system.

Elements of the organizer interface

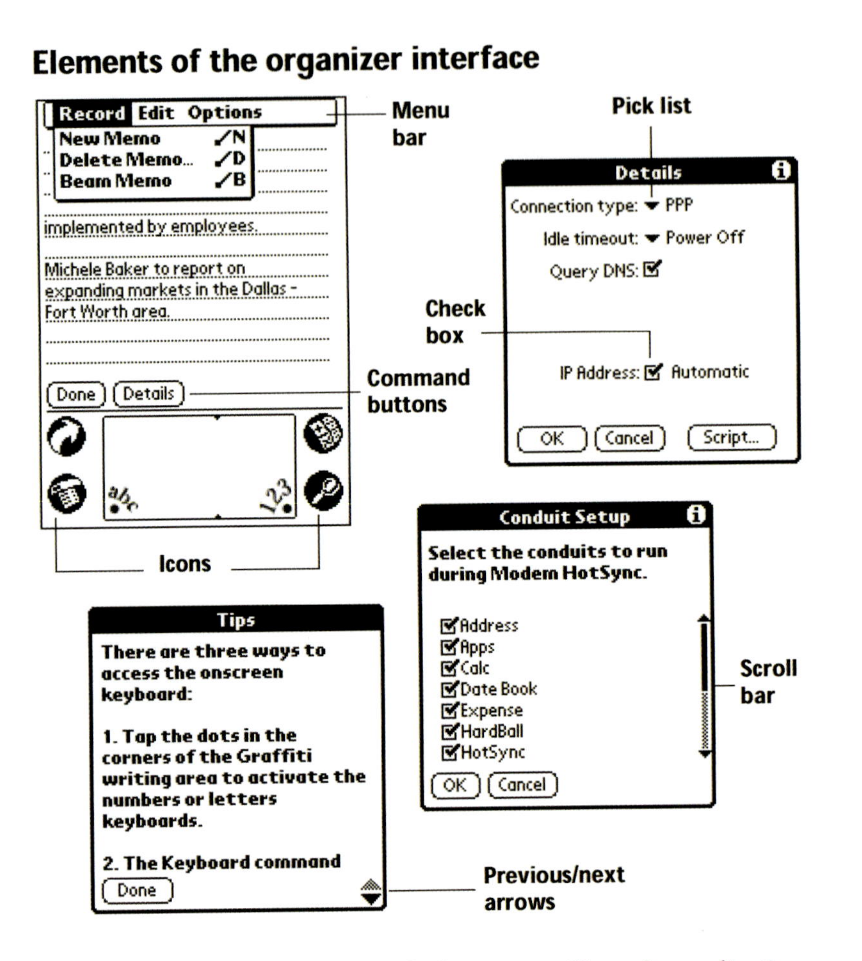

Menu bar A set of commands that are specific to the application. Not all applications have a menu bar.

Command buttons Tap a button to perform a command. Command buttons appear in dialog boxes and at the bottom of application screens.

Icons Tap the icons to open applications, menus, Calculator, and to find text anywhere in your data.

abc With the cursor in an input field, tap the dot to activate the alphabetic keyboard.

123 With the cursor in an input field, tap the dot to activate the numeric keyboard.

Rob Haitani

I developed "Zen Riddles" to articulate points in a way people would remember. The most core point was the riddle of "How do you fit a mountain into a teacup?" When I would present it, people would say, "Well, you have to shrink the mountain." If that's what you're thinking, then you're still thinking more is better—the PC thinking. What you really have to think is, "Why do you want to put a mountain in a teacup to begin with?" Ask the question about what really matters before you decide how to act.

Rob Haitani, 2001[22]

Interaction Design for Palm OS

■ A page from the manual describing the elements of the organizer interface

ROB HAITANI WAS developing the user interface of the Palm OS in 1995, when Newton had been out for about two years and it was clear that the initial excitement about the design was not going to be enough to make it a hit in the market. The conventional wisdom at the time was that products such as the Newton were not succeeding because they did not have enough functionality; if you are going to spend $700 on something it should do more, and you should pack it with features. Jeff Hawkins had articulated the goal of making a really simple product and defined his four design criteria of size, price, synchronization, and speed, and he was always there for the meetings when the design team was formulating their ideas for the new operating system. Rob led the team in building a consensus for simplicity and pushing back against the pressure for feature-laden functionality.

They tested Jeff's criteria in some customer research with focus groups, showing a form factor model to the participants, with the user interface on a Macintosh screen to give them a sense of what the interaction would be like.

First they showed the organizer on its own and said, "What do you think?"

People said, "That's interesting, the form factor is nice, it seems to be easy to use. How would I get the data into my PC?"

In the second stage they showed the cradle and said that the organizer could be synchronized with the PC and got a very enthusiastic response. In the third stage they said it could do wireless email, but very few people were interested:

> Wireless email was really hot back then. We're doing that now, but at that time it was not ready for prime time. We were asking people, "Would you like wireless email?"
>
> From our Silicon Valley bleeding edge mentality we thought that people would just be falling over each other to get it, but they were just shaking their heads. I remember very clearly one woman saying, "Well, I get about three emails a day. I log in the morning and I look at them; why would I want these in a portable device?"
>
> She didn't even understand what the concept was. That's when you really sit back and say, "Wait a moment, we've got to remember who our customer is."
>
> We're not the customers. We're geeks. We're the Silicon Valley propeller heads and not the normal people who will be using our products. Focus groups are most valuable when you have something that you can show not only the potential, but also the limitations, of the product. I remember thinking when we did our first focus groups with the PalmPilot, "Boy, the Newton must have just flown through these. Imagine a hand-held product, and it recognizes your handwriting. Would you like it?"
>
> The answer would have been, "Oh wow, that's great, I love it!"
>
> If you had a real prototype, most of the time it wouldn't have worked and it would have been really slow.

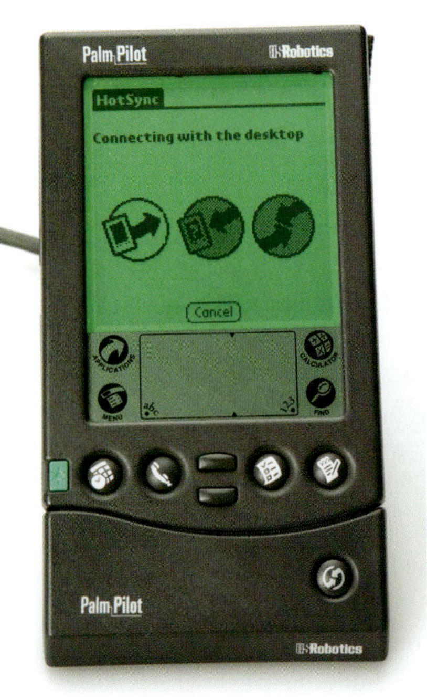

■ HotSync in cradle

The limits on size and cost that Jeff demanded forced Rob into using a monochrome display with only 160 x 160 pixels, posing a challenge for the interaction design. The 320 x 240 pixel display on the Zoomer had seemed incredibly difficult to manage, and yet Rob was now faced with the task of reducing everything on the screen to an even smaller size and still conveying the same amount of information.

Jeff defined the resolution and said, "Can we design an operating system on this resolution?" and I said, "Sure, of course, no problem!" and afterwards I thought, "Oh dear, it's going to be difficult to make this work."

You have to focus on what really needs to be conveyed on the screen. Ultimately this was a positive factor driving the user experience, because it forces you to be disciplined. For example, on this size of screen, instead of having a whole row of buttons, you can basically fit four buttons on the bottom of the screen, and the question is, "How can you decide which four buttons are on the screen?" You can either try to cram ten buttons in there and have this horribly cluttered interface, or you can decide which those four buttons are.

The calendar application was difficult on such a small screen. In the focus groups, people insisted on the importance of seeing a whole day, but even Newton, with its much larger display, only showed the day from 8:00 a.m. to 3:00 p.m. By using a font with a capital letter height of only seven pixels, Rob managed to create a screen that contained a row for each hour in a ten-hour day and still have room at the top and bottom for menu and controls. The screen was made to look higher by positioning the stylus pad for Graffiti handwriting recognition at the base of the display in an included rectangle.

Rob was starting to revel in a reductionist philosophy, and found that it allowed him to define the interaction design for the whole Palm operating system. After a while the ideas became ingrained in the attitudes of the original team of designers, who started to intuitively design to these four guidelines:

Less is more.
Avoid adding features.
Strive for fewer steps.
Simplicity is better than complexity.

That was the right approach to take in 1995, when the main problem with products was that they were trying to do too much. Products were not only too complicated, but developers were going in the wrong direction; they were trying to add more functionality and more features.

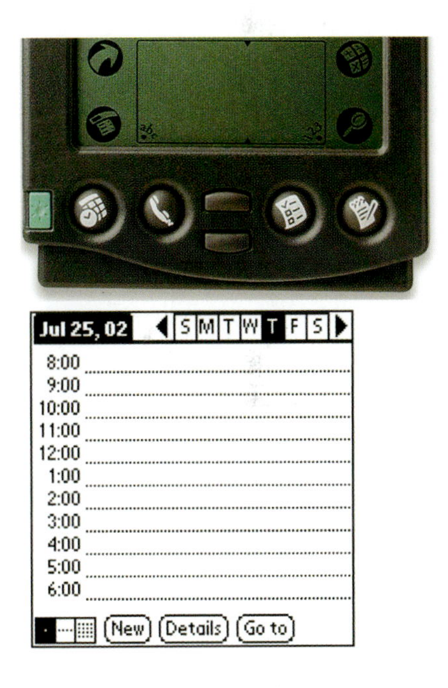

Four buttons and Graffiti pad ■
Calendar application in 160 x 160 pixels ■

The "Zen of Palm"

ONCE THE INITIAL products were launched, Rob developed ways of explaining his design philosophy that he called the "Zen of Palm":

> The "Zen of Palm" was not articulated as a design philosophy until the third-generation Palm OS. The concept was developed because we were growing as a company, and there were more and more people involved in the design; I got tired of saying over and over again, "No, no, we have to keep it simple."
>
> More people would join the company and want to add more features, saying, "Well, Microsoft is adding more features. . . ."
>
> It was developed as a way to teach people the philosophies that the core team knew instinctively. I was trying to articulate the ideas in a way that people could walk away and remember. I was sitting in my office at ten o'clock at night, preparing a presentation for the next morning, and I was trying to think of a funny way of capturing this. People had referred to Palm products as Zenlike, so I thought, "Okay, let's play on that theme!"
>
> I developed "Zen Riddles" that would try to articulate points in the way people would remember.

Rob put some presentation material together to show at developers' conferences and within the company. He created a chart that represented all of the features and how often you would use them. It had a few features at the top that you would use very frequently, and then it would dramatically drop off, forming a sort of bell curve. He then posed the question, "Which features do you put access to right on the screen?" He then showed the bell curve with the three of four most frequently used features at the top marked for inclusion on the screen, and all of the others forced below a menu or control. He illustrated this principle with an analogy:

> If you think about the way your desk is organized, you have some things on your desk, and some things in your drawers. Why is that? The things on top of your desk are there because you want to access them very frequently. Imagine if you had your mouse, or your phone,

or something that you access very frequently, and you put it in your drawer. Every time you wanted to use it, you'd have to pull it out of your drawer. It might be only one more step, and it might be only one second, but it would really drive you crazy over the course of a day.

Think about your stapler and staple remover. My stapler is on top of my desk, and my staple remover is in my drawer. The reason is that I staple papers more frequently than I unstaple them. You can argue that architecturally speaking the stapler and staple remover are equivalent and therefore should be in the same place. If you look at it intuitively and ask what you do more frequently, some of these decisions just naturally bubble up to the top. It all depends on understanding your customers, but not on a very complex level. It is not rocket science to suggest that you would be more likely to enter a new phone number than to delete one.

He emphasized the importance of instant access to data with the analogy of a watch, which shows you the time immediately. If you had to wait three seconds before you could see the time or had to a press a button to see the time, you would choose a different watch. If you need two or three steps to gain access to something that you only use occasionally, it is acceptable. This raises the question of how to hide the less frequently accessed functions? Do you use menus or modes?

One of the first answers to the problem of not being able to have a button for every function was, "What if we were modal about the buttons? What if you're in edit mode and some buttons appear, and you're not in edit mode and other buttons appear?"

The consensus was in favor of that approach. I didn't like the approach, but rather than argue in a room with a bunch of people in front of a white board, I said, "Alright, let me mock it up, we can test some people, and if I'm wrong, fine."

We mocked it up and tested people on a Macintosh, and sure enough people got confused. They said, "What happened to those buttons? They were there before."

That's where the reductionist philosophy comes into play. We said, "Well, we can't fit seven buttons on here. Do we really, really need to have this button? Could you have it in menus?"

"Well, now that I think about it . . ."

Stapler kept on the desk surface ■
Staple remover kept in a drawer ■

That was how we started to think about how you use the product, and which functions you need all the time.

Rob Haitani came to the same conclusion about modes for the Palm OS as Larry Tesler had for the desktop,[23] but he did not always succeed in reducing the number of steps to a minimum for the first iteration. He wanted to optimize the address book, where he had discovered from the user studies that the most important feature is looking up a phone number:

> It's ironic that the address book was the one application in which we didn't achieve the one-step solution. If you want to look up a phone number in a PalmPilot, you have to pull out the stylus, and you have to know how to use Graffiti in order to do it fast and efficiently.

There is an inherent conflict between the desire to reduce the number of steps for fast access and wanting to minimize the number of items on the top level to reduce complexity. That drove Rob into a pragmatic philosophy of just trying to do the right thing on a case-by-case basis. The conflict was resolved because there are only a very few features in any application that people use very often. Take for example a word processor or a spreadsheet; there are only two or three commands that you use over and over again. The applications are therefore designed so that the very frequently used features are on the screen, and a menu, or another form of additional step accesses everything else.

Rob articulates his design approach as a philosophy, but he also supports his philosophy with a very pragmatic design process: first understand the customer, then prioritize ruthlessly:

> One bit of advice that I gave to people designing the Palm OS was, "If you can really understand the one thing your customer wants to do most frequently, and make that a one-step process, then I guarantee people will like the product."
>
> Just say, "What is the one thing you want to do?" and even if you have to throw out conventions of logic, architecture, and hierarchy, you should make that one step. The more "illogical" your approach is, the less likely it is that it will blindly follow the conventional wisdom, and hence the more likely it becomes that you will be able to differentiate and create a successful product relative

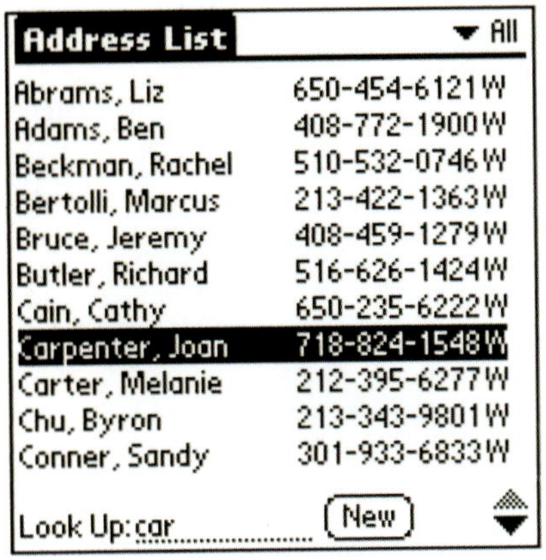

■ Selecting a number from the address book

to your competition. If you take the conventional approach, by definition you're not innovating. If you just say, "Here are all the features," and you lay them out in a logical pattern, then that's not going to be a successful product.

The Palm Product Line

The PalmPilot was announced in February of 1996, complete with the new operating system, Graffiti, built-in synchronization, $299 price tag, fast processing, and the shirt-pocket-fitting form factor. Jeff Hawkins launched it at a conference, with one of the premier demo slots, but his time was limited to twelve minutes. He remembers how the projector went wrong:

> I got up there and I started describing the product, and it's clear that I had the audience's rapt attention. No one had ever seen anything like this before. It's small; people want something like this. Then I put it under the overhead projector, and I started the demo. The second that I started the demo, the screen went blank, but the clock was still running. You had your twelve minutes, and that was it. So I had six hundred people in the audience, and no one could see it. We tried for a few seconds to get the system to work, and I said, "I'm running out of time."
>
> So, I walked to the front of the stage, I held it up, and I said, "I'm going to describe to you what you would be seeing if you could actually see the demo."
>
> It was almost better than showing the real thing. It was like telling a story. I said, "You can see this small product, and when you push this button, it's going to instantly change to this screen, instantly change to that screen."
>
> When they got the projector working again we were out of time, but the audience clamored that they wanted the clock to be reset. So we had a chance to do the demo again. I put it back on the projector and I demonstrated what I had just told them, and it was great!

That first year the PalmPilot had very good reviews and sold about three hundred thousand units, which was excellent for an innovative product in a category that had no track record of success. It was also enough to get the attention of competitors, particularly Microsoft:

> Microsoft decided that they were going to kill us. They had conferences with a thousand developers in the room, where they put a big bull's-eye on the wall and in the center of the bull's-eye it said "Palm." Steve Ballmer stood up and said, "We are going to kill these guys. Don't even think about working for them."
>
> All the analysts started coming to us saying, "Well, you know, this is really too bad, I'm sorry you guys are going to lose."

Microsoft also applied their legal muscle over naming rights. The Pilot Pen Corporation had sued Palm successfully in Europe, where the trademark laws are more restrictive than in the USA, over the use of the name "Pilot," so Donna Dubinsky and her colleagues decided to abandon the name and replace "PalmPilot" with Palm followed by a number in roman numerals.

Initially Microsoft was calling their competitive product "Windows CE," but then they announced that they were going to change the name to "Palm PC." Jeff decided to fight back:

> We said, "You guys can't call it that!"
>
> They said, "When you said Palm, you meant the tree; you didn't mean a hand-held computer. Your original logo was a tree; you didn't even think about hand-held computing."
>
> I said, "You guys are crazy."
>
> They're the mega-company, right? What are we going to do? So, we sued them in Germany. They were launching the Palm PC in Germany at the Cebit show, and we got an injunction. The marshals came on to the Cebit floor and removed all of Microsoft's materials. It was great! So we got them to change; they had to change the name to Palm-Size PC. Eventually they changed again to Pocket PC.

By this time Jeff and his team had developed another product called the Palm III, but he felt that he needed something dramatic to respond to the threat from Microsoft; more products in the Palm line with incremental improvements would not be enough. The Microsoft approach was to throw all these software engineers at the problem, so their first version of the PDA software had many more features than the Palm OS, but Jeff thought that they did not add much in the way of genuine value for the user. He puzzled over the best way to respond:

> I said to myself, "What can we do that they can't do?"
>
> The answer was, "We build the whole thing; they don't build it. They just make software, and they get some other party to build the hardware. Let's build a beautiful piece of hardware. They can't tell someone to make a beautiful piece of hardware."
>
> So, we decided that we were going to build the most beautiful, elegant handheld computer. We contracted with Dennis Boyle and his team at IDEO[24] to help do that, because that's the perfect type of project for them. I think that was the first project that I worked with Dennis. I came in and I described what I wanted. I said, "This is going to be the defining product. This is what all future PDAs are going to look like. We want the most elegant and stylish product."
>
> I actually forbade any new features in the software. The reason I did this was because when the product reviews came out, I didn't want to have a comparison like, Palm adds three features and Microsoft adds twenty features. I wanted the only thing they could say be, "Beautiful!" And it worked.
>
> It was an iconic product and still is to this day—an icon for the PDA. The strategy worked beautifully; our market share soared. People fell in love with the idea of this as personal jewelry, personal style statement, and we just left Microsoft in the dust, because they were arguing, "Well, we have more features for this and this . . ." No one cared, because we had this beautiful iconic product, the Palm V.[25]

Next, Dennis Boyle tells his side of the story of the development of the Palm V, and the definition of the physical attributes that made it so successful.

Photo Author

Dennis Boyle

Dennis Boyle grew up in a family of seven children, four of whom ended up as engineers or designers. His mother was in science and chemistry, and his father was an architect who worked for an apprentice of Frank Lloyd Wright. He was always pointing out good design. In spite of the fact that the classes did not mix easily, Dennis studied both industrial design and mechanical engineering at Notre Dame in Indiana. He went on to the master's program in product design at Stanford, where he met David Kelley, and they stayed together from then onward, building a consulting firm in engineering product design that thrived on developing products for startup companies in California's Silicon Valley, and which later became IDEO. Dennis continues his connection to Stanford, lecturing in the program where he studied and learned to design and build products. He is famous for taking a new prototype of a design with him whenever he goes to a meeting. He has perfected the art of iterative prototyping as a way of accelerating the development process. He has always been curious about ingenious ways of making things, as well as clever or amusing designs. Over the years he has collected interesting examples of objects from wherever his travels have taken him. His collection became a magnet for the engineers and designers at IDEO, as inspiration for innovation could often be found by browsing among his objects. In 1990 the value of the collection was institutionalized as the "Tech Box," a combination of parts and materials library, database and Web site, which is duplicated in all the major offices of the company.

Palm V
1:00
2:00
3:00
4:00
5:00
6:00
7:00
8:00
New
Details
Go to
APPLICATIONS

Dennis Boyle

Palm V

■ Palm V in recharging and synchronization cradle

Photo Steven Moeder

The talent that Dennis had for collecting things also showed itself in his habit of constantly acquiring the latest products on the market and trying them out. He was one of the first people to own an original PalmPilot,[26] and in spite of the fact that the first one had a lot of reliability problems, he became convinced that it was a great step forward because it combined synchronization with the PC, Graffiti, small size, and excellent interaction design for the operating system.

> I can clearly remember when I first became aware of the original Pilot in late April or May of '96. I had already tried a Newton, but it was just too big—it was not the right thing. Someone described it as a "high technology paving stone"; it was just too big.
>
> I said, "I'm not going to carry one of those electronic organizers unless it fits in my pocket and is more convenient." When I first saw the PalmPilot, I thought that it looked like something that I could really use.

Dennis patiently developed a relationship with Jeff Hawkins and Rob Haitani at Palm, building their confidence by showing them his many prototypes, and by his polite persistence. Jeff eventually decided to commission Dennis for the new version of the Palm series that became the Palm V. At the briefing meeting, Jeff flipped open a Motorola StarTac phone and was excited about the power of the design to captivate, saying that it just fit into your life because it was so elegantly thin and small. He pointed out that almost all of the sales of the organizers so far were to men, usually computer professionals in their thirties and forties, and asked, "How do we attract a bigger audience, and women in particular? What would be a much more natural fit for a wider group?"

The PalmPilot was nearly 20 millimeters thick. A goal of halving the thickness was high on the list, both to create a more elegant proportion that would appeal to a wider group of users and to make the fit to the pocket much more comfortable.

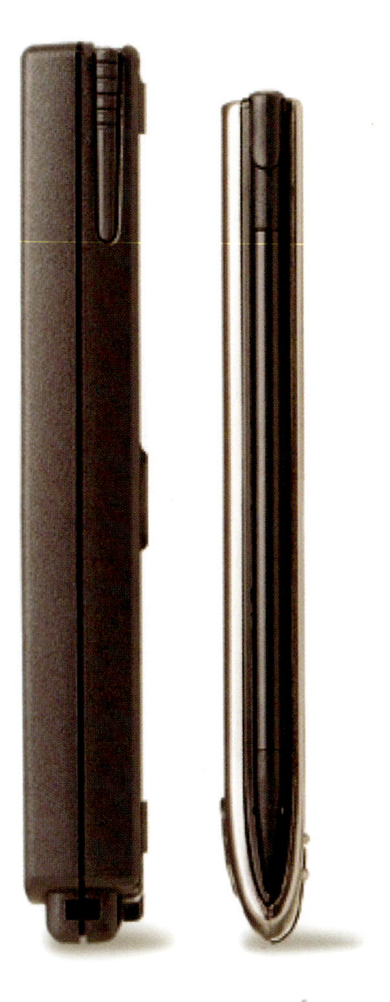

■ Actual size thickness comparison between PalmPilot and Palm V

> We wanted something that didn't broadcast that you were using a piece of technology, or that you were overly concerned with technology. We were looking for something more like a piece of jewelry or accessory—an elegant watch or something you might wear, or have in your purse, like a compact or something. We put together a design team that was half women, which worked out very well.
>
> To get down to what turned out to be 11 millimeters (we almost made the 10 millimeter goal), every single tenth of a millimeter was fought over in a big battle. It became clear that plastic was just not going to work at all for the case. We made models that proved you could feel the difference; you could feel a lack of tortional rigidity, and if you dropped them they would shatter. Metal came out of the analysis and investigations as being a great choice.

It was hard to find examples of handheld products made out of metal to use as a precedent, but they eventually located the people who made the camera bodies for the Canon Elf, and worked with them to make the aluminum stampings for the Palm V.

Dennis and his team noticed that people were making accessories for the original PalmPilot, and sticking them on with tape and Velcro, as there was no provision for attaching things in the design. This led to the idea for two identical rails, on either side, so that accessories could be attached. On one side you could keep your stylus, depending on whether you were right- or left-handed, and on the other you could attach a protective case or some other accessory.

The timing for the Palm V was perfect, as there was a fast-spreading desire for an electronic organizer that was inexpensive and conveniently small, and the Palm OS was gaining a reputation for ease of use, with the reassurance and convenience of synchronizing with a desktop computer. At that time there was very little competition, in contrast to the flood of competitive products that arrived in the following years. Over five million Palm Vs were sold, making it the highest-selling single model of PDAs.

Despite this success, Jeff Hawkins felt compelled to leave Palm and found Handspring.

Handspring

Back when Jeff Hawkins was inspired to start from scratch with the development of the PalmPilot, he needed much more in the way of resources and investment than if he had stayed with the original business plan of just writing software for PDAs. Donna Dubinsky, in her role as president of the company, was looking around for a major investor to provide the funds to develop and launch the Pilot and ended up selling Palm to US Robotics. The relationship worked out well, until US Robotics was in turn acquired by 3Com, which paid a high price for the modem business, without paying much attention to the fact that Palm was part of the purchase. A year and a half later the modem business was almost worthless, but Palm was worth quite a bit.

3Com was a networking company and had nothing to do with handheld computers, but they were happy that the success of Palm was making up for the losses of the rest of the company.

Palm V—front view ■
Handspring Visors, with ■
Springboard expansion slot

visor
CityTime
San Francisco 11:55 am
New York
Th 2:55 pm
London
Th 7:55 pm
Tokyo
Fr 4:55 am
Paris
Th 8:55 pm

They needed profits from Palm but were unwilling to invest because of financial pressures on the modem side, just at the time when the Palm business was growing fast and needed resources to expand to the next level. Jeff remembers the increasing tension caused by the lack of investment:

> We said, "Look, eventually Palm has to be separate from 3Com. It can be now, it can be three years from now, but we're in a very different business."
>
> We decided to leave when the management of 3Com made it clear that they would not spin out Palm. About ten people from the original team who had started Palm, including Rob Haitani, left with Donna Dubinsky to continue on what we'd started at Palm. The easy thing for us to do at Handspring would have been just to compete with our old company. We could have done better products, we felt we could out-market and out-design them, but we didn't want to do that. We did not want to kill our old friends, so we said, "What are we going to do that's different?"

Jeff had been convinced for years that the future of handheld computers would be in wireless communications, but the right technology to use was not yet obvious:

■ Handspring Visor Edge

Photos Steven Moeder

> At the time we started Handspring, it was very clear to me that eventually all handheld computers would have wireless communications in them. It was not clear to me at all that cell phones would be dominant; I didn't even know about cell phones at the time—it wasn't even in my vocabulary—but I knew that some form of wireless was going to be important. I wanted to try to figure out how to incorporate wireless into handheld devices, without committing to a particular technology.
>
> I felt that if Handspring built a wireless device immediately, we'd likely fail, so I wanted to build a mainstream organizer, but somehow add a strategy that would allow wireless. We decided to put in a slot in the device where you could plug in different radios. I actually built another wooden model at the beginning of Handspring, and it had a slot and all these different radios I could plug into it to see what it would be like. We thought it might be two-way pager, a Wi-Fi equivalent, or a cell-phone radio. Then we said, "Well, if we're going to do a slot, let's make it a generic slot, so people can put anything they want into it."

We created this expansion slot. It was a success and a failure at the same time. It was a success because we attracted a lot of people to create add-ons for the Handspring, with what we called the Springboard expansion slot. It was a failure because even though we sold a lot of PDAs with the slot, we didn't sell a lot of expansion products. We sold a lot of memory cards, but most of the other expansion things did not sell well, but we did use it as originally intended for learning about different radios.

eyemodule

Jeff was still relying on Dennis Boyle and the IDEO team to develop physical designs for the new organizers at Handspring, all of them including the Springboard expansion slot. First was the Visor, then a color product called the Prism, and later a thinner product called the Visor Edge, similar in concept to the Palm V.

Dennis was aware of the expansion concept from early on, and he decided to take advantage of the fact that he was helping to design the expansion slot and to develop the first example of a plug-in module in parallel; the plug-in was a camera called the "eyemodule." To stay true to Palm's philosophy of simple interactions, he decided to create a camera that you could plug into the slot, and it would immediately convert the PDA into a camera. He describes the interaction design solution:

■ Eyemodule being used in Handspring Visor to capture photo of flower in vase

> It was an attempt to have our own little business and take advantage of the platform. It was clear that cameras were going to be part of the future for handheld products, but in 1999 the technology for miniature cameras was immature. I am quite proud of the fact that you can take this module, and plug it in, and you have no action to do. When inserted, it starts up automatically and goes into the camera mode within five seconds. All you have to do if you want to take a picture immediately is to press the button, and a picture will come up.
>
> In order to create this simple-seeming result, there were several layers of complexity in the design solution, so I put together a multidisciplinary team. First we had to research and develop the

technology for the camera that would meet our price point and fit into the geometry of the slot. Next our human factors psychologists did some user studies about the way people thought about taking pictures on a PDA, and came up with a framework for the interactions with three stages—capture, view, and share. The interaction designers created icons for these three modes, so that they popped up on the bottom of the screen of the organizer. They were designed to fit into the visual and behavioral style of Rob Haitani's operating system and to use as little space as possible, leaving most of the room for the image that the camera was looking at.

For the "capture" component of the design, we created an interface to reside on the PC to allow you to sort and edit images, and to use the communications of the system to send copies to other people. We also put up a Web site to sell the "eyemodule" and to support customers, and we developed the packaging and user manual as well. Then there was the physical design of course, and the manufacturing, so we involved just about all the disciplines at IDEO in the process.

Jeff Hawkins was pleased that we developed the "eyemodule" in parallel with the Visor itself, as it turned into a very useful device to demonstrate the versatility of the expansion slot concept.

The next project for Handspring was the Treo, combining the PDA organizer with an email communicator and a cell phone.

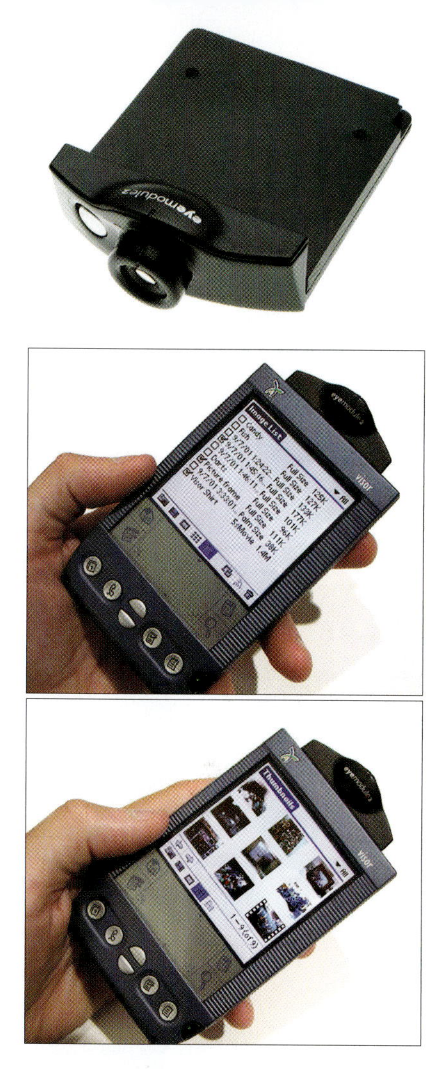

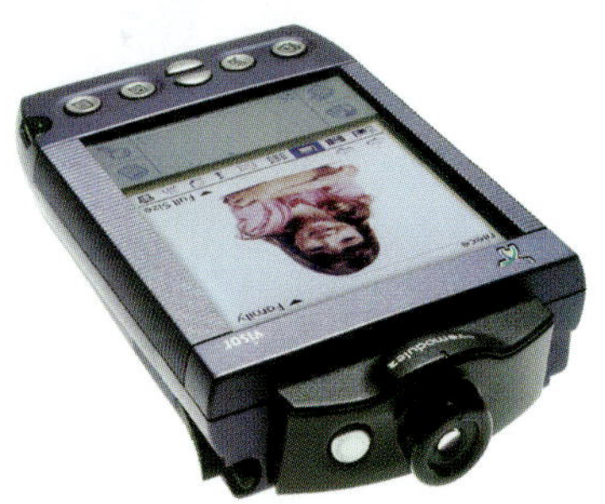

Eyemodule removed from Visor ■
Eyemodule in Visor—photo list ■
Eyemodule in Visor—thumbnails ■
Eyemodule in Visor—front view ■

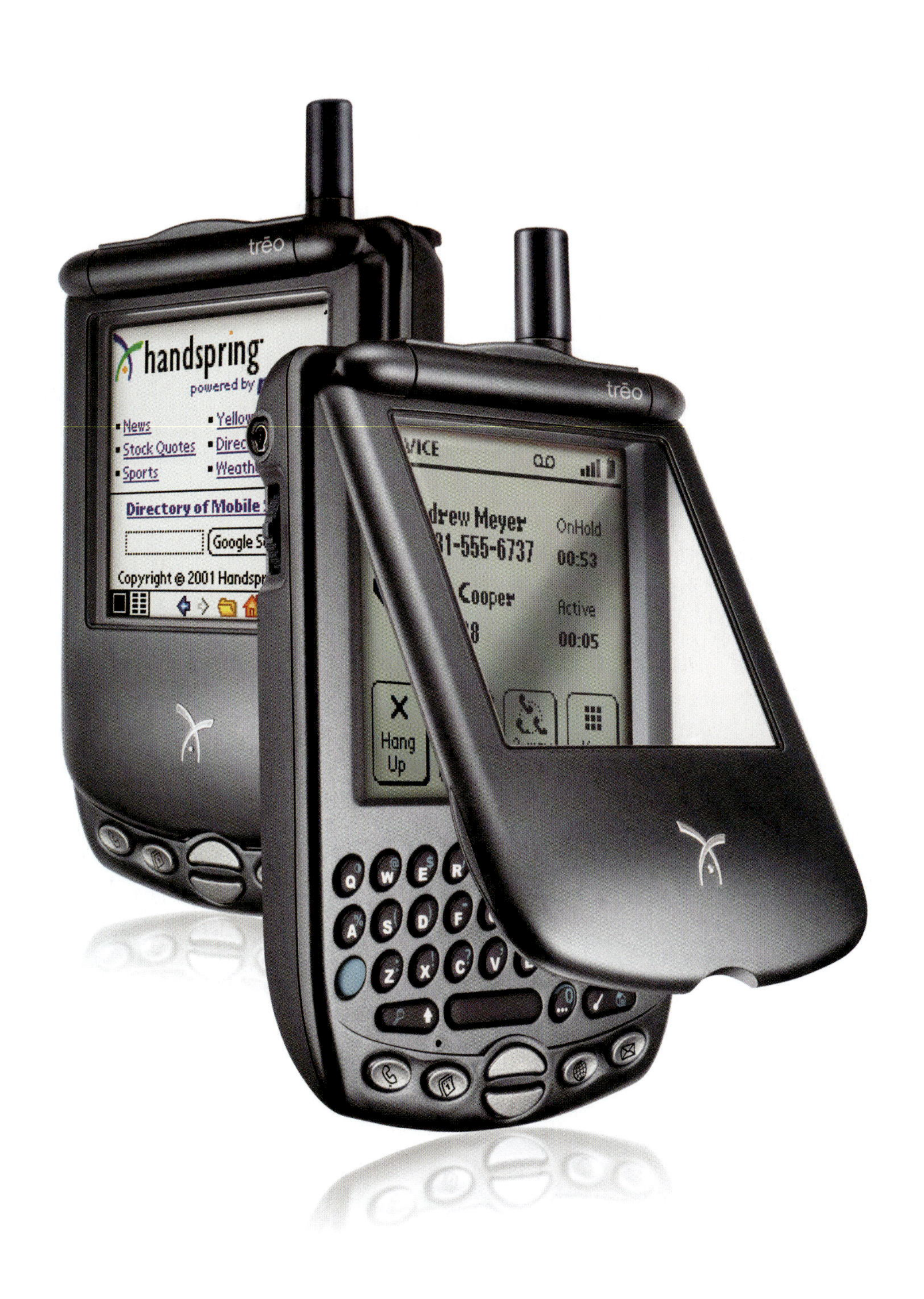
trēo
handspring
powered by
News
Stock Quotes
Sports
trēo
OnHold
00:53
Active
00:05
Hang Up

Combining PDA and Cell Phone

During the development of the Palm platform, the original research that Rob Haitani had conducted with focus groups had made Jeff Hawkins decide to postpone the integration of telephone and email functions into a PDA. Back then, although the technology had evolved to the point where it was technically possible, the trade-offs needed to make it happen were prohibitive. As Rob said, "It would be the worst phone and the worst organizer, combining the worst of all worlds."

Five years later, the technology was maturing to the point where the team at Handspring thought that the time was right to combine a PDA and phone, and that they could use the integration to advantage rather than having to make problematic trade-offs, so the Handspring Treo was conceived. Jeff describes the impetus for convergence:

> We were starting to realize that the cell phone was going to be the king in the world, and that it would become the design center for people's personal communication devices. We wanted to bring the benefits of the organizer, all that stuff we'd done there, to the cell phone. Up until then, there was no cell phone with a platform or third-party software.

■ Handspring Treo

Photo Courtesy of Handspring

The first Palm OS products were essentially organizers connected to PCs, and a cellular phone is a completely different animal. It was necessary to reinvent the user interface, using the same design principles. If you want to call someone, you just want to grab the phone and make the call, so Rob Haitani used his rules of ruthless optimization to look up phone numbers. He developed algorithms so that you could simply open the lid and type three or four letters, find one name out of a thousand, and be immediately connected.

One of the problems of integrating an organizer with a phone is that you want to look at your organizer while you are on the phone. If you are talking to someone, how do you schedule a meeting and continue to talk? That problem was solved by integrating a speakerphone, so that if you're on the phone you just press the spacebar to switch to speakerphone mode, allowing you to maintain a conversation and switch to any application in the organizer without having to put the phone to your head.

Another very simple design feature was a little switch on the top that let you turn your ringer off without taking the Treo out of your pocket or clip, thereby shortening the moments of embarrassment when you have forgotten to turn off your ringer in a public place.

When you are using a Treo for wireless email, you want to reply to messages as if you were using a full computer, demanding much more fluent text entry than for normal organizer tasks. Dennis Boyle remembers the surprising success of the miniature QWERTY keyboard:

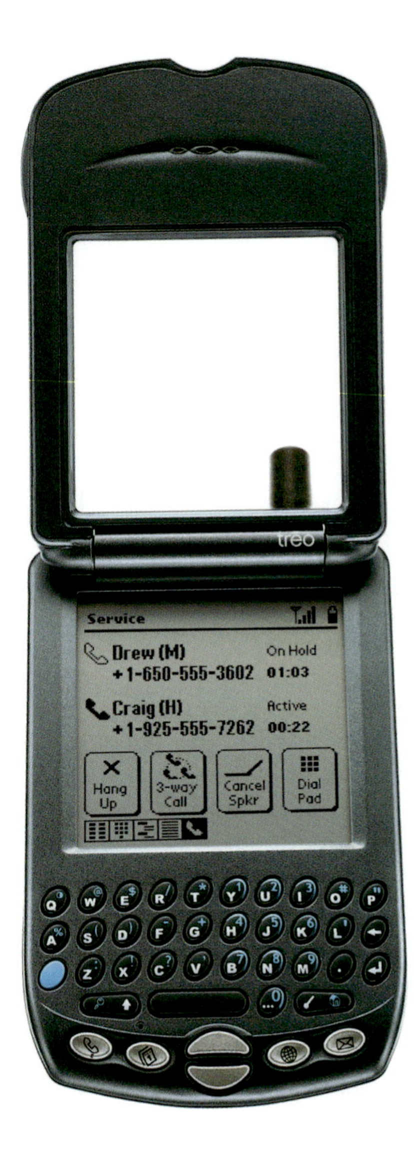

■ Treo with QWERTY keyboard

> When you compare Graffiti to entering text with buttons in some fashion, it shows how market needs change over time. There was almost no good way to enter text in a small handheld device. From the very beginning, with Apple, when they tried to do handwriting recognition, it turned out to be so poor that it became kind of a joke among writers and cartoonists.
>
> It was clear that people needed some sort of text input. Hawkins had the idea of meeting it halfway by developing Graffiti, a stylized alphabet that people could get pretty good at with a couple of hours of practice. It captured some devotees, and it was enough to get the business going, but it was still a very small percentage of the population who could even be bothered doing that.
>
> I remember that Handspring decided to put the Treo out with both a keyboard and Graffiti, because they didn't know which one people would choose; they decided to let them vote. The result was quite clear; a large majority went for the small keyboard. It doesn't seem intuitive, when you show it, people say, "How can you possibly type on that?"
>
> Then I just type out a little paragraph for them like this in a matter of seconds, and they say, "Wow, you get pretty good at that, don't you?"
>
> The human hand and eye can be trained quite quickly, and it seems like the little QWERTY keyboard, bad as it is, is such a standard that it requires no guesswork, and that attracts more users. The

success of the RIM BlackBerry products, followed by the keyboard version of the Treo, proved that some sort of little thumb keyboard could be effective. It broke through a "thumb barrier," if you will.

The keyboard was a very dramatic change in interaction style. Rob Haitani had always known that Graffiti was something you could learn and pick up, but also felt that at some point they would hit a wall in the number of people who would be willing to learn a different way of writing. There are people who just prefer keyboards. They want buttons; they want to press an *A* and get an *A* rather than deal with a stylus. The challenge posed by the keyboard was that it immediately projects an image of a much more complex product. How do you overcome that and keep the same essence of simplicity? Perhaps people are ready for more complexity.

Jeff Hawkins has an amazing track record of clear forward vision, but even he is uncertain enough to want to rely on iterative development, rather than expecting to be right first time:

In designing products, it's really hard to know what the best design center is. I always try to imagine the future, but usually that takes a couple of iterations. It took us a couple of iterations with the PDA and it took us a couple of iterations with the Treo.

The first design for the Treo was a clamshell. It had the keyboard, it had the screen, it had Palm OS, and so on. It was a reasonably successful product. We sold 350,000 of them and it won a lot of acclaim, but it wasn't a huge success. We didn't sell enough, and it wasn't gaining enough traction. But we took that knowledge and said, "Okay, let's do another tweak. Let's try to hone in further. What have we learned?"

The next try ended up being the Treo 600, which I think is much closer, and I believe it will have a long life. Its design center will have a very long life; I have not seen a replacement for it yet.

Jeff is sure that the cell phone is the dominant communicating device of the future, and he uses statistics to emphasize the point:

The cell phone has already won. There are six and half billion people on this planet. Somewhere between 1.2 and 1.5 billion of them have

Treo 600 with built-in camera

a cell phone. That is the number of people actually using cell phones today [in 2004]. The PC doesn't come close. Nothing else comes even close. It's done! Game over. A few years from now, I don't know what it will settle out to—maybe 3 billion? But it's incredible. Think about the impact on humanity. It's an amazing thing.

Throughout his career Jeff Hawkins has flip-flopped between designing computers and studying the brain, and in 2004, after the launch of his new book *On Intelligence*, he reflects on the connection between neuroscience and design:

Brains like familiarity, but they get bored. They are genetically programmed to want to discover new patterns. You don't want it too new because that seems dangerous. You want it somewhat familiar and somewhat new.

Think of music. The best music has some kind of essence of things you can recognize: a normal beat, harmonies, and melodic phrases, but you don't want to hear the same old, same old. You want something that's slightly jarring, and a little bit clever. The newness matters more than any other particular aspect of the aesthetic value. You want newness combined with cleverness.

Somehow new and old at the same time gives the best design. If a design is so new that people can't relate to it, then they reject it, even if they could theoretically learn how to use it because it's very clever. Styles are like this in general; if you have a new style for clothing, generally you don't want it to be too crazy. You want it to be just slightly different, enough that people say, "Oh, that's cool."

It's built into the human brain. We want familiarity, we want to be able to learn how to use it, but we also want some newness to it, and that's what makes us excited about it.

■ *On Intelligence* by Jeff Hawkins

How surprising that Jeff achieved his first great success with the PalmPilot by insisting on design simplicity in a complex world, but in 2004 he is looking for his next great success by combining PDA with cell phone, email communicator, and browser—not a simple combination:

I want to continually try to move toward the best single product I can build. It doesn't mean that doing multiple things is bad. People thought that the PalmPilot was successful because we only did a few things; that's not true. The things we did, we did well. People don't mind doing more things; they like it as long as you do them well. As long as you make it easy, intuitive, fast, and so on, they don't have a problem with that. That's the distinction. I think we can do a lot. And I think it's inevitable that the phone in your pocket will be most of the world's Internet connection, most of the world's communications, most of the world's email, most of the world's Web browser. It's going to be their music player, it's going to be their video player, eventually, in a number of years, it will be their PC!

In the next chapter, "Adopting Technology," we look into the reasons behind these paradoxes of familiarity and boredom, simplicity and sophistication. David Liddle discusses three phases of the adoption of technology, and the interviews that follow show some examples.

4

Adopting Technology

Interviews with David Liddle, Mat Hunter, Rikako Sakai, David Kelley, and Paul Mercer

TV
ON/OFF
POWER
VOLUME
VOL

SATELLITE ON/OFF
CHANNELS UP/DOWN
OK
2
3
5
6
8
9
LOCAL CHANNELS START AT 884

We interviewed some people with beautiful and very elaborate new media systems who were quite discouraged and quite unhappy with them. The solution from the manufacturers of consumer products was to produce the most dumbfounding, enormous remote controls. Thirty buttons was not a large number for those controls. There was a period of suppression of the adoption of the best of this technology simply because it was too complicated to use.

David Liddle, 2003[1]

■ Understanding how to use a TV remote is made easier by a friend

Photo Nicolas Zurcher

DAVID LIDDLE, PROJECT leader for the design of the Xerox Star, the founder of Metaphor Computer, and head of Interval Research, explains that a technology is adopted in three phases[2]—the enthusiast phase, the professional phase, and the consumer phase—and that these phases apply to the technology of a remote control just as much as to a computer. The maturity of a technology in this sequence has profound implications for designing interactions, as the nature of the design process changes as each phase is reached. Using the car and the camera as examples, David explains this process of adoption and its importance to an interaction designer.

The theme of camera is expanded to take a look at the way digital photography is being adopted, replacing previous technologies in processing and printing as well as in the camera itself. Mat Hunter was lead interaction designer in the team at IDEO that developed an "interaction architecture" for digital photography with Kodak, giving the company an early advantage in the market for digital cameras. He describes the development of the architecture and tells how "experience prototypes" were used to good effect.

Logitech
Pocket Digital

MINI

Connecting images together to form a panorama is an attractive function of Canon digital cameras and software. The story behind the development of the interaction design for Canon's PhotoStitch technology is revealed in an interview with Rikako Sakai, a human factors specialist and interaction designer from the internal design department at Canon.

We look at the output side of digital photography with Epson "printables," a conceptual project to design printers for digital photographs, thinking of the qualities of photography that could influence the designs to be different from normal computer printers, yielding designs that fit naturally into everyday life.

David Kelley is both a practitioner and a teacher. Tracing the development of interaction design from screen graphics to complete experiences, he explains how the design disciplines have adopted technology and proposes a future where designers act as integrators.

The iPod from Apple is a success story of the adoption of a technology in the consumer phase, including interactive product, computer application, and Internet-based service. Paul Mercer, an inventive software engineer with a background at Apple, as well as founder of Pixo and Iventor, tells the story of the iPod development in the context of his more general contribution to the creation of software tools for the design of portable devices.

- DigiCamera from Logitech

  Photo Courtesy of Logitech

- Driving controls from Mini Cooper

  Photo Courtesy of BMW

Photo Author

David Liddle

At the age of ten David Liddle saw his first computer. It was two stories tall and belonged to the Burroughs Corporation[3] in Detroit, where his father was responding to an emergency request for components on a weekend. While he was waiting for his father, the technicians taught him to count to 1023 in binary on his fingers, and explained Boolean logic to him. On the way home in the car he said, "This software thing is going to be big, really big!" He went on to study electrical engineering at the University of Michigan, and received his PhD at the University of Toledo while working at the same time on the design of a plasma display that sparked his interest in the potential for designing graphical interactions. He arrived at Xerox PARC in time to help with the POLOS project and design the display controller for the Alto. He went on to become the project leader for the development of the Star, the precedent-setting design for graphical user interfaces, about which he says, "As far as I'm concerned, the Star GUI was a great improvement over all of its successors!" In 1982 he left Xerox to found Metaphor Computer and, using the advantages of graphical interaction design for database access and program development applications, built Metaphor into a successful company, until IBM acquired it in 1991. In 1992 he was asked to set up and lead a new research laboratory, Interval Research, to stir up some new thinking for commercial possibilities. He assembled a stellar team of researchers, including interaction, graphic, and product designers, and media and behavioral people, as well as computer scientists. He is now a venture capitalist.

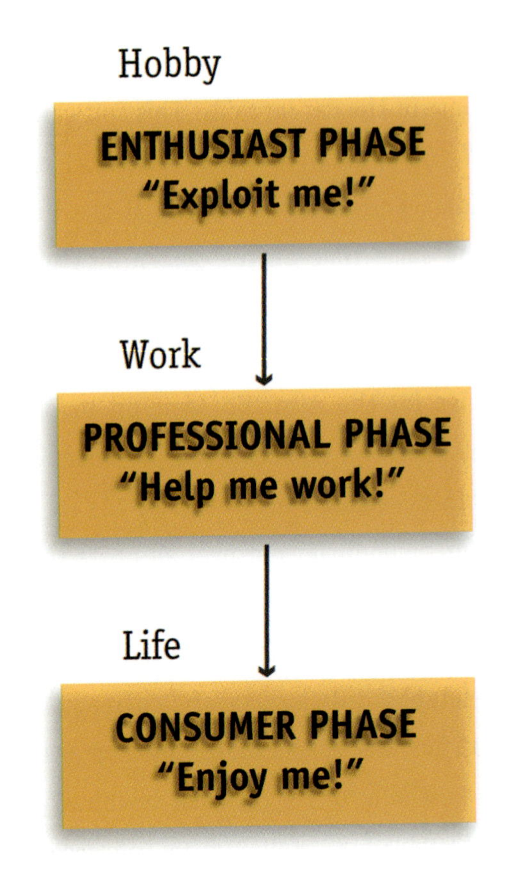
Hobby
ENTHUSIAST PHASE
"Exploit me!"
Work
PROFESSIONAL PHASE
"Help me work!"
Life
CONSUMER PHASE
"Enjoy me!"

David Liddle

Three Phases of Adoption

DAVID LIDDLE HAS a simple explanation of the development phases that a technology can be expected to go through, a process that has profound implications for designing interactions, as the nature of the design process changes as each phase is reached. Here is his explanation of the enthusiast phase, the professional phase and the consumer phase:

> In the twentieth century at least, the adoption of a fresh technology, ordinarily passed through thee stages, and seems to continue to do so now. Sometimes one of the stages may be very small.
>
> The normal progression is first to enthusiast users, who actually love and appreciate the technology in an aesthetic way, who enjoy exploiting it. The fact that it may be difficult to use actually adds to the fun, and it's certainly the case that competing variants of it will always be operated very differently. This was clearly true of automobiles, clearly true of cameras and all photographic equipment, true really of all the things like that that we might think of. The enthusiast phase is important because the enthusiasts take the

technology far beyond what the inventors and designers imagined could be done with it; they show the extremes of its potential. During this period there's always a great deal of ferment, quickly produced competing approaches. The controls for such a technology always vary a lot, because, for a while at least, people try to use them as the basis for competition. If you're an enthusiast, you're somewhat proud of you ability to manage all of the complexities and difficulties. Early automobiles broke down every four or five miles, and you had to stop and pump up the tires, or recrank the starter or something, but that was a good part of the fun. It was after all just a Sunday afternoon thing that you did.

Once enough enthusiasts have their hands on a technology, sooner or later one of them will say, "I can use this in my work!" They get a clever idea about how they're going to do something really practical with it. Notwithstanding that they enjoy its use, they decide to find a way to fit it into some practical part of their life, either literally their livelihood, or at least their home life in a practical way. As this begins to happen, there is a great change in the priorities of the developers of the technology. For one thing, they become more focused on costs and prices, not because it's going to become inexpensive, but because it will now be judged to some extent by how practical or useful it's going to be. The people who buy it, whether business people or consumers, are now saying, "Well, is that worth it for what I'm going to do?" There becomes a much more stabilized view about how much things are permitted to cost, and reliability and so on becomes important, but particularly we see the standardization of controls.

After a product has built up big enough volumes through this business phase, that's when suddenly one begins to reach a price point where it's practical for consumers to buy it. It goes from being the buy based on the aesthetic property for enthusiasts, to a practical return-on-investment kind of purchase by a professional, and now it becomes a very easy discriminatory purchase for a consumer, who feels it's practical and within their price range.

The enthusiast wants that product to say, "Exploit me! Look at my capabilities."

The business user wants the product to say, "Look at the productivity I can give you; here's how I'll change your activities."

The consumer wants the product to say, "Look at how I fit in with your style! Here's who you are. Use me and enjoy my capabilities."

In that stage the priorities for the product have dramatically changed, and one thing that we always see is that most of the important controls become automatic; for example, automobiles have automated safety functions, and cameras are automated to allow you to point and click. In this third stage we see prices that allow easy consumer decisions, the automation of the most subtle and important of the controls, and a great emphasis on the compatibility of the lifestyle of the purchaser with the image of the product.

Enthusiast, Professional, Consumer

DESIGNING FOR THESE three phases requires different skills and processes. Inventors are often good at coming up with the first version of a technology and can find the "enthusiasts" to adopt the technology by creating nothing more than an innovative solution. A single designer is sometimes enough, although great inventors, like Thomas Edison, employed a team of experts to increase their output.

The inventor, even when supported by a band of technicians, cannot develop the technology once it enters the "professional" phase. New design values apply when people adopt the technology for practical purposes. Now the design must be reliable, it must perform consistently, it must be priced to offer reasonable value, and above all it must be both useful and usable. This is a much more demanding set of requirements than necessarily applied to the enthusiast product. Large and complex organizations in companies for development of new products and services have evolved to respond to these needs. Teams of developers must include people with scientific, technical, and engineering skills to provide performance and reliability; people with business and value engineering skills to create solutions with the right balance between price and value; and marketing and human factors expertise to ensure the combination of usefulness and usability.

A design for the professional phase does not need to be easy to use, as people take pride in acquiring skill in their work; their learned skill separates them from the unskilled and allows them to feel expert. The design does not have to be enjoyable, as people tend to take their work seriously and are willing to try hard to be productive, even if the experience is unpleasant. Education for human factors professionals has evolved around this need for professional productivity, with methods that focus on evaluation of the way people use technologies in their work, both civilian and military. The version of this contribution in digital technologies is called human-computer interaction (HCI).

The makeup of a design team needs to change once again when a technology enters the "consumer" phase. Ordinary people will not buy products and services unless they like them and find them easy to use. There are plenty of examples of things that are not easy to use and cause frustration, but the basic value proposition must be there. The VCR is a good example of this, as the basic function of playing a tape is an excellent piece of interaction design: you push the tape cassette into a slot that is easy to see, the mechanism grabs it, and the tape automatically starts. Press the eject button, and the cassette is presented to you. By contrast, the functions needed for recording were badly designed for many years after the VCR was cheap enough to be accessible to consumers, with incomprehensible remote controllers, cryptic feedback, and little in the way of helpful automation. This classic example of bad interaction design persisted, resulting in all those examples of unprogrammed VCR displays flashing "12:00." Here the value proposition of playing the tape was enough to justify the purchase, but most people never used the device as a tape recorder because it was too difficult, until the designers eventually made use of the TV screen for output.

The design team has to be structured in a different way during the "consumer" phase in order to create solutions that are both easy to use and enjoyable. The same skills that were needed for the professional phase are still in demand, at an even more critical level, as the balance between price and performance is harder to achieve; but now it is also necessary to bring designers into the team who are capable of creating interaction design solutions that people want, that they find easy to use, that they enjoy, and that will give lasting satisfaction. In this situation interaction design fills the equivalent role for digital technologies that industrial design has filled for physical objects. Designs must work at every level but should be beautiful and delightful as well. Competitive advantage will accrue if they are behaviorally and aesthetically enjoyable.

Learning from Kids

DAVID LIDDLE DESCRIBES the techniques that the researchers at Interval developed to learn about the adoption of technology by studying the behavior of young people:

> One of the things we worked on very hard at Interval was developing techniques to try to understand—by age group and by background as well as simply by temperament—what kinds of products would be interesting, particularly information technology products, and how they spread from one such group or segment to another. We learned many interesting things about this, particularly among teenagers and young people of fourteen to twenty-four, but also in a lot of other age groups. We did a lot of work on this and found it to be part and parcel of how you thought about product design, human interaction design, graphical design, and so on.
>
> One very interesting thing that we learned came from our sending a touring tent along on the "Lollapalooza" alternative rock concert tour in the summer of 1994. This is a huge, multiday event, in each of forty cities or so. Besides the continuous performances, there are other little exhibits. We had a tent called "The Electric Circus" and we had a number of experiments in new media in this tent, and several hundred thousand people between fourteen and twenty-four passed through these exhibits. We interviewed a subset of them on video, or by questionnaires.
>
> We learned a number of interesting things, some of which are somewhat dated to that period of 1994, but let me give you a very

Backstage pass

interesting example. At this time, it was the practice of the Telecom industry to say, "We've got to start advertising things directly to kids in junior high school, or in high school, because then we'll have them as long-time customers. We've got to show them the value, how much fun it is to use the telephone in various ways, to interest them in various new telephone technologies and accessories."

That turned out to be completely wrong. At that time, if you were between twelve and seventeen, being on the phone a lot was a way of showing that you had a life, that you were in demand and interesting, and part of it. Your parents of course controlled what you did, but being on the phone was a clear way for you to be in contact with your friends. What we discovered was that once kids turned about eighteen, they were either in college or they were working for a living, but in any case they were not subject to anything like the same level of parental control. As a result, being on the phone a lot was a sign of NOT having a life. We got responses to the questionnaires saying things like, "Are you kidding? Why would I carry a cell phone around? Like, it would ring when I was at a rock concert or something!" or "Why do I need a message machine? Do you think I'm so lame that I can't miss a phone call? They'll call me back!"

In other words the idea that the telephone played a big role in their lives was exactly opposite to the image that they were now trying to construct. The question was, Is there an approach to telephony, to this kind of communication, that would be interesting to them, that wouldn't speak to their being restricted or at home alone with nothing to do but talk on the phone, that seemed to work with the idea of being out in the big outside world?

In Japan and in Western Europe, the great take-off among teenagers in the use of cell phones didn't come because they wanted to dial one another up; it came because they wanted to send messages, exchange ring tones, and do lots of other interesting things. In Japan you had this gigantic adoption of these surprising and strange techniques—capturing your own little photos; people standing round the block to have their photo taken such that it could be embedded in their cell phone—before there was easy data transport. The connection of telephony to messaging and games and other things like that was a part of what that age group saw themselves doing—a symbol of freedom and the completely fresh use of a technology rather than the earliest stages of "adult use" of a new communication device.

The insights from this kind of subjective research were used to seed projects at Interval, several of which developed into "spin-out" ventures, for example Purple Moon,[4] a company devoted to developing interactive media for girls.

David Liddle refers to the car and the camera as he explains the enthusiast, professional, and consumer phases of the adoption of technologies. This concept of phases helps to explain how interaction design has evolved and is a crucial idea to grasp if we are to be more successful in structuring both the education and the practice of designing interactions. Deeper looks at the examples of the car and photography follow.

BMW
Kommunikation
Klima
Navigation
Entertainment
12:23
6.6

The Car

Its cabin, too, is awash with innovation. A color screen is linked to the parking radar and shows how far you are away from a scrape. The iDrive switch—which controls the music, the navigation, the phone and the cabin's climate—is carried over from the 7. In the 5, though, its functions have been simplified. It is now an intuitive control, rather than a baffling one. It's still a lot more complicated than a few simple knobs, though. To change radio channels you need to push the "Menu" button, scroll down to "entertainment" with the iDrive knob, push the knob again to choose the correct radio frequency, and then swivel through to your desired station. Still, once you've read the owner's manual you're fine. Owning a modern BMW is like buying a new computer. Puzzling at first, but marvelous when you're up to speed.

- BMW iDrive

Photo
Downloaded from
www.bmwworld.com

From a description of the controls for BMW 5 series, new in 2004[5]

The automobile has had plenty of time to move through the three phases of adoption. The enthusiast phase lasted from the day in 1886 when Gottlieb Daimler fitted one of his petrol engines to a horse-drawn carriage until the launch of the Model T Ford in 1908; indeed, you could argue that the enthusiast phase continued much longer, particularly with the design of European sports cars that were unreliable enough to demand careful nurturing. The Model T was an amazing leap forward in design, making the car accessible to consumers as well as professionals, and establishing a dominant design for the basic control functions that is still with us.

You have to look at the peripheral interactions of entertainment, communication, or navigation to see examples of the struggle to create new controls that are easy to use. This is well illustrated by the quote above, about the BMW 5 series, where even this sophisticated driving machine is offering interaction design solutions for the functions on the central console that are not just difficult to use but that also create a safety hazard by diverting the attention of the driver away from the road ahead for a complex sequence of interactions—when the driver is looking forward, the central console is located in the peripheral vision zone.

At first the car was called the horseless carriage, and there was some confusion about the best approach to the design of the interactions. There was the tradition of interacting with the horse-drawn carriage, with reins and verbal commands and steering by guiding the path of the horse. Take away the horse and this made no sense! At least the front axle could be angled to steer, so the first question was how to turn it right or left relative to the body of the vehicle. Some coachbuilders tried selective braking for the right and left side. Others tried to build on boating traditions by devising tillers. Still others turned to the tradition of larger ships by designing steering wheels, which soon became the dominant design, providing direct manipulation at the same time as mechanical advantage for adjusting the steering linkage.

Then there was the question of how to start and stop. At first a pedestrian with a red flag was required to walk in front of the car to warn people of the danger approaching, but faster progress was soon wanted, and hand levers and foot pads were adopted for engaging and disengaging the engine, applying the brakes, and adjusting the speed.

The pattern of steering wheel, foot pedals, and hand controls has stayed almost the same since. Some variations still persist, like the islands of Britain, Japan, and New Zealand, where you drive on the left side of the road, mirroring all of the controls. Persistence is the key here, in that once a set of interactions as complicated as driving is learned by a large population, an escalating resistance to change sets in. The dominant design is in place, infrastructure is built up to support it, and it is difficult to persuade people to adopt another solution. A variation in gear changing has survived with the invention of the automatic transmission, but it has still not replaced the stick shift. Otherwise everything is the same; we still steer with a wheel, and both accelerate and stop with foot pedals. Even the details of the controls for signals and windshield wipers are now standardized enough that you can get into an unfamiliar make of rental car and know how to drive without confusion, at least with the controls that obviously matter to safety, even if the interactions for comfort and entertainment in the car are still confusingly different with different designs.

Changes in technology have had surprisingly little effect on the basics of driving. The value of electronic technology in cars continues to grow and was already more than a third of the total cost of a typical vehicle by the 1990s. Computer systems control instrumentation, fuel economy, emissions, and emergency behaviors like airbag activation and antilock braking. Most people are unaware how much of their driving experience has been subtly altered by this technology, which has invaded the vehicle transparently. We usually think of technology as expressed in the design of the personal computer, with keyboards, mice, and screens. It would be strange and frightening to have to sit in the front seat of a car with a keyboard, and steer by typing commands like, "15 degrees right in 35 yards—enter." The direct manipulation of steering is simple, effective, and enjoyable. Learning to drive takes time and patience, but once we have acquired the skill, we take pride and pleasure in the power of controlling the movement of this huge object that travels so fast. The design has evolved slowly by iterative steps, with each step making it a little easier, or a little safer, or a little faster, but the interactions have stayed substantially the same.

Even the instrumentation on the dashboard has remained analog, with simple rotating pointers in round dials, resisting the temptation to look more high-tech and digital. The car is a remarkable example of interaction design that matured early in the history of the product category, developing an approach that worked well for consumers as well as professionals. There was no need to change from a dominant design that remains satisfying to most people. For several decades, technologists have been predicting more automated ways of controlling cars, for example drive-by-wire to allow you to surrender control to the computer and tuck into a fast moving stream of traffic on a specially equipped highway. This may eventually be the future, but there is a huge psychological barrier against giving up control. We prefer the risks of death and injury on the roads to the idea of letting a machine take over, partly because we mistrust the computer—and also because we love to exercise our driving skills.

Digital Photography

David Liddle points to the camera to illustrate the three phases of adoption of technology. He uses the cameras that were taken into space by the early astronauts as an example of the "enthusiast" phase, saying, "The 35mm cameras used by the astronauts in the fifties, nearly required a PhD in optics to operate them."

- Nikon F3 NASA—Space Nikon—front
- Rear

> In the case of the 35mm camera, the design suddenly stabilized when it went from very expensive exotica to being broadly used by professional photographers and serious photographers. The viewfinder was in one place, you exposed by pushing with your right index finger, you wound the film with a lever with your right thumb, and you focused in a particular way. There was a stabilization of the controls.
>
> Today when you buy a 35mm camera, even if it has film in it, it will read the film speed automatically, set the exposure automatically, set the flash automatically, and actually a chimpanzee can take pretty good photographs with today's highly automatic 35mm camera.

They are dubbed "idiot cameras" because anyone can take a pretty good photograph, even without expertise in photography. Point and shoot—the consumer-phase technology—takes care of all the details and gives you the best shot that is technically possible in the circumstances. When the consumer phase arrives, it does not replace the market for professional solutions, but often expands it as more people realize the potential to improve over their amateur skills.

The experience of photography is much broader than the design of the camera on its own. There is a huge infrastructure supporting both professional and consumer photography in parallel. The professional side includes photographers who will take the pictures, processing and printing services, endless categories of equipment, and the gear to control lighting at every scale. On the consumer side there is an enormous network of processing facilities, most of them offering one-hour services to go from film to print.

Digital photography is replacing film and print photography in an industry that is already mature enough to have both professional and consumer versions of the technology, so we can see sweeping changes—and the opportunities for innovative solutions that accompany them—affecting the whole industry at once. In the interview that follows, Mat Hunter tells the story of developing an "interaction architecture" with Kodak for digital cameras and photography in the consumer market.

Photo Author

Mat Hunter

When Mat Hunter was studying industrial design in London, he chose to design a videocassette recorder for his major project. He turned the VCR on its back so that it could sit on the same shelf as the videocassettes in the library, and reshaped the remote control to avoid losing it in between the sofa cushions. He found a quote from George Bush Sr., president at the time, declaring his intention to make every American able to program their VCR: the obvious failure in meeting this goal made Mat wonder if the design of the VCR might be as much to blame as the educational system, so he decided to study interaction design at the Royal College of Art and to master the art of designing interfaces that would be easy and enjoyable to use. He joined the San Francisco office of IDEO in 1995 and was key to the development of an interaction architecture for Kodak. He transferred to IDEO London in 1999 and became head of interaction design. Both as a manager and designer, he has worked on a wide range of innovative fusions of hardware and software, including medical devices, interactive guitar tutors, Web-based education software, cable modems, and a system for reserving meeting rooms in offices. He has created exploratory concept projects for connected appliances, for example "social mobiles,"[6] an exploration that looks at the social impact of mobile phones. He has appeared in television programs on design and innovation on the BBC and Open University and is currently head of the London office of IDEO. He also plays guitar and drums in Amped Up, the office band.

11:08 AM 09/03/96
4/50

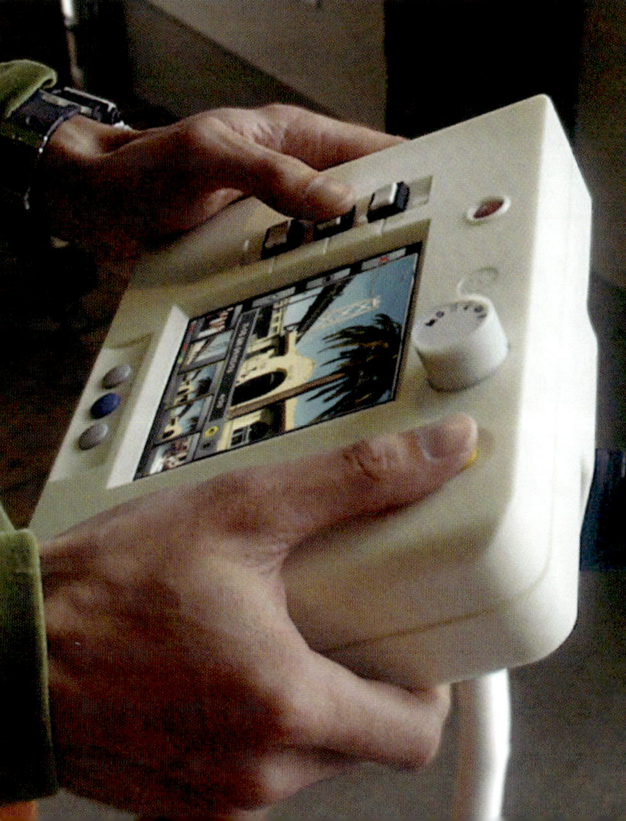

Mat Hunter

Interaction Architecture

Clockwise from top

- Screen for prototype
- Experience prototype
- Concept for future camera

Photos
Courtesy of IDEO

Mat Hunter was a key member of the team that developed an interaction architecture for digital photography, helping Kodak retain their strength in the consumer market, while attempting to bridge the gap from film-based photography. This case study illustrates some of the issues facing interaction designers as they design for the adoption of digital technology in an area that already has a strong consumer tradition but where a conventional technology is being replaced by electronics.

In 1995 Kodak commissioned IDEO to look at the design of digital cameras, but fairly soon it became evident to the team that they would need to expand the vision a great deal further than just the camera itself, because digital technology would change photography as a whole. Mat Hunter[7] describes this epiphany.

> George Eastman himself had said right at the beginning, "You press the button; we do the rest."
>
> He realized that actually it wasn't just the Box Brownie they were making, but also the whole service, the back end, for turning this

- User observations—sorting
- User observations—displaying
- User observations—storing
- Ceiva digtal picture frame

> captured Kodak moment into a print, or whatever else was the final artifact. What we had to do was take the digital camera, step back, and reassess why people wanted to take pictures in the first place. Then we would have to build up some picture of the ecology, you could call it, of products and services surrounding the digital camera that would be the replacement for the film and film processing, product, and service that Kodak had become successful with.
>
> We went and looked at how people took images and understood how they used them to capture special moments and to share memories with others. Perhaps it was a form of self-expression, photography as a hobby; sometimes it was merely to record very basic information. Underlying motivations were slowly extracted and synthesized, and these were used to inspire a range of products and services.
>
> For instance, if you want to share images easily, perhaps we should have a digital picture frame, and in this way, something very simple, much simpler than a PC, would sit on someone's mantelpiece. I would take a picture and send it over the Internet, over some sort of network, to the picture frame. And that way, Grandma could get to see the picture.
>
> Or what if you have much smaller personal communicators, where you can send and receive images? What would it be like? What role would Kodak have in that world? Would they actually make the device, or would they merely provide the underlying engine within the device?

Those initial scenarios for the potential of digital photography have come true since then. Ceiva[8] is one of the companies making digital picture frames, and image communicators are a standard offering from most of the cell phone service providers, with digital cameras built into the phones. A broad range of products and services is emerging to support this digital infrastructure for imaging. You can email images to an Internet site, and they will be printed for you and mailed back to you, providing a service that is analogous to the traditional Kodak print service; you can store your images online in some kind of online photo album. You can buy dedicated printers now, so that you can connect your camera directly to it without needing to go through a PC.

If we look back to 1995 and see this strategy that we were constructing and come forward to 2003, we see that this new ecology of digital imaging has been built, but it's been very slow. The old silver halide photography that grew up over a hundred years cannot be shifted overnight despite the fact that digital cameras have leapt off the shelves and are taking over more and more. Kodak realized that we wouldn't really be moving to digital imaging completely overnight, so once we had understood the larger ecology, they directed us to make our first priority to design excellent interactions for digital cameras.

It was fairly clear from other digital cameras that were just appearing that they would have things like small displays on the back of them so you could review the images. This immediately changed the nature of the camera, because previously cameras were purely about capture: now they were also about review. This means that you want to do things like delete images, group them, send them off somewhere, perhaps email them to people or to a printing house. Maybe you'd want to capture motion as well as still images. Perhaps you'd want to record a sound annotation, a sort of "voice note" on it. Suddenly this essentially rather simple device was becoming much more complex. We already knew that cameras could get very complex just dealing with the fine nuances of how to capture things. How complex would they become if suddenly they had all this other functionality?

The challenge from Kodak was, "Find a way to make sense of digital camera interactions!" The design team had to take another step back, and look at the fundamental modes of use. They were looking for a really cohesive user experience, something that would put Kodak out in front again. Kodak had already lost their dominant position in camera sales and was being overtaken by Japanese competitors in many areas, but they still had powerful organizations in the US and European markets, potentially capable of launching a whole new range of digital cameras. They could build a strong brand with a great reputation for ease of use, creating cameras for everyone, not just for technologists. Mat came to the conclusion that something more than a single camera with well-designed interactions was needed.

> We said that we had to build an "interaction architecture" because we weren't looking to build any one particular camera; we were still really working with the research team. Therefore, what we had to do was make an extensible system of design principles, values, and elements, so that the development teams would be able to find the bits that they needed as they were making their products and bundle them cohesively into a camera. What we hoped was that this would happen over many years, and there would some consistency across the cameras that were made as they evolved, as features were added or taken away. So it was something that was much more extensible than merely the design of one single camera.

The insights from the observations and research were gradually coalescing into concepts that were clear enough to use for design. Jane Fulton Suri,[9] a psychologist, was leading the human factors studies and research for the team at that time, and she remembers some of the challenges:

> Some professional photographers were already using digital cameras at that time, but there were no consumers with experience in digital photography. We were trying to push forward into the future, based on observing professionals and early adopters of the new technology, combined with an understanding of the way ordinary people thought about photography, plus projections of trends for the spread of digital equipment.
>
> I remember giving a high-end digital camera to one of the families that we'd interviewed, so that they could try it out for themselves. When I explained how to use the camera, the mother said, "Where's the film?" so I had to talk about receptors, pixels, and digital memory; things that most people know about now.
>
> Her next question was, "How do you know how many pictures you've got left?" so I had to tell her about the tradeoff between the size of each photograph, what you wanted to use it for, and the number of pictures that you could take. This was also a difficult issue for Kodak, as they were proud of their tradition of high-quality images supported by lots of carefully evolved metrics. It was hard for them to see the benefits of trading quality for other advantages, for example, taking a picture of the baby that would be small enough to transmit immediately over a phone line to a little screen on granny's mantelpiece.

Jane prepared a framework that summed up the opportunities for consumer digital photography under five headings:

1. Readiness to capture

The professional photographer travels with cases full of lenses, camera bodies, tripods, and lighting equipment. The team predicted that when digital photography is adopted by the general public, cameras will include a broad range of devices, from the traditional professional kit at the top end, through simple cameras with built-in lenses, to devices such as cell phones, or wearable cameras that would look like jewelry.

2. Information at capture

The real-time feedback of the screen on the back of the camera would emerge as a highly valued feature of the digital camera, so you could see immediately if the shot looked promising or disappointing. Information about when a picture was taken could also be recorded, along with the technical details of the image, and perhaps a voice annotation. In a future where GPS is inexpensive enough to be integrated into the camera, the information about where the shot was taken could make browsing and sorting a lot easier.

3. Creative control

In traditional photography, the composition of the shot and the choice of lighting happens in the camera, but there is another set of opportunities for creative control that happens later in processing and printing. The team realized that digital photography is not so sequential. Any time during the process, you can apply filters, pixilate, choose sepia, add picture frames, text, and so on. This realization led to this framework, expressed as five balloons around the user, rather than a linear journey through the experience.

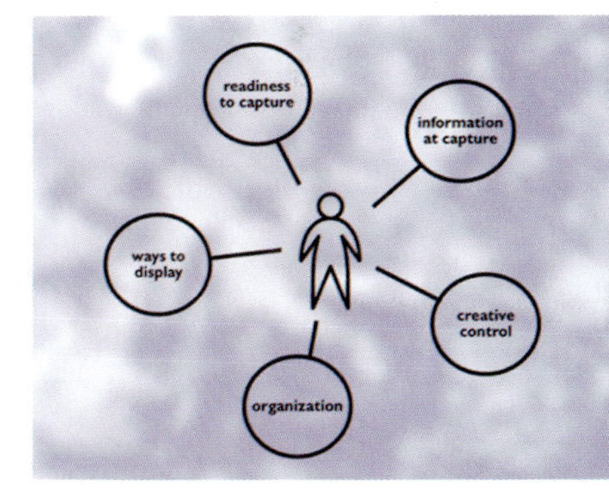

Framework for digital photography ■

4. Organization

There are well-organized albums of photographs that people use to remember an event or a trip, or to recount the story to their friends, but there are also countless boxes full of unsorted photographs in almost every home. Digital photography offers the opportunity to sort using the "information at capture," but also to recognize images from small thumbnails. iPhoto from Apple has made excellent use of our ability to scan tiny versions of images to recognize the one we are looking for, leveraging the fact that we remember images best by a visual representation rather than by which shoe box we put it in.

5. Ways to display

Pictures mean very little unless you can see them, so one of the great potentials of digital photography is to increase the diversity of means of display. Prints and transparencies are still valuable, and indeed a whole industry has grown up around printing, but there are also many new possibilities. Electronic displays include the television, computer screen, the electronic picture frame, the e-wallet, fridge door display, and cell phone, as well as others that will emerge in time. As digital images become more ubiquitous, it is interesting to see how we use them more habitually to illustrate a point in a conversation with a friend or to remember a piece of information. When the images are displayed electronically, they can be captured and shown at no incremental cost, so they spread into all sorts of unexpected places.

The system perspective

A system perspective was summarized by putting the camera at the center, with connections to the computer for editing, to the printer for output, to the television for display, to online resources and agencies for sending to other people and for remote printing, and to kiosks in public places for copying and printing.

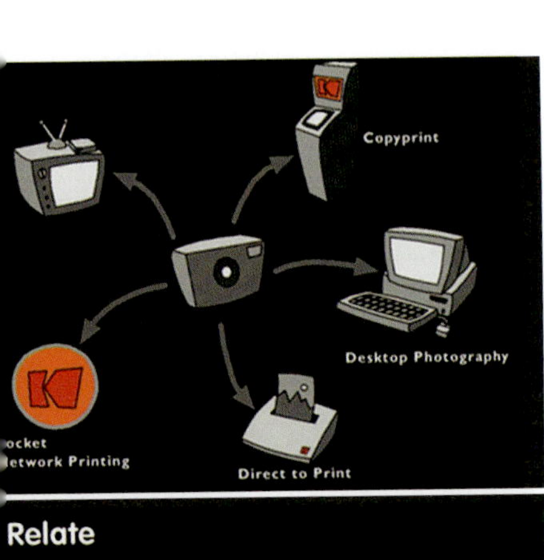

- System diagram
- "Relate" scenario 1
- "Relate" scenario 2

Scenarios

Scenarios were developed to bring the design opportunities to life. One was called "Relate" with a slogan "I can stay in touch anywhere, any time." The story was about a business trip to Belize, to check tourist amenities, yielding these highlights:

- Preview and review images
- Local image transmission
- Direct link to communication infrastructure
- Voice annotation
- Multiple display options
- Visibility of Kodak as the enabler

Another was called "Express" with a slogan "I can see in new and fun ways." The highlights from this one were:

- Emphasis on creativity at capture
- Stylus input for fine control
- Global effects pre-capture
- Limited manipulation post-capture
- Cards for loading effects
- Print output from service bureaus

These lists of highlights were used to develop patterns of value that would appeal to Kodak's customers and formed the basis of design for the interaction architecture for the system as a whole, as well as potential business cases for analysis. The elements of the interaction architecture for the cameras themselves were also starting to emerge, with the first creative synthesis of the concepts for the display screen, the mode dial, the filmstrip, and the navigational controls.

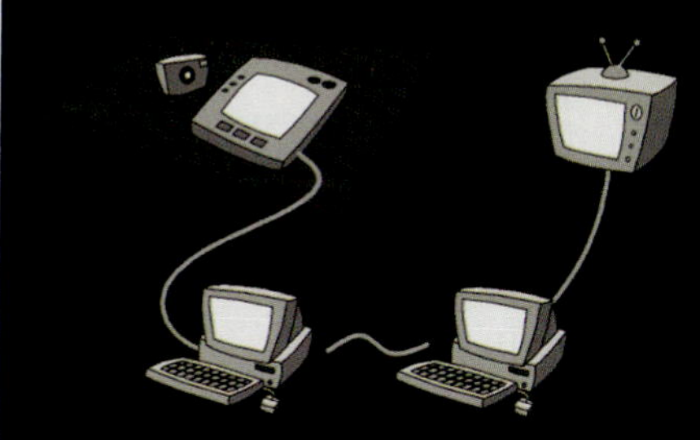

"Express" scenario 1 ■
"Express" scenario 2 ■
User experience prototype diagram ■

User Experience Prototype

Mat sums up another difficult challenge, caused by the separation of this research activity from the development teams that would want to use the "interaction architecture":

> Because we weren't actually designing directly with the development teams, we knew we had a few challenges. One was that we couldn't actually be sure of the technology we were using. We knew we had to make certain assumptions about the size of the display on the back of a camera and the processing speed that would affect the way in which it captured images and presented menus. We decided to think a little bit in the future and say, "This is the idealized camera experience, and we believe this technology will be obtainable within three to five years." Then we hoped that the development teams would be able to "down-sample" what we had done; they would take the essence of it, applied in practice to whatever screen display size or whatever processing speed they actually had.

They racked their brains for a way to communicate the interaction architecture that would engage the imagination of designers and engineers in the future. A book of guidelines would be the conventional approach, but however interesting and beautiful they could make a book, diagrams and text would not be a very compelling form of communication. They came up with the idea of creating a working prototype of an archetype for the interaction behavior, so that the members of the development teams could experience the behaviors directly.

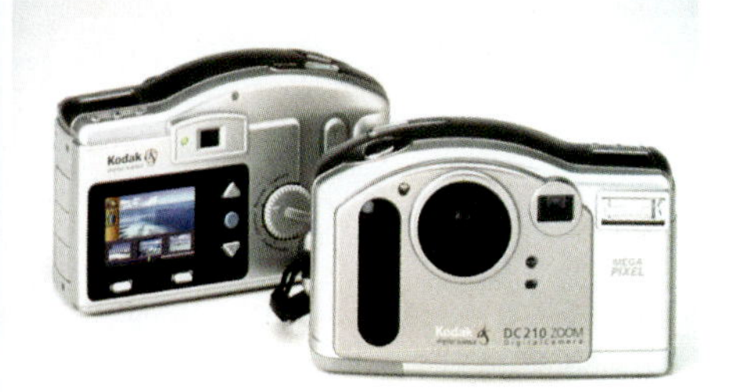

■ Kodak DC 210—first production camera

> It was a real live working specification. We called it a "User Experience Prototype." In physical form it was pretty big and ugly. It was a beige plastic box the size of a very large hardback book. We got a CCTV security camera and bolted it onto the front; we tethered it via a rather large cable to a tower Macintosh, the fastest we could get at the time, but achingly slow today, and built a working system.
>
> The whole point was that you shouldn't really look at the physical form; you should become immersed in what you could see on the display and what happens when you press the buttons and rotate the knobs. What we created in this device, therefore, was what we

believed to be the epitome of the user experience as you are interacting with a device. This is how it should behave, both logically and in terms of its animation and its time-based behavior. What was exciting was that when we finished this user-experience prototype and showed it to Kodak, they immediately got what we were talking about, both in terms of the logic and the spirit of the device. This was something that not only was logically easy to use, but it felt easy to use. It was responsive, it moved as if it were a very simple mechanical device. People could understand it.

The idea of the "user experience prototype" was working, and Mat was very gratified when Kodak said, "Make us four of them, please." They wanted to ship one out to Japan to the camera factory, so that the development teams based in Japan making the next generation could immediately immerse themselves in the specification. They used the other three to send to different parts of the Kodak organization. Only eight months later, the DC 210 was born, which was the first of this new generation of digital cameras, using the concepts in the interaction architecture.

The architecture had several basic elements. Firstly, there were three modes to make sure that the user wasn't overwhelmed with everything at once. These were "capture" for taking pictures, "review" for seeing what was already captured, and "send" for the possibilities of communicating the images. They decided on a rotary control for the prototype, and called it the "mode dial." It was big and prominent with icons printed on it, so that if you looked at it, you immediately had a good idea what the camera could do.

Second, there was the way in which the images that had already been captured could be shown on the display. In the previous designs from Kodak and the cameras from competitors, when the camera memory contained a lot of images, perhaps forty or fifty, it was very hard to navigate. It was important to be able to see, especially in the "review" mode, what was already captured, both the individual image and where it was relative to the other images:

Interaction architecture diagram ■
Design concept ■
Kodak DC 210 implementation ■

Rikako S

Rikako Sakai

I have been working for Canon for more than eight years. When I was involved in the development of PhotoStitch, I was working in the human factors department as a kind of human factors specialist. This was the first time I had worked on something related to digital cameras, since that engineering team hadn't asked us for help to improve their products, to make them user-friendly.

Rikako Sakai, 2002

■ Using Stitch Assist mode on a Canon Digital Elph camera

Photo Nicolas Zurcher

In 1996 Canon launched their first version of software for stitching images together to form panoramas or large tiled photographs. In order to use it, you had to take overlapping shots in your camera as best as you could, download them to your PC, and then stitch them together using the program. Kenji Hatori was the software engineer at Canon in Japan who led the team that designed the program. He said that initially they

> were thinking of a big feature that can be done by digital camera, not the traditional camera. The first idea came from a development team that investigated the algorithm of image stitching; they were investigating for a few years. When the algorithm was almost fixed, the product planning division thought it could be put into a product, but there was no UI. There was only algorithm, and the product planning division found the member who could implement the UI. There were several ideas, but the most impressive and biggest feature was the PhotoStitch idea.

This idea of automating the connection between adjoining photographs was first developed as a software product to reside within Windows, so the user of a PC could import overlapping images from a digital camera, or scans from prints or slides, and the algorithm would help them stitch the images together. There was no connection to the camera, so the photographer had to guess how to juxtapose the images with the right amount of overlap. This meant that the first version of the software only performed well if the photographs were carefully positioned, using a tripod and rotating at a defined angle for each shot. It was hard to use, both in the camera and on the screen.

In the second version they added a Stitch Assist mode in the camera, helping the user to take the best shots as they record the images. This integrated the physical controls on the camera with the software that would enable the stitching and made it much easier to use. As Kenji Hatori recalls:

> With the Stitch Assist mode, the user can easily take the panorama image. First, the user takes one image, and then the first image will remain to the left side of the LCD. The user can adjust the camera image to match the remaining image. The remaining image and the current image is transparent, so you can see the difference. Then the user can match the current image with the previous image.
>
> The Stitch Assist mode in the camera I think came from the PPD [Product Planning Division] and the camera engineers. They knew that the version 1 was already shipped. They looked at it and tried to use it and found that it was a little difficult to take such photos because the images had some common area. They thought the camera could assist the software. The concrete idea came from the camera hardware development team.

When the mode is selected, a guide appears in the viewfinder display to help you as you take one image, showing the position of the current image relative to the next one in the series. When the first image is recorded, it is repositioned to show about a third of its area adjoining the next image, so that the viewfinder display can easily be used to help align the new photograph with the one before. This gives you a preview of what you are trying to do and guides you through the process in a very fluid way. The actual stitching is still done on the PC after the shots are recorded, but without this real-time interactive help, it is very difficult for people to position each shot on their cameras effectively for

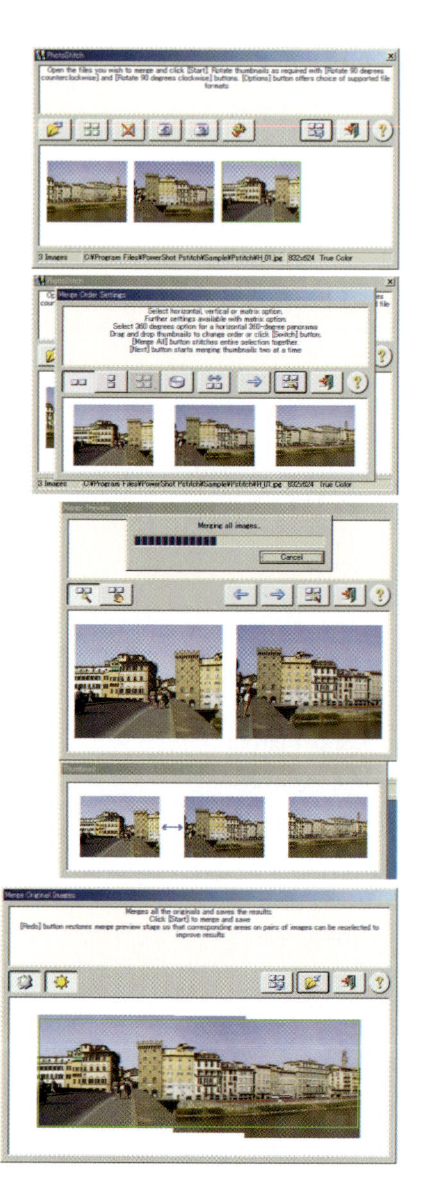

- PhotoStitch version 2—open files
- PhotoStitch version 2—merge order settings
- PhotoStitch version 2—merging all images
- PhotoStitch version 2—save result

completing a panorama. By building it into the camera itself, the experience is much more enjoyable both when you are shooting and afterward on the PC.

The second version also improved the merging process on the PC screen by adding a "merge all" feature, but people still found it difficult to make the final adjustments to the connected images. For version 3, Rikako Sakai joined the team from the Canon Design Department. She is an interaction designer and human factors expert, and she guided the engineering team through a process of user testing and the design of a much more intuitive user interface for the screen-based software. She added animated icons, tabs for the steps in the process, informative text messaging, and transparent overlays and indicators for the fine adjustments.

Stitch Assist—mode dial ■
Stitch Assist—first picture ■
Stitch Assist—second picture ■
Kenji Hatori, Canon software engineer ■

Merge Images Shot in Stitch Assist Mode
Click [2. Merge] to merge these images.
For images shot as a 360-degree panorama, click [Arrange], select [360 Degrees] and then click [2. Merge].
1. Selection and Arrangement
2. Merge
3.Save
Open...
Arrange
Switch
Clear
Rotate
Enlarge
Reduce
H_06.jpg
H_07.jpg
H_08.jpg
No. of Images: 3
512 x 384 True Color

Save Image
Click [Save] to save the merged image. To merge a different image, return to [1. Selection and Arrangement], click [Clear] and then [Clear All].
1. Selection and Arrangement
2. Merge
3.Save
Save...
Adjust Image...
Enlarge
Reduce
View the Saved Image?
No
Yes
Image Size: 1059 x 272

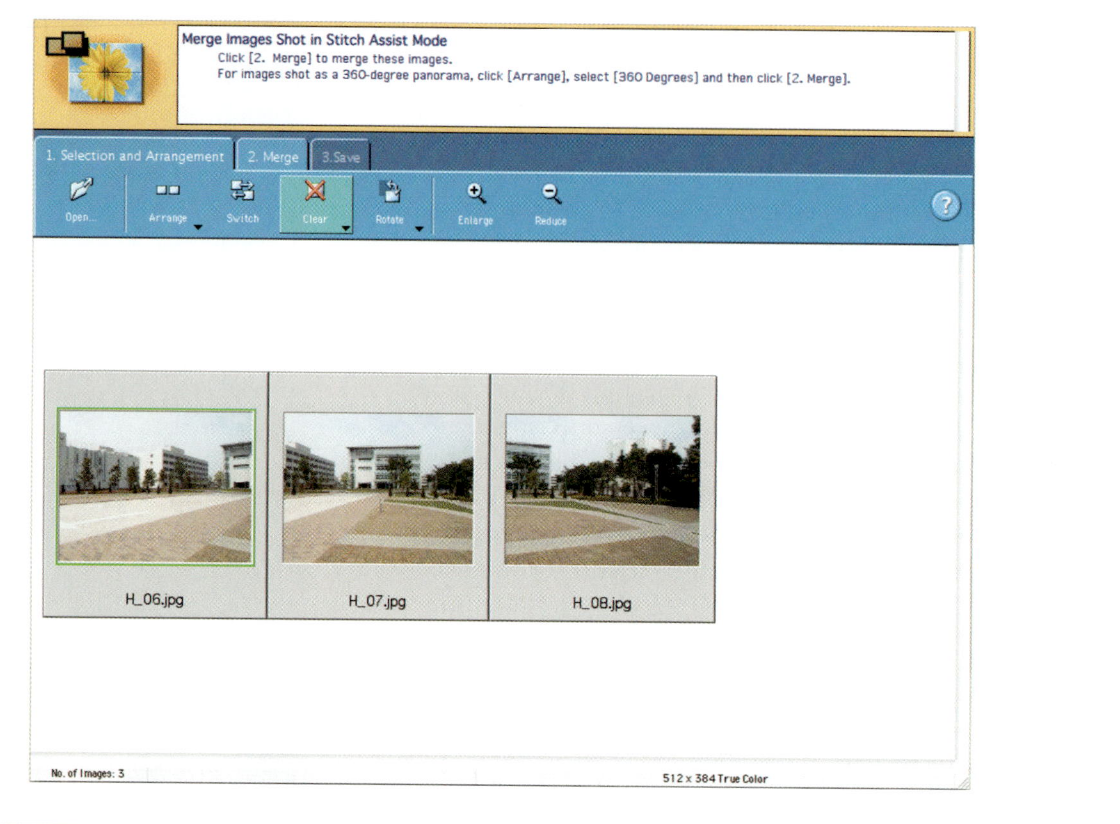

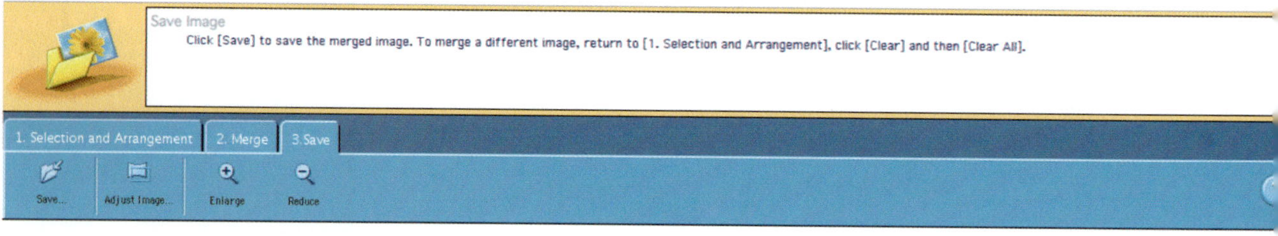

Canon PhotoStitch

After we shipped version 1, Product Planning Division and customers said it was not so good UI. It was not good looking. It had no color, only grey color because it was based on the Windows standard buttons.

Kenji Hatori

PhotoStitch version 3

- *Top* Selection and arrangement
- *Bottom* Saving

For the first two versions of PhotoStitch, the engineering team developed the design without working with interaction designers or human factors specialists, only requesting help from Canon's Corporate Design Center for the design of the screen graphics when the behavioral aspects of the product were already defined. When Rikako Sakai was brought in to help with the design of version 3, the first thing that she did was to set up thorough usability testing of the first two versions. She assembled the whole team who were involved with the project, including engineers and screen graphic designers, to observe how people used the products from behind a one-way mirror:

> Throughout the usability testing I found many problems with the old version, more than I imagined. In fact, before the usability testing, the engineers had already noticed some of the problems, and they told me what they had known before the usability testing. I added their findings and my findings on a checklist.
>
> After the tests, we realized that the biggest problem was its structure. The structure was not clear and visible to users at all, and there were too many operational steps to stitch downloaded photos. We also noticed some problems with the guidance messages. There

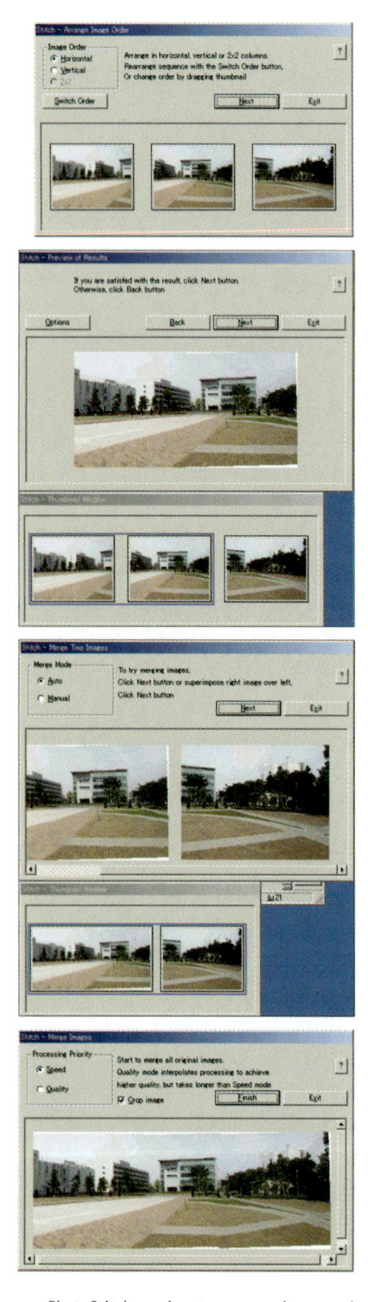

- PhotoStitch version 1—arrange image order
- PhotoStitch version 1—preview of results
- PhotoStitch version 1—merge two images
- PhotoStitch version 1—merge and save

> was navigational guidance on the user interface, but it didn't make sense to users at all, and it was not really helpful. The old version also had a help function, but it didn't make sense to users either, so once they had problems during the operation, they had no way to get out of their difficulties. I found some words were difficult to understand for users who didn't have much computer experience. With the guidance messages, there were some technical words. Also the surface design—the geographical user interface design—was not intuitive to beginners. Some icons didn't communicate distinct functions to the users. The entire GUI looked a little bit complicated.

Great strides had been made to improve the design in the second version, both by adding the Stitch Assist mode in the camera interface and by improving the basic algorithm for the stitching process. Rikako continued to work with the engineers who were writing the software and the designers of the screen graphics, but she was able to control all of the interactive elements for the new version of PhotoStitch, including graphical expression, text and help messages, as well as all the error messages and dialog boxes.

The navigation was improved by changing to tabs, so that the user could move backward and forward at will, rather than being forced into a linear step-by-step process:

> I made a lot of changes from the old version. The biggest change was adopting the tab user interface instead of the wizard. We had lots of arguments about this. At the time we developed the software, it was not so common to adopt a tab user interface for step-by-step operations. We had to design each operational step to be very clear to users. We also had to revise navigational messages at the same time. With the new user interface, when you import all the photos and you are going to stitch, the second tab will be focused automatically, so you realize that the second step is available to choose. That's a part of the new user interface that we created. Also, the revised guidance messages inform you what you have to do next with plain words. So, if by any chance users get stuck, the guidance will help them overcome their problems.

Another navigational problem was in starting the application, as it was buried among a long list of utilities offered by Canon for digital cameras, so Rikako developed distinctive icons to represent the application and viewer. Importing folders and images was supported through an "Open" command, but during the observations Rikako noticed that people were trying to select them on the desktop, and drag and drop them into the open application, so she decided to support that alternative. She also noticed that when people had a lot of images to be stitched, they often lost track of the order, so she added file names and numbers to the images as they were presented and reduced the size of the thumbnails to give a better overview:

> I also made some suggestions about improving the scaling functions of the viewer. One of the concerns with the old viewer was difficulty with getting the overview of an entire image. I made questionnaires during the usability testing to figure out how many steps the user actually needed to take to get an overview.
>
> With the new version, you can go back whenever you want to the full montage. This idea also came from the usability testing. During the usability testing, we observed users trying to go back and forth. Especially when users got stuck, they tried to get back to the previous step, so we decided to support that movement.

The icons were also improved, with a combination of individual icons on the buttons under the tabs, plus an animated descriptive icon next to the text prompt box to reinforce the indication of the tab selection:

> We also modified each icon to be more intuitive to beginner users. With the old version, the icons didn't make sense to the beginners, so I decided to improve all the icons and add text labels. The first time I asked Osami Matsuda, our graphic designer, to revise the icons, he refused to put text labels together with the icons because it doesn't look cool. But after the usability testing, we realized again that displaying graphical icons is not enough to communicate distinct information to beginners, so in the end, we decided to display both icons and labels.
>
> We discussed every detail of the icons. For example, I really wanted these clickable icons to look like buttons, like square

PhotoStitch version 3—merge images ■
PhotoStitch version 3—amend merge results ■
PhotoStitch version 3—view seams ■
PhotoStitch version 3—save image ■

> buttons or something like this, but the graphic designer didn't want to do that because it doesn't look cool. So, we fought for a while, and in the end I lost, but with the new version, when you put the cursor on a clickable icon, the icon changes its appearance into a button, and you can select it.

Linear green frames and borders are used to indicate active images, the overlapping areas, and to crop the merged image. Rikako was pleased that the engineers came up with these delicately designed indicators without prompting.

The success of the resultant version of PhotoStitch can be attributed to the combination of the Stitch Assist mode in the camera, integrated with the computer-based application:

> If you use the Stitch Assist mode with a digital camera that Canon made, this process is going to be very easy, because the order and orientation of the photo is automatically set by the software, so users don't have to do that by themselves.
>
> If you want to make some changes with the automatic result, you can choose the parts that you want to modify. I made a change with the user interface too. Another problem with the old stitching software was lack of information on how to fix the automatic result, how to adjust the overlapping areas. A navigational message described the process, but with technical words like "drag" or "click" that don't make sense to beginners. We noticed that the text message was not enough to explain this process, because dragging one photo image onto another was not a common task for all users. This was the most challenging part to improve in terms of interaction design, so we decided to include animations to support the text messages. When we tested version 3, we were convinced that this kind of animation was helpful to novice users. The animation describes how to drag one photo onto another. Osami Matsuda designed the behavior. I just asked him to add animations to reinforce the text messages. He did a great job!

Masaaki Sakai, the senior general manager responsible for Canon's Corporate Design Center, says that "the role of design is to be the interpreter of technology." He declares that design can help people adopt new technology successfully. It seems surprising therefore that the skills of the people in his department

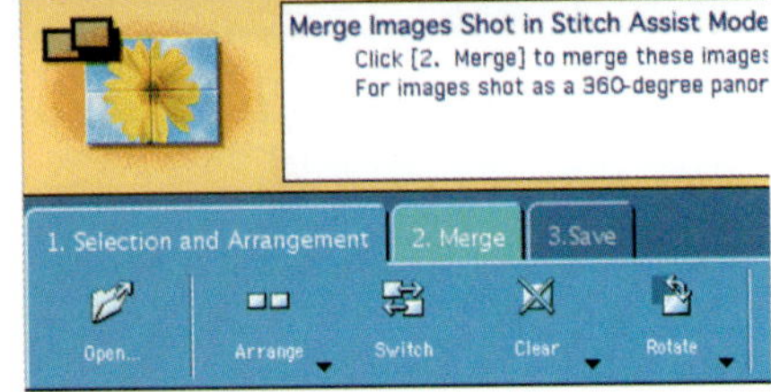

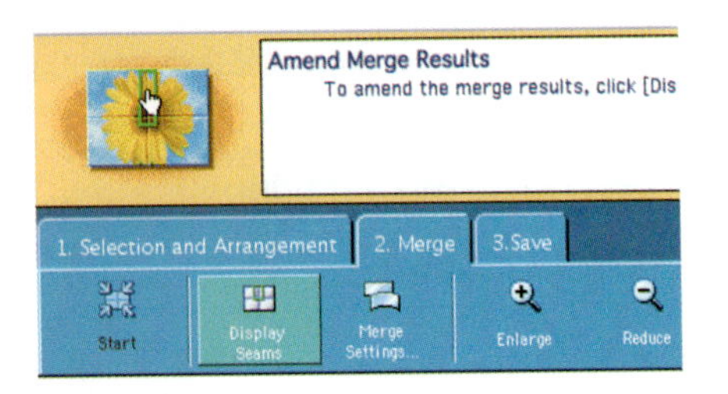

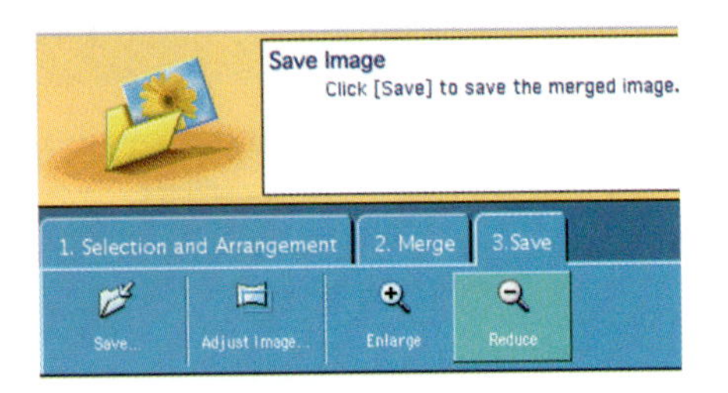

- Osami Matsuda, Canon GUI designer
- PhotoStitch version 3—merge icon
- PhotoStitch version 3—seams icon
- PhotoStitch version 3—file icon

were not engaged in the first two releases of the PhotoStitch software. Why was the algorithm applied to a standard Windows interface, in a foreign language, without reference to design and usability expertise? Perhaps the answer is typical of technology driven companies around the world, where so much effort is put into invention and patent applications, but there is an assumption that the inventors can design usable solutions themselves. In the earlier phases of adoption of the technology, this has often worked, as enthusiasts and professionals are patient and acquisitive. Once the adoption of the technology reaches the consumer phase, the skills of interaction designers and psychologists are much more likely to be essential for a successful outcome.

PhotoStitch version 3—completed three-image panorama

Printers for Digital Photography

■ "Drawer for drawings"

Photo
Hidetoyo Sasaki

COMPUTER PRINTERS HAVE a history of innocuous and self-effacing design, trying hard to fit into the background of the office environment as the undistinguished peripheral cousins of the computers that drive them. In the days of impact printers and needle printers, this attempt to hide was futile, as they generated enough noise to be agonizingly noticeable, and a lot of effort was put into designing sound reducing enclosures for them. Then the inkjet and laser technologies took over, and the designs could sit quietly on a shelf or in a corner—bland beige boxes performing their professional duties on demand.

Sometimes they needed attention from a person to clear a paper jam or replenish the ink supply, so design efforts were focused on making the diagnostics of maintenance comprehensible to people who had no training. Xerox pioneered this work in the early eighties, with a design strategy[11] for copier printers complete with color-coding for access, interactive touch screens, animated diagnostic diagrams, and simple sequential procedures for changing cartridges or finding paper jams. Since then, the replacement of consumables for printers by untrained

personnel has become commonplace, with diagnostics more on the PC display than the printer itself. Epson has done a particularly good job of designing these interactions.

As digital photography started to be adopted by consumers, printers took on new roles; now they were starting to live in the domestic environment, producing images that people cared about in a very intimate and personal way rather than just printing spreadsheets and pages of text. This raised the question of the design of the printers themselves; would they still be neutral designs, looking as if they had been borrowed from the office of yesterday, or would they start to evolve aesthetic characteristics that fit them to their new photographic tasks?

In 1998 Epson commissioned a conceptual design project called "Printables" to examine this question, to create designs that would be appropriate for printing photographs at home, and to build working prototypes of the ideas. The project was led by Naoto Fukasawa,[12] working with his team at IDEO Tokyo, in collaboration with seven of the Epson designers. The examples shown here demonstrate an aesthetic that fits the domestic environment of the consumer phase rather than the conventional appearance of printers as extensions of business computers.

- "Kinetic Deliverance"
- "Mysterious Thoughts"

Photos
Hidetoyo Sasaki

"Drawer for Drawings," designed by Shoichi Ishizawa

The printer is built into a simple piece of wooden furniture, made of cherry veneer on particleboard. The top can be used as a general-purpose surface or to support a connected laptop. The paper is inserted into a slot on the top, and the print is delivered into a drawer, which can also be used to store supplies of paper for printing.

"Kinetic Deliverance," designed by Mugio Kawasaki

A delicate paper tray, made as a wire frame rolling on tiny wheels, supports the print as it emerges from the simple block form of the printer. The tray moves with the image, celebrating its arrival and enhancing the transition between start and finish.

"Mysterious Thoughts," designed by Hirokazu Yamano

Draped in a white cloth, the printer appears to be alive as the print head moves back and forth, gently disturbing the surface of the cloth, with the subtle sound of the mechanism enhancing the mystery. The image gradually appears from under the edge of the cloth, as if from a slow motion version of a magician's handkerchief.

"Memory Developing," designed by Sam Hecht[13]

This design harks back to the days of photographic development using liquid chemicals. The paper tray that receives the digital print is shaped like a traditional developing tray, lending a sentimental familiarity to the characteristics of the design.

"Imperfect Perfection," designed by Naoto Fukasawa

In contrast to the predictions of the paperless office, digital printing has caused dramatic increases in the consumption of paper, mostly due to the fact that it is easy to print out a proof and then improve the on-screen original before trying another version. This printer is designed to support this pattern of use by mounting the printer on top of a recycling bin, so the user can inspect the proof and conveniently drop it in the bin if they are not satisfied with the result.

- "Memory Developing"
- "Imperfect Perfection"

Photos
Hidetoyo Sasaki

Photo Rod Searcey

David Kelley

Armed with an undergraduate degree in electrical engineering from Carnegie Mellon, David Kelley went to work at Boeing, in Seattle, where he was given the task of designing the lavatory "occupied" signs. He felt a little out of place in such a large engineering department, so when he discovered the product design program at Stanford University, he went there for his master's. The program was focused on innovation and understanding user needs, and what's more, they really built the products that they designed. It was a perfect fit for David, so much so that he has never really left, moving from student, to lecturer, and now tenured full professor in design. When he graduated in 1978, he started a consulting company with his friends from Stanford and soon became successful developing products, such as the first Apple mouse,[14] for Silicon Valley companies. David Kelley Design grew in experience and stature throughout the eighties, providing the ingenuity and technical expertise to bring many new product concepts to reality. In 1991 David founded IDEO, combining his engineering and innovation firm, which by now had offices in Chicago and Boston as well as Palo Alto, with the author's design firm, with offices in San Francisco and London, and Mike Nuttal's industrial design firm in Palo Alto. The combination of expertise on both the technical and human side of product development made IDEO immediately successful, and the company grew steadily in both size and influence. David handed the roles of president and CEO to Tim Brown in 2002 and now spends much of his time at Stanford, while staying connected to IDEO as chairman.

David Kelley

Interaction design started from two separate directions, with screen graphics for displays and separate input devices, but it got more interesting when the hardware and software came together in products. Then along came the information appliance, implying that technology would start to fit into our everyday lives, and when the Internet connected everything together, we found ourselves designing complete experiences.

David Kelley, 2004

Design Adopts Technology

■ Roller Controller input device for young children for Philips

Photo
Joe Watson

DAVID KELLEY HAS been involved with the development of interaction design as it is practiced at IDEO, and he has partnered with Terry Winograd[15] to teach classes in the subject at Stanford since 1995. Here is his summary of what it means to him.

> When I hear the words "designing interactions," I think of designing for people. When I was a student at Carnegie Mellon, I took Fortran. Fortran was a language for scientists, so you learned it and became an expert, but it really wasn't very interesting until you actually used it for something that resulted in work, something that made sense to someone. I see interaction design as the opposite of that. It's not something learned scientifically that you can then use for some technical purpose. Interaction design is using your technical knowledge in order to make it useful for people, to delight someone, to make someone get excited about the new technology they're using. I guess I would say that interaction design is making technology fit people.
>
> It started with screen graphics. Screen graphics are kind of like graphic design. Designers got all excited about the fact that they

could do things that moved. It used to be that you printed it and that was the way it was forever. Having something that would come alive and that you could actually change over time was exciting to them. It wasn't exciting to them, though, that the richness of the screen was so much worse than they were used to. They had all this paper and ink, and it was a real visceral feel to get the color just right, but then they took this big step backward to these pixilated graphics. It polarized the graphic design community into people who wanted to hold on to the richness of the inks and the paper, and people that said, "Hey, this is they way of the future!" It was more capable of doing interesting things, but it was less rich from a purely artist point of view.

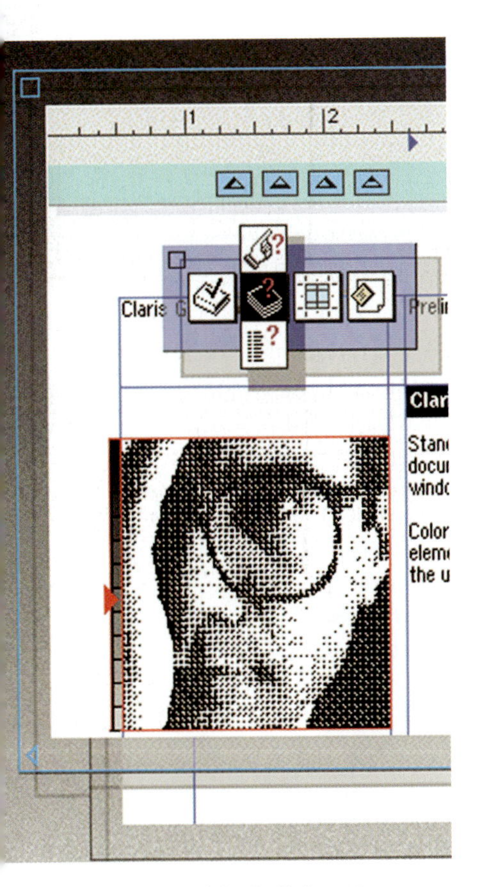

Screen design for Claris, 1989, showing concepts for transparency and flying menus

Input devices were the first aspect of involvement in the design of interactive products for David Kelley Design.

We have designed a lot of input devices. To begin with, input devices were really exciting to us because they were new to the world; nobody had ever made these things in the same way before. The excitement was that we were designing things that were going to be very personal, like the bar of soap that you take a shower with in the morning is such a personal thing. We started out trying to see what kinds of behaviors were natural, coming up with an idea, and then testing it.

We originally thought that a trackball was the best idea. If you picture that the surface of the table has a ball coming out of it and you could spin the ball, that seemed like a much more natural thing than sliding this mouse thing on the table. It was interesting learning what you had to be mindful of. For example, "What were you dragging on the table? Were you dragging your palm on the table, or was your arm extended and it wasn't touching the table? Where did you get the friction in the system?" I had not been involved in anything quite that tactile before.

In the early days of designing Apple's mouse, we spent a lot of time trying to get it to be accurate, in a one-to-one relationship between the movement on the table and the movement on the screen; if you moved it one millimeter on the table, the cursor on the screen would move one millimeter. We were crazy about accuracy because we were engineers. At some point along the way, we had a breakthrough when we realized that your brain was in the loop. If you draw a circuit diagram, there's the mouse on the table, and then the wire goes through your brain and then goes into the computer, so you didn't have to be accurate at all! Your brain would send a signal to your hand to move it to the right place; you could hit a space on the screen very easily because you've got all this processing power of your brain to take out the little inconsistencies and inaccuracies. This meant that we didn't have to spend so much money on technical precision, which allowed the mouse to be quite a bit cheaper than we originally thought it could be. As long as it was consistent, it didn't have to be specifically one-to-one proportional to what was happening on the screen.

David and his team fulfilled their wish to develop a trackball, but in an unexpected way. They were asked to develop an input device for young children by a startup company in southern California. The company had a contract with Sesame Street to create a controller that would be easy for their audience of three-to five-year-old kids to use. The designers enjoyed playing with the kids of that age group and prototyping various options for them to try.

When we tested mice and joysticks with kids, we found out that they had trouble watching the screen while they moved the device. Whenever they wanted to do something they would look down at their hand, so they couldn't watch the screen and look; it just wasn't natural for them. We played with lots of things, but none of them worked. Someone had the idea that if we use big muscle groups instead of just little hand movements, that they would be more comfortable looking up, which actually turned out to be true. So we went to a really big trackball where they were using their arms and shoulders, and then they had no trouble looking at the screen while they were activating it.

A significant development was the integration of hardware and software into products in which the way people interact with the product could drive the whole solution.

In the early days of Silicon Valley, we had a lot of design of screens and input devices, and they were mostly general-purpose things. It got real exciting when the hardware and the software

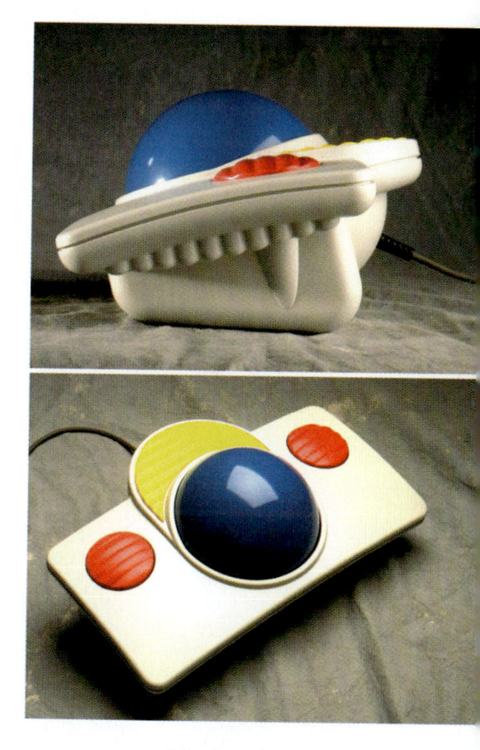

Roller Controller—side ■
Roller Controller ■

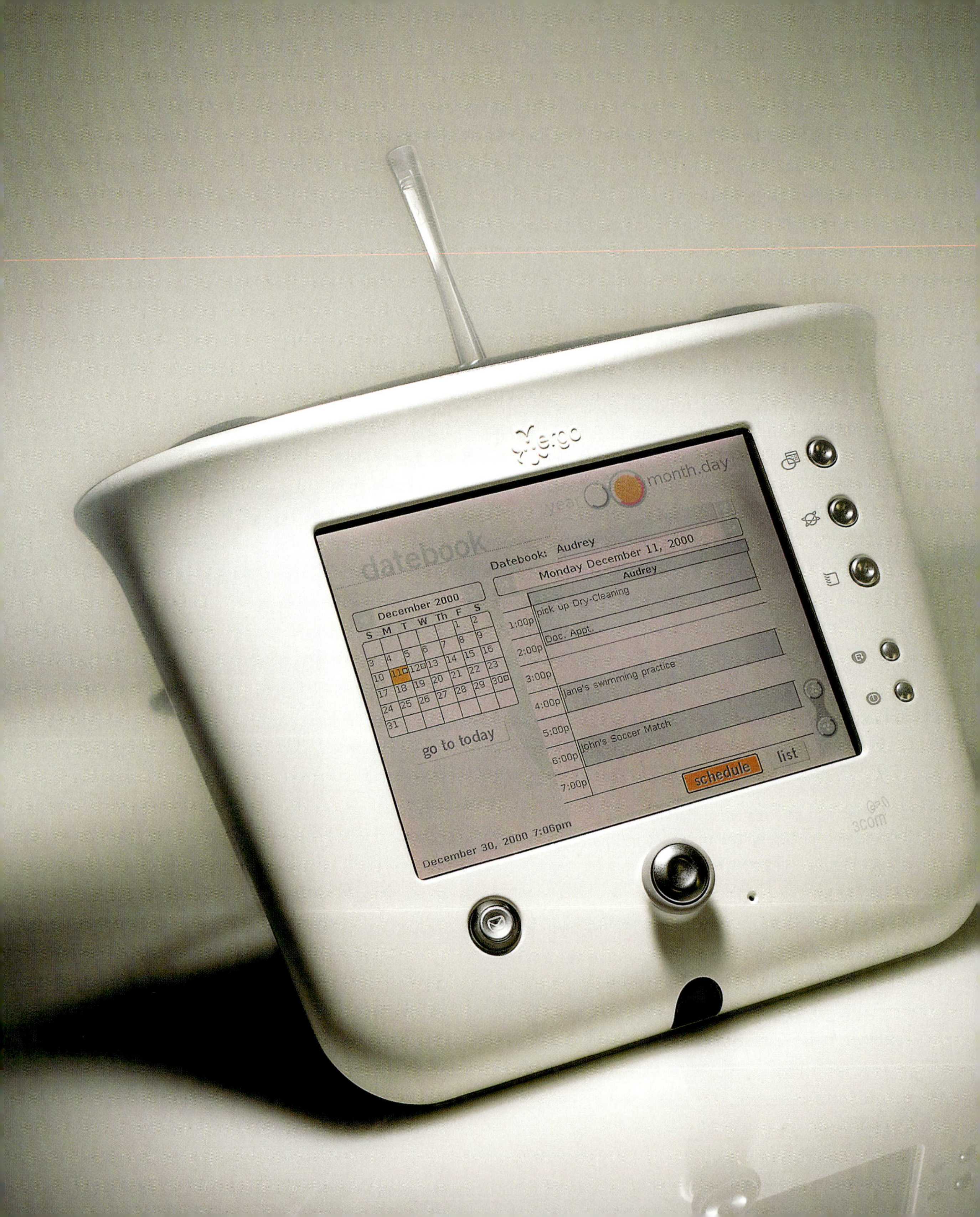
ergo
year
month.day
datebook
Datebook: Audrey
Monday December 11, 2000
Audrey
December 2000
S M T W Th F S
pick up Dry-Cleaning
1:00p
Doc. Appt.
2:00p
3:00p
Jane's swimming practice
4:00p
5:00p
John's Soccer Match
6:00p
7:00p
go to today
schedule
list
December 30, 2000 7:06pm
3COM

came together and we were really making products. Now you're talking about special-purpose things where you can design the controls, you don't have to use a general-purpose solution. This allowed things like the Palm Pilot, cell phones, and so forth to be quite exciting from a design point of view. You can make the displays of a size that were enough to do interesting graphics but were small enough to fit in your pocket. Things became more personal as they became more productlike, opening up a whole new explosion of possible products for us to design. Then behaviors really came into it.

Before, we had the approach of, "Word processing exists, spreadsheets exist, we're going to teach you that. You're going to conform to the way we, the software designers, expect it to happen."

As you got to products, we went the other way. We were looking at "What do people want to do? What's people's behavior like around telephones or their phone lists or other things that they normally use now?" so we could design the product to meet the behavior and the need rather than expecting that we're going to teach them a software program.

Then along came the information appliance, the idea being that technology-enabled devices would start to fit into the everyday lives of people in a similar way to appliances in the kitchen, like a toaster or a blender. This is the opposite concept to the general-purpose computer, in that the appliance is designed for a specific purpose and used only in that context. There are examples of the integration of technology in appliances, for example the toaster that uses "fuzzy logic" to brown more consistently. A digital camera can be thought of as an information appliance, in that it contains electronics to record the image as well as for automatic exposure and focusing, but people still think of it as a camera rather than a computer.

■ 3Com Audrey Internet Appliance

Photo Courtesy of IDEO

A heralded example of an information appliance that IDEO designed was 3Com's Audrey Internet Appliance. It was an Internet-access computer designed to be used in a communal area of the home, perhaps the kitchen, and the navigation was simplified to a single control akin to a radio tuning knob, with a push function to select. The simple controls, personalization for individual family members, and an "always on" approach to the

Internet connectivity, made it convenient to gain access to weather, traffic, sports, and a unified family calendar. Audrey periodically updated its information in the background, so it was available the moment you woke it up, without having to wait for the PC's long boot-up-and-connect process. It was launched with great fanfare at Comdex, just in time for the end of the dot-com boom, but was too expensive to survive the downturn.

David Kelley believes that the era of the information appliance is yet to come; he is not yet confident in the future of the idea, but he adds:

> The thing that will happen, I believe, is that the products will be smart enough, or integrated enough, that they will be able to react to us; that the product will know what's going on with us and will be able to do the right thing. I think that's different from the toaster and the blender; the toaster and the blender sit there, not knowing how we are, waiting for commands. I think information appliances, highly technological appliances, will know we're there and anticipate what we want just from the way we act.
>
> I think an automobile is a very good example of technology integrating into our lives to the point where we're not aware of it; it's seamless, and it works very well. The average person doesn't realize how many computers they are actually commanding when they drive a car. There are already examples where computing power can save your life. An airbag is a great example of that. It's up to the computer to know when to open that airbag, and your life is threatened if it doesn't, and we somehow accept that. But I don't think people sit around thinking, "Oh, I hope the computer works when the airbag . . ." The electronics, the mechanics, the fabric, the thermodynamics, and the physics are all kind of wrapped up together. It's a very sophisticated thing, but anybody who's been in enough of a fender bender that the bag goes off, just sees it as an ordinary machine that works quite well.

IDEO was steered steadily through the Internet boom, continuing with the same kinds of innovative development of products and places as before, rather than riding the wave of design for e-business. This proved to be a wise choice when the crash came, and the design organizations that had focused on the

Internet started to fade away. It was hard to find a U-Haul trailer to rent in San Francisco—people were leaving town in droves.

By 2004 Silicon Valley was returning to normal, and new people were starting to arrive, but at least the cost of living had returned from the dizzying heights of the boom to something that was merely outrageous. David remembers:

> Living in the valley through the Internet boom and bust was quite interesting, mostly for my students who became CEOs of companies overnight and then came back to chopping carrots in restaurants!
>
> The Internet is a really important technology and business tool. My belief is that, from a business point of view, it makes the market more perfect. You can find the people who want the products and services more easily. From a design point of view, it allows us to explain the features of our products more fully. Because the information is more complete, you can do more subtle things in products, and people have time to understand them. The Internet is disconnected from real time. If I'm interested in some special tulip bulb that only comes from Holland, I have a chance of being able to find out about it over the Internet.
>
> In my own life, I'm particularly interested in old vintage cars and trying to find them. It used to be, if you were looking for the right Alpha-Romeo, you had to stumble across it or hear about it from someone. Perhaps you would hear that it's in a garage in Argentina, and then you had to figure out if it's worth going to Argentina or not. Today, with the Internet, you know where all of those cars are, what condition they are in, and you can see pictures and so forth.

When you go to the hospital, you expect an unenjoyable experience. If it is a visit to the emergency room, it is traumatic by definition, but even for a routine checkup, there is uncertainty and confusion to contend with. David points to the design of the hospital experience as an example of products, environments, information display, and services all playing a part:

> You go into a hospital and nobody is around. There's a desk where there's supposed to be a person, and there's no one there, or

Place of Waiting

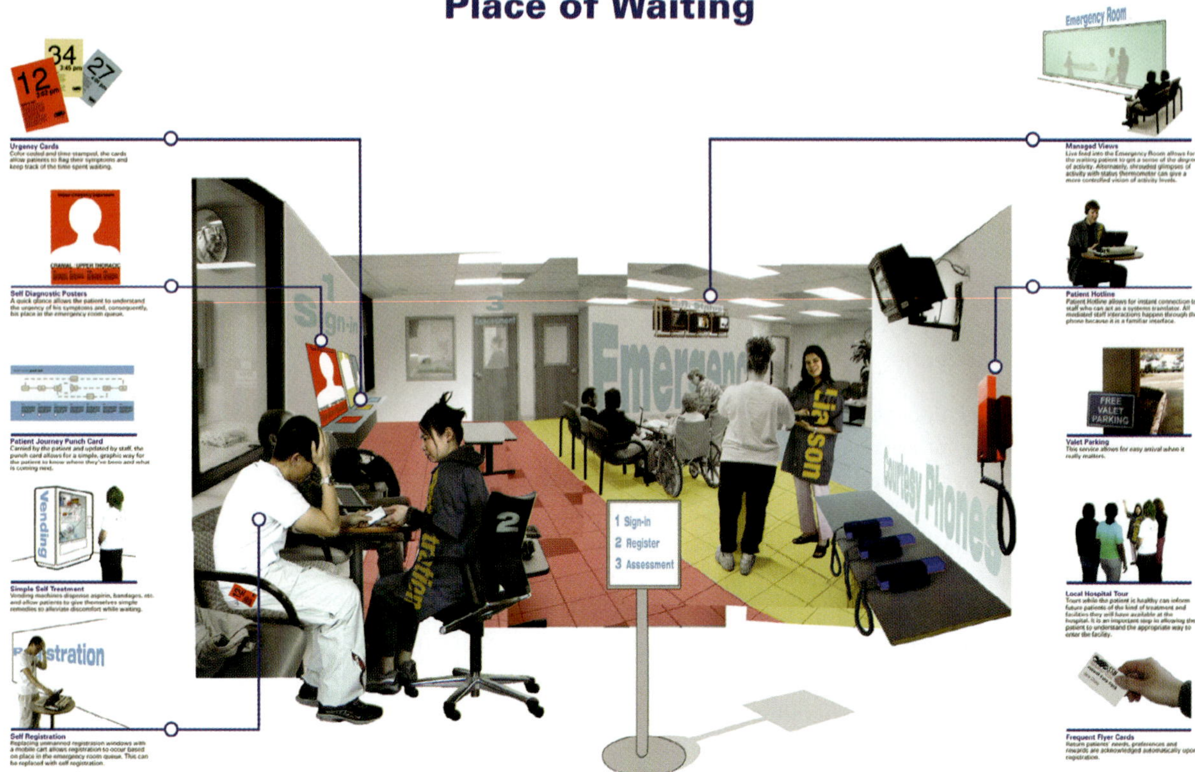

Place of Practice

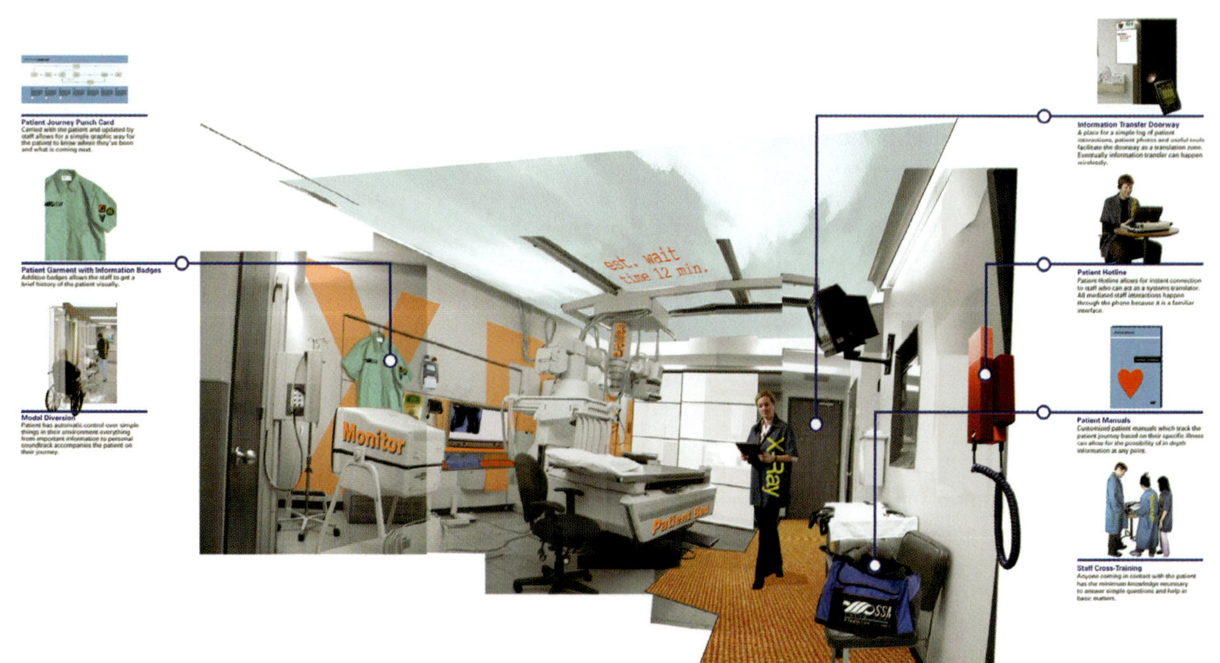

there's a big sign that says "triage nurse," and you don't know what "triage" means. You are thinking, "I just want someone to talk to, and to find out how I should be treated." It would help to just know where you are in the queue. You're the eighth person who's been in there, but are you going to go next? There's a tape running through your head saying, "I wonder what's going to happen next?" The more you can answer that question by giving people an expectation of what's going to happen, the better they feel about the experience.

David believes that the number of instances where it is important to design the complete experience is growing and represents a significant shift for design education and practice. He started his design consulting business in Silicon Valley in 1978, when the engineers and entrepreneurs were so focused on chips, printed circuits, and software that they used the word "packaging" to describe the physical objects that enclosed the technology. As products became more important, making those physical enclosures work well emerged as a key to success; mechanical and production engineering contributions were recognized.

David saw the opportunity to integrate the human design disciplines of industrial design, human factors, and interaction design with the technical disciplines of mechanical, electrical, and production engineering. He formed IDEO to combine experts in those areas into interdisciplinary teams for product development. This combination proved very successful for the development of products that included sophisticated user interfaces, and was key to the success that IDEO enjoys.

- DePaul Health Center for SSM Health Care 2001 patient care delivery model

The Internet expanded with the amazing surge of the dot.com boom, and everything was suddenly connected to everything else. Technology was being employed to enable services, so businesses had to design the experiences in a more holistic way. They could no longer simply produce products and train employees to offer the related services. David saw this as the next significant change for design:

I would say the most interesting thing that's happened for me personally as a designer over the last twenty-five years is the move away from the design of objects. I was a kid who grew up and took apart radios and cars and put them back together, and it was kind of physical. And then, of course, with the advent of this kind of electronic stuff, as an electrical engineer I got into that, but that was still physical, although you couldn't see the electrons moving. I was always focused on a thing, not so focused on the people who use it, though accepting that they were a necessary evil.

The movement away from designing the object itself to designing the experience, which everybody talks about, is really profound in my opinion. Designing experiences and services takes you away from the nuts and bolts, for a while anyway, and gets you into understanding people and their needs. I personally believe that technologists and engineers are even more motivated by doing something that has value to people than they are by technology. They think, "We're going to design a service or an experience that people really want and need, and their lives are going to be changed by it." This motivates them to do even better work, to push the technology even further, to work even harder, or knock themselves out to be more innovative, because they have more empathy for the person they are designing for.

Teaching designers to be integrators

At the time of writing in 2004, David Kelley was establishing a new design school at Stanford, dubbed the "d" school. Its goal is to provide an interdisciplinary program for the development of products, experiences, services, and spaces, with design as the core skill. There will be a kernel of resident design faculty, with visiting professors from other departments in the university, including business, social science, and technical areas such as computer science. David describes the philosophy of the new school:

We used to design objects, and we had machine shops to prototype them. We still need machine shops, but if you're going to design experiences and services, you have to have new prototyping tools to explain to people what it would be like with this new service, or how different it would be doing something if we had this new technology. Now we're using more storytelling. My students are taking improv classes and acting things out. They all know how to use some kind of quick and dirty video process so they can tell a story; they are becoming cartoonists so that they can do quick storyboards. Design is moving from understanding technology and building devices toward understanding people and telling stories. The challenge for teaching design is about designing experiences instead of just objects, and prototyping with video and storyboards, and acting things out.

Another issue for teaching design in university now is the difference between depth and breadth. Designers are inherently people who are good at breadth. They have broad interests, and they apply their skills broadly. That is why we teach breadth. But there is also the issue of depth. What are they going to be good at? The answer for us at Stanford is that they are going to be good at the process of how you bring all the experts together.

They are the experts in the methodology, so they hold the other disciplines together. Because of the complexities of the projects, you need a whole room full of experts in order to get anything interesting in the way of innovation. We decided that designers are going to be the people who integrate the technology and the process and are the glue that holds these experts together. They are empathetic to other disciplines, which translates to having breadth.

In 2004 the Apple iPod was a dramatic success story of the adoption of a technology in the consumer phase, including the integration of interactive product, computer application, and Internet-based service. Next, Paul Mercer tells the story of the iPod development.

Segment of David Kelley's mind map for the "d-school"

menu

iPod

The original iPod

Photo
Courtesy of Apple

THE IPOD FROM Apple shows how a physical product with a screen and controls can be seamlessly integrated with a computer-based application and an Internet-based service. When the first iPod was launched, the beautiful design was captivating, but the integration with iTunes really made the interactivity irresistible. It was so convenient to be able to use your personal computer to download music from the Internet, or copy it from your CD collection, and then sort your play list before you copied it onto the iPod. The first version had separate switches as controls, with wonderful tactile feedback, so the feel of using the product was delightful. Reliability and cost advantages made the designers change over to a touchpad for input in the versions that followed, in spite of the loss in tactile quality.

When Apple added their online music store, the design of the service was complete, and the success of all of the components in the system accelerated. People loved the object, they valued the connectivity between portable device and PC, and they found it hard to resist adding music to their library through the store, doing so without the guilt associated with Internet piracy. Other examples of "designing services" are covered in more depth in chapter six.

Paul Mercer's[16] team, at software startup Pixo, was responsible for the implementation of the user interface software for the iPod. In the interview that follows he tells the story of the development, as well as talking about the adoption of mobile devices and the changing nature of the design process.

Photo Author

Paul Mercer

"I built my own Timex Sinclair ZX81 computer in high school; it was $100 if you built it yourself from a kit rather than paying the full $150 to buy it preassembled. I'm a software guy, but this is where I broke out the soldering iron and built it myself." Paul Mercer showed an amazing aptitude for writing code when he was still very young and went on to hone his skill at Syracuse University, before being lured out to the West Coast by Apple at the age of twenty in 1987. Within a few months he found himself working on the next generation of Finder, the core of the Macintosh user experience, maintaining system 6 Finder while the underpinnings of the Finder (NuFinder) were rewritten in the then newfangled C++. In 1991 he put together a team to explore concepts for handheld Macintoshes and the software to go with them. Apple CEO John Sculley was impressed by working prototypes. By that time, though, he was committed to Newton and asked Paul to help move the Newton design from research to product. He built the core software framework for Newton and along the way came up with the little "poof cloud" that evaporates when you erase something on the Newton screen. In 1994 Paul left Apple to start his own company, called Pixo, as he wanted to develop the building blocks for the next generation of devices and user interfaces. Pixo grew to employ 150 people, with clients including Nokia and Samsung, in mobile phones, and Apple, for the implementation of the iPod. After eight years, Paul saw a new opportunity as more and more devices became wireless. He has founded a new company, called Iventor, to create enabling structures for ubiquitous computing.

iPod
Music
Extras
Settings
Shuffle Songs
Backlight
MENU

Look at a culture like Sony, where they spent decades refining their capabilities in industrial design and miniaturization, and they really took that to its zenith and were world masters at it. But now as the world has changed to include display devices in just about every product you can imagine, we're moving into an era where software is the primary differentiator of products, dictating the usefulness and functionality of a device. Look at something like the iPod, which has a very simple interface, and compare it to the myriad of other music players that are out there that don't measure up, that are very difficult to use even though we're talking about a screen of very few pixels.

Paul Mercer, 2004

■ iPod 2

Photo
Courtesy of Apple

Pixo

Paul Mercer was always passionate about building portable electronic devices. He translated his early experience on the Apple Finder into an effort to develop handheld Macintoshes. He developed working prototypes that were just a little larger than the production Newton that shipped two years later but used the well-understood and low-cost Macintosh technology. His idea was to leverage the Macintosh installed base, using a technology that had already been enthusiastically adopted and even had fanatical evangelists supporting it. He added networking capability to share files with the Macintosh on your desk and a notepad application to allow you to bring your files with you, view them and annotate them. He spent a lot of time trying to promote the concept inside Apple:

> I think Mac users will remember, during the nineties there was very little going on for the Macintosh. There were just minor

iPod
Playlists
Browse
Extras
Settings
Backlight
MENU

enhancements. The fundamental work of reinventing the core OS and the underpinnings was really floundering, and Apple spent a lot of money and resources trying to get out of that mess. I had a small role in that, and after Newton, one of my jobs was to help move the Macintosh architecture forward. This was difficult to do at a low level, because the Macintosh was so chaotically built. At the same time, I was still in love with the idea of a handheld Macintosh that ran on batteries. I thought it would be a very good move for Apple, technologically and marketwise. So with every regime change at Apple, I would bring out my working prototypes of the handheld and try to get Apple interested in building it.

There were several eras at Apple during which there was a lot of interest in building devices, so the hope of building little mini-Macintoshes lived on for a couple of more years before I finally gave up on the idea. Eventually I realized that the Macintosh technology, which was supposed to be a stepping-stone and accelerant to building devices, was getting old. The processor world was moving away from the Motorola MC68000 architecture, which the Macintosh was built on, toward the RISC-based architectures. So with that I realized, "Hey, that Macintosh magic, that capability at Apple is no longer necessarily a differentiating ingredient."

In 1994 I left Apple and started up a company, called Pixo. My goal was to create the building blocks for the next generation of devices and to build user interfaces for those devices.

■ iPod Minis

Photo Courtesy of Apple

The idea behind Pixo was to write modules of code in C++ that would enable flexible user interfaces and functionality. In the mid nineties, it was a major achievement for a device maker to go from programming devices in assembly language to using C and eventually C++. They were typically working with very poor tools for software, as they came from a culture of building devices based on hardware capabilities, not building software and user experiences. Paul describes the offering that made his new company successful:

Pixo was formed with the idea of creating fundamental building blocks at a low level, to enable more sophisticated software on portable devices. This meant that the building blocks had to be very low-cost, had to be easy to use, and had to be fairly powerful. On the one hand, we had to build that technology, and then in parallel we

iTunes

Search

Browse

Source
Library
Party Shuffle
Radio
Music Store
60's Music
My Top Rated
Recently Played
Top 25 Most Played
Aerial Ruin
Alex
Tunes Sampler

Artist	Album
All (227 Artists)	All (102 Albums)
"Aeterna fac cum Sanctis tuis- In te, Domine, speravi"	Airbag/How Am I Driving? [EP]
"Te Deum laudamus" Allegro	Al Green - Greatest Hits
"Te ergo quaesumus" Adagio	All Systems Gone
3-11 Porter	Another Late Night
A Plus	Another Late Night (Kid Loco)
A Tribe Called Quest	Arvo Pärt - Te Deum

Song Name	Time	Artist	Album	Genre
Airbag	4:46	Radiohead	Airbag/How Am...	Alternative...
Pearly	3:33	Radiohead	Airbag/How Am...	Alternative...
Meeting In The Aisle	3:09	Radiohead	Airbag/How Am...	Alternative...
Reminder	3:51	Radiohead	Airbag/How Am...	Alternative...
Polyethylene (Parts 1&2)	4:22	Radiohead	Airbag/How Am...	Alternative...
Melatonin	2:09	Radiohead	Airbag/How Am...	Alternative...
Palo Alto	3:44	Radiohead	Airbag/How Am...	Alternative...
Tired Of Being Alone	2:43	Al Green	Al Green - Great...	R&B
Call Me	3:03	Al Green	Al Green - Great...	R&B
I'm Still In Love With You	3:14	Al Green	Al Green - Great...	R&B
Here I Am (Come and Take ...	4:14	Al Green	Al Green - Great...	R&B
Love And Happiness	5:03	Al Green	Al Green - Great...	R&B
Let's Stay Together	3:18	Al Green	Al Green - Great...	R&B
I Can't Get Next To You	3:52	Al Green	Al Green - Great...	R&B
You Ought To Be With Me	3:20	Al Green	Al Green - Great...	R&B
Look What You Done For Me	3:06	Al Green	Al Green - Great...	R&B
Let's Get Married	3:23	Al Green	Al Green - Great...	R&B
Livin' For You	3:12	Al Green	Al Green - Great...	R&B
Sha La La	3:02	Al Green	Al Green - Great...	R&B
L-O-V-E	3:08	Al Green	Al Green - Great...	R&B
Full Of Fire	3:29	Al Green	Al Green - Great...	R&B
Belle	4:48	Al Green	Al Green - Great...	R&B
Future Love	6:19	Presence	All Systems Gone	Electronica...
This Is You	5:49	Presence	All Systems Gone	Electronica...
Been 2 Long	7:58	Presence	All Systems Gone	Electronica...
Matter Of Fact	5:22	Presence	All Systems Gone	Electronica...
Your Spirit	4:58	Presence	All Systems Gone	Electronica...
Keeping Count	6:03	Presence	All Systems Gone	Electronica...

1202 songs, 3.5 days, 7.13 GB

had to build examples of what the user experience might be. As the technology improved throughout the second half of the nineties, we steadily added things like color, audio support, and scripting capabilities.

At its heart, the idea was to democratize the level of capability that the Macintosh gave developers and to bring it to the world of devices. It was very easy for our customers to look at Pixo and say, "Ah, you have these great building blocks, and we can pick and choose, save some time, and save some money in building our product."

That really wasn't what Pixo was about. We created the building blocks to help build products cheaper and faster, but our ultimate aim was to help people build better products, such as the iPod.

iPod and iTunes

Apple was one of Paul's customers, coming to Pixo for help in creating the system software toolkit for iPod and implementing the user interface to Apple's specification. Paul has great respect for the culture and leadership at Apple:

■ iTunes

Photo
Author's screen capture

> I think if you look at the culture of Apple, it's a company that's had twenty-five years of building personal products, and in the last few years they've had a very astute individual at the top who can really dictate in many ways, or arbitrate, what's good and not good. I think that culture and management capability at Apple makes it unique in this industry.
>
> The answer to the question "Why is the iPod so great compared to the competition?" is really the same answer as to why the Macintosh is still different from Windows or anything else before it. I think it's really this culture of being able to build good products.
>
> Apple started working on music very slowly and built the business up deliberately over a period of years. They started by acquiring the technology. In September 2000 they acquired a company called SoundJam to build iTunes, and then turned that into the iTunes franchise, starting first on the Macintosh. The ability to generate music, to let the user rip that music, that's the root of the

application—you've got to have it. Apple invested in iTunes, built that up and improved it over the years.

In November 2001 Apple shipped the first device that synchronized with iTunes. The fact that the two were deeply integrated together, and the fact that the integration was through a high-speed bus like FireWire was another necessary ingredient of being able to get the content and then move it to the device. If it took ten times longer to move, the iPod would not have been a success in 2001.

Then in 2003 Apple launched the iTunes music store. This again was something that did not exist before at a consumer level that was mass-marketable. There were MP3 players before Apple shipped the first iPod, and there were music stores before the iTunes music store, but Apple was the first to make it mass-market capable. They applied the ineffable "Apple magic" to make that possible, whatever that is. If you could put it onto five bullet points on a piece of paper, you could probably make a fortune explaining it to people.

It took Apple a couple of years before iTunes for Windows was actually developed and shipped; they took their time in doing it. They were practically moving in slow motion if you look at it with hindsight, but the industry has not been able to match it. Now they are moving into color displays, and eventually they'll move into video, as Moore's law continues giving us its bounty.

Paul is very interested in the subtleties that make up a culture in an organization to allow creative design. He is a developer of what he calls "building blocks," or toolkits, that he intends should be used for the design of solutions that are easy to adopt, but he is aware that culture is based on a subtle synthesis of attributes, rather than just the use of the tools. It is not just what you do, but also how you do it:

■ iPod Shuffle

Just because you have the building blocks, doesn't mean you'll build great products. You witness what Microsoft has done. They have the fastest computers in the world running their platform; they've got a scientific staff, a research staff that's really unparalleled today. Many of the great computer science and user experience researchers of the last twenty years are now working for Microsoft. And yet, what is missing there that does not allow them to be the first to build iPod and iTunes and the next generation of products?

What is missing there? I think it goes back to the culture. Even at Pixo, where we were a very small company, where we didn't get beyond 150 people, we had that culture. If you don't set that tone in the beginning, it's very hard to alter those forces.

There have been some reports in the press crediting Pixo for the design of the iPod, but Paul is very clear that he only provided the building blocks; he did not invent or design the iPod. He does not want to take credit for what Apple accomplished, and waxes enthusiastic about the phenomenal job that they have done in carrying forward the promise of devices, but he is still puzzled by the competitive advantage that Apple has maintained:

Now, keep in mind, the iPod is very simple-minded, in terms of at least what the device does. It's very smooth in what it does, but the screen is low-resolution, and it really doesn't do much other than let you navigate your music. That tells you two things. It tells you first that the simplification that went into the design was very well thought through, and second that the capability to build it is not commoditized.

The fact that nobody has been able to build this thing, to duplicate the capabilities, seems at first sight surprising. It means that the building blocks may be difficult to come by, and that the design sense, to create a simple and easy-to-adopt solution, does not exist in most of these product development organizations worldwide.

It is very curious, because the iPod has been out there for about three years now, essentially unchanged in terms of its core software design. The dozens of products that have come out since have not been able to catch up to it. People always want to beat the champ—why are you in this business if you don't want to dethrone the champ? Nobody's really done that. It's very curious that over the years and all of the money that Apple has made, that the competition hasn't figured this out.

iPod Nano ■

The Interaction Design Challenge

Paul has recently started a new company, Iventor, with a mission to democratize the design of better user interfaces for portable devices. He wants to create tools for developers that will enable better interactive experiences for more people. He sees the shortage of good interaction designers as a worldwide problem. There is tremendous pressure on the consumer side, as people welcome devices that are well enough designed to be easy to adopt, but the culture and skills of design are the limiting factor. There is a real business need to solve some of these user interface problems:

> The world has changed a lot in the last few years. Everything is connected now; everything is wireless. We have P2P technologies; we have very high-speed wireless now, practically to the level of ubiquity. I think we're ready for another generation of technology and user interfaces for devices. I think in the years to come you're going to see portable devices take off in many more directions and be much more pleasant to use.
>
> Today, when you get a new cell phone, you might love the industrial design, you might love the radio on it, and you might love the battery life, but I don't know anybody who loves the software on their cell phone; it just does not exist. Getting something into your calendar, downloading a number from your address book is a nontrivial exercise in any cell phone today.
>
> One of the great frustrations of working in the device world, particularly in the wireless device world, is that the ability of a designer to develop and launch a good product is not fluid right now. In the PC industry, anybody with a good idea and some talent can go and build something, and put it up on the Web or launch it as shareware. That kind of opportunity does not yet exist in the mobile world, because the cell phone industry is built around state-sanctioned monopolies of the airwaves, which has resulted in each carrier building controlled economies around their network. This structure does not award innovation, particularly software innovation, and consequently, you have seen very stilted development of software on phone handsets. This will change soon since the software stack

> and the usability challenges are getting too difficult for the handset industry to address. You will see companies such as Apple and Microsoft, with deep system software and user interface experience, come to the fore.
>
> A core piece of technology that we're bringing to the puzzle is the idea of much more robust, managed code, or virtual machine-based environments. You don't need to write code that is specific to a particular piece of hardware any more. We've got enough horsepower now, even in the simplest of devices, to be able to develop in the abstract, driven by user needs rather than hardware capabilities. You will have much better building blocks and a better vocabulary for building devices, giving a new level of prototyping and development speed, and a level of robustness that does not yet exist in the industry, allowing very cool applications.

If Paul Mercer's Iventor is able to create a set of tools that will enable a level of interaction design that is only offered by a few elite products such as the iPod today, we may see a surge in the adoption of portable devices, starting with the already ubiquitous cell phone, and expanding into other devices that we can carry around, whether they are cameras, music players, or communicators.

Will you want a single device that can do everything—a cell phone that includes a PDA, camera, music player, video player, and communicator? Or will you prefer several devices with more limited functions that you can wear like jewelry or carry one or two at a time? Both options will be out there during the period of confusion that comes with the adoption of new technologies, until consumers vote with their pocketbooks.

5

Play

Interviews with Bing Gordon, Brendan Boyle, Brenda Laurel, and Will Wright

I think one of the reasons why games have led the way in interaction design in some respects is because the objective is to have fun. There's not a productive outcome, so all of the seriousness that we bring to work is not present in the design of these things.

Brenda Laurel, 2001[1]

■ Child's play

Photo
Author

PEOPLE PLAY TO learn as well as to have fun, but they stop playing immediately if the toy or game gets boring. Toys and games are designed for enjoyment, to give rewards of pleasure and entertainment from the moment that they are first encountered to the day they are discarded. That presents a rigorous discipline for the designers and implies that we have a lot to learn from understanding how to design interactive play. There is no need for patient tolerance while the design creeps gradually through the professional[2] phase. For toys and games, the design leaps immediately from a short enthusiast phase to the consumer phase, and if it fails to please, it dies a swift and certain death.

This chapter looks at the attributes that make the design of interactive play succeed. Bing Gordon, a founder of Electronic Arts, communicates his mastery of the video and computer game industry, explaining a taxonomy of games and interactive formats. Brendan Boyle of IDEO leads a team of designers who are dedicated to inventing toys and games, and he helps us see the design of play in physical products, most of which include embedded technology. Brenda Laurel tells of starting Purple Moon to create games for preteen girls, and brings a point of view from theater, research, and academia, as well as a lifetime of experience with games. Will Wright is a founder of Maxis, an Electronic Arts subsidiary, and creator of the Sims. He tells the story of the development of the best-selling computer game in history, which he claims is more of a hobby than a game, and gives a lucid account of the attributes behind well-designed play.

Photo Author

Bing Gordon, cofounder of Electronic Arts

Electronic Arts (EA) was founded in 1982 with the slogan "We see farther," implying that interactive technology was becoming an important part of entertainment and improving rapidly to facilitate play. Trip Hawkins[3] left his job at Apple to lead the company, starting work in an office overlooking the San Francisco airport landing path, with Bing Gordon and six other founders. W. Bingham (Bing) Gordon had studied for his BA in literature and drama at Yale University and then moved to Stanford Business School for his master's. He joined EA in a marketing role from the advertising firm Ogilvy and Mather and has been a key figure in building the success of the company ever since; he is now chief creative officer and executive vice president. He says, "I've failed at many jobs in Electronic Arts, succeeded at some, and have been here since the beginning." He is a mentor to studio producers and development teams, helping them to maintain an edge in creativity and innovation. The head office of EA is now in a large glass-covered block, not so far from where they started in 1982. When Bing shows you around the development areas, he points with pride to the creative junk that overflows from the developers' cubes, and greets everyone he meets with an easy humor. EA was the first video game publisher to treat its developers like rock stars, referring to them as "artists," giving them credit and publicity for their work, and sharing the lavish profits of the company as it grew. This strategy made it easy for them to attract the best designers.

Bing Gordon

Starting Electronic Arts

■ Lion cubs playing

Photo Natphotos

Bing Gordon recalls the ideas that inspired the founders of Electronic Arts:

> One of the first precepts of Electronic Arts, that interactive entertainment was going to be as big as traditional music and video entertainment, was driven by our belief that "play" is a core human value; even a core mammalian value. We used an analogy that lion cubs learn to hunt and fight by playing together. We asserted that interactive virtual world gaming would be a way that people could train in a bunch of different ways, socialize, and get the same kind of richness that one can get in many aspects of real life, but without the risks. We imagined that people using technology could have the same kind of fun that lion cubs have when they're tussling in the Savannah, and also the same kind of utility, knowing that lion cubs that didn't become effective tusslers weren't going to eat. We also started with the assumption that some day technology was going to give us enough of a platform, that we would be able to put people in virtual worlds that looked as good as motion pictures. Twenty years later, technology has lived up to our hopes on that front.

Before Christmas in 1982, Tim Mott[4] was the ninth cofounder to join the team, as VP of technology. Trip Hawkins had chosen the name "Amazin' Software" for the company when he started, but none of the other founders liked the name, so in the fall of 1983 they held an offsite meeting to brainstorm for a better name. "Soft-art" sounded good, but it was too close to something that was already registered. Bing Gordon suggested "Electronic Artists," but there were some objections to that, as they wanted their developers to be thought of as the artists, rather than the company itself. Tim Mott suggested the modification to "Electronic Arts," and they had consensus.

With the new name agreed upon, they commissioned a local design firm[5] to design a corporate identity, resulting in a design for the logo that combined a square, circle, and triangle—the visual building blocks of graphics, rasterized to indicate technology. Bing played interesting tricks with the logo, hiding the shapes on the game covers, so that spotting them became a game in itself.

Tim Mott and Bing Gordon became close friends as they worked to make the company successful. Tim describes some of the challenges:

> At the time, the technology to support games was really primitive, as were the games themselves, but it was clear that sometime in the next twenty years, we didn't know when, the gaming technology would be able to support very rich interactive entertainment experiences. We set about building a company, a culture, and a set of processes, on that assumption. It was really a struggle for a long time, because what we were interested in doing wasn't yet possible, as the hardware simply wouldn't support it at consumer prices.
>
> When it comes to designing a game, one of the things that we figured out really quickly was that the intrinsics of the product really make a difference. It doesn't matter how much money you spend promoting a movie, if it's not a good movie, it'll fail at its second weekend after release. The same thing's true of a game; it doesn't matter how much money you spend promoting it and marketing it, if it's not a good game, within weeks if not days, word of mouth gets around that it's no fun. When people pay for an entertainment

■ Original Electronic Arts logo

experience, they're not only paying cash, but they're also making a commitment to spend time, and they don't want to waste time doing something that's not enjoyable.

From the very beginning, we built Electronic Arts around people and with people who were just crazy about games. You couldn't get a job in the company as a designer, a marketing person, a sales person, or an engineer, without being crazy about games. We spent a lot of time with people who were avid game players, figuring out what they liked and didn't like. We did extensive Beta testing and a lot of focus group research. We built a process that enabled us to incorporate feedback from potential customers and consumers into the design of the game itself.

The user-centered approach that Tim had developed when he was working at Ginn and Xerox PARC, combined with his mastery of technology and programming, served him well in guiding EA toward interactive entertainment. His aptitudes were perfectly balanced by Bing's talent for marketing and his ability to attract and retain the very best game designers. The two of them were major contributors to the amazing success of the company, which had grown to annual sales revenue of over two billion dollars by 2002.

A Taxonomy of Games

BING HAS DEVELOPED a taxonomy of video and computer games, categorized by the interests of the players, their age, and their gender.

The interests of the players

Nowadays people choose categories of video games primarily based on their interests. That was not the case for the first decade of Electronic Arts, because there were so few competent video games that most people who played at all tried all the best games. Their attitude was: "Finally, it's October, there hasn't been a good new game in over two months. Now that there's one out, I better play it even though I'm not so interested in that kind of game." From the mid nineties onward, there have been more than enough really competent and entertaining games to fill the top twenty slots, so people have started to play games that line up with their interests. About half of all games are now sold to people who choose specialized categories—car games, simulations, war games, sports games, strategy games, or story and adventure games, as well as many subgroupings.

The age of the players

Bing explains that there are three ages of gamers, the preadolescent, the teen, and the grown-up. These ages have different preferences, and sports is the only category that is popular in all three groups.

Preadolescents

> Kids who are not yet adolescent really want only two things in life. One is muscle, and the other is to find freedom from the control of their parents and teachers.
>
> If you ask a ten-year-old boy, "Why do you play video games?" he answers, "At school, my teacher always tells me what to do, at home my parents always tell me what to do, or maybe my older brother or sister. With video games, no one tells me what to do; I'm the boss."
>
> These kids are yearning to grow up. When you see a ten-year-old boy and say, "Oh my, you've grown two inches over the summer," his chest puffs up with pride, and it's like, "Yeah, and you ought to see my muscles now."
>
> When they are playing games, they want to be Arnold, Deuce Staley, a WWF wrestler, or a muscle-bound Def Jam guy. They want to experiment with having huge amounts of power, and they want to feel like they are earning the virtual power with their hands. They play fighting games, wrestling games, games of physical mastery and skill, and some of the action character games with a lot of spinning, punching, and jumping. If they play sports games, they want to play primarily as a muscle character. In football they will choose to be the running back, so that they can run over tacklers and throw blockers aside; or as defenders they want to take the quarterback and plant him into the ground up to his waist.

Teenagers

The job of teenagers is to explore identity, so they like playing story games. They want to compare and contrast their own lives with parallel alternatives, because they think they've got to pick a direction by the time they're eighteen or nineteen. There are many fifty-year-old guys who get a beard, grow their hair long, exchange wives, change cars, send the kids off to prep school and start wearing tie-dye, but all teenagers think that they have to make a final choice before they grow up.

Digital virtual reality gives them a chance to play out scenarios in multiple lives. They can be Frodo, Brett Favre, or a mayor, and do it all quickly. They can use the "What if?" powers of computers to start over and try to be a different kind of Frodo or a different Brett Favre. In sports games, they want to play to see what it's like.

"Well, what if I was John Madden as a coach? What if I played like Brett Favre instead of like Jeff Garcia?"

They can try out alternate futures for themselves.

Adults

In our business, we only used to reach grown-ups between eighteen and twenty-five, but now it's more like eighteen to fifty, as the Nintendo generation ages and the baby boom generation is looking for new things to do with their savings. Adults like to justify their leisure with self-improvement. They play games for mental stimulation; if they're stuck in a rut, self-improvement shows them a way to get out of it.

Kids play flight simulator and say, "Did you see that explosion I caused? That was awesome."

Adults play flight simulator and say, "I was going to have to pay $2,500 for flight school, but ha! For only fifty dollars, I now have improved my flight rating up to . . ." Or, "I'm a football fan. Now, if I'm playing Madden Football, I'm a much better football fan." They can justify the play, and explain the value of time well spent.

The gender of the players

Gaming has been mostly male. Bing thinks that is partly because males lined up as the early adopters of computer technology, but also that in the early days of computers, the representations were mostly abstracted like Space Wars or Pacman, and it is easier to depict violence with abstracted representations than it is to show cooperation and relationships between people. Relatively recent games like the Sims[6] are played by about the same number of females as males and span generations as well. Bing describes a shift in attitudes:

> In the last five years, we have had female protagonists in popular games. Up to 1995, boys would not play with a female character; they wouldn't play with a Wonder Woman action figure or a doll, but girls would play with male action figures; they'd play with GI Joe.
>
> Starting in about the mid nineties, for the first time we saw boys willing to play with girl action-characters in toys, and in the late nineties the game Lara Croft: Tomb Raider; The Angel of Darkness came out, and a lot of boy gamers wanted to play that. There's a bit of lowering of sex identity boundaries. It's now okay for boys to experiment a little more broadly. I think the younger generation of gamers takes for granted technology-based communication, Internet and email, but also new kinds of sexual identity.
>
> Back in the nineties there were some lines of games that were targeted primarily for girls of specific ages. There were also educational games for girls. The problem with purely educational content is that kids grow through it very quickly. The best educational product ever made is the word processor; seven-year-olds can use it, and seventy-seven-year-olds can use it. By contrast, kids can blow through a "learn to spell three-letter words" game in a month, so paying thirty dollars for that game is a little like buying a Gucci product for your fast-growing child; parents figure that out.
>
> There were some well-meaning people who tried to do technology-based edutainment for girls back in the nineties and they were miserable commercial failures. One that was wildly successful for a short time was a Barbie line of games. They weren't leading edge design, but they were using what is perhaps the best girl-only franchise license of all time. It sold well for a couple of years, and then stopped selling.

Interactive formats

EA tries to put their games out on multiple platforms, so if, for example, they create a James Bond game, it goes out on a PC format, a Macintosh format, a console format, and on a handheld format. Bing admires the sixth sense that people seem to have about the interactive format that suits the game best. Even if they launch all of the formats on the same day, players know which they think is the best one. Some of that certainty comes from the way they understand the technology, some of it is precedent, and some of it is the social context. He describes the differences between the formats:

> Video game consoles are usually played by two people sitting on a couch, ten feet away from the TV. If you're playing a video game solo, you're practicing for when a friend is going to come over, or maybe wasting a little time improving your manual dexterity. You get a video game so you can have friends over on the couch. The social experience of a console game is; "I just kicked your ass! Ha, ha, ha. Want a beer?"
>
> You get a handheld game so that you can waste time during mobile moments. In the car, the kids who normally say, "Are we there yet?" are now concentrating on something else. It might be in the car, or on the bus to school. The social message of a handheld is, "I'm by myself, I'm putting up a virtual telephone booth around me, leave me alone."
>
> The PC is primarily a solo experience, played from about eighteen inches in front of the screen. The interface on the PC is much less about manually dexterity than the console. The social message of a PC is, "I'm by myself in a nice place, I'm kind of surrounded by this monitor, so if I talk to anybody it'll be through the computer." When potential customers see that there's a James Bond game coming out, they say: "Is James Bond about, 'I'm going to kick your ass,' or is James Bond about, 'Leave me alone while I'm traveling,' or is James Bond about, 'I'm going to immerse myself in a solo experience'?" And it turns out that most people think; "James Bond, hmm. You've got guns, you've got good guys and bad guys; I'm going to do that on my console with a friend."

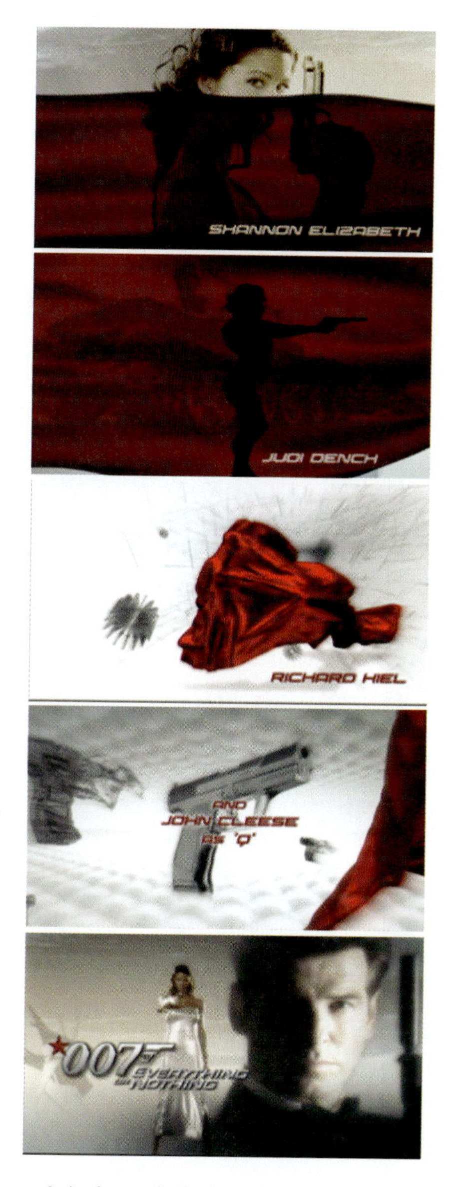

Series from trailer for James Bond 007 game, Everything or Nothing, from EA

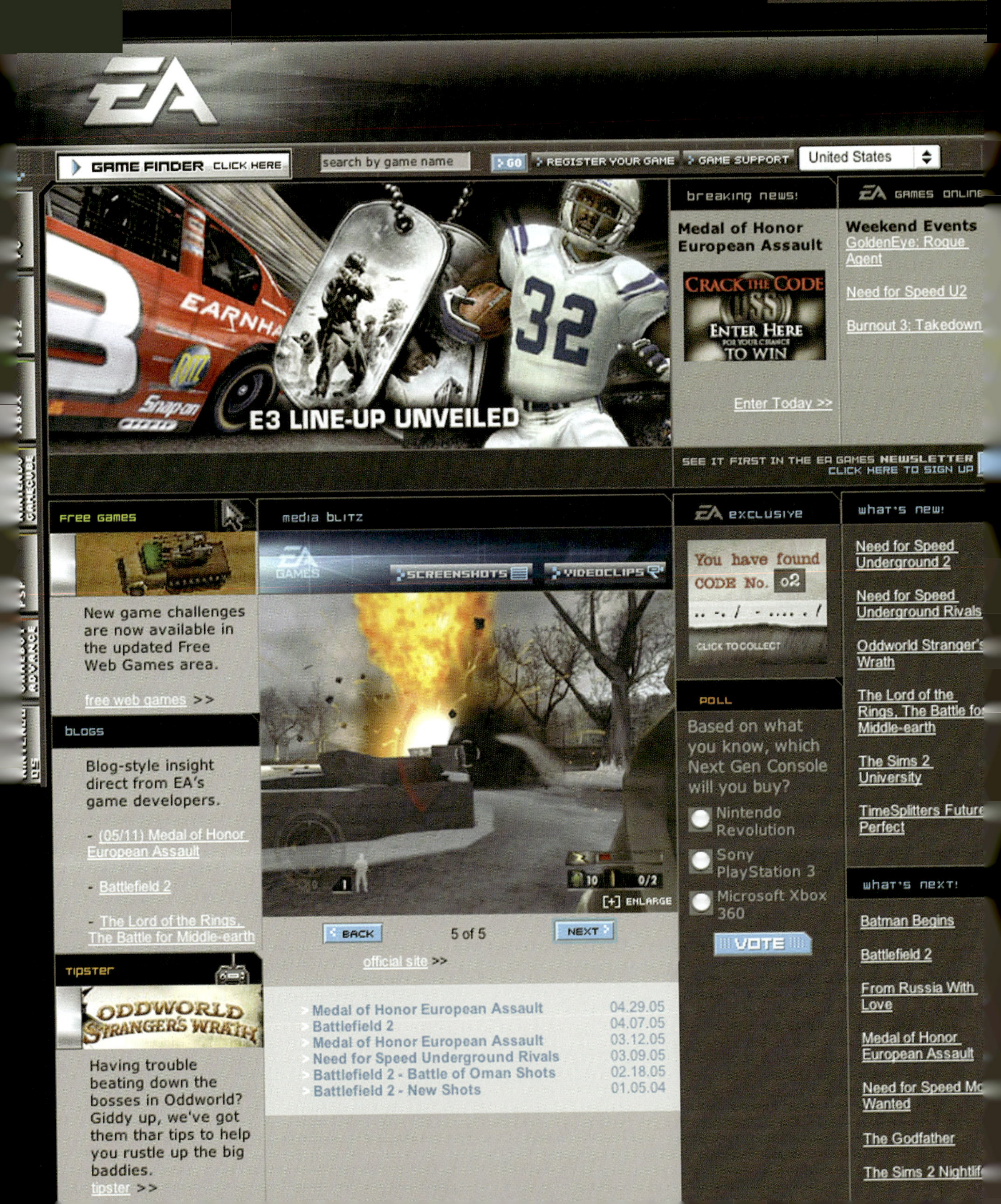

NIC ARTS
SUPPORT | LOGIN
FIND A STORE | EA STORE
GAME FINDER CLICK HERE
search by game name
GO
REGISTER YOUR GAME
GAME SUPPORT
United States
E3 LINE-UP UNVEILED
breaking news!
Medal of Honor European Assault
CRACK THE CODE
ENTER HERE
TO WIN
Enter Today >>
GAMES ONLINE
Weekend Events
GoldenEye: Rogue Agent
Need for Speed U2
Burnout 3: Takedown
SEE IT FIRST IN THE EA GAMES NEWSLETTER
CLICK HERE TO SIGN UP
Free Games
New game challenges are now available in the updated Free Web Games area.
free web games >>
blogs
Blog-style insight direct from EA's game developers.
- (05/11) Medal of Honor European Assault
- Battlefield 2
- The Lord of the Rings, The Battle for Middle-earth
Tipster
ODDWORLD STRANGER'S WRATH
Having trouble beating down the bosses in Oddworld? Giddy up, we've got them thar tips to help you rustle up the big baddies.
tipster >>
media blitz
SCREENSHOTS
VIDEOCLIPS
[+] ENLARGE
BACK
5 of 5
NEXT
official site >>
Medal of Honor European Assault 04.29.05
Battlefield 2 04.07.05
Medal of Honor European Assault 03.12.05
Need for Speed Underground Rivals 03.09.05
Battlefield 2 - Battle of Oman Shots 02.18.05
Battlefield 2 - New Shots 01.05.04
exclusive
You have found CODE No. 02
CLICK TO COLLECT
POLL
Based on what you know, which Next Gen Console will you buy?
Nintendo Revolution
Sony PlayStation 3
Microsoft Xbox 360
VOTE
what's new!
Need for Speed Underground 2
Need for Speed Underground Rivals
Oddworld Stranger's Wrath
The Lord of the Rings, The Battle for Middle-earth
The Sims 2 University
TimeSplitters Future Perfect
what's next!
Batman Begins
Battlefield 2
From Russia With Love
Medal of Honor European Assault
Need for Speed Most Wanted
The Godfather
The Sims 2 Nightlife

Brands

People also have strong associations with brands. Apple is the brand approved by mothers and art directors, who are more interested in education than entertainment. Bing describes the psychographic of Nintendo as:

> Plush doll entertainment. We've got bright colors, we've got round surfaces, this is something you don't feel bad about your six-to-twelve-year-old playing; a great experience on Nintendo is the best of children's literature. But if they're old enough to enjoy Harry Potter, they might be too old for Nintendo.

Within the game console category, Sony has a reputation for creating the leading edge of consumer electronics and owns the No. 1 brand. They offer entertaining, high-quality and innovative products, so when in doubt, people choose the Sony PlayStation. By contrast, Microsoft has moved into games with the Xbox and gained a reputation for appealing to gamers who are more rebellious. Bing thinks that is surprising:

■ Electronic Arts
Web site
May 2005

Image
screen capture

> That's pretty weird, because you wouldn't expect a conversation that goes like this:
>
> "Hey, Ballmer and Gates are going to make a video game system."
>
> "Who's it for?"
>
> "Well, it's for slacker rebels who like guns and don't like sports."
>
> "Huh? That doesn't sound as big as the video game system for everybody."
>
> "Well no, it's not as big."
>
> Two-thirds of video gamers own multiple video game playing platforms, and they have very little confusion about which game they ought to buy on which platform. A gun game that's a little edgy might be a toss up between Xbox and PlayStation. For a cute game, they might choose Nintendo if they have it, or another platform. Games with a lot of data, or games that you want to play with more than two people are likely to be personal computer games.

Number of players

Over the last twenty years, there has been a trend toward socialization in games. EA does regular focus groups with randomly selected children in junior high schools. Bing describes a sudden shift in attitudes:

> Junior high schoolers who played games were all loners until 1987 or 1988; they walked into a room, and you could tell through a two-way mirror that you might want to take an Air Wick with you if you went into the room.
>
> Then there was a sudden change, and we had a lot of class presidents starting to show up in the focus groups. At first we thought it was random, but then we realized that every junior high school was starting to have kids who were opinion leaders about games, whose social role was to know what was going on with games, and that conferred as much status as being the quarterback on the football team.

When EA Sports launched on the Sega Genesis in the early nineties, two-player games started to get more popular, and since then about half of the games sold are used predominantly in two-player mode. In 1994 the launch of DOOM set a precedent for two-player games on personal computers, and by the end of the millennium, multiplayer games were getting popular, with an increasing number of versions running on servers:

> As you know if you've ever done paintball, two-player paintball isn't a whole lot of fun. But with thirty-two player paintball, you get to a critical mass, and it's fun. I call those *n*-player games. You've got one-player games, two-player games, a little bit of four-player games, and *n*-player games. Ninety percent of the handhelds are one-player games, 50 percent of the console games are one-player games. For PC games, as connecting to other players via the Internet is easier, one-player games are probably down to 30 percent.

Input Devices

The three ages of gamers have different needs for input devices. The preadolescents like plenty of physical controls, so that they can exercise their muscles and feel the power. Adults are just the opposite, as they are interested in self-improvement and mental stimulation, and a daunting physical interface puts most of them off. They think, "Forget about it. That's not who I am, that's not what I want to do. It's too complicated, and I don't want to go through the learning curve."

In order to appeal to broad audiences, the video game console makers tend to add a little bit of complexity every few years. That keeps the controls familiar to existing audiences but adds some novelty. There is a catch there, in that newcomers may be put off by something that appeals to the loyal player. Bing describes the quandary:

> Someone who sees an ad on TV says, "Ooh, those graphics look good! I want to play!" Then they pick up a controller and think, "It's going to take me fifteen years to use this thing."
>
> People who've been playing for fifteen years go "Yeeah! Huh? All right. Great!"
>
> For mass-market games like Lord of the Rings, we start the game in a mode that bypasses the physically daunting controls. We might start by saying: "Kill these Orcs just by pushing X. Ah, you seem to be succeeding. Oh, that's perfect. That's excellent! Ooh, you are awesome. Let's try something new. Now, push triangle. Look at the way you split that shield. Oh, that's just awesome. X again, X again, you got it? Okay. Triangle again! OOOOH, you're perfect, you're awesome. . . . Now let's try the circle. Ready?"
>
> You try to gradually get people through the learning curve. If an expert comes along and says, "Yeah, yeah, I can do that. Where's the super Orc? This is easy, perfect, perfect, perfect! This is so easy."
>
> Then we can say, "Maybe you should be playing in expert mode."
>
> Then it's, "Ah, X, X, X . . . good? Hey, where'd my perfect go? Good? Fair? Whoa, okay, I gotta pay attention."

Electronic Arts has also explored the market for specific input devices. Between 5 and 10 percent of the people who buy car-driving games will buy a steering wheel, and 15 percent of the people who buy flight simulator games buy the control column and pedals. There are consoles for fighting games with oversized buttons and floor mats that people use for dance steps. To sell easily, specialized input devices have to be priced at $29 or less, which means that they are not very physically robust and electronics are minimal. For example, force feedback is too expensive to meet these criteria. Bing explains the underlying limitations:

> If an input device is more than $29, the cost of making you more expert in the game is too high. The game itself costs you fifty bucks, and you may play it for a hundred hours, so you don't want to spend another $50 to be 5 percent better; however, you might spend $3 to be 5 percent better. On the other hand, if somebody's going to spend $500 for a fighting game, or if they're in tournaments in a fraternity where they're plunking down $20 every Friday and Saturday night, being 5 percent better could mean a difference of $500 in winnings a year, and therefore they would explore alternate input devices. There just aren't many people for whom the price-performance of more customized input devices pays off.

During his first two decades of steering the development efforts at Electronic Arts toward success in the marketplace, Bing Gordon has amassed a deep and intimate knowledge of the way people play and the games that they enjoy. He has become a treasure trove of market research information and understanding, so that whenever the designers in his R&D organization show him a prototype of a new concept for a game, he responds immediately with an erudite explanation of who will play with it and why they will enjoy it. He offers an evaluative filter for new design ideas but is not the actual creator or inventor of the new concepts. For that he relies on his ability to attract the best and most creative game designers to work with him.

Next we meet Brendan Boyle, who specializes in coming up with the concepts in the first place. He leads a design team at

IDEO through the process of inventing new toys, games, and products for children. His focus is on creating a stream of ideas for new designs, and he has evolved a process for moving quickly from concepts that are harvested from brainstorms through rapid prototypes and trying the designs out with kids to communication pieces that can be used to demonstrate the concepts to the experts inside toy and game companies. The chosen designs are then licensed, so that Brendan and his team can see their designs on the market carrying various brand names. He takes us through his process for inventing toys and games and describes three examples.

Photo Author

Brendan Boyle

You can find Brendan Boyle sitting at a tiny desk, close to the rest of his group of creative designers at IDEO. He kept the desks small and close together so that people in the team can see and hear one another easily as they talk about inventing toys and games. The intimate setting also leaves space for a little shop for physical models and mockups right there in an adjoining room, and another area for electronic prototypes. Equipment for making videos is scattered around the studio. Just outside there is a low, round table with little chairs, surrounded by all sorts of playthings; that is where the kids come once a week to try out the new prototypes. Brendan was always taking things apart when he was young, and sometimes managed to put them back together as well. His older brother Dennis[7] could help with the reassembly and demonstrate a path toward design. Brendan graduated with a degree in mechanical engineering and then went to Goodyear, where he learned to design wheels. He found his niche in the product design program at Stanford and went on to work with David Kelley, designing products that ranged from a yogurt container to a tablet computer. He had entrepreneurial ambitions, so he branched out with a business partner, founding Skyline to develop some ideas he had for toys. He discovered that there was a well-established culture of invention in the toy and game industry and went on to become expert in the field. When Skyline was successful, he brought it back into IDEO.

TYCO

Brendan Boyle

Children . . . may have more fun with pots, pans, and a wooden spoon than the latest hot toy or game. In a market sense, the words "toy" and "game" mean a plaything that an adult is willing to purchase, rather than just an item that a child wants to play with, which would include almost anything.

Brendan Boyle 2004

Inventing Toys and Games

■ Focus play group

Photo
Nicolas Zurcher

INVENTING A TOY or game is a rigorous process. Brendan has ten people in his team, dedicated to understanding play and focused on coming up with new ideas that have a chance of succeeding in the marketplace. They spend a lot of time brainstorming, yielding a stream of new concepts. He describes how they build prototypes of the designs that are close to the intended result, so that they can try them out on kids to see if they like them:

> We do a lot of prototyping; if you visit us you'll see that we've designed our space to be like a big project room. We wanted very small desks to take up less room, and then have a bigger tinkering lab in the back. We have an electronics lab and a mechanical lab—a place that's only twenty feet from your desk to walk back and start building something.
>
> We do a lot of proof-of-concept models that we won't show to anybody; we're just trying them out ourselves to see if an idea has merit. We set up brainstorms on a regular basis, and we also try to get out to the toy stores once a week just to see stuff that's happening. People think that things stay the same month after month

in a toy store, but that couldn't be farther from the truth; it's such a charge to see what's going on. You can spark new ideas by going to stores on a regular basis, like Toys "R" Us, Wal-Mart, Target, and the specialty stores.

One of our cornerstones is having kids in to play with our stuff. We commission a group of five to seven kids every six weeks. We have them in once a week and try new things with them, both things that we're working on and things that we've bought and tested. We call it a "Focus play group"; we have a couple of adults, the same ones for the whole time, so they start to build a little trust. They sit down, ask them a lot of questions about what they're into and what's interesting, get a conversation going, and then try some new things.

The only rule we have is, "Anything you're not interested in, just tell us, and then we'll move on to something else."

That is a little bit different from structured play at a preschool, kindergarten or elementary, where they'll say, "We're going to do twenty minutes of painting and then we're going to do twenty minutes of this."

The more you work with kids, the more you realize that they have a very serious side; they have issues that bother them, they have pressures, they have all sorts of things. It may seem an obvious thing to say, but they're little people!

A trap that a lot of designers fall into is thinking, "Oh yeah, I remember when I was a kid; I remember what was cool," but you just can't. If you try to think back to your earliest memory, it's most likely to be an amalgam of a bunch of memories that have come together.

Once an idea has got past the hurdles of proof of concept, prototyping, and testing with the target audience, it is time to start concentrating on trying to sell it. The designers make little videos, often similar to TV ads, to demonstrate the play values of the ideas. Brendan spends much of his time maintaining the relationships with the people in the industry who may be interested in licensing the concepts. It is not as simple as getting into a toy company and saying, "Hey, I've got a new idea!" You have to gradually build their confidence in your process, professionalism, and integrity before you ever get to the invention concept. Until that trust is established, they are hesitant to even look at an idea. They may already have a similar concept in their portfolio and worry that the inventor will sue them for copying, not believing that there was a preexisting or parallel design.

Brendan and his team members also have to understand what a Mattel or Hasbro will need to sell to their client, probably Wal-Mart or Target. They have to be grounded in unit cost, understanding what a toy or game can sell for:

> People want to pay the same for a toy or a game today as they did ten or fifteen years ago; it can do more and more, but it should cost the same. It seems that $20 is a magic price point for a birthday gift, and about $10 for an impulse purchase. This pushes us to do more and cost less. We have to leave a lot of great things on the design room floor, just because of the price point.

When this process is successful, the toy company licenses the concept from the invention team and sends it off to their vendors for development, and manufacture. There is a well-established network of offshore facilities for manufacturing, engineering development, and detailed design. The vendors used to be most often in Hong Kong, but there are a growing number of other options now in Asia. The turnaround is typically around six months, with the target always being the all-important Christmas season.

Brendan and his team spend a lot of time coming up with ideas, but just as much time trying to sell them, because the hit rate is so low. Even today, though they have licensed over 125 items, he is still amazed when someone buys a concept, because everything needs to line up. You have to have a great concept, the company has to have the right timing for it, and the business opportunity has to fit their strategy.

> Children will play with anything that is available to them. Play includes learning, imagining, pretending, competing, discovering, socializing, and almost everything that kids do; they are just interested in what is enjoyable and fun, without noticing that they learn from playing. They may have more fun with pots, pans, and a wooden spoon, than the latest hot toy or game. In a market sense, the words "toy" and "game" mean a plaything that an adult is willing to purchase, rather than just an item that a child wants to play with, which would include almost anything.

FOOTBALL

Companies in the toy and game industry are always looking for a big hit to drive the fourth quarter, because everyone is looking for the hot toy. Some examples of the big hits of the past are the Hula Hoop, the Cabbage Patch Doll, Teddy Ruxpin, Furby, and more recently Tickle Me Elmo. Sometimes a new design that looks like a short lived hit when it is launched, rockets up on a high trajectory of popularity, but never plunges to earth; this is called an "evergreen" and is the goal for every toy invention team and every toy company. The nearest that Brendan and his team have come to an evergreen so far is the Aerobie Football, which has been on the market for over ten years. There are between fifty and a hundred evergreen toys, including, for example, Mr. Potato Head, Slinky, Silly Putty, Yo-Yo, and Twister. Brendan hopes and expects to eventually create something that gets on the evergreen list.

Here are three examples of Brendan Boyle's designs:

Aerobie Football[8]

■ Aerobie Football

Photo
Nicolas Zurcher

When Brendan started Skyline with a partner from the Stanford Business School in 1992, their first success was the Aerobie Football, which is still selling today, more than a million footballs later. The first idea was to have a foam football with four fins on the bottom, just tiny ones that would be self-teeing, to make it easy to stand on end for kicking. They were thinking of Charlie Brown, remembering that Lucy would always pull the ball out, and he would fall over, but they thought he would have been able to kick the ball without Lucy if it was self-teeing.

When they were prototyping the fins, one of the mockups had twisted fins by mistake, and when they threw it they noticed that the twist made it easier to throw a tight spiral. They went back to the drawing board, accentuated the propeller design, and reduced the fins to just two. It worked! They were able to license the football idea quite quickly, and it came out eight months later; this gave them something to point to, which helped their credibility with the toy companies.

Finger Blaster[9]

BRENDAN RECALLS THE development of the Finger Blaster, a dart made of foam that is light enough to be harmless, but can fly far and fast:

> I think foam ball came out in 1969. Indoor foam play was the whole idea, and now it's become almost a word in the English language. You can find foam footballs, soccer balls, and various kinds of projectile. We did an item that has its own cult here at IDEO, called the Finger Blaster. It's a really fast-flying foam dart that had a built-in shooter in it. The first built-in shooter was a rubber band, and the manufactured one is a nice molded part. I remember taking the first prototype home and shooting it past my wife. I was really proud of this invention; it just zinged by her head, and she said, "Brendan, that's a terrible toy, don't sell that to anyone!"
>
> I knew at that moment that there might be some potential resistance from moms, but we'd probably have a big hit! She still hates the toy to this day! My son, who's now eight, shoots the thing better than I do, so it's become an outdoor toy for sure. They've sold millions of them.
>
> There were foam darts and shooters, and then the Super Soakers came into play. You can buy a pressurized squirt gun that shoots twenty yards, with eight gallons of water that you can carry around.

■ Finger Blasters

Photo
Nicolas Zurcher

Fib Finder
EXTREME
Totally Truthful
All facts
Smooth Talkin'
Way To Go
Lookin' Good
Such a fake
No way, friend
I don't THINK so!
False hood
You've got to be kidding!
It's ALMOST TOO Late!
ALL TIME FIBBER

Fib Finder[10]

When designing physical games, or toys for that matter, it helps Brendan and his team to compete for notice when they include a bit of technology, because they are always compared with the internal groups at Mattel and Hasbro, who also have talented and experienced designers.

Brendan enjoys the game examples particularly, because they bring people together:

> Games are an interesting category. I like designing games because they are all about social interaction. You are getting kids together, or families together, not in front of the TV, but in the family room, sitting round a table or on the floor. That's kind of a wonderful feeling.
>
> We did the Fib Finder game, a unique lie detector, which gives a good impression of telling if kids are telling the truth or not. It was fun when we tested it, seeing girls aged eight to eleven, with what we call a "high giggle factor." It was this slumber party laughter. They were having such an enjoyable time because the questions that we wrote were open ended, so that they would find out new things about each other. That was very satisfying!
>
> It's that whole quest of getting folks playing together and talking. It's most popular with girls, because they are less into video games. We're doing a boys' version of the Fib Finder called High Voltage, where again you have a lie detector. This one gives you an electric shock, a mild one; well really it's a fake one, but it feels like it. Again, it's made successful by the proper kind of questions that get boys thinking and chatting. It's the software where you really want to put your thinking.

■ Fib Finder

Photo
Nicolas Zurcher

The question of designing play that appeals to girls as well as boys, and games that are particularly for girls, is addressed in the next interview with Brenda Laurel. When at Interval she focused on this question, working on an extensive research project to understand gender differences in the context of play and used the information to form a spin-off venture called Purple Moon that developed interactive media for preteen girls.

Photo Author

Brenda Laurel

Brenda has been dubbed a "digital diva," a reputation that she has earned by living in the world of theater at the same time as the world of computers, showing designers and engineers how to think about the people that use their products and how to use enactment to inform design. Currently she is chair of the Media Design Program at the Art Center College of Design in Pasadena, where she is teaching students how to use improvisation to think about designing interactions and experiences. She is also a Distinguished Engineer and director of the Experience Design group at Sun Microsystems Laboratories. Brenda Laurel is a researcher and writer whose work focuses on designing play, interactive narrative, and the cultural aspects of technology. Her career in theater and design spans over twenty-five years. She holds an MFA and PhD in theater from Ohio State University and has published on numerous topics, including interactive fiction, computer games, autonomous agents, virtual reality, and political and artistic issues in interactive media. Her first book, *Computers as Theater,*[11] was published in 1991, and she has edited two compilations, *The Art of Human-Computer Interface Design*[12] and *Design Research.*[13] She has worked as a game designer, producer, and researcher for companies including Atari, Activision, and Apple. In 1990 she cofounded Telepresence Research to develop virtual reality and remote presence technology and applications. Brenda was one of the first people to join Interval Research in Palo Alto, where she examined gender and technology, leading to her helping to found the spin-off Purple Moon, a company that developed interactive media for girls, where she served as VP of design. When the dot-com boom turned to bust, Purple Moon was snatched up by Mattel.

utopian
entrepreneur
brenda laurel
WORK

Brenda Laurel

I was a utopian entrepreneur. Maybe I still am. But for a time, I was also Cmdr. B. Laurel, a Navy test pilot, and I rode a modified F-14 into the desert floor. I've made the 60,000-foot downward spiral in some of the F-14 Phantoms and F-18s of the computer game industry—Atari, the old Activision, Epyx. This last time it felt different—I think I was fonder of the plane. My F-14 was Purple Moon, a company I cofounded, which was devoted to making interactive media for little girls. It was a dream come true. The ironic thing about this flameout was that I got into doing games for girls precisely because I was so tired of seeing things explode.

From the start of Brenda Laurel's *Utopian Entrepreneur*[14]

■ Book cover for *Utopian Entrepreneur*, by Brenda Laurel

Cover design Denise Gonzales Crisp

Games for Girls

Can a design for a girl be the same as the one for a boy? Are there real differences between the sexes, or have we just grown up to expect them? When Brenda Laurel joined Interval Research, she decided to try to answer those questions. David Liddle explains his point of view in sponsoring this research:

> When we were at Interval we made a decision to ask some questions that had traditionally been thought of as out of bounds. This had to do with gender preferences in electronic media. We looked at this across all age groups, but with a particular focus on preteens. At that time, we found a very marked difference between boys and girls in the use of any kind of computing capability.
>
> This was before the emergence of the Internet. At that time, it was quite striking that there was an enormous $10 billion industry producing video games for boys, but there just was no segment of any

significance that was serving girls. We did quite a bit of field research. I was so lucky to get Brenda Laurel to come to work with us at Interval, and she led a really excellent research project, which we called Safari because it was meant to be the search for the big game that girls would play. We did a couple of years of research in that area, with ultimately probably a thousand kids.

The first step was to understand more about the way the brain works. The politically correct silence about gender difference has started to fade away, and there has been time for a lot of research into brain-based gender differences. The most marked difference is that girls have better linguistic and social skills than boys, while boys tend to find three-dimensional graphical manipulations easier.

Brenda explains the connection between maps and video or computer games:

■ Brenda Laurel

We did a massive amount of literature searching first. We found a lot of stuff, especially in the area of brain-based sex differences that are statistically significant; small, but large enough that they get amplified by cultural narrative. For example the story that women can't read maps well as men has to do with a brain-based difference in how males and females tend to prefer to navigate. You see women turning maps upside down because they want to have a body orientation toward the direction that they are moving.

When you looked at traditional computer games, in the early days at least, you had the left to right scrolling thing going on. That's a mental rotation like turning the map upside down, if you're trying to put yourself in the position of the actor or the agent, and then you've got the translation from the plane of the keyboard to the plane of the screen. Gosh! That kind of explains some things.

Brenda had been immersed in the electronic game industry since the seventies and had helped to create many computer games, enjoying them as she went along. This convinced her that there was no underlying reason that girls would not play with computers but made her want to find out how to create games that girls would really like. She called Christopher Ireland[15] in to help with the gender study:

We looked at play preferences in terms of favorite toys and got kids to take pictures of their play activities and bring them in. We looked at gender signaling in toys. How do you know this is for a girl or for a boy? The fun part there was mixing up signaling traits in the same toys. For example we made a pink furry truck, and we learned that pinkness overrides truckness. We did a diary with bullet holes in it, and found that it is still a diary and a boy won't use it. We ended up with this little hierarchy of what you can get away with in gender signaling. We made the choice, based on the differences that we saw there, that we were going to aim the games specifically at girls rather than do the politically correct thing of gender-encompassing games.

The research was yielding a strong point of view about how to create designs for the big game for girls that the name "Safari" had implied. David Liddle was eager to set up spin-off companies to commercialize products based on the intellectual property that Interval was creating. This would be essential if Paul Allen, the cofounder of Microsoft, was to have a return on the hundred million dollar investment promised to Interval for ten years of operation.

Purple Moon was funded through Interval but structured to behave independently, in a similar pattern to the typical Silicon Valley startup company. Brenda was a founder and member of the board of directors, as well as the development leader as VP of design. She worked with Christopher Ireland to consolidate the findings from the research and translate them into design principles for use in developing products for preteen girls.

After a stage of advanced development inside Interval, the company was formed and in 1997 launched three interconnected businesses: interactive CD-ROMs, the purplemoon.com Web site, and an array of Purple Moon collectibles:

We made the decision early on that we wanted to create a world with characters that girls could affiliate with, where girls could have emotional rehearsal space for the social lives that they led, hoping that they would find that they had more flexibility, and that they would have more elasticity in their own lives. It's really fun for them to think, "Gee, how would that have gone if I'd done it a different way?" They could always rewind, make a different choice, and see what would happen instead.

CD-ROM and Purple Moon collectibles

Rockett
New Adventure
Select Adventure
Save My Place
End
soft
LOUD
Purple Moon
Miko
LOVES
NAME
BEST FRIENDS
FUTURE CAREER
BEST AT
BIRTHDAY
Make a Face
Color Skin
Fab Fashions
Color Top
Make A Friend

In the other series of games, the Secret Path series, we looked at the inner fantasy world. We learned by interviewing girls that they usually placed that kind of activity in a more natural romantic setting. We got some surprises there. I always thought that there'd be lots of nurturing and taking care of animals and flowers and things, you know this sort of stereotype that we have.

The girls that we spoke to told us that, "No, I go there to be alone, and if anything I want the animals to take care of me. This is where I get taken care of. I'm going to get information from fairies or secret beings in the woods. I'm going to explore on my own. It's not a place I take my friends."

Girls told us that video games were boring. They have this predisposition toward narrative play, in fact narrative construction. When we talk about constructive play, we think about hammering things and making snow forts and stuff, that's a stereotypically "boy" form. Although girls do those things, they are much more interested in the kind of constructive play where we make up a family, or make up a couple of sorority sisters, so that there's an ongoing narrative; that was the piece that was missing for them in traditional games. They are not overtly competitive, so getting a high score, or having a game that yields a score, or has you play against the clock, is intrinsically not as interesting as monkeying around in the lives of some characters and seeing how you can change what happens.

- Purple Moon screens

  Left column
  Rockett's New Adventure at school and her way of thinking

  Center column
  Coloring the steps, to find the magic stone and put it in the purse

  Right column
  Creating a new friend, and giving her character hair and clothes

The choice of CD-ROM for the game component of the product line turned out to have limitations, as the e-commerce surge was just getting started, and CD-ROMs were giving way to online games. From the beginning, Brenda had been interested in bridging the gap between media, hence the combination of computer-based game, Web site, and the physical manifestations of the little dolls and the characters. She wanted Purple Moon to be a participatory place for the girls who used it, so that they could appropriate the characters and the situations and rework them to construct personal relevance and meaning. The Web site was a successful vehicle for this and turned into a very social space.

They were doing this before there were any off-the-shelf, e-commerce infrastructure packages, so they were desperately trying to build their own shopping site in order to support the activity, and that was an expensive proposition. In the end, it turned out that the Web site was the most successful part of the whole project; the CD-ROMs primed people to go to the Web site and enjoy the social interaction, supported by the material from the CD-ROMs and the new stuff that they could pick up online:

> A part of the interactivity that you had to really probe the game to find was that you could always go to the lockers and look in a character's locker. Since everybody was worried about girls snooping, we had a thing where when you open the locker the child would welcome you, "Hi, I'm Jessie." It wasn't like you were peeking in their locker. The contents of the locker, including journal entries and pictures and stuff, would change depending on how you had played the game so far.
>
> The Purple Moon site was one of the few sites in those days that didn't feel lonely. The first thing you saw on the screen was who was there. There was an internal postcard system, like an internal email system, so that we could protect kids from predatory behavior by adults. There was always a sense that it was populated by both characters and players, and that these two worlds could blend there, that they were intermingled.
>
> We were very proud of the strength of the community that formed on the site. In fact, when the Paul Allen Group suddenly pulled the plug on the company, we put a "Farewell" screen over the front of the Web site. About three weeks later we got some additional funding to bring it back up, so that girls could connect with their friends and they wouldn't be lost forever. During the time that it was down, we got about three hundred new registered users. Girls hacked into it, or they had bookmarks inside of the site, so it was successful even in death. It stayed very well populated even when Mattel was handling it, and they weren't really servicing the properties with new materials.

Brenda was deeply disappointed that Purple Moon did not survive, and if you read *Utopian Entrepreneur*, you will feel bitterness behind her account of the events that made her describe it as a "flameout." The design principles are still with her, and with the other people who were involved, so perhaps one day soon we will see an emergence of electronic games that are deeply valued by preteen girls.

Playing with Purple Moon collectibles

Will Wright is another designer who has succeeded in creating games that appeal to girls as well as boys. He has designed a series of computer games that combine the characteristics of hobbies with enjoyable play, culminating in the Sims, which is the best-selling computer game to date. Next he tells the story of developing his series of simulation games and explains the structure and aesthetics of computer-based play.

Photo courtesy of Electronic Arts

Will Wright

Will Wright is the best-known guru in game design, partly because the Sims is the best-selling game of all time for personal computers, but more significantly because he is so articulate about what he does and how he does it. He remembers the books he has read, and quotes the titles and authors as he talks. He thinks through the reasons behind his design decisions and presents an analysis in simple and accessible terms. His manner is direct and unpretentious, and although he normally seems serious, there is often a twinkle in his eye. Will bought an early Apple II in 1980 and found himself immediately sucked into writing programs and building simulations. His first game was published in 1984, and the first version of SimCity was developed a year later, running on a Commodore 64. He founded Maxis in 1987, with managing partner Jeff Braun, and created a series of simulation games, culminating with the Sims. The games in the series have earned a reputation for intelligent and creative design, with a sense of social responsibility. If you add up all the different games, they have sold more than 8 million copies worldwide. Maxis had a down period after going public in 1995, with the pressures of quarterly profits forcing them to try to build too many titles. They ended up being acquired by Electronic Arts and were rescued by strong management, allowing Will to focus on what he does best. They are now a self-contained division, employing around 160 people, building on the success of the Sims by developing new versions that can be played both locally and online.

U.S. NAVY
SIMS
Who Owns the Sun?
BRUCE STERLING
ONE CITY, TWO VISIONS
Energy & Land Use
Burchell and Listokin
DRAW FROM YOUR HEAD
人世祭事
THE WAY THINGS REALLY WORK
Captured by Aliens
Joel Achenbach
are we alone in the cosmos?
TUFTE
VISUAL EXPLANATIONS
MAPS OF THE MIND
ENTERING SPACE
GOLF

Will Wright

Models

■ The shelf in Will Wright's office

Photo Author

"As a kid I spent far too much of my time making models!" says Will Wright, as he sits at a round table in the middle of his spacious office. The habit has not left him. The table is covered with an architectural construction toy that he is playing with. He clips the wall segments into the floor grid and patiently builds a multilevel structure with rooms and windows. The toy is his own invention, designed and prototyped in his spare time. There are models everywhere you look. A black military helicopter hangs from a fishing line, silhouetted against the brilliant blue California sky outside the window. The long bookshelves on the wall are littered with plastic construction toys formed into a dinosaur and a sphere, more helicopters, and memorabilia of Maxis products. There is a model of a DNA strand next to the electric scooter that Will uses to zoom around the building.

His life has intertwined these physical models with the more abstract modeling of software constructions. He thinks about everything that he encounters as a potential model, abstracting

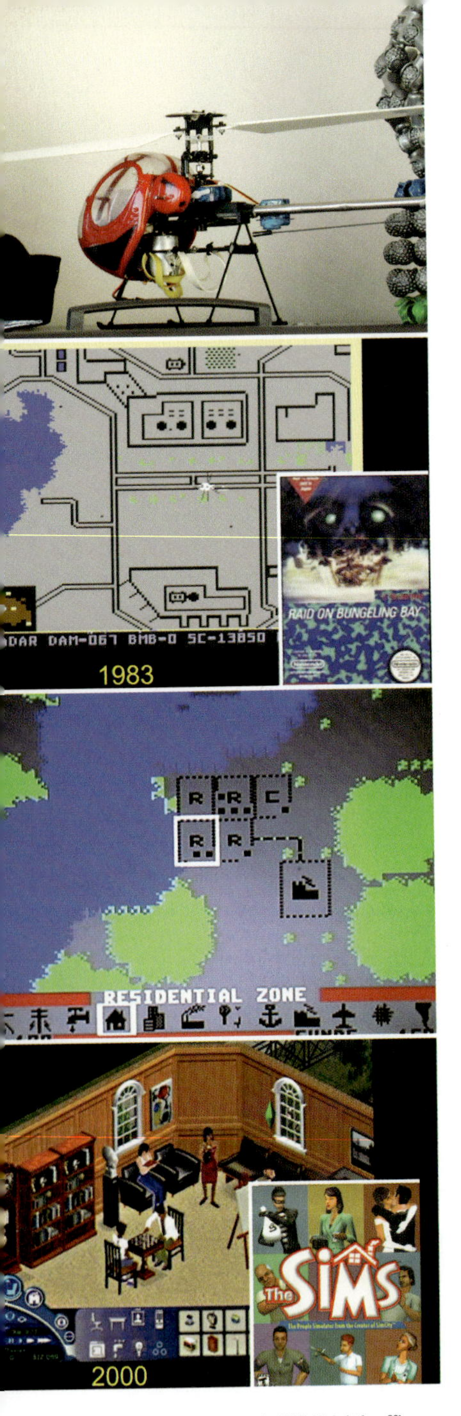

- Model helicopter in Will Wright's office
- Raid on Bungling Bay (1983)
- First version of SimCity (1985)
- SimCity (2000)

behaviors into sets of rules and probabilities that can be modeled as a computer program. He spends his days guiding his team to write code, describing more and more sophisticated models of people and their social interactions. His games have the compelling qualities of soap operas, but rather than leaving you an inactive couch potato, they engage you in the action, becoming an addictive hobby as well as a game. In his spare time he develops robots with his teenage daughter and enters them into the local "robot war" competitions.

When I was a kid, I was very fascinated with the process of building models of little aircraft and tanks, but also as I built them, I was a big student of World War II history. It would bring me to understand and spark my interest in these different things that I was modeling. I started transitioning to models that actually had behavior, that were mechanical and would move around and do things, and I got very interested in home-brew robotics.

When the first personal computers came out in around 1980, I bought an early Apple II. The original idea was that I was going to use this to interface to my robots, and in fact I started doing that, but I got totally sucked into the software side of it, especially simulations. The idea occurred to me that you could build virtual models inside the computer, not only as models of the static structure, but also as models of the process; these models could have behaviors and dynamics. At that point I decided what I wanted to do. I wanted to learn to build these models, and that's when I started pursuing it as a career and went from there into the game industry.

The first game I made was around 1983. It was called Raid on Bungling Bay. It was one of these stupid shoot-up things, flying a helicopter over these islands bombing everything. It was on the Commodore 64 and was published in 1984. There was a lot of piracy back then, so it didn't do that well in the States, but in Japan it was one of the first American games put on the Nintendo, the very first Nintendo system, and there it sold about a million units. When I was designing that game, part of it involved me creating this landscape that you would fly over and bomb. It was a landscape of islands with roads and factories and things, and I created an editor for doing that, where I could scroll around and put down the roads and things. I found that I was having more fun designing and building these islands than I was bombing them in the game, so I took that editor and I kept working on it.

I started reading some of the theories about urban dynamics from Jay Forrester.[16] I started programming traffic models and then growth models into my editor. All of a sudden the subject of city planning and urban dynamics became utterly fascinating to me, because I had this little guinea pig on the screen in front of me, so that I could test out theories. I could actually program in the theory and see what would grow out of it, what would happen. I began to think that other people would enjoy doing this. If they had a little toy city to interact with and build, I thought that they would enjoy it as much as I would, and that's where the idea for SimCity started.

Will developed his first version of SimCity in 1985, to run on a Commodore 64. The publishers kept saying, "When's the game going to be finished?" They were expecting a more definite win-or-lose ending to it, like all games had at that time. He kept trying to tell them, "No, it's more of a toy, and less of a game," so they lost interest in it and never published it. In 1987 Will met Jeff Braun at a pizza party and got talking about ideas for games. Soon they were poring over the Commodore 64 and Jeff was falling for SimCity. This was the start of a long and fruitful partnership, as Will's talent for game design was perfectly complementary to the entrepreneurial energy that Jeff contributed. They started their own company to publish SimCity for home computers and called it Maxis. Jeff provided the space, setting up the office in his apartment. He was tireless in his development of the business and in 1989 made a copublishing deal with Broderbund. Sales started slowly, as the game was much more intellectual than anything else on the market, but a breakthrough came when *Time* wrote a full-page article about it, and it was soon the hit of the industry. SimCity did very well for Maxis; it paid for a lot of mistakes as they were growing the company:

> We did a lot of other Sim games. The next game I worked on was SimEarth, modeling the earth for the last four billion years. It was inspired by the work of James Lovelock, who wrote about the Gaia hypothesis,[17] and in fact he worked with us as an advisor on the game.

SimCity (1989) ■
SimEarth (1991) ■
SimAnt (1993) ■
The Sims (2000) ■

File
Speed
Options
Disasters
Windows
Newspaper
Help
Oct 1991 ‹Oakland› $20,000
Query Tool
Fire Storm
SIGN
RCI
Chris's house
Caldecott Tunnel
Hwy 24
Lake Temescal
Eubanks 7
Hwy

The next game I did was called SimAnt; it was actually based on the work of Edward O. Wilson, who is the premier myrmecologist in the world. He had just published this very large book called The Ants[18] that won the Pulitzer Prize that year. Ants have always fascinated me because of their emergent behavior. Any single ant is really stupid, and you sit there and try to understand what makes it tick. If you put a bunch of these little stupid components together, you get a colony-level intelligence that's remarkable, rivaling that of a dog or something. It's really remarkable, and it's like an intelligence that you can deconstruct. Ten- and fifteen-year-olds really got into SimAnt; it was really successful with that group. Most adults didn't play it long enough to realize the depth of ant behavior and mistook it for a game about battling ants.

For about six months after SimAnt, Will Wright started formulating ideas that were more about social models of interactions among people and would emerge eventually as The Sims. There was a lot of pressure from the market for a new version of SimCity, but Will was more excited about his new direction, so he asked a colleague who had collaborated with him on SimEarth to take on the sequel. In due course a prototype for the next generation of SimCity was delivered, but it was designed from a bad perspective and included some unstable code from SimEarth. The reluctant Will was forced to drop everything else and take over the project, so for the next year and a half he worked on SimCity 2000. He introduced an isometric perspective that made the landscape three-dimensional and augmented the interface without altering the successful elements of the first game. It was released for DOS in 1994, and quickly became the best-selling game on the market:

■ SimCity 2000 Oakland Fire Scenario

When we did SimCity, a lot of people started sending us letters about the game, wishing that we would add x, y, and z. I had this huge stack of letters in my office, and I read all of them, to find out what people wanted. At the same time the technology had progressed quite a bit from the original SimCity, so I started looking at what we could do with the model, how we could make the game more compelling, more visceral. The major difference was that there was three-dimensional terrain. It had much more of a 3D feel. We had deeper levels of infrastructure: we had three different types of road rather than just one road. We had a whole national model around it—there was a context for your city and the neighboring cities.

With the successful sequel yielding a stable income stream for Maxis, Will was interested in expanding beyond the Sim series. One of his new ideas was for an open-ended adventure game combined with a flight simulator. It was called The Hindenberg Project and was based on the famous airship that exploded in 1937. He assembled ten theories about the cause of the accident and made the players discover which theory applied to their game. This involved a new type of probability model but also built on the model of landscape inherent to SimCity. The concept ran afoul of the politics of the Nazi era, as the Nazi logo was on the tail of the airship, and even if they had removed the logo, people would have associated the ship with the Nazi era.

Even though this experiment did not move forward, it gave Will and Jeff a hunger for expansion and diversity that led them down the path toward taking Maxis public. The first step was to seed the company with some venture capital. The next was to bring in a top manager with a business background and Disney experience. They moved into the sixth floor of a new corporate office block in Walnut Creek, a fast-growing satellite town in the San Francisco Bay area. Maxis went public in the middle of 1995, raising $35 million from the offering, and reported $6 million income for their first public year. From the outside they looked strong, but the treadmill of being beholden to the shareholders and to Wall Street was starting to cause some anxiety on the inside. Jeff Braun wanted a break from the intensity of eight years of growing the company and started to phase himself out of day-to-day operations. Sales of SimCity 2000 were starting to decline. What were they going to do next?

Will embarked on developing a game called SimCopter, where the players could fly a Schwitzer 300 helicopter around a city that was exported from SimCity. "You are flying this rescue helicopter around a city, and you're rescuing people and putting out fires and chasing criminals." The idea was fun, but time pressure was increasing, and the resources at Maxis were being spread impossibly thin. The new management insisted on shipping four games by the end of 1996: SimTunes, SimCopter, SimPark, and Full Tilt Pinball. The stress levels for the developers shot up, and although they did manage to ship something resembling a finished product for all four games, nobody was happy about all the corners that were cut. Will was particularly disappointed, as he felt that the design for SimCopter was coming along nicely, but it had to be released before it was ready. Poor sales for all four games proved the point.

The situation only got worse in 1997. Maxis tried the acquisition route, buying a small game company from Texas called Cinematronics to develop dungeon adventure games such as Crucible. They also tried children's software, a sports brand, and even full-motion video, with a game called Crystal Skull featuring a star from the TV show "Miami Vice." There was an atmosphere of frenetic experiment without enough resources to make any single effort successful, and morale plummeted. In midyear they reported losses for the previous year of nearly $2 million. In desperation, the management turned to Will to develop another version of SimCity, hoping that an upgrade with three-dimensional graphics would provide a road to recovery, as 3D graphics were the newest fad in the industry at that time. Unfortunately, when Will analyzed the available technology, he discovered that 3D was not yet ready for the microscopic details of cities and landscape that were essential to SimCity. The management did not want to hear this bad news and insisted that they go forward with a 3D implementation, leading to the display of an embarrassingly inept version of SimCity 3000 at a trade show. They knew that they would ruin the reputation of the Maxis brand if this version were to be released.

Enter Electronic Arts, the dominant interactive entertainment company in the industry. EA had been making overtures to Maxis for some time, as they were looking for ways to improve their offering in the PC market, but Maxis executives thought of them as competitors rather than saviors. By mid 1997 the prospects for Maxis were desperate enough for this attitude to change, and

negotiations started. Electronic Arts acquired Maxis for $125 million in stock, but Will was very worried about the deal. He knew that there would be layoffs, and his experience with professional management had so far been a bitter disappointment. EA appointed Luc Barthelet, a straight-thinking and straight-talking Frenchman, to run Maxis as general manager. Luc took a fresh look at the people, resulting in the removal of almost all the top-level management and sales staff. He took a fresh look at the portfolio and declared a focus on "top ten products," causing quite a few of the development staff who were committed to second-tier products to leave. He cut back to a few development teams and divested Cinematronics, leaving a core development staff of the highest caliber.

He brought Lucy Bradshaw with him to focus on SimCity 3000, and together they took a long, hard look at the progress so far. They canceled the problematic 3D requirement and focused on improving the game-play experience from SimCity 2000, building on Will Wright's successful formula, enhancing the maps and zoom features, as well as adding more sophisticated parameters. They showed the game to a positive reception in 1998, and with the EA purse behind them, they were able to wait until it was satisfactorily finished in every detail before releasing it in February 1999. It was soon at the top of the charts.

■ Sims wallpaper

Image Courtesy of Electronic Arts

The Sims

Luc Barthelet realized that Will Wright was probably the best game designer in the world but that his talent was being frittered away, without adequate focus or staff. As soon as SimCity 3000 was safely under Lucy's leadership, he started a search for the best possible talent to work with Will, and set him up with an open-ended brief to create the next innovative leap forward. Will had been eager to develop a new game that was about people and social interactions, based on contemporary life. He explains:

■ Lucy Bradshaw
■ Luc Barthelet

> Most games are striving to get as far away from contemporary life as possible, wanting to be fantasy, science fiction, or military, or whatever. If you go to a bookstore and look at what the books are about, you have a few books over here about military history, and you have a few over here that are fantasy books, but the majority of the books center around contemporary life. It's the same with prime-time television. You go into a software store and it's the exact opposite; there's almost nothing about contemporary life.

In a 1994 interview in *Wired* magazine, Will said:

> I'm hoping to strike out in a slightly different direction. I'm interested in the process and strategies for design. The architect Christopher Alexander, in his book *Pattern Language*,[20] formalized a lot of spatial relationships into a grammar for design. I'd really like to work toward a grammar for complex systems and present someone with tools for designing complex things. I have in mind a game I want to call "Doll House." It gives grown-ups some tools to design what is basically a doll house, but a doll house for adults may not be very marketable?[19]

How wonderful for Will to be able to focus on this idea that had been in his mind for so long, and to have such a good team to move it forward. By this time the concept had matured beyond the doll house metaphor into The Sims, a game that would build on the processes and strategies that people use in everyday life. The Sims is about social interactions among people. You create characters and make them do things. It is like writing your own soap opera, setting up situations for stress, or conflict, or love, and then playing them out. As you move up the levels of the game, you can move from mundane shopping trips and visits to the bathroom, to design clothes for your characters and places for them to live. It soon becomes a hobby:

> When SimCopter completed, I started building a product team around The Sims and pursuing that idea in earnest. The Sims has had a level of success that is just amazing. At some point we realized that it was the best-selling personal computer game in history. We were reaching a much broader demographic, across gender, across age, across computer experience. We had a lot of very casual players who did not normally play computer games.

A frequent vector for The Sims to spread would be that the hardcore gamer, usually male, would bring home the game and play it, and their spouse, or their sister or girlfriend, would watch them, and then say, "That looks interesting," and they would start playing it. There was also a very wide age range from ten-year-olds to fifty or sixty. A lot of grandparents would play it with their grandkids. We were actually hitting a group of people that ten years before would not have been online—they would not have been subscribing to CompuServe—but by then they had Net access.

The original idea for The Sims was to make a doll's house that boys would want to play with and a strategy game that girls would want to play. The intersection of those two gives you a strategy game happening in a doll's house.

We noticed that when we were designing The Sims, a certain degree of abstraction in the game is very beneficial. You don't actually get very close to the characters. You can't quite see their facial expressions, but everybody in their mind is imagining the facial expressions on the characters.

In computer game design, you're dealing with two processors. You've got the processor in front of you on the computer and you've got the processor in your head, and so the game itself is actually running on both. There are certain things that the computer is very good at, but there are other things that the human imagination is better at.

The Sims probably has more sex than most games out there. It's PG sex and it's more kind of titillation than realization, but The Sims is basically in a social space, and it's about the way these people relate, and they get married, and they can have kids. They can hang out in the hot tub together, and they can play in bed.

A lot of players will do experiments on the Sims, to the point of torturing them, or seeing what it takes to kill them, or seeing how upset they can get them. It turns out that the people that are doing these clinical experiments on the Sims, on their psychology, turn out to be more female than male.

A lot of games that allow user customizability only do so in a very difficult granule, like the first-person shooters. You can write mods for them, but it basically involves C code and knowing how to program. With The Sims we have all these levels that you can customize. At the simplest level, you can make a new costume, and all you need is a paint program. At the next level above that you can make a new object and it's a bit more involved.

Doll's house play kit ■
A degree of abstraction ■
PG Sex ■
Customized Experiments ■

The Sims was released in 2000, and since then Will has developed an online version. The ease with which people can create unique versions of people, their objects, and environments, made it an ideal game for an online community. The game itself is interesting and compelling, but the community that built up around it brought it to the next level. People can upload their designs, share them, and have databases online where they collect things that they have created.

The collections are made more interesting by the intelligence of the inanimate objects in the game. Inspired by the work of Christopher Alexander, Will embedded the behavioral rules for good architecture into the elements that make up a house, so that a balcony is an appropriate width for example. This makes designing a house in the game both easier and more successful, so that the open-ended quality of the game is not entirely without the wisdom of experience. The bylaws of architectural structure and object behavior are built into the individual items. Another way of thinking about this is that the objects in the game are designed to be intelligent, so that they can attract both the players and the characters in the game. This releases the characters to concentrate more on their emotionally driven behavior, such as falling in love or violent disagreements.

■ A landscape of play

The Landscape of Play

Will describes gaming as a landscape populated by mountain peaks. One peak is media-based role play, with a story line and a strong plot, for example adventure games such as Myst. A second peak is about skill and achievement, including sports games and first-person shooters. A third peak is about creative simulation, where people develop a hobby and build communities around their hobbies. Another peak is based on strategy, where simple decisions lead to entertaining consequences and situations. You can map the position of a particular game in this landscape and see the strength that it has relative to competitive titles:

The genres that are currently popular are peaks on that landscape. These are areas that prove to be fun, that someone found in all the possible game-space. What happens generally is that somebody discovers a peak, and it grows and grows. Maybe it's real-time strategy, then everybody else says, "Oh, there's a peak over there, let's go and design a game like that."

In fact, there are thousands of other peaks that nobody has explored. Occasionally you'll see an unusual, groundbreaking game jump out in the middle of nowhere, but it usually fails, not because the concept was bad, but because the execution wasn't good enough. The Sims was kind of waffling between simulation, strategy, and a role-playing game. It couldn't decide which peak to live on because really it was a new peak somewhere among the three. Most of the game sites eventually decided it was strategy, so they put it in strategy, even though it is a simulation, and even though it is very much about role playing.

A lot of games are built around a movie model, where there's a beginning, middle, and end; perhaps there's some dramatic climax, or you're defeating evil. The Sim games are more like a hobby where you kind of approach, and you have a shared interest with other people, and you can take the aspects that interest you most and really focus on those. With an electric train set, a lot of people build a model and are totally into the scenery, or making sure the mountains are perfect. Other people are into the switching logic on the track, or the village, or the actual trains that they collect, so you can come to a hobby like that with your own specific interests, and you can really focus on that, and customize the hobby to yourself.

I am interested in developing metrics to look at a community for a game, and figure out where it is positioned relative to this landscape. You can learn a lot if you watch a person playing the game and apply the metrics. You can predict what they would enjoy, and what advancement ladders they are aiming for in the game. You should be able to find content that would be interesting for that person, and download it into them transparently. It could even be a peer-to-peer transfer like Napster. Then as they play the game more and more, the game learns what they enjoy and offers new content, perhaps new characters in the game, new objects that they could buy, and new situations.

When people play these games, especially the open-ended games, they are in fact creating stories. Whatever happens to them in the game is the story, so that the path that they take through this game is defining some kind of story arc. The computer could start helping to support that story if it could recognize the arc, based on the experience of watching a million people moving through the game. For example, it could see that you're buying a lot of spooky things and you're making a haunted house, and then it could start collaborating with you on that story. It might even test you in the game, so if your character walks into the next room, and it can't decide if you're doing a horror or a comedy, maybe it could put a cream pie and a chain saw in the room, and wait to see which one you pick up. I can imagine a system where the player becomes the game creator, and we're providing them the tools.

With The Sims online right now, that's one of the concepts that we're pursuing. In The Sims, you have a build mode. You can buy new objects, place them wherever you want, put up walls, and design a house. We're also doing a lot of incremental objects, at a fairly low level, that are game components that the user can place. These are things like dice, or one-way doors with secret buttons, or conveyor belts. They are things that in combination you can use to create a lot of different games. In some sense we are hoping that the build mode in The Sims becomes a kind of game creation system, and then the real competition in this online game will be who can make the best game using these components.

Designing Games

A STARTING POINT for designing a game is to engage players in deciding what their goals are. They may know in advance, if they've seen the game being played or heard about it from a friend. If it is a driving game with stock cars, they know that the goal is to win the race. With the Sim games, the options are much more open-ended and diverse. In SimCity, the game designer doesn't tell the player the exact goal. There is no instruction to build the biggest possible city in twenty years, or to make the residents happy. Each player decides what his or her goal is; that decision is as important as anything else that happens in the game. Players might say, "I want to see how big a city I can build," or "I want to see if I can eliminate crime in my city," and then they pursue that.

The game designer also has basic choices about speed and scope at the beginning of each project. Will describes this as the "Granularity of the interaction, which is often how you are actually making a decision that's going to alter the outcome." The "choose your own adventure" books have very large granules, where you may make one choice in a chapter. The first-person shooters are the finest granules, where the software is sampling the input device sixty times a second.

There is also the significance of the space that the user is navigating while playing the game. Some games, like the Sims, have very open-ended spaces; others, like the shooters, have very constrained spaces. An analogy for the dramatic interest or challenge associated with that space is trying to climb a hill to get to a destination on top. Some hills have very smooth, gradually ramped sides that are easy to walk up, and others have cliffs that are very hard to climb. How quickly does the game get difficult? Is it smoothly ramping up in difficulty, or does it have dramatic moments with real significance to you?

The pleasure in playing a game is influenced by the structure of the feedback. When you first play a game, the very first thing you encounter is a five-second feedback loop between you and the computer, based on the control structure. The controls must be understandable to get you past that first potential barrier, and have to be fun to use or you will lose interest in the game. At each one of these interaction loops, you may succeed or fail. Once you succeed at the first feedback loop of five seconds, you can start playing at the next loop, which takes longer than a minute. Once you are successful at that one, then you can go to the next one, and so on:

> Frequently the really important thing for the designer to concentrate on is not the success side of these interactions, but the failure side. If you can make failure a big part of the entertainment value of the game, people get a blast out of it. You look at kids playing with blocks; they build a tower and it falls over and they laugh, and they build it again and it falls over. At some point, if they build it and

they run out of blocks, they'll knock it over on purpose. This is designing the playability of the game.

Look at Pac-Man for example. With Pac-Man you come up to the machine, and you have buttons, and you start pressing the buttons. Very quickly you learn the mapping between the buttons and the movement of your character on the screen. If you haven't learned that, the rest of the game is going to be unplayable to you, but you learn it very quickly. Then you learn that these guys are chasing you and if they touch you, you die. Now you know how to move, and you know that these guys are going to eat you. Then you're starting to play the game a little bit longer and you're able to avoid the guys, and the next thing you notice is, "Well, I'm not going to progress anywhere until I eat all these dots." At each one of these stages success buys you access to the next level of game play. When you're playing the game, you're using all three of those overlaid. I'm moving the guy with my skill of pushing the buttons; at the same time I'm avoiding the bad guys trying to eat me, and thirdly I'm trying to eat all the dots while doing the first two things.

With a game like The Sims, the very first level is, "How do I make my character move around and interact with objects?" You learn that you click on an object, and it comes up with a menu and you select an item. Then once you know that you can move your character around and interact with objects, you start noticing that they have needs. They need to go to the bathroom, they need to eat, and they need to have social interaction with other characters. Each of those has a failure state; if they don't eat, they'll starve to death; if they don't go to the bathroom, they'll soil the carpet. At that point you start learning to keep all of the needs in the green. Once you've done that, you've actually bought some free time, so you can start pursuing the economics of the game. Every game has these overlapping loops of interaction. We're mapping these complex things into your instincts and your intuition.

- Gardening analogy
- Train-set analogy

Every game that Will Wright has created seems to have combined an academic and a metaphoric inspiration. SimCity was triggered by Jay Forrester's theories about urban dynamics and came to life with mixed metaphors of elaborate train sets and gardens:

Most people, when I tell them that SimCity is really about gardening, they understand it, but they've never thought about it. In fact you're tilling the soil, you're planting the seeds, and wonderful things pop up, and you have to weed the garden. The process of playing SimCity really maps much more to a garden than it does to a train set.

The Sims combines the inspiration of Christopher Alexander's *Pattern Language* with the metaphor of the doll's house. Will uses the metaphors to help his thinking flow, and also believes that the result makes the players more comfortable with the process of playing the game, although they may not realize it at the time.

New technology dictates limitations and opens opportunities for game designers. Computer graphics capabilities have dominated the industry in the past, but as the visual possibilities approach realistic appearance, the balancing qualities of motion and sound design will be more significant. Competition has been driven by the development of the technology for the highest frame rate, the graphics cards, and chips. We are now to the point where you can buy a $200 or $300 console with the processing power that only military flight simulators had twenty years ago. Now the weakest element is much less likely to be graphic and much more likely to be behavioral, so the behavioral technologies are going to be a big focus over the next ten years.

Will sees the augmentation of reality as a significant opportunity and possible next step for the industry:

> The heads-up display thing just never went anywhere, and I think you have to actually try one out to realize why. In fact the immersion is less complete using these things than it is in a dark room, at a high frame rate, with DOOM on your computer in front of you.
>
> Now I think that the augmented reality idea has potential. This is the idea that there are computer overlays on top of the real world. For example, I might be wearing a set of glasses that can project computer images, and mix them with the real world.
>
> I can imagine something, probably more like fifteen or twenty years out, where you have two kids wearing these things, and they're out playing in the dirt. They're talking to each other, and all of a sudden, little army men appear in the dirt running around having battles. The kids are playing in the real world, but with this computer partner helping their imagination. So the two kids are saying, "I'm

> going to have a fort here, my fort's over here; I just sent five guys down that hill." In fact both kids are seeing the five guys running down. It's a shared point of imagination for the two kids, so that their two imaginations run in sync. The computer in that sense is a third playmate. If you look at little girls playing with a dollhouse, that's pretty much what they're doing; they're saying, "This'll be the mummy, this'll be the daddy, let's have this happen," so they're both building up this whole other world through their imagination that's overlaid on the actual artifact of the doll house.

What can we learn about designing interactions from Will Wright? First we can learn about how to play. Games only survive if they are enjoyable, a characteristic that is sadly missing from so much interactive software. We can learn from Will's explanation of how to engage the imagination of the players and build in a series of experiences that make them successful a little bit at a time, while keeping the path toward another step visibly open. We can learn that the controls must be fun to use, so that you can immediately understand how to use them but can also feel yourself improving as you practice and gain skill. There needs to be a path from inexperienced to expert that allows you to gain fluency and the rewards of skill without having to stop on the way and start again. This usually involves controls that have a direct effect on the outcome, like a steering wheel or joystick, but could possibly be more cryptic and mysterious, like a typewritten instruction or numeric code, if the context of the game makes the indirect quality part of the play.

These questions of engagement, feedback, and controls are all about designing the game right. What about designing the right game? This is where Will's patient perseverance and thoughtful analysis are so unique. He shows us how to think strategically about how to position ourselves in the overall landscape of play and how our design should relate to the other designs that are around it. He shows us how inspiration from academic curiosity and research can inspire an idea of what the next right thing can be. Whether it's Jay Forrester's urban dynamics or James Lovelock's Gaia hypothesis, you can feel how these abstract ideas inform his approach to the design, while at the same time giving him great pleasure in discovery. He ferrets out these authorities because he is fascinated by the subject matter, and uses his creativity to capture the qualities of ideas that will be relevant for his game.

He also shows us how to use a simple metaphoric idea to retain a focus on what is right. The ideas of gardening for SimCity and doll's houses for The Sims are used to test each new notion for the qualities that define the right game. Coming up with these simple ideas in the first place is in itself a form of synthesis that can feel like a creative leap, but is probably formed from a complex subconscious set of experiences and intuitions. The ability to do this well is a mark of a great designer.

We can also learn about the pleasures of designing code, the software that makes the game exist. Will reveals his delight in a good algorithm when he describes the beauty of unraveling many possibilities from the simplest of structures:

> One of the real measures of a beautiful game design, I mean the aesthetics of the design itself, goes back to the question of emergence. You ask yourself, "What is the simplest possible system that I can build, that for you is going to decompress into the most elaborate set of possibilities?"
>
> I'm compressing a large set of possibilities down into a few algorithms of computer code. When I hand you that computer code and you start running it, you can then decompress it in your play experience to this rich set of possibilities. If your experience is very unique relative to another player and very meaningful to you, but still based on this very simple rule structure that I built—that to me is aesthetic elegance in game design.

6

Services

Interviews with Takeshi Natsuno, Live | Work (Chris Downs, Ben Reason, and Lavrans Løvlie), and Fran Samalionis

Main Menu
IM
Messaging
iTunes
MEdia Net
MEdia Mall
My Account
My MEdia
Address Book
Exit
Select
cingular
Janet Smith
480-555-2323
Speed No.82#(P)
Category: General
468 Cedar St.
Shady Dell, AZ
Back
Edit
cingular

You are what you use . . . not what you own

Slogan from Live|Work Web site[1]

THE TELEPHONE SERVICE is one that many of us take for granted, having used it every day for most of our lives. But is it designed? Everything is designed in the sense that someone decides how to do something or make something, and that set of decisions is developed into a recipe or a prescription for doing and making. For services, the development of the prescription has until recently been thought of as a marketing and training function rather than a design function. Now services are becoming more and more enabled by technology, and that means that they have to be designed by an interdisciplinary team, just like products that contain technology.

■ Modern cell phone service—menu and address book

Photos
Nicolas Zurcher

A modern cell phone is a good example of a service where design decisions are making the difference between success and failure. The evolution of telephones is used to illustrate the design of services, starting out with a contrast between early phone services and modern ones. Takeshi Natsuno, managing director in charge of strategy for the *i-mode* cell phone service from DoCoMo in Japan, explains the phenominal success of his venture. A cautionary tale is included about the difficulties encountered when trying to operate a vending machine with a cell phone using the *i-mode* service.

In the rest of the chapter, the three young founders of the London-based service design consultancy Live|Work explain their philosophy and process for designing services, and Fran Samalionis, a leader of the service design practice at IDEO, expands on this process with examples.

The Phone in the Hall

THE INTERACTIONS NEEDED to make a call were simple in the early days of telephony. You walked into the hall and found the phone hanging on the wall, between the hat stand and the mirror with the gilded frame. The earpiece was connected by a thick woven cord, and was hanging on a hook-switch made of metal, which was spring-loaded to click upwards and make the connection to the line as soon as you lifted it. You pressed it against your ear with one hand, while you rotated the handle of the ringer a few times with the other hand to get the attention of the operator, speaking into the mouthpiece on the front of the phone.

"Could you connect me to Mrs. Smith in Shady Glen, please?"

"One moment please: is that the Mrs. Smith on Main Street or on Cedar?"

"Cedar, please."

"Thank you. The phone is ringing now."

These interactions were simple enough, so that it was not very complicated or difficult to design them satisfactorily. The physical design of the phone supported some of the interactions. It was satisfying to turn the handle of the ringer, differentiating between routine and urgent by the speed and duration of the rotations. You could hear well because the earpiece was big enough to allow the dished shape to seal over your ear. The horn-shaped mouthpiece collected the sound waves from your voice, and the hook-switch was shaped to invite you to hang the earpiece up on it again when you had finished your call. The service was defined, and thus in a sense designed, by training the operator to respond politely to customers, to know how to deal with emergencies or errant behavior, to make the connections by plugging jacks into the patch board, and to connect to the long-distance operator.

■ Telephone for operator-assisted phone service

Photo
Ryan McVay

A Modern Cellular Phone Service

CONTRAST THIS WITH using your cell phone in the new millennium. If you want to talk to Mrs. Smith in Shady Glen, you may have her name and number in the address list in you phone, in which case you can look up her number and then dial it. Here is an example of how that works:

Turn on the phone, wait for it to boot, go to menu, select "contacts," choose "find contact," thumb 7 four times to enter the first letter of her name, s, *scroll to "Smith on Cedar," select, and send.*

If you know the number, you can dial it yourself.

Turn on the phone, wait for it to boot, enter the seven digits on the numeric keypad, and send.

If you want to find the number through a human operator, you can do it, for a price, by dialing the number for assistance. Alternatively you could look the number up on the Web-based listing, connecting to the Internet through your phone; the interaction sequence is too long and complex to list here in detail, making it not surprising that most people never get to the point where they can take advantage of the browser access features on their phone. A typical cell phone has options for messaging, music, games, organizer functions, personal preferences, as well as phone book, calls and Web-based services, supported by an instruction manual of around a hundred pages.

The cell phone itself is a little technological miracle in the palm of your hand, complete with high-resolution color display, an array of buttons, a pointing device, electronic circuitry and storage, main and backup batteries, transmitter and receiver. The design of the interactions is based on a confusing hierarchy of overlapping systems. Each call is supported by the infrastructure of the network of cells, as well as the overall telephone system of lines, exchanges, optical networks, microwaves, and satellites.

Ideally all of this should be transparent to the user who just wants to make a call, but in practice it often becomes annoyingly visible. The service provider is designing an offering in a competitive environment, leading to an escalating range of features that soon become impossibly complex. The service provider is separate from the handset vendor, as the handsets take longer to develop than the services and are more intimately linked to the electronic behaviors of the input and output devices and the chips that drive them. Once you connect to Web-based services, each individual site or service that is accessible through the phone has interactions that are designed by separate teams of people. They try to provide a version of their offering to fit the scale of the interactions that work well on the phone, but they often do this with very little knowledge of the details of the interactive capabilities of the cell phone. With all this complexity in play, it is not surprising that the modern cell phone is difficult to use.

Development of Phone Services

The telephone grew up as a consumer product, with the design driven by the simple goal of allowing one person to connect to another. In the early days, the service providers increased their revenue most effectively by attracting new customers, so the interactions were designed to be simple and easy to learn, facilitated by human operators. As time went on, people formed the habit of using the phone, and feature-creep set in. First there was the rotary dial, so you had to find out the numerical address of the person you wanted to talk to. Then push-button dialing arrived, and it was possible to add features accessed through the star and hash keys, such as voice mail access and conference calling. Although business phones soon became blindingly complicated, sporting banks of autodial buttons and lots of intricate functions, the phones at home stayed reasonably simple for a long time. ATT was very successful at habituating their customers, using a strategy of keeping local calls free, so that kids were used to making long and frequent calls to their friends before they left home and started to pay for long distance. In a typical American family, the phone was almost always being used when the kids were at home. Contrast this with Britain, where every second is paid for, and parents limited their spending by forbidding the use of the phone; when the phone rang, it was probably because someone had died.

The phone left its tether behind with cellular services, and competition between providers became much more confused. Sometimes it was based on performance, sometimes on price, and sometimes on features. Complexity jumped up a notch with the *i-mode*[2] service in Japan, which went from zero to 33 million subscribers in only three years. The service offered Internet access on the phone, with interactions that, though not very easy to learn, were mastered by teenagers as well as adults with enough patience; many Japanese people have long commutes in crowded trains, with time to puzzle over the interactions with screens and button pushes, but where it is too embarrassing to talk out loud. This was paralleled by the use of short message service (SMS) in Europe, dubbed "texting," and instigated first in Finland by Nokia. It is amazing to watch the young expert users of phones, whether in Tokyo or Helsinki, typing words deftly with their thumbs on a ten-key numeric pad. They are the elite operators of modern telephones, leaving most of us in a fog of confusion, condemned to simplistic numeric dialing.

There is very exciting potential for a personal communication service that handles voice, data, images, and eventually video. For now, the designs are struggling to leap from the enthusiast phase to the consumer phase, without the intervening professional phase to sort things out. There is confusion at several levels in the service hierarchy, as the technology evolves. The industry feels a bit like the computer business did before the desktop emerged as a standard design approach.

In 2005 we are seeing a competitive collision between PDAs[3] and cell phones, as the PDAs add telephone functionality, and the cell phones include many of the functions of the PDA, with access to the Internet becoming standard for both platforms. The design of the interactions for the PDA has evolved from the PC, adapted to accommodate miniaturization, while the design of the interactions for the cell phone has evolved from simple calls, adapted to add functions. The PDA is easier to use, but fewer people own them, so the telephone platform is starting to dominate in spite of the challenges posed by the interaction design.

Within the telephone platform there are still widely different standards and layers of complexity. The basic difficulty is that the layered structure takes away the possibility of creative control from a single source. The underlying layer is the infrastructure, but that is fragmented by the contributing technologies; cellular networks, microwaves, satellites and so on supplement landlines of many types and speeds. Next is the handset layer, with the individual instruments containing displays and speakers for output and buttons and microphones for input. There is not yet a standard way of arranging these interactive elements, so the designs vary widely in ease of use and speed of learning. On top of that are the layers of the service providers, both the phone service itself, and the data access services for messaging, email, and all of the Web-based services. Each of these data access layers is hoping to find customers across more than one service provider, so the interactions are at best a compromise between the user interfaces on the various service providers, and at worst completely new and different. The Web access layer also suffers from the scalability problem, as the interaction design is a scaled-down version of a Web-based service that was initially designed for normal, computer-sized screens and keyboards. Only a few of the Web-based services design a special version of their interaction for the phone-based display and control limitations.

All of this complexity makes for phone services with bad interaction design, and there are great opportunities as well as challenges in designing phone services that people can enjoy and learn quickly.

STARBUCKS COFFEE

Designing the *i-mode* service

THERE IS A PEDESTRIAN plaza outside Shibuya station in Tokyo. It is flanked on one side by the railway line and on the other by a star-shaped convergence of roads. The surfaces of all of the surrounding buildings are obscured by an endless array of brightly illuminated, mostly animated signs. Five jumbo screens are playing different advertisements and music videos at the same time, with the sound tracks blaring a cacophonous combination that blends into the roar of busses and taxis passing in front of you and the buzz of conversation of people around you. Several thousand people are waiting patiently on the plaza for the traffic lights to change and the traffic to stop. At that moment, the main mass of humanity surges across the roadway in a solid wave heading for the sidewalks on the other side, but there are also some who cut diagonally across toward a different street, moving swiftly and purposefully, like shooting stars. On the station side of the plaza sits a bronze dog, with front legs splayed and hind legs folded, looking attentive and eager in the permanent freeze of statuary. The dog is the meeting point where you can wait for your friends before heading into the narrow streets of Shibuya to eat, shop, or perform your best karaoke song.

■ Shibuya crossing

Photo
Author

As you wait, you notice that most of the people around you are using their cell phones, but only a few are actually talking to someone else. Most of them are holding the phone in front of them, looking at the screen and pressing the buttons—some with fingers of their other hand, and some single-handedly with their thumbs. A man is looking up train times, a girl is checking what's on at a cinema, and two boys are each holding their phones in front of them, playing a game with each other as competitors. The chances are that they are using the *i-mode* service from NTT DoCoMo, giving them access to Internet-based services as well as messaging and normal cell phone use.

More than a quarter of the total population of Japan subscribes to the *i-mode* service, an amazing success story for a service that is only a few years old. How was the service designed to succeed so dramatically? What makes people want it and recommend it to their friends?

Keiichi Enoki and Mari Matsunaga

THE ENTREPRENEURIAL LEADER of *i-mode*, behind the scenes at NTT DoCoMo, is Keiichi Enoki. He had established his reputation as an outstanding leader within NTT by the nineties and in 1997 was given the task of starting a new mobile phone service by the company president Koji Oboshi, who went on to become chairman. The idea was originally suggested to the president by McKinsey, the business consulting company, and a McKinsey team stayed with the program as external advisors. Oboshi-san took the unusual step of asking Enoki to start a completely new venture, appointing him as general manager of the Corporate Sales Department of a business that did not yet exist, and asking him to find and hire his own team, both from within and outside NTT. In the West we would call this a "spin-out," where the mother company keeps the ownership by providing the venture capital but gives the appointed leader enough freedom to escape the weight of the corporate structure and culture of the parent. This allows the kind of startup behavior that is so fertile for innovation, with a small team of dedicated individuals who are highly motivated to succeed and able to take advantage of the money and technology of the parent, without being encumbered by large size and a complex history.

■ Keiichi Enoki and Mari Matsunaga

In those days, the market for mobile phone services in Japan was assumed to be only for business people, but Enoki-san had a vision of a much larger opportunity based on observing the behavior of his own son and daughter and their friends. His daughter Kyoko was a high school student with a passion for email. She was always exchanging email with her friends, even itching to check her messages during family meals. Her father wondered what it was that engaged her so strongly. His son Ryo was in junior high and never needed to refer to the instruction manual when he got a new video game or program for the computer. Enoki wanted to create a service that would be valuable and accessible to everyone rather that just targeting the businessman. He expressed his vision as designing the service so that "even children will use it!"

The first task was to put together the perfect team for the new venture. He advertised the available positions inside NTT DoCoMo, and forty people applied. He was looking for individuals with the right background and skills who would respond to new challenges as well as working well under stress. Helped by McKinsey he set up "stress" interviews with twenty-four of the candidates, to test their response to pressure situations, and selected five people with business and technical backgrounds, two of them in their early twenties. This rigorous interviewing process helped Enoki form his ideas about what the new service should be like, as he was forced to answer questions from the applicants, and as he went along found himself more and more confident about his answers.

His vision became clearer: the service should appeal to young people and amateurs as well as people with jobs and commutes. He could see that there would be new opportunities to achieve this if messaging and Internet access could enhance the normal phone service, but it would have to be designed in a way that would appeal to impatient youngsters and technophobic adults. None of the people he had found inside NTT DoCoMo would find it easy to think about the nature of content and services that might have this appeal, so he decided to look outside. That was when he thought of bringing in Mari Matsunaga, who knew how to make magic with very few words in a classified employment ad.

Mari Matsunaga has been dubbed "the mother of *i-mode*" by the Japanese press and was recognized as "Asia's Most Powerful Businesswoman" in 2000 by *Fortune* magazine, for her contribution to the success of the business. She has a combination of panache and drive that has allowed her to break through the gender barrier and achieve popularity and recognition as a leader and entrepreneur. She graduated from Meiji University with a degree in French literature and joined Recruit, the company that owns and runs a multitude of magazines full of classified ads. She served as chief editor of magazines such as *Employment Journal* and *Travail*, and honed the art of communicating meaningful messages with very few words—a skill that would become of crucial importance in the confined space of the screen on an early cell phone. She is a member of Japan's Tax Advisory Council and appears regularly on TV shows. She has written a delightful book about the development of *i-mode*.[4]

Enoki-san arranged a dinner meeting with her through a mutual friend, and after a few minutes of small talk came straight to the point, asking her directly to join his team to take responsibility for the information content that would appear on the small screen. Mari was shocked by such a direct request. She had no love for mobile phones, thinking of them as an "electronic chain" around the neck of the user and the cause of many interrupted meals and social occasions. She was a notorious innovator, however, and enjoyed new challenges every few years. She had been at Recruit for more than twenty years and was finding it increasingly difficult to find new motivation there. Enoki-san was a persistent suitor, following up the day after their dinner with a card of a Van Gogh painting and the message, "Please work with me." The next time they met, he told her about his children and the inspiration that they gave him for innovation in his new venture. She responded with a suggestion for a part-time assignment that would allow her to contribute without leaving her job at Recruit permanently, but he insisted, "If you decide to join us, I want you to come over to DoCoMo officially and be totally committed to the business." She was fascinated by the design challenge of trying to create a new medium that would appeal to young people within the narrow limits of a tiny screen. The challenge combined with Enoki-san's vision and determination made her decide to join the team and lead the development of content in July 1997.

■ *The Birth of i-mode*, by Mari Matsunaga

In her book she describes some of the most significant events in the design of the interactions for the new service. For example, she demanded a display with eight characters across and six lines, to allow the display of a calendar for both weekdays and month views. This was technically challenging both for feasibility and cost, as at that time cell phones had two line displays showing phone numbers and the time of day. She suggested that an *i-mode* button be added to give direct access to the Internet. She also encouraged the inclusion of a shorthand of iconic characters, equivalent to our "emoticons." There are now more than 180 icons as well as the normal characters in the alphabet. Each icon shows a message—the heart mark, for example, to send a message of love and the smiling icon to show that you are happy. High school students had been using icons on pagers and SMS before the development of *i-mode*, so Mari thought that they would appeal to young people. The difference from the other phone service providers was that they mandated these icons to all the handset vendors.

The *i-mode* dream team was coming together well, but there was still a gap in expertise about the business opportunities for Internet-based services. Enoki-san had originally expected to start with SMS and then gradually migrate to Internet-based services, but the SMS business had grown explosively in Japan, leaving no room for a new service in that market. That meant that they would need to succeed with Internet-based services right from the start and expertise in that area would be essential. Mari Matsunaga had taken Takeshi Natsuno under her wing when he was a student intern at Recruit and knew that he had the right expertise, so she got in touch. He immediately saw the potential and was instantly an enthusiast. He remembers the conversation:

> When I was in a management meeting in my startup in 1997, I suddenly got a phone call from Matsunaga-san. She told me, "Now I will quit my company and I will join NTT DoCoMo."
>
> My response was, "What are you talking about? You are not like the people at NTT. NTT is a symbolic company as traditional, conservative, noncreative telecom people, so why have you decided to do so?"
>
> She replied, "I don't know what kind of things I can do, but it seems to be very, very interesting and fun. I don't know the detail because it's too technical."
>
> I felt that this was very interesting. She told me a little bit about what she was told by the NTT guys, and it was really exciting. If I could combine my ideas about Internet services with the power of the cellular phone, the success possibility would be very high. So after a long talk with Enoki-san, who was, and still is, the leader of this *i-mode* project, I finally decided to join NTT DoCoMo.

Next, Takeshi Natsuno tells the story of the development of the *i-mode* service.

Takeshi Natsuno

Takeshi Natsuno met Mari Matsunaga when he was a student intern at Recruit, while studying political science and economics at Waseda University. He was already facile with computers at that time, inventing ways of compiling mailing lists of Recruit readers and automating the production of address labels. When he graduated he joined Tokyo Gas, a very traditional energy company, and worked in city planning. This taught him about the basic theory of city and infrastructure planning. He was an excellent worker, both diligent and ingeniously innovative, and the company identified him as a potential leader. They sent him to the United States to study at the Wharton Business School in the University of Pennsylvania. "I learned a lot at Wharton about how to apply the Internet to the real business. If I didn't go to Wharton, you don't see *i-mode* right now! I learned a lot about the Internet even before the launch of Yahoo, even before the commercialization of Netscape. What is the business potential of the Internet itself? I don't care about the technological possibility, but more about the business opportunities." When he graduated and returned home, he realized that not many people in Japan understood how to make the Internet useful for real business. This provided an irresistible temptation for his entrepreneurial instincts, so in 1996 he left Tokyo Gas to start up a new Internet business. His idea was to offer free Internet access funded by advertising. This was before Internet service providers (ISPs) became commonplace, and it was too early to succeed, making him willing to try the *i-mode* experiment.

Takeshi Natsuno

We have successfully introduced the Internet way of thinking rather than the telecoms way of thinking to implement this service.

Takeshi Natsuno, April 2002

The *i-mode* Service

■ Examples of *i-mode* phones

top left
First generation

top right
Second generation

bottom left
Third generation

bottom right
Fourth generation

Photos
Author

TAKESHI NATSUNO JOINED the team and worked through the business issues that were facing the fledgling new division, now separate from the rest of the company and called the "Gateway Business Division." He prepared a business plan, outlining the potential of the concept, emphasizing the importance of choosing the right content to be available from the Internet, and proposing a strategy for attracting potential information providers:

> The history of implementing *i-mode* was not so easy. First we started to recruit talented people, but even with these talented people, still the toughest thing I had to overcome was how to migrate these people to the Internet way of thinking from the legacy way of thinking, because you see before we introduced *i-mode* service, we have been so accustomed to voice business, which is totally telecom business. In the voice business you don't have to worry about the third-party players, because you can just create these handsets, and set up tariff, and sell it to subscribers; that used to be the business. After the introduction of the service to access the content through

> the Internet, we need support from the Internet community, otherwise, we couldn't have any kind of content, and in this network service, content is king. Without content, subscribers cannot understand what is the benefit of this *i-mode* service.
>
> To set up a win-win relationship with our content providers, which means third-party guys outside of our community was very, very important, and I started to set up a business model to make them profitable, finally leading to our profitability. My biggest mission was to find third-party content providers. I adjusted our technology to accommodate the third-party guys; I adjusted my business model to accommodate them, and I adjusted our marketing activities to their benefit. That was the essence of the *i-mode* introduction, and the small thing we can do as operators was how to design terminals, handsets, how to make the branding. These things were totally up to us, so we made our heavy, heavy effort how to make phones cute enough, attractive enough to all the ordinary people rather than techy guys. That's why the phones from us are very sophisticated, with rich capabilities to show content; all these things are very important to make our third-party communities happier and happier. That means our subscribers will be happier and happier, and that finally means they will pay more money to us.

■ Cover of *i-mode Strategy* by Takeshi Natsuno

Enoki-san initially intended to develop a service that was more like SMS in Europe, as that was already proving to be successful in Japan, so the first business plan was based on using the SMS infrastructure to deliver information as well as messages. This turned out to be limited by scant network resources, as SMS was already booming, so a new approach was needed. In August 1997 the engineers proposed using the Internet. Takeshi was an enthusiastic supporter of this direction, as he saw the possibility of leveraging the huge existing network of information providers. The challenge would be to persuade them to develop scaled-down versions of the information that they provided, redesigned to fit the limitations of the small screens on the cell phones:

> When we started our project in 1997 there was no WAP. I thought that if I can use HTML, that is the best, and only if I cannot use HTML I should find a different standard. Even at that time I got proposals from startups in the United States to use different markup languages, but I thought, "Why do you need that?"

The very, very important lesson we learned is that a de facto standard is very different from a de jure standard. For the telecom industry, to set up a de jure standard is usual business. De jure standard is to decide something as a standard and then use it. De facto standard is to choose a dominant technology from a set of possible technologies. One technology would dominate and be very popular in comparison to other technologies. That is a de facto standard, so we have to understand the difference. At that time, we were told from other people, "You are using proprietary technology," but the reality was, and now it's proven, that we were something different from the other companies inside the wireless industry, but in the Internet industry, we were the de facto standard, and they were something different. This is comparing the small fish and the big fish, and the big fish and the whales. In reality we were not proprietary.

After the decision to go with HTML was confirmed, Takeshi developed a business model for a balanced collection of content providers. Rather than thinking about the details of the content itself, he set up a content portfolio:

The meaning of content portfolio is simple. I wanted to set up an image of what the design of the service itself should look like. To have a variety of content does not necessarily mean a simple image, or design of the service to end users, so to have some message as a product, as a service, or design of the service, I started to write up a content portfolio. By having this content portfolio, I can balance which part would be weaker, which part would be stronger, and which part we should persuade more. We cannot create content by ourselves, so managing our content portfolio would give a target for us.

He set up four different categories for the content portfolio, and then the difficult work of persuasion started:

I set up four different categories, naming first e-commerce as transactive content; second, information-based content; third, database-based content, and fourth, entertainment-based content. As I got agreements from the companies, I listed their name into this content portfolio. By taking one and a half years, I got support from 67 companies and I started *i-mode* service on February 2, 1999. At that time to have 67 content providers was remarkable, but already

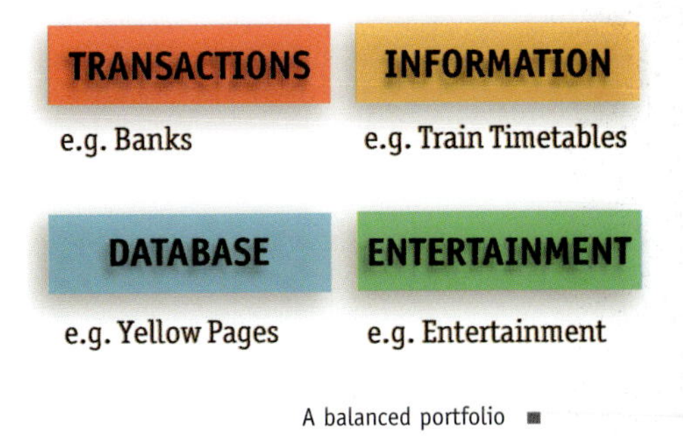

A balanced portfolio ■

now I have more than 2,000 official content partners, and more than 50,000 independent content providers, so now nobody will say 67 was enough.

Once the plan for the content portfolio was in place, Natsuno-san became a whirlwind of energy, working to persuade the content providers to commit to the service. He started with the e-commerce companies offering transactions, as he knew that those applications would have a long lead-time. He approached banks, credit card service providers, and security protocol companies. Soon he had ten banks, two airline companies and two e-book stores signed up:

> In terms of the ratio of my content providers at the starting point, transaction content was the richest segment. My method to persuade this e-commerce arena was like this. I started with the banking industry, because I knew that the banking industry was the toughest to be persuaded amongst all of the e-commerce guys. After I got agreements with some of the advanced banks, I went after some of the normal e-commerce guys, like the airline industry and brokerage companies, and e-book stores, city stores, and ticket companies.
>
> I said, "Some banks have already decided to introduce our service, so why do you worry so much about security, when they have already agreed?" In my strategy, if you got some support from the most conservative guy, it's much easier to get support from all other guys.
>
> The entertainment category had different interests. For them to get revenue from the end user was the final goal. I got support from Bandai as the first entertainment provider, but it took me almost six months to get other entertainment industry companies interested, as there were only a small number of subscribers at that time. Six months after the launch I started to persuade entertainment guys by saying, "I already have 1 million subscribers. Why are you not doing any business with us?" So the order [of which category you talk to first] is really, really important.

It was easier to find participants in the database and information content areas, as they already provided Internet-based versions of their products. Newspapers, recipe providers, timetables, and yellow pages companies were all willing converts, as all they had to do was develop algorithms to scale down the content to fit the small screen.

He developed a strategy to offer the potential content providers a guarantee of support, clearly stating that NTT DoCoMo would support their business and would never be competitive:

> I said, "We will focus our efforts on the design of the service, the design of the handset, the design of the user feelings, and the design of the marketing approach." In this way all other people can easily join us. The image of a "concierge" came from discussions with Mari-san and led to the message that we just wanted to make this cellular phone as a very, very nice agent to each person, like a butler. "I just want to make it a satisfactory personal and useful supporting tool for your life." She presented that concept as the image of the concierge.
>
> To realize the really useful and really enjoyable service, the handset design is very important, because the handset can represent your taste. Of course, this is a very technical tool, but at the same time you have to have this tool all the time. That means that you can show your lifestyle by the selection of the handset. What kind of handset you are using and what kind of content you are using reflect some of your life. That's why we are always making a really heavy effort for the tiny details of this handset design. This kind of latch is very important. Feel is very important. The shape, how round it should be, is very important. The little things are very important.

Natsuno is very clear about the business model, where the handset design is only part of the full value chain. It extends from the handset up to the network service, and only then up to the Internet-based content provider. A single company cannot dominate the whole of the value chain. In the case of the *i-mode* service, they are in the middle, unable to create the content, or to design the handset:

> I cannot jump into the world to download Java applications from the network to the phone, but already one tenth of the Japanese population is doing that. Why? They have user experience to download something from the network already, even before the introduction of the *i-mode* Java phone, so I'm always taking care to

"A useful suporting tool for your life!" ■
Details of early *i-mode* phone ■
Details of later model ■

adjust the speed of evolution of each different layer to form the total value chain.

This extended value chain poses a difficult challenge for the service provider. In order to offer a satisfying interactive experience to the customer, they want to influence the parts of the chain, or layers, that are outside their direct control. The most direct experience for the user is in the user interface of the phone itself, and this is where the *i-mode* service development team made great efforts to influence the design. Natsuno describes their achievements, which were surprisingly successful, considering that they were an unproven new service:

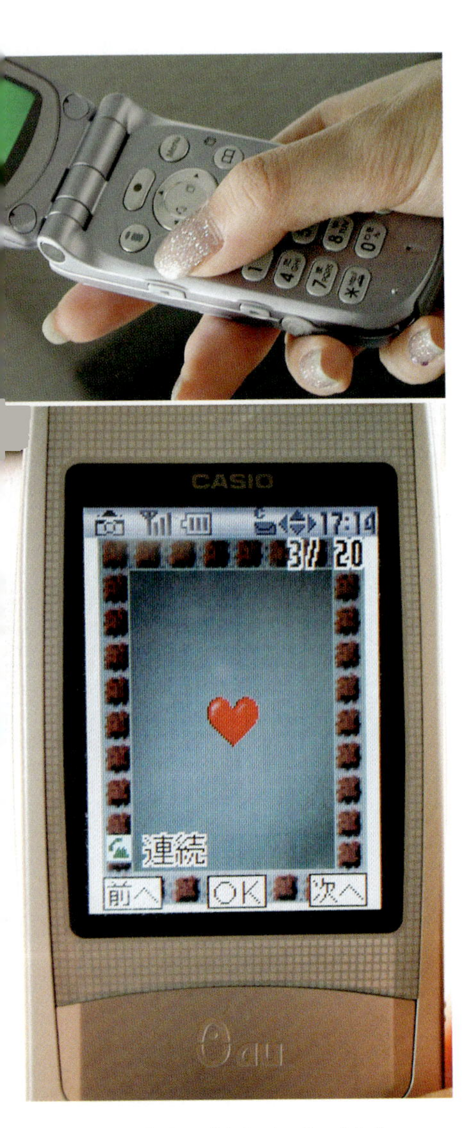

■ Early model showing *i-mode* button
■ Love message

> The user interface of this phone was and is very important. The user interface of the browser and phone should be easy enough for everybody! This is not a PC. Not so many people really read manuals, and even though we have thick manuals with all the phones, and my staff is always working very hard to publish very good manuals, not so many people really read that. The very basic concept of UI development is how to make everything intuitive.
>
> When we first designed *i-mode* phone specifications, we requested our handset vendors to have an *i-mode* button to launch the browser, and four directional keys to navigate in the browser. I don't mandate the circular design for the four keys. Some vendors are using a jog dial, which is fine. I didn't want to limit the creativity of the vendors, so I only provided the minimum specification we should need. All the remaining controls are the same as a simple phone.
>
> Another great feature of *i-mode* was icon-based communication. We developed more than 180 icons, in addition to the normal characters in the alphabet. Each icon shows a message, like the heart mark that always shows you some kind of love message, and the smiling icon shows that you are happy. Even before *i-mode* there was a big boom for high school students to use pagers and short messages over the phone using icons. We thought that without icons we could not get support from very young ladies and young boys and girls, so we took these features into our service. The difference from our competitors was that we mandated these icons to all our handset vendors, so that now 32 million people can communicate with one another using these icons.

As an additional feature, I wanted to make this browser resemble the browser on a PC, with the possibility to use bookmarks or favorites to jump into your favorite Web site; and also you have a cache function in the browser side. In the user experience, the PC browser was not only for the technical people. The Netscape guys and the Microsoft guys really made a heavy effort to make their browser easy to use, so to take advantage as a follower for the wireless industry side from the PC side was a very natural way. The bookmark function, the cache function, and the URL inputting function were all very necessary functions for this phone.

By 2002 Takeshi Natsuno had risen to become managing director of NTT DoCoMo, in charge of *i-mode* strategy. In the first three years of operation, the *i-mode* service grew to more than 33 million subscribers, with 12 million of them being Java phone users. This means that a quarter of the Japanese population was using the service, with one tenth of the population using Java programs on the phone. During the 2001–2002 fiscal year, *i-mode* earned close to $6 billion in revenue. He sums up the reason for this amazing success:

When I first introduced *i-mode* phones, the capability of the phone was just to browse the Web and to send and receive e-mail. With the second generation you started to download color graphics, ringing tones from the network. With the third generation, thanks to Java capability, you can customize the function of your phone to your needs. People customize their phones as karaoke machines: they see the script here and sing a song to practice.

Many people ask me why *i-mode* is so successful and the others are not. We have successfully introduced the Internet way of thinking rather than the telecoms way of thinking to implement this service, and this can be a great message for all the operators in the world and all the industry players in the wireless industry in the world.

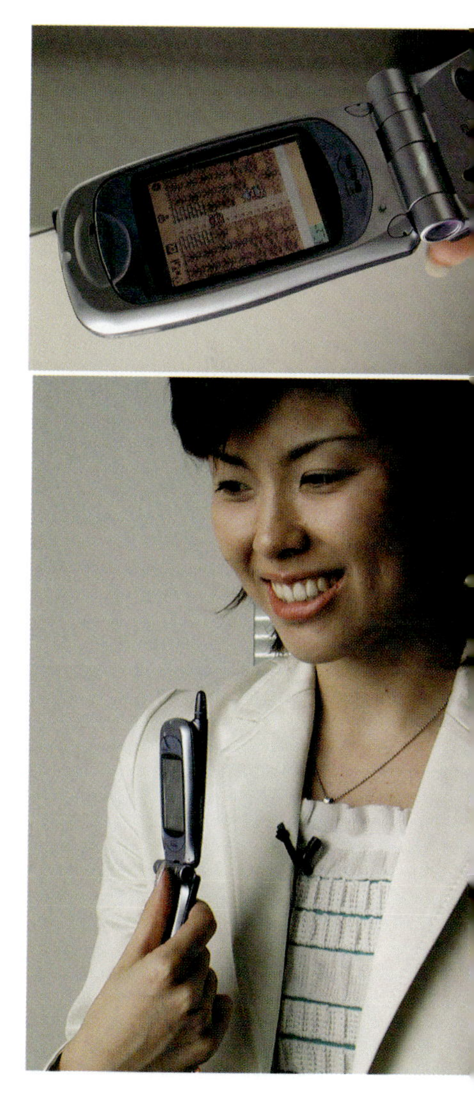

i-mode game ■
Playing downloaded ringing tones ■

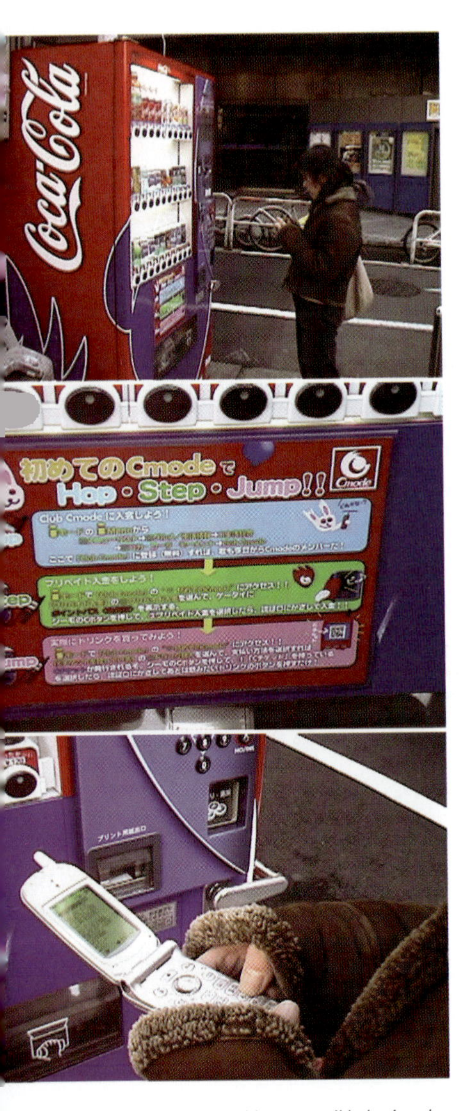

- The drink machine, accessible by *i-mode*
- Instructions with an out-of-date address
- Searching for the new address

A Cautionary Tale of a Soft Drink

CHIHO SASAKI, AN interaction designer and human factors researcher at IDEO Tokyo, had heard about the possibility of using an *i-mode* phone to interact with a vending machine and make a purchase. Without knowing about the upcoming interview with Takeshi Natsuno, she decided to make a test, to find out if the interaction was well designed. On a chilly November morning in 2002, she set out to find a Coca-Cola machine that was offering the *i-mode* service. Chiho took a video camera to record the event, and Kaoru Ishihara came as the observation subject. Kaoru seemed the perfect person, because as office manager, she was responsible for the operation of the computer equipment and was very technologically savvy. Here's what happened:

Minute 1

Kaoru reads the instructions on the front of the Coca-Cola machine, which give a Web site address for the *i-mode* access to Coca-Cola vending machines. She thumbs in the address using her numeric pad to enter the characters.

Minute 2

Unfortunately the address printed on the machine is out of date. Kaoru spends five minutes searching for the new address. She finds it and goes to the site.

Minute 5

When you enter the site, you need to make it a favorite in "my-menu," so that's what Kaoru does. She's shivering a bit in spite of the warm coat and scarf.

Minute 10

The software promises to send a reply message by email, enclosing a barcode for customer identification, which the Coca-Cola machine will be able to read.

Minute 13

Kaoru waits for the email, but there is no sign of it. Then she remembers that she has her junk mail filter on, which could be rejecting it. She goes into her preferences set up and turns off the junk mail filter. No, there's still no sign of the email!

Minute 15

She calls Coca-Cola customer service, using one cell phone to make the call and another to check the email. The customer service agent sends a message, but it is the address of a link site, not the barcode.

Minute 17

The link site asks her to enter her name, address, home address, phone number, *i-mode* address, and birthday. She completes the form.

Minute 21

An email containing a barcode comes through; the excitement warms her up a little! She presses the button on the machine for *i-mode* purchase. The display on the machine asks for a cash deposit to cover the purchase. Then she is asked to put the cell phone up against a window on the machine so that it can read the barcode. Nothing happens! It requests backlight on the cell phone. She turns on the backlight, and it reads the barcode!

Minute 30

She tries again. The machine recognizes the bar code, accepts cash deposit, tells balance, allows purchase and offers receipt. Lights flash. She chooses a hot drink!

This cautionary tale shows a fatal disconnect between the designers of the Coca-Cola *i-mode* service and their customers. Not even the most patient person is willing to wait so long for interactions, even in setup mode. How ironic to be asked to use coins to pay for the account!

Ten minutes have passed ■
You have to laugh ■
Calling customer service ■
The first barcode arrives ■

- Cash deposit needed
- Backlight for phone display requested
- A drink is delivered
- Drink up!

The story illustrates vividly the point that Takeshi Natsuno makes about the telephone service provider only being part of the value chain. NTT DoCoMo has enough influence with their handset vendors to be able to get a single button to access the Internet, but they have very little influence on their content providers. Most telephone service providers around the world are not in a strong enough position to even be able to influence the handset designs, so the chances of implementing a unique interaction design advantage are even less.

The challenges of designing services are mostly about this sort of complexity, where no single organization has direct influence over the entire experience. The best hope for avoiding design failures is that everybody in the various development communities starts to use a process that looks at what people want and need as a first priority.

Next, we meet three young designers who have set out to make the design of services their specialty, by founding a service design consulting firm called Live|Work.

Photo Author

Chris Downs, Ben Reason, and Lavrans Løvlie (*left to right*) of Live|Work

Live|Work is a service innovation and design company based in London. Chris Downs, Lavrans Løvlie, and Ben Reason are the founders and principals. Chris says, "We are children of the Web. Before our generation, interaction designers were dealing with interfaces. We started making Web sites in 1994, so we have our heads wired to think about networks. When you deepen an interaction beyond an interface and think about the network, you eventually end up at the service." Ben had been working as an interaction designer at Razorfish and Oyster in London and Chris and Lavrans were designing Web sites, but they were all so involved with the technical and business aspects of the design solutions that they realized they were designing the whole service. Chris met Lavrans when they were studying for their master's in the interaction design program at the Royal College of Art in London and decided that they shared an interest in designing services, so in the summer of 2001 they boldly set out to form a new kind of design consulting company. They spent long evenings and weekends talking about what service design could and should be and defined a point of view that they could tell people about in conference presentations, teaching in design programs, and on their Web site. They put together some case studies, and started working with Orange, the UK-based cell phone service, and in Italy with Fiat and Telecom Italia, through the Interaction Design Institute Ivrea.[5] A new design discipline was being formed and finding voice. By designing from a service instead of a product perspective, they are promoting use over consumption.

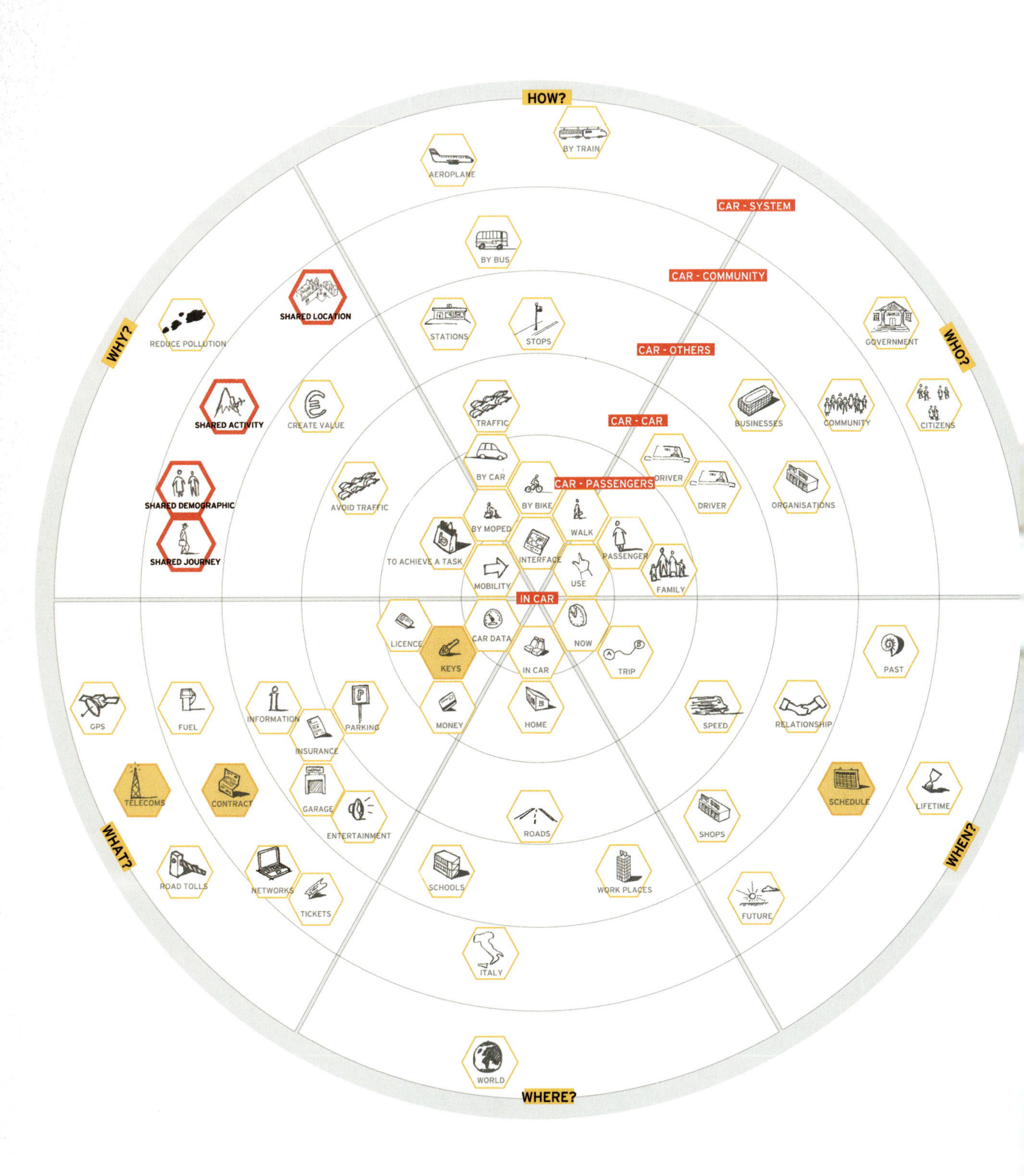
HOW?
WHO?
WHEN?
WHERE?
WHAT?
WHY?
CAR - SYSTEM
CAR - COMMUNITY
CAR - OTHERS
CAR - CAR
CAR - PASSENGERS
IN CAR
BY TRAIN
AEROPLANE
BY BUS
STATIONS
STOPS
TRAFFIC
BY CAR
BY BIKE
BY MOPED
WALK
INTERFACE
MOBILITY
USE
TO ACHIEVE A TASK
AVOID TRAFFIC
CREATE VALUE
REDUCE POLLUTION
SHARED LOCATION
SHARED ACTIVITY
SHARED DEMOGRAPHIC
SHARED JOURNEY
GOVERNMENT
BUSINESSES
COMMUNITY
CITIZENS
DRIVER
DRIVER
ORGANISATIONS
PASSENGER
FAMILY
NOW
TRIP
PAST
SPEED
RELATIONSHIP
SCHEDULE
LIFETIME
SHOPS
FUTURE
CAR DATA
IN CAR
HOME
ROADS
WORK PLACES
SCHOOLS
ITALY
WORLD
LICENCE
KEYS
MONEY
INFORMATION
PARKING
INSURANCE
GARAGE
ENTERTAINMENT
GPS
FUEL
TELECOMS
CONTRACT
ROAD TOLLS
NETWORKS
TICKETS

Live|Work

Starting Live|Work

"Service Ecology" poster for Fiat Multi+ actors

Illustration
Live|Work

When the three founders of Live|Work talk about designing services,[6] they exude an infectious enthusiasm. They think of services as things that people use rather than own, and from that idea they are building a new consulting practice. There is a strong idealism underlying their point of view, as they want to promote use over consumption, and hope to shift the desire for consumption toward the desire for use. To achieve this shift, they believe that government and consumer businesses will have to create future services that surpass the quality and desirability of the products that people own today.

Chris Downs tells the story of putting the company together:

> We started in the summer of 2001. I knew that there was something in these two guys that meant that if the three of us got together something special might happen. We decided that our common interest was designing services. Coming from Web and interaction backgrounds, we were working a lot with new business startups and dot-com companies. We knew that we'd been designing services for

COMMUNITY
BY CAR
NOW
WHO?
HOW?
WHEN?
SHARED
ACCESS
WHY?
WHERE?
WHAT?
SHARED
LOCATION
IN CAR
ACCESS
IF A COMMUNITY SHARES A CAR
IN A PARTICULAR LOCATION
THEN WHAT ACCESS MECHANISM
DO THEY USE TO GET INTO THE CAR?
COMMUNITY
BY CAR
SCHEDULE
WHO?
HOW?
WHEN?
SHARED
TIME
WHY?
WHERE?
WHAT?
SHARED
ROUTE
ON THE ROAD
INFO
IF A COMMUNITY SHARE CARS
BASED AROUND A ROUTE
THEN WHAT INFORMATION IS
USED TO SHEDULE THE JOUR
COMMUNITY
BY CAR
FUTURE
WHO?
HOW?
WHEN?
SHARED
COMMUNICATION
WHY?
WHERE?
WHAT?
SHARED
ACTIVITY
ITALY
TELECOMS
IF A COMMUNITY SHARES MOBILITY
INFORMATION & COMMUNICATION
THEN WHAT IS THE NATURE THIS
FUTURE MOBILITY NETWORK?
COMMUNITY
BY CAR
RELATIONSHIPS
WHO?
HOW?
WHEN?
SHARED
RULES
WHY?
WHERE?
WHAT?
SHARED
DEMOGRAPHIC
SCHOOLS
CONTRACT
IF A COMMUNITY SHARE MOBILITY
BASED AROUND A DEMOGRAPHIC
THEN WHAT RULES MANAGE THE
COMMUNITY REALTIONSHIPS?

the last few of years, but we hadn't really been talking about it. So we said we need to be a "service design" company.

Designing services is something we felt we were already doing, but we didn't have a name for it. No one was saying we were designing services. It was sometimes called a customer experience, but we thought it was slightly deeper than that. Customer experience might only be part of the whole service story. The concept of full service takes into account all the stakeholders, thinking about what the back-end system is having to do, what the motivations of the staff are, and the motivations of the competitors. The customer experience is part of that.

Lavrans Løvlie admits that they were very surprised that they could not find any other service design companies out there to learn from, so they had to spend their first few months trying to decide what services could be in a design context:

> We needed to have a language to speak about services in a native way; we realized that we wanted to have a connection to the academic community, so that we could test our thinking rigorously; and we needed some big clients that would buy service design projects.
>
> We've been building service design from a series of different academic disciplines. We've looked at academic theory about how value-nets operate; we've been drawing on anthropological work from human-computer interaction, and we've taken everything we could from interaction design, and put all this together in what we call "service design."

■ "Service Ecology" poster for Fiat Multi+ relationships

Illustration Live|Work

Four touch-point examples *overleaf*

Ben Reason is keenly aware that services themselves are nothing new, and that in some sense they have been designed as long as they have existed:

> Services have been around for a long time. There's a branch of science and ecology that's talking about Gaia systems as services. People have been starting to understand natural systems as services that are provided to the species that live on the earth's surface. Rivers and seas provide cleaning services for water, the atmosphere provides fresh oxygen services. These things work in a very service-like way in that they're ongoing, and there is a very symbiotic relationship between species.

4 Touchpoints: Multi+Access

IF the Multipla becomes a community vehicle,

THEN users need to be able to personalise their access devices.

Fiat Multi+ How Mobility Services could inform the design of the Fiat Multipla

5 Touchpoints: Multi+Rules

IF the Multipla is used as a service vehicle

THEN there needs to be a mechanism for recording rules.

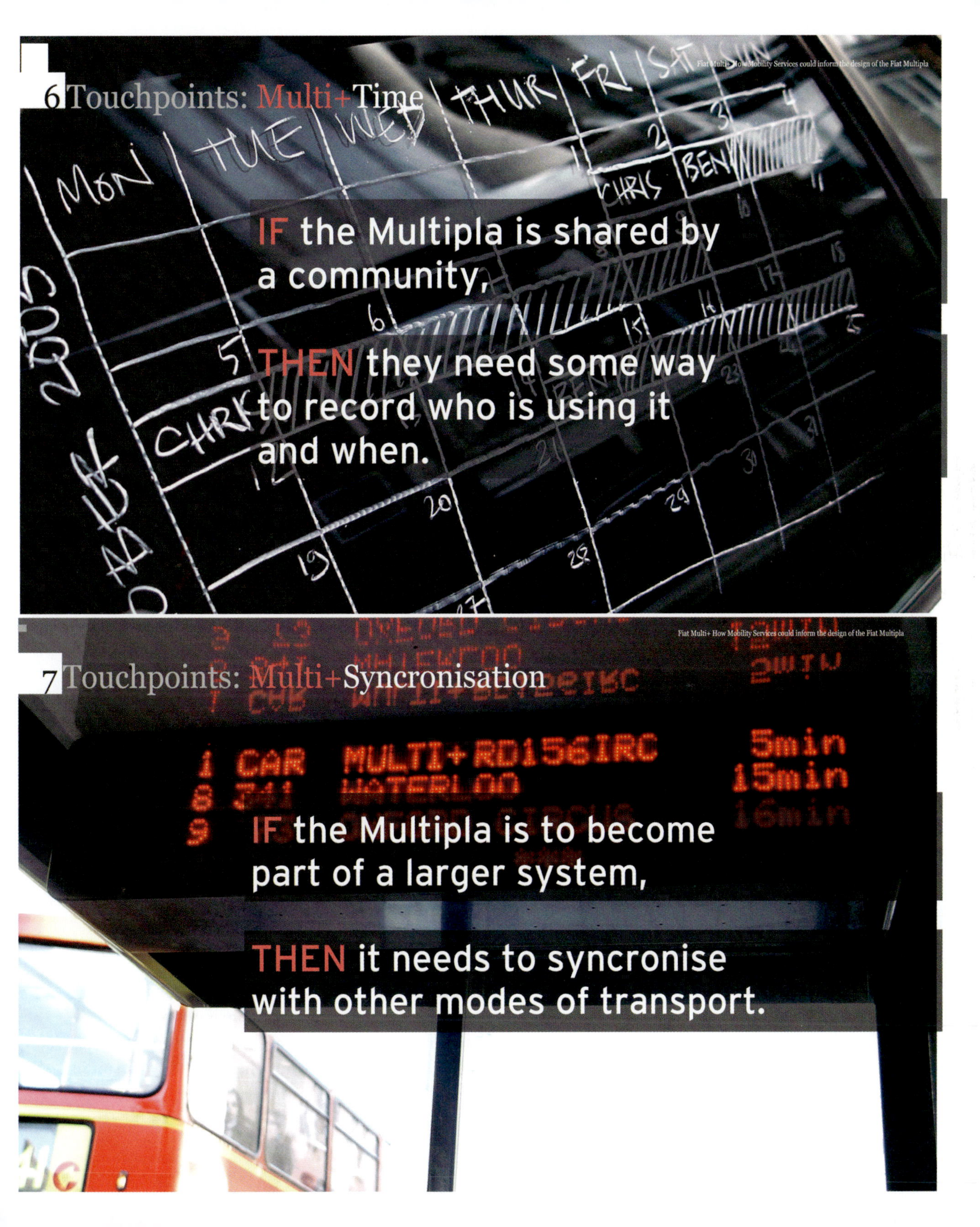
Fiat Multi+ How Mobility Services could inform the design of the Fiat Multipla
6 Touchpoints: Multi+Time
MON TUE WED THUR FRI SAT SUN
CHRIS BEN
IF the Multipla is shared by a community,
THEN they need some way to record who is using it and when.
Fiat Multi+ How Mobility Services could inform the design of the Fiat Multipla
7 Touchpoints: Multi+Syncronisation
1 CAR MULTI+RD156IRC 5min
8 341 WATERLOO 15min
IF the Multipla is to become part of a larger system,
THEN it needs to syncronise with other modes of transport.

I don't think we know much about sustainability in relation to designing products, so I think it would be presumptuous to say that we do for services, but there is a school of thought about services for sustainability. For example, we picked up an economic argument about the responsibility of the provider from *Natural Capitalism*,[7] the book by Paul Hawken, Amory Lovins, and Hunter Lovins. We've been exploring the design edge of that argument and finding out how complex it is, but there's definitely something in terms of the flow value, as a model, in contrast to the consumption of things and waste of things.

Designing Services

WHEN YOU BROWSE the Live | Work Web site, you notice a link to "View the Glossary." Click on it and you find this introduction:

> Service Design is a new mix of existing practices, new terms, current values, and evolved methods and skills founded in the traditional design disciplines. As part of our research, we take part in defining this practice. Here are some of the words we use a lot at the moment . . .

As of May 2004, there were eight terms in the glossary, four of which are concepts about designing services; the other four are keys to the processes employed by Live | Work. The definitions of the terms are included below, supported by comments from the interview with Chris, Lavrans, and Ben.

■ Live|Work Web site

1. Service design

> Service design is the design of intangible experiences that reach people through many different touch-points, and that happen over time.

The value you receive from a service is usually intangible. Try touching your banking service or showing it to other people. Lavrans explains that his ultimate goal is to try to design those intangible things. He feels that the challenge is demanding enough to take a lifetime of effort. Chris responds:

> Yeah, you've defined that challenge pretty well, in that you can't express yourself through your bank account, but you can express yourself through the choice of car you drive. Services are developed. Services are run and operated throughout the world, but they're not often designed. They're not crafted to the same level of expertise that products, interactions, and interfaces are. As designers, we know how to inscribe cultural meaning into objects and interfaces, but we don't know how do inscribe cultural meaning into a service. I'm proud of owning a Rolex watch, but I'm not proud of having a bank account.

2. Service ecologies

> A service ecology is a process we use to establish a systemic view of the service and the context it will operate in. We map service ecologies in order to map the actors affected by a service and the relationships between them, reveal new opportunities and inspire ideas, and to establish the overall service concept. Ultimately, we strive to create sustainable service ecologies, where the actors involved exchange value in ways that are mutually beneficial over time.

The idea of ecology implies a complex system but also has connotations of sustainability. Lavrans explains:

> We all understand we can't produce and use and throw away more and more things—it's just obvious! Services in themselves, since they are not about ownership of stuff but about paying for a value you receive, should be more sustainable. We think service ecology is a good name because like a natural ecology, you can't ever completely analyze it. It's just impossible to count how many leaves are on a tree, but we can try to make some sensible choices about how we can put all these things together.

The complexity of service ecology is well illustrated by a cell phone service, where there are many interdependent providers: the handset manufacturer, the mobile phone operator, and the third-party service providers offering online services. Chris expands on the banking example:

> Service ecology thinking acknowledges multiple partners over time, in a way that a product doesn't. Like ecology, a service relies on value

exchanges between actors in a network. There's a value exchange between a customer and a bank. Understanding that there has to be an equal amount of value in trust, emotion, and intrinsic value in a relationship if it's going to be sustainable. If all I ever give the bank is money, the only thing they'll ever give me back is money, and I therefore assume that banks are only interested in money. If we can find a way of helping people exchange more than money with their banks, they might get something more back.

3. Touch-points

Service touch-points are the tangibles that make up the total experience of using a service. Touch-points can take many forms, from advertising to personal cards, Web interactions, mobile phone and PC interfaces, bills, retail shops, call centers, and customer representatives. When we design services, we consider all touch-points in totality and craft them in order to create a clear and consistent unified customer experience.

The time dimension helps the designer to map and understand the potential touch-points in a service. It helps to think of the analogy of a journey through the service experience and, as Ben explains, the important moments within the journey:

> We have an interesting metaphor of on-ramps and off-ramps to services, so you're not talking about the main road of content flowing through, but how people access it, how they leave it, what they do with it when they're finished with it. It's only when you build up enough touch-points around the service that it starts to feel multidimensional.

Chris thinks of these on-ramps and off-ramps as the transitions between the touch-points within the service:

> Every service has a bill. Every service has an interface. But the way you transition in between those things is where the brand of the service can live; in-between experiences can be designed. As interaction designers, we might design a calendar on a mobile phone. As service designers, we provide the calendar on a mobile phone as one of the touch-points, but we also think about how the customer became aware that the calendar could exist on a mobile phone. We also think about the signing up process, the process of them first

entering their details, and then think about billing and receiving a bill for that service.

4. Service envy

We can think of products as serving two basic needs: to perform the function they are engineered to do, and to confirm and communicate the owner's set of values. The second function is crucial. Products help us identify ourselves through a complex product and brand language. If we want to make people desire services more than products, then services will also have to communicate these values, and we have to create services that help people tell one another who they are. Our major challenge is to enable people to express who they are through the use of services instead of through ownership of things. We must create service envy.

Chris believes that the ability to create service envy should be the ultimate goal for the service designer:

> How do you design a service that people can use, not only obtain the functional benefit of the service, but use the expressive value? How can I express something about my character through the services that I subscribe to? For example, being able to say in the pub, "I fly Virgin!" means something.

live|work

Streetcar:
Creating Service Envy?

5. Evidencing

We often start mapping assumptions about a future service and animate these ideas as tangible evidence; both negative and aspirational futures are embodied as designed touch-points. We focus as much on the effects of possible designs as the design of the service itself. Therefore, evidence can often be a newspaper article describing the results of the service, and other third parties' response to an innovation. This type of "archaeology of the future" enables us to make early qualitative judgments about the implications of a design. Evidencing can be done as a workshop or as more focused production of touch-points. Ultimately it allows customers and collaborators to "play back" their own assumptions as concrete experiences rather than abstract evaluations.

live|work

Orange
Tangible Evidence

Service envy ■
Evidencing ■

Experiences can be enacted, but the communication works much better if the actors are using props that form evidence in the mind of the onlooker. Chris talks about "faking it," by which he means that quick and informal techniques can be used to create the evidence:

> Faking is a state of mind, and it's something we use right across the process. We might fake an advert or we might fake a piece of CCTV footage of somebody using a service as evidence that this service already exists. Faking and evidence are things that we use together quite a lot. We fake bills as evidence that a service exists.

6. Experience prototyping

> How can we prototype the experience of using services that are intangible, may take place over a lifetime and have multiple touch-points, media, and modes? We look at prototypes of a service experience as an equivalent to the way a product or architectural model prototypes the object. We design multiple service touch-points, set the scene, the place and the time of a service experience, and establish a way for participants to suspend their disbelief, in the way that theater is able to temporarily transport an audience. We use experience prototypes to do rapid service prototyping, involving customers, experts, and clients in developing and refining services.

The goal of experience prototyping is to get a very intimate and subjective idea about what the experience of using a service could be. The prototype is experienced over time, and over the network touch-points. Ben emphasizes speed and economy in the techniques that are chosen:

> We came across a great phrase in Italy—"rapido, piccolo, economico"—which is an Italian description of entrepreneurial process. This description matches our ideas for experience prototyping: doing things very fast and as cheaply as possible, like using eBay, as well as small-scale things that you can do immediately; not putting off a project because you don't have a certain piece of equipment that you think you need. For example, when we were working on a project in Italy, we couldn't get the Italian voice interaction prototyping tool that we'd been promised to work, so we ended up using answer phones and pretending we were machines.

7. Service experience models

> For product designers, the model is invaluable as a way to develop, refine, share, and present their designs. Service models represent intangible experiences, and need to employ formats to convey the experience and the functions of the service in an immediate way. They allow us to evaluate the viability of the services qualitatively, as well as sharing the concepts with potential users, colleagues and decision makers. The service models, supported by a business case, will often be the material needed to decide whether a service should go into development, or whether it needs further development, or even shelving.

The concepts of evidencing, faking, and experience modeling all come together in a service experience model. This is the way in which a proposal for the design of a new service can be described, evaluated, and improved through iterative development. Chris emphasizes the techniques that reduce the scale of effort needed to create a convincing model:

> Making services, or faking services, needs a lot of touch-points to be delivered over time, so we have to find a really quick way to build the service experience model, and faking is much quicker than trying to design. If you try and fake a bill, it will take you a lot less time than it would if you tried to design a bill. As a designer, you would be quite precious about the details, but if you're making a forgery, you're more focused on getting the content right and getting it out. So as part of the "rapido, piccolo, economico" process we think about faking stuff, and it really frees us as designers. We don't care so much about the details—we just get it out.
>
> If you set something up as a mock-up or proposal and put it in front of somebody, you're inviting a particular kind of comment. The interaction is already established around the idea that this is a mock-up. If you can fake something so that people believe just enough that it's real, the conversation is about the experience of the object. If I brought to you now a model of a mobile phone that's quite clearly a model, you'd start to tell me that there's a problem with the weight of it, there's a problem with some of the form. If I were to show you a list of SMS messages to and from my thirteen-year-old niece using this mobile phone, we would be more likely to start

talking about the value of mobile telephony; we wouldn't care so much about the details in the object.

8. Service blueprinting

In our definition, a service blueprint describes a service in enough detail to implement and maintain it. The blueprint is used by business process managers, designers, and software engineers during development and works as a guide to service managers that operate services on a day-to-day basis. The blueprint informs service managers about the features and quality of the service, ranging from the flow of use to technical infrastructure and brand management.

The blueprint is the implementation phase of the Live | Work process. Lavrans explains that this is the time to reconnect to the other design disciplines:

> The further you go towards actual market launch, the more you use classical design disciplines, like the details of the form, usability testing, all those things that have to be in place for it actually to come out and be useful and wonderful.

The examples of designs already completed by Live | Work and in the public arena show evidence that they are off to a good start in establishing a service design agency. They have successfully articulated a language and process for the task, made strong ties to academia by teaching at the Interaction Design Institute Ivrea (IDII), and are working for a growing list of clients, as well as the examples shown here from Fiat. The "ShareWay" project shown in the six illustrations that follow was developed as part of their teaching program at IDII.

Fran Samalionis has pioneered the practice of service design at IDEO, both in San Francisco and London. She has collaborated closely with Live | Work on projects and helped them establish their point of view. Next she expands on the service design process, and describes a case study of designing a service for an online bank.[8]

THE SERVICE STAKEHOLDERS ECOLOGIES PROTOTYPING POSTERS

Valentina Novello & Peggy Thoeny - Interaction Design Institute Ivrea (2003)

The SERVICE

SHAREWAY is a free and safe ride-sharing service offered to citizens by local authorities, with the help of other citizens willing to be useful. It provides people living in rural areas or small cities with a new form of mobilitiy.
SHAREWAY is designed to compliment the public transportation system and to offer an attractive alternative to personal vehicles.

The goal is to make local travel easier and more flexible for citizens, both those who want a lift and drivers who suffer from current traffic congestion problems, giving and getting rides in total security.
Therefore, we established strictly followed rules respecting privacy: to subscribe to the service both drivers and passengers have to register, filling the form with their personal data, and have a mobile phone.

This service provides the subscribers with a membership card and a blinking light. Drivers will display the light on their dashboard so that it is visible from the outside, showing their availability to give a ride. Passengers who wish to get a ride will wear the it.

When driver and passenger meet, they will show their cards to each other and will call the service free number to register the ride, dialing on their mobile phones the id numbers written on each card.

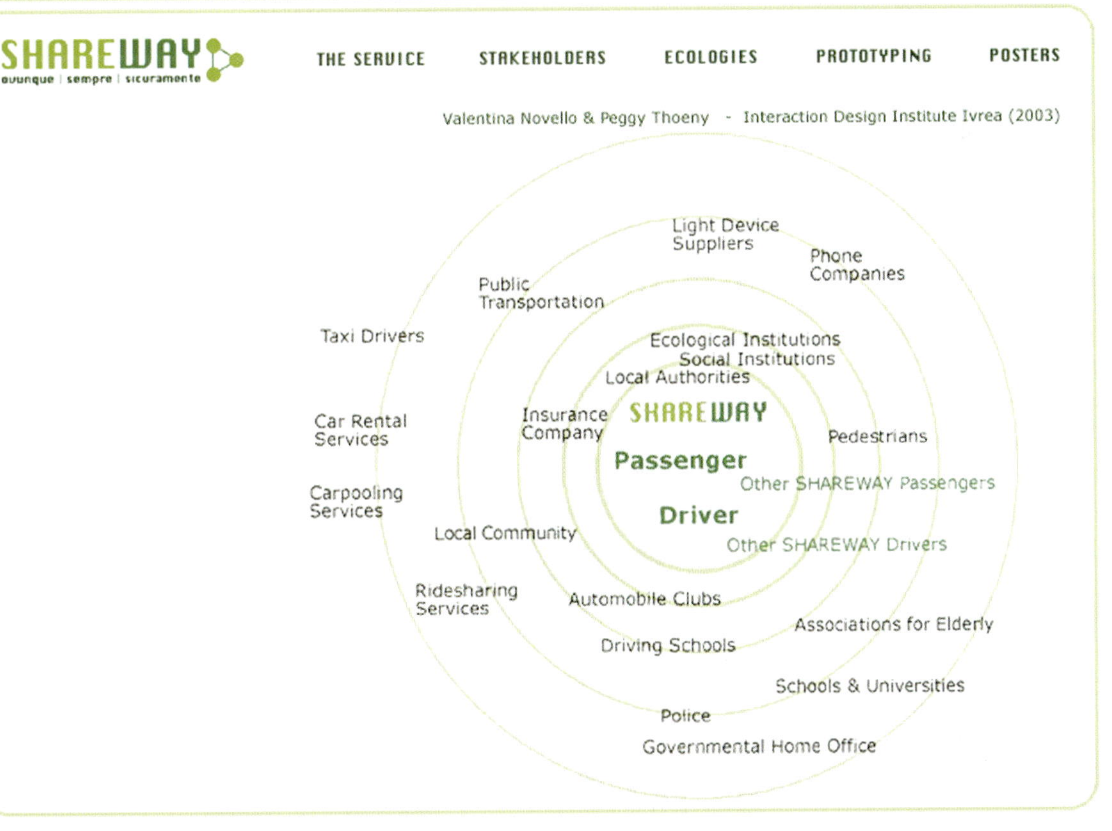

THE SERVICE STAKEHOLDERS ECOLOGIES PROTOTYPING POSTERS

Valentina Novello & Peggy Thoeny - Interaction Design Institute Ivrea (2003)

POSTERS

I go wherever I want.

What about a coffee downtown?

Hitchhiking? No, thanks.

Buses on strike?
Sudden invitation?
Awful weather?

Going to work?
Now it's fun!

SHAREWAY
ovunque | sempre | sicuramente

THE SERVICE STAKEHOLDERS ECOLOGIES PROTOTYPING POSTERS

Valentina Novello & Peggy Thoeny - Interaction Design Institute Ivrea (2003)

POSTERS

I go wherever I want.

What about a coffee downtown?

Hitchhiking? No, thanks.

Buses on strike?
Sudden invitation?
Awful weather?

Going to work?
Now it's fun!

THE SERVICE STAKEHOLDERS ECOLOGIES PROTOTYPING POSTERS

Valentina Novello & Peggy Thoeny - Interaction Design Institute Ivrea (2003)

POSTERS

I go wherever I want.

What about a coffee downtown?

Hitchhiking? No, thanks.

Buses on strike?
Sudden invitation?
Awful weather?

Going to work?
Now it's fun!

THE SERVICE STAKEHOLDERS ECOLOGIES PROTOTYPING POSTERS

Valentina Novello & Peggy Thoeny - Interaction Design Institute Ivrea (2003)

POSTERS

I go wherever I want.

What about a coffee downtown?

Hitchhiking? No, thanks.

Buses on strike?
Sudden invitation?
Awful weather?

Going to work?
Now it's fun!

Photo Author

Fran Samalionis

Fran Samalionis is a leader of the Service Design and Innovation practice at IDEO. She argues that IDEO has earned permission to innovate in service design, as the next step in a history of combining skills and resources. "We started in product design by bringing engineering and industrial design together, with a focus on people. Then we introduced interaction design, which adds the dimension of time. Relatively recently we added the design of environments to our capabilities, with the dimension of space. Now it makes sense that IDEO can innovate in the design of services, because we understand how to create tangible contexts for intangibles, in different channels, that people interact with over time. Our philosophy is to keep our 'head in the clouds and feet on the ground'—the clouds helping us with original and innovative thinking and the ground ensuring our ability to implement the results." Fran joined IDEO in 1996 as a human factors specialist and has worked in both London and San Francisco. Her background was in astronomy and electronics, and she has a master's degree in ergonomics from University College London. When she graduated, she worked with Philips Semiconductors as a product manager for application specific integrated circuits. While at IDEO San Francisco, Fran managed the development of customer experiences for several startups, and a project to help the San Francisco Museum of Modern Art welcome its visitors. Fran has led projects with Egg, an online financial services provider, and numerous telecommunications companies in Europe. She has worked on the human factors of the design of game controllers, medical products, and of a self-propelled underwater camera.

acela
2006

Fran Samalionis

Some customers are so used to an existing product, it does not even cross their mind to ask for a new solution.

Dorothy Leonard,[9] Harvard Business School

Service Innovation

■ Amtrak Acela exterior, café car, and axonometric of first-class car

Photos Courtesy of Amtrak

FRAN SAMALIONIS LIKES to collaborate with Live | Work on service design projects whenever she can and has been a mentor to Chris, Lavrans, and Ben as they have developed their ideas. She sees the need for innovation in services being driven by competition, market dynamics, regulatory issues, technology developments, and social issues:

> One of the things that a lot of companies tend to forget is that, whether they're focusing on a business driver or a technology driver or a customer driver, they need to bring the other dimensions along with them; the market is littered with failures that illustrate that point. For example, interactive television failed because the developers forgot that television is a very "sit back" interaction, rather than a "sit forward" interaction.
>
> Another example was the introduction of offset mortgages. This is a relatively new service in UK banking, combining financial services products such as mortgages, loans, and savings accounts, so that you can offset the interest rates across those products; the mortgage

interest rate applies to your savings account and to your credit card. You can also choose not to receive interest on your savings account in order to take that interest off your mortgage. It's a brilliant business idea, but completely unintuitive to customers. A lot of banks are using massive advertising campaigns to educate customers on what it could mean for them, but they are talking about interest rates, which is confusing, and there is no emotional connection for people.

Fran is an enthusiastic proponent of empathic human factors research techniques as an integral component of every project:

> Customers have got far more demanding than they ever were. They're tuned in to the experience economy and being always on, everywhere, and personalization. And yet on some level researchers have lost the ability to get them to articulate what it is they need. Traditional market research has been overused, and they are unable to tell you anything new; they just regurgitate the last marketing campaign.

She explains the value of using these research techniques for designing services and uses a diagram to explain the relationship between empathic research and traditional market research in the context of "subjects," "truth," and "inspiration." Market research uses large numbers of subjects, or participants, in order to reveal statistically viable truth, but it is unlikely to yield inspiration. Empathic research methods, on the other hand, if skillfully used, can yield much inspiration from small numbers of subjects. Whether the inspirations are true or not depends on the quality of judgment of the researchers.

Process

> You start with observations—customer observations and other stakeholders in the service ecology as well. From those observations you develop insights and then craft the insights into a framework. The framework bounds the problem for you, reducing the complexity, and from that framework you can start to generate lots of ideas. You

don't just leave those ideas floating in the ether, but ground them very quickly into prototypes, of many different levels and fidelities. Through iterative prototyping, you work toward the most effective solution.

In service design it's not just getting in tune with the customer. We have to consider all the other different stakeholders in the mix. That probably includes the business perspective, brand perspective, technology, operations, and the relationship between the business and competition. It may also include some viewpoints of stakeholders who are less obviously part of the service on first analysis but turn out to be very important, for example industry commentators. We use the same empathic techniques to understand customers and to understand those different perspectives.

We are looking for insights from these observations. An example of a business insight could be the "J curve" on a financial product, its profitability over time, and what the business needs from the underlying product behind the service. In technology, it could be the map of available technologies and a systems approach: how the technologies will interact with each other, what they can support, what they can't support, and how you can make movement between channels seamless. On a customer perspective, it could be their behavior around money or what motivates them. You need to pull all these different insights together into a framework to reduce the complexity and bound the problem.

One of the frameworks that we found most useful in service design is a customer journey. That journey starts from, say, becoming aware of the proposition, and then moving on to engage with it, and then potentially moving on to join it. There's some value that the consumer gets from the proposition, like feeling smart, and eventually they may move on to advocacy. This can potentially become a virtuous circle.

THE FRAMEWORK OF a customer journey helps you think about the experiences and touch-points that exist before and after the most obvious parts of a service. This is applied to the design of the Amtrak Acela[10] train service, where the most obvious part of the service was literally a journey, but the design team identified a surprising number of additional steps on the total customer journey, as shown overleaf.

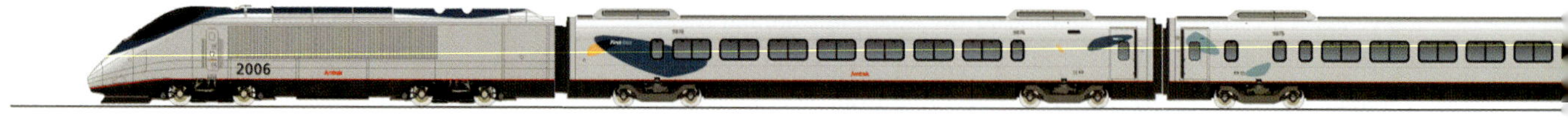

Steps	*Physical Aspects*	*Digital Aspects*
1. Learning	Advertising, Travel Agent, Word of Mouth	On-line, Phone info., Intranet
2. Planning	Station Staff, Travel Agent, Brochure, Phone	On-line, Phone info.
3. Starting	Other form of transportation	Radio – up to the minute info.
4. Entering	Station Architecture	Signage
5. Ticketing	Ticket Office, Travel Agent	On-line, Phone info., kiosks
6. Waiting	Waiting Room, Station Facilities	Signage, On-line services
7. Boarding	Doors and Luggage Storage	Auto Doors, Dynamic signage
8. Riding	Seats, Meal Services	Info., Media, Comms
9. Arriving	Station Architecture	Signage
10. Continuing	Other form of transportation	-

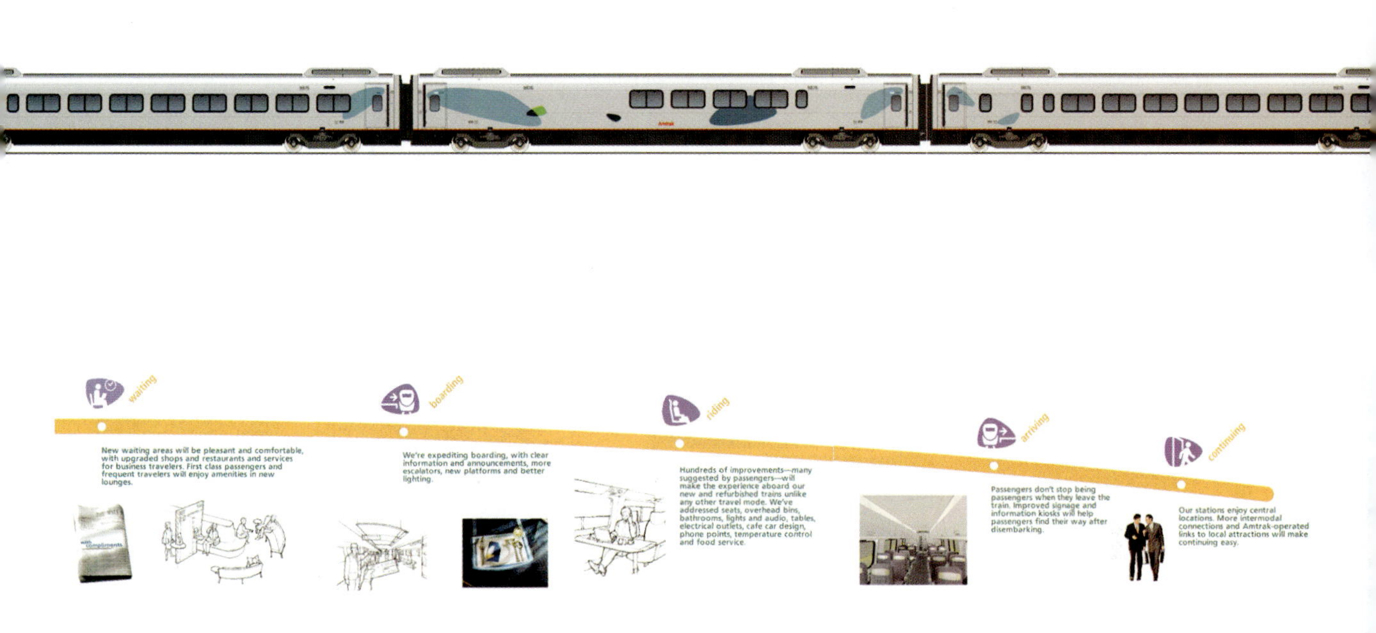

The chart opposite summarizes the overlapping of the physical and digital touch-points for designing the service. Notice that the traditional idea of designing a train, both interior and exterior, only applies to the boarding and riding steps in the journey, and the opportunity to enhance the experience with digital technology applies to all of them, albeit in an unknown form for starting and continuing.

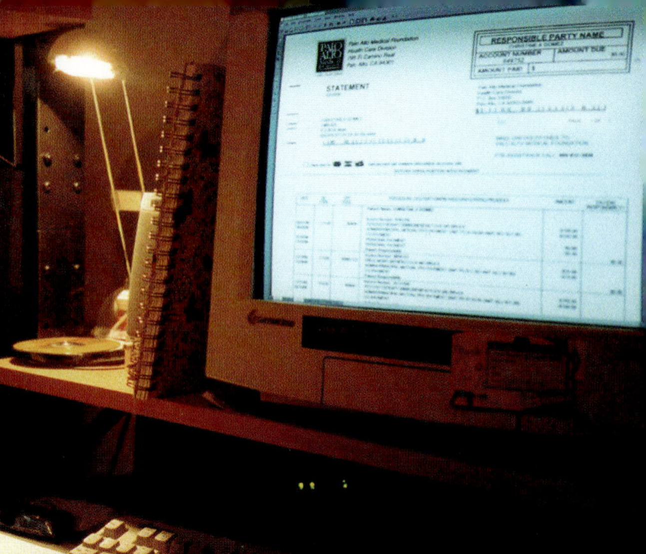

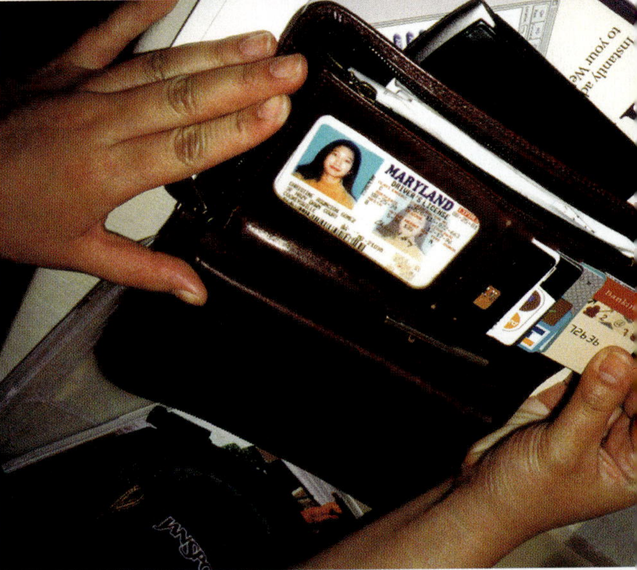

PETTY CASH RECORD

DATE | Acct Number | Description of Transaction | PAID OUT PAYMENT/DEBIT | PAID IN DEPOSIT/CREDIT | Cash Balance

TOTALS

Record all payments or credits that affect the Petty Cash Balance

A Case Study: Juniper Online Bank

WHEN FRAN SAMALIONIS was in San Francisco in 1998, she was project leader for a "Customer Service Strategy" for a startup company called Juniper Financial. She tells the story of this project to illustrate the service design process:

> Juniper was an online bank. A bunch of guys that had come out of Bank One[11] had decided that they wanted to do a startup. When they came to us, they were running around trying to solve every conceivable customer problem. What they really needed was some clarity and a point of view about what they could offer as a service provider. We took them through our process, moving from observations to insights to frameworks, and then through to prototyping.
>
> We started with a broad range of observations, picking a fairly diverse range of people in America, across different coasts, different ethnic backgrounds, and different incomes, because we were looking for different attitudes to money.
>
> One technique was to trace a bill through a home. This was interesting because at that time in the US, people were still using checkbooks to pay their bills, unlike the UK, where everything is set up for payment by direct debit. Using a checkbook meant that people had to be in tune with their bill cycle, otherwise they would be horrendously late paying their bills. People used different mechanisms. Some would move the bill around the home. It lands on the doorstep, it sits by the door for a while, then it moves into the kitchen, onto a little pile. From the kitchen the pile moves into the bedroom and sits there for a while. Eventually, when it gets a certain size, it moves into the study, where somebody can sit down and go through the ritualistic task of writing checks and paying their bills.
>
> Some people would create a space on a shelf that was a certain size, and when the bills filled up that space, they knew that it was time to sit down and pay them. They were using their environment to gently remind them to pay their bills. This kind of observation became very interesting when we were looking for insights to inspire a proposition for Juniper.

■ Observations of Zina, a well-organized person who already uses online banking. She says, "I like to find efficient ways to do things."

Photos
Courtesy of IDEO

These observations helped the team to understand the physicality of the behaviors associated with finances and banking. The next level up was to search for insights into attitudes about money in a more general sense. They found some people who had a very holistic perspective, both in attributes and over time. Some were very goal-oriented but not interested in managing money. Some would micromanage every aspect of their finances, and others only thought about what they could spend it on. Fran describes the four-quadrant framework that they developed to categorize these attitudes:

> We started to develop those insights into a framework, and at some point that framework successfully summarized the psychographics of the consumers. The dimensions of the two-by-two matrix were based on a vertical axis describing the view that the user had about their finances, with a long-term view at the top and a short-term view below. The horizontal axis defined how engaged they liked to be with managing their money, with low engagement on the left and high engagement on the right.
>
> In the top right hand corner, you've got somebody who is highly engaged and takes a long-term perspective on money. These were the holistic people; we called them the "pathfinders." Below them, in the bottom right, were the highly engaged micromanagers, and they became know as "organizers." Next-door to them, in the bottom left, were the people who were just thinking about what they could use their money for, and they became "onlookers" in terms of managing their money. Above them you've got these people who were not particularly engaged but had a long-term view; these are the "dreamers"; money for them was just a means to an end—it was all about the dream. That framework became very powerful as a decision tool within Juniper. It gave them a perspective on who their prospective customers might be and what their behaviors and needs might be. We could also look at the competition and analyze which type of customers they were going after and how they were addressing these customer needs.
>
> In overlaying the competition onto this framework, you could start to see that hardly anybody was chasing the customers in the "dreamer" segment, but selling the dream in financial services used to be massively overused and had been dead for a long time! In the

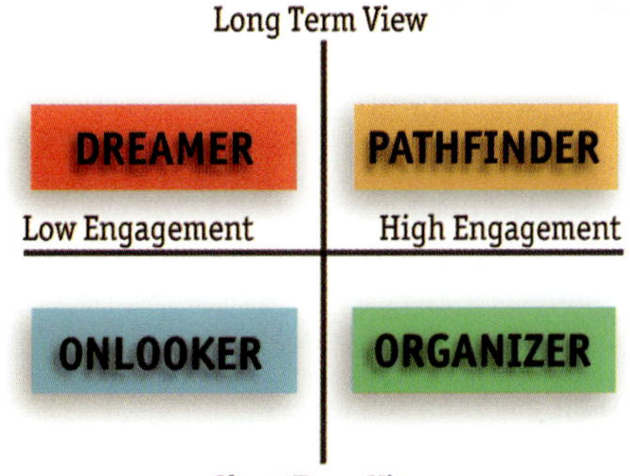

Framework of attitudes about banking

"pathfinders" segment, there are one or two competitors like Fidelity, who offer a holistic perspective that those customers want. There were also some banks offering services in the bottom right "organizers" corner, geared up for things like credit card surfing, for people who were always micromanaging and looking for the best rate.

The "onlooker" quadrant was quite crowded, but what we'd learnt about onlookers made us believe that most of the competition in that quadrant weren't really addressing the needs of the customers appropriately. They had confused lack of engagement with finances with an inability to understand finances, so they had tried to develop services with "dumbing-down" of finances. Actually, onlookers are not engaged because they are engaged in other things: they are far more into their family, or their career, and money is just something that sits in the background. Once we understood not just who those customers were but also what the competition was offering them, it was very easy for Juniper to say, "Okay, right, we don't want to sell the dream, we're not geared up to help pathfinders. We're a startup online bank; we're not really interested in organizers because they don't stay around long enough to make a viable business. That leaves us quite naturally sitting in this onlooker space. Although onlookers with a low engagement may be difficult to persuade to come to Juniper, once they're there, they will also stay around for a while."

The analysis worked brilliantly as a decision-making tool and also as a starting point for design. We could understand not just what an "onlooker" was like and what their needs and behaviors were, but we could also understand them in contrast to other the needs and behaviors of other types of customer.

When we started prototyping the Web touch-points for Juniper, we knew that onlookers aren't engaged in managing their finances, so we wanted to give them the ability to dip in and out of the site—to just dip in, get the right information, and then get out again. The other thing we knew was that the Web at the time felt literally like a web of information; you could disappear quite quickly into it, moving from hyperlink to hyperlink. We knew that that was not appropriate for "onlookers." We wanted to give them a sense of place. Transacting, banking online, was still very new, and there was a lot of nervousness around the virtualness of the bank, so anything that could give onlookers a sense of place was really valuable.

Fran Samalionis working on a framework ■

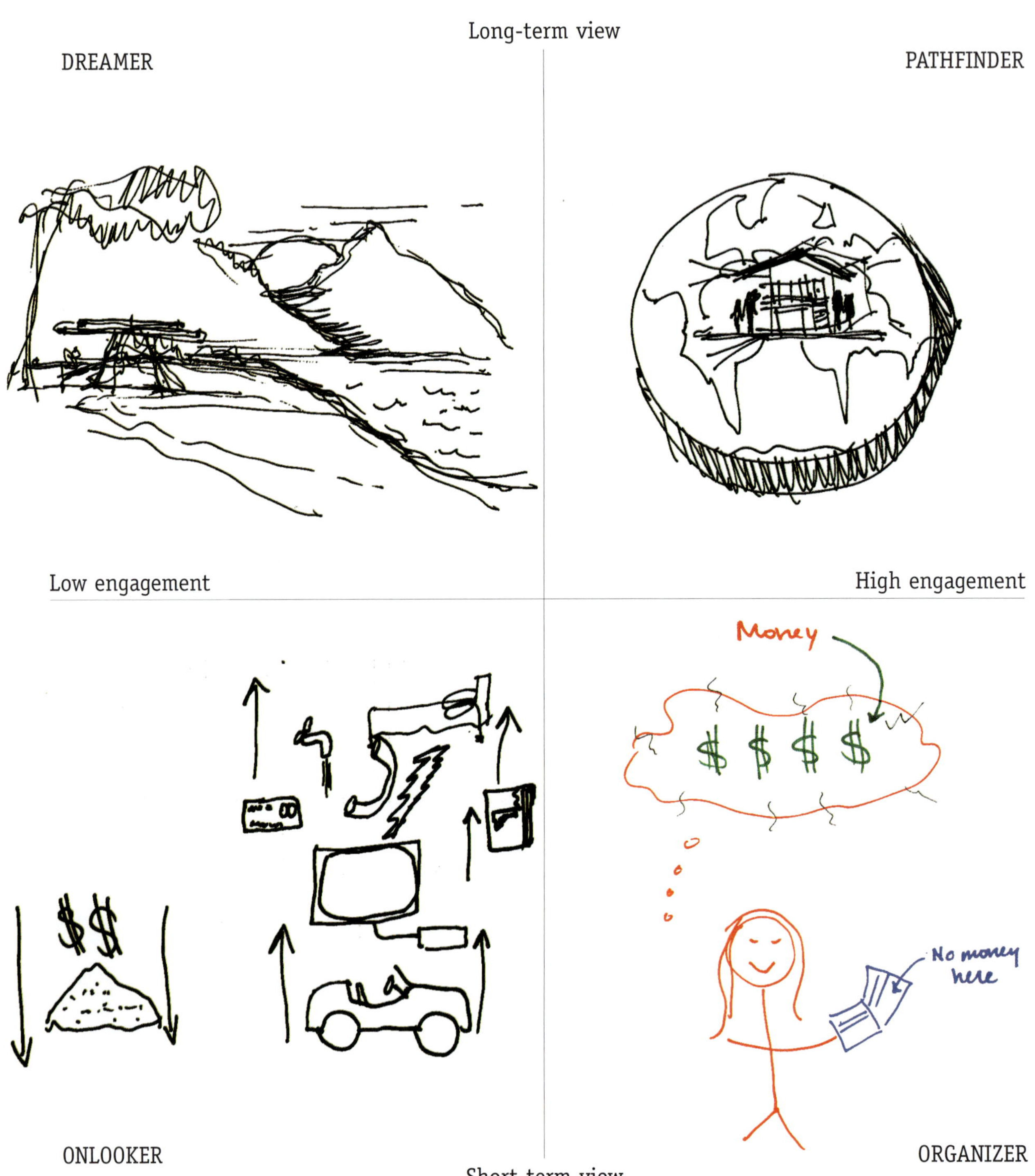
Long-term view
DREAMER
PATHFINDER
Low engagement
High engagement
Money
No money here
ONLOOKER
ORGANIZER
Short-term view

A method that was very helpful in establishing this framework during the research phase was to ask the participants to draw their money. Two members of the team had already spent time with them in their homes identifying different aspects of their lives that they associated with their financial situations, and asking them to sit down and make a drawing of their money helped to bring out their feelings at a more emotional level. As they started to draw, they talked about themselves in a more open way, and it became much clearer what they would want from a bank. Fran describes some examples:

> One "pathfinder" drew her family in a shelter, and that shelter sat on a coin, but the face of the coin was the whole globe, so you can see her holistic global perspective. For one "organizer" it was all about the money; she drew a bubble above her head with dollar signs in it, and she was holding an empty wallet, indicating that she remembered the complete picture and had no need for cash. One "dreamer" drew an island paradise, which was his ultimate money dream. An "onlooker" drew a pile of gold coming in and all the stuff that he could spend his money on going out; there were all these icons of the things that he would spend his money on, like a car, and a TV, and so on.
>
> When we looked at what people were drawing, there was a good face validity with the psychographic matrix that we had developed. It was not necessarily statistically significant, but it became very easy for us to take somebody's drawing and to understand, "Oh, yeah, no, they're a pathfinder," or "They're an onlooker." We had about thirty or forty people at Juniper draw their own money, and they became very intrigued by our diagnosis in terms of what quadrant they sat in.

■ Framework populated by drawings of money

The research gave the team a good understanding of the kind of Web experience that would be most appropriate for "onlookers." They designed a navigational structure so that some parts of the navigation were persistent throughout the whole experience and then built the rest of the page. There was a column on the left containing a list of all of your accounts, with the amount in each. The design team called this a dashboard, because you could get a reading of the full financial picture at a single glance. You could interrogate any item in the list, and the

Bill Jones sign off

Message Center
Paycenter -132.00
Profile

House Checking ∞	2,000.00
Checking	3,000.00
IN 05/14/00	256.00
OUT 05/14/00	512.00
Mastercard	-753.00
House Deposit (SA)	6,000.00
IN 05/14/00	1000.00
OUT 05/14/00	
College CD	10,640.00
8.62% 12/12/00	
Boat CD	6,120.00

Message Center

Saving for your child's education

SPECIAL REPORT

Tax incentives and rising fees are spurring a new trend among parents. Saving for your child's education from their first birthday. Click to see how america is saving

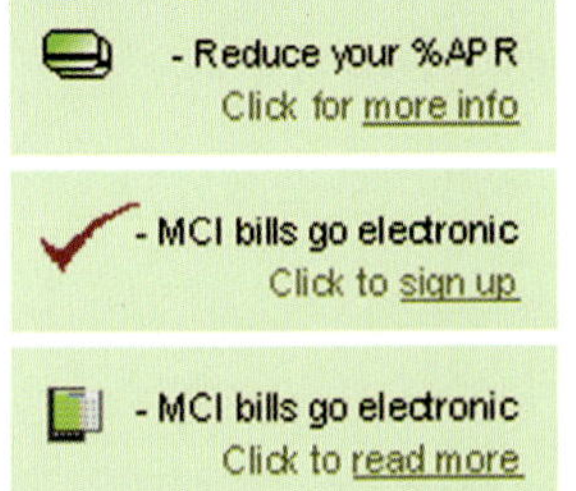

Notifications Services

Today	2:15 pm :	ATM/Debit Card "House Checking" is reported Lost/Stolen. Click to replace.
Monday	4:45 pm :	Your PG&E bill is due. Click to Pay this Bill.
Monday	1:45 pm :	Your Checking Account "House Checking" balance is below $500.00 OK
Friday	4:40 pm :	Your Checking Account "House Checking" balance is approaching $500.00 OK
Wednesday	4:40 pm :	"College CD" account (CD) has completed its term. Click to extend, or transfer.
05/12/00	9:00 am :	Your Checking Account "House Checking" balance is approaching $500.00 OK
05/10/00	11:00 am :	Your Checkbook "Checking" is running low. Click to Reorder.

Bill Jones sign off

Message Center
Paycenter -132.00
Profile

House Checking ∞	2,000.00
Checking	3,000.00
IN 05/14/00	256.00
OUT 05/14/00	512.00
Mastercard	-753.00
House Deposit (SA)	6,000.00
IN 05/14/00	1000.00
OUT 05/14/00	
College CD	10,640.00
8.62% 12/12/00	
Boat CD	6,120.00

Checking Services

Current Statement
September 00
Page 1 of 7

Total out	512.00
Total in	256.00
Initial balance	2,208.58
Current Balance	1500.00

Date	Description	Credit	Debit
4/12/00	Check # 00556132		12.28
6/12/00	Check # 00556132	85.21	
7/12/00	Check # 00556132		12.28
7/12/00	Check # 00556132	85.21	
7/12/00	Check # 00556132	85.21	
7/12/00	Check # 00556132	85.21	
8/12/00	Check # 00556132		12.28
9/12/00	Check # 00556132	85.21	
9/12/00	Check # 00556132	85.21	
9/12/00	Check # 00556132	85.21	
9/12/00	Check # 00556132	85.21	
10/12/00	Check # 00556132	85.21	

main area of the screen would give you all of the details about that item. The link between the dashboard and the details, in the same overall visual space, made you feel that you were in the same place all the time. Everything was served up to you in the same frame. Most of the time, you just wanted to dip into the Web channel to understand, "Am I on track, what's my account balance?" If you did want some more detail, it was offered to you in the same space.

The designers started with sketch paper prototypes, developing ideas for the interactions with the dashboard, and how different frames might appear and what sort of information structure needed to be in those frames. Soon they wanted to try some experience prototypes, so they moved onto the screen. In this case they leaped straight into the design of HTML pages, using Macromedia Dreamweaver to simulate a Web experience. This had the important advantage that they could take assets developed during the experience prototyping and deliver them to Juniper for use in constructing the site. As the design moved forward they built up a library of interaction assets and were able to quickly prototype different configurations and transitions, forming experiential examples of the whole interaction.

■ Sketch designs using Macromedia Dreamweaver

Fran describes the solution to the problem that "onlookers" had with paying their bills on time and the dangers of cross-selling:

> One of the things we knew about "onlookers" was that, because they're not particularly engaged in finances, they're often late in paying their bills. What we wanted to do was find a way to help them, much like we saw in the observations, when people would stack their bills as a gentle reminder to pay them; we wanted to create that same gentle reminder online. We created a message center, where we could send little alerts about how things were progressing or transacting on their accounts. They could configure those alerts, as different people had different ways of staying in rhythm with their bill cycle. The message center was a good place for this to happen, as it was coordinated in one place, although they could also receive alerts on their phone or through their email.
>
> We started to understand how Juniper could benefit from "cross-selling." There are many places where it's inappropriate to cross-sell a

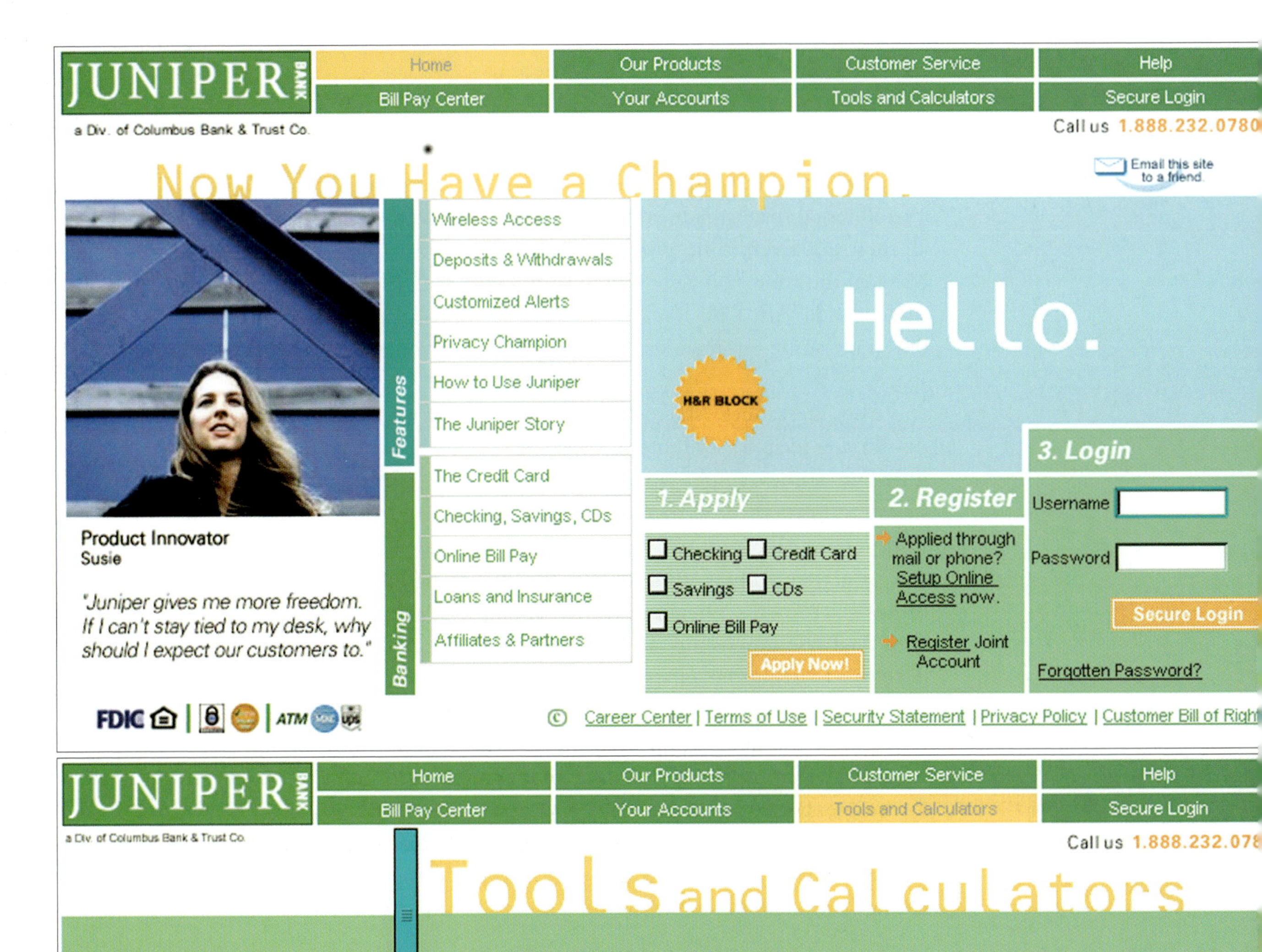

JUNIPER BANK

a Div. of Columbus Bank & Trust Co.

Home | Our Products | Customer Service | Help

Bill Pay Center | Your Accounts | Tools and Calculators | Secure Login

Call us 1.888.232.078

Tools and Calculators

Juniper has provided a growing set of tools and calculators to help you manage your finances and your financial future.

Tools

Simply enter your street address, city, or zip code to find an ATM, Mail Boxes Etc., or UPS location nearest you. Or access Juniper's e-Wallet for online comparison shopping and eas online purchasing.

Calculators

Juniper offers a collection of easy-to-use calculators to help answer your financial questions about paying off or consolidating debt, saving for college or a home, determining the right insurance for your needs, and many more. Select the category of interest at left and choos from a list of available calculators.

Tools

- ATM Locator
- Mail Boxes Etc. Locator
- UPS Locator and Tracking
- Forms Center
- Go Shopping

Calculators

- Credit Card
- Savings
- Equity Loans
- Mortgage
- Auto Financing
- Insurance
- Budgeting

customer from one product into another. For example, if they had a query about their account, or even a complaint about their account, trying to cross-sell them after you've resolved that query is dangerous and probably damaging. All the good will you've created during the phone call is lost if you add a sales message at the end. But the message center, where Juniper is being helpful with alerts, and where customers are used to receiving information about their accounts, became the perfect place to position cross-sell.

Another touch-point in the design of the online service was about the information for the customer's personal profile. Everyone is nervous about the intimate information that is held in a virtual bank, but "onlookers" are not just nervous, they are inclined to forget their password or which answer they gave to those personal questions that are needed for verification. The design made that information immediately visible from the same dashboard, protected by being in a secure part of the site that only customers had access to, so that they could click on "profile" to see all of that information and have a chance to change it. This proved to be reassuring to customers and strengthened their relationship with Juniper.

Final Web site

- *Top* Homepage
- *Bottom* Tools and calculators

The design team also recommended the radical proposition of getting rid of charges for late payments. They accepted that "onlookers" would be late payers, but also that these same people would be attracted to a service that forgave their lateness. The design helped to mitigate the risk by providing the reminders, but constructed the business risk model to account for a proportion of late payers. Juniper went on to introduce no over-limit fees and a low late-payment fee. This brought in a lot of customers in the group that Juniper[12] was targeting.

7

The Internet

Interviews with Terry Winograd, Larry Page and Sergey Brin of Google, Steve Rogers, and Mark Podlaseck

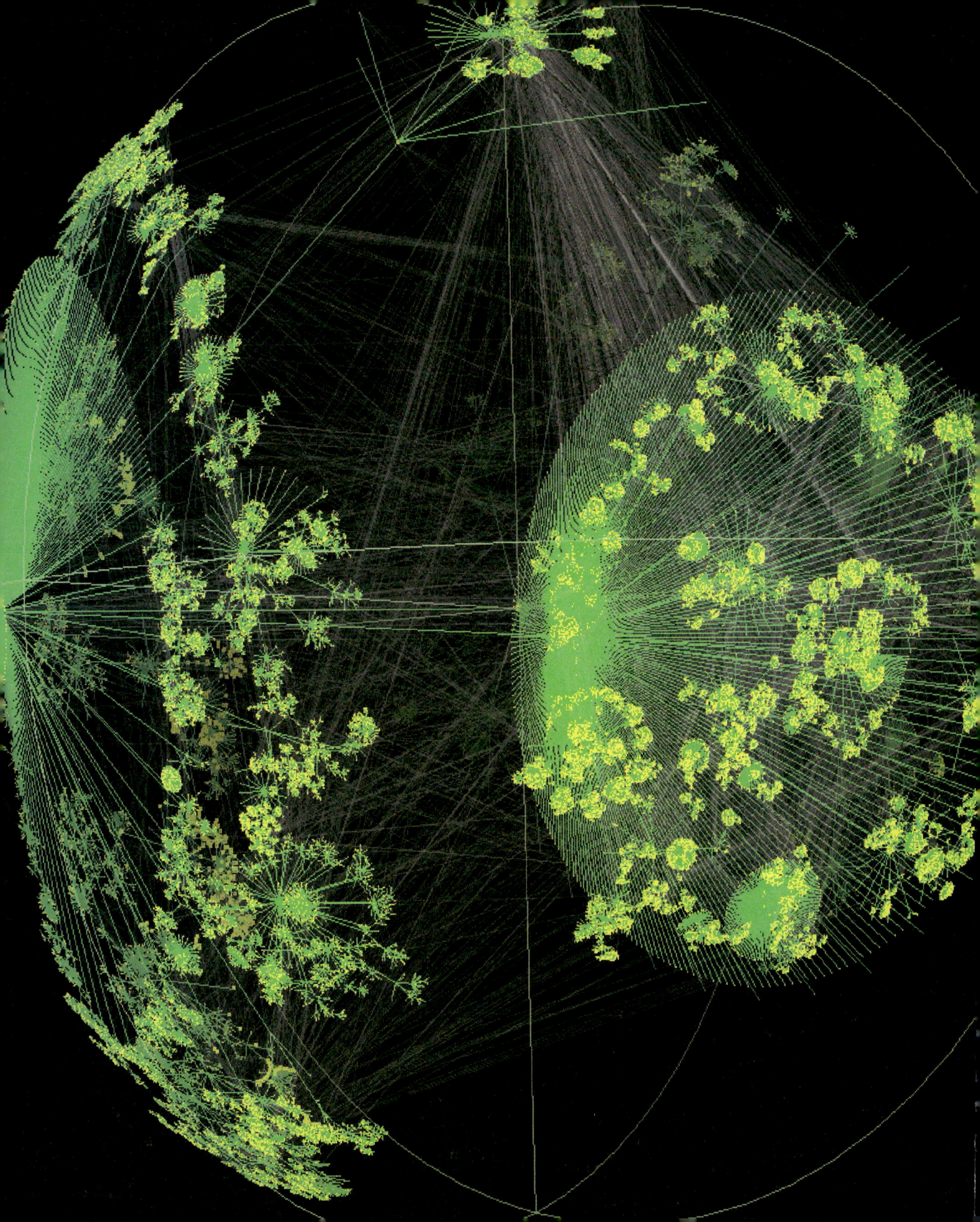

I did a calculation in the mid nineties of the number of documents that the seated user at home could get to within a minute and found that over a period of four years the number increased by a factor of ten thousand. One order of magnitude came because the disks are bigger, and three orders of magnitude came because of the Internet. That's a huge change in a short time. If I want to know, for example, whether "foodchain" is spelled closed up, or if there's a space between food and chain, I can whip over to my workstation, type it in both ways, find the number of people on earth who have used it each way, and know definitively where the majority usage is. I would never have known that before, and it happens in almost the same amount of time that it takes me to search my own memory. It's as if I have a strap-on cortex!

Stu Card,[1] March 2002

■ Representation of the stucture of the Internet

Download Young Hyun of CAIDA, using graph visualization tool code-named Walrus

THE KIND OF enhancement to our abilities that Stu Card revels in is enabled for most people by using the Google search engine. This chapter features an interview with Larry Page and Sergey Brin in the spring of 2002, when they were still in their twenties and there was no talk of going public any time soon. They were making light of their achievements and engagingly modest about their designs, but it was already obvious that they had successfully resisted the dot-com madness and had survived through the crash and the period of "dot-gone."

Professor Terry Winograd teaches computer science at Stanford, and he was advisor to Larry Page when Larry and Sergey were developing their first prototypes; in the first interview of the chapter, he talks about the reasons behind the extraordinary success that Google has enjoyed and gives an

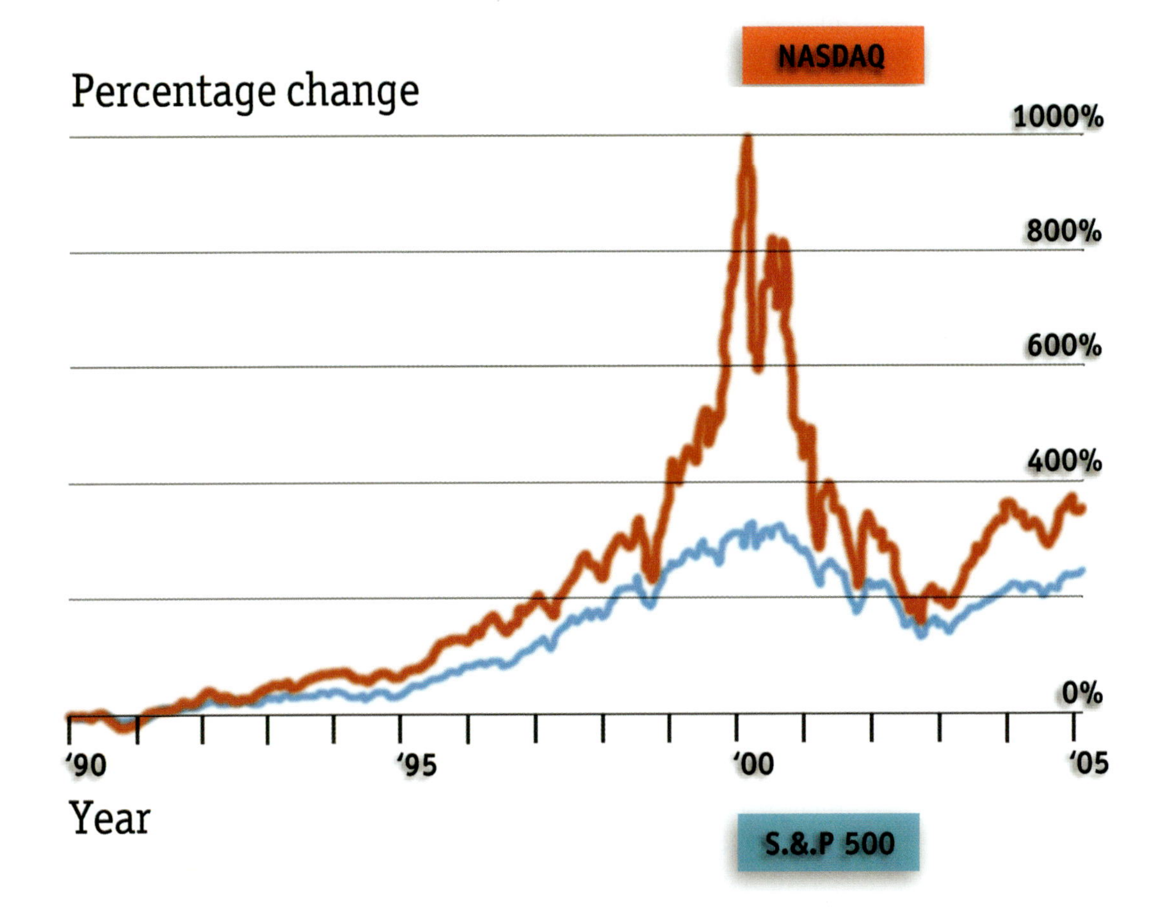

NASDAQ
Percentage change
1000%
800%
600%
400%
0%
'90
'95
'00
'05
Year
S.&.P 500

overview of the development of the Internet. An interview with Steve Rogers, head of production at BBC New Media, discusses the design of the BBC homepage, which is shown as a case study. Mark Podlaseck, who researches the navigation of large databases at IBM, describes in his interview the rationale behind his beautiful design for the "glassengine," a Web site that allows you to browse the music of Philip Glass.

This chapter only touches a tiny part of the design of the Internet, which is a gigantic subject worthy of many books, but it offers some illustrative expert opinions and examples.

Dot-com madness

Do you remember the heady days of the dot-coms? You had to be living in the San Francisco Bay area to appreciate the full extremes of the craziness. Silicon Valley was powering along, to keep pace with the need for server farms, routers, and of course chips, chips, chips. Up in San Francisco, the area between Market Street and the bay was being redeveloped at breathtaking speed, housing an endless flood of startup e-commerce businesses and Web design consultancies. The business plans for the startups often projected no more than banner ads as a revenue stream, and still they were generously funded by venture capital. Townsend Street was dubbed "Multimedia Gulch," housing design shops such as Razorfish, Sapient, and Scient, which were surfing the wave of change as every company in the USA added a Web site, and many of them added an e-business arm to their portfolio. Junior designers were commanding six-figure salaries and being charged to clients at $2,000 a day. Rents in town were skyrocketing, driving away the residents who were not benefiting from inflated salaries. It was nuts!

■ Dot-com bubble

Source: Bloomberg Financial Markets

With a little common sense, it was easy to see that the design boom was not going to last very long. The wave of change that accelerated demand was only going to continue until all the companies had their first Web site or their first e-business. Once that was in place, they would only need a low level of design effort for maintenance or an update several years down the line. It was also easy to see that many of the e-commerce business ventures were founded on speculation rather than realistic revenue projections. Investing in market share was only going to pay off for the small number of enterprises that would end up dominating in the areas where there was a genuine value proposition to build on.

At last the crash came. The downturn was much more dramatic in San Francisco than elsewhere, because Multimedia Gulch and Silicon Valley had been the center of the madness. When people move to another town, the least expensive way to take their things with them is to rent a U-Haul trailer, load it up with all their stuff, and pull it behind their car: it was hard to find a U-Haul trailer in San Francisco after the crash, as the traffic was one-way outbound! Property started to be more available, the rents fell, local unemployment soared, and lots of investors were deeply distressed. Why did the madness continue for so long before the crash came? Perhaps it was because there was a genuine revolution going on, and that moving into the information age is as significant a change as was the arrival of the industrial age. Life really is different because of the Internet, and the interviews in this chapter show us an inkling of the design implications of the change.

How have the Internet and the World Wide Web emerged from the downturn? The Internet as a whole continues to be a communication medium, dominated by email and chat, while the Web is the part where people look for information as well as buy and sell things. The communication component of the Internet is closer in some ways to other communications services, like telephone and mail. There is convergence there as well; we call it email because it is easy to see the similarity to snail-mail, but now we also have streaming audio, allowing us to use the Internet for telephone calls and to listen to the radio. Phones have built in cameras, so people send images to one another. Streaming video is just around the corner for the Internet, so we can expect a surge in video calls and TV watching soon.

The Web was the part that took off with such flamboyant growth, and is now the extraordinary new world of information that is instantly accessible to everybody with a browser. In the preceding chapter, Takeshi Natsuno described the content portfolio that he created to understand the "Internet way of thinking" as it could be applied to a cell phone service. He named information-based content, database-based content, and entertainment-based content." In the transaction category he thought first of banks, credit card companies, and security companies. For the information and database categories, he was looking for news, yellow pages, recipes, timetables, and so on. For entertainment he looked for online games and found Bandai as his first content provider in the category. When we look from an overview position at the successful companies that have emerged from the downturn, it is interesting to see if Natsuno's portfolio seems relevant, or if his categories are only applicable to the specifics of a Web access provider that is also a Japanese cell phone service.

Terry Winograd starts by explaining the difference between the Internet and the World Wide Web, and comparing them to ubiquitous computing.

Photo Craig Syverson

Terry Winograd

Terry Winograd is a professor of computer science at Stanford University, where he has developed an innovative program in software design, with a focus on human-computer interaction design (HCI). His BA was in mathematics in 1966 and his PhD in applied mathematics at MIT. He went on to teach and study in the Artificial Intelligence Lab at MIT before moving to Stanford in 1973. He consulted with Xerox PARC with the goal of getting computers to understand natural language but became frustrated with the slow progress in the field. "A reason to have computers understand natural language is that it's an extremely effective way of communicating. What I came to realize is that the success of the communication depends on the real intelligence on the part of the listener, and that there are many other ways of communicating with a computer that can be more effective, given that it doesn't have the intelligence. At that point, I shifted my view away from what would be thought of as artificial intelligence to the broader question, 'How do you want to interact with a computer?' Then I got interested in what makes interactions with computers work well or fail and what makes them fluent. That's been the direction of my work." In parallel with his teaching at Stanford, he has also consulted with Action Technologies, Interval Research, and Google. His most recent book is *Bringing Design to Software*,[2] a compilation of contributed chapters and interviews, with interleaved profiles each describing a successful project related to the contributed material. He is also a founder and past president of Computer Professionals for Social Responsibility.

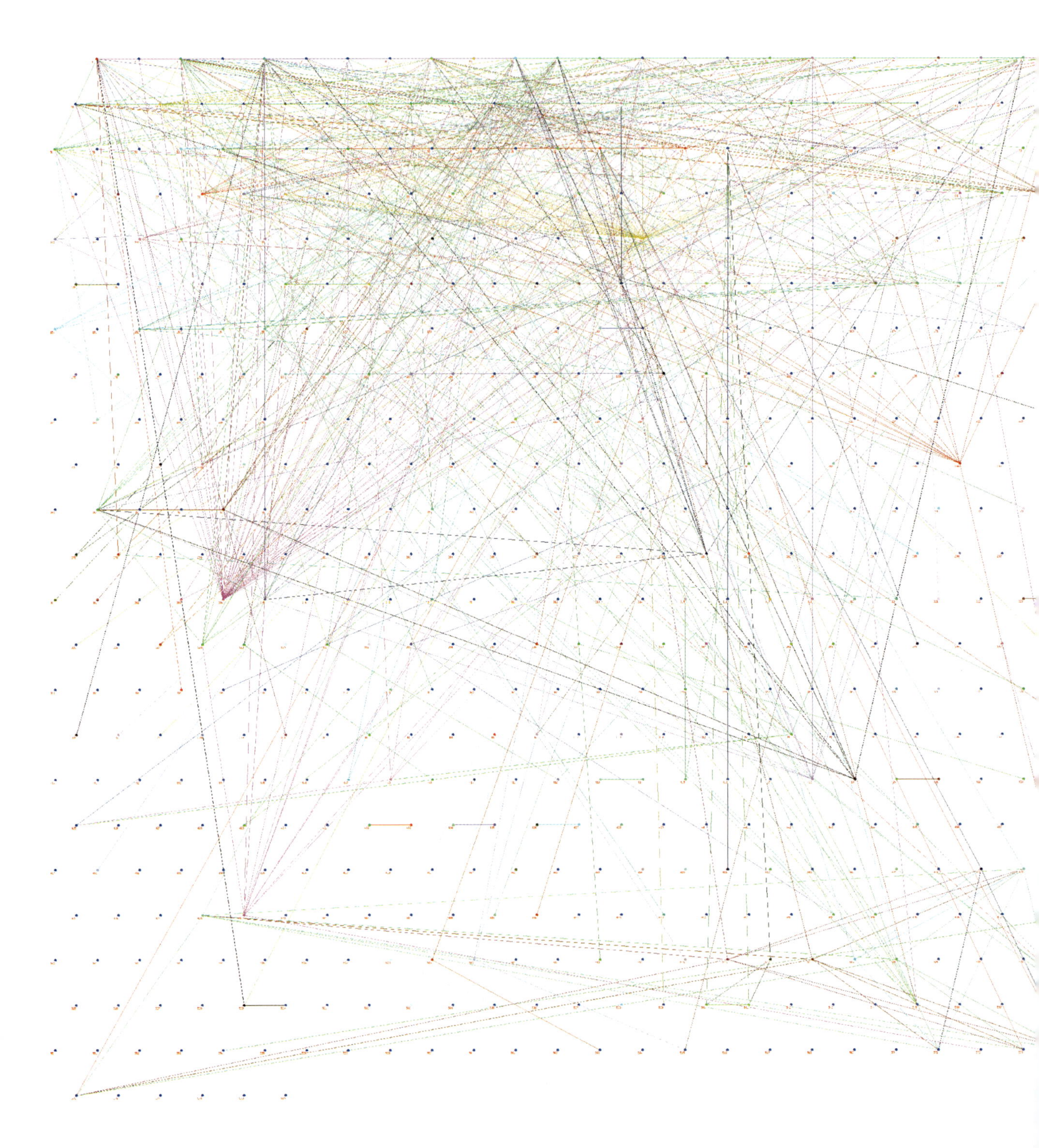

Terry Winograd

The Internet or the Web?

■ Map representing Web sites as nodes, with joins indicating links between sites

Download Seraphim Proudleduck statistics

A lot of people wonder what the difference is between the Internet and the World Wide Web, usually referred to as the Web. Terry Winograd defines two differences, one technical, the other social-historical:

> At the technical level, the Internet is a set of protocols for communicating between machines, sending information around. One particular protocol, which got built on top of those protocols, is called http, the HyperText Transfer Protocol. That was the protocol that created the Web. If you want to be technical, applications that use the http protocol are using the Web, while others that use other protocols on top of the underlying Internet protocols are just part of the Internet. By that definition, ordinary email is not part of the Web, as email is transported through the Internet, but not via the Web. But then you may use a Web-based reader to read it on the Web once it's gotten delivered, so it's confusing. Now, protocol differences may be interesting for techie people, but it's not a very interesting distinction for most people.

Terry thinks of the other distinction more in a social context. The Internet was first developed by a collection of people who were computer-savvy, mostly computer programmers or scientists, so it was designed and optimized for that community. The Web also started that way, as physicists, who were using it as a way to communicate their preprints and papers among themselves, created the http protocol. Then a surge of growth started to expand the Web, and the dot-com boom took off. Every business realized that they needed at least a Web site and possibly an e-commerce arm to stay competitive. There was a sudden shift from the specialist technical community to a new commercial consumer space full of business opportunity.

> I think that, as a social phenomenon, this was a tremendous explosion that was different from the underlying social phenomenon of the Internet.

■ Early time-sharing on Univac
■ Xerox Alto

Ubiquitous computing versus the Internet

The way that people interact with computers has shifted over the years, although not as rapidly in some ways as people expected. When Terry started working with computers, you punched decks of cards, put them into card readers, and waited for them to return printouts. He had his first chance to experiment with interactive timesharing at the Artificial Intelligence Lab at MIT, where he had a machine, he did something, and it did something right back. There wasn't this gap of giving it a bunch of stuff and waiting for a result.

Then, when he was given an Alto at Xerox PARC, he had the chance to use a graphical user interface, allowing him to use the visual space of the screen to let the computer know what he was doing by pointing. Terry explains the next vision:

> The desktop and the mouse have really dominated the way we interact with computers, pretty much for the last twenty years. We think of it as sitting down, interacting by doing things with our hands, primarily typing, because that's a very efficient way to get large quantities of text in, and also by pointing, dragging, moving, and drawing, and so on.

There is a next vision, which has been put forward and explored but certainly hasn't taken over. Mark Weiser, who was also at Xerox PARC at a somewhat later period than I was, developed a notion he called "ubiquitous computing."[3] The basic idea is that people don't want to interact with computers. People want to get something done. They may want to write documents, they may want to draw pictures, they may want to turn the lights on and off. Whatever they do, the fact that there's a computer involved in an interaction is instrumental. It's not the purpose; it's the way they get things done.

The question Weiser was asking was, How can we make computers become invisible? How can we interact with environments, rather than interacting with computers, where the computers now become the medium through which we interact? That includes a lot of different kinds of devices, so instead of sitting in front of a computer, or holding a computer and doing something to it, you simply operate in a space. You're in a room and you're doing things. You're writing on a board, you're moving around; you're doing whatever it is that is important for you, in terms of why you're there. The computers are in the background both helping you get things done and providing "affordances"—ways that you can make things happen.

The idea of ubiquitous computing is to move away from the desktop toward multiple devices. Rather than thinking about using a computer, you think about using a room, a world, or a whole environment of computers. You move away from simple one-to-one interactions toward more implicit interactions:

What you do with the computer, and around the computer, is being interpreted, and that can help you, but that can be difficult. The fantasy is the Star Trek computer.

You say, "Computer do this, computer do that," and it just happens. That's very hard to design.

The reality, which is what the research is really on, is how to put computers into the tangible real world we're in and have them do things that don't require the inference and intelligence that people have.

One of the initial points in Weiser's work on ubiquitous computing was to envision a spectrum of computers. He called it computing by the inch, by the foot, and by the yard. Computing by the inch was something called the PARCtab, which was the predecessor of today's

Mark Weiser
Star Trek bridge

- "Inch"—PARCtab
- "Foot"—Microsoft tablet PC
- "Yard"—large wall displays in the Gates iRoom at Stanford

PDAs.[4] By the foot was a little tablet, which was a predecessor of things like the Microsoft tablets.[5] And by the yard was big displays on the wall. The goal was not to have to choose one, but to be able to smoothly integrate among them.[6]

There were two really different strands operating and developing in the nineties. One was, as I said, the move away from the desktop toward ubiquitous computing. The other was toward more connectivity, toward more things that happen on your desktop, while being connected to everybody else in the world's desktop, and servers, and so on.

These trends are complementary. Most of the stuff that's gone on in the Internet doesn't challenge the basic interaction desktop metaphor. What's new of course is what's going on that screen, who's putting it there, and how you're interacting with it.

Interval Research took the interaction design direction that was more toward ubiquitous computing and tangible interfaces at a time when, for financial commercial reasons, the direction that was really happening was the other one, which was the Web. Everybody was eager to put things onto the Internet, get them off the Internet, send information, find information, sell things, and buy things. I think there were a lot of ideas that would have developed much further, if all of the resources and attention hadn't shifted in massive focus to what we could do on the Web, and as we saw a few years later, that was a bubble that has now been corrected.

From direct manipulation to "being there"

Terry suggests that we interact with the world around us in three main ways; manipulation, locomotion, and conversation. In manipulation you move things around with your hands; for locomotion you move yourself from place to place; and in conversation you say something and another person says something back. Terry explains the relationship between those three interactions and computers:

> If you look at computers, all three of those metaphors are present. The early ordinary timesharing system was conversation. I type something in; it types something back.
>
> The Xerox Star and the Macintosh—that whole line of interfaces—is manipulation, and in fact Ben Shneiderman coined the title "direct manipulation" for it, as you actually move things around.

As the Internet became popular and shifted to the Web as we now know it, the metaphor shifted toward locomotion, even without much change in the technology.

I used to say things like, "I'm going to retrieve a file from somebody else's computer and bring it up on my screen."

That's manipulation: I retrieve it; I bring it up.

Now I say, "I'm going to go to their homepage." I'm doing exactly the same thing. I'm retrieving a file from their computer and I'm bringing it up on my screen, but I've shifted my thinking away from doing things to moving. There's a space—there's a place.

One of the things that made the Web very appealing and effective in many of its applications was the shift to a metaphor of locomotion and place, where I think of it as a set of places I can go to and be in rather than a set of objects I can do things with.

The location metaphor goes along with the initial Web as primarily a read-only medium. Most users could see things, but you can't easily change things. That is changing today with what people call "Web 2.0," a style of Web programming that integrates the full power of direct manipulation into Web-based applications, along with the use of Web-based information services.

Technical people understand networks, routers, servers and all the rest of the hardware that makes the Internet and the Web work, so they have a conceptual model that looks like a system diagram of hardware components, supporting software structures and protocols. Most of the people who go online don't think that way; in fact, they don't even know what hardware is where. They think of the Web in terms of sites and pages that belong to some person or organization. If you say,

"Well, is there a server? Where is that site?"

"It's at Somebody.com. It's on their site."

They don't think of it as being on a server in some computer center, they think of it as being at Somebody.com. In their mind, the geography of the sites has to do with what pages are connected to Web addresses. That is a geographic conceptual model, but it is completely different from the physical one of networks, routers, and servers.

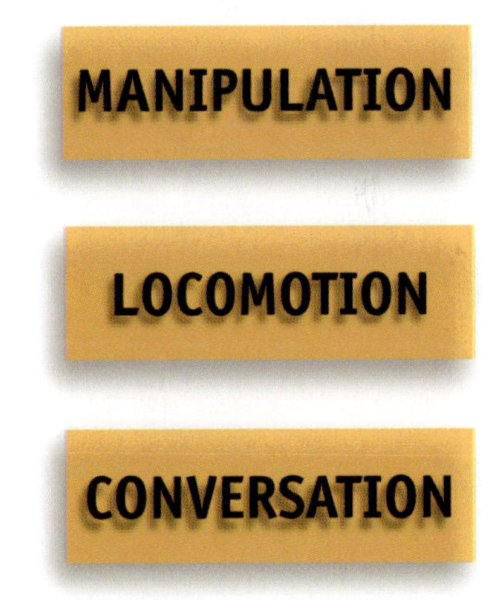

Three main ways that we interact

- Buying a book on Amazon
- Trying on clothes

The immediacy advantage

> When you compare the Internet to earlier forms of communication, it has one obvious huge advantage, which is its immediacy, which is independent of geography. No matter what I do on the Net, it could be having an effect anywhere in the world, basically at the same instant, microseconds. There are a lot of things for which that's really important and where it made a big difference. I think the fallacy was in assuming that that's what everybody wanted for everything, and therefore all kinds of transactions, all kinds of communications would just shift there, when of course no medium is right for everything. And I think people have learned that for certain kinds of things Internet communication is really wonderful, used all the time, and for other kinds of things, it doesn't work.

Shopping is an example. If you want to buy a book, and you already know the title and the author, and you just want to order it fast, something like Amazon is wonderful. You type it in, order with one click, and soon it arrives. Buying clothing is quite different. Looking at pictures on the Web is not the same as touching the clothes and trying them on. Terry explains that it is a communication issue:

> I think one of the interesting things about the Internet is that it's very new, but it's not new. Obviously it provides a technology; it provides a speed and ease of communication, which is very different from what it was before, but in the end it's a communication medium. People have had new communication media over time, over many centuries, and there are certain things that people care about that they will then adapt to whatever new medium they have.
>
> When you look at the original idea of the Internet, if you actually go back and look historically, it was for people to be able to run programs on somebody else's computer. So I could be at MIT, which was one of the early branches of the Internet, somebody could be here at Stanford, and they could run my program while sitting at their terminal at Stanford. Things like email weren't even part of that original notion. They got sort of tacked on as it went, and when they did, people realized that the real power of this networking was the communication part.

If you look at the Internet as a whole and ask what is most used, of course it's communication through things like email and chat. Those have been really dominant applications. In the future I think we're going to see many more applications that depend on the high bandwidth of sending video images. Right now video is still a second-class citizen because technology doesn't make it really easy, really smooth, really efficient and cheap. I think that the video phone, which never worked in it's earlier incarnations, is going to be much more successful. I think we will see a lot of video applications, a lot of video surveillance, video distribution, and other ways to make use of the extra bandwidth that's coming with broadband.

Online communities have worked very well in certain kinds of niches. There are online communities of people who are sharing and helping each other, who don't necessarily live in the same place, and maybe aren't physically able to get out and see each other, and really get a tremendous benefit out of that. But, in general, it hasn't replaced your company, your neighborhood, your school; the kind of communities that are really built on a richer set of interactions that include linguistic and visual communication; they're built on a sharing of a physical space. I think we're still inherently physical animals, and what we do in a physical space really effects us on a psychological level, even if in some abstract sense you could say it's the same information that we would get over a screen.

Google

During the 2002/3 academic year, Terry Winograd took a sabbatical from Stanford to spend a year at Google. He already knew Larry Page and Sergey Brin very well as they had been his students before they founded Google, and Larry was his advisee. He was excited to be there, because this was the first company that he had consulted with that was having a major impact on the marketplace. The others had been research laboratories, and he enjoyed the direct connection to the needs and demands of serving hundreds of millions of people and trying to understand what kinds of things they use and do. He compares it to the academic situation:

From a human-computer interaction research perspective it was incredible. We struggle and struggle in our lab at Stanford to set up

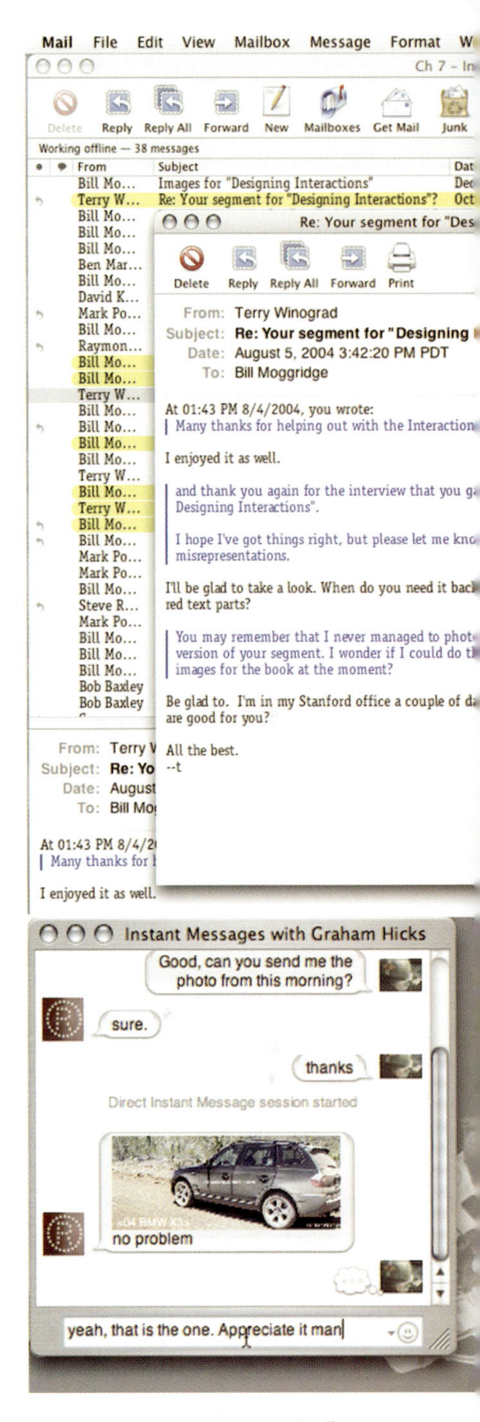

Email ■
Chat ■

an experiment with twenty or forty people. At Google, they can run an experiment with a hundred million people by just sticking something on the Web. So it's been a very useful experience for me in broadening out my sense of how things work.

I think they've been very successful for a number of reasons, but largely because they've respected what it is they think users can do and what users want. I think that's a big lesson from Google. They don't say, "Here's what we're going to force on you, here's what we think we can sell you."

They really started from a point of view of, "Here's what we hope will be useful. Let's find out. Let's try it." Certainly the culture is very user-empirical driven. For a lot of questions, the answer is, "I don't know, let's put it up and experiment and see what people do."

Here is another example of a process that combines the focus on people with prototyping. Throughout this book, as with Bill Atkinson and Larry Tesler designing the Macintosh pull-down menus, we keep seeing examples of successful design that combine efforts to understand the needs and wants of users with rapid iterative prototypes to test the concepts. The dramatic difference in the Internet age is that the prototypes can reach millions of users immediately. Terry also observed that Larry Page had a surprisingly diffident attitude to money:

In the early years of Google, Larry Page, who was my student, used to come in, and we'd chat. I'd worked with him some on the algorithms they used for the search, so he'd come in and he'd talk about what they were doing with the algorithms and how they were improving the search and so on, and I'd say, "How are you going to make money?"

At that point there were no ads, it was just a straight search engine. They were providing it as a free service. He would do his little smile and say, "Well, we'll figure it out later."

I think that really got it off on the right foot. The starting point was not, "How do you make money on the Web?" The starting point was, "I have an idea for a search engine that's going to be better. Let's get it out there and see if people want to try it. Then, we'll figure out later where to go with it."

So when they started putting ads on, instead of starting with, "What's the way we can maximize advertising revenue?" they said,

"What's the way we can give something that's useful to users without getting in their face too much?"

The use of small text ads in place of banners and pop-ups was driven by a sense of thinking what it's going to mean to the user. I've heard commentators complain that Google is too much driven by the technologists, that the people who are running it care more about having good technology than whether it makes money or not. I think that's still true, although it has certainly moved into the world of making large amounts of money.

Google established its position by providing quality, because when they started out, they were not the only search engine. People used Alta Vista, people used Lycos, and there were several other search engines. Google, by being respectful, that is, by not dumping stuff in people's face, and also by providing better-quality results, gradually took on more of the market. At this point they have a very large share, and it's growth was self-feeding in the sense that people who used it told their friends, and more people used it, and it built up a momentum.

The obvious big threat to anybody in the computer business is Microsoft. Microsoft has the same advantage they've had in every other area they've gone into: they own the desktop. So right now when you want to search on Google, you go to the browser and you search. But there's no reason Microsoft couldn't put a search box into Word and Excel and so on, which goes to their search engine, and you don't have to go to the browser. They've got your eyeballs on their applications, and they can control much more where you go. I don't think Google feels threatened that other search engines are going to beat them on quality. They're getting better. All of them are getting better, and everything improves, but Google got a good head start, and they have a lot of smart people developing better quality. I think the real questions that are going to come up are how this integrates into these larger pictures, like who owns the browser? Who owns the desktop? As we know, that's been played out in many other areas in court in the commercial field.

Photo courtesy of Google

Larry Page and Sergey Brin

Larry Page and Sergey Brin founded Google together in 1998. Larry is now "Co-Founder & President, Products" but was the CEO for the first three years, growing the company to more than two hundred employees and profitability before he found Eric Schmidt to take over as CEO and chairman. Larry was brought up in Ann Arbor, Michigan, where his father was a computer science professor at Michigan State University. He was passionate about computers from the age of six and graduated with honors from the computer engineering program at the University of Michigan, where he built a programmable plotter and inkjet printer out of Legos. He went on to the PhD program in computer science at Stanford University, where he met Sergey Brin. Sergey, originally from Moscow, graduated with honors in mathematics and computer science from the University of Maryland and is now "Co-Founder & President, Technology" at Google. He is fascinated by the challenges of extracting information from the huge unstructured world of the Internet and has published more than a dozen academic papers. He was working on "data mining" at Stanford when he met Larry. After lots of stimulating arguments, they found they shared a passion for understanding information structures and started working together. They were looking at the structure of links and accidentally ended up with a method that could improve the ranking of results, so they said, "Why don't we build a search engine?" Their interview was in the spring of 2002. At the time of writing, in late 2004, they have successfully taken Google public, with strong financial results and a share price that has pleased their owners.

Web Images Groups News Froogle Local more »

Advanced Search
Preferences
Language Tools

Google Search I'm Feeling Lucky

Advertising Programs - Business Solutions - About Google

©2005 Google - Searching 8,058,044,651 web pages

Larry Page and Sergey Brin

From its humble beginnings in Larry Page's and Sergey Brin's Stanford dorm room six years ago, the company has become the latest mecca for clever engineers and a $2-billion-a-year growth machine.

Fred Vogelstein, *Fortune* magazine, December 13, 2004

Successful Searching

SERGEY BRIN AND Larry Page met at a spring gathering of new Stanford University PhD computer science candidates in 1995, when Sergey was twenty-three and Larry was twenty-four. This is what they say about the encounter:

■ Google homepage June 2005

> SERGEY We met for the first time when Larry was visiting Stanford, when we were recruiting him as a prospective PhD student for the Computer Science Department, where I already was.
>
> LARRY And I thought Sergey was very obnoxious!
>
> SERGEY I also thought Larry was obnoxious, and I definitely haven't changed my mind. We went on a trip to San Francisco, where we were taking the prospective students, and Larry and I got into continuous arguments all the way, about the value of the real estate, about building codes, about any number of possible things.
>
> LARRY We had interesting and stimulating arguments!

By the end of 1997, they had collaborated to develop technology that would become the foundation for the Google search engine. They started with an interest in data mining, the study of patterns and relationships in data, and went on to develop

PageRank, a software tool to compare one Web page with another. They added a search engine called BackRub, named for its ability to analyze the "back links" pointing to a given Web site:

> SERGEY I was working on data mining, which broadly stated is analyzing large amounts of data for patterns and relationships.

> LARRY I started gathering all the links on the Web, and Sergey naturally fell into this thing of, "There's all this good data to look at," so we started working together. We've been working together since. We sort of accidentally stumbled into designing a search engine. We didn't intend to do a search engine at all. We were doing data mining, we were looking at link structure, and we ended up accidentally with a method that could rank results better, so we said, "Why don't we build a search engine?" Once we decided to build a search engine, we thought that there were a lot of things that we could do that people aren't currently doing. We set out to build a prototype that would let us experiment. One of the things we were working on was link structure and looking at which links were important on the Web. We evolved this thing called PageRank which let's you determine the importance of pages based on the links to them.

PageRank does not count links; instead, it uses the vast link structure of the Web as an organizational tool. It interprets a link from Page A to Page B as a "vote" by Page A for Page B, and then assesses the importance of a page by the "votes" it receives. It also analyzes the pages that cast the votes, so that votes cast by pages that are themselves "important" weigh more heavily and help to make other pages important.

> SERGEY This was just a way to compare one Web page to another Web page. Web pages are very different from one another. You have something like the White House homepage versus I have a page that tells you what I had for lunch on a particular day; we have a café at Google, so all the lunch menus are online. The relative significance of that page is very different from the White House homepage. Compared to almost any other medium, the difference is much greater. Even though you have some books that are much more important than other books, with Web pages it is a much more exaggerated difference. PageRank was a way of comparing one page to another,

and in the end the way we evaluated it was to do little searches. For example, we'd see how all the Web pages that mentioned the word "University" ranked up. We noticed that you've got all the major universities at the top, with Stanford and Harvard and so forth, and of course we'd always compete because everybody wanted their alma mater to be at the top.

Once we did these little experiments, just trying to figure out how good PageRank was, we realized that this was a pretty good way to search. Search had originally been a validation test of PageRank. It turned all the way the other way round, and search became our primary focus, with PageRank becoming one of the tools that made it work well.

LARRY It's a good example of how, when you're doing research, you don't really know what you're going to end up with. We had no intention to build a search engine. We sort of stumbled into it, and we've been working on it ever since.

SERGEY Next, we just continued to play with the technology, to make it a little bit better. We pursued it with purely scientific interest. At some point, we started having a demo up so that everybody on the Web could use it. In the old days of the Web, people just put stuff up and everybody would play with it. It started getting traction; people liked it, and we started talking to the existing search companies, asking, "Well, wouldn't you like to use this technology?

They were kind of interested, but the talks didn't really go anywhere, partly because we weren't that motivated, as we were interested in the purely research aspects. At the time, search engines like Excite, Lycos, and Infoseek were already becoming portals, emulating Yahoo, so they weren't that interested.

Eventually, what had been our little demo prototype, really ballooned out of control. We had to keep accumulating lots of hardware from all over the department. We had to borrow it from different groups.

LARRY We would hang out at the loading dock, waiting for equipment to come in, and then we'd bug the professors.

SERGEY We'd borrow it. Sometimes we wouldn't really mention it because we figured they would never miss a machine or two. This was in order to accommodate the traffic and also the experiments we wanted to do.

1999 special logos
During beta testing ■
"Uncle Sam" search ■
Halloween ■
Thanksgiving ■
Holiday season ■

- Original storage
- "Corkboard" computer
- Google servers
- Al Steremberg, founder of www.wunderground.com

LARRY We had to download the entire Web, and store it and process it.

SERGEY It was more than just the two of us. There were two other people working on it: Scott Hassan, who went on to found the company eGroups that got purchased by Yahoo, and Al Steremberg who founded The Weather Underground.[7] That's one of the main weather Web sites. It's pretty funny that out of that group there are three companies.

LARRY To download the Web you start with a Web page, actually we started with my homepage, and you just follow the links. It's like you're surfing. You just follow the links from that page, and keep doing that until you have the whole Web. It's very much a discovery process.

SERGEY You record everything as you go, and you do it at a rate much faster than a person would; a thousand Web pages per second or something. At the time we didn't do it nearly that quickly.

Larry and Sergey continued to work on search technology during the first half of 1998. They bought a terabyte of disc memory at bargain prices, maxing out their credit cards to do it, and built their own computer housings in Larry's dorm room. Sergey set up a business office in his room and started talking to potential partners who might want to license search technology that worked better than the other options available at the time. They failed to interest the major portals of the day and therefore reluctantly decided to make a go of it on their own. All they needed was a little cash to move out of the dorm and pay off the credit cards, so they wrote a business plan, put their PhD plans on hold, and went looking for investors. They managed to raise a million dollars in funding from family, friends, and angel investors to start Google.

On September 7, 1998, Google was incorporated and moved into its first office, in the garage of a friend in Menlo Park, California, a mile from Stanford University. The garage came with a remote control to open the overhead door, a washer and dryer, and a hot tub. There was also a parking space for the first employee who joined them, Craig Silverstein, who became director of technology. By the end of the year they were answering ten thousand search queries a day, in spite of the fact that they were still in Beta testing. In December *PC Magazine* included Google in the list of "Top 100 Web Sites and Search Engines" for the year.

LARRY We spent a lot of time on the name for the company because we figured that would be important for people to be able to remember it, and for it to be reasonably short. We wanted a name that was fun. Yahoo is a good example of a fun name. We were looking at all sorts of information. We wrote programs to look at domain names. Eventually we ended up with this list of large numbers, and at the top of the list is googol. It seemed like a fun word; it's pretty short, with six characters, and it means ten to the one hundred, a one followed by a hundred zeros. That's pretty much what we wanted to do. We wanted to do really big things! We did have this unfortunate incident where we misspelled it.

SERGEY That's true, it was before the Google spellchecker!

LARRY We didn't have the spellchecker, but it turned out that domain name was available, and the one spelled correctly was not. It's okay, everyone spells it the way we do now!

By early 1999 they were answering half a million search queries a day, and had grown to a group of eight people. They were already too big for the garage, and moved another mile to an office on University Avenue in Palo Alto. Their first commercial search customer, Red Hat, signed on partly because of their commitment to run their servers on the open-source operating system Linux. By the middle of the year they had secured $25 million in equity funding from two of the leading venture capital firms in Silicon Valley, Sequoia Capital and Kleiner Perkins Caufield & Byers. In August they moved again to the heart of Silicon Valley and officially launched their Web site in September. By the end of the millennium they were performing three million searches a day and had proved that they were more than just a university research project.

The Google headquarters was starting to express a unique company culture. Lava lamps in every possible color were oozing and blobbing contentedly on shelves. The boardroom was a

2000 special logos
March 17, St. Patrick's Day
June 18, Father's Day
July 4, Independence Day
November 7, Election Day
November 15, Shichi-go-san

Google

cluster of mobile office chairs around the ping-pong table. People worked on simple desks made of wooden doors propped up on sawhorses, but they were equipped with the most sophisticated computers.

Offering employees a free lunch in the company canteen encouraged the exchange of ideas. Charlie Ayers, the company chef, who had become well known while cooking for the Grateful Dead, prepared delicious meals. Part of the parking lot was roped off twice a week for roller hockey games, encouraged by Sergey's passion for roller blades. He often arrives at work on his blades, wearing a crumpled and sweaty tee shirt emblazoned with the Google logo. He grabs a fresh new one from the store to start the day.

After the initial venture round of funding, Google managed to eke out their resources until they were able to become self-sufficient and profitable.

> LARRY Sergey was very focused on building a profitable company.

> SERGEY We really wanted to be profitable. It was as much an ego thing as anything, I just felt it was lame to have one of these big unprofitable Internet companies.

■ Google lobby

Photo
Author

In the first quarter of 2001, Google was answering more than a hundred million searches per day, and the demands of running the company were growing all the time. Larry set out to replace himself as chief executive, and successfully recruited Dr. Eric Schmidt, chairman and CEO of Novell and a former CTO at Sun Microsystems, to join Google as CEO and chairman of the executive board. Schmidt focused on building the infrastructure for the company to continue along the path of rapid growth and sought the best possible balance between speed of development and high standards of quality.

> LARRY Our growth is based on the quality of our service. We've done almost no marketing. We don't spend any money in order to get people to use Google. A friend tells them to use Google or they read about it. Some of our competitors were spending over a hundred million dollars on TV advertising. We didn't do that, which was good for our business.

Our revenue started with text ads [as opposed to banner ads with intrusive graphics], which I think was a good break for us. The reason people like this is that they usually just click on search results, and as those are just text, we decided to just have text ads that are relevant to the search results. At the time I remember our sales team was very upset with me; I had to argue with them everyday about this. We've actually had very nice pick up with this kind of program in advertising. The ads are good for our users; if you search for golf clubs you've got some place to buy golf clubs, that's a useful thing for the user. The advertiser makes money and so they pay us some of it. It's not a very complicated decision to say, "I'm an advertiser, and I'm making $3.00 on every user that Google sends me, so it's OK for me to pay Google a $1.50 fee."

By the beginning of 2002 the size and scope of searchable information available through the Google search engine had grown to three billion Web documents, including an archive of Usenet messages dating back to 1981. New services were added as tabs on the home page, without cluttering up the design. These included searching news headlines, images, and catalogs.

- Craig Silverstein, Google's first employee
- Dr. Eric Schmidt, CEO and Chairman

LARRY We've added a lot of services. It's a design challenge to add services without increasing the complexity, and we've spent a lot of time on the design. We have tabs now so that you can search for images, or you can search over groups. We have about 300 million images and about 700 million messages on groups. Those were pretty significant enhancements, but it was a complicated design process, to give you access to those features without complicating your normal tasks. We went to a tab design that really helps you with that, so that you can easily do your search on images or groups, and know that those things are possible, but not in such a way that impedes your normal activities.

SERGEY I think one of the other interesting things that we do is that, in a normal Web site, when you add a new service, you deploy it right there on the main site and see how well it does, and then keep it there or take it off. In our case we really insist on initially deploying a new service (like we did with images, or right now we have catalogs, or news search, things like that) off the main page. We insist that they get a lot of traction on their own, without the benefit of that top-page promotion. If they have user pickup at that level, we will go ahead and bring them up as a short cut or convenience to users.

It's really a different way of thinking about it. We're not trying to thrust services on to users; it's only when they actually find the services we are producing useful that we'll give them a more convenient way to get to them. There's huge variety in the kind of needs people have. The diversity of people's search needs has gone up over time. When we started the company, the top ten queries accounted for 3 percent of the searches, but now the top ten queries account for under half a percent of the searches. The diversity of people's needs has gone up over the last few years and I think it will continue to do so as the Internet grows.

On August 19, 2004, Google went public. Larry and Sergey look like mature and purposeful young men as they peer at you from the cover of the December issue of *Fortune*. The subtitle raises the question, "Is this company worth $165 a share?" and the feature article inside argues both sides of the answer. Four months after the IPO the stock is worth about double the initial value, and advertising revenues are growing healthily. It remains to be seen whether they emerge as a real competitor to Microsoft or fade away more like Netscape. Whether you bet on a positive future for them or not, it is certainly amazing to reflect on how far they have come. Recall Terry Winograd's question of only five years earlier, "How are you going to make money?" It is poignant to think of Larry's little smile and his answer, "Well, we'll figure it out later."

One has to remember that they started Google at the height of the dot-com madness, when venture capital was flowing to people with any harebrained idea and the business model for most of the startups was revenue from banner ads. This made most of the dot-com sites horrible to read, as you were constantly bombarded by the animated advertisements. Browsing was like standing in Times Square. Larry and Sergey resisted the temptation to ride this wave, staying focused on developing real value for the users of their product and making their product perform. The approach certainly worked.

When you browse www.google.com it is easy to find out a lot about the company; they are very open in their approach to

2001 special logos
March 9, Indian Festival of Color ■
April 22, Earth Day ■
July 14, Bastille Day ■
August 15, Korean Liberation Day ■
December 10, Nobel Prize centennial ■

sharing information. Take a look, for example, at the "Letter from the founders,"[8] which explains why Google is not a conventional company.

The first sentence of the company overview says that Google's mission is to "Organize the world's information and make it universally accessible and useful." Larry sums up the philosophy behind this statement:

> The perfect search engine would understand exactly what you mean and give back exactly what you want. I think the main issues with search are not so much around interaction. I think it has more to do with just pure quality in understanding. We like to say that we're focused on the ultimate search engine. The ultimate search engine would basically understand everything on the Web, it would understand exactly what you wanted, and it would give you the right thing or the right things. We're a long way from that. In computer science we call that AI-complete, meaning that it requires artificial intelligence; it would have to be smart. If you had the perfect search engine, you could just stop working, because it would just do anything; it could answer any question. We have a long way to go before we can get to that, but we will continue to make advances that really are significant for people.

■ Nasdaq launch—Larry Page signs

Google Truths

Under the heading "Our Philosophy," Google publishes "Ten things Google has found to be true":

1 Focus on the user and all else will follow.
2 It's best to do one thing really, really well.
3 Fast is better than slow.
4 Democracy on the Web works.
5 You don't need to be at your desk to need an answer.
6 You can make money without doing evil.
7 There's always more information out there.
8 The need for information crosses all borders.
9 You can be serious without a suit.
10 Great just isn't good enough.

These ten things form a manifesto, both for the design of their product and for the development of the company. The first three are about the design approach, so here they are in full, augmented by some comments taken from the interview. The others are more generally about business issues, so if you want to see the full text, look on the site.

1 Focus on the user and all else will follow.

From its inception, Google has focused on providing the best user experience possible. While many companies claim to put their customers first, few are able to resist the temptation to make small sacrifices to increase shareholder value. Google has steadfastly refused to make any change that does not offer a benefit to the users who come to the site:

- The interface is clear and simple.
- Pages load instantly.
- Placement in search results is never sold to anyone.
- Advertising on the site must offer relevant content and not be a distraction.

2004 special logos
January 1, Happy New Year
January 15, Spirit on Mars
February 3, birthday of Julia Gaston
February 14, Valentine's Day
February 29, Leap Year

By always placing the interests of the user first, Google has built the most loyal audience on the Web. And that growth has come not through TV ad campaigns, but through word of mouth from one satisfied user to another.

Sergey is self-deprecating about the design of the site, and it is true that the typography of the home page is not likely to win any awards in graphic design annuals. The most important qualities of the design derive from the focus on performance and Sergey's insistence on a simple and quiet design. There is a dramatic contrast between the open white space of the Google homepage, and the throbbing and pounding of typical pages with animated banner ads. The embellishments of the logo for special occasions also provide some charm and humor.

Sergey makes light of his initial design and talks about the importance of user testing:

> Originally I was the Web master and I designed the page, and I wasn't about to spend a lot of time on it, so I just put a search box in there, a search button, and the logo. Eventually we added a little bit of stuff about the company, but it was still quite small and compact, and we realized how powerful that was. It actually matters when you go to the homepage of a search engine: you don't want to spend a lot of time trying to find the search box. You want people to be able to come there, and right away use it for what they want. After that we made a conscious decision that we were going to take things off that page. If you look at the amount of white space, it has actually gone up over time, even over the last couple of years; we've made a number of revisions to it that have made it even lighter, less cluttered. I designed the basic logo originally, and we had a graphic designer tweak the font. The logo is one of my proudest accomplishments. The coloring was very important; the original thought behind the logo was that it was meant to be playful in terms of the coloring, but also with a 3D very solid quality to it, so that it would be both friendly and reliable.
>
> One thing I've learned over time is that it is very hard to predict what will make the designs for our products great to use, so actually we do a lot of testing. We have people come by our offices, and we have a whole test lab, where we look at them through one-way

mirrors and things like that. One of the really important things to us has always been to have our own Web site. Other companies just try to provide search services to others, but for us, having our own Web site has allowed us to have a direct interaction with users. It has allowed us to run tests, and to be able to really learn about how people use the site.

For example, we always wondered about how many search results we should display. I have my default, I always show fifty search results, so I thought, "Why would you want to have just ten?" It turned out in testing that people really wanted just ten. Sometimes your personal bias really colors your way of thinking. I don't know that we've fine-tuned it between nine, ten, or eleven, but once you're in that range, ten is a number that people deal with pretty well.

2 It's best to do one thing really, really well.

Google does search. Google does not do horoscopes, financial advice, or chat. With the largest research group in the world focused exclusively on solving search problems, Google knows what it does well and how it could be done better. Through continued iteration on difficult problems, Google has been able to solve complex issues that stymie others and provide continuous improvements to a service already considered the best on the Web. Innovations like Google's spell checker and the Google Toolbar, which enables users to search using Google from any Website, make finding information a fast and seamless experience for millions of users. Google's entire staff is dedicated to creating the perfect search engine and work tirelessly toward that goal.

We all know how hard it is to be efficient and productive if we are being constantly interrupted by meetings, phone calls, or urgent emails. The culture of a development organization is often in danger of similar types of distraction at a larger scale. Think of Apple in the years when John Sculley was CEO, when there was little focus, and the development organization was creating a huge array of new products; it took the return of Steve Jobs to bring

2004 special logos
May 9, Mother's Day
June 8, Venus transit
Summer Olympics in Athens
September 7, Google's sixth birthday
September 23, Birthday of Ray Charles

back a cohesion and effective concentration on a narrower set of objectives. Similarly with Palm, it was Jeff Hawkins's insistence on doing a limited set of things really well on the Palm OS that led to such a successful design.

Larry and Sergey spent years relentlessly focused on the well-defined and simple goal of being the best at search. They had to accept that the perfect result is not possible every time; here they talk about how the impossibility of achieving their goal gave rise to the "I'm feeling lucky" button:

> LARRY We are trying to build a search engine that's so good that you don't even need to look at the results. It's a kind of interaction design thing, that instead of looking at the results you could go directly straight to the first result. You never even see the results; if you type Stanford you just got the Stanford homepage. It doesn't quite work yet. It's not the case that you always get the best thing first, because we're not perfect. We want to be fun about it and not over-promise, so if you click on the "I'm feeling lucky" button, that means that you think you're going to get the right thing. Most people don't necessarily know what it means, but it becomes an interesting conversation topic for people, saying, "Now here's Google. What does this 'I'm feeling lucky' button do?" It has a lot of marketing value I think.

> SERGEY It's kind of a fun thing to have on our site, but it also keeps our engineers target sights in view for what we want to do, which is to always keep the one result on top, the correct one every time. It's impossible to do this every time but you can always do it a greater percentage of the time than before; it's like Xeno's paradox, get half as close to the goal.

3 Fast is better than slow.

GOOGLE BELIEVES IN INSTANT GRATIFICATION. YOU WANT ANSWERS AND YOU WANT THEM RIGHT NOW. WHO ARE WE TO ARGUE? GOOGLE MAY BE THE ONLY COMPANY IN THE WORLD WHOSE STATED GOAL IS TO HAVE USERS LEAVE ITS WEBSITE AS QUICKLY AS POSSIBLE. BY FANATICALLY OBSESSING ON SHAVING EVERY EXCESS BIT AND BYTE FROM OUR PAGES AND INCREASING THE EFFICIENCY OF OUR SERVING environment, Google has broken its own speed records time and again. Others assumed large servers were the fastest way to handle massive amounts of data. Google found thousands of networked PCs to be faster. Where others accepted apparent speed limits imposed by search algorithms, Google wrote new algorithms that proved there were no limits. And Google continues to work on making it all go even faster.

The search time is displayed prominently at the top of every result. For example when I type an esoteric query about a little known aluminum trailer into the search box, the header says:

Results 1–10 of about 167 for Southland Runabout Trailers. (0.29 seconds)

By contrast if I try the well-known publisher of this book, the header says:

Results 1–10 of about 5,620,000 for MIT Press. (0.16 seconds)

How amazing that both results arrive so quickly! It does make you feel that the whole world of information is at your fingertips, and it must also please the people at the MIT Press to be above the five million mark. Sergey and Larry comment on the time question:

> Sergey We measure the time from when a user has some information need until we've satisfied it. That includes going to the Google homepage, finding a search box (which is pretty easy to find on the Google homepage), actually getting the results, so that computation is pretty fast, being able to look through them and to pick one out. Obviously, having right ones there is the most important thing.

> Larry The "snippets" are another example that save the user time. The summaries that we generate are actually specific to the search. In the little two-line summaries we give you, we show you where your search terms match in the document. That requires extra work for us, but it saves you time in deciding which things to click on; actually it might even have what you are looking for in the summary itself.

2004 special logos
October 4, SpaceShipOne wins X Prize ■
October 31, Halloween ■
November 2, Vote ■
November 25, Thanksgiving ■
Season's Greetings ■

These three "truths" are serving Google well as design principles or guidelines. Larry is also interested in a future where dialogue is intrinsic to the interaction design:

> I do think that in terms of interaction, there's lots of things we can do to make Google better. Right now, if you type a query, you get back some search results, some images, or some discussion information. Potentially, there are a lot of more kinds of data that you could get. You might want to have a dialogue with the search engine, so that when you type a query, it replies, "Did you mean this, or did you mean that?" The challenge with those things is that they haven't so far been useful enough to warrant the extra communication. We have people who try all sorts of different things, and it's really hard to predict what is going to work well. Mostly it's really important to be able to try out many different things quickly. You can pretty much tell whether they go to work after you've done a simple prototype.

BBCi

The BBCi homepage[9] contrasts strongly with Google. The BBC is a publicly owned organization, funded by license fees that are decreed by government, so it is beholden to the general public, whereas Google is a business aiming to develop a product that will please individuals. This leads the BBC to try to maintain a strong sense of local community and social responsibility, but Google strives to design for the best results, while remaining politically and socially neutral.

The BBC has a long tradition as a media provider, so the content of their Web-based offering is inextricably intertwined with their parallel media offerings in TV and radio, and the BBC brand is dictated by the public's preconceptions of the organization. Google, on the other hand, has a razor-sharp focus, as defined in their second truth, "It's best to do one thing really, really well—Google does search."

Steve Rogers was responsible for leading the team that designed a new homepage for BBCi in 2002, and in the interview that follows, he takes us through a case study of the design development. He contrasts the priorities for a portal like BBCi with a search engine like Google:

> Google has made an enormous impact. They did the same in the Internet world as Palm did in the PDA world; they looked at that whole business, which was becoming bloated and unusable, and said, "Okay, what's important about a search engine? What do I actually need this thing for? Let's strip out everything else, get rid of it!" What's important about a search engine is that it loads fast; it gets you what you want—that's it!
>
> Three things are important about a portal like BBCi. First, you want to recognize where you are and feel comfortable; second, it should answer your needs personally, but not necessarily everyone else's in the world; and third, you want to get through it to your destination quickly.
>
> A search engine succeeds by saying, "We don't have anything here, but we can find you everything you need."
>
> A portal for a site like the BBC says, "We can find you exactly what you need. We think that we've probably got the answer within the BBC, so we're going to make it as easy as possible for you to get that answer. And, by the way, if you can't get that answer within the BBC, we're also going to make it as easy as possible for you to find it anywhere." This means including a search engine as an option within the portal experience.

Photo Author

Steve Rogers

Steve Rogers is head of production for BBC New Media and in 2002 was responsible for leading the team that designed a new homepage for BBCi. He studied transportation design, but lost interest in becoming a car stylist when he realized how narrow the specialization was. He moved into industrial design instead and found a job with Philips Electronics, where his main task was designing VCRs. This triggered a fascination with user interface design: "When you've designed fifty or a hundred video recorders, you realize there's very little wrong with the way a video recorder looks. There's one thing wrong with a video recorder: no one can use the thing!" He was able to work on enhancing the interaction by using the TV for displaying control information. His expertise in interaction design gave him the chance to set up the Philips Multi Media Center in California's Silicon Valley to look at the impact of digital media on product design. This was at the beginning of the dot-com boom, so there were a lot of exciting innovations in the air. His center hosted a stream of visitors from Philips Design, with the remit of demonstrating future technologies, for example, a portal that he developed that gave the user the chance to personalize their home page. At the height of the dot-com boom in 2000, Razorfish offered him the opportunity to lead their product development team with a goal of integrating hardware and software, but the crash came all too soon, and he was only there for one year. When the opportunity to develop BBCi came up, he welcomed it.

Steve Rogers

We wanted to create a page where users would feel at home and that they would adopt as their own homepage. It had to have character as well as appearing to respond to them: or even mould itself around them. . . . Just like a pair of shoes really.

Quote from *The Glass Wall*[10]

BBCi

Well-worn boots from Doc Martens

Photo
This image, and the others in this Steve Rogers interview, are taken from *The Glass Wall*, the documentary book about the BBC homepage redesign, 2002

STEVE ROGERS HAD been suffering at Razorfish during the downturn and hating the fact that his job had become one of managing the process of downsizing. He felt that he had learned a lot about the design of online services and understood the business model. He was interested in getting closer to the creation of actual content and wanted to understand where content comes from, how it is created, and how you build the stuff that drives the whole system. The BBC seemed the perfect place to do that:

> I was phenomenally excited when someone phoned me up and said, "I'm not sure if you're interested in working for the BBC?"
>
> Given the state of Razorfish at the time, my first answer was "yes," and the second answer was "and, what is it to do?"
>
> Then to find out that the opportunity was to build and head up design navigation within BBC New Media was just a phenomenal opportunity. Fantastic!
>
> The BBC has one of the most visited, one of the most successful Internet sites in the world. It has over a million pages of content, which is just massive. One of the statements within the BBC at the moment is, "Move from monologue to dialogue." This means moving from an old world broadcast environment, where you're talking at the

Mandy's mood board

BBCi homepage

Voice mapping über map

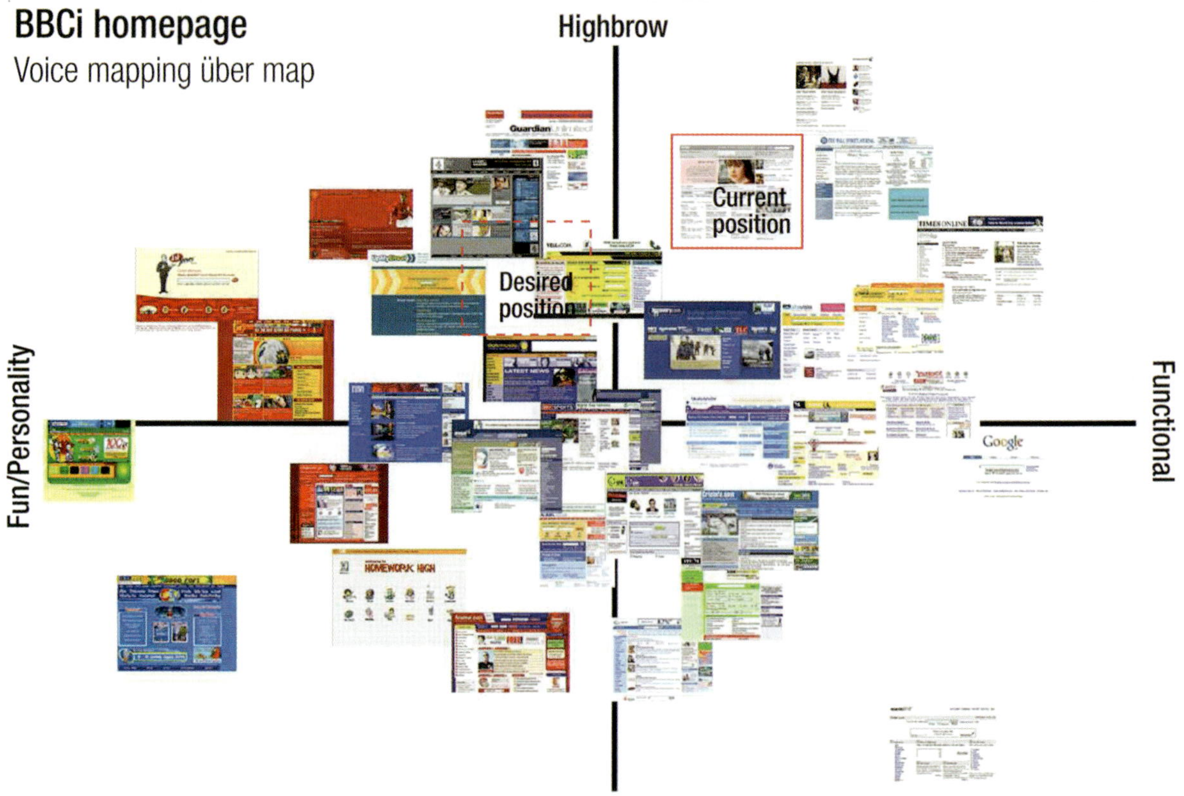

audience, to a two-way dialogue with an audience; you can really understand what people want to get from the design.

A policy goal of the BBC is to help people become engaged in the digital world, so they want to build engaging services for people who are not used to the Internet, or to any other digital media. For the design of the BBCi homepage, that means trying to make it really intuitive to explore the site, making sure that people have the opportunity to find what they want easily. It also means helping them engage in dialogue by offering a simple way to comment on something they've seen, or send an email. Live chats and message boards are offered and connected with the BBC programs, so there is more two-way traffic.

There is a popular community site called "h2g2," which is built by the audience. At the other end of the scale, "Video Nation" makes it possible for people to publish short films, diaries, and stories about their own life. The goal is to encourage dialog across the UK as a whole. Steve talks about the implications of this for interaction design:

- *Top*
  A mood board describes one of the personae
- *Bottom*
  A map analyzes positioning

> If you are enabling interactions between people and BBCi as a service, you've got to do it in a way which people understand and actually want to engage with. One of the things that we've spent a lot of time doing is understanding our audience, understanding who it is that's likely to get involved in the sort of communities that we have. If you take a typical Web community, it's not a typical BBC Web community. A typical BBC Web community might be around gardening. It might be around antiques, all sorts of rather unusual topics for the Web. We have to visit people, talk to people, do a certain amount of ethnographic research, start to build personas, understand what those personas mean, start to live those personas. One of the luxuries we have at the BBC is that we're not reliant on advertisers to tell us what to do. That allows us to build a best practice in things like user-centered design, so if we feel it's appropriate to involve users in the process, then we really do it.
>
> One of the things that's very key to the BBC is that it seems a safe place, so parents will allow their children to use it; so we've got to be damned sure that it really is. It's not at all easy. At the moment, almost all of our chat rooms, and certainly all the chat

The history

The BBC homepage has been through three major changes in its life, most recently the launch of BBCi in November 2001. Along the way it has seen many ideas and concepts for new brands and radical layouts.

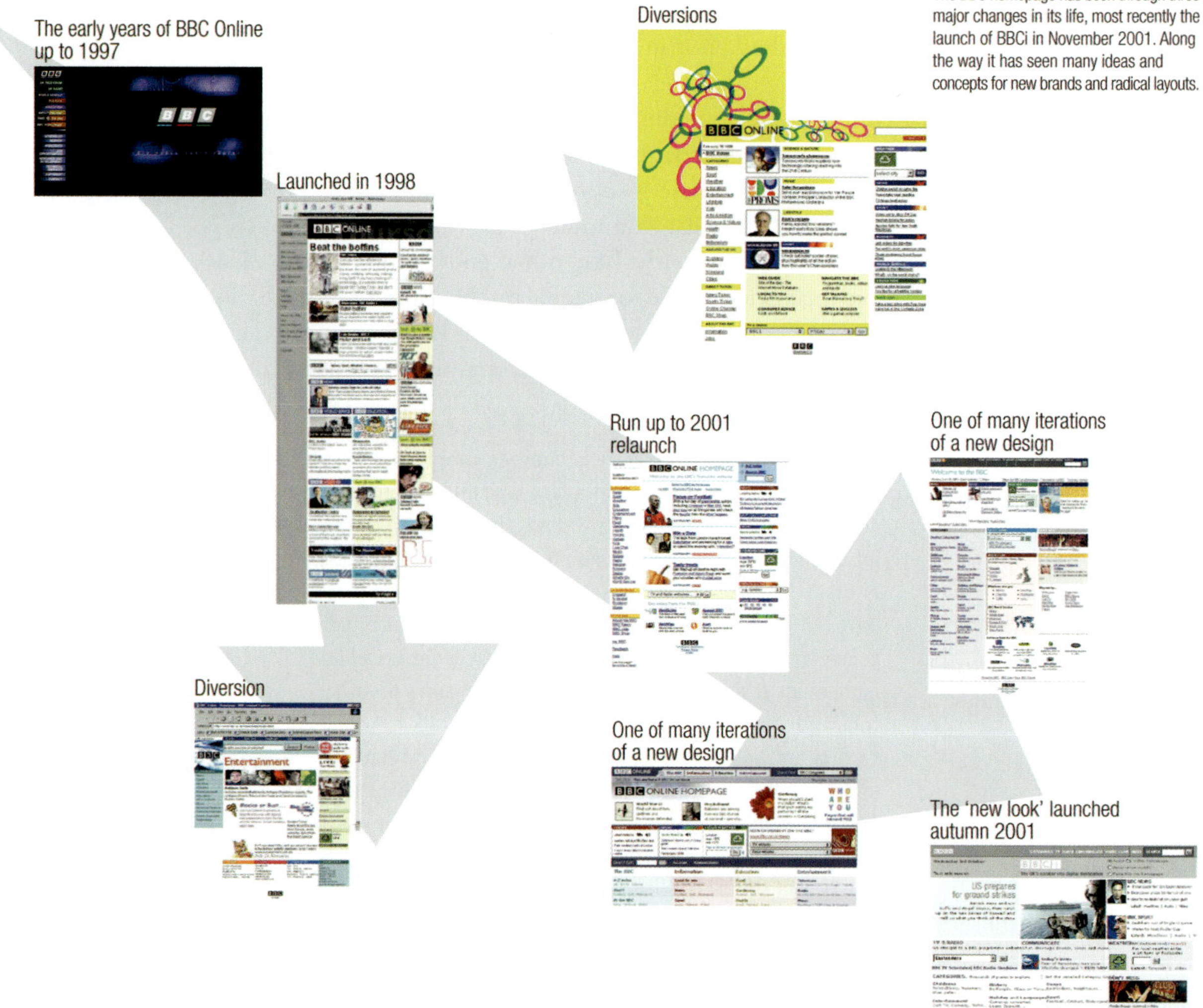

rooms that are aimed at young people, are fully moderated, so that parents know that if their children are using a BBC chat room, there are BBC staff watching what's going on all of the time. With the more grown up chat rooms, something like gardening, we start to allow the community of the chat room to moderate itself, but still with BBC moderators looking over what's going on at regular intervals.

The Homepage

THE "BBC NETWORKING CLUB" was started in the mid nineties to experiment with the Internet. It created the first BBC homepage, which looked a bit like a parish magazine. Other areas of the BBC Internet, like BBC News and a lot of the entertainment sites, soon realized that the Internet is a medium worth taking seriously and moved their designs forward, but the basic navigation of the site stayed as it was. When Steve Rogers was given the chance to apply for his job at the BBC, the first thing he did was to look at the homepage.

■ The historical development of BBCi

I looked at the basic skeleton and navigation of the site, and it was atrocious; it was awful. The content was wonderful, but the site was fragmented and very difficult to get around; it had no clear voice. At the interview, when I was asked what I thought of it, I said, "It's not very good. The navigation really isn't very good, and there doesn't seem to be any focus."

Luckily, that was what they all thought too, so it was not difficult when I arrived to say, "We need to get things moving and changing very, very quickly."

The old site had four or five ways to get to the same information. It had incredibly differing ways of indicating something was a link to somewhere else. It also had a frightening amount of information. It is a tough information architecture challenge to develop a site that needs to get across as much information as a massive destination site like the BBC. If you then duplicate links three or four times, you've just made your task three or four times harder.

One of the first things we did was look at that and say, "Realistically, for a site this size, we need some anchor points."

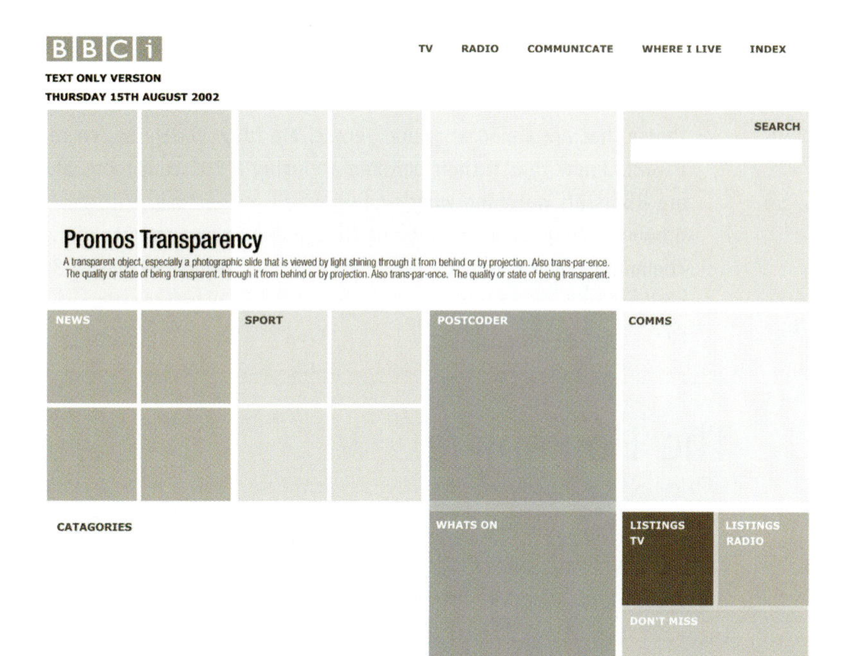
BBCi
TV
RADIO
COMMUNICATE
WHERE I LIVE
INDEX
TEXT ONLY VERSION
THURSDAY 15TH AUGUST 2002
SEARCH
Promos Transparency
A transparent object, especially a photographic slide that is viewed by light shining through it from behind or by projection. Also trans-par-ence.
The quality or state of being transparent. through it from behind or by projection. Also trans-par-ence. The quality or state of being transparent.
NEWS
SPORT
POSTCODER
COMMS
CATAGORIES
WHATS ON
LISTINGS TV
LISTINGS RADIO
DON'T MISS
WORLD SERVICE

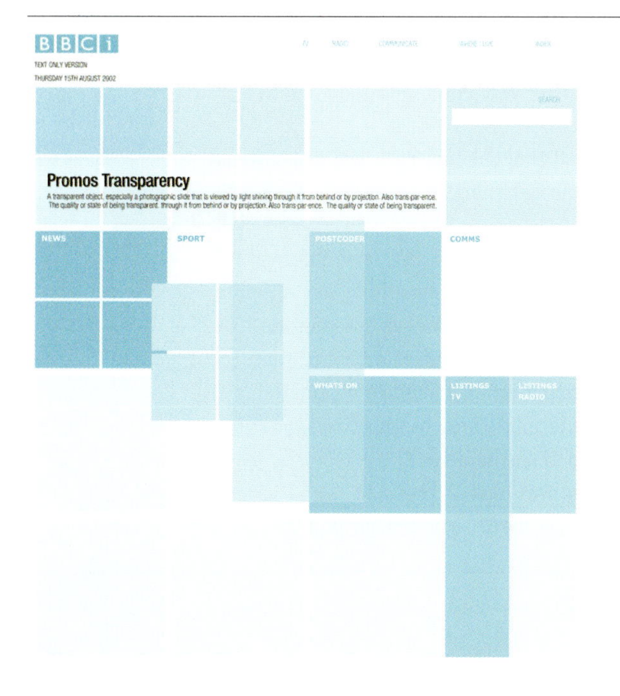
BBCi
Promos Transparency
NEWS
SPORT
POSTCODER
COMMS
WHATS ON
LISTINGS TV
LISTINGS RADIO

BBCi
TV
RADIO
COMMUNICATE
WHERE I LIVE
INDEX
TEXT ONLY VERSION
THURSDAY 15TH AUGUST 2002
SEARCH
Promos Transparency
COMMS
CATAGORIES
WORLD SERVICE
LISTINGS TV
EASTENDERS
BBC ONE
BBC TWO
BBC CHOICE
BBC FOUR
EASTENDERS
BBC ONE
BBC TWO
BBC CHOICE
BBC FOUR
EASTENDERS
BBC ONE
BBC TWO
BBC CHOICE
BBC FOUR

We introduced a toolbar, which was effectively an anchor point for the user, so that stayed on every page on the site. We gave it a visual language that was almost like a browser or a widget, the "browser" of the BBC environment.

This global toolbar is subtly designed in neutral grey, forming a header across the top of the window. It always allows you to return to the homepage, to search for specific destinations, or to jump straight into the main categories. The enormous archive of over a million pages makes navigation difficult, so a good search capability is essential. A lot of the archive is old news, but still interesting for research, and the BBC wants to offer the British public the opportunity to access it. There is a specific archival search within news but not within the rest of the site. The search demonstrates that you are looking at UK information, thus differentiating itself from search engines like Google. So for example, if you put in "Football," you will find soccer, and if you look for Hampshire, you will find Hampshire in the UK, not New Hampshire. It also has very carefully structured parental filters built into it, so that children can search safely, and BBCi is seen as a "trusted guide." Steve uses the analogy of a pair of comfortable shoes to communicate the aesthetic values of this sense of trust.

- *Top*
  Grid for layout of homepage
- *Bottom*
  The color of the images in the promotional material drives the color of the page

If you go to into a shop to buy yourself a pair of Doc Martens, they're not actually that comfortable. Once you've worn them every day for about six months or so, then they start to mold themselves to your foot, and they are comfortable. If you leave them in the cupboard for another six months or a year, then pick them up and put them on again, they're still comfortable because they are still adapted to you. One of the nice things about digital technology is you can do that same thing.

We also wanted to make sure that the graphic language of the site said that it was trustworthy, said that it was professional, but at the same time was at least somewhat engaging and intimate. That's one of the reasons why the clearly dominant main promotional image at the top of the page is always a very personal image. We have a very elegant looking structure, which is then supported by a very intimate image, appealing to people's soul, to their emotions. It's very often a picture of a person, often a face close-up, or if not, it's always a very emotive image.

BBCi
CATEGORIES TV RADIO COMMUNICATE WHERE I LIVE INDEX SEARCH Go
Text only | MAKE THIS YOUR HOMEPAGE
BBCi
Wednesday 20th November 2002
SEARCH THE WEB
SEARCH
the Web BBCi only
POPULAR SEARCHES RIGHT NOW ARE:
• bitesize
• eastenders
• fantasy football
Why search the web with BBCi?
"Sex Bomb"
That's what they're saying about Ainslie on the message board... but which Fame Academy student do you support? Have your say!
Vote to help your favourite along the road to success.
Would you like to be in the limelight? Get top tips from the professionals at OneMusic.
NEWS
Audio | Video
• Race to contain tanker disaster
• Forces chief deals strike warning
• Cervical cancer vaccine success
News in 43 languages عربي | TÜRKÇE
SPORT
Audio | Video
• England wait on Crawley
• Gabbidon out for Wales
• Broadhurst secures Tour place
TV
• BBC TV schedules
• Digital TV
• A-Z of BBC programme websites
RADIO
• All BBC radio
• Launch radio player
• Radio schedules
WORLD SERVICE
News in 43 languages عربي | TÜRKÇE
• Arabic
• Chinese
• English
• Hindi
• Russian
• Spanish
• Urdu
• Others...
DON'T MISS
THE CHANGING FACE OF TV & RADIO
YOUR BBC
• Contact us
• Help
• Jobs at the BBC
• About the BBC
WHERE I LIVE
To get information for a different location, enter a postcode or town
GO
e.g. HR4 9AR or Hereford
Weather for SE5 8UT
light rain
min 7°C max 11°C
View the 5 day forecast
Your local BBCi site:
• London
What's on for London: South:
Cinema, Clubs, Music, Comedy, Theatre, more...
Your BBC local radio station:
• BBC London 94.9
• Schedule for BBC London 94.9
Your local school league tables:
• Primary schools
• Secondary schools and colleges
COMMUNICATE
Your thoughts, your views
From antiques to holidays and gardening, share your ideas on the Lifestyle message boards.
BBCi DIRECTORY
A B C D E F G H I J K L M
N O P Q R S T U V W X Y Z
Business & Money
Small Business, Money, News, Programmes, Work & Careers...
Children's
CBBC: Club, Art
CBeebies: Games, Stories...
Education & Learning
Schools, Colleges, Revision, Languages, Subject Listing...
Entertainment
Comedy, Drama, Films, Games, Lottery, Teens...
Health
Fitness, Healthy Living, Medical Conditions, Nutrition, Parenting...
History
Ancient History, Great Britons, Historic Figures, Pyramid, War & Conflict...
Lifestyle
Antiques, Food, Gardening, Holiday, DIY...
Music
News, Reviews, TV/Radio, Gigs/Concerts, Listen...
News
Business, Local, UK, Weather, World...
Science & Nature
Animals, Birds, Genetics, Robots, Space...
Society & Culture
Communicate, Crime, Disability, Religion & Ethics...
Sport
Cricket, Football, Motorsport, Other Sports...
View all categories...
BBC Shop
Buy BBC products
CBeebies
Play and learn with CBeebies
Learning
BBC Learning resources for all
CBBC
Access your favourite shows
MAKE THIS YOUR HOMEPAGE

"Digital patina" is a way that the design of the homepage expresses the fact that it is adapting itself to you. This is achieved by an algorithm that selects any of the areas that are separately "cookied" on the page, and changes the intensity of the colors. The areas that you visit frequently pump up slightly in intensity, and the areas that you use less often fade a little. The effect is random, so that it is not predictable or repetitive. The result is that, after you have used the page for a while, the areas that you are most likely to be interested in become more prominent on the page without you having to do anything.

> We chose to cause the effect of "digital patina" through the gradual fading in color, because we wanted to make sure that anywhere you wanted to go was still as easy as it would anyway have been. We wanted to say, "Actually, this is somewhere that you've been to more often." At that point it really feels like your page.

This example of the design for the BBCi homepage shows how a Web portal can provide a gateway to more than one medium, helping people navigate and choose what TV to watch or radio to listen to. At the same time, it offers an adaptable quality that is uniquely facilitated by the Internet, allowing people to access local events, weather, and community, with the "digital patina" developing an appearance that reflects a pattern of personal preferences.

■ BBCi homepage at launch in 2002

The example that follows, in the interview with Mark Podlaseck, also connects to media and provides personalization, but in a very different way. The site www.philipglass.com/glassengine is designed to help you find any piece of music composed by Philip Glass that you want or need, based on attributes that you can navigate by direct manipulation, with the gratification of being able to hear what you have chosen in streaming audio. Before reading the interview, please try the "glassengine" Web site yourself.

Photo Steve Bryant

Mark Podlaseck

The design for the Glass Engine started as a skunkworks project. Philip Glass had worked with Mark Podlaseck on another project a few years before, and he decided he wanted a Web site. This was in the middle of the dot-com boom, so he asked Mark who would be a good designer for the project. They went to various agencies, but no one was willing to talk about anything less than a million-dollar project, so Mark thought, "I'll take a stab at it." Mark works at IBM's T. J. Watson Research Center, in upstate New York, and his research director was sympathetic, believing that there are a lot of large databases giving people navigational problems; a Web site for Philip Glass might offer a solution that could be generalized for access and browsing, as well as having high-profile cultural appeal. Mark originally studied English literature and then shifted to computer science. He got his first job as a system programmer for IBM in 1988 and soon transitioned into design. He was always ambivalent about whether his first love was cultural or technological in bias, so when he found himself at IBM Research working on a program to help Philip Glass, he felt that he had found his niche. The connection between composer and designer/programmer had come about five years before. Mark had brought in the set designer Robert Israel to create three dimensional and theatrical effects for a CD-ROM version of IBM's first interactive annual report. Robert was also designing sets for Philip Glass, so he made the introduction. The three of them later collaborated on a project for interactive opera called *Ghost Dance*.

FILM SCORE **Mishima**

Score for Paul Schrader's film about the life of Japanese w
section.

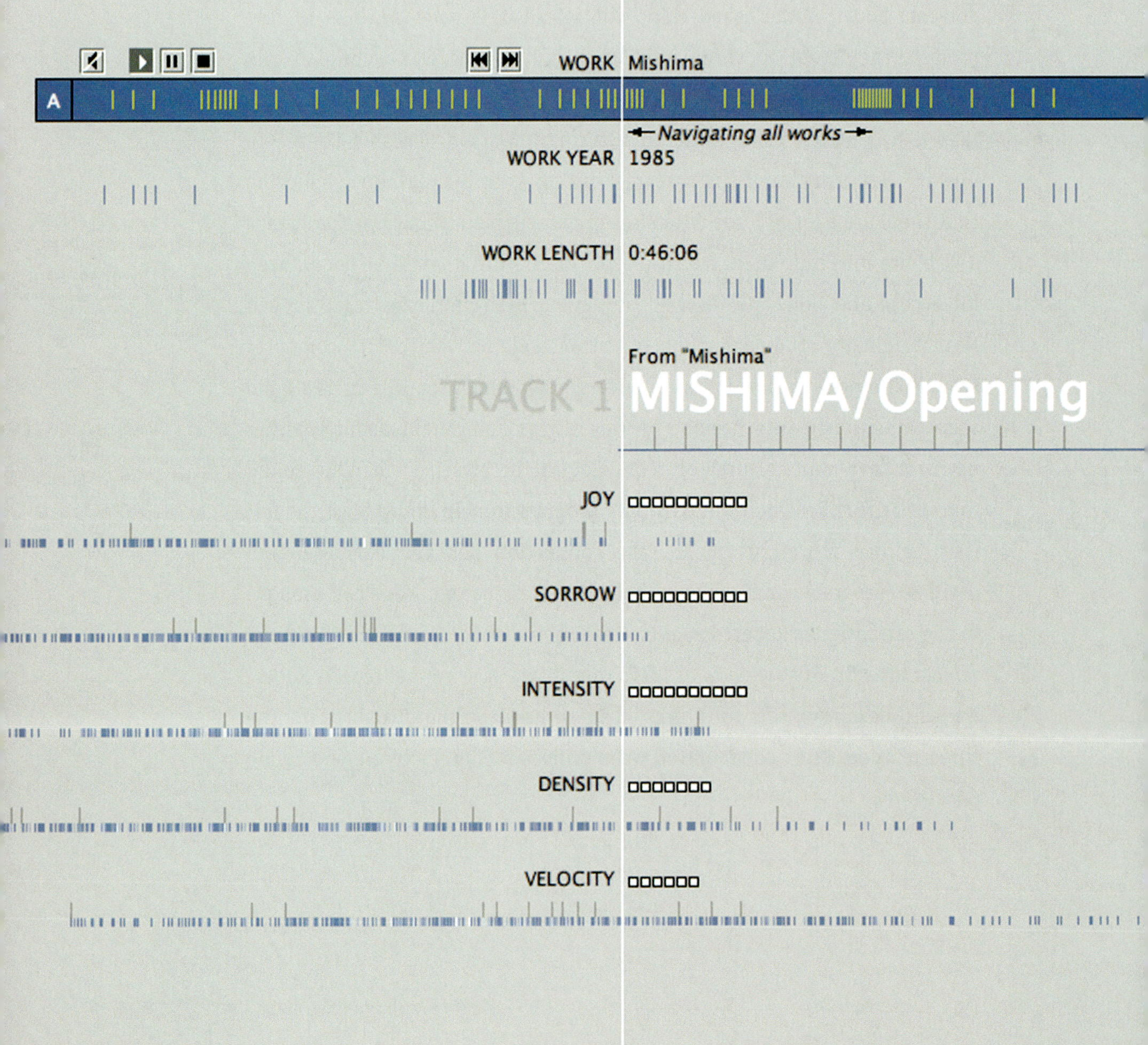

Mark Podlaseck

Glass had described a musical scrollbar which people could use to navigate his works chronologically. We had jokingly referred to this as "Radio Philip Glass," but this nickname captured two important qualities: its simplicity and its fundamental quality as a listening device.

Excerpt from "This Is Not a Catalog: Philip Glass's Works Online"[11]

The Glass Engine

■ Selecting and listening to Philip Glass's soundtrack for the film *Mishima* by its title

TRY GOING TO www.philipglass.com/glassengine. The first screen has a bold red button labeled "LAUNCH," three iconic operating instructions and two iconic "warnings," plus some text about compatibility and answers to frequently asked questions. At the bottom of the page is a request for feedback from the designer, Mark Podlaseck, with an email contact link.

Click on the "LAUNCH" button, a dialogue box tells you that the program is loading, and then suddenly you are there. Philip Glass music is flooding over you, and your screen is filled with the simple and elegant browsing interface that helps you discover the range and richness of more than sixty Glass compositions. The screen is a neutral gray all over; there is no button bar, address bar, favorites bar, status bar, or links to Amazon: you are just in a magical musical place. The title tells you that the introductory sequence is the first track from *Mishima*, the score from Paul Schrader's film about the Japanese writer Yukio Mishima. It plays for just under a minute. There is a delicate white vertical cross hair in the center, and a series of horizontal bars, labeled with the attributes of the music:

FILM SCORE Mishima

Score for Paul Schrader's film about the life of Japanese wr
section.

WORK Mishima

WORK YEAR 1985

WORK LENGTH 0:46:06

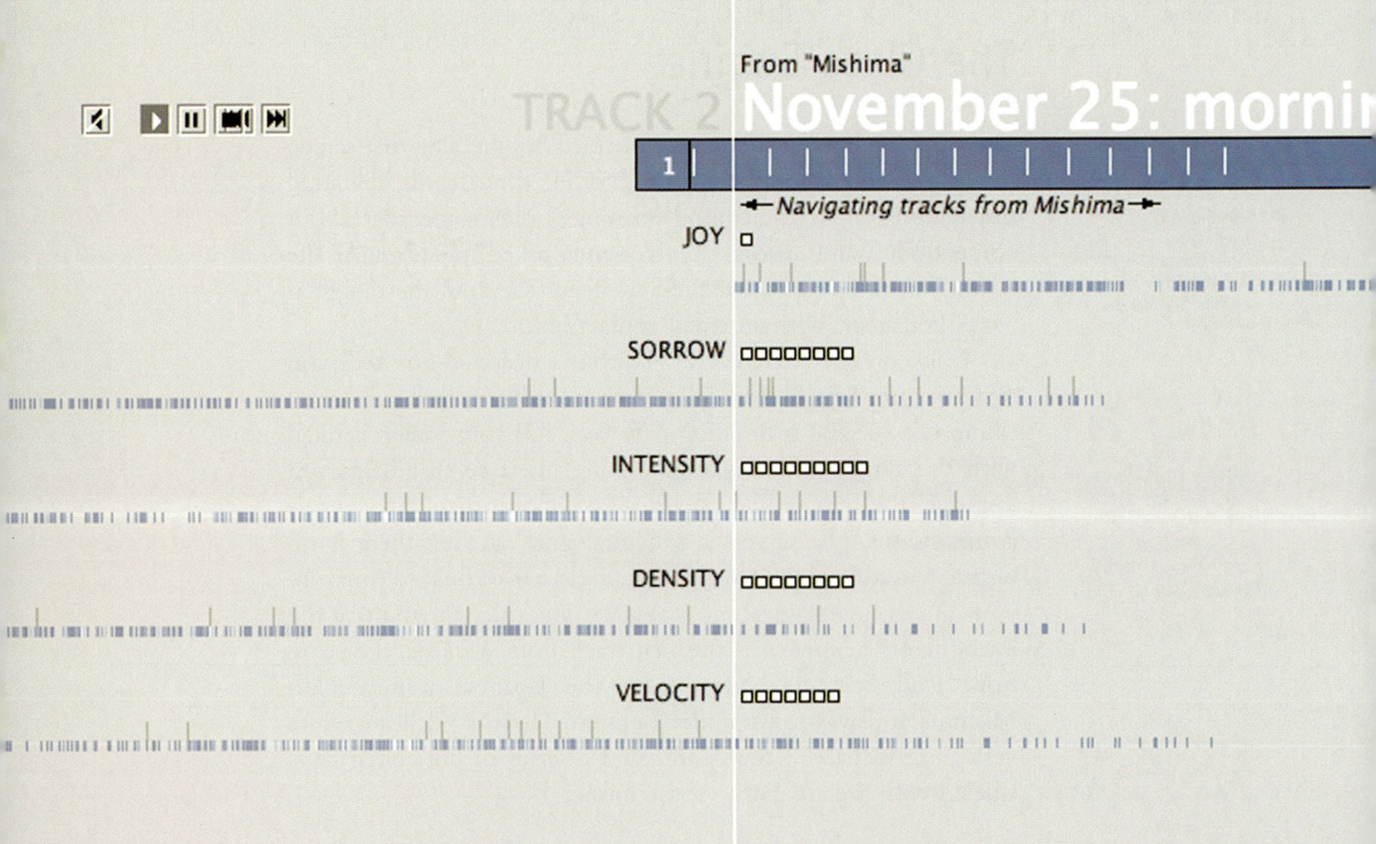

We had this idea of a number of spectrums that represented these various attributes, and we started looking at analog devices for navigating the spectra. First we looked at TV or radio, that nice feeling of flipping through a series of arbitrary content without having to make any decisions. Just pushing a button up or down, and something is always playing, and you stop at something you like.

It seemed like the idea of making these micro-decisions; "I don't like it, I don't like it, I do like it," was more appealing than, "I'm looking for something with these qualities," and having to deformulate these qualities and navigate in, and then find out there's nothing with the qualities in there. It was the idea of scrubbing or surfing across a characteristic to see if there's something there you like. We give someone the full representation, "This is everything that's here; you won't find it anywhere else if it's not here. Start browsing!" The sliders give you direct control, but they are also interlinked, so that they connect to pieces of music that are composed and actually there.

Perhaps you would like to hear more of the *Mishima* work, and you notice that one of the horizontal bars indicates the tracks, so you click on it. It highlights to the darker blue, showing that it is selected, and the cursor changes to a two-way arrow. As you move across to the second track, all of the other horizontal bar indicators slide deliciously to the right or left, sorting themselves into the attributes for the new track. This one, "November 25: morning," is sad (low on the joy scale), sorrowful, intense, dense, and fast (fairly high on the velocity scale). It's interesting that several of the other tracks are high on both the joy and sorrow scales—how ambivalent these musicians are! But the music does seem to trigger both of those emotions.

■ Navigating sequentially through the tracks of *Mishima*

Navigation

All of the sliding bars contain the full selection of over sixty works by Philip Glass, and each work is represented by a vertical stripe. You can browse to choose any of the pieces based on the attribute of the sliding bar, and the sliders are linked so that they will magically move to show you the other attributes of the piece as you roll over it on the active bar. Mark explains:

> The idea was, "How do you represent a bunch of different attributes in a way that if you learn the representation of one, it works for all the rest?" The goal was to have a consistent encoding. Once you unlock the key for one, they all work in exactly the same way. It is a set of dimensions, or characteristics. In most multidimensional browsing or visualization, you start with 2D space and you say the X is here, the Y is there; now the Z is going to be the color of the space, and the ZZ is going to be the size. You end up having these different encodings for different attributes.
>
> We used an analog radio dial to explain this to people, especially the business people, to say that there's something great about it. If you're in a new city you can go to the radio and say, well I like NPR, those stations are usually at the bottom. You go to the bottom of the dial, and you don't hear anything you like. But it's not as if there's nothing left; you just keep on moving until you find something.
>
> I drew a picture of what I wanted the thing to look like. And it was a bunch of little colored bands, each one representing a piece of music, and I thought, "I like this!" As I started explaining it to people, the radio thing kicked in. The way to think of this is as a radio. That was what got people to understand it much quicker than, "This spectrum represents one characteristic, this spectrum represents another characteristic, and so on." How to navigate, and all that stuff, fell out much later.

■ Philip Glass
■ Traditional radio dial tuner display

This browsing structure works well if you are already in a category that you understand and want to roam around in a layered structure to explore qualities. Picking up on the analogy of the radio, you have already decided that you want to browse among public radio stations rather than "country" radio stations, so you choose that part of the dial. To find a good song on the

Web, you normally choose a category or genre first, but once you are in "country" for example, all you are allowed to do is dive deeper into another hierarchical tree of structured choices, like "bluegrass" or "hot country," and there you find a very limited list. This forces you to wade out and back in again, without the chance to browse based on different attributes.

The qualitative browsing structure that Mark has designed for Glass could be generalized for any other attributes where qualities are more relevant than categories. Choose a category first, and then explore through layered attributes.

> When we show it to IBM customers, the first comment they have is, "This is really cool for classical music, but I can't imagine using it for sleeping bags." So just recently we drew up a set of pictures to show how you can navigate sleeping bags. It is basically the exact same thing, but we used pictures of sleeping bags, and all of a sudden people said, "Oh! Now I get it." They really needed to be shown how to make the jump.
>
> The attributes of sleeping bags are the weight, the cost, the lowest temperature you can sleep in it at—those kinds of things. It shows a picture instead of playing the music. So it also has constant feedback, so you're never only in navigation land, you're always hearing or seeing the content at the same time; you're always experiencing something. Wherever you slide to you're always seeing the sleeping bag, instead of having to make a decision about, "What brand am I interested in?" or "What temperature am I interested in?" You are always looking at something.

In the case of Philip Glass, the motivation was to help people choose music to license as well as to enjoy. Glass has more than seventy works recorded, comprising over five hundred tracks. He makes some income from commissions, but his earnings come more from licensing existing pieces.

As part of his research for the design project, Mark Podlaseck sat with the people behind the licensing desk for a couple of days and heard them receive phone calls such as this: "I'm looking for something. I have this commercial that has these qualities, and I'm looking for something like this." That research helped him to decide what kind of attributes would be relevant for the Glass

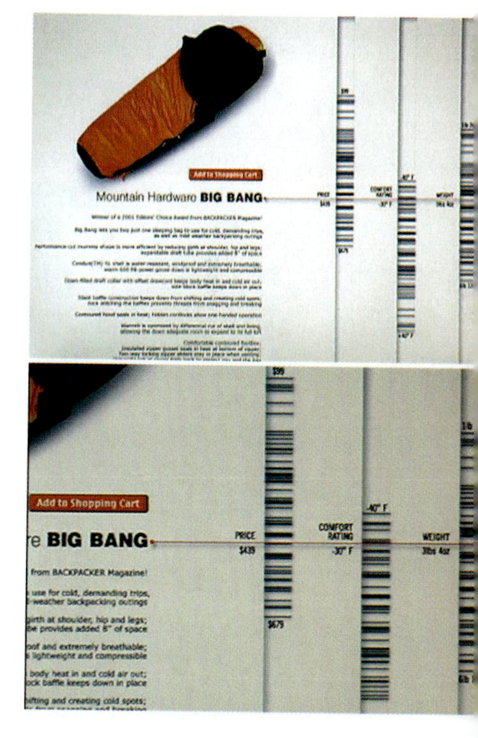

Sleeping bag navigation
Detail of sleeping bag attributes

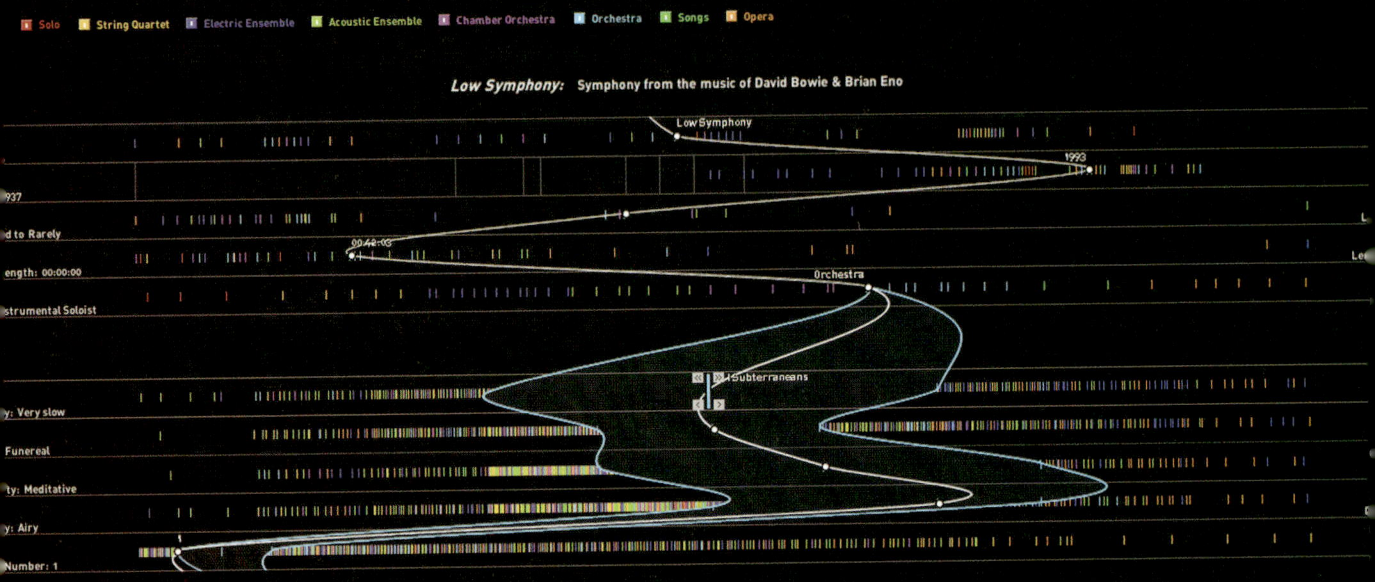

Solo String Quartet Electric Ensemble Acoustic Ensemble Chamber Orchestra Orchestra Songs Opera

Low Symphony: **Symphony from the music of David Bowie & Brian Eno**

Low Symphony
1993
937
d to Rarely
00:42:03
ength: 00:00:00
Orchestra
strumental Soloist
Subterraneans
y: Very slow
Funereal
ty: Meditative
y: Airy
Number: 1

Sections From *Low Symphony*

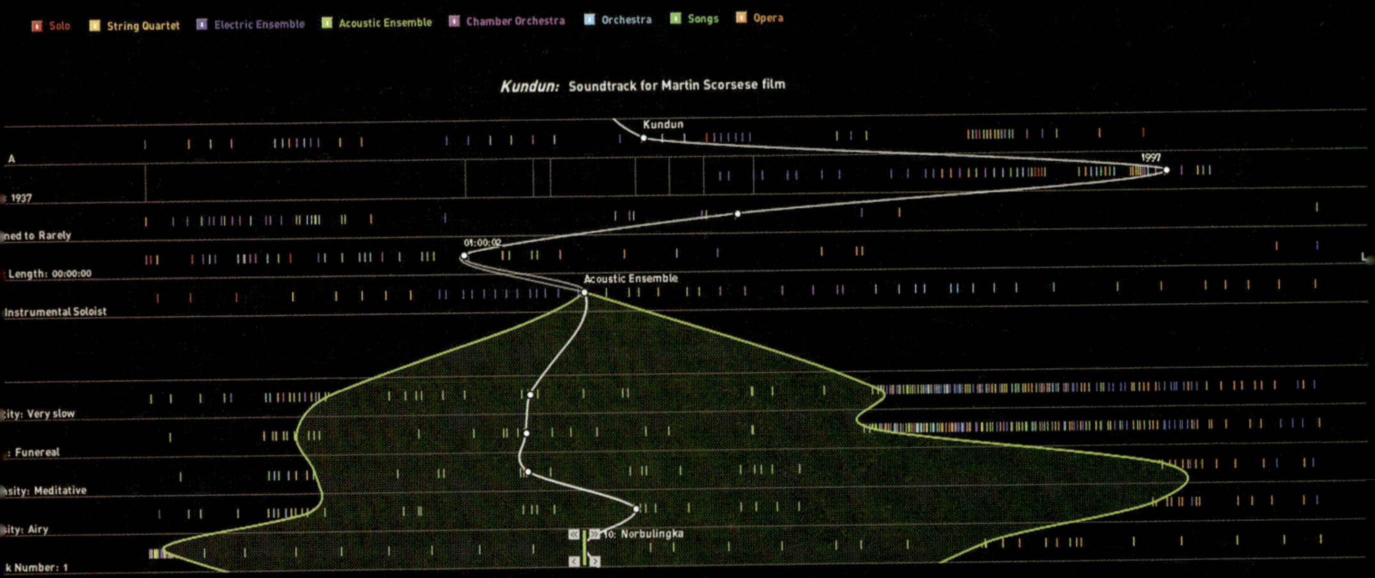

Solo String Quartet Electric Ensemble Acoustic Ensemble Chamber Orchestra Orchestra Songs Opera

Kundun: **Soundtrack for Martin Scorsese film**

Kundun
A
1997
1937
ned to Rarely
01:00:02
Length: 00:00:00
Acoustic Ensemble
Instrumental Soloist
city: Very slow
Funereal
nsity: Meditative
sity: Airy
10: Norbulingka
k Number: 1

Sections From *Kundun*

Engine, and he also worked with Philip and his musical team to develop a list of the kinds of things people would look for.

The first design had a parallel coordinate representation of various lines crossing the dimensions, and you manipulated the line. Mark prototyped it in Shockwave and then put it in front of some users:

> When I started designing this particular project, I was designing it for myself as a listener of Philip Glass. That was my first approach; if I was at this Web site, this is what I would want. Once we had a prototype, putting it in front of people was a complete shock, because this was perfect for me, and then to see other people use it; it was like, "You IDIOT! Can't you see that you can get to the music by moving this thing?"
>
> It was extremely painful. It's funny, because most projects, if you're designing for financial analysts or something, it's not you, so it's easier to think about being in the other person's shoes. You can remove yourself because it doesn't interest you that much. But in this case, I wasn't able to achieve that kind of distance immediately, and that was the hardest part.
>
> We had a couple of reactions. One would say, "Whoa, this is very scientific!" It looked like a scientific visualization, and that was probably inappropriate to the music. The second thing was that people started navigating using the rollover technique to access the music directly. They played with the cursor and figured that each colored line represented a piece of music. I was trying to decrease the cost of commitment to zero, both for selection and listening. I assumed that if it was zero, or close to it, the information that was revealed during rollover would be superfluous. I was convinced that no one would bother to roll over pixel-wide hot spots in order to read titles like "Symphony No. 2; 3rd Movement" when they could play the same piece for half the effort! I was dead wrong about that.

Early design with attributes in fixed locations, and the line manipulated

Top
Selecting and listening to a track from Glass's *Low Symphony* by "Velocity." In the bottom half of the screen, the line opens up to show the boundary conditions for the tracks from this symphony.

Bottom
Navigating Glass's soundtrack for *Kundun* in the traditional manner, that is, track by track.

For the second iteration, Mark and his team solved the rollover dilemma by separating the cursor manipulation from the music, only allowing the pointer to be used for adjusting a characteristic that is interesting. When the cursor was used to select one of the horizontal adjustment bars, the normal selection pointer was replaced by a two-way arrow, indicating that the cursor could manipulate the value, instead of pointed at

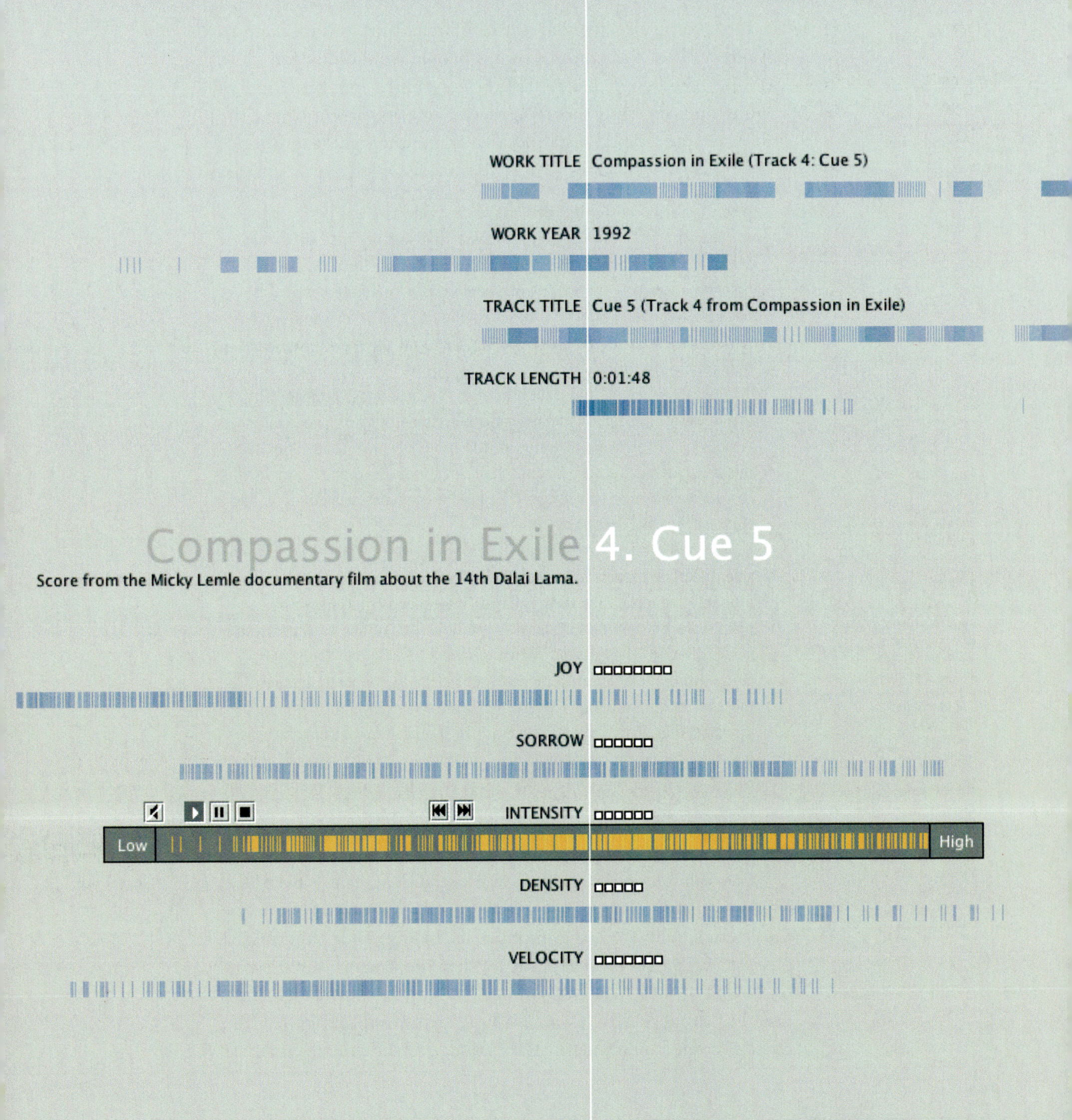
WORK TITLE Compassion in Exile (Track 4: Cue 5)
WORK YEAR 1992
TRACK TITLE Cue 5 (Track 4 from Compassion in Exile)
TRACK LENGTH 0:01:48
Compassion in Exile 4. Cue 5
Score from the Micky Lemle documentary film about the 14th Dalai Lama.
JOY
SORROW
INTENSITY
Low
High
DENSITY
VELOCITY

something. This breakthrough led to the elegant graphics with the horizontal bars and central hairline. Mark is very modest about the design, and is surprised that it looks good enough to be the work of a professional graphic designer. He remembers showing a version with a black background to a designer friend, who said, "It's very nice, but it needs a gray background. Simplify it." So he turned the background gray.

The earlier versions had colors representing various categories of the music, yellow for opera, red for symphonies, but that started to look fussy in the dense areas of overlap between the categories, so he decided to simplify:

> We ended up with this monochromatic thing. I think this is much more appropriate to the music, because there's so little to look at, and it allows you to focus on what you are listening to. The most satisfying designs for me are those that are paired down to the bare essentials of what is being communicated; there are no excess gestures, pictorials, or experiences. It's just completely about that thing. That to me is the ultimate pleasure—laser-sharp focus!

■ Final design: browsing by intensity. The endpoints of the bar ("Low" and "High") can be dragged to filter out, for example, all high-intensity tracks. Manipulating the endpoints on multiple bars enables complex filtering and queries like "I want to hear only the slow, melancholy, low-intensity tracks."

Until recently, rendering bits into human-readable form has been restricted mostly to displays and keyboards—sensory deprived and physically limited. By contrast, "tangible bits" allow us to interact with them with our muscles as well as our minds and memory.

Nicholas Negroponte, a founder of MIT's Media Lab

■ The drummer surrounds himself with stimulants for all of the senses, and an electronic keyboard (from Yamaha)

Photo
Steven Moeder and Craig Syverson

We all have five senses; how sad that our connection to computers is "sensory deprived and physically limited," as Nicholas Negroponte so aptly phrases it. Visual displays are gradually improving, but our sense of touch is limited for most of the time to the feel of the keyboard and mouse. Sound exists as a dimension in the interface but so far has not taken the prominent place that seems possible. Smell and taste are not yet present. And then, what about dimensionality? Can we go beyond x, y, and z, and make more use of the time dimension? Although we already have some examples of animation and time-based behaviors, we could go so much further, if we think about making full use of multiple media.

This chapter explores the opportunities for interaction design to become multisensory and to take advantage of multimedia. We start with a plea to break away from the status quo and design for better use of our vision and touch. Then we look at the work of some remarkable innovators. An interview with Hiroshi Ishii, professor of the Tangible Media Group at MIT Media Lab, introduces the concept of "tangible bits." Durrell Bishop, an interaction designer based in London, talks of interfaces made up of things that are physical and connected. Joy Mountford tells the story of pioneering the use of QuickTime, when she was Head of the Human Interface Group in Advanced Technology at Apple, and her research into audio at Interval. Bill Gaver, researcher and interaction design teacher, talks about designing sound, discusses the psychology of affordances, and shows some examples of concepts that have subtle psychological relationships with the people that use them.

"Visions of Japan" Exhibition at the Victoria and Albert Museum, London 1991–92
- Room 1, Cosmos—"The Realm of Cliché"
- Room 2, Chaos—"The Realm of Kitsch"

Vision

WHY SHOULD YOU be chained to your computer? You sit for so many hours at a time, staring at that small rectangular display of information: it is always the same focal length, with no relief for the eyes; it makes no use of your peripheral vision; it is so dim that you have to control the surrounding lighting conditions to see it properly. Why not break away, and wander in smart environments covered in living displays, or carry a system with you as an extension of your senses, augmenting vision?

In 1991 there was a wonderful exhibition in London called "Visions of Japan,"[1] based on a concept by the architect Arata Isozaki. You moved through three large spaces, each celebrating a theme. The first was "The Realm of Cliché," which presented various entertainments. There were examples from such arts as the tea ceremony, flower arrangement, incense connoisseurship, calligraphy, martial arts, and popular and classical performing arts, to sexual pleasures, and the traditions of the underworld.

The second space was "The Realm of Kitsch," which examined the nature of competitiveness in games and sports. Competition is the basis of baseball, golf, the Japan Broadcasting Corporation singing contest, pastimes like pachinko, and the majority of other topics of daily conversations.

The third theme was "The Realm of Simulation," and this space demonstrated a dramatic expansion of the potential for visual display. The entire floor and walls of a high-ceilinged rectangular hall were completely covered with moving images. Some of the time they were separated into individual images making a collage of screens, and some of the time they were huge panoramas, stitched together to form a single image. One movie was recorded in the concourse of a mainline railway station in Tokyo at rush hour, so that as you moved through the space, you were part of a sea of Japanese commuters, hurrying in every direction to find their trains. The images on the ground were projected from the ceiling, so that the visitors to the space became part of the display screen, covered in moving images themselves, as they stood transfixed or moved slowly forward.

Here is a quote from Isozaki's description of this theme in the catalog:

> Electronic devices of innumerable kinds have spread throughout society, transforming its systems and practices from within. Television, video recording, pocket-size audio devices and giant video displays, compact computer devices, like television screen hookup game equipment and personal computers, are irreversibly altering our ways of life.
>
> The images produced by these systems are displayed on screens but they are completely separated from the real things themselves—processed, edited, and otherwise qualitatively changed, often into something completely different. That process can be manipulated, creating impressions of convincing simulation.
>
> The constant bombardment of such simulated images could cause those images to flow back into the real world, blurring the line between real and simulated. Perceptions may become completely reversed, producing the sensation that reality is only part of a world of simulation.

This idea of "blurring the line between real and simulated" was demonstrated very convincingly by the exhibition, but the audience were passive receivers of the experience, like cinema-goers; there were no interactive enhancements to their lives.

There is a considerable body of research into collaborative work making use of large electronic displays. For example, Terry Winograd has set up an interesting program called the "Stanford Interactive Workspaces" project[2] to explore new possibilities for

Room 3, Dreams—"The Realm of Simulation" ■
Arata Isozaki ■

people to work together in technology-rich spaces with computing and interaction devices on many different scales. The focus is on augmenting a dedicated meeting space with large displays and concentrating on task-oriented work such as brainstorming meetings and design reviews. The implementation of these high-technology solutions has been slow in coming. Part of this is due to the high cost of the equipment, and the immaturity of the software solutions. Perhaps there is a more basic reason based on the nature of our vision: we see clearly in a narrow focus, but we also have a powerful capability of perception with our peripheral vision. Terry Winograd describes us as spatial animals:

> There have been a variety of projects to try to take information and make it into something that feels like a real space. People are spatial animals; our brains evolved through millions of years of operating in the world, starting in the savanna or wherever it was. One direction has been to make abstract spaces, which capture the structure of information in a way that feels more like a real space.
>
> I remember some of the early demonstrations from SGI that took your file system—your ordinary hierarchical file system—and turned it into a bunch of buildings spread around on a landscape, so an area corresponded to a file directory, and you could zoom into a building to find a document. I think it was interesting, but in general did not work well, because the abstraction that was supported did not match one's intuition spatially. Your brain ended up spending a lot of time trying to figure out what all that stuff was doing, when none of it was relevant. It wasn't really a physical space, it wasn't really a tiger coming to catch you, it was just some node opening up, and you don't want to put the cognitive resources into dealing with that. So the trick—and I think it's a challenge—is to match the spatial representation with the cognitive structure of what you're doing, so that it actually makes sense and it isn't just a separate layer of window dressing on top of it.

Multidisciplinary design teams at IDEO[3] have evolved a solution to this quandary called the project room. Design projects are assigned a dedicated space, which is filled with all of the information generated during collaborative work, relevant reference materials, mockups, prototypes and so on. As you enter one of these rooms, you are engulfed in the richness of information. Most of the vertical surfaces are made up of large foam-board surfaces, covered in printouts, images, articles, handwritten notes from brainstorms, and multicolored "stickies" embellished with sketches and notes. Horizontal surfaces are stacked high with reports, magazines, books, and lots of the objects that inform the context of the project. If you are a member of the design team, you will probably have spent much of your time working in that space with your colleagues. If you are away from it for a while and then return, it is amazing how you can just stand there for a few minutes, and find that all your memories and insights about the project come flooding back. Perhaps that is because of the nature of our peripheral vision combined with the way our brains work, but we have not yet found ways to make good use of these abilities when we are using visual display technology.

When it comes to the technology that you can carry with you, the concept of "augmented reality" has replaced the expectation of "virtual reality" that was so popular for a time. Moving into a completely separated virtual world may still be attractive for entertainment or fantasy, but to ignore the real world is giving up too much for many applications. The heads-up display for fighter pilots has been augmenting vision with additional information for decades, but the versions of that concept that have been tried for the windscreens on cars, or the equivalent for eyeglasses, have not yet been designed well enough to attract a significant audience.

Our eyes are so important to us, promising a lot of opportunities to improve what we see and the way that we see it.

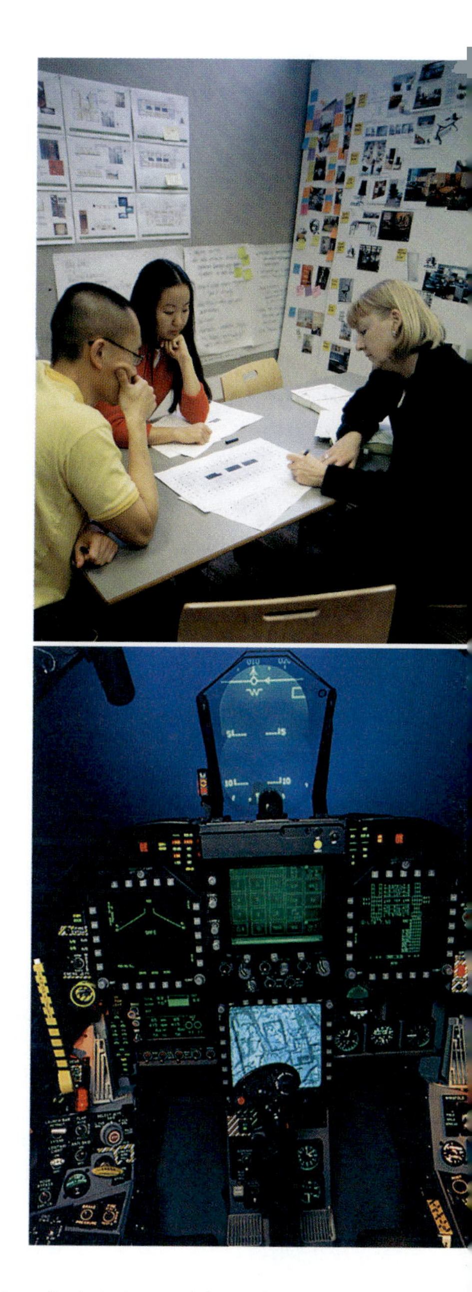

Members of a design team work in a project room at IDEO, full of visual reminders of information ■

The cockpit of an F2 fighter (1999), with heads-up display ■

Touch

CONSIDER THE TACTILE qualities inherent in the design of a spoon. An elegant shape may be the first thing that appeals to you when you are looking at cutlery on a table or in a store, but the difference between a spoon that you enjoy using repeatedly and one that you come to ignore is much more than love at first sight. Touch and feel means a lot with a spoon—the way that the edges of the handle feel when you pick it up, the weight and balance in the hand, the feel of the bowl as it touches your lips, the way it slides into your mouth, plus the quality and surface texture of the material. The tactile qualities of an object mean a lot to us.

A telephone handset has a similar level of tactile intimacy as a spoon. You feel it in your hand, pick it up and put it against your face, pressing the earpiece over your ear to hear the strongest sound. A cell phone also has the interactive complexity of lots of keys for input—too small to operate accurately without a good snap-action tactile feedback. Turn off the ringer to avoid interrupting others, and you can feel the vibrator telling you that a call has come in. The cell phone is an example of the convergence of digital and physical interaction; in one product the design for sight, sound, and touch are all crucial.

■ The touch of a spoon compared to the touch of a handset

Photos
Nicolas Zurcher

When you are designing for generic computers, there is limited opportunity to work with touch, as the medium is normally limited to visual display and sound for output, plus keyboard and mouse for input; it is only when you are designing one of these input devices that tactile feedback and the qualities of touch are essential ingredients of the solution. Hiroshi Ishii and Durrell Bishop are both doing something about breaking the touch barrier, adding the dimensions of physical feeling to the interface. In the interview that follows, Hiroshi Ishii describes his tangible user interface (TUI) and introduces projects that are being designed by the members of his Tangible Media Group at the MIT Media Lab.

Hiroshi Ishii

“This is a small weather forecast bottle that I wanted to give to my mother on her birthday, but as she passed away in 1998, it became my tribute to her. It contains the weather forecast of Sapporo City, my hometown in Japan. Let me check what the weather is like. Now you hear the sound of the bird singing; this means tomorrow becomes a clear day. If you hear the rain sounds, tomorrow becomes a rainy day. Information is brought to you from the Internet, but it is a very different interface from using Microsoft Internet Explorer or clicking with a mouse.” As he demonstrates his weather forecast bottle, Hiroshi Ishii is standing in the MIT Media Laboratory, where he is professor of the Tangible Media Group. He is surrounded by projects, prototypes, and demos, which explore the design of seamless interfaces between people, digital information, and the physical environment. With degrees in electronic and computer engineering from Hokkaido University in Japan, he came to MIT to found the Tangible Media Group. His team seeks to change the “painted bits” of GUIs to “tangible bits” by giving physical form to digital information. Ishii and his students have presented their vision of tangible bits at many academic, industrial design, and artistic venues, emphasizing that the development of tangible interfaces requires the rigor of both scientific and artistic review. Before MIT, from 1988 to 1994, he led the CSCW Research Group at the NTT Human Interface Laboratories, where his team invented TeamWorkStation and ClearBoard. His boundless enthusiasm for tangible interfaces carries him around the world to make presentations and demonstrate prototypes.

PingPongPlus

Hiroshi Ishii

At the seashore, between the land of atoms and the sea of bits, we must reconcile our dual citizenships in the physical and digital worlds. Our windows to the digital world have been confined to flat rectangular screens and pixels—"painted bits." But while our visual senses are steeped in the sea of digital information, our bodies remain in the physical world. "Tangible bits" give physical form to digital information, making bits directly manipulable and perceptible.

Hiroshi Ishii[4]

Tangible Bits

■ "Tangible Bits" exhibition at the ICC Gallery in Tokyo

Photo
Courtesy of NTT InterCommunication Center (ICC)

Hiroshi Ishii stands in the conference room adjacent to his project space at the MIT Media Lab. He is eager to explain the concept of tangible bits, and has already prepared some hand-drawn posters to illustrate what he wants to say. He starts by talking about basic interactions, leading in to a comparison between graphical and tangible user interfaces:

> This diagram shows very simple structures. Interaction requires two key components. One is the controls, through which people can manipulate access to digital information and computations. Also, it's very important to have external representations that people can perceive, to understand the results of the computations. Today I would like to extend this model of interaction to explain first graphical user interface, then I'd like to talk about the main topics of tangible user interface.

GUI Graphical User Interface
input
output
remote control
intangible representation
physical
digital
information / computation
TUI Tangible User Interface
input
output
e.g. digital shadow
control
tangible representation
intangible representation
physical
digital
information / computation

GUI—graphical user interface

This diagram illustrates the graphical user interface that was originated by the famous Xerox Star work station in the early eighties. The graphical user interface provides a variety of components, like windows, menus, or icons, but it represents these components as intangible pixels. The basic medium of the representation is pixels on the computer screen: that is intangible. To control these representations, the graphical user interface provides generic remote controllers, like a mouse or a keyboard. One of the key features of graphical user interface is the separation of intangible representations from general purpose remote controllers, which enables flexibility and malleability.

TUI—tangible user interface

This diagram illustrates the tangible user interface, which my group has been working on for the past several years. The key idea is giving a physical form, a tangible representation, to information and computation; this differentiates our approach from the graphical user interface. The tangible representation is tightly coupled with the computation inside the computer, but the representation is physical, so that it also serves as a control mechanism, allowing people to directly grab and manipulate. By doing so, they can control the internal computation or digital information. So the coupling of tangible representation and control is one of the key features of the tangible user interface.

One of the problems of physical representation is that we cannot easily change a shape, or a color, or a form dynamically, using current technology. Therefore, we usually couple a tangible representation with an intangible representation, like a video projection or a sound. We then try to create the illusion that these two representations are coupled perceptually, so that people can get dynamic output or feedback, either video projection or sound, coupled with these tangible representations.

In short, an important key feature is to give physical form to information, so that you can have multiple forms of control of the information, especially multiplex control. This also contributes to helping people simultaneously work in collaborative situations.

- GUI—graphical user interface
- TUI—tangible user interface

Illustration
Hiroshi Ishii

Abacus

Hiroshi picks up an abacus. It is a simple and elegant design, over a foot long and about three inches wide, with a dark rectilinear frame well polished with use. The counters are simple double-cone-shaped wooden beads that slide on slim wooden dowels. He handles it with the easy familiarity of a long association and talks about the meaning it holds for him:

> Here is an abacus, the simplest form of digital computation device. All of the information is represented in the array of the beads, in a physical way, so that people can directly touch, manipulate, and feel the information. This coupling of manipulation and control is very natural in this kind of physical device, but in the digital domain, the graphical user interface introduces a big divide between the pixel representation and the controllers like the mouse.
>
> Another important feature is the affordance. This is a simple mechanical structure; by grabbing this device when I was a kid, it immediately became a musical instrument, an imaginary toy train, or a backscratcher, so I could really feel and enjoy the beads. This also serves as a medium of awareness. When my mother was busy doing the accounting in our small apartment in Tokyo, I could hear the music the abacus made, which told me that I couldn't interrupt her to ask her to play with me. Knowing other people's state through some ambient sound, such as this abacus, teaches us important directions for the next generation of user interfaces. This simple historic device taught us a lot about new directions, which we call tangible user interface.

■ Abacus

Photo
Webb Chappell

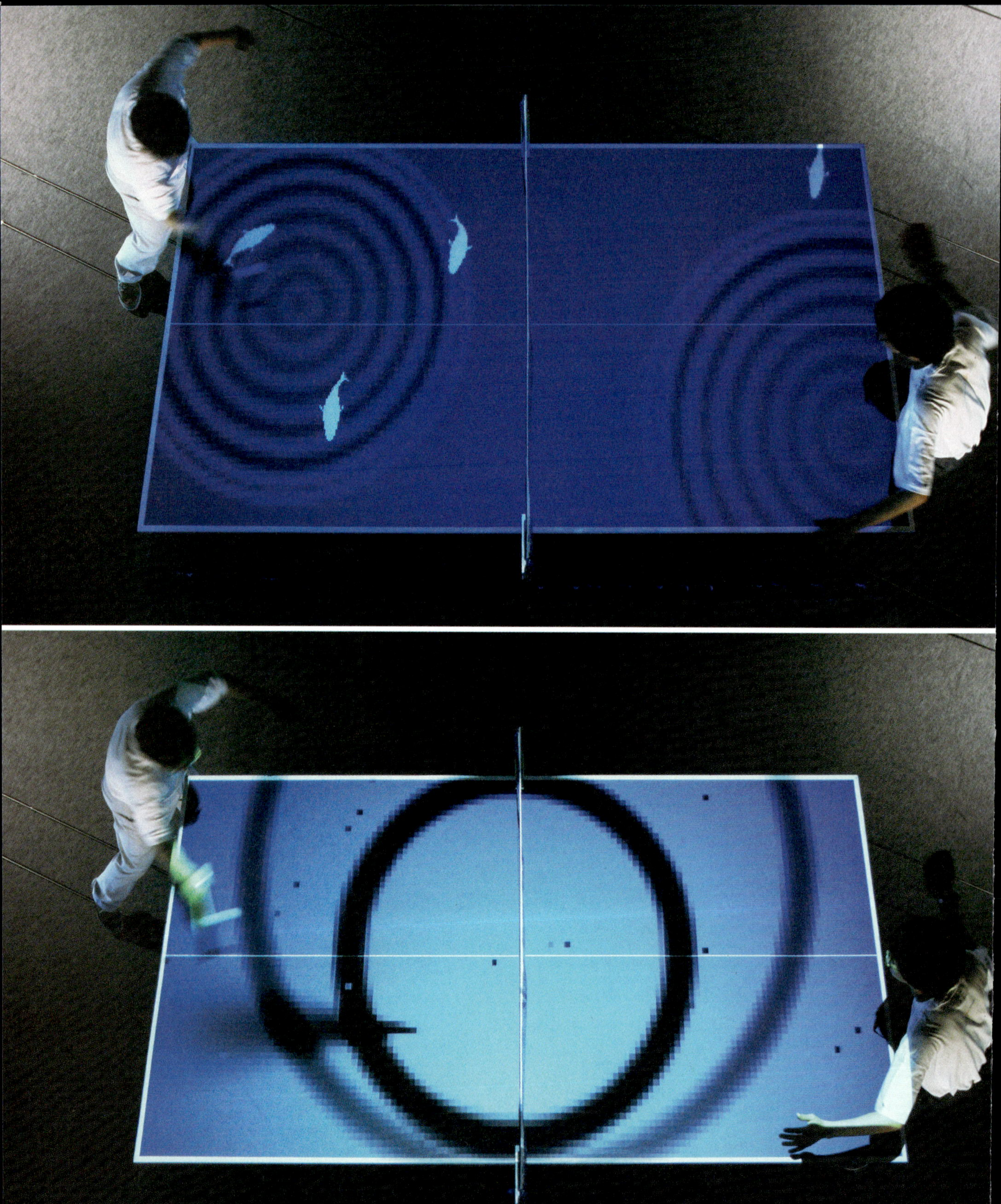

Ping Pong

His next prop is a Ping Pong paddle. It emanates an aura of antiquity almost like the steps of a medieval building, well worn to the point of deformity and covered in pock marks and scratches; when he holds it in the play position, hand and paddle suddenly become one, and it melts into his body as an extension of his arm and hand:

> Ping Pong is one of my favorite sports; that's why we designed PingPongPlus.[5] Ping Pong really allows very engaging interactions, using full body motion, speed, vision, and other kinesthesia.
>
> We can learn a lot from this Ping Pong paddle about how interaction design should be really invisible and transparent. Well-used paddles become transparent, so that the player can concentrate on the main task, playing Ping Pong, trying to hit the ball. A good fit to the body is really critical to make the interface transparent. To make a good fit, you have to choose the right form, size, and weight. This physical object changes the form after intensive use for twenty years; you can see the dent left after twenty years of playing, capturing the traces of my physical body, in this case the right hand grip. The coevolution of these physical tools changing their form seems to suggest how we can design the interface to become transparent and also to become extensions to the human body, for both digital and physical domains.

■ PingPongPlus using sensing, sound, and projection technologies

Photo Courtesy of NTT ICC

musicBottles[6]

In the corner of the project space there is a shelf completely covered with transparent glass bottles. There are all sorts of shapes and sizes, but they are all attractive and interesting to look at and touch. Next to the shelf is a display consisting of a black horizontal surface, with an illuminated translucent disk set into it. On the disk there are three bottles with glass stoppers in place. Hiroshi reaches over and gently removes the stopper from one of the bottles, triggering the sound of a jazz pianist; then he does the same with the other two bottles, adding bass and drums to the trio, after a time turning off the sound by replacing the stoppers:

> Let me introduce the musicBottles project, which is using simple glass bottles as containers and conduits of online digital information. People have been using this kind of glass bottle for more than five thousand years. We extended the meaning of the container into the digital domain, and also the simple affordance of opening and closing it. This is a jazz trio. Let me play these glass bottles: she's a pianist, and bass, and drums.
>
> The importance is not the music, but the possibility that you can put anything you can imagine into any existing glass bottles in your home. You can see a variety of glass bottles behind me; some bottles contain stories, some bottles contain a genie, and you can also imagine perfume bottles that contain a chanson, or whisky bottles which contain a story of Scotland, for example.

- musicBottles: each bottle represents an instrument, turned on by removing the stopper

  Photo Courtesy of NTT ICC

With another three bottles he demonstrates a performance of a classical music trio. He then goes on to talk about the original weather forecast bottle, described in the introduction to his interview, which was inspired by his desire to communicate with his mother in Sapporo, Japan.

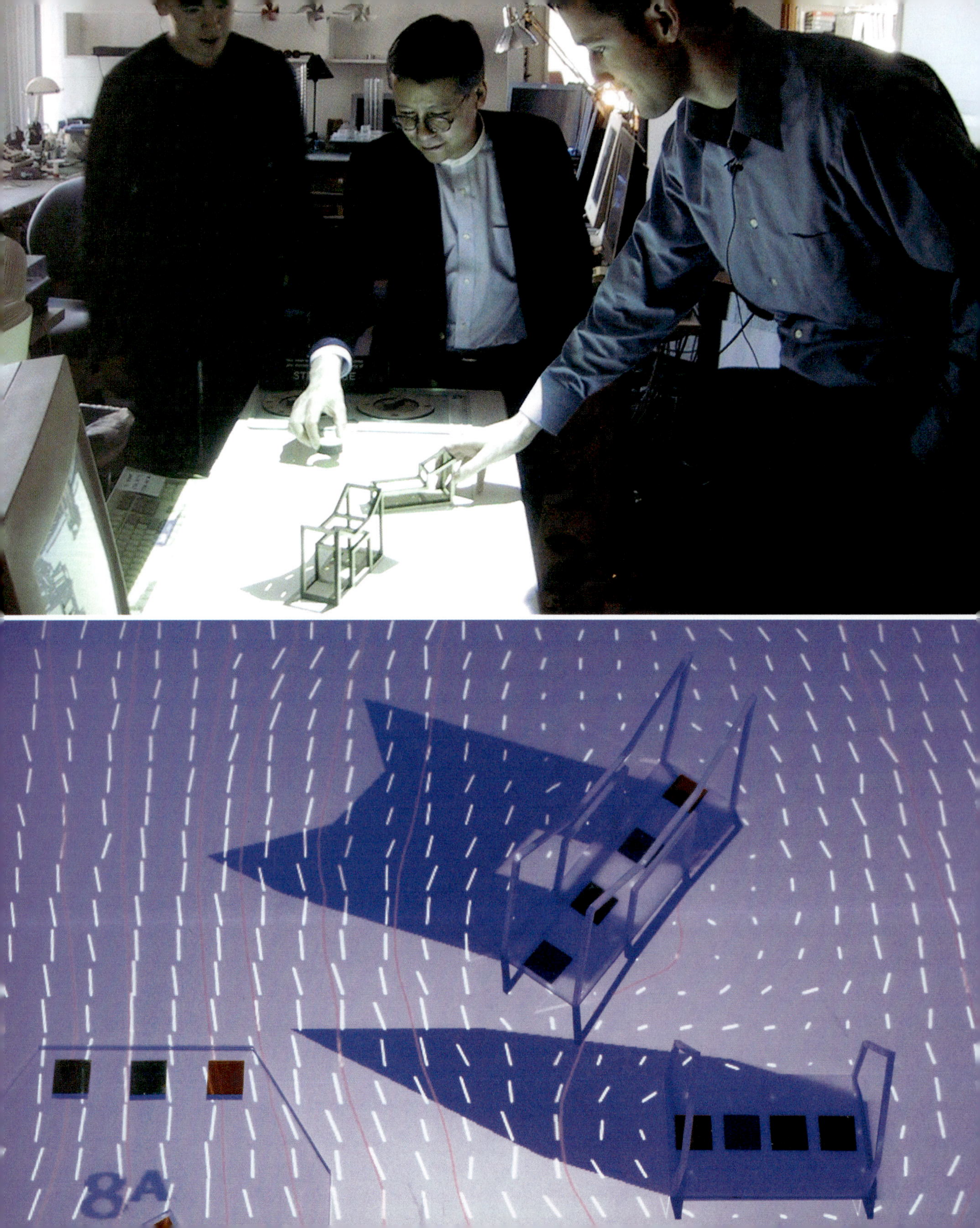
8A

Tangible Media Group

Hiroshi Ishii was developing these ideas about tangible interfaces at NTT before he came to MIT as an associate professor in 1995. Since then he has been in full flow, with a team of students to help, led by a select group of graduates. This has given time for his lab to accumulate a wonderfully rich set of demonstrations and prototypes, making you feel that the whole world could be made up of magical connections between atoms and bits, with every physical object illuminated by projected information and offering controls for unseen systems.

James Patten is a graduate research assistant exploring tangible interfaces for business supply chain visualization. He shows a tangible tabletop interface covered with a projected diagram of business processes, where the little wheels on the surface act as knobs to allow you to play what-if? games with inventory control. There is a flat panel display at the back of the table, giving several different kinds of information about the process. As you rotate the wheels, you can see the parameters changing, represented by numeric values and little vertical bars, like thermometers. They are projected onto the table surface from above, so as you manipulate the wheel, the image falls onto your thumb, distorting slightly. It makes you feel that it should hurt, as the red column rises, but you can only feel the knob. Another surprise occurs when you drag the wheel away from the node on the diagram: it pulls the virtual graphic with it and then suddenly detaches itself: the graphic snaps back, and your control connects itself to another node with new parameters.

■ Urp, an application of the I/O bulb, is a digital urban planning workbench

Photos
top: Author

bottom: Courtesy of NTT ICC

James moves on to demonstrate Urp,[7] an urban planning workbench. He positions physical architectural models on the surface of the table, and virtual shadows are cast according to a computer simulation of the time of day and season. The rotary controls to the side allow you to control a virtual clock, seeing the shadows and reflections when you adjust the time; a variation in the position of a building, or its size and shape, allow you to avoid any problems of overlap. Another simulation demonstrates air currents around the buildings in different wind conditions, so the planners can avoid those blasts of chill air that you sometimes encounter when you come round the corner of a large structure. Perhaps urban planners always feel that they have a supernatural level of control over people's lives, but there is something about using Urp to change these parameters in real time, which makes you feel power surge through your fingertips!

Next we move into a closetlike space that is overflowing with technology. There are projected images on two walls as well as the table and computers off to the side. This is the "Illuminating Clay"[8] project, where landscape models can be constructed using a ductile clay support. Three-dimensional geometry is captured in real time using a laser scanner, and from this information, simulations such as shadow casting, land erosion, visibility, and traveling time are calculated. The results are projected back onto the clay model, combining the advantages of physical interaction with the dynamic qualities of graphical displays. Ben Piper was another graduate student who was working on this project, and he explains:

> One of the prime aims of this interface was to allow objects from the designer's environment to enter directly into the computational simulation, rather than having to build objects digitally before adding them to a model.

The process is visually captivating, with rich colors, and multiple versions of the digital information arrayed on and around the physical model in a framework of rectangular windows. Ben demonstrates the molding of the clay to change the landscape, rotating the model to examine sections in different planes, and the addition of objects representing buildings. The real-time feedback for the experiments is so immediate that you can even use your hand to try out the impact of a large structure or a new hill.

- "Sandscape" project demonstration (Sandscape is a later iteration using malleable sand)
- "Illuminating Clay" project demonstration
- "Illuminating Clay"—additional projections

Returning to the main area of the lab, we find Brygg Ullmer, a PhD student, sitting in front of a computer workstation with two flat screens. The surprise is that there is no keyboard or mouse on the surface in front of them; instead, there is a metal rack and a collection of bricklike modules by the side of it. Brygg explains that in this project, called "Tangible Query Interfaces," he is using physical objects to represent databases and express queries to those databases. He picks up a cylindrical object that looks as if it could be birthday cake from a bakery, until you notice that the decorative fringe is technical components rather than icing, and the words on the top say "REAL ESTATE." He explains that it represents a database of about five hundred homes in the Charlotte area of North Carolina. When he places it on the rack, it brings up the information about the homes on the screens—one as a geographical view and the other as a scatter plot view. He picks up the objects that look more like technology modules, saying that they represent parameters for the database, such as price, lot size, or square footage. Each module has a glowing indicator light, a screen on the front displaying a label and histogram, and two sliders that can be used to select a range within the displayed variable.

He puts the price module into the rack; the system recognizes it and brings up all of the houses in the system that fit within the chosen range. He moves the sliders to experiment with the prices and see their location in town. There seems to be a strong cluster of expensive houses in one area, but the inexpensive ones are more randomly scattered. He then adds another module containing lot size and demonstrates "AND" as well as "OR" relationships, depending whether the modules are touching each other or not. He adds a third parameter (the square footage) and experiments with the values and the order, which define the axis on the graphical representation. Soon he's reduced his list to a small number of houses that might be really interesting to him. He can extend the complexity of the manipulation of the database by adding a second rack, more query modules, and by moving the whole system back and forth on the table surface to change the values. You get the feeling that he can play his house hunt like a musical instrument or a construction toy, with the tangible quality of the interface adding a richness to the interaction that could make you feel more deeply connected to the information.

Hiroshi Ishii and the valiant band of graduate students in his Tangible Media Group are building connections between media and adding tactile qualities to the interface between people and computer systems, demonstrating that multisensory and multimedia interactions can be fun and help us do things better. Durrell Bishop wants things to be themselves, whether they are in the physical or digital world. In the interview that follows, he explains how he wants to design affordances to communicate potential behaviors, so we can express what interface elements are by designing them as physical objects that have digital properties.

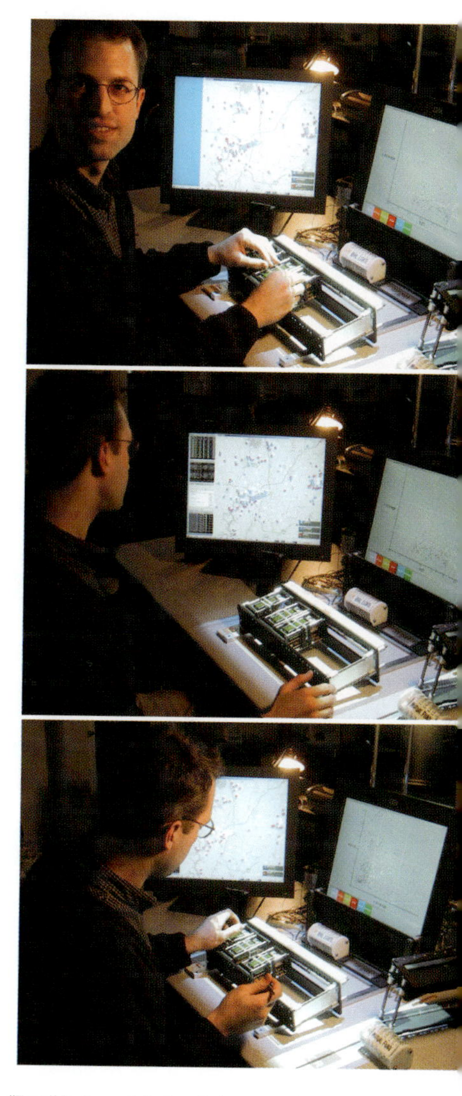

"Tangible Query Interfaces" demonstration, allowing queries to be posed to a database of information about real estate

Photo Durrell Bishop

Durrell Bishop

Durrell designed the game Tea Diving for a CD-ROM included in an issue of the design magazine *ID*, keeping it compact, at less than 2MB. The first screen shows a box with a diving figure and a mug of tea, plus the description of the diving kit. Next is the "easy to assemble electronics," a screen with a printed circuit board and components that you have to drag and drop into place before it will "work." Once the task is complete, you are in the game. Little clothed figures fall from the sky and splat on the ground if left unattended. There is a large cookie that you can use as a paddle to rescue them, and you can bounce them into the huge tomato ketchup bottle: they emerge from the sugar pourer in swimming trunks ready to dive, and if you can bat them into the tea mug before they hit the ground, the side of the mug scrolls a message to the sound of cheering. The game exemplifies the impish humor that Durrell brings to his designs. He originally studied industrial design in London, and after a period of freelance design and photography, joined IDEO. In 1991 he returned to the Royal College of Art in London for a master's in interaction design and stayed on to continue research at RCA and with Interval Research in California. Later he designed games with Dancing Dog and then set up "itch" in partnership with Andrew Hirniak. After another spell with IDEO in London, Durrell branched out on his own again in 2004, helping his clients get the most out of highly interactive products and media.

TABLE TOP
DIVING KIT
INCLUDES :
full instructions
easy to assemble electronics
sample programme
adjustable variables
interactive postcard
COMPETITION DIVING IN YOUR OWN HOME
STEP 1. ASSEMBLE CIRCUIT BOARD
4.00
1. Select components
score...16 @ itch.co.uk
score...14

Durrell Bishop

Things Should Be Themselves!

■ Tea Diving game by Durrell Bishop, designed for the Web site for *ID* magazine, size 231KB

Durrell Bishop wants to design objects that are self-evident, whether they are physical or virtual. He looks at electronics and notices that the shape of the objects does little to describe what they are actually doing; it is hard to see the difference between a radio and calculator by their design. Consumer electronics modules are almost universally black boxes of a standard size, so that you can only tell the difference between them by the graphics that label the product and designate the buttons, and the buttons themselves are part of a text-based language; the legend above the button tells you what it is, and the button is no more than an action on a word. Perhaps the product has an instruction manual, but that is also text-based, so the conceptual model that establishes itself in your head is a series of instructions to help you manipulate labels.

What a contrast there is between these objects, which are supposed to be interactive, and the real world around us, which is full of self-evident things, like knives and glasses and gloves. These

- Corkscrew and record player
- Kitchen implements
- Supermarket checkout
- VCR compared to Monopoly

are objects that we immediately recognize and understand through the mechanical properties that they display by their shape:

> The mechanical world has got a lovely solution to this. Mechanical objects are usually descriptive of what they do. Here we have a corkscrew just to open a bottle of wine. The idea of pulling out the cork and the shape of the corkscrew fit together; you see it in your head the same way as you do it. When you see the object, it reminds you of what it does. Also with an old record player, the physical elements have properties which you can see and perceive how to act on them: the arm moves across, the disk spins finding a track, you look for the grooves and find the spaces. The whole product forms a fairly simple and a very descriptive system.
>
> I really like the kitchen. The kitchen is full of products designed by different people. Each of them is descriptive of what it does, but they all work together. At one end you've got things grown on trees, and at the other end you've got electrical appliances. Recipes work with them; they are like the manuals on how to use all these different items together. When you walk into a kitchen for the first time, you can probably guess where things are. This is a far cry from electronic boxes; as we all know, networking between different devices is one of the great nightmares!

The game of Monopoly is a visual description of a system that seems about as complex as a videotape recorder, but the VCR is the most frequently mentioned scarecrow of interaction design difficulty—so few people get past the play function and actually record successfully. Monopoly does a good job of making the functions of the game self-evident. The graphics lay out the possibilities clearly, and the physicality of the players' pieces and the dice let you know what is happening at a glance. As the game progresses, the houses express ownership for one player and risk for the others. There is a physical representation of the different elements of the software of the game. That is exactly what you would love to have in a VCR. You want to know what is on the tape, where things are, how much space there is left, whether it is recording, and who else in the family is using it. What would happen if the design principles of Monopoly were applied to an electronic product?

Durrell uses money as another example of physical objects that represent meaning:

> Here is a coin. Yes, mechanically it has certain properties. It's hard to copy; it fits in your pocket. But it has three other interesting properties; they are pretty much social properties. It has value; yes, it's written on it what the value is, and its size and shape denote that to some extent, but the real idea of value is not a physical thing. It also has country; it belongs to a nation. But most of all, and strangest of all, it has ownership; the ownership isn't represented on it at all, but we totally accept it, and it's mostly defined by the distance it is from you. If I'm holding it, it's mine; if it's in my pocket, it's mine. If I place it far enough away, we start questioning whose it is, but we don't think about this as a pointer to money; it's not a tag for money—it is money.

It may be possible to make virtual items, both space and objects, seem just as real as physical items by designing them to say more about themselves. If each of the items that you are designing is self-descriptive, both the environment itself and the physical objects in it, you can expand the connections between virtual and real.

> If a recognizable physical object has a pointer to a window or folder, some form of container in a computer space, then perhaps the physical environment is just as real as the screen environment; in fact, they are one and the same thing. Any object picked up physically, which you can see has been augmented with additional information, can be taken to a tool, perhaps a reader, or to a screen, and you can see the same object in its other representation; the screen is only another representation. In this case, the objects are tagged, with the tag pointing to a file, an application, or a folder on a computer.

Durrell is constructing a physical world, which describes the computer space, using both three-dimensional objects and virtual characteristics to define the interface. A first reaction to this may be that it is artificial, but the artifice is only describing what goes on inside the computer, in the same way that the screen is only describing what is inside the computer. Folders give us pointers

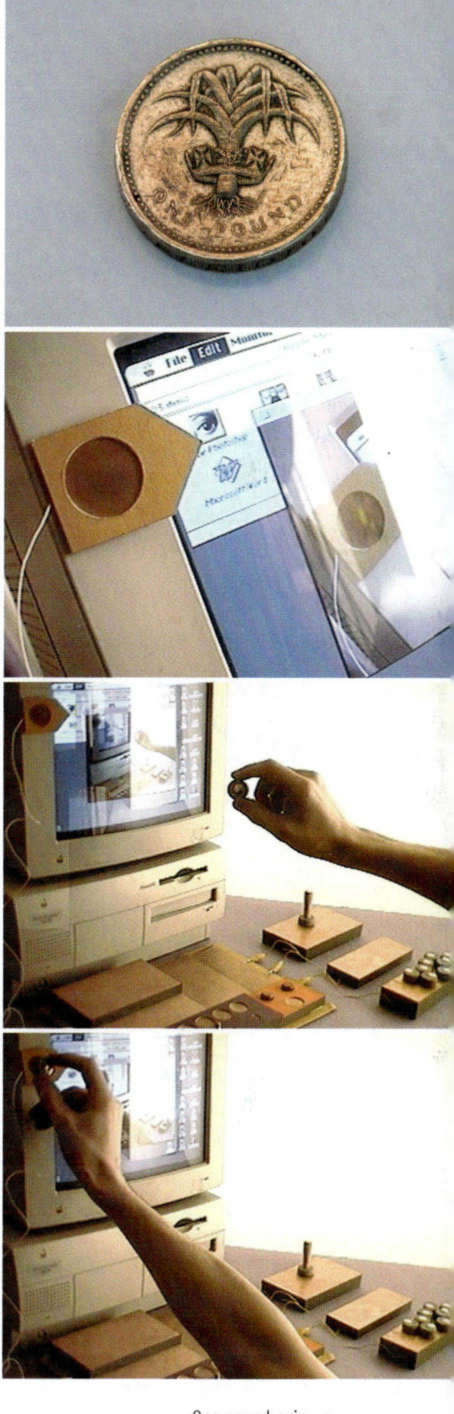

One-pound coin ■
Video editor—augmented object reader ■
Video editor—augmented object to screen ■
Video editor—augmented object reading ■

icon of friend for emails, home movies, telephone number

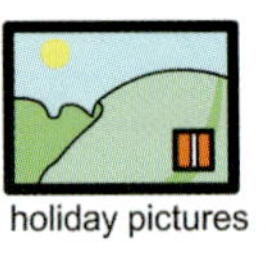

holiday pictures

bull dog clip emails and letters

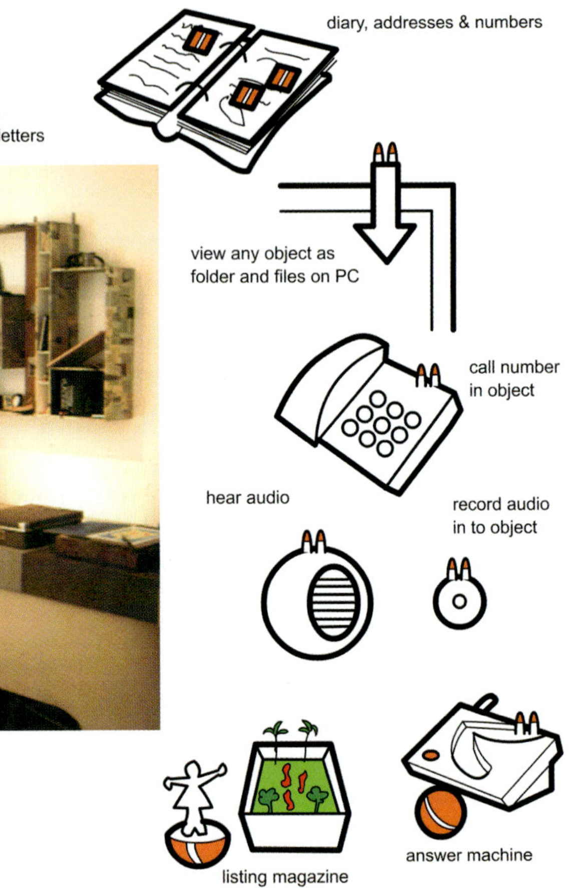

diary, addresses & numbers

view any object as folder and files on PC

call number in object

hear audio

record audio in to object

listing magazine

answer machine

2 radio stations

joke collection

gift with pointer to birthday card animation

audio messege board

strange application listening in on the room

sticky tags (IDs)

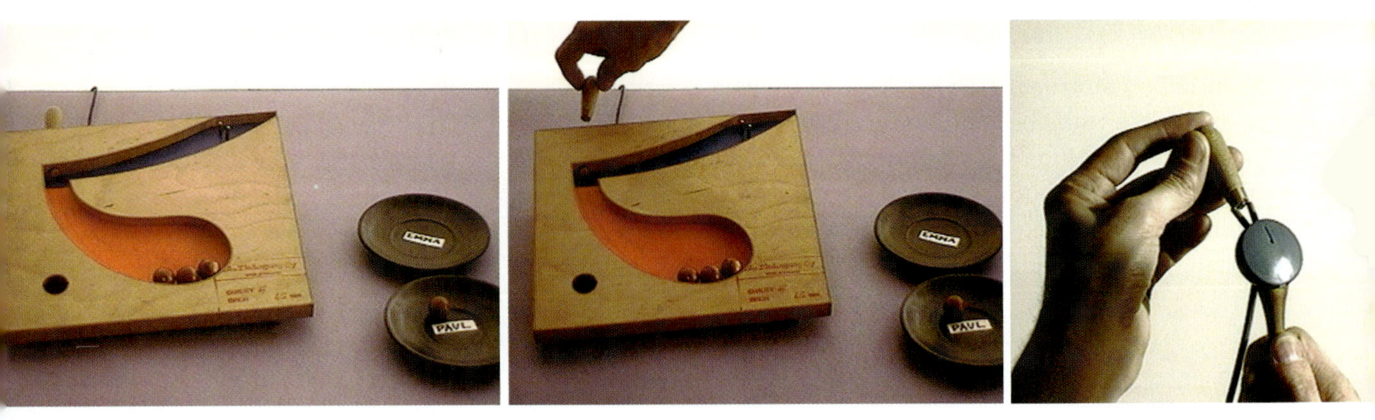

to locations in storage, so why not use a physical object to point to the same space? A successful metaphor like the desktop is useful because it reminds us of some familiar item with equivalent behaviors and lets us operate in a way that is at best intuitive, or at least easy to learn. The physicality of objects can offer the designer many more possibilities for representations that are both familiar and exhibit relevant behaviors. The freedom from the confines of the computer screen also promises a stronger relationship to our perception of reality, just as we think that money really is money, rather than just being representations of value. Computing can break loose of the desktop and become more ubiquitous, not only in the transparent way envisaged by Mark Weiser,[9] but also in ways that present people with more-relevant and better-designed representations of the functionality and behavior available to them.

Durrell likes to build working examples to communicate his ideas, and he uses a smart telephone answering machine to illustrate his concept for physical representation:

■ A collection of tagged objects

Below
Telephone answering machine, showing recording of outgoing message

Photos, drawings
Durrell Bishop

> So let's have a look at this telephone answering machine. It's an application. As you can see in the physical version we made here, the messages drop out, but there is an extra object, that's the outgoing message. You need a way of putting audio into it, so we have another tool, that's a microphone. Any object taken to a microphone lets you put audio into that object. It just puts in an outgoing message. What sort of other objects do we have? Well, in this case, there's a speaker. When any object is taken to a speaker, [the system] looks inside that object on the computer, and plays the audio from it. There's a bulldog clip here. It's got a tag on it? What does that do? The bulldog clip is kind of an abstract thing. You need to attach it to something to have any meaning. So I put a microphone on it, I put a message in, and I put a paper on it saying, "Letters from John," and I leave it out for somebody. I started out to make my own icons and my own physical objects on the machine.
>
> A nice result of this design was the idea of friends as products. After all, you get given letters from people, you get given emails, you get given bits of video hopefully; you know about addresses and birthdays. If there is a way of collecting all these together and

- A bulldog clip takes messages from a microphone
- The clip is labeled by a handwritten title
- A frog represents a friend
- Opening the friend's folder

representing them, then all you really need is an object, representing the person, that you keep; that then becomes the item that you pick up and take to different tools to find things.

Here we have a little plastic frog that's got a friend's name on it. If we take him to the computer, it opens up the computer representation of him, i.e., a folder. Inside that folder is a series of files. I can now pick a piece of video to send to him and drag it into the folder, and take the object off the computer. Now I put a piece of video into a small plastic object; if I take it to a camera, maybe I'll see that piece of video; if I take it to the telephone, it might dial him.

This got really exciting to me when someone asked, "Are you simply augmenting objects with new types of properties?" Do we start seeing things, and start assuming they have video in them?

Picking up tagged objects is only one possible way of describing the potential for interactions with a computer system. As technology becomes a larger part of our everyday lives, we can expect to see different kinds of interaction emerging, specifically developed for each of our activities. Durrell was given an opportunity to develop an exhibition for LG, the Korean consumer electronics giant, and he used this to create another kind of connection between physical objects and an underlying computer system—this time in the context of home entertainment. He built a wall[10] with objects representing a CD player, television, radio, door entry system and a home banking terminal. A display screen was mounted on a rolling trolley arm, so that you could slide the screen over the objects.

The screen knew where it was as it slid along a wall. Behind it we placed a series of five products, each of them working, and each of them looking at a different aspect of the relationship between the physical object and what a screen might do.

At one end was a CD player, mounted on the wall. It had three buttons: you could go up a track, down a track, or eject. By putting the CD in it, it played, so it was very limited in terms of its mechanical interface. If you slid the screen over it, it opened up an application that gave a visual description of the controls for the CD player; you could see what was on the CD and you could shuffle the tracks.

The next product on the wall was a television represented by a clothes brush, and the clothes brush simply reminded you of the fact there was a TV. When you put the screen over it, it launched television. It had four buttons on the screen, as in Britain most people only had access to four channels at that time. I liked the fact that the clothes brush became a television, just because that was how you perceived it.

Next was a radio. In this case the electronic components for the radio were elsewhere, and all you were left with was a representation of the interface—a ruler, with blackboard paint on it that you could move in sixteen steps, and a pencil. By sliding the ruler down, it picked up a preset station, and you could read from the blackboard paint what it was. To set the stations up, you moved the screen in front of it, and it launched the 1950s GoldStar radio, allowing you to change that preset on the ruler.

Then there was a doorbell. In this case it was pair of eyes on the wall. You slid the screen across and you got a video image from a source elsewhere in the exhibition, as if it was a video monitoring system for your entrance door.

The last one was a home bank. A little display on it showed you your current account. If you slid the screen over that, it showed you your current account over time. If a little light flashed indicating that an email had come in, you could slide the screen across that particular element to read that email.

The whimsicality of this design, engaging though it is, may take away from the seriousness of the intent. Durrell is experimenting with the potential of new products that combine the properties of the environment, the Internet, and applications in a physical representation that you can perceive and that you are likely to remember. The connection between a clothes brush and a television may seem peculiar, but it engages both your spatial memory, and your associations with analogy and humor. Durrell sums it up:

What's important to me is that there are different items, which sit in an environment, and you can remember what their properties are. You can see the potential of an action, for example, the potential of how far something might move, and it doesn't actually matter what the

LG home entertainment wall—GoldStar radio
Radio image distorts as it is tuned
Wall with screen in radio position
Wall with screen in TV position

- LG home entertainment wall—CD player position
- LG home entertainment wall—TV position
- LG home entertainment wall—banking position
- Homebank splash screen

> object looks like, as long as you can remember it easily after seeing how it behaves.

Durrell Bishop is passionate about expanding the dimensionality of interactions, adding to the two-dimensional, screen-based representations of events and behaviors a third dimension by pushing into the three-dimensional world of physical objects. His ideas of representing the potential of actions by adding twists of humor and surprise make sense in the context of the way the human brain works, as proposed by Jeff Hawkins.[11] Jeff postulates in *On Intelligence* that the brain is essentially predictive and that we remember things either because we have experienced them repeatedly or because something surprising or unusual pushes the memory out of the ordinary and makes it stick. The lateral thinking of humor can make this difference; both the representation of Durrell's friend as a plastic frog and the television as a clothes brush contain enough surprise to make them memorable, so we can easily predict their behavior next time we encounter them.

In the next interview, Joy Mountford tells of her passion for expanding the dimensions of interactions by making fuller use of media and the senses. She has achieved dramatic success in this, as she pioneered the inclusion of moving images in computer interfaces; she starts by telling the story of the development of QuickTime.

Photo Tom Gruber

Joy Mountford

"Never in my wildest dreams in England did I think I'd do anything that had to do with high-speed aircraft!" says S. Joy Mountford, as she describes her job designing displays and controls for military aircraft and the space shuttle when she was at Honeywell. It had been flight that had brought her to America in the first place, as she had won a scholarship in aviation psychology and learned how to use some flight simulators with horribly complicated control systems that pilots had to cope with. Her undergraduate degree was from University College London, and her graduate study was in engineering psychology at the University of Illinois. "We did a lot of what is now called 'task analysis' of man-machine systems. My professor was very methodical; I think it took us a whole semester to do a task analysis of just being able to get into your car and put the key in the ignition." This rigorous training helped her as she gained experience in high-tech industries. She found her niche as the creator and manager of the Human Interface Group at Apple Computer, the team that invented, among other things, the initial use of QuickTime. From Apple she went on to join Interval Research, leading a series of musical development projects. Now she is founding principal of Idbias, an interaction design partnership, consulting in the development of novel and enjoyable ways for people to interact with the technology that surrounds them. Joy has been designing and managing interface design efforts for over twenty years. She frequently teaches, lectures, and presents at conferences, always delivering an inspiring performance.

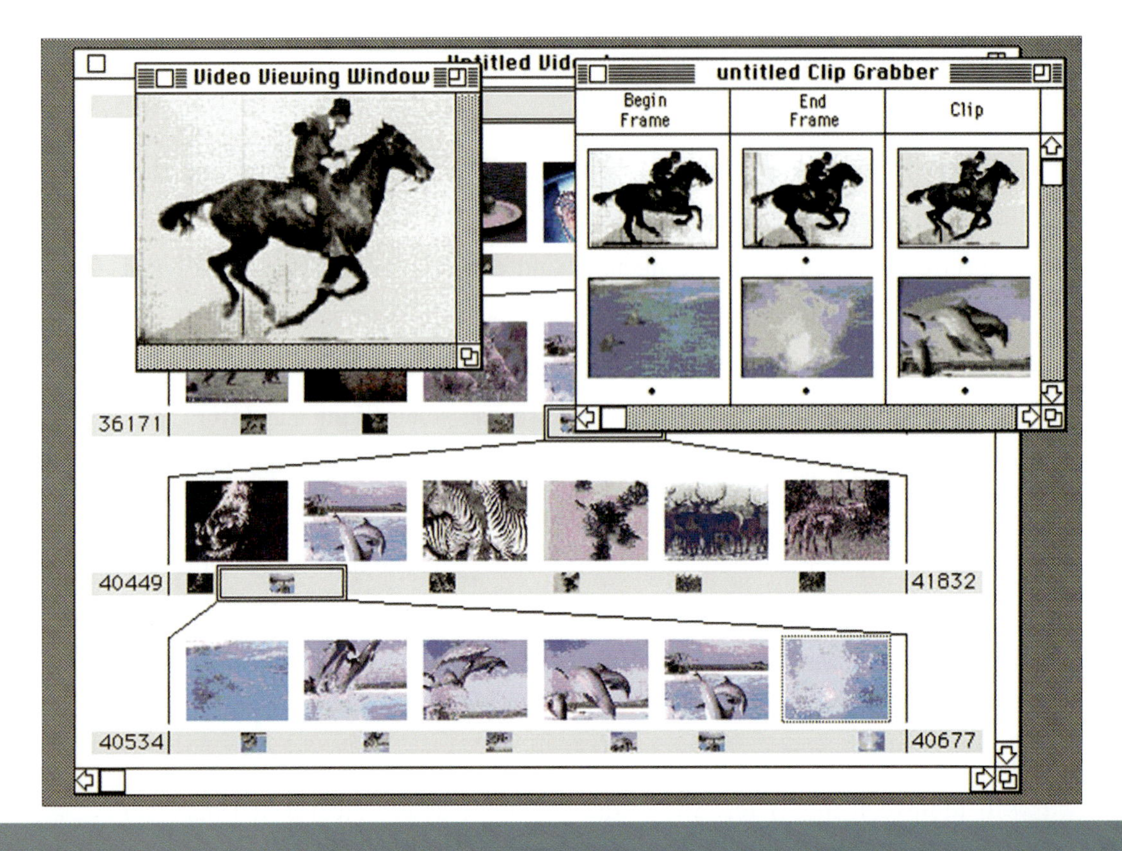
Untitled Vid
Video Viewing Window
untitled Clip Grabber
Begin Frame
End Frame
Clip
36171
40449
41832
40534
40677

Moto-small30.mov
00:01:19

Joy Mountford

QuickTime

- Early QuickTime compared to 2005 version

Screen capture

Before she went to Apple, Joy Mountford was working at Microelectronics Computer technology Consortium (MCC), which was sponsored by a consortium of companies developing intelligent systems to compete against the Japanese fifth-generation computer effort. She gained experience in artificial intelligence and visual displays, but she was worried that she did not know enough about graphic design. A SIGGRAPH[12] conference opened her eyes to the simulation concepts that were making displays look almost photo realistic in the seventies and early eighties. She realized that her future was not going to be limited to intelligent systems; she must include the design of how they worked with people.

> A friend of mine suggested that I look at an interesting company called Apple Computer. The only thing I'd seen about Apple Computer was in *Time* magazine, where the vice president was wearing a black leather jacket, which I thought was very cool at the time.

> In preparing for my interview, I was very shocked when I used a Macintosh for the first time. It did not seem to be able to do anything with its small screen, floppy disks, a one-button mouse, and only a black-and-white display. I said, "I feel very sorry for those people. All they have is this tiny little box. And it doesn't do anything. It just does word processing and spreadsheets." I had got used to high-end Symbolics machines with very large screens. I'd always used a three-button mouse, and I'd always used high-resolution, 3-D graphics systems. My friend, thank goodness, persuaded me that there was a future for it, so I persuaded myself to go and work there.

■ Joy Mountford in 1987
■ Mike Mills in 1991

Joy was happy at Apple once she got there and found that the place was full of interesting and enthusiastic people. She put together the Human Interface Group, and one goal was to help release the human interface guidelines in 1986. The purpose of the guidelines was to provide helpful rules for Apple's many developers, both internal and external, so that there would be a consistent interface for all users.

At that time, most people were still using computers only at work, for things like spreadsheets and writing documents. The market for personal computers at home was just starting to grow. A more significant shift was taking place in the workplace, as the people buying the products were changing over from being IT professionals to the office administrators. They helped initiate a wave of change that was good for Apple, as their competitive advantage was desktop publishing. Inside the company, Joy recalls, people were looking for the next new wave of change:

> When I got to Apple, the question every week was, "So, what's beyond the desktop?" At that point, of course, we had files and folders, derived from the familiar metaphor of everyday office work. People had some familiarity with the elements of the metaphor, so they felt more comfortable beginning to use a computer that looked and behaved sort of similarly to the real world. However, based upon my past experience, I was very frustrated with that, because I thought, "Why would I want to do just paperwork on a computer?" What fascinated me was, How are you going to do something unique on a computer? Not just the replication of the real world. What would

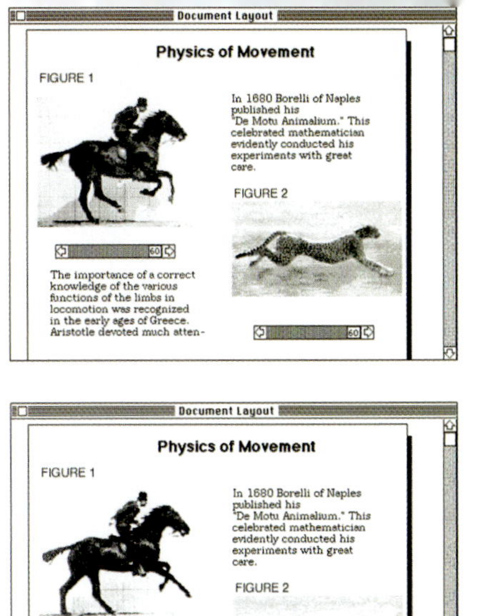

really captivate people who spend time with computers over the wonders and beauties of things like books and paper?

The idea that began to obsess me was how we might include pictures, sounds—even movies. In about 1988 I attended a conference where I heard a paper on dynamic documents presented by Professor Michael Mills. I was very intrigued. So I managed to persuade Mike to spend his sabbatical with us, starting in 1989, and he went on loan from the Interactive Telecommunications Program at New York University, where he was a professor.

Mike Mills came for his sabbatical and was soon smitten with the opportunities to put his ideas into practice.[13] He had always been interested in time-based events, particularly in how they represent spatial relationships. The challenge for the Macintosh in the late eighties was to build a toolbox that would support time-based events, so that all the different computers of varying processor speeds would play time-based media consistently. Mike ended up staying at Apple for six years and worked with Joy and her team on a wonderful series of prototypes that became the seminal work contributing to what we now know as QuickTime. Joy recalls the early work on what they were calling "dynamic icons," or Dicons:

The first thing I remember about this was that Mike managed to put together a series of illustrative prototypes using VideoWorks, which was the precursor to Director. VideoWorks enabled you to write a big score, so that you could sequence exactly the events that occurred within a transaction. This was the first time that anyone could see something occurring over time within the interface, rather like just playing back a little movie. The little movies that we put inside documents often used the original Muybridge illustrations of horses running or people running. So frame-by-frame we could play back a sequence of someone moving. This brought the document to life. Hence the team started working on dynamic documents.

I remember a day when Jean-Louis Gassée, president of the Apple Products Division at the time, was in an executive staff meeting. I knew where he was and what was going on, and when he took a break I managed to waylay him in the direction of the cube where Mike Mills was working. I persuaded him to put his head over the wall

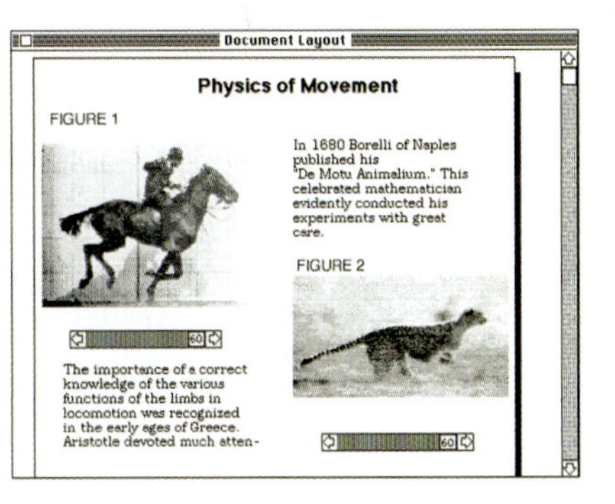

Demonstration of QuickTime using Muybridge images

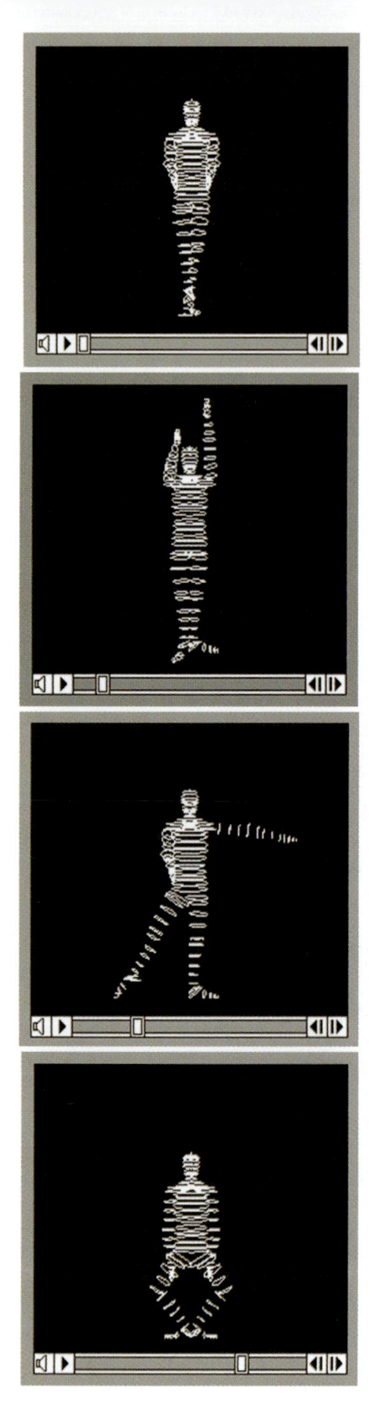

■ Skeletal figure animation sequence

just long enough to see the first dynamic document. He saw a skeletal structure of a couple of movies, as it were, playing, a half inch big, with some text all around them.

He stopped, and he said, "Now I know why my grandmother wants a computer!"

I remember at the time thinking, "What an extraordinary thing for him to say!"

I had never even thought of my grandmother using a computer, let alone why it would captivate her, and why what we had done with movies meant that. Looking back, of course, he had a lot more insight than I did. It began to change what a computer and all the documents on a computer were about. Something moved, something came to life, something played. And it showed something more than just another version of a paper document that you could read better and print. We were very excited. That began a series of four or five years of building successively on the first illustrative prototypes, to bring more and more control and playback capabilities into Simple Player to control time-based events, which we now know as QuickTime.

This was the first step toward bringing video into the personal computer interface and turning the PC into a multimedia device. It also had important implications for interaction design, in that it allowed prototyping of time-based events, which is the whole point of interaction and designing for it. At that time it was very hard to demonstrate the intention of an interactive behavior. Hypercard was released in 1987. It was wonderful for click-through behaviors, and we used it for some simple animations. But we needed something more powerful to explore new metaphors. Designers were using paper animation techniques, such as flipbooks, to explain their ideas, but it was hard to convert those into the details of code. When QuickTime arrived, it was suddenly easy to generate design alternatives for behavioral animations in a medium that could also form a specification for software.

Joy remembers Mike and his team[14] working on the controller—the user interface for controlling the video player on the computer. They put together lots of illustrative samples of prototypes to show alternate ways that you could control the video:

There were many options to consider: how to control something, how to label it, how to shrink it, how to increase its size, and so on. One of the things that we now had using VideoWorks was a way of showing all of the different options that we could provide people. In addition, we could actually imagine different styles of controllers, different mechanisms, just a very subtle thing like, how would you indicate start and stop?

Would you just want to start and stop? No.

Would you like to go faster or slower?

Of course there are real-world metaphors from video players, which probably most consumers had in their homes, so we used some of those elements, but it was a different medium. If a document was dynamic, then the video was inside a document. There were many unanswered design questions.

We were beginning to show people illustrations of what people might want to do with documents that included time-varying dynamic information, such as movie events. Meanwhile, there were programmers working directly within the toolbox to create enabling technologies such as 32-bit QuickDraw, which was essential to enable time-based data. They came by our offices and studied our prototypes. We began to be a place where people came to look at what a new type of document might look and behave like.

People were asking, "Well, after 32-bit color QuickDraw, what do we do? We will need that toolbox to support more events—more movie based events, with a clock that will support them across different machines."

In addition, it took a team of engineers in the Macintosh Product Development group to bring all the functionality of QuickTime together to create a viable product. We had realized to make our vision work in the way we wanted, we would need API programmers to understand how critical the interface would be for the overall product success. We also hired programmers to help build increasingly in-depth working prototypes. This allowed us to better show some of the subtleties that we were evangelizing within the interface.

At the time QuickTime was being developed, very few people were familiar with film and video-editing tools and techniques. iMovie has made video editing popular, in a similar way that word processing and laser printers brought publishing to the desktop. Now people are far more familiar with incorporating video and being able to edit clips of their children. At that time, access to a video-editing suite was expensive and daunting, and the operators of the equipment seemed to have incredible skills. Mike and his team were among this elite, coming from a film background at the Interactive Telecommunications Program at NYU. They developed what they called a "playback head" as part of the video controller interface. They were familiar with jog shuttle controllers, which are used to freeze and move forward and backward to sequence a particular segment within a movie. Joy recounts the dilemma that arose:

> They invented a graphic element called a "hand controller," which was an image of a graphical hand that appeared on the controller interface and could be grabbed to move the video, just like a jog shuttle can be spun. You could move it forward and back while it was on the controller. It had a very similar kind of feel—not a similar look, but a similar feel—to the jog shuttle. We had those hand controllers working in the lab, and we were building more capabilities borrowing from the movie-editing world. We actually patented the "hand controller." The patentable idea was that by making a vertical movement of the mouse, you could cause the open hand to "grab" onto the controller thereby locking in a frame rate, changing it from a jog shuttle to a slider. So instead of having two separate controllers, you could have both jog shuttle and fixed speed in the same controller, which was a clever kind of idea.
>
> I also had a team working in my group doing user studies, who said, "We're not too sure about this hand controller. We think we should do some user studies."
>
> We began to bring people in for studies, and we asked them to do a series of movie-editing tasks using the hand controller. I think about 80 to 90 percent of the people that we interviewed really disliked the hand controller. They felt it was like a disembodied hand that appeared from nowhere and grabbed the video. They didn't know why it was a hand. The personification—the anthropomorphizing of the interface—was not something they really enjoyed. So despite the fact that we'd taken the time to program up all of these very sophisticated controller ideas, I also spent a fair amount of time "managing them out" of the controller that actually shipped with QuickTime. The resulting Simple Player controller, indicated in the

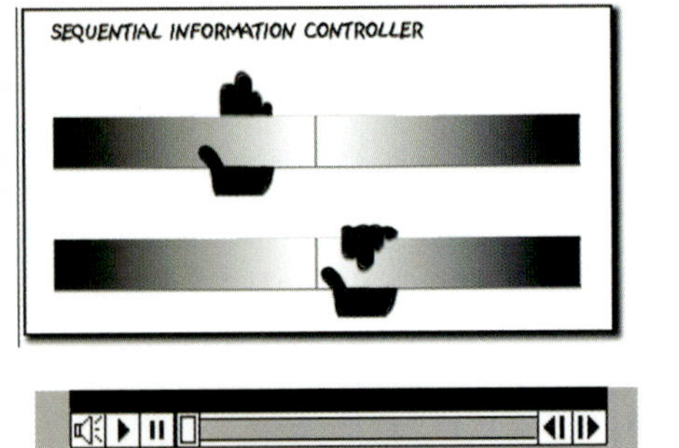

- "Hand controller" concept
- Simple QuickTime controller

drawing, really only allowed for video playback and audio level control.

Yet again, this story emphasizes the tendency of designers just as much as engineers to design for themselves, for their own skills and familiarities, rather than for the audience for whom the product is intended. User studies might have a different result now, as many more people have engaged with the idea of video editing.

The QuickTime starter kit shipped in the fall of 1991, and Mike Mills and his team spent the year leading up to shipment working full-time with the product teams to make sure that the vision and simplicity of use were preserved. Afterward they returned to Joy's group and continued to develop the next stages of QuickTime, with projects for creating videodiscs and toolkits for transitions.

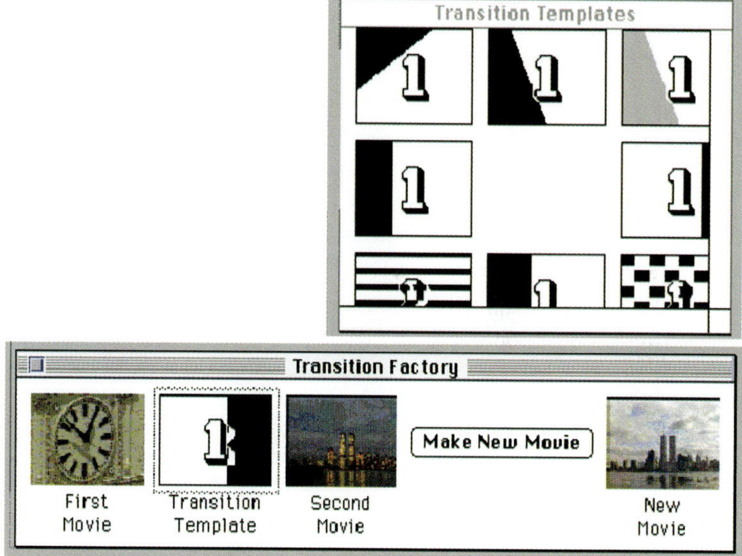

Transition templates ■
Transition factory ■

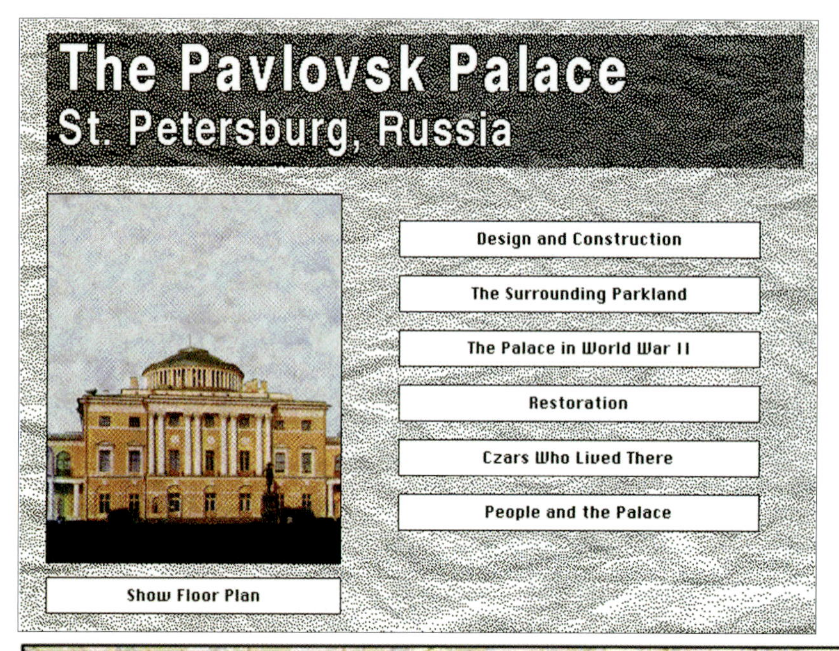
The Pavlovsk Palace
St. Petersburg, Russia
Design and Construction
The Surrounding Parkland
The Palace in World War II
Restoration
Czars Who Lived There
People and the Palace
Show Floor Plan

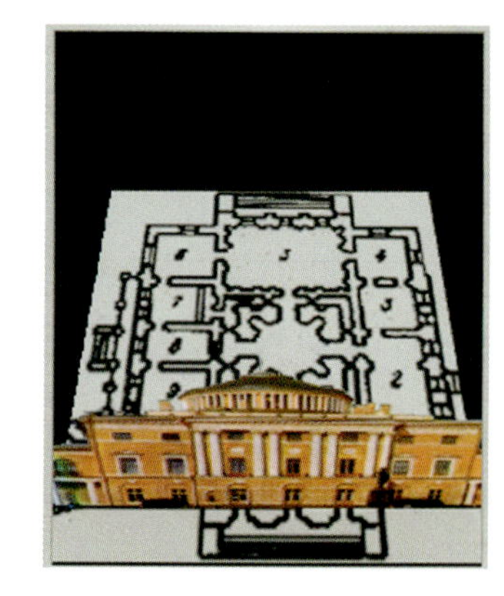

QuickTime VR

Joy Mountford has maintained strong connections to academia throughout her career. Every now and again she teaches a course at one of the interaction design programs around the world. She started the International Interface Design Project at Apple and continued it at Interval and now runs it for Mattel and Microsoft: this sponsored project assembles interdisciplinary teams of students to work on a project, bringing the results together for a show, critique, and celebration. She has also been a regular employer of graduate students as summer interns.

> I think it's a wonderful opportunity for both the company and also the graduate students to work together and learn different things from each other. I've always had a large number of interns coming in each summer, since they provide a whack on the side of the head! They do wild and wonderful things.

One summer she hired an intern, Dan O'Sullivan, who was also from the ITP/NYU graduate program. He started his own project without explaining to her what he was trying to do. He had a video camera pointing at an object, seemingly doing the same thing day after day.

■ Pavlovsk Palace, showing the menu screen, the transition from front view to floor plan, and the QuickTime VR rendering of the interior

Screen capture

> I got pretty annoyed with him because it seemed like we weren't making any progress. He was using a rotating mount from a security camera, taking images upwards, downwards, sideways and all around. He had figured out a way to take hundreds of still images, and sequentially be able to record an entire room. He was rotating the camera, taking an image, noting its position, moving the camera, taking another, and successively going all the way around and recording each image position. He had been photographing image after image after image and then referencing all the images. Simultaneously he had become friends with Michael Chen, who had developed the virtual sphere, which was a coding technique for changing the orientation of an object in 3-D space by using only a one-button mouse. So Dan decided to systematically map all his images referenced as overlapping tiles onto the virtual sphere, but from the inside looking out.

At this point, I thought, "Yes, but still why would I want to do that?"

It felt a little bit like he had been obsessing about just proving that he could control the head of the camera and record the image. But what he had done is make it possible to navigate a composite image of the entire room. You could move around the camera's view of the room just like you could manipulate a 3-D view of an object with the virtual sphere.

Simultaneously the Human Interface Group had released a version of the virtual sphere code, which allowed for a one-button mouse to change orientation of a three-dimensional object. It was as if the object was encased in a translucent ball, and the user could reposition the ball in any direction, letting you to look at it from any vantage point. Joy and the team also realized that by combining the virtual sphere with Dan's large set of images, they could offer the appearance of direct manipulation in virtual space. The catch was that for Dan's images, instead of being outside looking in toward the object, you wanted to be at the center of the sphere looking outward, which they achieved by using a variation of the same basic code, but putting themselves in the center of a virtual room. They called it a "navigable movie," and Joy started thinking how to promote the concept:

Content, as we all know, is very key to the success of ideas like this. Sadly, Dan's first example showed his kitchen, which really wasn't that interesting, so I decided we'd try and use some interesting content that would really make people sit up and pay attention.

We did a couple of wonderful projects, which were very high risk and exciting. One was created by additional team members from the Interface Group,[15] who went up to the top of the Golden Gate Bridge. It was, I believe, the only time the Macintosh had ever gone to the top of the bridge. There's a very small elevator, which carries you all the way up the outside of the bridge support structure, and it's only big enough for one person. There was no room for the Macintosh, so it had to be strapped to the outside of the elevator.

The Macintosh, camera, and rotating camera mechanism all were on a platform because the camera had to be steady when it was recording all of the incremental images. The platform was bigger than

Camera and HDD mounted on the elevator ascending the Golden Gate Bridge

the elevator, so it had to be mounted on the outside of the elevator while taking pictures. And, in addition, it had to have a very long power cord, which went all the way down from the elevator at the very top of the bridge to the ground.

Once the images were safely on the hard drive of the Macintosh, they used the "navigable movie" program to wrap them together into a continuous virtual space. When it was finished, you could look all around, into Marin County, over to San Francisco, and you could actually look down and see the long power cord beneath you. John Sculley demonstrated the resultant movie at MacWorld in January of 1992.[16]

The audience, mostly of developers, literally kind of drew their breath in. People had never seen something that could move around like that, and to see all those different points of view was very exciting on a window on a Macintosh.

Another project that we did to attract attention to this new capability was filmed in Russia at Pavlovsk Palace. This project explored the inverse of the navigable movies, looking at an object from every angle around it. I wanted to film a Fabergé egg to examine it from every direction. I'd gone to see Fabergé eggs in museums and had always been very disappointed because they were too far away from me, and I couldn't ever see them from any other point of view than the one they're showing me in the glass case.

When I saw a Fabergé egg in person, I felt, "Well, it's really not as compelling as I thought it was going to be. I mean, in these beautiful books I have at home, they look a lot better."

I commissioned a large structure to be built by Peace River called the "Object Maker," which was almost like a CAT scanner.[17] The camera could be positioned and moved around in three-dimensional space—well, nearly three-dimensional, as you couldn't quite get underneath, because it had to be held somehow. In any case, the camera was controlled very cleverly and gently, and it allowed us to photograph a 3-D object from viewpoints all around it. We could do the inverse of a navigable movie, to enable you to move your viewpoint around the object just as you can move the camera view within a room.

Inspired by the Fabergé egg, the team[18] built a virtual world of a Russian Palace so that the viewer could appreciate the surrounding beauty of the room in which such objects would have existed. The

■ Object Maker scan of cup

team went to Pavlovsk Palace and filmed Maria Feodorovna's[19] bedroom, with its beautiful painted ceilings and inlaid wood floors. These truly panoramic interesting floors and ceilings all made for an interesting rich 3-D scene. Within the room was a china case, which contained some of the things that she used and collected. The team went to work and created a magnificent virtual palace, including navigable views all around her bedroom, plus the additional special close-up view of the navigable china cup that could be viewed from all angles. It was an excellent example of two QuickTime capabilities coming together very effectively and about a place we are unlikely to be able to ever visit. The Human Interface Group distributed a navigable movie controller kit on CD to Mac developers, which was programmed and designed by Mitch Yawitz.

"Navigable movies" were the birth of what later became known as QuickTime VR. Joy and Mike and the team[20] were very successful as evangelists. Joy knew how to promote the concepts; she had the knack of choosing memorable subjects and the drive to make things happen on a large scale. Mike was inventive with his prototypes and demonstrations, and they were so compelling because they really worked, even if the scale was small, and the code was not yet robust. Meanwhile Jonathan Cohen was actually programming up a storm, creating a pioneering special effect editing tool called "Transition Factory." This enabled direct editing of audio and visual effects, which helped make the content examples work very smoothly and look good. So the audio component of media was ever present in Joy's mind, even during the early days of QuickTime.

The Bead Box

JOY WAS FURTHER fascinated by the possibility of expanding to other time-based media events and their uses in computers. This led her to move beyond video to its essential but undervalued cousins: audio and music. She felt that sound should be used more in interface design, integrating music, voice, and more sophisticated sound effects. People are easily attracted to moving images but often forget the evocative effect of the movie soundtrack. David Liddle offered her an opportunity to delve deeper into designing a series of audio products and projects within an innovative research environment, so she left Apple Computer to join Interval Research.

> When I got to Interval, we began to think of ways that we could extend the audio domain to more people. Needless to say, we started thinking about music, and one of the things that we also found out was that 70 percent of the population think they're amateur musicians, which is pretty high (I wonder if 70 percent think they're amateur moviemakers?), so I felt that there was a large potential audience out there. Music also blurs boundaries across gender, language, and is highly expressive. It extends from very young to quite old. People are interested in different types of music at different ages, but we all have a visceral connection to music, and sometimes a physical one, which might be to dance or play air guitar. Children often have expensive music lessons that their parents pay for, and they stop taking those lessons when they hit the teenage years, twelve or thirteen, and they often don't play music very much after that. They do, however, listen to it, but they don't necessarily play. However, currently at clubs now, people participate in DJ performances, which is an interesting genre, where they're playing samples of sounds, but also twisting and warping and playing them slightly differently each time, even though it's all preprocessed and preselected audio.

Joy led a team at Interval called Soundscapes to study the creation and use of music. She discovered that many people who want to make music, including professional musicians, are unable to read musical notation. A lot of people buy synthesizers and sit

OSCARS ATLAS
BY HENRIK DRESCHER

at home jamming without being able to read music; they communicate with others through their music but have no written language. This study led them to design the "Bead Box," a device for people who want to make music but have not mastered a conventional instrument notation or the meaning of a score.

The Bead Box had a grid of holes on its surface, five wide by four high, into which people put beads. The beads were made with resistors that tagged them uniquely, so that the box could detect their identity and location when they were put into the holes. Each bead triggered a sample. Along the horizontal axis, the density of the sounds increased as you moved a bead to the right, by adding to the richness of sampling. On the vertical axis, the pitch of the sample was higher as you moved a bead upwards. A virtual "playback head" would scan the holes and play the sounds corresponding to the beads in the plugged holes. A person could create a collage of different sound samples by placing beads and vary them dynamically by removing and repositioning the beads. Joy describes the experience:

■ Bead Box

Photo
Nicolas Zurcher

> If you had no beads, nothing happened. If you put one in, it would go "boink," and the playback head would keep moving, so there was silence until the head came back to the beginning and went "boink" again. So, it could go "boink," or "boink boink," and then you could try to move it to add to the density, so it would be "boooing, boink, boynnk."
>
> With one bead, it's not that interesting, but with multiple beads that changes. The head keeps moving, looking for and playing beads when it reaches their positions. Because of the silences and because you now have two, three, four, however many, you now trigger different sample effects, which have different overlapping decays, which all contribute to the effectiveness of the resulting music. And because you can also change the pitch, it's as if you're playing a tune while dynamically changing how it sounds. What really intrigued me was how much variation of the audio or music mix you could actually create, even with the simplest samples and changes. It was really quite addictive, and it became almost an art to see how wonderful your music could be with just three beads.

> The reason we picked a bead to represent a sound is that it is something very small, that is, a collectible, that you could hold or wear—rather like a solitaire pendant. You could see the piece that you wanted to move as a tangible object and put it somewhere and control that space. People were very keen on playing with the music box. They liked the music they created, and the box was also attractive, having embedded lights that showed through the translucent beads when the head read the sound sample for that bead. One of the most compelling illustrations of using this was actually a Yiddish recipe, said by the grandmother of one of the designers. All it said was "Take the meat. Mix into the bread." You could take each one of the beads, and make "Take the meat" more dense, less dense, higher or lower. It started to sound like a piece of music, although no one actually knew the source was her grandmother's voice saying, "Take the meat. Mix into the bread."

The initial prototypes used a translucent material for the beads, so that as the scanning head/beam went by the beads would light up. In a darkened room you could see a delicate glowing pattern of red, orange, and green shades as the scanner moved under the bead connectors and played sounds collaged together as music. By now they were confident that they had designed a captivating experience for their own ears and eyes, but Joy wanted to see if it would actually work for different age groups. They collaborated with a research firm to test the design with four-year-olds, eight-year-olds, and teenagers, both boys and girls, in three different states in the USA. For the younger children they used samples made up of body noises; for the older children they had a variety of rock and roll sounding songs, but with no lyrics:

> To our absolute amazement, all the different age groups liked it, which actually turned out to be not such a great thing, because now we didn't know who our target user or population should be. Accidentally, we had children being picked up by their parents, and then children told the parents what they had done, and the parents said, "Oh, I would like one of those." The parents suggested adding personalized samples of audio to it. They were coming up with things like, "Oh, if I could only have a bead with my child saying, 'I love

you Mummy,' or my husband saying, 'I love you darling,' "—just a small, little, evocative personal expression that they believed could be within a bead that they could hold, or hang around their neck, or carry around in their pocket as a keepsake. We carried this sort of idea a little farther and made a particular place on the grid for a bead that you could press in and record a three second phrase. Now you could be part of this rather interesting blend of audio effects, with a personal meaningful message in the mix as well. Imagine someone saying "I love you" just at the right moment.

The research results showed a compelling product that appealed to young and old, but the challenge of evolving a successful business solution was still ahead. The design would need to be developed to allow manufacturing at the right price and focused on a specific sales channel. The team at Interval consulted experts in business and marketing for the toy retail market. This is a difficult space, where the offer has to be simple enough to be understood by a child or parent walking down the aisle of a toy store. This design was too abstract and innovative to succeed in a conventional channel and would have needed a gradual process of distribution through a marketing process that gave time for acquaintance, such as schools, or a captive audience where people could see and hear someone playing the Bead Box.

Joy Mountford had come from Apple, where the whole structure of the organization was dedicated to creating products that are launched into the real world and sold as physical products and software. She was proud of the success of such product innovations as QuickTime and found it satisfying to see it used by so many people for such a wide variety of purposes. On the other hand, Interval was set up with a main purpose of generating influential ideas from research, like Xerox PARC, but there was also a hope that the research would lead to successful new products or industries, launched to the real world by setting up spin-out companies.

The story of the Bead Box shows how difficult it is to make this happen. This wonderfully talented team of researchers came up with an engaging concept, developed prototypes through several iterations, and then validated it in extensive market research. The initial setup for the R&D team at Interval was highly interdisciplinary. The Bead Box lived in a new business area and was hard to position, given known product practices. Having more and earlier input from business or marketing folks in the retail toy space might have helped the product succeed.

It is interesting to compare this approach with the model adopted by Brendan Boyle,[21] where the concepts for new toys and games are developed in large numbers to a very rudimentary level before being offered for license to the major companies with specific distributional channels and market understanding. It is hardly surprising that research institutions like Interval or PARC have found it difficult to connect to the market, as even startup companies, or specialist invention companies, have only a small percentage of business successes. Joy had moved from Apple to Interval and had the opportunity to develop products that would be well researched, and based on a deep understanding of latent user needs and opportunities for innovation. The Bead Box project succeeded in this, but it was not particularly well positioned for retail and business issues necessary for success in the market.

Joy has always been intrigued with finding the right balance between corporate development and research environments; she sees it as an ever-evolving challenge, but believes that a symbiotic relationship can benefit both. Soon after she joined Apple, Joy went to a conference in Key West, Florida, and there met a student named Bill Gaver, who was studying with Don Norman at the University of California, San Diego. Bill had written an interesting paper outlining ideas of "auditory icons," so Joy immediately offered him a job as an intern within her group at Apple. Bill's internship resulted in the Apple Human Interface Group releasing the first ever SonicFinder (1986), which associated all Finder operations with a size-proportional and unique natural sound. After the SonicFinder was no longer supported, people complained about the quiet Finder! This early work from Joy and her team just goes to show how much all time-based media should be designed to work together to make for the most compelling interactive experiences at the user interface.

The interview with Bill Gaver that follows covers his journey from designing sounds, through research into affordances at EuroPARC, to becoming a senior research fellow at the Royal College of Art in London, where he explored the possibilities of technology in a context of aesthetics and cultural consequences.

Photo Author

Bill Gaver

In the early eighties Bill Gaver was a graduate student in psychology with Don Norman,[22] studying sound perception. When Don asked him to make a presentation about how sound might be used in computers, Bill reviewed his work so far and concluded that by thinking about the dimensions of sound-producing events, you should be able to make very simple mappings to events in the interface. That idea led to his work on auditory icons. He was studying at UC San Diego and earned his PhD in experimental psychology for work on everyday listening. He wrote a paper outlining the concept of auditory icons for a conference in Florida. There he met Joy Mountford. She liked his ideas and immediately offered him an internship at Apple, where he developed the SonicFinder. He later became interested in broader issues concerning mediated social behavior, helping to develop an audio/video communications network at Xerox EuroPARC, and also developing experimental systems that support social activities over a distance. His work as a senior research fellow, then professor of interaction research, at the Royal College of Art, London, explored the use of technologies to make aesthetic, social, and cultural interventions. He was one of the founders of the Equator Project, a six-year Interdisciplinary Research Collaboration funded by the Engineering and Physical Sciences Research Council (EPSRC), to investigate the integration of the physical and digital worlds by developing innovative systems. The initial research involved design-driven research techniques called "Cultural Probes" to uncover people's values and activities. In 2005 he was appointed professor of design at Goldsmiths College, London.

Bill Gaver

Designing Sound

■ History
Tablecloth with teapot

Photo
Andy Boucher

When Bill Gaver was invited to Apple as an intern in 1986, he made contact with people in the Finder software group, and started talking with them about the possibility of adding sounds to the Finder. It became a kind of underground project within Apple to make the "SonicFinder" actually work, and Bill pushed ahead with adding sounds to the real software, rather than building prototypes in HyperCard first, proving the exception to the rule that prototyping is essential to rapid progress.

> What I could have done was just show images of icons and have them make sounds, but it wouldn't really have done anything. I met John Meier, who was one of the chief programmers for the Finder, and he helped me; he was incredibly patient in walking me through the Finder code and helping me add sounds. What that meant was that I had a real working Finder, so people could use it in their day-to-day lives to do their everyday work, and the thing would make noises at them.

At that time, two schools of thought dominated work on the psychology of sound. One was trying to understand more about how music works, and the other was learning some of the basic ways the ear picks up sound. The research at the time tended to focus on attributes like frequency and pitch, or amplitude and loudness, or the spectrum and timbre of sounds. The SonicFinder was based on Bill's insight that people, when they listen to sound in the world, do not listen to the dimensions that the psychologists were interested in.

> If you think about how we hear sounds in the everyday world, we listen to events in the world; we hear cars going by, we hear people walking up and down stairs, slamming a drawer, or putting a book on a table. All of those things are quite complicated from the point of view of normal psychological ways of thinking about sound. At some point I realized that we could start to build a new psychology of sound by trying to understand what the dimensions of sources are that people hear and what the acoustic information is that conveys information about those sources.
>
> You could try to understand how people hear the material of an object when it's struck, or how big something is—things like that. That sets up a new way of thinking about the dimensions of sound. When I started thinking about using sound in interfaces, it became pretty clear that if interfaces were going to have graphical representations of real-world objects, they could have auditory representations of those objects as well. In other words, if you click on a file icon, it would make a sound that a file would make if you tapped on it. If you dragged a file around the desktop, it could make a sound as if it was a physical object being scraped across a surface: that underlaid everything I did with the SonicFinder.

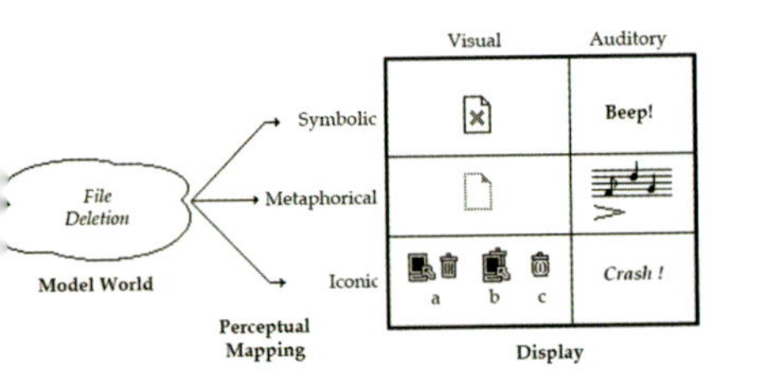

- Diagram of SonicFinder
- Bill Gaver in 1995

The SonicFinder was an auditory overlay on top of the graphical interface for the Macintosh, and Bill's strategy was to add corresponding sounds to the main interaction events. For instance, when you clicked on a file, you would hear a tapping noise, with the kind of the file being indicated by the sound of the material, and the size of the file by sound of a small or large object. The sounds were not just repeated monotonously, as they changed with the secondary properties of the objects. Scrollbars made tapping sounds to indicate how far they were from the top or the bottom of the document. The sounds of windows opening and closing were slightly more imaginative, associated with events that do not exist in real life. The sound of pouring water indicated how far a copying operation had progressed, so as you copied files, you would hear a "glug, glug, glug" sound that would increase in pitch the further along it got, setting up an analogy between filling a file with information and filling a container with water.

Bill explains the qualities of sound information:

> It's important to realize that sound conveys very different information than vision does. The way vision works is that light comes from a source and bounces around off surfaces; every time it hits a surface, some bits of it are absorbed by the surface, so what's reflected back is modified, and that gives rise to information about color and texture and so forth. Our eyes pick that up, so our vision allows us to get information about surfaces laid out in space.
>
> Sound works very differently. Sound is created when objects start to vibrate, and the way they vibrate depends not just on their surfaces, but also on their internal configuration, as well as certain details about the interactions that cause them to make sound. Once a sound is created, it bounces around the environment before it reaches your ear, but it seems to convey less information about the environment than it does about the source.
>
> Once you start thinking about mapping sounds to events in the interface, you're in the business of conveying different kinds of information than you would visually.

The sound made by tapping an object can be in harmony with the visual representation of an object, but it will tell you about different things; it can communicate emotional qualities, rich with connotations. Bill was very interested in the information that sound could convey, and he remembers visiting a famous sound effects artist at Lucasfilm, who had worked on *Indiana Jones* and *Star Wars*.

> I showed him videos of some of the interfaces I'd built at the time, and he looked at me after I was done and said, "You know, a lot of these sounds seem created for humorous effects."

And I thought, "What? What do you mean, humor?"

It was a dimension that I hadn't considered for my sounds. I had never consciously thought about the sounds being humorous, or sober, or serious or what have you. Later he told me that when he created sound effects, he was less worried about the information that the sound might convey than he was about their emotional connotations. If there was a chase sequence in which two single-engine planes were flying after each other, he would work to make the engine of the good guy's plane sound confident and good and wholesome, whereas the bad guy's plane might sound a bit ominous or sinister or aggressive. All that was a foreign language to me, but it really opened my eyes to a different aspect of sound than I had been thinking about.

I don't know how to think consciously about how you create emotional tones with sounds. That's something that I believe is a sort of design and artistic thing about how you hear and how you can craft sounds. It's impossible to be neutral about these things, so the SonicFinder sounds did have emotional connotations. I think I tried to fit with the prevailing emotional tone of the Mac interface at that time, which is a bit happy, a bit jaunty, kind of friendly.

A particularly impressive sound signature in computers is the start up sound for the Mac. It was created with very little memory and processing power, but it is very elegant. Bill Gaver's SonicFinder did not stay around for very long, though it was circulated widely by informal users: it seemed to get lost in the shuffle when he finished his time at Apple. Sounds for the Macintosh remained minimal and unsophisticated until Cordell Ratzlaff set about designing a better solution for Mac OS 8.5, working with Earwax to create a set of "Finder sounds."[23] Bill was philosophical that his work took such a long time to have an effect:

I'm fairly convinced that the people who did the Finder sounds probably never saw and heard the SonicFinder, even if they had heard about it. It took about ten years from the original SonicFinder before Finder sounds were released. I think it's a good example of how the kind of research we do folds into a sort of background consciousness, and then reappears later, sometimes without people even realizing it. I take that as a hopeful sign.

Affordances

BILL WORKED ON the SonicFinder for a year and a half at Apple, first as an intern and then as a consultant. After that he moved to Cambridge, England, to work at Xerox EuroPARC, where he got interested in other aspects of psychology, in particular, affordances.

In 1979 the perception theorist J. J. Gibson wrote his book *The Ecological Approach to Visual Perception*,[24] which changed the way we think about how people perceive the world. He asserted that perception is designed for action, claiming that our whole evolution has been geared toward perceiving useful possibilities for action, and that rather than recognizing separate properties like length or mass, we perceive complicated combinations of these things that have validity for us to do something with or about. We see surfaces for walking, handles for pulling, space for navigation, tools for manipulating, and so on. He called the perceivable possibilities for action "affordances."

Bill explains the relationship between interaction design and the affordance offered by a flight of stairs:

> People have studied empirically the affordance for stair climbing, where it turns out that if you have a given leg length, then the depth of a stair and the riser height will be more or less optimal in terms of the biomechanical energy you spend to climb. There is an affordance for stair climbing that can't be measured just in terms of the physical dimensions of the world, or the capabilities of a person, but has to be evaluated as a complex relation between the two. That offered an interesting way to look at how interfaces convey information about what you can do with them, so that's what I turned my attention to for a number of years.
>
> I tried to peel back the notion of affordances to its real essentials. There are a lot of misunderstandings in the design community about affordances; people think of it as an expression of what you can do with an object, or simply that you can do something easily with an artifact. When you take that stance, you beg the question of whether those things are mediated by culture and whether the kinds of mappings that people are learning are arbitrary. Gibson really meant for affordances to be a statement about

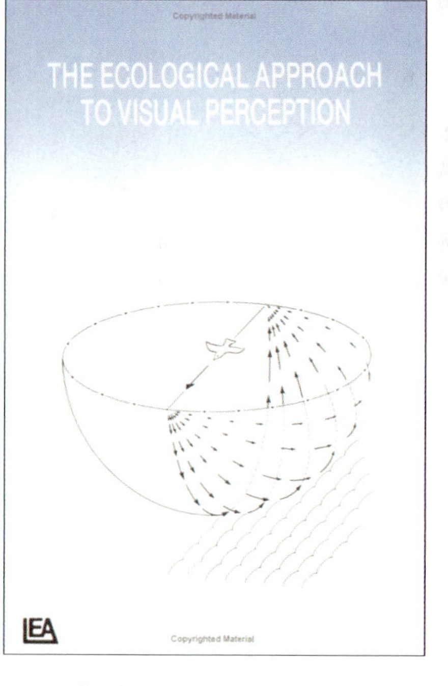

J. J. Gibson's book about affordances ■

perception, so for something to have an affordance, you need to think more about the biophysics of a situation and combine that with fairly low-level perceptual information—in other words, information that can be conveyed through light or sound about the physics of a situation, without a lot of mediation by culture or learning.

I've tried to show that once you take a very basic metaphorical leap in the interface to thinking about the interface being a physical environment rather than being a kind of command-line-driven conversational metaphor, then all of a sudden people can start to deal with items that are shown graphically as if they are physical objects. Then they start to attend to the information being conveyed that gives them hints about what they might be able to do with those objects.

For instance, you could take the scrollbar that sits on the side of a window on most interfaces, which allows you to move the view of the window. It's difficult to understand how you would know what you might do with the scrollbar. You can start by saying that usually the handle of a scrollbar is shown as a kind of separated, bounded object within the interface, and that at least gives people some information that they might be able to interact with it in some way. The tendency might be to click on it or select it. When you do that, it's likely to move. So all of a sudden, there's perceptible information, not only about the affordance of grasping something virtual, but also about the potential for moving it. Now people can start to explore the affordance of movement. When they do that, they see the view on the window change, and now they have information that the handle moves a connected surface.

Equator Project

Bill got more and more interested in the subtleties of the subjective and qualitative relationships that people have with both digital and physical things. In 1994 he moved to the Royal College of Art in London. There he explored the use of technologies to make aesthetic, social, and cultural interventions in people's lives. He was interested in expanding the scope of the ideas and associations that people have when they think about what digital technologies can do to products. He tested the ideas by making working functional products that people can try out and live with over a period of time. He wanted to test whether the things that he thought would be interesting and valuable to them actually turn out that way.

He was involved with a large project called Equator, a six-year interdisciplinary research collaboration, funded by the Engineering and Physical Sciences Research Council (EPSRC), to investigate the integration of the physical and digital worlds by developing innovative systems. There were eight computer science, sociology, and psychology groups participating from British universities, and Bill's group looked at new technologies for the home. They built a series of prototypes to see how weight sensing could be used to get partial information about people's activities in the home. Bill describes some of these prototypes.

History Tablecloth

The History Tablecloth uses weight sensing, measuring how long things have been left on the surface. Things that have been left on it for a long time develop a kind of halo under them, which points them out and highlights them—sections of the tablecloth glow. Objects that have only been there for a short time are not highlighted.

> Ethnographers in Nottingham have done a number of studies of the home, where they've focused on the way that people use surfaces—tables and shelves and so forth—as a way of organizing flows of information. We built on that by saying that one of the problems is that you can't see the history of objects in the home, so the history tablecloth works by looking at when things are placed on certain areas of a table, and indicating how long they've been there.
>
> The way we're building it is quite interesting. We've started working with a woman who has experience with printing electroluminescent material directly onto flexible substrates, and we're working with a company to develop it. Not only do we have a very flexible display, though very low resolution, but each of the elements of the display can be quite complex and fine because it's screen-printed. The end result should look a lot like a kind of lacey

tablecloth, but segments of the tablecloth will light up to highlight things have been on it for a while.

The tablecloth appealed to us because it started to capture a kind of aesthetic for the home that we thought was particularly comfortable. Instead of having purpose-built—obviously electronic devices that you're meant to use as furniture—it becomes an accessory that you can put over your existing furniture.

Key Table and Picture Frame

The Key Table also uses weight sensing, but to get a sense of people's emotions from the way they put things down on it, much as slamming doors are a crude measure of mental state. The table measures the energy or the force with which you throw something down, and then it maps that to your mood. If you come in through your front door in a bad mood, you are likely to throw your keys down onto the table violently, whereas if it has been a good day, you will probably place them there gently. The table triggers reactions to emotional entrances in a variety of ways; for example, a picture tilts at an angle to warn other inhabitants to tread carefully.

■ Key Table and Picture Frame

Photo
Sarah Pennington

The Key Table is a less well-developed design than other pieces we developed. It's much more of an experiment, more of a kind of lighthearted stab in a sort of direction. We originally wanted the Key Table to contain an automatic drinks mixer that would dispense the appropriate alcoholic beverage for your mood: if you came in and you were happy, it might give you a piña colada, but if you were in a bad mood it would give you a double whiskey. There are people in Sweden who built an automatic drinks dispenser that looked at your brainwaves and mixed you a drink, so we probably could have made that concept work, but the picture frame seemed to us to be quite a light-hearted and nice way to indicate mood.

How-To
AA

Drift Table

The Drift Table is about the size of a coffee table. It has a small round display in the middle of the top surface that looks like a kind of porthole. On the display, you see a slowly drifting view of the landscape of Britain looking from the air. It feels as if your room is floating at a height of a few hundred feet, and you are looking down through a hole in the floor. If you put things on one side of the table, the imagery starts to drift in that direction, and adding weight causes it to "descend," zooming in on the landscape below. A display on the side of the table shows the location of the aerial image.

> The table suggests a "hole" in the home connecting physical and virtual space. In the end, you can't really tell whether it's an interesting idea unless you make the thing; so we have. We've built a table now that contains a high-end PC, a bunch of hard drives, load sensors, stamp chip and so forth, all of which sits within the table. When you put the cover on, it's just an elegant object, which shows an image drifting gently by.

■ Drift Table, from installation to navigation

Photos
Bill Gaver, Andy Boucher, Sarah Pennington, and Brendan Walker

The Drift Table has been built, exhibited, and tried out by people extensively. It has a magically gentle entertainment value, both soothing and engaging.

Bill Gaver talks with intellectual rigor about the meaning of affordances in the context of biophysics and perception, but as you make the metaphorical leap with him toward understanding the potential for designing interactions as a complete physical environment, you are quickly drawn into the possibility of objects conveying information that is full of associations and emotional qualities. His explorations in this direction, as well as those of Hiroshi Ishii and Durrell Bishop, are closely related to the work of Tony Dunne and Fiona Raby, as they explain in the interview that follows in chapter 9, "Futures and Alternative Nows."

9

Futures and Alternative Nows

Interviews with Tony Dunne and Fiona Raby, John Maeda, and Jun Rekimoto

We're not interested in futures, as in technical futures or scientific futures or technological futures, but more in alternative nows: how things could be right now if we had different values. It's about the psychological approach to design; psychological need and complex need. Instead of need being purely functional, we are looking at the idea of a more emotional and psychological need.

Dunne and Raby[1]

■ Energy Futures, London Science Museum, 2004: a scenario from Dunne and Raby shows children growing meat to provide energy to operate a TV

Photo Jason Evans

Tony Dunne and Fiona Raby suggest an "alternative now" that belongs more in the aesthetic mists of the arts than in the pragmatics of functionalism. They explore complex pleasures and existential design with a delicate wit that makes you smile on reflection. You will discover in the interview that follows that their work has a lot in common with the "aesthetic, social, and cultural interventions" of the Equator project, explained by Bill Gaver in the previous chapter, perhaps partly because they have worked together with Bill at the Royal College of Art in London, forming a node in a community of ideas about technology and design.[2]

If we return to David Liddle's explanation of the three phases in which technology is adopted[3]—the enthusiast phase, the professional phase, and the consumer phase—we can see the "alternative now" proposed by Dunne and Raby as a sophisticated extra layer within the consumer phase. The most obvious type of consumer adoption of technology is when prices fall far enough for everyone to be able to make use of a technology, and the design has been developed enough to make it easy and enjoyable

for people who want to use it. David Liddle gives the example of the 35mm camera, where the technology for automatic exposure, focus, flash, film wind, and so on, are well enough evolved for anyone to be able to take the best possible snap in the circumstances. The "alternative now" that Dunne and Raby offer is something beyond the obvious functionality of the consumer product: they look for more complicated pleasures that hover on the border of the subversive and artistic, but always offering some comment on humanity. What could you do with the camera to offer food for the soul as well as materialistic gratification?

John Maeda[4] has produced a wonderfully rich body of work as a digital artist and designer, and the designs coming from the students and researchers at his Aesthetics & Computation Group at the MIT Media Lab have been stellar. In 2003 he suddenly decided to start again and create a new group called the Physical Language Workshop (PLW), plus an associated research initiative called "Simplicity," with an "alternative now" that seeks to return to simpler values and behaviors in the digital realm. Perhaps this is the start of the digital equivalent of the Arts and Crafts movement inspired by William Morris in reaction to the Industrial Revolution,[5] or perhaps more like the Bauhaus in rethinking design. Will John lead us toward something equivalently inspirational for the information revolution? In his interview he describes the start of his search.

■ Illustration for *Cartier* magazine of John Maeda's hand, repeated many times

Image Copyright John Maeda, 2005

Jun Rekimoto[6] is building a more direct future, concerned not so much with alternatives as with enabling some of the many promises of interactive technology. As director of the Interaction Laboratory at Sony in Tokyo, he is leading a group of computer scientists and designers to develop a future that offers alternatives to the graphical user interfaces on the devices that we use today. In his interview, he talks about the research that he is doing to make the concept of "ubiquitous computing" a reality.[7]

Photo Author

Fiona Raby and Tony Dunne

"We are interested in using design as a medium, to ask questions and provoke and stimulate people, designers and industry," says Tony Dunne. "We are exploring things that exist somewhere between reality and fiction," adds Fiona Raby, as they explain their philosophy of design. When you first meet them, Tony and Fiona seem shy, almost diffident, but they soon communicate their passion for complex pleasures and existential design. They have their own studio[8] in London, where they consult, write, and research. They use products and services as a medium to stimulate discussion and debate among designers, industry, and the public. Many of their projects are collaborative; they work with industrial research labs, academics, and cultural institutions. They were founding members of the Computer Related Design (CRD) Research Studio at the Royal College of Art in London and were based there from 1994 to 2002. In 2004 Tony was appointed as head of department and professor of interaction design, and Fiona as tutor. They describe the work of the department in three overlapping areas: "technology as medium"[9] looks at the aesthetic and functional potential of new technology by playing with it and experimenting directly with the material; "technology as product"[10] imagines new services and products and considers how they fit into preexisting social, cultural, economic, and technological systems; and "technology as critique"[11] makes the social and ethical implications of different technologies tangible and, as a result, debatable. They see the Interaction Design Department as a place where people who are frustrated with the limitations of their original disciplines can gather to figure out which bits of what discipline—from anthropology and architecture to computer science, fine art, and design—can combine to create better, more human, electronic products, media, and services.

Tony Dunne and Fiona Raby

Complicated Pleasures

TONY DUNNE AND Fiona Raby spend a lot of time looking at newspapers, searching for the odd story about a real event that is surprising or unexpected. They are constantly collecting examples of reality that seem stranger than fiction, as they find this can provide inspirational raw material for thinking about emotional responses. For example, they recently found an article about a father whose daughter died, and when she was cremated, he had her ashes turned into diamonds, and then gave the diamonds to different members of the family. They found that story interesting because it explored the relationship between the idea of a person and precious objects. A real company was offering this as a service, but if they had proposed the concept as an art project, it would have seemed very poetic, strange, and unrealistic.

Another example was a very small Japanese car that had been equipped with powerful sound system and a bank of switches controlling simulations of different engine noises. The driver could choose whether to sound like a Ferrari, a monster truck, a Harley Davidson motorcycle, or a range of other options. The appeal of making a tiny car sound "wicked" shows irrationality, but it is also an example of something that people love to do. Dunne and Raby like designs that pander to the bad side of people—the side that is complicated, irrational, and contradictory. If you filled the material world with objects that reflected those values, they wonder, how different would it look from the material world that surrounds us now, as our lives are so often filled with things that exude niceness and rationality?

They talk about this borderline zone between pragmatic design and emotional experience, giving examples to illustrate their ideas:

TONY I think what we're researching, really, is the idea of complicated pleasure. The pleasures you get from reading a book or watching a film are the kinds of things we're exploring in relation to products. How can you design products that provide complex and complicated pleasures, that stimulate our imaginations, create dilemmas, make us think, and rather than smoothing out our lives, actually create glitches?

Our interactions with purely physical objects, like glasses and tables and things like that, are very sensual and physical, giving pleasures that have to do with the body; a sense of gravity, a sense of balance, and so on. With electronic products, the pleasures are more likely to happen in the imagination.

For instance, one product we really like to use as an example is the "Truth phone," which is a real product manufactured by an American company. It's basically a phone that has a built-in voice stress analyzer. When somebody calls you on it, you get a read-out of the likelihood of whether they're lying. So when you use that phone, you're thrown into a dilemma. You wonder why the person is lying to you. Is the technology accurate? That kind of narrative is a complicated pleasure that could only arise from an electronic product.

FIONA Also, there's room for interpretation, where people can reinterpret something. That's exactly what we're interested in. Leave space for interpretation in an object but enough clues with which to pick up a story. Perhaps it's not our story, but it will enable people to create other stories from the object. It all comes from the idea of looking at how people behave. We assume that there are certain behaviors, or ways you feel about other people, that we can empathize with. We play with empathy a lot.

Placebo Project

For the Placebo Project in 2000, Dunne and Raby developed a collection of electronic objects to explore mental well-being in relation to domestic electromagnetic fields.

They designed and built eight prototype objects to investigate people's experiences of electromagnetic fields in the home and placed them with volunteers. They suggest that once electronic objects are taken home, they develop private, or at least hidden, lives. Occasionally you can catch a glimpse of this life when objects interfere with one another or malfunction. Many people believe that mobile phones heat up their ears or feel their skin tingle when they sit near a TV, and almost everyone has heard stories of people picking up radio broadcasts in the fillings in their teeth. The interesting question is not whether these stories are true or scientific, but rather how people develop narratives to explain and relate to electronic technologies, especially in this case the invisible electromagnetic waves emitted by electronic objects.

The Placebo objects were designed to elicit stories about the secret life of electronic objects, both factual and imagined. Homes for the objects were found through a variety of means, including advertisements in a London listings magazine, workshops at a museum, a window display in a department store, and an article in a national newspaper. Potential adopters filled out application forms detailing any unusual experiences with electronic products, their attitude to electromagnetic waves, and their reasons for choosing a particular object. They were interviewed when their allotted time with the adopted object was up, and a photographer captured images to support what they were saying. In the written introduction to the project, Dunne and Raby say:

> Designers cannot always solve problems; we cannot switch off the vast electromagnetic networks surrounding us. Although we cannot change reality, we can change people's perception of it. Like a medical placebo, the objects in this project do not actually remove or counteract the cause for concern, but they can provide psychological comfort. The Placebo Project is definitely not scientific: although

aware of ethnographic and anthropological methodologies, we chose to adopt a more informal process in this case. We wanted to prove that people are more receptive to radical ideas than industry acknowledges, and to test our ideas about aesthetic meaning and electronic technology. We accept that the group of adopters was self-selecting. We also accept that they are probably exceptional people, but they are real people, and anything we discovered was grounded in reality rather than fiction.

Their interest in electromagnetic fields was first aroused when they came across an article of underwear on the Internet called a "personal protection device." There was a male and female version. The underwear was normal except that it was covered in silver nylon, supposedly to protect you from radiation while using the computer: of course, this had no real protective effect, but was a placebo.

Dunne and Raby became interested in the notion of the placebo as a way of making relationships between people and spaces more ambiguous and open-ended. They did not think of these kinds of objects as designs for mass production, but rather as tools to think critically about how our technological lives are being shaped by industry and business. They liked the idea that these products would be available for rent, providing a service in the form of a reflective experience. Living with them for a while might encourage the borrower to think about the environment in a different way, especially in relation to electromagnetic fields:

> Take the placebo knickers for instance, if you wear these knickers for a day, and go about your ordinary life, would you deal with the world in a totally different way? Would you think about the electromagnetic environment differently? Would you become paranoid, or would you find some strange aesthetic pleasure in your adventure? What kinds of new narrative experiences might you have?

Each of the objects in the Placebo collection tries to provide a particular way of negotiating a relationship to electromagnetic fields. They talk about two of the designs:

"Personal protection device" (his) ■
"Personal Protection Device" (hers) ■

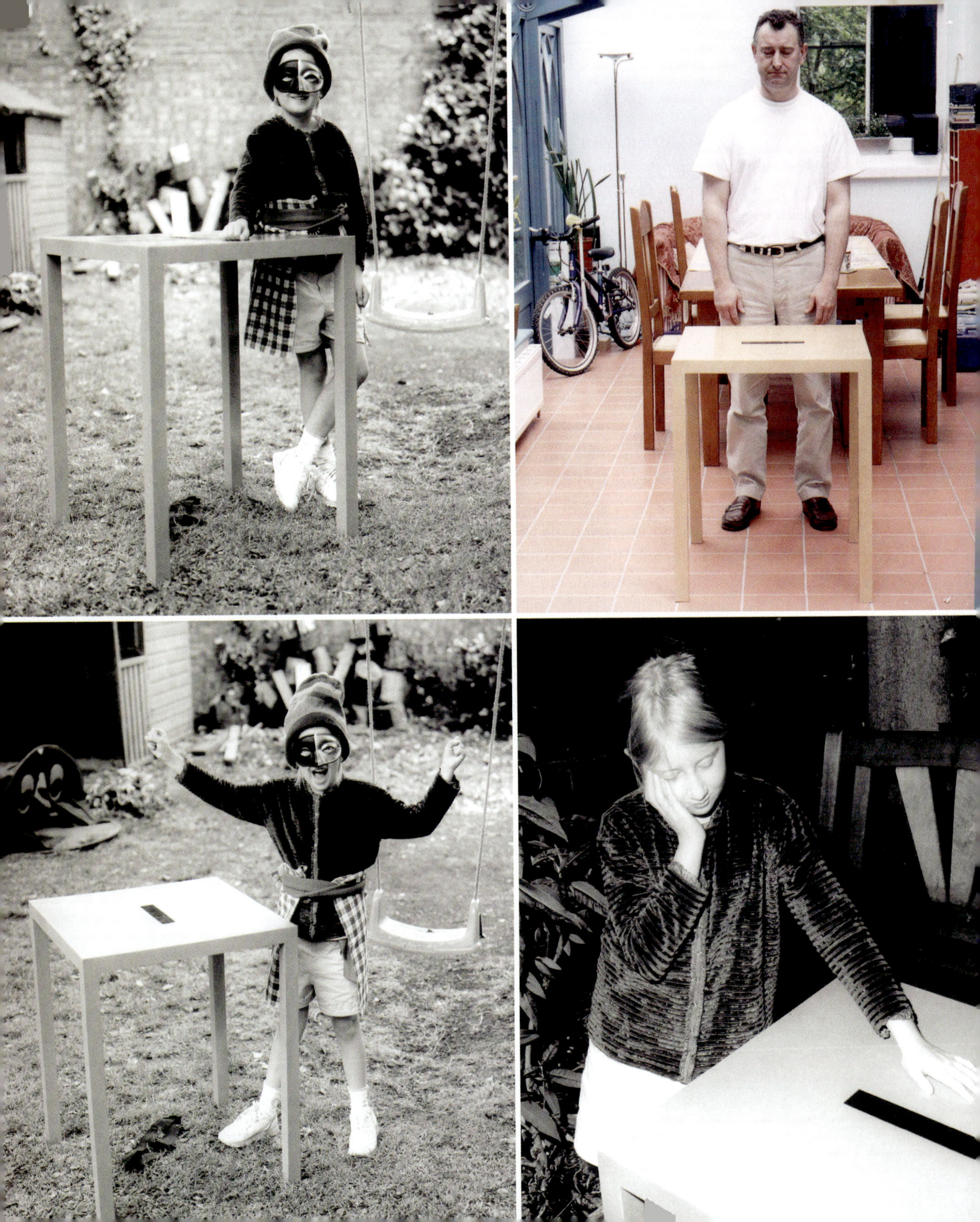

Placebo Project example: GPS Table

TONY An example of embedded behavior is the GPS Table, a small table with a global positioning system sensor inside it. The top surface contains a display, which shows its exact position. When it's indoors, it often can't communicate with the satellite, so it just says, "lost." Some people see that as a weakness in the design—that really it should be able to communicate all the time and give its position, but we see that as its function, because by being lost, it asks the owners to help in some way. Do they take the table out into the garden and let it communicate and fulfill itself, or do they try to comfort it, or live with it in other ways, because somehow this table is unfulfilled and frustrated?

FIONA What was also nice about the table was the different way in which people reacted to it. Lorna was looking after a child at home, so she was always in the house. It made her think a lot about her relationship to the table in the home and the satellites going round. When she thought about the table, she became humbled by it; suddenly, in an every day moment, she would feel that she was really small; this tiny person on the planet.

TONY She also talked about the table being physically there, but electronically absent. So she really understood the object as existing in two spaces; the space of the room, and this kind of hyper invisible electronic network. We are discovering that people are subtle in their appreciation of interactivity, and their relationship to electronic products.

■ Placebo Project, GPS Table—a table that displays its exact position in the world

Photos
Jason Evans

VDH 192X

Placebo Project example: Nipple Chair

FIONA The Nipple Chair uses electromagnetic sensors in the back of the chair, so if you're sitting in a field, the nipples will vibrate and you become very aware that your body is being penetrated by this field. We saw it as a very paranoid object, but Neil had a totally different interpretation of it. He actually loved and collected gadgets. He had a whole cupboard full of objects that he would never use; he would just collect them. He would get them out and look at them and love them, but he was totally perplexed by the chair. I asked him if he thought the chair was a gadget, and from the minute I mentioned it, he was constantly upset by the thought that it could be termed as a gadget. He kept changing his mind as to whether it was or wasn't a gadget. It was very strange.

TONY One of the reasons he said it wasn't a gadget was that you couldn't control it. The chair just did what it did. The nipples vibrated when it picked up the field. He said if you could adjust its sensitivity, or it had another function like telling the time, it would definitely be a gadget. He saw it as an autonomous object that he just had to live with, or cohabit with. We thought of it as a paranoia-inducing object that would make him nervous and scared of the electromagnetic fields in his house, but he actually used electromagnetic fields to animate the object and interpret the object's behavior, as though it had moods or it was playing with him.

When he came in from work, for instance, he would walk across his nylon carpet and build up a big static charge. The object would sense that and become very excited, and he would say the object was pleased to see him when he got home. He knew exactly what was happening, but he enjoyed these stories that came out of living with it. His friends came around and he wanted to show it getting excited, but sometimes it wouldn't; he also liked that unpredictability.

■ Placebo Project, Nipple Chair—the nipples vibrate in response to electromagnetic fields

Photos Jason Evans

FIONA He found it a little frustrating, because he'd want to show it off. He put something on it and it was supposed to move, but it didn't. I think he found pleasure in the fact that he couldn't control it as much as he wanted to. That was his complicated pleasure in the situation.

Animals for Energy
Nicholas Boyd
Avoiding emotional attachment to animals purchased for use as energy
JONES FAMILY
HYDROGEN
JONES FAMILY
HYDROGEN

Existential Design

At one point Dunne and Raby were thinking of "existential computing" as a category that would be interesting to explore, but on reflection they dropped the label as it was too connected to the world of computers. They are interested in products that behave existentially and are enabled by electronic technology but are not thought of as computers. They want to treat people as responsible individuals who make their own decisions about what is right or wrong, good or bad:

> The role of design seems to be to make the world a better place. It's as if designers have all sworn an oath never to think a bad thought. We seem to have this blind optimism about the future and about technology. Designers somehow automatically think that design is neutral and implicitly good.

Tony and Fiona encourage designers to consider both positive and negative scenarios when thinking about how new technologies become absorbed into everyday life. They see a new role for design as a medium for debate.

Two of their recent projects illustrated this approach. One was an exhibit aimed at children in the new Energy Gallery in the London Science Museum. Another was their biotechnology project, "Consuming Monsters."

Energy Futures, London Science Museum, 2004

- *Top left* Teddy bear blood bag
- *Top right* "Animals for Energy" manual
- *Bottom left* Electrolyser Backpack
- *Bottom right* Company uniform for family energy producers

Photos Jason Evans

Energy Futures, London Science Museum

Tony One of the main messages the museum wanted to put across was that in the past it's been impossible to predict the future of energy. They told us that many predictions had been wildly wrong, so we put forward three different energy future scenarios, speculating on the social impact these futures might have on the life of a child, particularly trying to capture the imagination of a child.

Fiona All the material from the museum was a little bit dull and biased toward hydrogen and hydrogen cars . . . so we did our own research, and found some very fascinating ideas about energy.

Teddy bear blood bags

TONY In probably the most unlikely scenario of all, we found out about a meat-eating robot being developed at the University of South Florida called Chew-Chew. It's designed to eat slugs using a technology called microbial fuel cells. They have living bacteria that break down food and convert nutrients into electrical energy. So we thought, "Imagine if this technology took off. How would things change?" It really sparked our imaginations. What would it mean? Animal and blood products as energy.

FIONA Maybe you would feed meat to domestic products like TVs and lamps; perhaps rodents, worms, or even human blood?

TONY Would humans and animals be exploited in new and horrible ways? Or would laws be passed to protect them? To replace batteries, we made an FM radio that uses a blood-bag in the shape of a teddy bear to power it. We use the language of design to make it more friendly and acceptable.

Poo lunch box

■ Energy Futures, London Science Museum, 2004: poo lunch box energy pack

Photo Jason Evans

FIONA In another scenario we were inspired by a seminal book called *Cradle to Cradle*.[12] It told a story about rural farmers in China using biological waste on their paddy fields. When someone comes around for dinner they are expected to donate a "gift" before they leave, returning the nutrients from the meal back to the soil.

TONY How would social behavior and etiquette change if the main source of energy was human sewage?

FIONA But this isn't science fiction; we were told people living in Denmark can leave their poo out for the bin men. Apparently the world's largest chicken poo power station is in the UK.

TONY In this scenario one of the objects we designed was a poo lunch box. Perhaps children would be expected to bring their waste home from school in their sandwich box. Poo would be too valuable for the school to keep, as it would be needed at home.

JONES FAMILY
HYDROGEN

Hydrogen

Tony The most likely use of hydrogen is as fuel for cars, but even there we wanted to hint at underlying motivations, showing that technology does not always bring the best out in people. In our hydrogen scenario we looked at how over-competitive parents might exploit their children, a return to child labor.

Fiona We used Jeremy Rifkin's book *The Hydrogen Economy.*[13] He suggested that energy production could be decentralized. Energy consumers could become energy producers, and local communities could produce their own energy. We imagined households as competitive producers, competing against their neighbors and needing to market their company and family brand. Everyone in the family might have to wear uniforms displaying the family logo.

Tony When a child reaches a certain age, say eight years old, instead of receiving a birthday card they get a contract which they have to sign, camouflaged as a birthday card. This commits them to producing a certain amount of hydrogen every week; of course any extra becomes pocket money.

Fiona You could actually say this is quite an ethical stance, as it makes children aware at a very young age of their energy liabilities, how each one of us, individually, needs to take on some responsibility.

■ Energy Futures, London Science Museum, 2004: hydrogen-producing family

Photo Jason Evans

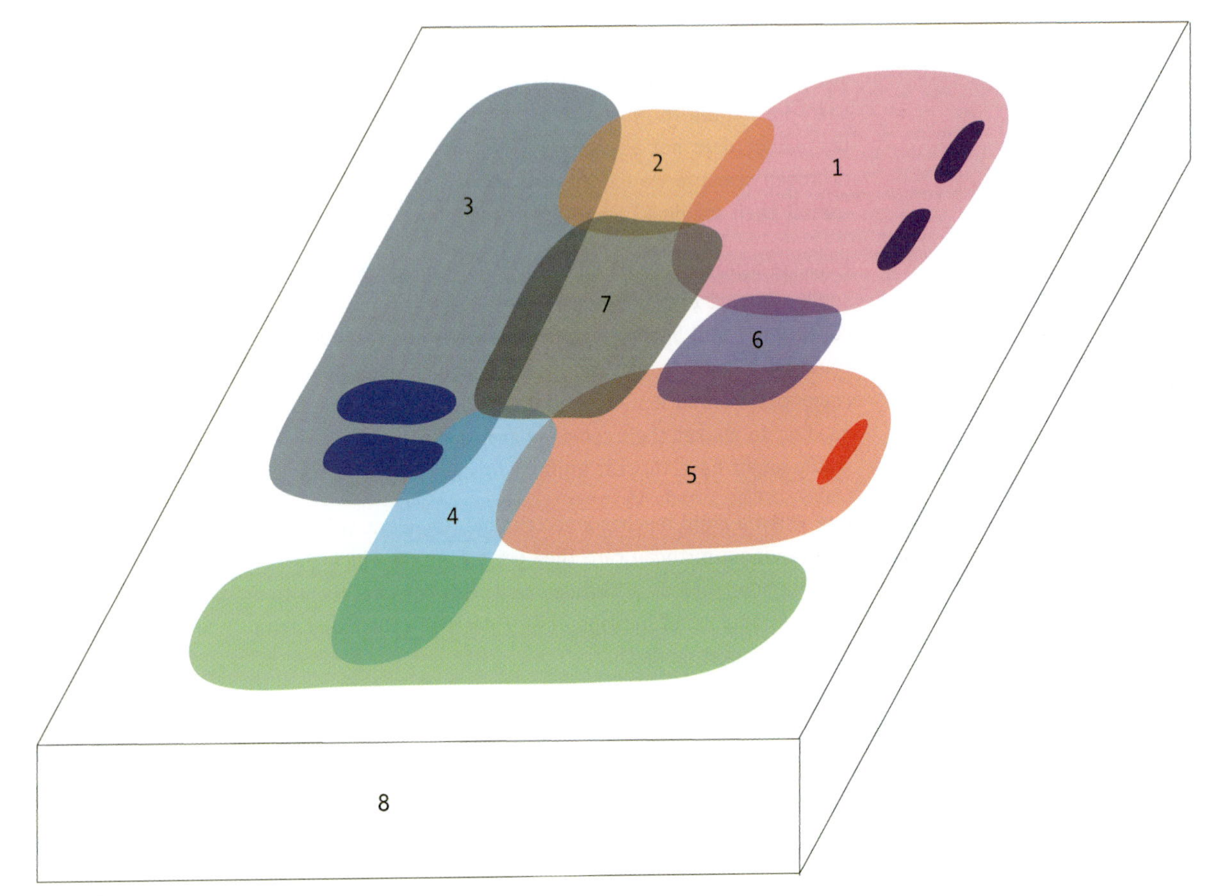

BioLand

1. IVF Land (Passion Conception Centre)
2. Clonetopia, BioBank, Utility Pets,
3. Immortality Inc
4. ForEverAfter
5. GM Love
6. Future Perfect (Prescription Pets, DNA Detectives, Counselling, and Toy Shop)
7. Clinic
8. Underground Laboratories

Consuming monsters: big, perfect, and infectious

In their biotechnology project, Dunne and Raby demonstrate how hard it is for everyone, even specialists, to grasp the implications of biotechnologies for our everyday lives.

> FIONA When people participate in the biotech debate, they participate as citizens. They take a very philosophical point of view, saying, "Yes, this is right!" and "No, this is wrong." They argue very passionately about how the world should be in general terms, but when they step off their soapboxes into their everyday lives—washing the clothes, taking the children to school—they buy things that totally contradict their ethical or moral positions. Their behavior seems at odds with their beliefs.
>
> TONY The aim of the project is to move the debate from the level of responsible citizenship to that of consumer choice. In this way we will be confronted with real desires. We may not wish to acknowledge them, but they will inevitably influence the shape of the future, whether we like it or not. We gathered together examples of biotechnology that have already entered—or are about to enter—everyday life in the form of products and services. We then mapped these onto a notional landscape called BioLand, an existential shopping mall, probably on the outskirts of some town.
>
> FIONA The idea is to use the planning and design of this new hypothetical mall and the qualities of the shopping experience as the debating ground.
>
> TONY Essentially it's a big shed; the laboratories and storage will be underground, and on top sits a thematic consumer landscape, with departments called IVF Land, Immortality, and GM Love. In the center there is a hospital or clinic.

■ BioLand: an overview of the existential shopping mall concept

Illustration Dunne and Raby

BioLand is a substantial project, with many products and services on sale. Tony and Fiona talk about Utility Pets as an example of the type of products that you might buy there: this was a project designed by Elio Caccavale, an industrial design master's student at the Royal College of Art.

Utility Pets

TONY Elio's project is about xeno-transplantation; using pig organs as replacement organs, your DNA can be genetically engineered into a pig, when it's an embryo.

FIONA So you have this little baby piglet with your DNA intrinsically part of its DNA. Who is going to be responsible for the well-being of your pig? Are you going to give that responsibility to a laboratory or pig home? Or would you want to take responsibility yourself? After all, it's your health; that heart growing inside the pig might eventually be inside your body. Does this mean that pigs may enter domestic space and become part of the family? Elio found out that pigs are very intelligent and that they love to watch TV, offering a perfect way to introduce pigs into domestic space.

TONY If you have these spare organs, that are being well looked after in this healthy pig, you may just as well enjoy yourself, and keep up your forty-a-day habit.

FIONA It really illustrates the separation between our actual behavior and our utopian delusions.

Utility Pigs, by Elio Caccavale.
- *Top and middle left* Smoke Eater
- *Bottom left* Pig Memento Mask
- *Right* Pig watching TV

Photos Jason Evans

TONY Elio designed a special device which allows you to keep smoking in the same room as your pig, but stops the pig suffering from the dangers of passive smoking. So what happens when your pig has to donate its organs? What are the psychological pressures of grief or guilt? It has been known that people with transplants have dreams that come from the previous organ owners; would people suffer from pig dreams? Elio created a device that, when you wake up in the morning, reassures you that you are not a pig and are unlikely ever to become one.

FIONA It puts you in touch with your friend, which now is an intricate and essential part of your body.

In contrast to Tony and Fiona's search for the subtle and emotional complexities of existential and ambivalent expression, John Maeda describes how he is searching for a new simplicity in the design of interactions in the future.

Behavior-Based Robotics
Arkin
DIGITAL IMAGE PROCESSING
DESIGN OF EVERYDAY THINGS
SOFTWARE DESIGN
DIGITAL MANTRAS
The Aesthetics of Music
For You
Learning C

John Maeda

“Recently I placed some desktop patterns on my Web site that have found an enthusiastic audience. I made these images to celebrate ‘food’ as the letters F-zero-zero-D. Kind of cliché I realize, but nonetheless an enjoyable task of eating and creating.” John Maeda had created these images for an exhibition that celebrated the sensual pleasures of looking at beautiful images and tasting delicious food, combined with whimsical social commentary. He seems boundlessly prolific, as an interaction designer, computer artist, and teacher; you can feast your eyes on his retrospective book *Maeda@Media*.[14] He was raised in Seattle, the son of Japanese immigrants who toiled for sixteen-hour days in their tofu factory. He demonstrated talents in both art and technical subjects. He studied engineering at MIT, and he followed his future wife to Japan, where he studied product design at Tsukuba University. His graphic design talent kept surfacing, and he found a niche creating work that was both artistic and technical, for example, the series of “Reactive Books,” small-print pieces accompanied by software, about sound, time, the keyboard, and the mouse. Recognition started to arrive, with awards flooding in, including Japan’s highest honor, the Mainichi Design Prize, and the USA’s highest honor, the National Design Award. Soon he was a professor at the MIT Media Lab, directing the Aesthetics & Computation Group. He has recently made a fresh start with the Physical Language Workshop, plus an associated research initiative called “Simplicity.” He has a variety of work archived online at his personal Web site www.maedastudio.com. There are some misconceptions that MAEDASTUDIO is a large company, but it is not; it is the name he gives his desk at home.

John Maeda

Images from FOOD Exhibition, 2003

- "Amber Waves" French fries
- "Rebirth" anchovies

Images
John Maeda

Dr. Maeda, an associate professor of design and computation at the MIT Media Lab and an award-winning graphic designer, has spent eight months putting forward his own one-word vision of the future: simplicity. There is too much needless complexity in the world, he argues. Technology, which was supposed to make our lives easier, has taken a wrong turn. In 20 years we've gone from the simplicity of MacPaint to Photoshop. While the first fostered a creative explosion, the second gave birth to an industry of how-to books and classes. And such complexity is commonplace, Dr. Maeda says. Despite the lip service paid to "ease of use," "plug and play," and "one-click shopping," simplicity is an endangered quality in the digital world, he adds, and it is time to break free from technology's intimidating complexity.

Jessie Scanlon, New York Times, May 20, 2004[15]

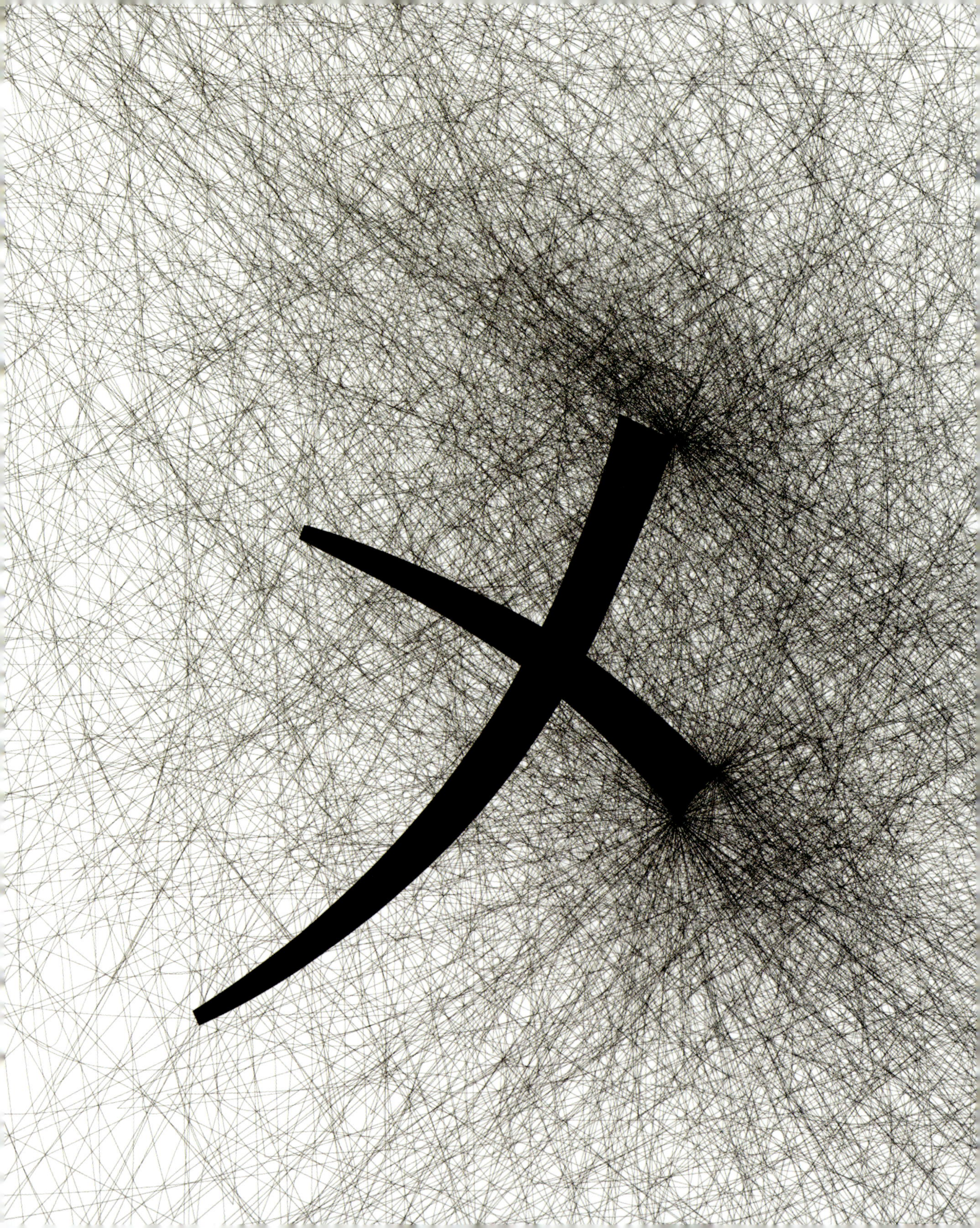

Simplicity

John Maeda came back to MIT as a junior professor in 1996. In Japan he had become very successful in graphic design and also in interactive design. He had been lucky to be advised by Naomi Enami, Japan's pioneer of interactive media:

> You are one of the few people in the world that can make these interactive things that are captivating and beautiful, but are they any good? How do you know they're any good if you have nothing to compare them with? You have to go into education to build the people who will one day come and destroy you.

John took that to heart, and spent seven years at the MIT Media Lab building the Aesthetics & Computation Group, which was devoted to redefining how media looked and felt, and thereby destroying John's predominance, as his students have graduated and become stars themselves. He started to wonder what to do next:

> I came to a realization that I could keep doing this. I could keep on making a unit that was able to create these people, but what if there was something I could do instead? What might that be? I kept asking myself, "What are the basic, most simple problems?"
>
> One of the questions that I've been recently faced with is the fact that digital tools today are too complex; they're too expensive; I have to buy all the upgrades. If I upgrade the OS, I have to buy all the software. These little bits of money are okay, but they're bothering me now, and I want to make a change.
>
> "How do you change it?" I was asking myself. Well, the answer may be by doing something that seems impossible, that is to rewrite all the software that is out there as simple, freely available, extensible modules that live on the Web. We already have a painting program, a photo-editing program, a drawing program, we're going to make a movie-editing program. It's basic, simple software, designed simply, engineered simply. And what this means, I hope, is that any school anywhere will be able to use this software in their own curriculum, free.

■ The final image in a series in which John Maeda manipulated the Japanese kana character for "me"—in this case by exploding one of its serifs

Image
John Maeda

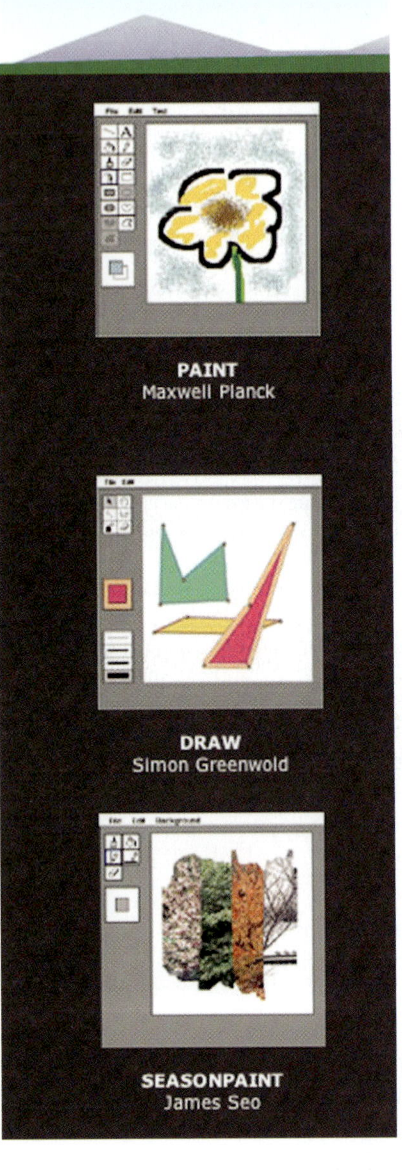

■ Simplicity—Treehouse Studio applications

He argues that open-source software is not truly open unless people can access the code and easily alter it themselves. Even though John is a good C programmer, he is unable to extend or change Linux, in spite of the fact that it is called open-source. At time of writing in 2004, a group of his students are working on a basic technological infrastructure[16] for a kind of Bauhaus for the twenty-first century. The goal is to create a completely networked, interconnected system for visually and tactically oriented people who are constantly communicating with one another.

In order to provide connections to the new infrastructure, the team is building a gallery system for online exhibitions and a café to meet people:

> I don't like chat rooms, but people use them, so I thought, "What if we had a chat room about food? Virtual food." So in this system, I can meet people online in a restaurant; we can order food, we can click on it and eat it right now. People ask why would we buy virtual food? If I said Wolfgang Puck designed a pizza, you'd wonder, what is that pizza, so I think there is a possibility of selling virtual food online. Then you can imagine, again, different designers and artists from all over the world designing food for the restaurant and being able to sell the designs.
>
> Also we want to pour the bits, the visual landscape, out into the world in different ways. We are working on a flexible display system to display any geometry, and a physical conduit—this is very old-school stuff, basically a box that allows easy connection to the outside world—to make an open hardware specification for this kind of device.

John is influenced by the idea that core information connectivity is needed to provide the infrastructure behind the products that people actually come in contact with. He respects the iTunes approach from Apple for this:

> I remember I thought that Steve Jobs was kind of a fool, around 1999 or 2000, when he was putting in information-server services instead of new hardware. It was like, "Oh my god, he's making this iDisc, iWhatever, what an idiotic thing!"

But then I realized that—I'm not sure if it was intentional or not—he was building enterprise-class systems that were robust and secure. And because he had that base, he could do something like iTunes. He could embed the content into the player. Nobody could do that unless they had infrastructure for a global network. That's when I was thinking, "Well, that makes so much sense!"

Members of the Physical Language Workshop are trying to re-architect how we draw on the computer, to get more people to understand it from basic principles. The MIT thinking used to be that programming was important and tools that allowed you to bypass the code were bad. Now John thinks that tools are good, but only if you are in control of them. Any good architect has to be able to sharpen a pencil by hand; in the digital world, there is no equivalent because everyone clicks the mouse the same way. The difference will occur in how the tool is held in the mind, which will mean that the programming of the tool is going to matter more. This appreciation of tools is deeply rooted in John's experience. When he first moved from MIT to the product design program in Japan, he recalls:

It was a place where they were so behind; there were no computers. I liked that because it was so antitechnology. I began to sort of blossom because it was then that I realized, in all the drawing lessons and all that, that I couldn't "undo" anymore. It's an amazing thing when you realize that you've made a mistake, you're reaching for the "undo" command, but you can't. I sort of reformed myself there.

I was doing product design in 1991, but at the same time I had very good friends in communication design and graphic design. We used to always hang out, so I would always bridge the gap. I would go to the different conferences and events and study product design but was also practicing graphic design as a hobby, and then I began to do very well all of a sudden. I began to achieve awards, get connections to really amazing teachers, and meet the design leaders in Japan.

I came to the conclusion that product design was not going to be able to change very fast. I thought Mechatronics was very interesting, in products like the Bang and Olufsen stereo, which opens when you

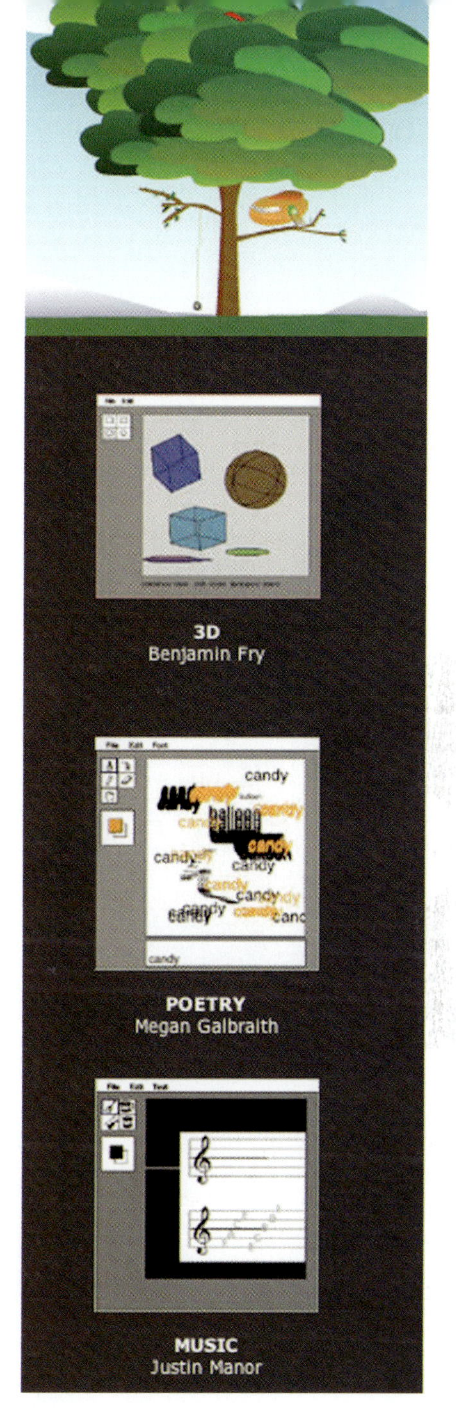

Treehouse Studio applications ■

approach it as if by magic. I realized that there just weren't the parts there yet. There weren't the micro-motors, there weren't the sensor arrays we have now, and most importantly, there weren't these amazing embedded processing systems that we have now today. I didn't realize all these specifics, but I knew that, "Well, I can't do what I want to do in solid form yet, so why not just do it in graphical and virtual forms?"

I noticed also, especially in Japan, that many product designers had lost their mojo; maybe they had lost hope because there was someone in the States who had proven that industrial design wasn't working properly any more, and they had to do this new sort of cognitive science approach. I thought that a lot of people were headed down this very straight and narrow research-ish path. To me it's always been about the sort of passion of the whole activity, and that's why things like Bang and Olufsen are indeed magic. They aren't giving any specific affordances, but just have a magical moment, and I don't mind magical moments at all.

■ Beosound 3200 with the magic doors
■ *Design by Numbers*

John has created lots of magical moments for the people who enjoy his books and the archive of designs on his Web site. He works alone to create that material at his desk at home, with the support of his wife and four daughters. *Design by Numbers* was his first major book, published in 1999 by the MIT Press. He had thought for a long time that knowledge of programming was important for every young design student, because it shapes the digital landscape. He was thinking of writing a book called "Java for the non-Java inclined," to give people easier access to programming:

I went to buy a compiler or something, and tried to install it, and I couldn't get it installed. I realized how hard it is to program. Whereas, if you went back to the eighties, it was much easier to program because that's all you could do. You turn the computer on, it's blinking; it can do nothing unless you program it. People today don't have that experience any more.

Design by Numbers was an attempt to say, "Okay, what if I didn't like to program? I liked to draw and I wanted to learn how to program by drawing?" I wondered if there was a language for people who were more visually oriented than mathematically oriented, so

Design by Numbers was about simple premises. Your drawing area was 100 by 100 pixels; there was no color, it was only gray; all the numbers were from zero to one hundred. If you wanted a black square, you made it one hundred. If you wanted a gray square it was fifty, white was zero. Drawing on a computer is not hard, but it can be tedious. I led you through to the level that let you set the paper to a certain level of gray, set a pen to black, and draw a line, all with some numbers. With just those three capabilities you could sit and draw a picture of your friend using numerical expression.

You might wonder, "Why the heck would you do that, because it's much easier to draw it by hand?"

My point was, "If you can draw it by hand, draw it by hand. There are certain things you just can't draw by hand efficiently, so use the computer for those."

That was *Design by Numbers*. After I finished it, I was quite happy.

Almost immediately after he had finished, he was asked to write another book, this time a retrospective of all his work. His approach of working alone, writing and designing every page, made this a daunting task, but something in him drove him to agree, because he felt that only by making a full compendium of his past work could he free himself of it, and be able to think in a fresh way:

I embarked on this 480-page book for which I designed and created everything, and it literally brought me to a very bad point; I can never drink caffeine any more, because it has become very dangerous for me. Yeah!

It was good to do it. It's called *Maeda@Media*. It showed to me my own limitations, I think. This whole idea that I could play basketball and baseball and swim or whatever—I hit my extreme physical limitations. People like Paul Rand, they didn't actually design their entire books; they had assistants, staff, or whatnot.

When you browse through *Maeda@Media*, you can enjoy the design of every page for its perfect visual integrity relative to all of the other pages. This cohesiveness could only have come from the intensity of the single authorship, from many long days and nights with too much caffeine, when every choice of layout, font,

Reactive Books ■
Reactive Books display ■

John Maeda

MAEDA @ MEDIA

Foreword by **Nicholas Negroponte**

and color came from the same mind. The nature of the work presented in the book is very diverse and spans a long period of time, but you can feel a level of integration in the design that could not have been achieved by "assistants, staff, or whatnot."

This effort cleared Maeda's mind and allowed him to go back to first principles and think about "simplicity." His ambition is to create a new Bauhaus:

> In recent years, maybe recent means decades, many people have tried to bring back the idea of the Bauhaus in the digital realm, the Digital Bauhaus, reverse Bauhaus, I'm not sure. Everyone wants to bring it back. I believe it's important for there to be a moment of crystallization in this global creative community that we have, which happened in something like the Bauhaus. Why was it possible then? Why isn't it possible now? I'm not sure, but I've always thought it's because of physical constraints. I think the fact that there were fewer people working in the field, and, furthermore, family structures were different, I could say, "Goodbye family. I'm going to Paris to study painting for four years. See ya! I'll be back." You can't do that any more.
>
> The thing about the Bauhaus that cracks me up is that the early classes were taught by two instructors. One was the master craftsman, and the other was the master artist or designer, and the artist and the craftsman taught together. What happened is, as the Bauhaus created graduates, they began to hire their own graduates, but they weren't masters, they were junior masters; they were hybrids that could be both craftsman and artist/designer. Then they began to fire all the master craftsmen, because they were just people who make things, and they couldn't defend themselves in the political landscape. That struck me as a sad symptom of the triumph of politics over content.
>
> I think most people are attracted to the Bauhaus as an ideal dream; we humans crave to be inspired. I look to the Bauhaus as just one inspiring moment with many uninspiring things around it. Is it possible to build another inspiring moment in digital media? There has to be; otherwise, we should all just stop—pull the plug!

■ *Maeda@Media* book cover

Image John Maeda

John's idealism in putting together the Simplicity team is founded on the desire to educate at a basic level. He wants to create a new set of tools, freely accessible to children, which will help them develop the creative skills of artists and designers.

John Maeda's First Law of

simplicity

"A complex system of many functions can be simplified by carefully grouping related functions."

John Maeda's Second Law of

simplicity

"The positive emotional response derived from a simplicity experience has less to do with utility, and more to do with saving time."

> I'm putting all my ideas in a space of basic competency in the visual domain. In schools there's an emphasis on reading, writing, and arithmetic, developing a narrow aspect of your brain. There's nothing to test how creative you are! I'm trying to build these infrastructures to get more and more people everywhere interested in the idea that communication, expressed in a visual or tactile experiential way, actually enhances life, and that is something that won't be in our future the way things are moving, but I want to bring it back. I want to force that future to occur; gently, of course.

Will it be possible to reinvent the structure of software, to create basic software that is designed to be simple and engineered to be simple? It is an ambitious task for a small group of graduate students and a professor, however intelligent, accomplished, and dedicated they are. Perhaps it is impossible, but we will have to wait and see. Watch closely, because something significant is likely to emerge from the future of the Simplicity program. John is determined, even if he feels the need for a disclaimer:

> Well, about the future, I think that anyone who says they know the future is on drugs or something. I mean, I don't know what the future is; I don't claim to. I claim that we can make our own future, and I'm making that future.

While John Maeda is leading his little band toward "simplicity" by creating a new Arts and Crafts movement or a new Bauhaus,[17] in Tokyo a dedicated research scientist called Junichi Rekimoto is trying another kind of rebirth. He is building an Interaction Laboratory for Sony, akin to the Xerox PARC of the seventies, but more focused on pragmatic results for the many businesses of Sony. His future is more directly about enabling some of the promises of interactive technology that are emerging as outgrowths of the main flow of innovation. In the interview that follows, he describes the work of his group at the Computer Science Lab (CSL).

John Maeda's Third Law of

simplicity

"When the richness of an experience is increased in a manner that facilitates the perception of the overall intent, but all means don't skimp. Add more!"

John Maeda's Fifth Law of

simplicity

"A material's failure to comply to a specific application provides indication that its more natural usage lies elsewhere."

John Maeda's Seventh Law of

simplicity

"The more care, attention, and effort applied to that which is less, the more it shall be perceived as more than it really is."

John Maeda's Fourth Law of

"The more you know about something beforehand, the simpler it will ultimately be perceived."

John Maeda's Sixth Law of

simplicity

"In order to 'feel,' you gotta have noise. Too much noise, and all you've got is noise."

John Maeda's Eighth Law of

simplicity

"Recognize not only the absolute laws of the physical universe as important constraints, but also the artificial laws as of equal importance when striving for simplicity."

Photo Author

Jun Rekimoto

"My name is Jun Rekimoto, and I am working on the interface of the future, and I am also directing the Interaction Laboratory in Sony Corporation. When I was a high-school student, I was quite impressed by the Xerox PARC work, especially Alan Kay's article in *Scientific American*,[18] and then I decided I wanted to go into this field." Sony Computer Science Laboratories (CSL) was established in 1988. It is tucked into the Tokyo cityscape in an unobtrusive office building, just a few minutes walk from Sony headquarters. The intimate connection between the lab and Sony development is more than physical; CSL has produced a stream of research that is pragmatically connected to the business of the company. Jun seems young to be running the Interaction Laboratory, with a dozen researchers and designers in his group, but he speaks with authority and thoughtfulness that makes you immediately appreciate his leadership qualities. He studied at the Tokyo Institute of Technology, but his first experience with computer programs was at the age of ten. He worked for another computer company in Japan for about eight years, and then moved to Sony, establishing the Interaction Laboratory in 1999 to investigate the future of human-computer interactions and digital lifestyles. He is interested in designing interactions for portable computers, situated in the real world and augmented by computer-based information. He envisages the ability of the computer to assist the user without having to be directly instructed. Before the end of the decade, he expects that such computers will be as commonplace as today's Walkmans, electronic hearing aids, eyeglasses, and wristwatches.

SONY
SONY

Jun Rekimoto

Recent progress in hardware technology has brought about computers that are small enough to carry or even wear. These new computers, however, preclude traditional user-interface techniques such as a graphical user interface (GUI) or desktop metaphor. To overcome these shortfalls, human computer interaction (HCI) technology is rapidly changing, resulting in a transition akin to the switch to GUI in the 80's.

Dr. Rekimoto's Web site[19]

The Interaction Laboratory

■ Jun Rekimoto demonstrates connections between PDAs, laptops, and wall screen

Photo Author

The Interaction Laboratory is full of prototypes. The large central space is dark enough to allow the contents of electronic displays of all types to be easily seen, but with enough ambient light so that furniture and objects are also visible. Jun Rekimoto and his team of researchers have individual offices behind frosted glass walls, so that you can see through them to the glow from the external windows beyond. As he takes you around, demonstrating prototypes, introducing his colleagues and explaining his ideas, there is an unmistakable air of excitement and feeling of energy.

The work of his Interaction Laboratory scratches the surface of the future while at the same time staying connected to the realities of the present. Here are his descriptions of summaries of four of the projects:

ActiveInk computational ink[20]

Perhaps you are asked to create a very complicated three-dimensional scene, using a sketch interface. ActiveInk is computational ink, which

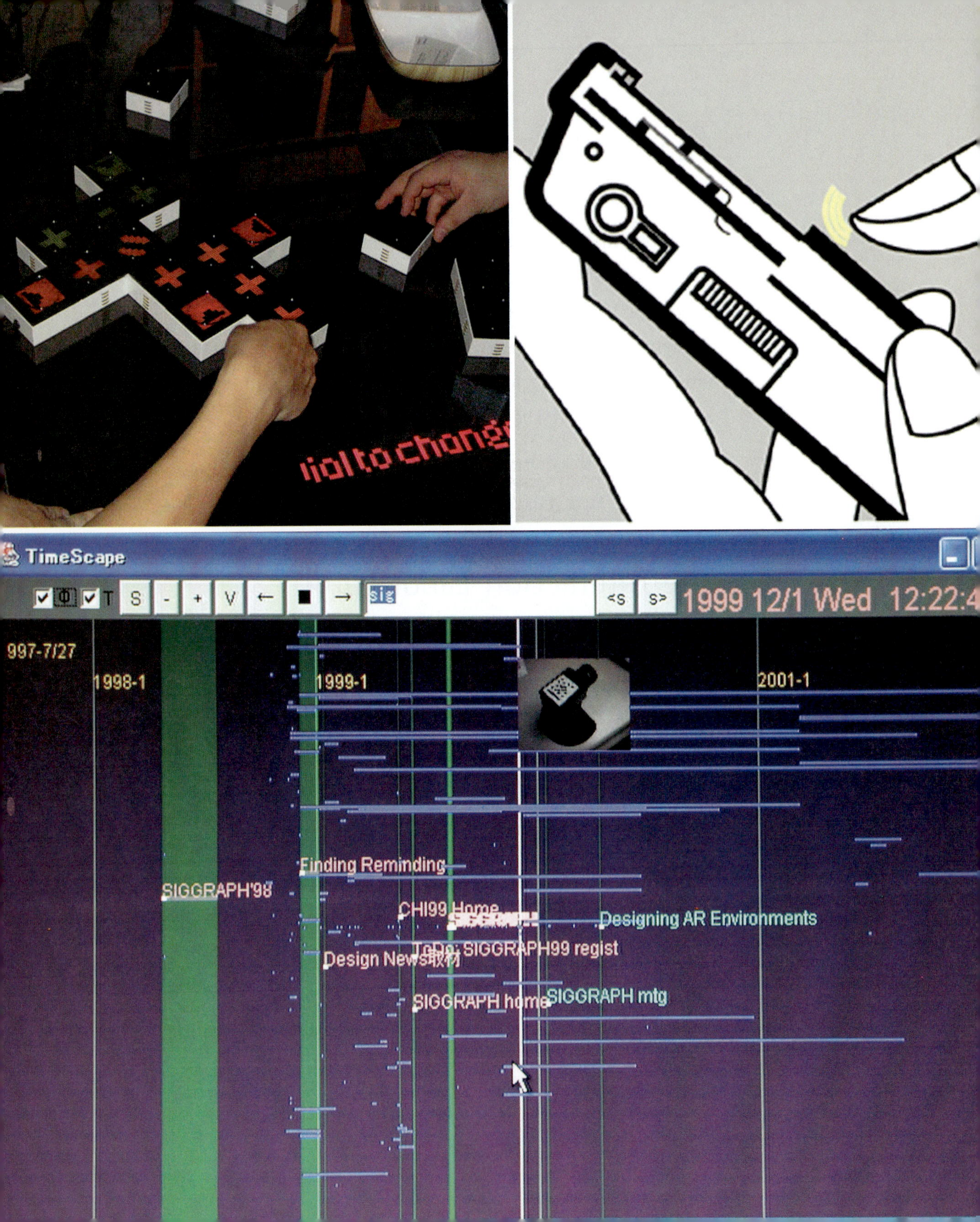

TimeScape
sig
1999 12/1 Wed 12:22:4
997-7/27
1998-1
1999-1
2001-1
Finding Reminding
SIGGRAPH'98
CHI99 Home
Designing AR Environments
ToDo: SIGGRAPH99 regist
Design News取材
SIGGRAPH home
SIGGRAPH mtg

means that if you draw a picture and want to draw a sky, you want to use blue paint and maybe mix in white paint. This is the traditional way, but with this system you can use sky ink. It has the ability to do sky. If you paint with this ink, a cloud will emerge automatically, or you can mix sky ink with fire ink, and you will see different types of surfaces.

BlockJam interactive music cubes[21]

This interactive music toy system is made up of modular cubic-type blocks. When you put the blocks together, the music can be changed according to the physical configuration. Each of the types of cubic object has a connector, and each cube has a computer, so you can snap them together and create a configuration, like Lego blocks, and the system understands which blocks are connected. Each block has several functions, such as timing or rhythm, or changing sound, so if you create a differently shaped object, you get different types of music. This gives a tangible interaction interface to invisible information such as music.

You can become a composer; one box can do a simple rhythm, but you can combine with other boxes, the resulting rhythm is much more complicated, so you can get infinite kinds of music sequences.

- *Top left* BlockJam interactive music cubes
- *Top right* TouchEngine touch panels
- *Bottom* Time-Machine Computing navigation system

Photos Courtesy of Sony CSL

TouchEngine tactile feedback for touch panels[22]

If you press the glass surface of a touch screen normally, you cannot feel anything, and only sound or visual feedback is available. With this tactile feedback system, a very small actuator vibrates the surface of the glass, so that you can sense a subtle feeling on your finger. It feels almost like pushing a physical button, so this is a tactile interface. The feedback is programmable, so stronger feedback and weaker feedback could explain the various system situations.

Time-Machine Computing navigation system

His fourth example is a project to look at alternatives for organizing information and the possibility of escaping the tyranny of hierarchical folder structures, which are difficult for novice users to navigate. If you take a picture for example, it may belong to a particular project, or it may belong to a photo album, so the same object belongs to two or more categories. Rekimoto and his team have chosen time as a concept for organizing information, so that the computer archives all the activity and lets the user go to any point in time. This means that if you want to look at documents from yesterday's meeting or last year's meeting, you can simply go to the date of the meeting, and you will see your desktop as it was at that time.

> Time is the most universal type of information available. If you take a picture, the photo album or the JPEG file will have the time information, and if you create a document, it also has a modification time. So if the system allows you navigate using time, you can find the document. You can also find a picture that is close to the document's creation date. So you can browse through only using time. And there is almost no cost to archive such time information. The other possible information such as location is rather difficult to always capture with currently available technology.

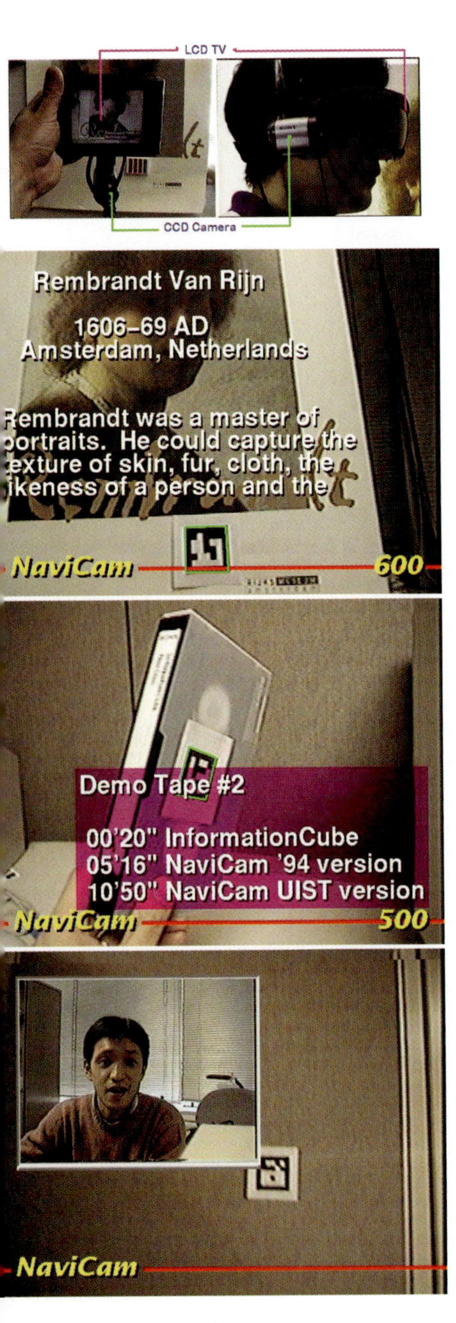

Using NaviCam

Augmented Reality

WHEN JUN REKIMOTO first joined Sony CSL, his research centered around augmented reality. He developed the NaviCam system, consisting of a small handheld computer with a camera and the ability to recognize barcode markers in the real world. It was capable of reading symbols and obtaining information and then providing information back to its user. Here is a quote from a *Business Week* article about it:

> It took a few moments before I could get the camera on Sony Corp.'s next-generation personal digital assistant to lock onto the bar code outside an office at Sony's Computer Science Labs. But once I did, the Navicam device came to life. Almost instantly, the top half of the display showed the name and photograph of the researcher inside. Below, I could read a description of his research interests. For more detail, I scrolled down the screen with a pen-input device. Another button let me switch the display from English to Japanese.

NaviCam is the first version of a new product category: smart portables that sense their surroundings. Wandering the spacious halls, I could learn what scientists were up to without disturbing them. And if I wanted to find a particular office, the Navicam led the way.[23]

The narrow definition of "augmented reality" is that the real view that someone sees is augmented by a computer-generated overlay of some kind, so three-dimensional matching is needed. Rekimoto thinks about it more broadly, suggesting that it encompasses any computer that can be aware of the real-world situation, such as location or nearby people or objects, and then create useful information, which is given back to the user. He emphasizes the opportunity based on location:

One of the most important situations is location, and there are a lot of different technologies—such as GPS or WiFi beacons—that are available. I think in the near future all mobile devices will be aware of location and will create person-centric information. Maybe the boundary between the telephone and the small mobile computers will be very vague. Maybe there will be a mixture of PDAs and telephones, because cellular phones are a very closed system, and we cannot create exciting applications without permission from the telephone carrier. On the other hand, PDAs are real computers, so we can create any application, but there is no wide-area connectivity. Maybe in the near future, IP mobile telephones can be a promising technology, and we can create a completely open-ended cellular phone, like a computer and a cell phone.

The small size of a cell phone is very significant in making it attractive to carry. Compare the huge brick of the early models with the continuing tendency to develop smaller and smaller phones; each generation seems to shrink, even when the smaller area available limits the sizes of buttons and screens. Jun Rekimoto therefore accepts that people will continue to want to use small screens, so in order to realize his vision of ubiquitous computing, he is searching for ways to leverage connectivity, allowing cell phones to seamlessly connect to other computers with larger displays, converting themselves into pointing devices and input or information transfer devices.

Pick-and-Drop
Gogh
Impressionism

Ubiquitous Computing

Pick-and-drop

AT THE MOMENT, if you have a PDA and wall screen or desktop computer, it is not easy to create a connection between them without checking an IP address, or doing something similarly technical. Jun has invented pick-and-drop as a more direct way of transferring information from one platform to another, so that you can simply pick an object up in one computer and drop it into another:

> I first used three different types of computers, Macintosh, Windows, and UNIX, so I had to use three mice on my desktop, and also three different keyboards. This was very, very complicated. I suddenly thought about why I have to use three mice. When I am dealing with physical papers, I only have to use one pencil for different kinds of sheet. If a particular pencil in the real world were connected to a particular piece of paper, the world would be very complicated.
>
> For the computer, it is assumed that the user has just one computer, but soon we will be using many different kinds of computers, so the fundamental design is different. So then I created a pen-operated computer, which allows the user to only handle a single pencil (stylus) using multiple computers.
>
> I am an Asian person, so I am very accustomed to using chopsticks. I can use chopsticks to move food from one dish to another, so I wanted to do a similar interface in the computer environment.

■ Jun Rekimoto demonstrates pick-and-drop

Photo Author

The demonstration of pick-and-drop in the Interaction Lab allows you to use a stylus to select an icon on one computer, which then disappears from the screen. When you tap on the screen of another computer, the icon appears on that screen and the file has been transferred. It works like "cut" and "paste," but it feels more like the file was virtually attached to the stylus than to a virtual clipboard.

> We want to grasp digital objects—such as icons from the computer screen—to hold them in the real world, so I use a kind of gesture

> that tells the system that I want to pick up this information. It is invisible, but I can conceptually think that I am holding the digital object. Then I can go to any other computer and gesture again by tapping to release the object.
>
> I remember that I am holding it using my short-term memory, so it is not a practical idea to pick up an object in Tokyo and drop it onto a computer in New York. We can also think about a stylus with a tiny display, so I can look at what I am holding, or maybe a sound, or small vibration can indicate the object is here.
>
> Maybe a small computer—such as a cellular phone—can be acting as a pointing device for the nearby environment. You can make a cellular phone call, attach to a nearby screen, pick up some information, and then drop it onto another computer. This small cell phone-computer can also act as a remote controlled mouse.

This drag-and-drop approach is much more direct than anything we use today between separate devices. Even a memory stick requires several steps to transfer the data.

Jun believes that in the near future people will be using combinations of multiple devices, posing a challenge for interaction design, as most interfaces so far have been designed in the context of a single computer. He thinks that it will be possible to build on the concept of direct manipulation across platforms, leveraging the familiarity with drag-and-drop that people have experienced with the graphical user interface:

> I think direct manipulation is still very important, even for the ubiquitous computing environment, because we are directly manipulating physical objects, and the GUI takes this metaphor into the digital world. In the near future we can live in a mixture of digital space and physical space, but still I think that directness is very important.
>
> A computer must be aware of the surrounding environment or location or any other objects, so it must sense the situation and know how to behave, maybe automatically, based on the situation. So this is not a totally direct concept, but I think the mixture of directness and context-sensitive computing is the future.
>
> For example, if you want to do a presentation in an unfamiliar conference room, you have a cellular phone, and you simply approach

the screen, and the screen automatically becomes your presentation screen, and you can control the presentation material without any command structure, but simply by using your cellular phone. All of the necessary network connection or security establishment can be done automatically by sensing proximity, because you are very close to the screen. This is maybe the simplest example.

Gestural interfaces

Gestural interfaces are likely to be a preferred form of input. As well as the use of gestures for pick-and-drop, Jun Rekimoto is developing a finger sensor, so that a table surface can be aware of your hand motion without your touching it, using a very weak radio field around the table. You can imagine a world of augmented reality controlled by gesture. For example, if the message from a restaurant is irritating, you turn it off with a subtle "cutting" motion of the hand. You can tell a store with bad advertising by the fact that people are making little cutting gestures as they walk by.

We saw efforts to develop gestural input languages with the early tablet computers and PDAs described in chapter 3, "From the Desk to the Palm," but the Go and Momenta computers and the Newton were all ahead of their time, so it is hard to know if the gestural aspects of their design will prove successful in the future. Stu Card has thought about the underlying interactive potential enough to articulate an opinion about gestural interfaces:

> The problem with gestures is that they require recall instead of recognition. You have to be able to remember all the gestures, so you need to make a rule that, though it's okay to use gestures, you can only have a small universal set.
>
> Another rule is that the gestures should be mimetic rather than symbolic. It's okay for me to have a gesture that says I want to move this book over into the bookcase here, or I want to make it go farther back in the space. For example, if I take this book, put the mouse over it, and flick it in this direction, that will send it back one tier into the space; that gesture is a mimetic abbreviation of what I would do if I was carrying it all the way back and placing it on the tier. It's not a symbolic thing that has an arbitrary meaning to it.

> If we build a gestural language like that, we can build a system in which we can very rapidly manipulate items around a world, and in which you can very easily remember what all of the commands do. In a gesture of this sort, we combine the specification of the argument and the specification of the command in a single stroke. I can't think of how you could get any faster than that.

Ubiquitous computing enabled by sensors and receptors

Jun Rekimoto forecasts a near future in which everyone emits some kind of signal or carries some kind of sensor, so that our personal preferences and messages travel with us, and the environment is able to adapt to us in a way that we choose. Similarly, he predicts that the environment will emit local information, so that stores or restaurants are telling us about themselves and can be interrogated if we wish.

Simply by moving around, we will automatically get access to information, between ourselves and other people, as well as between ourselves and the places that we are near. Durrell Bishop describes a scenario of an augmented environment with a similar vision of the future:

> Imagine that John walks into a shop looking for holiday. He looks through a brochure and he sees something he's interested in. "Ah-ha, a holiday in Turkey." He takes out his reader and it transmits just locally. He strikes the holiday with his reader, and then chooses a screen to view it on. Here he is picking a tagged object—an augmented book—that has been broadcast to the shop. The shop may have got the data locally, or it may be going to Turkey to the hotel to find the data, and put it up on the screen. John feels that he has a tool with him that lets him get at augmented objects, at the digital world behind things, and lets him connect together material and outputs.
>
> In another example, John is walking down the street and looking for a flat. He goes down to the newsagent, he looks in the window, and he sees some flats for rent. He takes out his reader and strikes the card in the window. Looking at the screen inside the shop, he now sees pictures of the flat.
>
> I believe that this is the sort of thing that is beginning to happen, and I know of examples where people are trying to find the equivalent of HTML for physical objects.

Durrell Bishop's scenario meshes perfectly with the research direction that Jun Rekimoto is following, and they are both building prototypes of these ideas that they are passionate about. Their vision of the future also follows the path toward ubiquitous computing advocated by Mark Weiser and described by Terry Winograd in chapter 7, "The Internet." This all combines to indicate a way forward that connects the physical and digital, and offers us the chance to design interactions that are full of the richness of form and movement, freeing us from the feeling of being constrained by our computing devices.

10

People and Prototypes

The author's own ideas about how to design interactions, with help from his friends and colleagues Jane Fulton Suri and Duane Bray

Prototype early and often, making each iterative step a little more realistic. At some point you are likely to experience that wonderful "Ah ha!" feeling that comes with a creative leap, but that is only an indication that you have moved forward in the detail of the aspect of the design that you are focusing on right then. You will only know that the design is good when you have tried it out with the people who will use it and found that they are pleased, excited, motivated, and satisfied with the result.

- Various people

Photos
Courtesy of IDEO

IN THE INTRODUCTION I told two stories of personal experiences that lead me to start working toward a new design discipline, eventually called "interaction design," and said that I would talk more about my personal point of view in this chapter. One of my motivations for embarking on this book in the first place was the hope that I could move beyond being an interaction design practitioner and find a way of explaining it to other people. The title of this chapter gives me away; I believe that if we think first about people and then try, try, and try again to prototype our designs, we stand a good chance of creating innovative solutions that people will value and enjoy.

To "understand people and use prototypes for speed" is a good pragmatic summary of a way of answering a "how?" question, but it does not answer questions of what, why, or where. In the first section of this chapter I try to answer these other questions about interaction design from my perspective as a practitioner. Please forgive me if my theoretical explanations are limited; my excuse is that I am a designer. I can easily tell you what to do but find it difficult to articulate the rationale, and yes, I will try to give a reason for that difficulty.

1 2 3 4 5 6
7 8 9 10 11 12 13
14 15 16 17 18 19 20
21 22 23 24 25 26 27
28 29 30 31
DELL
DELL

I am helped by two of my friends and colleagues in telling a more complete story about people and prototypes. Jane Fulton Suri was the first human factors psychologist to join my design team. She has pioneered the integration of human factors into the design process at IDEO. She helps me explain the methods that we have developed to learn about people and derive insights from that knowledge to inspire design. She also explores the use of prototypes for understanding existing experiences, investigating design ideas, and communicating design concepts.

Duane Bray leads the interaction design discipline at IDEO, so I have enlisted his help for an analysis of prototyping techniques. We talk about how prototyping fits into the design process, explain the different sorts of prototypes that are useful for the various categories of interaction design, and try to predict how that will change the practice of design in the future.

In the final section, about process, I characterize the difference between designing something new and designing a new version of something. With this contrast in mind, I propose a general method for designing interactions successfully.

Examples of prototyping environments at IDEO

Clockwise from top left

- Machine shop *Photo* Roberto Carra
- EE Lab *Photo* Author
- Video prototypes *Photo* Author
- Animation software *Photo* Craig Syverson

DILBERT
BY SCOTT ADAMS
EVERYONE GRAB AN ODD-SHAPED PIECE OF FOAM AND SIT DOWN.
scottadams@aol.com www.dilbert.com
WE'LL CONTINUE THE DESIGN PROCESS BY POINTING TO THESE BRAINSTORM NOTES AND MAKING INSIGHTFUL OBSERVATIONS.
12/12/01 © 2001 United Feature Syndicate, Inc.
THE NOTES ARE ALL YELLOW.
SWEET JEEPERS!!! YOU'RE ALL ENGINEERS!

DILBERT
BY SCOTT ADAMS
WE'VE HIRED THE WORLD'S MOST INNOVATIVE DESIGN FIRM.
scottadams@aol.com www.dilbert.com
WE'LL OBSERVE THEIR SUCCESSFUL METHODS AND STEAL THEM FOR OUR OWN. HEH HEH HEH.
12/10/01 © 2001 United Feature Syndicate, Inc.
MAYBE THEIR SECRET IS HIRING SMART PEOPLE.
I'M HOPING IT INVOLVES EASELS.

Designing Interactions

Design is the conception and planning of the artificial.

Richard Buchanan, 1995

What Is Design?

Dilbert cartoons about design

- *Top* Process
- *Bottom* Intellectual property

Cartoons by Scott Adams, courtesy of United Media

IN THE FOREWORD, Gillian Crampton Smith summarized the design of interactions as being about shaping our everyday lives through digital artifacts—for work, play, and entertainment. Her essay gives us a very good understanding of the special attributes of interaction design when we compare it to other design disciplines, and if we are already fluent in our understanding and appreciation of design. However, it assumes that we know the answer to the question, What is design?

If you ask a designer for a definition of design, you are often answered with a smirk, a joke, or a change of subject, as design is notoriously difficult to define, and designers are much more at ease learning and knowing by doing than they are explaining. In 1995 the British Design Council put out a little book called "Definitions of Design," which was arrived at by asking fifty people—designers, children, and others—to give their personal definitions. The result was surprisingly uninformative, but entertaining. Here are four examples:

I believe design is an intention, purpose, plan: and that good design is therefore by inference, where such plan has been well conceived, well executed, and of benefit to someone.
Milner Gray, Designer

Design is all around us—either we control it—or it controls us.
Wally Olins, Chairman Wolff Olins

Design is the difference between doing it, and doing it right.
Mark Fisher MP, Co-chairman, All-Party Group on Design

With art—if you like, you can be really weird. But in design you have to think about what other people will like.
Ghisli, age 10

These quotes, like an impressionist painting, give you a sense of what is meant when you look from a distance, but they are not satisfying as definitions. This vagueness remains an accepted fact of life for design. If you visit the current Web site of the British Design Council,[1] the rhetorical question, What is design? is posed, and the answer given is, "Design is everywhere—and that's why looking for a definition may not help you grasp what it is."

The most satisfying definitive description of design that I have encountered is the statement by Charles Eames in conversation with Madame Amic. Here are the questions and answers from that conversation that seem particularly relevant to designing interactions:

■ Charles and Ray Eames with a model of the exhibition "Mathematica," 1960

Q. What is your definition of "Design?"
A. A plan for arranging elements in such a way as to best accomplish a particular purpose.

Q. Is design an expression of art (an art form)?
A. The design is an expression of the purpose. It may (if it is good enough) later be judged as art.

Q. Is design a craft for industrial purposes?
A. No—but design may be a solution to some industrial problems.

Q. What are the boundaries of design?
A. What are the boundaries of problems?

Q. Does the creation of design admit constraint?
A. Design depends largely on constraints.

Q. What constraints?
A. The sum of all constraints. Here is one of the few effective keys to the design problem—the ability of the designer to recognize as many of the constraints as possible—his willingness and enthusiasm for working within these constraints—the constraints of price, of size, of strength, balance, of surface, of time etc.; each problem has its own peculiar list.

Q. Does design obey laws?
A. Aren't constraints enough?[2]

Core Skills of Design

Good design comes from the successful synthesis of a solution that recognizes all the relevant constraints, and the nature of the constraints defines the difference between design disciplines.

CHARLES EAMES WAS right about constraints; they are key to understanding design. Scientific disciplines rely on the ability of the practitioner to become expert in a narrow field, learning how to focus by excluding extraneous information and thus learning more and more about less and less. Here are five core skills of design:[3]

1. To synthesize a solution from all of the relevant constraints, understanding everything that will make a difference to the result
2. To frame, or reframe, the problem and objective
3. To create and envision alternatives
4. To select from those alternatives, knowing intuitively how to choose the best approach
5. To visualize and prototype the intended solution

I describe a process that includes this list at the end of the chapter. The five skills can be applied in the listed order, but the process is iterative rather than linear and does not necessarily follow a sequence. The most productive approach is often apparently unstructured, where members of the design team may suddenly dive into a prototype, renew some research activity, look

- Pinball machine
- The mind is like an iceberg

at people afresh, reexamine some of the constraints, or create new alternative concepts. The process does not look like a linear system diagram, nor even a revolving wheel of iterations, but is more like playing with a pinball machine, where one bounces rapidly in unexpected directions.

Tacit knowledge

Design thinking harnesses tacit knowledge rather than the explicit knowledge of logically expressed thoughts. Designers operate at a level of complexity in the synthesis of constraints where it is more effective to learn by doing, allowing the subconscious mind to inform intuitions that guide actions.

Perhaps the mind is like an iceberg, with just a small proportion of the overall amount protruding above the water, into consciousness. If we operate above the water line, we only have a small volume to use, but if we allow ourselves to use the whole submerged mass, we have a lot more to work with.

If a problem has a large number of constraints, the conscious mind starts to get confused, but the subconscious mind has a much larger capacity.[4] Designers have the ability and the training to harness the tacit knowledge of the unconscious mind, rather than being limited to working with explicit knowledge. This makes them good at synthesizing complex problems with large numbers of constraints; it also makes them bad at explaining or defining what they are doing or thinking. They will describe process and results because they are not consciously aware of their own rationale.

This is the reason that design education relies on a project-based approach of "learning by doing." The normal academic structure of learning is based on the conscious mind. You learn by understanding, with information that can be explained, elucidated and justified. A PhD is earned by contributing to the body of knowledge, by which we mean explicit knowledge. Designers learn by an atelier process, working on projects; the teacher advises on process as the designs are developed and criticizes the result, but neither teachers nor students are asked to explain the reasoning. When a problem is complex, with lots of constraints, it is much easier to recognize a good solution than to explain it.

These are typical evaluation criteria for a student design project:

1 Creativity/innovation
2 Aesthetics/quality
3 Human factors/values
4 Performance/technology
5 Completeness/presentation

Design disciplines

The nature of the constraints defines the design discipline. If you ask why people choose to be product designers, graphic designers, or architects, the answer will be less about their abilities and talent than about the kinds of constraints that they like to work with. Did they like everyday things, two-dimensional images and typography, or the built environment? Once you have been through a long educational process of projects and moved on to expand your experience in practice, it becomes more and more natural and normal for you to collect and understand the appropriate constraints for your design problem. Product designers know about how people relate to physical objects and how to manipulate metals and plastics. Graphic designers learn about how we see images and understand information and how to manipulate marks on paper. Architects become expert in the way we relate to space and learn how to develop structures for people to inhabit.

Designers are both enabled and controlled by the constraints that they learn about and come to understand; they are fluent with their tacit knowledge, in their own media, and in the contexts that they are familiar with and understand. This makes it difficult to develop a new design discipline in response to new kinds of constraints, but design problems are changing all the time. In the introduction I told the story of my own experience facing the complexities of designing a laptop computer and how this triggered my effort to start a new design discipline that we ended up calling "interaction design."

I think it is worth looking at the need for this new discipline as a step on a hierarchy, which forms a continuing trend of increasing complexity.

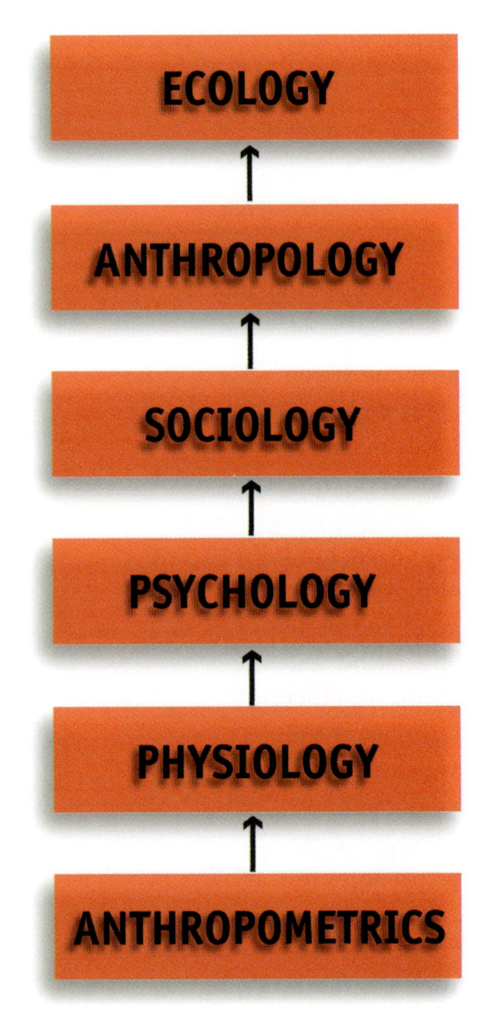

The interdependence of living things, for sustainable design

The human condition, for global design

The way people relate to one another, for the design of connected systems

The way the mind works, for the design of human-computer interactions

The way the body works, for the design of physical man-machine systems

The sizes of people, for the design of physical objects

This hierarchy shows the increasing complexity of the relevant constraints, if you consider each type of design problem from the point of view of the user. The hierarchy is based on the type of human factors that is relevant to the design context in each level of complexity, starting with the simplest at the bottom.

A Hierarchy of Complexity

WHEN I GRADUATED from college as an industrial designer in 1965, I expected to spend my life designing mass-produced objects to be manufactured in metals and plastics. Thinking about what people want from an object was a predominant consideration for the design, but there was an assumption that the most complex aspect would be to think about the subjective and qualitative values that would help the designer to create an appropriate aesthetic, so most of the research into what people wanted was aimed at discovering those subtle values that could inform an intuitive design process. The overall complexity came from synthesizing this understanding with all of the functional attributes of the design, such as performance, assembly, manufacturing, price, distribution, marketing and so on. These constraints demanded collaboration between experts in all of the fields that make up a multidisciplinary team, but with the roles clearly understood, individuals could operate successfully in separate disciplines, as long as they were willing to work together, even though failures were often encountered in companies when communications between discipline based departments were not strong enough. Designers were expected to be fluent with anthropometrics, as that was needed for the design of objects.

Anthropometrics—the sizes of people

FOR THE DESIGN OF PHYSICAL OBJECTS

The constraints are complex enough to demand the core skills of design, but the problems are well understood and have been evolving slowly since industrial design emerged as a new discipline in response to the Industrial Revolution. Designers have to understand basic human factors, but it is reasonable to expect that anthropometrics, or the sizes of people, are the most relevant. Thanks to the human factors work at the office of Henry Dreyfuss, anthropometric information for the designer is easy to find, by referring to the book *The Measure of Man*,[5] or the reference cards in *Humanscale*,[6] which present the salient dimensions of people of different statures, gender, age, and ethnic background.

Physiology—the way the body works

For the design of physical man-machine systems

The next level of complexity comes when you need to consider actions as well as objects. If the design context includes what the person is doing as well as the things that they are using, the constraints need to include the way the human body works, or physiology, as well as the sizes of people. When you are designing a chair for work, you must consider the danger that long periods of sitting may cause back strain, which demands that you understand the structure of the human spine and the muscles that support it; this is not a constraint when you are designing a casual couch or a bar stool. When you are designing a racing bicycle, you need to know about the way the frame can be fitted to the body to yield the maximum power. When you are designing a keyboard for long hours of typing, you need to understand about tactile feedback for the keystrokes, and repetitive stress for the carpal tunnels.

Once we delve into the specifics of an active context like this, the designer may find that the issues are too complicated to understand and act on intuitively; this is when the partnership between designer and a human factors specialist, in these examples a physiologist, becomes essential. The basic complexity of design constraints still demands subconscious synthesis as well as collaboration between everyone in the multidisciplinary team, but a special connection is needed between designer and physiologist, to allow them to be innovative in the human aspect of the solution.

Cognitive psychology—the way the mind works

For the design of human-computer interactions

Enter the chip! Electronics started with computers, gradually invaded everyday things and places, and are now almost everywhere. This is where we pick up on my stories of designing the laptop and the digital watch, as it is more and more difficult for the designer to understand intuitively about people and what they need and want, as the context is no longer just physical and biomechanical.

When you are concerned about the constraints that will matter to people when you are designing computers and things that are enhanced by electronic behaviors, you need a much more rigorous understanding of the way the mind works. When the design context includes machine intelligence as well as human intelligence, the design team will benefit from the expertise of a cognitive psychologist and will also need designers who are skilled at designing interactions. At this point in the hierarchy, we have arrived at the contents covered in the first five chapters.

Sociology—the way people relate to each other

FOR THE DESIGN OF CONNECTED SYSTEMS

Connecting everything together caused the next leap in complexity, when the Internet made connectivity a part of many design problems and solutions. Communications technologies like telephones and broadcast media have been with us for long enough to settle down and become familiar, but the sudden explosion of the Internet added the potential of connectivity to objects and services. Sociologists can help members of a design team understand the implications of this and to operate in the more abstract realm of designing services, where you are affected more by relationships among people as well as between users and objects or interfaces. Although services have been around for a long time, the sudden expansion of technology enabled services—and hence service design as a discipline—is still very new. We can see this by the freshness of the ideas expressed in chapter 6, "Services."

Forget your ego, and leave your discipline behind. Let's do this together!

The addition of the expertise of sociologists to a design team is especially important when the nature of the constraints is systemic. When we are designing connected systems of products, services, and spaces, which are used in real time, the brain of any designer who tries to absorb all of the constraints is likely to explode. We are better equipped to face the complexity as an interdisciplinary team, with a collective consciousness, and the ability to create designs as a group or team rather than as individuals.

Cultural anthropology—the human condition

For global design

Any designer who has developed a product for a global market has had to face the complexities that come from cultural variations. Some people eat with chopsticks and others with cutlery. And colors have strong symbolic meanings that are specific to particular societies. Cultural anthropologists can help people in a development organization understand the nature of cultural differences, which probably will not be intuitively obvious to them without some direct experience of the variations. There are also variations of culture within a single market, as different groups of people have unique anthropological characteristics, based on their occupation, background, or interests.

Ecology—the interdependence of living things

For sustainable design

At the top of the hierarchy is ecology, where designers need to understand the issues that will affect the environmental condition of our planet as well as the interconnected social and economic systems that we need to sustain. At first thought, sustainable design seems to be in direct opposition to the nature of the consumer society that industrial designers and interaction designers strive to enhance, and is thus a challenging subject for designers to come to grips with. Organizations and processes are emerging that allow the design team to understand and analyze the implications of their designs on sustainability, including the use of materials, energy, and the full lifecycle from "cradle to cradle."[7] This knowledge is still immature, making design for a sustainable planet an intuitive rather than exact science so far. The designer can intuitively synthesize a complex set of requirements, but the right information has to be there to draw on. Sustainability is still at the level of complexity where the science is not yet well established.

Why a Design Discipline?

When you go to design a house, you talk to an architect first, not an engineer. Why is this? Because the criteria for what makes a good building fall substantially outside the domain of what engineering deals with. You want the bedrooms where it will be quiet so people can sleep, and you want the dining room to be near the kitchen. The fact that the kitchen and dining room should be proximate to each other emerges from knowing first that the purpose of the kitchen is to prepare food and the dining room to consume it, and second that rooms with related purposes ought to be closely related in space. This is not a fact, nor a technical item of knowledge, but a piece of design wisdom.

Mitch Kapor, "A Software Design Manifesto" (1990)[8]

DESIGNERS GET THE love because we control the part that people want. I feel privileged to be a designer, because people like what I do (if I do it well). I also feel a little embarrassed to accept the accolades and the appreciation, as I know that I rely on all the other people who contribute the information that makes the successful synthesis possible. Mitch Kapor is right that designing a dream house is the output of design wisdom rather than technical knowledge. You enjoy your favorite article of clothing because it seems to be designed just for you, and it makes you feel good to wear it. I have a relationship with my favorite objects based on their aesthetic qualities more than their utility or price/performance ratio.

Mitch Kapor ■

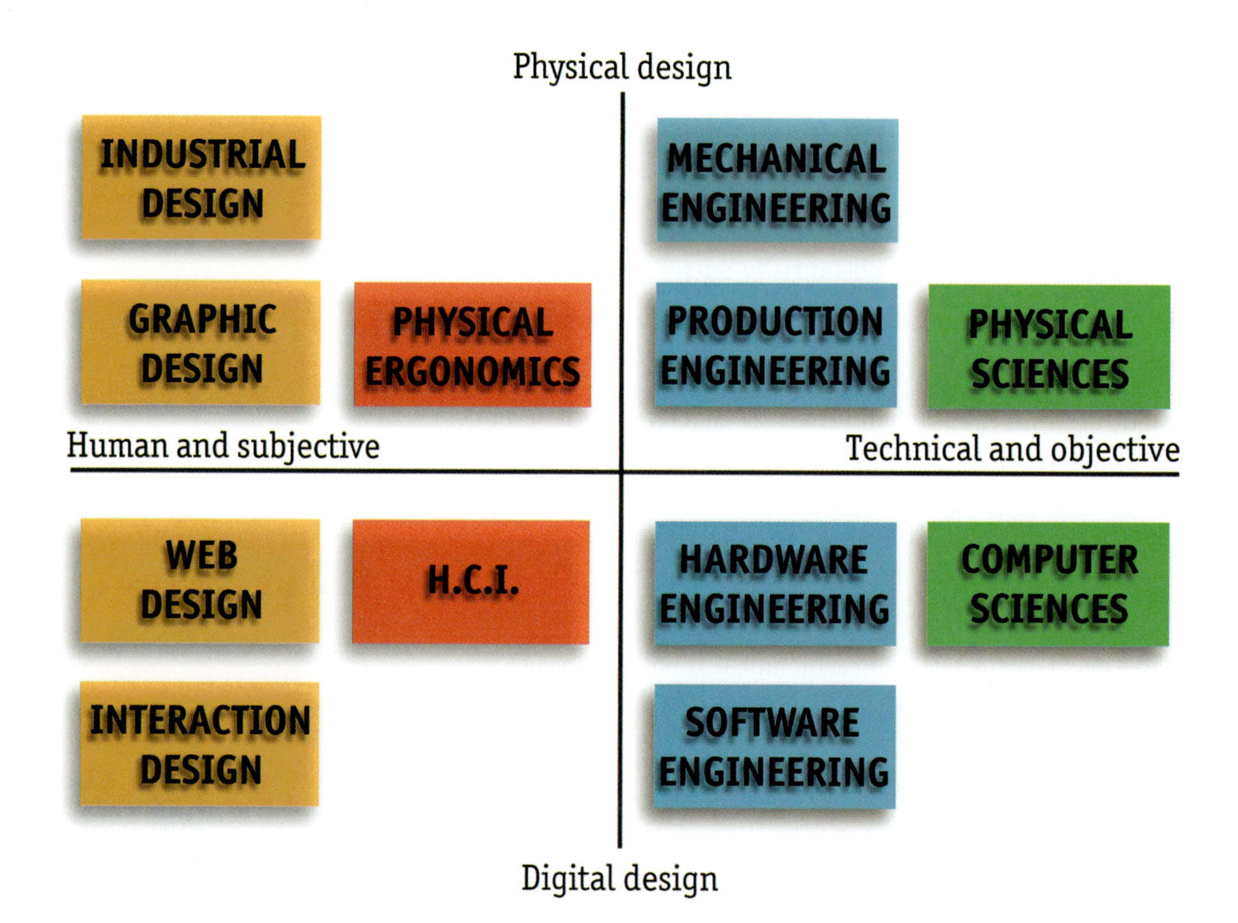

The diagram shows four quadrants, with the horizontal axis dividing human and subjective qualities from those that are technical and objective, and the vertical axis separating physical design contexts from those in the digital realm. We can position the development disciplines in four columns: the design disciplines, human sciences, engineering disciplines, and technical sciences. We see the need for interaction design as a discipline that can create solutions with human and subjective qualities in a digital context.

Designers rely on all the other disciplines, in that everything else has to work before design has a chance. First you have to be able to afford it, whether it is a house, a car, or a piece of software. Then it must perform: the building withstands the wind and rain; the car takes you where you want to go; and the software is stable. It must be useful, sheltering us, transporting us, and achieving the goals of the program. It must be usable, with stairs of the right tread sizes, steering wheel of a familiar size, and software that we can understand. Only when all of these attributes are already satisfied, after much effort from all of the contributors from the various disciplines, will the question of delight become important. Design wisdom has the power to please, but only in a context where the demands of all of the constraints are obeyed.

It can all go horribly wrong, of course, because the risks of living in the subconscious are so high. Operating at a subjective level, it is difficult to tell whether we are synthesizing the right set of constraints or whether the information is accurate. Your architect may be so interested in the magnificent material for the kitchen counter that the wisdom of space is lost, a difficulty that makes it risky to commission the design of your dream house, rather than buying one that already exists. At least with a car you can take it for a test drive as well as read the consumer reports. Interaction design is so new that there is very little established wisdom so far, and the chances are still low that you will be able to find a solution that satisfies all of those functional constraints, let alone give you aesthetic pleasure.

Where Does Interaction Design Fit?

A NARROW DEFINITION of interaction design is: "The design of the subjective and qualitative aspects of everything that is both digital and interactive, creating designs that are useful, desirable, and accessible." The designer is working in the artificial context of bits, pixels, input devices, users' conceptual models, and organizing metaphors. This is the version of interaction design that I practice—that I needed to learn in order to move up the hierarchy of complexity. This is a narrow version of interaction design, related to the experience and background of other design disciplines that deal in aesthetics and qualitative values, like industrial design, graphic design, and architecture. It is the equivalent of these disciplines in that the first concern of the designer is the values of the people who will use the design—the aesthetics, subjective and qualitative values, and human factors. The designer creates a solution to give pleasure and lasting satisfaction, and hence to fit the market, business, and social requirements.

A narrow definition of interaction design is: "The design of the subjective and qualitative aspects of everything that is both digital and interactive."

A broad definition of interaction design is: 'The design of everything that is both digital and interactive."

There is another, much broader, view of interaction design: "The design of everything that is both digital and interactive." It includes the design of all the interactions that are enabled by digital technology, whether by computers, chips embedded in products or environments, services, or the Internet. This broad view of interaction design includes the work of human-computer interaction (HCI) professionals, computer scientists, software engineers, cognitive psychologists, sociologists, cultural anthropologists, and designers. It includes everyone who has the knowledge and tools that allow them to "create or contrive for a particular purpose or effect"[9] in this digital context, sometimes as an individual, but usually as part of an interdisciplinary team.

It is natural for people outside the design and development disciplines to see this broad view, as they react to the resulting designs in terms of the experiences they have as users of interactive software, devices, and services. If they think about the design at all, they are likely to see the whole result, as they don't understand the individual roles of particular disciplines. This book is structured around this inclusive vision of what interaction design can be and has presented the thinking of many experts in the field from very varied backgrounds, chosen for their contributions rather than their closeness to my personal view of the discipline.

Is Interaction Design Here to Stay?

The decades ahead will be a period of comprehending biotech, mastering nature, and realizing extraterrestrial travel, with DNA computers, microrobots, and nanotechnologies the main characters on the technological stage. Computers as we know them today will (a) be boring, and (b) disappear into things that are first and foremost something else: smart nails, self-cleaning shirts, driverless cars, therapeutic Barbie dolls, intelligent doorknobs that let the Federal Express man in and Fido out, but not 10 other dogs back in. Computers will be a sweeping yet invisible part of our everyday lives: We'll live in them, wear them, even eat them. . . . Yes, we are now in a digital age, to whatever degree our culture, infrastructure, and economy (in that order) allow us.

Nicholas Negroponte, MIT Media Lab, 1998[10]

Nicholas Negroponte

We seem to be well on the way toward fulfilling these predictions that Nicholas Negroponte describes with such colorful images. Even if you doubt that we are already in a digital age, it is clear that we are marching relentlessly toward a condition where everything that can be digital will be digital.[11] What does this mean for interaction design?

In June of 2002 I was in London at the time of the display of work of the graduating master's students at the Royal College of Art, and I was looking at the projects from the interaction design department. I was impressed by the fact that most of them were both digital and physical; the students were designing smart objects rather than computer-based software. I was moving from the work of one student to the next, looking in some detail at the individual designs. Suddenly I looked up at the whole room, and discovered to my surprise that I had drifted into the area occupied by the projects from the industrial design department, never noticing a difference in the nature of the work. Just as the interaction designers were designing smart objects, the industrial designers were designing objects that were smart, finding it natural to include electronically enabled behaviors. It made me wonder if this was evidence of the beginning of the end of interaction design as a separate discipline.

Practitioners in the technical design disciplines adopt new technologies earlier than their counterparts in the human disciplines, as is explained by David Liddle in chapter 4, "Adopting Technology." This would lead one to expect that a similar migration might have already happened in engineering. Computer science emerged first and gave rise to new disciplines for the design of hardware and software. Eventually every engineer expected to use electronics and software in the natural course of development, so engineering education included learning about circuits and programming languages. However, this did not mean that the new disciplines of hardware and software design merged back into the traditional engineering design disciplines, but rather that all aspects of engineering design make use of technology, and all engineering designers can operate to some extent in the digital realm. It seems likely that a parallel to this will exist in the human disciplines, with all designers thinking it natural to include digital solutions as aspects of their designs, accepting the constraints and opportunities offered by new technologies. At the same time there will continue to be interaction designers who have a more in-depth knowledge and expertise about designing interactions and remain the experts in the field. I think interaction design is here to stay.

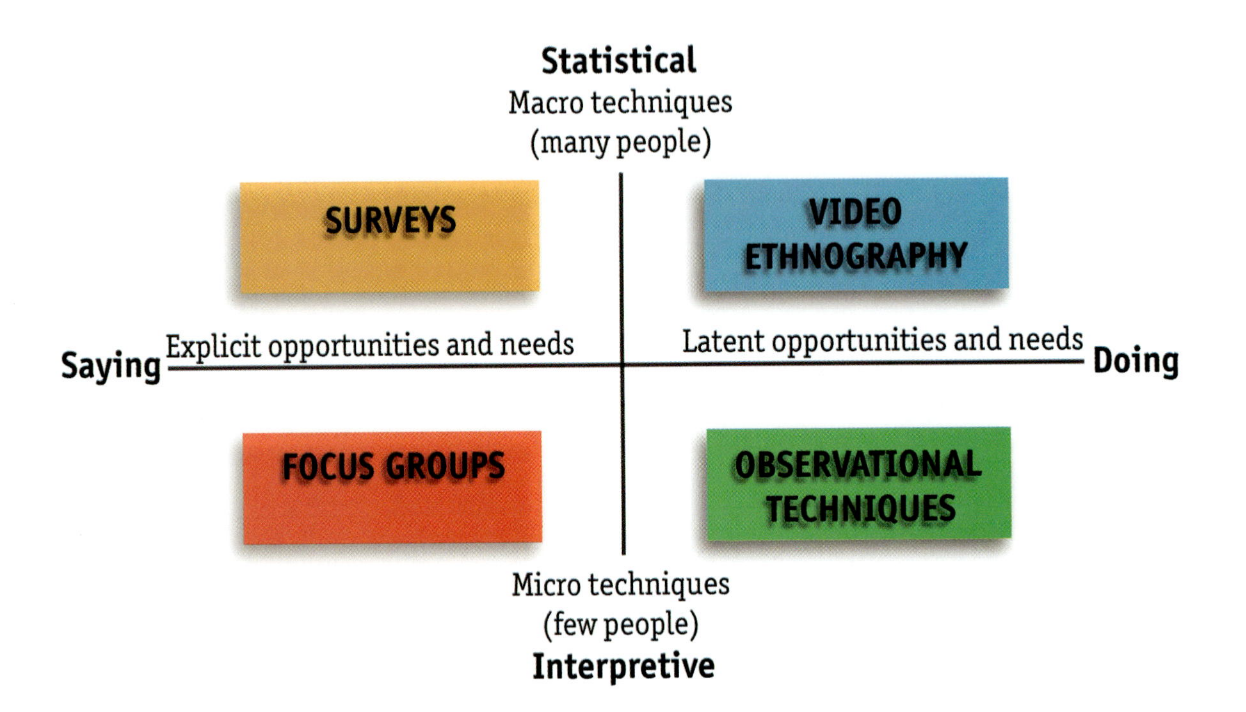

The diagram lays out different kinds of research methods, showing a horizontal scale that characterizes design opportunities and user needs, from explicit (left) to latent (right). The vertical scale indicates the difference in techniques from macro (top) to micro (bottom). Traditionally, market research was developed to find out what people want by asking them directly through large-scale surveys or more in-depth focus groups; these methods work very well to find out what people say they want.

If your goal is innovative design, your product or service has not even been thought of, so by definition it cannot be explained to research participants. This is where methods are needed to discover latent needs and desires that will help the members of the design team define potential opportunities. The examples on the diagram are video ethnography techniques on the macro scale, where stop frame video is set up to watch a space or task to reveal patterns of use. On the micro scale, the example is observational techniques, where members of the design team go to wherever the design context exists to see what people really do, as opposed to what they say they do.

People

It is essential to the success of interaction design that designers find a way to understand the perceptions, circumstances, habits, needs, and desires of the ultimate users.

Jane Fulton Suri, 2005

Latent Needs and Desires

In the mid eighties I was struggling to come to grips with what interaction design could and should be and how we could learn to bring our expertise in subjective and qualitative values to the realm of electronics. My first principle in design is to think first about the people part of the design: Who are the users? What do they want from the experience? What will give them satisfaction and enjoyment? In the seventies I had developed a tradition of going to look at what really happens in the context of each design problem. When I or one of the other designers in my practice was designing a marine radio for fishing boats, we went out on the boats to see how they used existing marine radios and talked to them about what was important for them. When we were designing a device used in hip surgery, we put on the green gowns and masks, went into the actual surgery, and watched what happened to try to think of ways that a new design could improve the situation.

"Observation" was the label we used for the best way to learn about people in the context of a particular design problem, implying that you needed to look at what people really do in a situation, rather than rely on the conventional technique of asking them about what they think and do. When you are trying to

understand the latent needs and desires of potential users before a design is created, it is important to learn about their existing habits and context of use—things they are rarely able to tell you about explicitly. You will gather clearer and more vivid knowledge of these by experiencing them firsthand.

Over the years, the human factors people at IDEO have evolved many new techniques beyond the simple observations that we started with, and now we have amassed a set of fifty-one methods, published as a deck of cards.

51 Ways of Learning about People

I GOT TO KNOW Jane Fulton Suri[12] in 1986 when she came to San Francisco to study for a year at UC Berkeley. This was a sabbatical for her, after a decade of human factors research and consulting in Britain, where she worked with a group that specialized in consumer product safety. She was interested in being more actively involved in design:

- Jane Fulton Suri

Photo
Skylar Reeves

> I'm always too late! I want to do some good in the world, but I'm only getting to influence bad designs after the damage is already done. For example, I've learned a lot about a lot of people who have had toes cut off by rotary lawn mowers. I would much rather have been working with the people who designed the mower, so I could have helped to make it safer in the first place, and saved the toes.

I thought this was a chance to integrate human factors expertise into my specialist team of designers, so I asked Jane if she would be willing to join the group in San Francisco when her course of study was complete. She accepted and started to work with the designers. At first they simply asked for her reaction to their ideas, but they gradually grew to appreciate the thoughtfulness and value of her contributions and started to ask her to help right at the beginning of each project and be involved throughout. By 1991 her contribution was clamored for by all of us, so we made a commitment to include a contribution from human factors specialists on every project, and expanded the

IDEO METHOD CARDS
IDEO METHOD CARDS
IDEO METHOD CARDS

human factors staff. As time went by, she and her human factors colleagues drew upon a vast range of methods for understanding people and their experiences. They soon evolved a substantial portfolio of tools and techniques. When the number of methods was approaching fifty, one of the team, Maura Shea, suggested that they represent them as a deck of cards.

The idea of the methods cards[13] is to make a large number of different techniques accessible to all members of a design team and to encourage a creative approach to the search for information and insights as their projects evolve. The intention is to provide a tool that can be used flexibly to sort, browse, search, spread out, or pin up. I find myself using the cards after a typical project briefing meeting, working my way through the pack as if in a game of patience and selecting the most useful set for that particular project in its various phases. When I meet with the team, I deal the set I've chosen and talk about why they might be useful in this context.

■ IDEO methods cards

Photo
Mark Serr

Each of the fifty-one cards contains explanatory text about how and when the method can be used and a brief example of its application to a real design project, with an illustrative and sometimes whimsical image on the other side. The cards are divided into four categories, ranging from the objective to more subjective—Learn, Look, Ask, and Try: "Learn" from the facts you gather, "Look" at what users do, "Ask" them to help, and "Try" it for yourself.

It is generally most valuable to apply, or sometimes modify, a range of different methods for any given project. The most useful set will depend on whether the purpose is primarily a *generative* one of defining design opportunities for particular kinds of users or a domain of activity, or an *evaluative* one of refining specific design ideas as they develop. In an evolutionary project, where the new design will be closely related to something that exists, techniques that yield explicit information about a particular product and usage may be valuable. If the project is revolutionary—the design will set a new precedent—methods that help the designer understand a broader domain of activity and related latent needs may be more appropriate.

Here are four examples of the methods from each category:

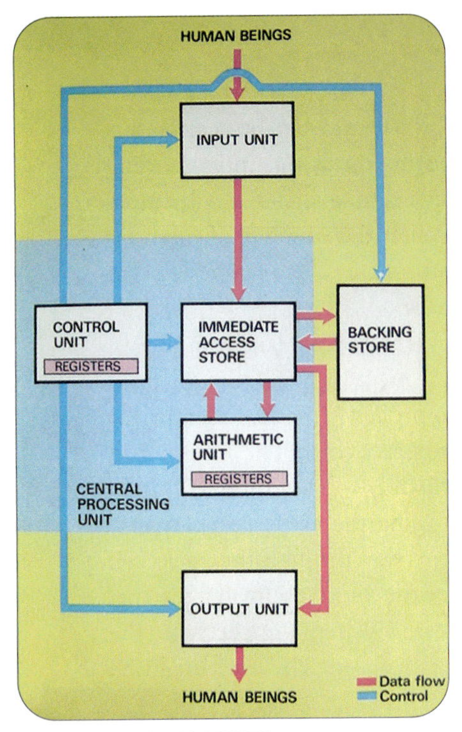

FLOW ANALYSIS

COGNITIVE TASK ANALYSIS

HISTORICAL ANALYSIS

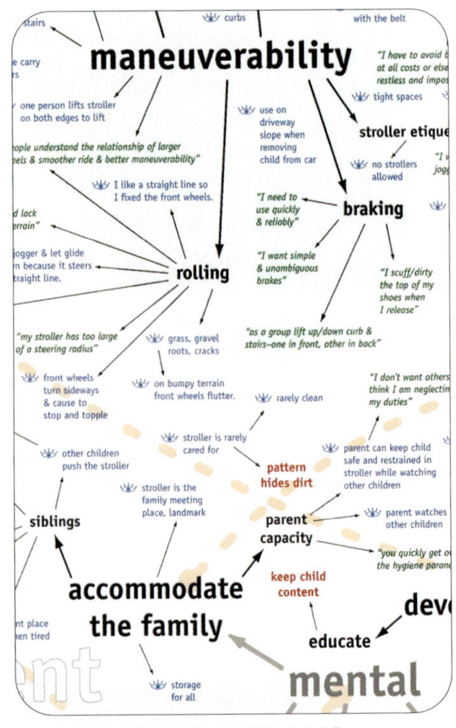

AFFINITY DIAGRAMS

Learn

ANALYZE THE INFORMATION you've collected to identify patterns and insights.

FLOW ANALYSIS

How — Represent the flow of information or activity through all phases of a system or process.

Why — This is useful for identifying bottlenecks and opportunities for functional alternatives.

Example — *Designing an online advice Web site, flow analysis helped the team to gain a clearer sense of how to make it easy to find your way around the site.*

COGNITIVE TASK ANALYSIS

How — List and summarize all of a user's sensory inputs, decision points, and actions.

Why — This is good for understanding users' perceptual, attentional, and informational needs and for identifying bottlenecks where errors may occur.

Example — *Logging the commands that would be involved in controlling a remotely operated camera helped the team establish priorities among them.*

HISTORICAL ANALYSIS

How — Compare features of an industry, organization, group, market segment or practice through various stages of development.

Why — This method helps to identify trends and cycles of product use and customer behavior and to project those patterns into the future.

Example — *A historical view of chair design helped to define a common language and reference points for the team members from the client and consultancy.*

AFFINITY DIAGRAMS

How — Cluster design elements according to intuitive relationships, such as similarity, dependence, proximity, and so forth.

Why — This method is a useful way to identify connections among issues and to reveal opportunities for innovation.

Example — *This affinity diagram shows what's involved in transporting young children, and helps to identify the opportunities to improve the design of a stroller.*

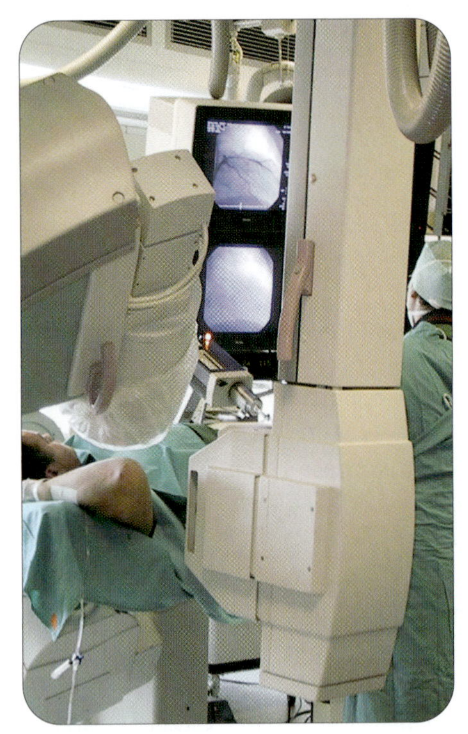

FLY ON THE WALL

A DAY IN THE LIFE

SHADOWING

PERSONAL INVENTORY

Look

Observe people to discover what they really do—not what they say they do.

FLY ON THE WALL

How — Observe and record behavior within its context, without interfering with people's activities.

Why — It is useful to see what people do in real contexts and time frames, rather than accept what they say they did after the fact.

Example — *By spending time in the operating room, the designers were able to observe and understand the information that the surgical team needed.*

A DAY IN THE LIFE

How — Catalog the activities and contexts that users experience for an entire day.

Why — This is a useful way to reveal unanticipated issues inherent in the routines and circumstances people experience daily.

Example — *For the design of a portable communication device, the design team followed people throughout the day, observing moments at which they would like to be able to access information.*

SHADOWING

How — Tag along with people to observe and understand their day-to-day routines, interactions, and contexts.

Why — This is a valuable way to reveal design opportunities and show how a product might affect or complement user's behavior.

Example — *The team accompanied truckers on their routes in order to understand how they might be affected by a device capable of detecting drowsiness.*

PERSONAL INVENTORY

How — Document the things that people identify as important to them as a way of cataloging evidence of their lifestyles.

Why — This method is useful for revealing people's activities, perceptions, and values as well as patterns among them.

Example — *For a project to design a handheld electronic device, people were asked* to show *the contents of their purses and briefcases and explain how they use the objects that they carry around everyday.*

CONCEPTUAL LANDSCAPE

COLLAGE

FOREIGN CORRESPONDENTS

CARD SORT

Ask

Enlist people's participation to elicit information relevant to your project.

CONCEPTUAL LANDSCAPE

How — Ask people to diagram, sketch, or map the aspects of abstract social and behavioral constructs or phenomena.

Why — This is a helpful way to understand people's mental models of the issues related to the design problem.

Example — *Designing an online university, the team illustrated the different motivations, activities, and values that prompt people to go back to school.*

COLLAGE

How — Ask participants to build a collage from a provided collection of images and to explain the significance of the images and arrangements they choose.

Why — This illustrates participants' understanding and perceptions of issues and helps them verbalize complex or unimagined themes.

Example — *Participants were asked to create a collage around the theme of sustainability to help the team understand how new technologies might be applied to better support people's perceptions.*

FOREIGN CORRESPONDENTS

How — Request input from coworkers and contacts in other countries and conduct a cross-cultural study to derive basic international design principles.

Why — This is a good way to illustrate the varied cultural and environmental contexts in which the products are used.

Example — *A global survey about personal privacy helped to quickly compile images and anecdotes from the experiences of the correspondents.*

CARD SORT

How — On separate cards, name possible features, functions, or design attributes. Ask people to organize the cards spatially, in ways that make sense to them.

Why — This helps to expose people's mental models of a device or system. Their organization reveals expectations and priorities about the intended functions.

Example — *In a project to design a new digital phone service, a card-sorting exercise enabled potential users to influence the final menu structure and naming.*

EMPATHY TOOLS

SCENARIOS

NEXT YEAR'S HEADLINES

INFORMANCE

Try

Create simulations and prototypes to help empathize with people and to evaluate proposed designs.

EMPATHY TOOLS

How Use tools like clouded glasses and weighted gloves to experience processes as though you yourself have the abilities of different users.

Why This is an easy way to prompt an empathic understanding for users with disabilities or special conditions.

Example *Designers wore gloves to help them evaluate the suitability of cords and buttons for a home health monitor designed for people with reduced dexterity and tactile sensation.*

SCENARIOS

How Illustrate a character-rich storyline describing the context of use for a product or service.

Why This process helps to communicate and test the essence of a design idea within its probable context of use. It is especially useful for the evaluation of service concepts.

Example *Designing a community Web site, the team drew up scenarios to highlight the ways particular design ideas served different user needs.*

NEXT YEAR'S HEADLINES

How Invite employees to project their company into the future, identifying how they want to develop and sustain customer relations.

Why Based on customer-focused research, these predictions can help to define which design issues to pursue for development.

Example *While designing an Intranet site for information technologists, the team prompted the client to define and clarify their business targets for immediate and future launches.*

INFORMANCE

How Act out an "informative performance" scenario by role-playing insights or behaviors that you have witnessed or researched.

Why This is a good way to communicate an insight and build a shared understanding of a concept and its implications.

Example *A performance about a story of mobile communications shows the distress of a frustrated user.*

An article by Daniel Pink in *Fast Company*[14] captures one way the cards can be used at the outset of projects.

> Fast Company decided to give IDEO's Method Cards a workout. In a conference room at the company's Palo Alto headquarters, we presented an IDEO team with two scenarios to see how they would begin wrapping their minds around a design problem. We weren't looking for an end. We were looking for a beginning—the initial steps that would set the course of the eventual design. Here's what happened when IDEO let the cards out of the box.
>
> *First deal: A carmaker, recognizing that people are living longer and better, wants to develop a car that appeals uniquely to drivers over 65 years old. How can the carmaker better understand the concerns of this group of prospective customers?*
>
> Five IDEO staffers—Jane Fulton Suri, David Gilmore, Kristine Chan Lizardo, Annetta Papadopoulos, and Aaron Sklar—listen as I read the scenario aloud. Then they open their boxes and begin sorting and shuffling the cards. Some they toss aside. Others they lay faceup in front of them. Our first-floor conference room is flanked by a wall-sized window that looks out on a sidewalk. To the pedestrians passing by, it looks as if we're playing pinochle.
>
> Gilmore, a British expat who once designed coins for the Royal Mint, holds up a card from the Ask suit. It's called Unfocus Group. To grasp the underlying design issues, Gilmore would assemble a diverse collection of people to talk about cars. He'd include healthy and active senior citizens, seniors with health problems, seniors who love cars, and seniors who don't. Fulton Suri, another Brit transplanted to the West Coast, chimes in: Why not also include a driving instructor and a state trooper for their perspectives? "And maybe they can help build something," she adds. She fingers the Experience Prototype card from the Try suit. Perhaps the grandmas and the smokeys could suggest a prototype car feature that IDEO could quickly construct and let them test. Fulton Suri also selects Empathy Tools. To simulate what it's like to have limited mobility and dexterity while driving, IDEO designers could don clouded glasses, slip on heavy gloves, or bandage their legs before taking a test-drive. "Of course, not everybody over 65 has those problems," she says. But the carmaker could end up introducing some new features for one age group that everyone might value because of the simplicity and elegance of the design.

Gilmore emphasizes the Emotional Dimension card. Cars have "life trajectories," he says. Like furniture and certain pieces of clothing, they carry memories of a particular stage of a person's life. So he'd have seniors craft a personal history of the cars they've owned and what those vehicles have meant to them. Buying your first car is a rite of passage. But, Gilmore wonders, what does it feel like to buy what could be your last car?

Second deal: A national television network seeks to reinvent its struggling nightly newscast and to update a format that has been largely untouched for a generation. What are some ways to uncover new approaches to the nightly news?

Lizardo starts things off by shouting, "A Day in the Life!" A card from the Look suit, it asks the potential users to document everything they do in a given day. The goal is to discover how people actually spend their time—and how that affects when, where, and whether they watch the news. Fulton Suri, eyeing the four cards fanned out in her left hand as if she were playing poker, sees and raises Lizardo. She suggests pairing her approach with another card: Behavioral Sampling. IDEO would give subjects pagers and then contact them randomly throughout the day to ask what news and information is available to them at that moment and what they've encountered in the past five minutes. Surveys and focus groups don't yield this sort of texture nor do they set the problem in context. And in this room, as elsewhere at the firm, context is king.

So is serious engineering. Two of the six people in this room are mechanical engineers, each with four patents to her name. One is Lizardo. The other is Papadopoulos, who offers the Foreign Correspondents card. She would enlist IDEO staff in different countries to watch the nightly news where they are and contribute their observations. Along those lines, Sklar wants to broaden the inquiry by using Extreme User Interviews, a card from the Ask suit. He'd try to understand the center by interviewing those who occupy the edges: "someone who doesn't have a TV, someone who gets all their news from the National Enquirer, someone who watches TV constantly."

Minds click. Ideas fly. How about Affinity Diagrams? How about Word-Concept Association? Says Fulton Suri: "Just the fact that I've got them in my hands is making my brain think about all sorts of different approaches." A breakthrough, it seems, is in the cards.

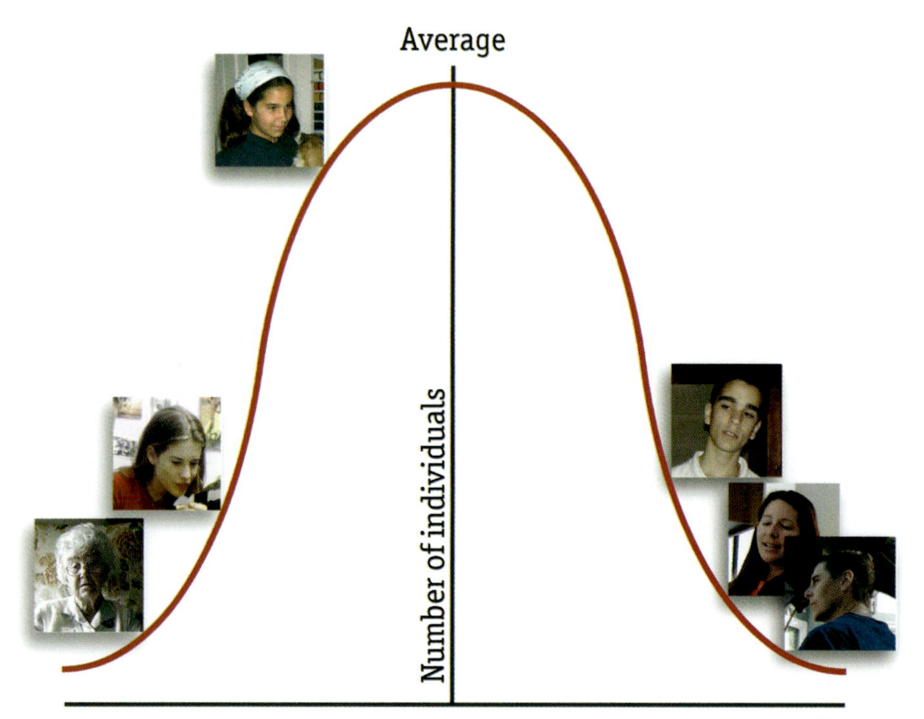

Remember the extremes

People vary in many characteristics that might be relevant to our design: interests, experience, learning pace, lifestyles, wealth, work styles, living situations, and so on. We maximize our chances of success by considering the full range of people we are designing for.

Many such attributes are distributed according to this kind of bell curve, where a relatively large number of people cluster around its average value, with numbers tailing off gradually to a few people represented at each of its extremes. When we want to learn about people, it is important to include some who represent critical extreme values of the relevant characteristics, to avoid the trap of designing only for the average.

A very simple example—if we design an ATM interaction to time out after the average time people take to input their PIN number, we will inconvenience the full 50 percent of users who take longer than average! Far better to design the system to accommodate all but the slowest 2 percent.

The kinds of techniques exemplified by the methods cards can be used to counteract our natural self-centeredness and better inform our intuition. It is very difficult to be a good designer without having a big ego. After all, we need to believe enough in our own ability to synthesize the right solution intuitively, while at the same time admitting that we may not readily have the most lucid explanation of the rationale. That may be why we find it much easier to design for ourselves than for other people. Good friends like Jane Fulton Suri, who offer all those methods for understanding users, their habits, and contexts, are invaluable for keeping us focused on other people, even inspired by our insights about them, so we don't slide back into the world we know and understand.

It is relatively easy when we are ourselves typical of the intended users. There are lots of examples of successful products that have been designed based only on the intuitive judgment of the designers thinking about themselves. The computer industry emerged in this way. Enthusiastic early adopters enabled the early phases, and they were thrilled to use the interactions designed by engineers for themselves. For twenty-five years Hewlett Packard was a company of engineers who worked in labs, designing equipment for engineers who work in labs. It was much more difficult for them when they started developing general purpose computers for a broader consumer market and needed to design interactions that would be easy to use for ordinary people. Nike attracts designers who are interested in athletic activities, so it becomes natural for them to design footwear for themselves.

Designers are often self-absorbed in this way. If you are sitting at a computer, working to complete a deadline for a project, it is easy to stay where you are, to design a solution to satisfy your own needs and aspirations, one that you find amusing or engaging and that fits your own idea of beauty. If you stay at your desk, your design is unlikely to represent the full range of people who will use the result of your work, but if you leave your desk and bravely open yourself and your design ideas to influence by potential users and usage contexts, you will produce work that more successfully reflects the needs and desires of a diverse set of people.

DU PONT

Prototypes

What I hear, I forget.
What I see, I remember.
What I do, I understand.

Lao Tse, Chinese philosopher, b. 604 BC

Language is convincing.
Seeing is believing.
Touching is reality.

Alan Kay

A New Prototype Every Day

- *Top*
  Gossamer Condor, 1977
- *Bottom*
  Gossamer Albatross, 1979

Paul MacCready is well known as a designer of innovative air and land vehicles, but it was the creation of the Gossamer Condor[15] that made him famous. In 1959 a British industrialist named Henry Kremer offered £50,000 for the first human-powered aircraft that could demonstrate the same degree of aerodynamic control as the early Wright fliers, by tracing a figure eight around two markers four-fifths of a kilometer apart. After frustrated attempts by various enthusiasts, in 1977 the Gossamer Condor was the first craft to succeed, pedaled by the cyclist Brian L. Allen. Paul MacCready led the design team, adopting a rapid prototyping approach to the development. The plane was built of a delicate skeleton of thin tubes and tensioning wires, covered by transparent plastic sheeting that was taped in place. This proved a very flexible kit of materials, allowing the design to be changed as often as once a day, and a new prototype to be built. This rapid prototyping technique was so effective that the craft was an easy winner in the competitive tests, and a later generation of the design went on to be flown by pedal power for great distances, including a crossing between England and France.

Larry Tesler told a similar story of creating new prototypes every day in chapter 2, "My PC." He and Bill Atkinson were designing the pull-down menu structure for the Apple Lisa, working around the clock. Bill would work nights and Larry would work days. During the night Bill would make prototypes of user interface concepts, written in a robust enough code to support some form of testing. Then Larry would run user tests during the day. Larry would give Bill a report at the end of the day and tell him what he had learned from the tests. Then they would brainstorm for ideas and decide what to try next, so that Bill could go off and spend the night programming. In the morning he would bring in a new prototype and then go home to bed. They used this method for several intense weeks until the specification was solid, and it was during this time that they designed the arrangement of pull-down menus across the top of the screen that is so familiar today.

In both these examples, the designers achieved dramatic breakthroughs by generating their ideas every day and advancing them by a combination of prototyping and user evaluation. In Paul MacCready's case, the ingenuity was in choosing materials that would allow daily changes in the design just by retaping the plastic or repositioning the structure of tubes and wires, so that the pedal power provider could try out another design. Bill and Larry generated new ideas by brainstorming every evening after the user tests of the day, relying on their experience and ingenuity to come up with the ideas for the next step; then Bill built a prototype, designing as he went along. Some nights may have been futile, but the tests on the following day showed if it was time to say goodbye to an idea. Other nights were spectacular breakthroughs, as Larry said in his interview[16] when describing the creation of the pull-down menu structure for Lisa. The user tests the following day proved the point.

There may not be many design problems where the development of a new prototype every day is possible, or even wise, but the surprising lesson that we can take away from these stories is the advantage of prototyping early and often, trying things out as quickly as possible and more often that we think in advance that we would dare. The risk of failure puts up a barrier to trying the first ideas, as we know that they are almost bound to be bad or wrong in some way. If we can shrug off the fear of that risk and get into the habit of trying things out as soon as we can, we will fail frequently, but the reward is that we will succeed sooner.

Interaction Design Prototypes

Pro-to-type *n.* 1. An original type, form, or instance that serves as a model on which later stages are based or judged.

American Heritage Dictionary[17]

THE DEFINITION OF a prototype in the *American Heritage Dictionary* seems particularly apt as a description of a design prototype in its broad inclusion of "type, form, or instance," and also in the inference of a cyclical process where later stages follow before judgment is passed. In the context of designing interactions, perhaps we can narrow the definition to "A representation of a design, made before the final solution exists."

This is still a very broad and includes a lot of possible types. When the design process is nearing completion, the prototype will need to represent a combination of the way the design looks, feels, behaves, and works. If the context includes the experience as well as the product, we will also want a representation for understanding, exploring, or communicating what it might be like to engage with the design. The "experience prototype" for Kodak, described by Jane Fulton Suri and Mat Hunter in chapter 4, "Adopting Technology," was the right approach to integrate and communicate the interaction architecture concept, but the team had worked on the problem for long enough to know exactly what to prototype. The uncertainties were already resolved by the research efforts and iterations that had gone before. Jane had articulated the framework that summed up the design opportunities for consumer digital photography. Mat had developed the key design ideas of modes, filmstrip, and so on; thus the design ideas were already mature. The design team had already developed and discarded many prototypes before they were ready for the version that they described.

In a paper called "Experience Prototyping,"[18] Marion Buchenau and Jane Fulton Suri divide prototyping techniques into three categories: those that help you to understand existing user experiences and context, those that help you to explore and evaluate design ideas, and those that help you to communicate ideas to an audience. The paper starts by introducing the background to the thinking:

Introduction

> Increasingly, as designers of interactive systems (spaces, processes and products for people), we find ourselves stretching the limits of prototyping tools to explore and communicate what it will be like to interact with the things we design.
>
> "Prototypes" are representations of a design made before final artifacts exist. They are created to inform both design process and design decisions. They range from sketches and different kinds of models at various levels—"looks like," "behaves like," "works like"—to explore and communicate propositions about the design and its context.
>
> As such, prototyping is a key activity within the design of interactive systems. Several groups of designers and researchers, perhaps most notably at Apple Computer, Xerox PARC, and Interval Research, have been active both in pushing the boundaries of prototyping beyond the range of traditional methods[19] and in developing understanding of the value of different forms of prototype. For example, Houde and Hill[20] discuss various functions for prototypes as being essentially about the "role" an artifact will play, its "look and feel" and how it will be implemented. Other work has explored issues such as different levels of fidelity,[21] prototypes for different audiences[22] and models or use in the context of participatory design.[23] Further, prototyping as a design practice is now promoted within the business community as a key element in innovation.[24] Building from this foundation, designers at IDEO are working to expand internal prototyping practices to embody the concept of

■ Marion Buchenau

"experience prototyping" as an integrated part of the design process. In this paper we will discuss what we mean by experience prototyping, why we think it is important and then look at its application within three key design activities—understanding, exploring and communicating—through examples from design projects.

What is "experience prototyping"?

First, let's think for a moment about what we mean by "experience." With respect to prototyping, our understanding of "experience" is close to what Houde and Hill call the "look and feel" of a product or system, that is "the concrete sensory experience of using an artifact—what the user looks at, feels and hears while using it." But experience goes beyond the "concrete sensory." Inevitably we find ourselves asking questions about the "role" which Houde and Hill define as "the functions that an artifact serves in a user's life—the way in which it is useful to them." And even more than this, when we consider experience we must be aware of the important influences of contextual factors, such as social circumstances, time pressures, environmental conditions, etc.

By the term "experience prototype" we mean to emphasize the experiential aspect of whatever representations are needed to successfully (re)live or convey an experience with a product, space or system. So, for an operational definition we can say an Experience Prototype is any kind of representation, in any medium, that is designed to understand, explore or communicate what it might be like to engage with the product, space or system we are designing.

Here are some quotes from the paper that describe the three categories, supported by an example of each taken from the paper, and others from the previous chapters. The first category is about understanding existing user experiences when you are collecting constraints and trying to understand everything that will make a difference to the result.

spyfish
front
50
m
240°
W

Understanding existing user experiences and context

Experience prototyping here is applied to demonstrate context and to identify issues and design opportunities. One way to explore this is through direct experience of systems—the prototyping goal is to achieve a high fidelity simulation of something that exists, which can't be experienced directly because it is unsafe, unavailable, too expensive, etc.

The questions to ask in this stage are: What are the contextual, physical, temporal, sensory, social and cognitive factors we must consider as we embark on design? What is the essence of the existing user experience? What are essential factors that our design should preserve?

An example from the paper is for the design of the control interactions for a remotely operated underwater camera:

The ROV Pilot experience

This example used a proxy device to provide the team with specific insight into an experience that was not readily available to them.

The project involved the design of a pilot's interface for an underwater remotely operated vehicle (ROV) and its cameras. It was important that designers grasp and deal with some of the cognitive confusion that would arise for the operator. There would be problems for operators steering a tethered vehicle with six degrees of freedom, as well as multiple cameras—which can be positioned independently from the ROV itself—while trying to find a target in a vast undifferentiated space with limited visibility.

- H2Eye Spyfish underwater camera ROV, 2002

Photo Jason Tozer

In the initial project phase, the design team created a task analysis, based on interviews with pilots and literature research which was useful to them, but did not communicate the realities of ROV operation very effectively. For the first experience prototyping exercise, one of the designers used a rolled-up sheet of paper to limit her peripheral view while searching for a target—a Post-it note in her work space.

To get to the more problematic cognitive and functional issues, the team developed a game in which one player, A, stood in a room which was empty except for multiple chairs (portraying underwater obstacles), and one of them held a chocolate bar, the target. Player A held a video camera connected by a long cable to a remote TV screen where the live picture was viewed by player B. Player B gave verbal instructions to player A to move right/left, forward/back, and up/down and gave separate verbal commands to direct the camera.

After a few yards of cables wrapped round A's legs and the chairs as well as B's frustration at making mistakes, "Aargh! I meant camera right not move right," the design team and the client had personal insight about many important issues. For example, it was obvious that a critical need was clear feedback to support a mental picture of the vehicle's path through space, feedback about the tether condition, and the need for a clear distinction between controls for the vehicle and for the camera.

As a follow-up, the team asked a participating retired ROV pilot about the validity of the simulated experience which, to his surprise, portrayed a quite accurate picture. He provided additional information, mainly about contextual factors (e.g., different levels of experience, underwater conditions, support tools like maps) which might change or influence the portrayed experience. The ability to share this experience prototype provided verification and enrichment of the simulated experience with a real life event. This further enhanced the participants' understanding of the pilot's problems and created a shared reference point between all members of the design team as the work moved forward.

The success of the game with two players was dramatic because each of the team members who tried it experienced a prototype of the difficulties that formed the crux of the interaction design problem. It was also ingeniously quick and inexpensive to do, with the whole team going through the exercise in a single afternoon, but notice that the inspiration for design of the prototype itself came only after an unsuccessful try with the rolled-up paper.

Other examples

There are several stories in the earlier chapters that belong in this category of understanding existing user experiences:

Guided fantasy

In chapter 1, "The Mouse and the Desktop," Tim Mott and Larry Tesler explained their devising a "guided fantasy" process to learn what people would want for a text-editing system. They put editors in front of a blank display with a keyboard and a mouse and asked them to walk through an imaginary editing session using that hardware. They explained that the mouse could be used to position a pointer on the screen and that the text would be on the screen. The editors described the process that they used at that time with paper and pencil, and together they imagined typing in the text and creating a manuscript, and then editing that manuscript using the mouse and keyboard in the same way that they would use a pencil.

Draw your money

Another example is in chapter 6, "Services." Fran Samalionis asked people to draw their money for the design of an online bank. After observational research, the participants were asked to sit down and make a drawing of their financial situation. This helped to expose their feelings and their mental models. As they started to draw, they talked about themselves openly, providing a clear view into the way they felt and thought about money, and hence the kind of services and support an online bank could offer them. This technique could be valuable in a more general service design context, as it helps to describe a complicated system and to establish a framework.

■ Children's picture communicator for Maypole project
■ Prototypes operated by equipment in backpacks

Exploring and evaluating design ideas

The second category from the paper is useful during the design development process, when alternatives are being created and envisioned:

> The main purpose of experience prototyping in this activity is in facilitating the exploration of possible solutions and directing the design team toward a more informed development of the user experience and the tangible components which create it. At this point, the experience is already focused around specific artifacts, elements, or functions. Through experience prototypes of these artifacts and their interactive behavior we are able to evaluate a variety of ideas—by ourselves, with design colleagues, users or clients—and through successive iterations mold the user experience.

An example from the paper is for the design of a picture communicator for children, where children used working prototypes for an extended period of time. Despite heavy backpacks containing batteries and drivers for the prototypes, the children were happy to integrate picture sending and receiving into their daily activity.

Children's picture communicator

Part of the process of design exploration involves checking out ideas with potential users. For example, in the EEC funded "Maypole" project's exploration of community communications[25] the goal was to create prototypes which would give children an experience as close as possible to that invoked by the intended design solution. Usually, user tests focus on fairly specific functional performance issues. Such tests also generally involve conditions that are not typical of the ultimate use situation, for example they frequently involve outsiders (e.g., as observers or "Wizards of Oz" when some functions need to be simulated by a person). This makes it difficult to answer questions about experience such as: How will people feel about the system we are designing? Will it change the way people behave or think about an activity? Is it compelling to them in their own context? A true experience prototype for users—providing a really relevant experience—seems to require a level of resolution and functionality such that it can be "let loose" into an everyday context and more fully integrated into people's lives.

For the Maypole project, Nokia built working sets of picture communicators that the design team was able to distribute to children who could take them away and play with them unsupervised for days at a time.[26]

These prototypes required a power pack and transceiver unit that the children had to carry around in a backpack, yet the experience of being able to take pictures and send and receive them to and from friends proved so compelling that the users almost forget about that inconvenience.

As an observer of user evaluations, one knows very quickly if the designed experience is a good one. If it is, people get so involved in the experience that they forget about the limitations of the prototype (e.g., a tether to the computer running the software, or an extreme weight or size hindrance because of limiting prototyping components).

Kids are notoriously tolerant of heavy backpacks, but they are also good at rejecting offerings that have no value to them, so this experience prototype showed the potential of the main proposition of sending and receiving images, as well as allowing the designers to try out the interactions.

Scrollbars

The exploration and evaluation of design ideas is central to the iterative design process, so it has come up again and again in earlier chapters. As one of the many examples, think of Bill Atkinson in chapter 2, "My PC." In collaboration with Larry Tesler, he honed the art of combining prototype designs with experiments and user trials. He proved that a combination of trial and error and a lot of experiments could lead to successful user interface design. He frequently built new prototypes and tried them on different people.

He gave the example of the directional ambivalence of the arrows on a scrollbar. Which way should the arrows go, and where should they be? When you scroll toward the bottom of a document, the document moves up, so there's some reason to think of a down arrow, and some reason to think of an up arrow. What do people expect? When people see an arrow, which way do they think it will move? He found, by prototyping and testing, that it mattered much more where the arrow was, than whether it went down or up. If the arrow was at the top, people expected to see more of what was above, whereas if it was at the bottom, they expected to see more of what was below.

HyperCard

Bill Atkinson was also the creator of HyperCard, which became one of the most valued tools for prototyping interactions in the eighties. As he explained in his interview:

> The most important thing is to start with the user interface, so we use what I call "String and baling wire" prototypes. These are software programs that have no depth to them, which would easily crash if you did anything other than the prescribed course of actions, but with which you can feel what it would be like to use this program.
>
> The process of going from one of these mockups to a rigorously crafted software application that can withstand users banging on it and trying all sorts of weird things is a big jump. It is a different medium. The most important thing with that first medium is to be able to try different ideas and iterate quickly. Prototyping environments, like high-level authoring systems or Smalltalk, are very useful because you can put things together quickly. I found that when people made a HyperCard stack, they could put a prototype together in an afternoon and get it to do what they wanted. If they wanted to craft this result into a robust application that a lot of people would use, they could use the HyperCard as an example, and they could sit down with their C compiler and write the software in a different medium.

Testing mouse designs

HyperCard was the program used by Bill Verplank to test and evaluate alternative designs for the Microsoft mouse, also described in chapter 2, "My PC." He devised five tasks to test a range of experienced and naive users trying out the various prototypes and existing mice. A tapping task measured the tradeoff between speed and accuracy for the most common mouse usage, that is move and click, by asking the user to click twenty times back and forth on pairs of targets ranging in size. Next, subjects were asked to trace their way through a maze, revealing the ability to steer. A task to test precision asked the user to position the cursor exactly in the center of arrays of dots, and then to click. Writing the word "TAXABLES," with one character in each of eight boxes, required repeated short strokes with the button down and then up. The final task required typing, then pointing, then typing, then pointing—again and again—measuring homing time as you move from keyboard to pointing device. These human factors trials allowed quick evaluations of a wide range of design concepts, and the combination of user testing and rapid prototyping was a key to the success of the project.

Faking

Bill was able to break the evaluation of the mouse designs into simple individual tasks, but sometimes the exploration and evaluation of design concepts is in a much more intricate context. Take for example the service design problems described by the team from Live|Work in chapter 6, "Services." They say that service touch-points can be faked with quick and informal techniques. Experiences can be enacted, but the communication works much better if the actors are using props that form evidence in the mind of the onlooker. This evidence can be faked using quick and informal techniques to simulate an advert, a piece of CCTV footage, or an invoice. This type of "archaeology of the future" allows qualitative judgments to be made early in the development process about the implications of a design. It allows customers and collaborators to "play back" their own assumptions as concrete experiences rather then abstract evaluations.

Service experience model

They use prototyping to get a very intimate and subjective idea about what the experience of using a service could be. The prototype simulates the experience of using services, which are intangible, take place over time, and have multiple touch-points, media, and modes. The concepts of "faking evidence" and "experience modeling" come together in a "service experience model." This is the way in which a proposal for the design of a new service can be explored, evaluated, and improved through iterative development.

Communicating ideas

The third category in the paper from Marion and Jane is more about communicating results:

> The role of experience prototyping here is to let a client, a design colleague, or a user understand the subjective value of a design idea by directly experiencing it. This is usually done with the intention of persuading the audience, for example, that an idea is compelling or that a chosen design direction is correct.

An example from the paper is for the design of a Kiss Communicator. This was a research project, looking for ways in which emotional content could be exchanged through an intermediating technology. The pair of prototypes let people have the hands-on experience of creating, sending, and receiving subtle sensual messages.

The Kiss Communicator

> In this example, "getting into the mood" became a significant set-up task for successfully communicating the proposed experience.
>
> The Kiss Communicator was a concept prototype built to explore ways of using technology to communicate with another person in a subtle, sensual way. The intention was to keep the nature of the physical object as simple as possible, so the interaction was more about the experience of the message.
>
> Designed to facilitate the exchange of emotional content between people separated by physical distance, the Kiss Communicator used wireless technology to transmit the digital equivalent of a personal gesture, such as a wave, wink, or a kiss. Each Communicator connects only with a specific corresponding module, resulting in a secure and intimate one-on-one exchange. To let a partner know that you are thinking of her or him, you squeeze the Communicator gently. It responds with a slight glow to invite you to blow into it and create your "message" in the form of an animated light sequence as the

■ Kiss Communicator

device responds to your breath. The "message" shows while you blow and if you are happy with it, you simply relax your grip and it is sent to the corresponding Communicator. On the other end, the partner Kiss Communicator indicates that there is a message but waits until its owner squeezes it to play back the light sequence.

There are some important conditions necessary to really appreciate the experiencing of this prototype: an intimate relationship, two distant people, sending a gesture, etc. Now imagine sharing this concept with clients in their business suits in a conference room. To help set the scene for the experience in this formal context the designers now usually preface the hands-on experience of the prototype with a short video sequence which shows a pair of the devices being used by a dreamy couple who are working apart. Using conventional devices like soft focus and a romantic soundtrack, the video creates, at least temporarily, an atmosphere that is more appropriate. This situation exemplifies how traditional and more passive communication techniques (like video) and experience prototypes can work hand-in-hand, with the goal of sharing a new user experience with an audience.

The design process, like other creative endeavors, leaps from synthesis to idea without rationale. Inspiration is hard to trust for the recipient, so the designer relies on showing the result to convince the audience. The proof is in the prototype. Seeing may be believing, but "touching is reality," as Alan Kay said.

The demo that changed the world

We see a prime example of the power of the prototype to communicate in the very first interview in the book. When Doug Engelbart demonstrated his interactive system in real time, in front of an audience at the Fall Joint Computer Conference in 1968, the computer science community moved from skepticism to standing ovation in an hour and a half, and the ideas of direct manipulation of a graphical user interface became lodged in the communal consciousness.

Doug sat at a console in the middle of the stage, with the twenty-foot screen behind him showing the view from the video feeds. The overhead camera showed his right hand using a mouse to point and select with, a standard typewriter keyboard in the center, and a five-key command pad under his left hand. The prototype of the graphical user interface was communicated and the dominant design was in place.

Inventing toys and games

We see another example in chapter 5, "Play," when Brendan Boyle describes his process for inventing a toy or a game. A team gets good at producing results if they are dedicated to understanding play and focus on coming up with new ideas that have a chance of succeeding in the marketplace. They spend a lot of time brainstorming, which yields a stream of new concepts. They build prototypes of the designs that are close to the intended result, so that they can try them out on kids and see if they like them. Having the kids play with the prototypes is essential to inform the iterative processes of prototyping. When they have confidence in the design, they make new and improved versions to communicate to the companies that they hope will license the design, presenting them as working prototypes, supported by videos that show young players enjoying them.

Dynamic documents

Joy Mountford described a dramatic example of the persuasive communicating power of a prototype in her interview in chapter 8, "Multisensory and Multimedia," in the story of bringing QuickTime to the personal computer. She was at the stage when her team had a series of illustrative prototypes running demonstrations of what looked like little movies inside documents. She managed to waylay Jean-Louis Gassée, president of the Apple Products Division at the time, and show him the prototypes. He saw a couple of movies playing, with some text all around them. He stopped, and said, "Now I know why my grandmother wants a computer!" From that moment forward he was convinced of the value of dynamic documents.

Pick-and-drop

The Interaction Lab at Sony's Computer Science Laboratory in Tokyo is full of working prototypes, which Jun Rekimoto uses to communicate his vision of the future of interactive technology. For example, when he wants to communicate the value of being able to move information between a PDA and wall screen or desktop computer, he shows that you can simply pick an object up in one computer and drop it into another. The demonstration of pick-and-drop in the Interaction Lab allows you to use a stylus to select an icon on one computer, which then disappears from the screen. When you tap on the screen of another computer, the icon appears on that screen and the file has been transferred. It works like "cut" and "paste," but instead of imagining a virtual clipboard, it feels more like the file was virtually attached to the stylus. This "drag and drop" approach is much more direct than anything we use today between separate devices. Even a memory stick requires several steps to transfer the data.

Jun believes that in the near future people will be using combinations of multiple devices, posing a challenge for interaction design, as most interfaces so far have been designed in the context of a single computer. He thinks that it will be possible to build on the concept of direct manipulation across platforms, leveraging the familiarity with drag-and-drop that people have experienced with the graphical user interface. His prototypes communicate the potential.

Prototyping Techniques

The categories that Jane Fulton Suri and Marion Buchenau devised help us think about why we want a prototype, so the purpose is the first consideration to drive the choice of what kind of prototypes to use. It is striking that there is such a wide variety of types of prototype, fueled by the increasing complexity of design contexts. I therefore thought it worth looking at the different types of prototyping technique as a separate topic and mentioning a few that I have found particularly useful.

Prototyping techniques are much more likely to change over time than user research methods, because they depend on our rapidly evolving technology rather than on our slowly evolving selves. The tools that we use to build a prototype are constantly changing, with new possibilities emerging all the time. I therefore look first at techniques, as people can choose their currently preferred tool.

I have enlisted help from Duane Bray to put together this discussion. He is another of my friends and colleagues based in the San Francisco location of IDEO, so first let me introduce him.

■ Duane Bray

Photo
Skylar Reeves

Duane Bray

Duane Bray studied to be a print graphic designer at the University of Florida. When he was designing posters and books, he discovered that he was much less interested in paper and inks than he was in navigational structures; how do you find your way around a book or perceive a poster? Then he got a job as a "digital designer" and found himself confronted with the challenge of designing screens for early online applications, where he could control the experience that unfolds for the user by manipulating the underlying structure. This was interesting enough to make him want to go back to study, and he returned to the University of Florida for a master's in "electronic intermedia."

He joined IDEO in San Francisco just as the group of interaction designers there was starting to flourish and rose to become the head of discipline for the whole company. In this role he is responsible for helping the community of practitioners to develop shared skills and a common philosophy about their work.

He has found that the strongest common bond that the members of this community bring to their work is a passionate interest in designing experiences, particularly temporal ones. He structures interdisciplinary teams for projects to allow the interaction designers to work with the other disciplines in a flexible way, sometimes contributing an understanding of navigation and flow, or perhaps an expertise in creating beautiful interface animations and behaviors. He is used to explaining the "what, why, and how" of designing interactions, and he thinks of interaction design in three main categories:

1. Screen-based experiences

The earliest to emerge was screen graphics, or pixel-based experiences, where the designer manipulates pixels to express software interactions. This is similar to the more recent skill needed to design for the Internet, as Web sites are also designed as screen graphics.

2. Interactive products

The second version is where the physical object is integrated with the electronic hardware and software. If a screen is embedded, the designer must consider the relationship to physical controls and the overall form factor. If there is no screen, the design relies on ambient feedback, using light, sound, or movement.

3. Services

The third is in the design of services, where the interactivity occurs between a company and the broader relationship with the customer, blending time-based interactions with multiple channels—spaces, products, the Web, and so on. This blurrs the boundaries between interaction design and organizational psychology.

When we look at the prototyping techniques that are needed for each of Duane's three categories, we find that the menu of possible techniques is almost complete by the time we have discussed screen-based experiences, as the other two categories usually also use pixel-based visual displays for output. The other categories add some requirements for additional techniques, as the means that the designer can use to enhance the users' experience are more than screen-based.

The categories are discussed below with some examples.

1. Screen-Based Experiences

In the early days of graphical user interfaces, the visual skills of a professional designer were usually applied to the design of icons, or the visual representations of behaviors such as window structures or tool bars, or perhaps at a more basic level to design typefaces. In these cases the pixels were a disappointing limitation, as seventy-two little squares per inch gives much less opportunity for artistic expression than the fluid forms of metal type, or the free flow of three hundred dots per inch. Designers, like Duane and I, who are attracted to this pixel-based world, find ourselves interested in the underlying behaviors combined with the limited pixels, so that we can create time-based user experiences as well as static graphics.

When the use of the Internet exploded, and every company realized that it needed a Web site, much of the early work was done by graphic designers. For the first iteration, they often translated a company's page-based print collateral material directly to the Web, just to establish a presence on the Internet. The limited resolution degraded the graphics and did little to exploit the behavioral advantages of the Web. Soon companies like Razorfish emerged, specializing in designing solutions for the new economy that were more than paper solutions applied to screens. Web sites started to be designed to deliver experiences that were more sophisticated, taking advantage of animation and the behavioral possibilities.

Initially design for software was quite distinct from design for the Web, but once they both started to understand how to design behaviors as well as pixels, they blended together much more. Duane describes a more current trend:

> The other thing I think the Web is starting to do is blend the boundary between the Web and interactive media, because the Web now can be a much more dynamic medium than it was before, especially with things like Flash and dynamic HTML. It has given people the ability to think about creating narratives, more like film and video. Instead of being a very static, print-based experience, as it was in the mid nineties, the Web has become animated. It can be designed more like software or interactive media.

EXAMPLE

Paper prototyping—in very early, sketch-based prototypes like these, designers can still simulate the user experience (note the use of the smaller post-it to represent a pull-down menu), but ineffective solutions can simply be placed in the recycling bin.

Here are some prototyping techniques that can be used in the design of screen-based experiences, first in the early phases of exploration, and then in the design of the images and behaviors on displays.

1.1 Screen-based experiences: Early exploration

In the early stages of understanding existing screen-based experiences and exploring ideas, the techniques that are useful are shared across all of Duane's categories. They are chosen to help members of a design team generate and share concepts as quickly as possible, and are driven more by the behavior of people than the specifically screen-based nature of the output. This group can therefore apply to all three categories.

The techniques in the "Try" category of the methods cards fit into this group, as do the examples used to clarify the first group in the "Experience Prototyping" paper. They were the game to understand the interaction context for the underwater remote operated camera, the "guided fantasy" devised by Tim Mott for the design of a screen-based publishing system, and the exercise that had people draw their money during the early phases of the design of an online bank.

Don't forget paper

You can do such a lot with paper. Designers are often too quick to start working in the final medium of their project. For a design where they know the result will be on a pixel-based screen of a particular resolution, they often leap straight into that medium. They can then find themselves sucked down into the details of "pixel pushing," when they should still be experimenting with the basic constraints of usability and perceived value. Paper is accessible and so versatile. You can quickly sketch, lay out, and evaluate interaction design concepts for basic usability, making it possible to rapidly organize, articulate, and visualize interaction design concepts.

You can also demonstrate the structure and behavior of a screen interface using paper mockups, separating the different components of the interactivity. Elements of the interface that will be separate on the screen can be attached to separate pieces of paper, like for example a pop-up or flying menu. You can

EXAMPLE

Designing a handheld media device, the design team used scenario cards to prototype early concepts, asking potential users to evaluate them.

sketch out ideas, by hand or with a graphics program, and then assemble them on a background of appropriate size and content. This allows you to demonstrate the possible behaviors by hand manipulations, with no need for time consuming scripting for animations, and because these lo-fi prototypes are not precious, they invite more honest comment and critique by users than "perfect looking" screens rendered in Photoshop. You can talk this through with colleagues, or show it to stakeholders, and you will find that the speed with which you can make changes and the informality of style help communication. If there is a particular piece of animation that you want to describe, you can make up a little "flip book" to communicate changes over time.

Remember the whole journey

The context of a particular design solution is often too narrow. Designers tend to explain their work within a limited framework that has been imposed from somewhere else. Perhaps they have focused on the constraints within the screen design, without understanding what happened before or after, or in a more systemic context. The idea of the whole journey is very useful to challenge the limits of a context. When we go back to the basics of the experience that a person has as a whole and think about what happens from start to finish, we often find areas of design opportunity.

Prototype techniques that are useful for this more expansive approach tend to push beyond the screen and are therefore more related to role and enactment than specific screens, so we will return to them in the group of techniques associated with designing services. Even within screen-based experience design, however, the journey notion can help to extend a context over time and force us to consider the different situations that will occur.

1.2 Exploring, evaluating, and communicating design ideas

The prototyping techniques that you need for designing screens have to combine two-dimensional graphic representations with changes over time. The graphics are usually structured as pixels, but there are some exceptions, such as liquid crystal displays, where there are fixed image elements that are on or off. These

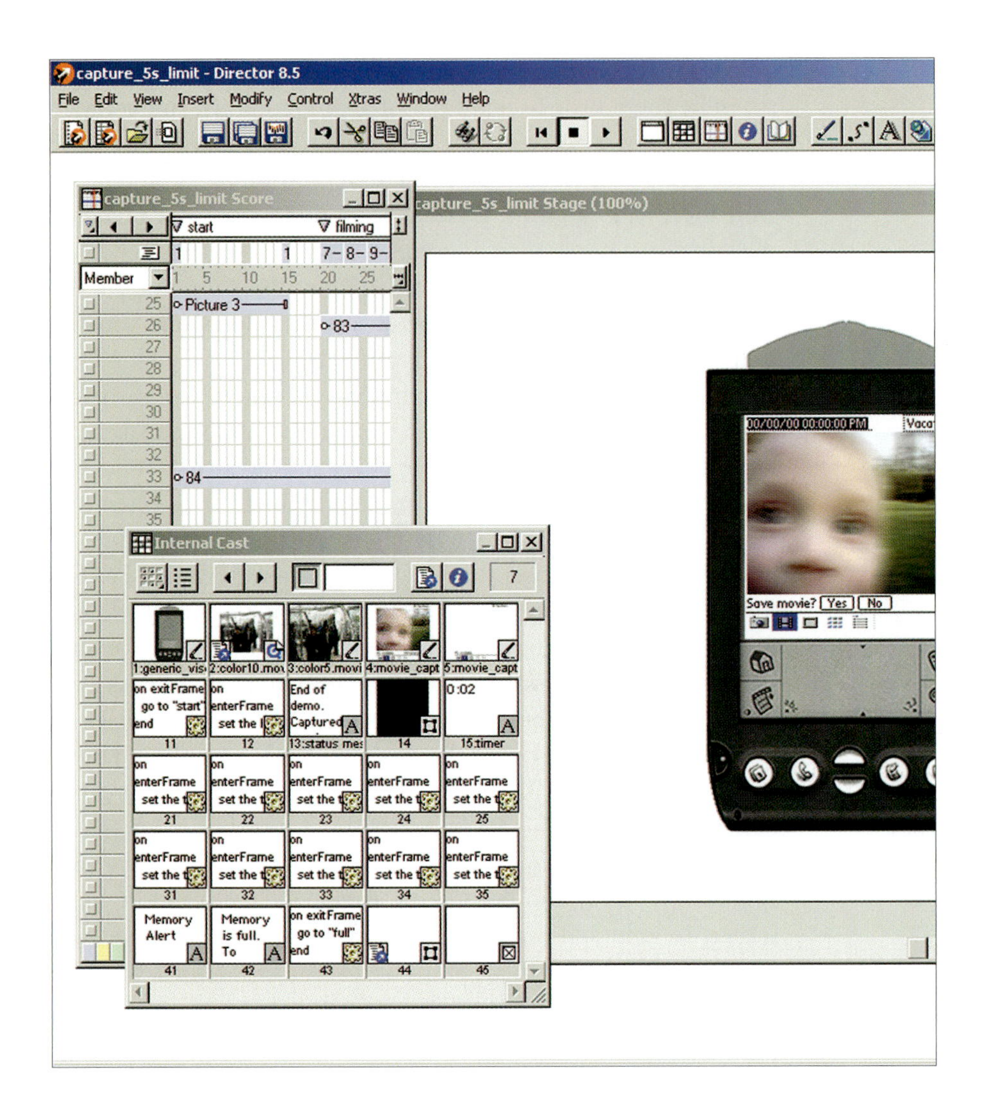

EXAMPLE

This interactive simulation is being created using MacroMedia Director, another iteration in the design development of the camera interface for a PDA. The prototypes were used to develop the design and test users, redesigning the approach until the right balance had been reached between the interactions that were consistent with the Palm operating system resident on the PDA and the interactions that would be familiar to users of digital cameras.

simple requirements have been met by a large number of prototyping tools aimed at designers, including HyperCard, Supercard, Visual Basic, VideoWorks, and Macromind Director.

Director became the clear choice for designers as soon as it was launched, and the company, now called Macromedia, went on to develop a range of tools for prototyping, including more recently tools like Dreamweaver and Flash, for prototyping Web sites. Tim Mott was instrumental in the early success of the company, after he left Electronic Arts, and he talked about his contribution in his interview:

> After I left Electronic Arts I ran a small multimedia company called Macromind. Over a number of years we turned that into a larger multimedia company called Macromedia. The mainstay of the product line was a design tool called Director. When I got to the company the mantra was, "We've got to make Director easier to use, and less expensive, and then we'll be able to turn every secretary in every office into a multimedia designer and producer."
>
> It seemed like a good idea at first, but we realized that, independent of the tool, not every secretary in every office had the design sensibility to become a multimedia producer. In fact, the users of that product were, and needed to be, professional multimedia designers.
>
> We reversed the strategy. We went out and talked to the users of the product, and found that they didn't care that it was difficult to use because it was so much better than anything else they had. What they cared about was additional functionality. I spent a lot of my career trying to figure out how to make things easier for everyday use, and then I found myself back into the business of building rockets for rocket scientists!
>
> Subsequently the company worked on products much more limited in functionality, and that were much easier to use, and could address the needs of a broader audience. You see some of that today in PowerPoint for instance; there are limited media capabilities in PowerPoint, and it's pretty easy for anyone to learn to use, but you wouldn't find a professional multimedia designer using PowerPoint because it doesn't have anywhere near enough capability.

Director established Macromedia as the primary company to deliver prototyping tools for interaction designers. Today that

EXAMPLE

An axonometric view of the layers in the screen design can help to explain the structure, clarifying the difference between the control layer at the front, the content layer at the back and the system layer in between. This example from 2001 shows a Web-based user interface from an IT application service provider (ASP) aggregator.

trend continues, but more and more interaction designers are using Flash, rather than Director, as their prototyping tool of choice. PowerPoint or Keynote are enough for early sketches and simple transitions.

Live prototyping

There is a recent trend for prototyping tools and methods for interaction designers to converge with the development tools and techniques used by software engineers who are writing code. Most of the techniques described so far have been useful for prototyping the design of the experience and have not been directly connected to the world of software development. Whether the interaction designer was using paper, Supercard, or even Macromedia Director, a translation was needed for the development engineers to make sense of the design and start to develop algorithms and code. The translation was usually in the form of a specification document of some sort, to transition from design to development, but this tended to leave plenty of opportunity for errors and misunderstandings, so the final implemented product would often fail to match the early design. Duane explains the trend that is called "live prototyping":

> Prototyping tools have been moving closer and closer to real-world code. An example of that is Flash, a tool that has a scripting language associated with it, but unlike the "designer friendly" English language based scripting language, it is something that is much closer in syntax to a true programming language. For example, someone who knows Java can easily use Flash. Tools have been created for "rich Internet applications"—for example, Macromedia Flex and Lazlo—that allow people with software development experience to create Flash applications, without ever actually using the nice-looking graphical interface, just working at the XML code level.
>
> Director and Flash used to use a sequential timeline of the screens, as well as describing what happens on individual screens. As the coding has become more sophisticated, what you end up with is this long movie format, with one frame and a whole bunch of code that updates that frame as you interact, so it is much closer to a real software application.

Photo Credit

EXAMPLE

Prototyping tools such as Dreamweaver or Flash can be used to try out screen behaviors for Web sites, incorporating animations, sound and video, in a realistic equivalent of the final result. A Web site like this from Isse Miyake (www.isseymiyake.com—2003) could be prototyped and tested with these tools.

> You see examples on the Web, where people are able to take Flash tools, or Flash applications, and embed them within a Website, forming a product that can actually be shipped. You also hear more and more about companies that are willing to accept a "Flash front end" that accesses a database and that becomes your prototyping tool. The boundary between prototyping tools and the development world is blurring.

This chance to access real databases using prototyping tools is a huge leap forward for interaction designers. "Live prototyping" can give you the opportunity to run user tests with large numbers of participants as you develop the design, so that each attempt teaches the lessons of reality and gives the designer the chance to try again with the knowledge of what worked for people.

Terry Winograd pointed to an example of this in chapter 7, "Services," when he took a sabbatical from Stanford to spend a year at Google. He was excited to be there, because this was the first company that he had consulted with that was having a major impact on the market place. He enjoyed the direct connection to the needs and demands of serving hundreds of millions of people, trying to understand what kinds of things they use and do, and marveling at the ease with which it was possible to try out prototypes with enormous numbers of users.

Live prototyping and the evolution of prototyping tools are all about moving closer and closer to the implemented result. The culture of software development, where people share sample code or comment on their code as a way to build communities, has parallels in the prototyping world. You can easily go online and find people sharing code as a way to help one another out, so people are learning prototyping tools in a similar way to how they used to learn new programming languages.

EXAMPLE

A cell phone is an example of a product where screen interactions are integrated with physical and tactile behaviors. This Sony CMD-J5 Dualband Mobile Phone from 2001 shows a combination of lively screen graphics with various controls, but the audible and vibration aspects of the interface cannot be seen from the photographs.

2. Interactive Products

THE SECOND OF the three categories of interaction design that Duane Bray defines is in the context of products. The need for a new kind of design is triggered by the ability of everyday objects to "behave," enabled by interactive technology. This is the version of interaction design where the physical object is integrated with the electronic hardware and software, and people are interacting with ubiquitous computing devices, sometimes not thinking of them as computers at all but rather as products that are responsive or intelligent in some way.

To prototype the behavior of an object, you need tools and techniques that can simulate behaviors of the physical things that are both digital and interactive. For generic computers, whether desktop or laptop, the physical objects are input devices—keyboards, mice, track pads, tablets, and so on—where the traditional prototyping techniques of product design work well enough as long as user testing is cognizant of the interactive tasks that will be required, as with the tests for the Microsoft mouse described above.

The new challenge for interactive products occurs when the physical object and the electronic behavior are integrated. The cell phone has a screen and push buttons, but it also has rotary controls, or perhaps a jog shuttle, slider switches, acoustic feedback, ringing tones, and a vibration behavior for the silent mode. How do you prototype all that? The techniques are similar to those used for mechanical engineering and electronic hardware and do not need to be specific to designing interactions. Simple mockups are useful in the early stages of the design, using any tools that are at hand, perhaps random objects taped together, mockups constructed from foamcore board, or Lego, using the MindStorm robotic invention system to add some behaviors.

Sometimes it is important to engage team members in radical design ideas before they are fully resolved. For example, in an exploration of television remote controls, the designer wanted to explore the specific experience of switching channels, while

ignoring other aspects of functionality or look and feel. He was especially interested in exploring the implications of a more intuitive and multisensory design solution. He created what he called "behavioral sketches" which were simple electronic circuits containing a few lines of code (Basic Stamps™), encased in off-the-shelf soap dishes. Two experience prototypes were controlled by a tilting gesture, switching channels up or down, one with visual feedback with moving bands of light and the other with tactile feedback using vibrations. By tinkering with the simple software program, he was able to quickly develop and test subtle iterations of product behaviors and user experiences.

The photograph opposite of the workbench associated with the "musical mobile" shows a typical collection of hardware components for prototyping simple electronic circuits, combined with the prototype parts for the physical form of the device. The integration of these prototyping techniques with the screen-based methods requires ingenuity, but nothing completely new for the experienced prototyper. The advent of programmable chips like the "Basic Stamp" has made the prototyping of interactive products accessible to interaction designers.

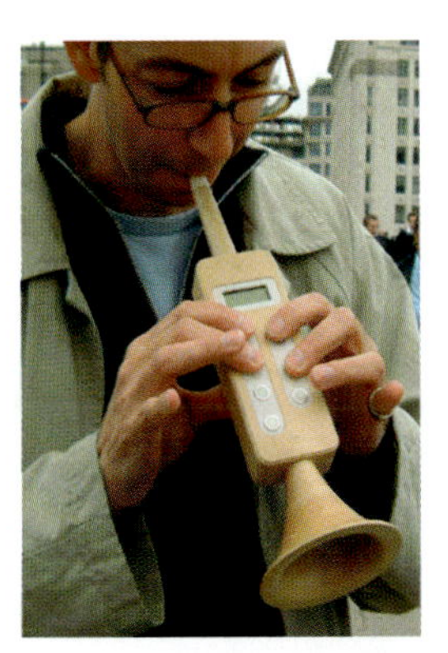

EXAMPLE

This "musical mobile" was one of the Social Mobiles in a research project, which commented on the social problems that are caused by mobile phones. The phone requires you to play the tune of the phone number that you want to call. The public performance that dialing demands, makes you look somewhat ridiculous, so you have to be a pretty confident that it is appropriate to make a call in that time and place. The prototypes were built using the electronic hardware in the photograph and simple code on programmable chips.

NOKIA
[My Locker]
Games
Ringtones
Pictures
Take Me Home
Help
Add to My mMode
Share This Page
Exit
Options
NOKIA
[Spotlight]
Site of the Day:
Corbis Gallery
Latest & Greatest
Special Offers
People's Choice
Pam's Picks
Options
Exit
NOKIA
[mMode Home]
My mMode
Spotlight
mMode Guide
Games & Tones
Mail & Messaging
Search
Where I've Been
Options
Exit
NOKIA
[My mMode]
ESPN Leaderboard
Wired Magazine
Media Line
New For You
New to My mMode
Manage My mMode
My Account
Options
Exit

3. Designing Services

THE THIRD KIND of interaction design described by Duane Bray is the design of services, where the interactivity occurs between a company and the broader relationship with the customer. The design of services has usually in the past been thought of in terms of training the employees who work for the service provider, but as technology enabled services have become more prevalent, interaction design is increasingly needed to create successful solutions. The need to articulate processes for the design of services is a recently emerging challenge, so chapter 6 of this book is devoted to the subject. Duane sums it up this way:

> The service category to me is an interesting one, because there may be outcomes which you would look at and say that they are very specifically something that an interaction designer would do, but often there is something there which is about designing the relationship or the interaction that a company has with its customers. That is much less tangible.

■ AT&T mMode service

Photo Courtesy of IDEO

As an example, Duane was working on the design of a new service for AT&T Wireless, called "mMode." The company was facing the challenge created by the late arrival of cellular phone services in the USA. Europe and Japan had been evolving mobile phone services over a long enough period for people to get used to the new types of functionality on offer, but in the USA the situation was suddenly changing. Cell phone coverage had been incomplete enough to drive competition on the basis of the ability to make a call, so that people were thinking about their mobile phone as only useful for voice conversations. Suddenly they were offered a phone with a camera in it, so that they could send pictures to people, or they could trade stocks on the phone. It was necessary to reposition the phone as a much more multipurpose lifestyle tool. The team developed a design philosophy for the new service that could be applied to the whole offering, whether it was text messaging, data-services, or photography. Duane describes the prototyping techniques:

With live prototyping, we have the ability to embed prototypes in the real world in the way that they would be as finished products. We can also connect them to actual data, so that they can make use of real-world content. For the AT&T Wireless project, we prototyped a new way to have a user interaction running within the cell phone's browser. We were able to create an initial prototype of the experience and put it up on a server that we could point our mobile phones to, to prototype and test as if it were the running service.

Because our prototyping tools are becoming more sophisticated, we were using XHTML and using the same tools as the in-house developers, so there was no effective difference between the prototype and the finished product, either in appearance on the phone, or in the reality of the code; it was just a matter of who actually owned and created that code. For the prototype it was us, and for the final product it was the software developers at AT&T Wireless.

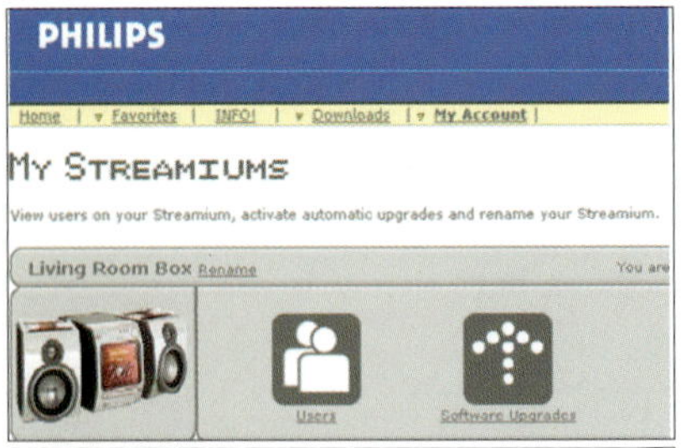

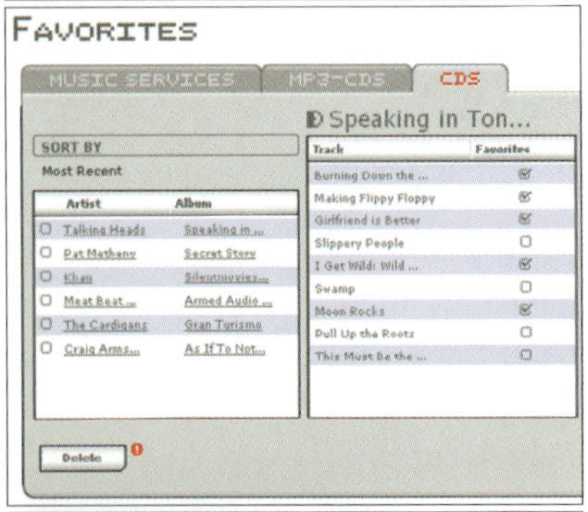

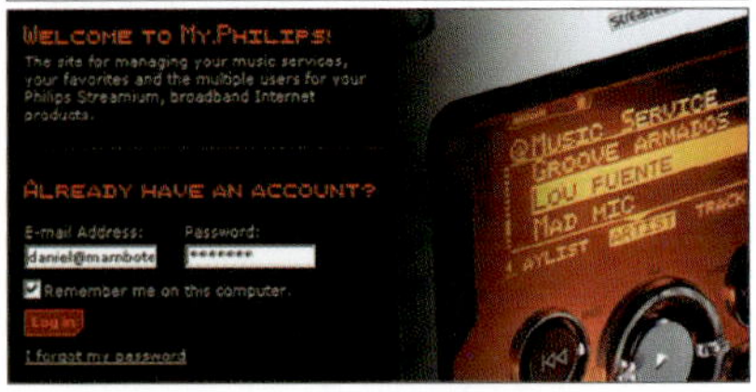

When you are designing a complete service, your contexts and constraints are intrinsically complex. They are formed by the combination of all the individual interactions, whether technology-based or human-to-human, which make up the various touch-points within the service. This makes the use of live prototyping even more valuable, as the results of testing the prototypes are much more likely to be realistic.

Duane also cites the example of his helping the team work on a service called Streamium from Philips, which allows people to access digital content for entertainment, including music and video:

We prototyped a version of it in Flash that was remote control-driven, for TV or Media center use. Just testing the user interface of browsing categories was not very effective. One of the challenges of this user interface was that there is such a wealth of content out there, including so many digital radio stations, so many different playlists, and all these different archives. What you want to be able to experience in the prototype is not the subset of that world that you might be able to think about or code in. You actually need the reality of the scalability of the actual content that is out there. A live prototype is needed to go out onto the Internet, access the content, and update it dynamically. From a user experience

- Philips Streamium—personalization
- Philips Streamium—favorites
- Philips Streamium—splash screen

perspective the prototype was the same as the final product, although Philips did not develop the final version in Flash.

There is often a disconnect between the design process and the real world. We like to have a small and comfortable set of parameters to work within. For example, if we are designing a new operating system, we don't actually prototype the situation when you have ten thousand files to work with. Lack of scalability often hurts our design solutions. With the Philips example we allowed scalability to intrude into the design process by accessing the real-world material.

Designers and developers are converging

Live prototyping is not the only trend that is pushing software developers and designers together. Another is called "Xtreme programming" (XP). This approach to software development adopts some of the principles of human-centered design. A "client" is appointed as an end-user advocate to work within the team, and the developers use both collaboration and iteration techniques that are similar to the design process. Duane enjoys the convergence:

> When we've worked with clients where Xtreme programming exists, the developers are pre-wired toward understanding and embracing the process that we're using; the process of going out into the world and understanding end users, and turning those into insights and opportunities. They try things out repeatedly, knowing that they are not perfect the first time and learning from the imperfections as they evolve. They collaborate, realizing that the value of the team is greater than the value of the single individual contributor. That process is sometimes very alien to traditional software developers, who work in isolation on a piece of the whole.
>
> One of the big challenges in software development is the notion that code is precious; once you've got something in code, you can't possibly throw it away if it's inappropriate, because too much value has been put into it. That used to be one of our philosophical disconnects with software developers.
>
> In Xtreme programming, people code in pairs for a particular iteration and rotate the pairings over the process of development, so you are cross-pollinating the entire team. This gives you collaboration and cross-pollination happening at the same time. You build

> constantly! One statistic that I read was that an Xtreme programming team of forty people might have eight to ten builds of their product in a day. The idea is that you always make something that you can use, even if it's only the tiniest piece of a feature. You always make something that can be validated. Validation is against the "client," who represents the end user, or it could also be sent out for end user validation.
>
> It is a way to say, "We believe that this product has all of these features, and needs to do all of these things." You are testing the reality by iterating on as many of those components as you can, and seeing how they work. Then you can either eliminate the feature, change its importance, or modify it based on what you find out. This set up makes the train of thought of the programming team mirror what is happening in human-centered design, so designers don't have to be evangelists for user validation, or iteration, or collaboration; it's there!

Space matters

The design of the work environment itself affects the way that people can collaborate and cross-pollinate ideas. In order to develop the kind of collaborative pattern required for the Xtreme programming model, and also for interdisciplinary design teams, one has to provide open and flexible workspaces, with furniture that is easy to move, and portable equipment, such as laptops that can communicate wirelessly. Not many of the major software development companies are providing environments like this. One of the reasons that Microsoft has such an enormous campus of buildings is that every developer has his or her own office. If you look through the halls, you see endless rows of offices, where each person can close the door and feel free to work on their individual piece of the puzzle.[27] There's nothing about the design of the space that helps people come together. Duane describes the contrast between this and the offices of Xtreme programmers.

> I visited a client where they're trying to use some of those principles. There you see shared offices where between two and four people are working together. They delineate the individual space where their computer is, but they also have public space in each office where they come together. The same client also has very public open spaces,

where people can come together to collaborate, share, work around a computer or whatever. When you look at what the people are doing there, you see something that looks exactly like the offices of an interdisciplinary design team. They are using the same principles! I think that if schools of thought like that become more and more adopted, we are going to see a world where design and development can work hand in hand much more easily than they have in the past.

We know that we can do that successfully at IDEO; it is in our culture. It will be great to find ways of doing it in collaboration with our clients, to create that sense of telepathy.

Process

▪ A community of design practitioners from IDEO looking through stereo glasses

Photo
Joe Watson/IDEO

As a designer, I am much better at synthesis than analysis, so I am short on good theories about designing interactions, but I can tell you in practice how I do it. To finish my story, here is a description of the process that I have evolved for designing interactions, working with my colleagues as a community of practitioners. I have done my best to explain why interaction design exists, and how interaction designers contribute to the development process. I have stated my belief that if you are going to create good designs, you first have to understand people—what they need, want and enjoy, as well as how they think and behave. I talked about my conviction that the practice of designing interactions is enabled by prototyping, that we arrive at good designs by prototyping early and often, by trying out ideas as quickly and frequently as possible, and by taking them to the users for responses and evaluations.

Is this focus on people and prototypes enough? Can we rely on just those two simple strategies to create excellent designs? I'm afraid not, as the constraints will come from the full context of the design problem, not just the people. Even so, a focus on the people is important enough to be the best place to start and is particularly valuable when we are designing something new; if we are designing a new version of something that already exists, we have to be sure that we have a full understanding of the "state of the art"—the constraints that defined the previous result.

Designing Something New

THE KEYWORDS OF "people and prototypes" are needed most when you want to design something that has no precedent, where innovation is the only possibility. The essential first step will be to start from understanding the latent needs and desires of the people who will use the design. You are not just designing for the average person either; you will need to understand the viewpoints of the full range of people who will interact with the outcome, from the slowest to the fastest, the most naive to the most expert, and the least experienced to the most fluent. They will probably be surprisingly different from you, so it will only be by understanding them that you can avoid the trap of designing for yourself.

The keywords of "people and prototypes" are needed most when innovation is the only possibility.

The context of the design problem is not just the people. You will need to understand as much as possible about everything that will affect the solution: what it is for, how it will work, how much it will cost, and so on. Each of the team members will need to listen and learn from all of the other experts to find out as much as they can about the context in a short first burst of discovery, but without worrying about not understanding everything.

You, that is, the collective "team you," will need to stop researching and let your tacit understanding of the problem help you come up with design ideas, creative leaps, and first solutions. Prototype as quickly and roughly as possible, just enough to communicate each concept to one another. Then evaluate the designs. They are most likely really bad solutions, so try again. If the ideas seem a little better next time, you can make the prototypes a bit more descriptive. Perhaps the evaluation this time will be with end users as well as your peers. That will probably be a shock: "Why don't they think more like me?" Try again! Prototype early and often, making each iterative step a little more realistic but minimizing the time and effort invested each time, relying instead on the learning that feeds your subconscious each time you try. At some point you will know that you have arrived at a good design, both from your shared intuitive judgment and from the way the people who are evaluating your attempts react. When their response changes from critique to involvement in the result, you can start to hope that you are on the right track.

Designing a New Version

IF YOU ARE designing a new version of something that already exists, "state of the art" is the most useful starting point. The chance to set a precedent with something completely new is rare. In most cases you are designing a new version of something that is already there, so you can research what has been done before, learn the lessons from previous attempts, discover guiding principles, and extract knowledge from the precedents. There is design wisdom out there, but it takes time to shake out.

Thinking about the people that will use the design is just as important, and the process of working through iterative versions of your solution with prototypes and evaluation will still be the best and fastest way to get to a good design. The difference is that you need to spend more time and effort understanding what has already been done in the first place, so that you are building on the state of the art rather than trying to reinvent solutions that others have developed before. The research phase that comes before the first design solution or creative leap must be thorough; your team must catch up with everything that has already been done.

Look at the competition, try the previous designs, research the literature, understand the design principles, compare and criticize alternative versions, get to the point that your shared mind is so full of the existing designs that you can drop them back into your subconscious, and know that whatever you come up with will automatically build on the past. Once you have reached that state, you can move back into the iterative design process of thinking about other people, coming up with an idea, building a prototype, and trying it out.

I hope that this book is in itself a good summary of the state of the art for designing interactions and that the collection of interviews will help you discover relevant constraints for your design contexts. When I look back at the material, I am conscious that it takes time to establish a state of the art. The chapter about designing services has very little in the way of notes referring to

If you are designing
a new version of something
that already exists,
"state of the art"
is the most useful
starting point.

- Bruce Tognazzini
- Jakob Nielsen
- Don Norman

well-established principles and knowledge of the subject, because at time of writing, technology-enabled services are only just emerging as an opportunity area for interaction design.

In contrast to services, the design of the personal computer has had time to mature, and there are plenty examples of well-expressed explicit knowledge on the subject. The first two chapters tell stories of the emergence of the dominant designs for personal computing, through the accounts of a few of the people involved. The state of the art for designing interactions with personal computers has been developed by many more people than these. There has been time since the creative confusion of the original invention to articulate the user interface design principles clearly and simply. Take, for example, the work of Bruce Tognazzini, who has explained "The First Principles of Interaction Design," by listing twenty-two principles on his Web site.[28] Bruce founded the Human Interface Group at Apple, where he wrote and performed for the video "WorldBuilder"—expounding the design principles for Macintosh software. He went on to Sun and is now with the Nielsen Norman Group.[29] He has published two books[30] on interaction design, making him a "must read" for any designer who wants to work on screen behaviors for desktops. This set of design principles and constraints is wonderful for us now, but it took a long time to articulate after the original innovation achieved by Larry Tesler and Bill Atkinson. And, by the way, the other members of the Nielsen Norman Group have done a lot to clarify the constraints of interaction design. Jakob Nielsen is known as the guru of Web page usability, and Don Norman has done wonderful work bringing an awareness of usability issues to the design of objects both physical and digital, from "The Psychology of Everyday Things"[31] to "Emotional Design."[32]

These are just a few of the luminaries who have helped designers, and those people who are affected by the designs, to understand more about the new constraints of designing interactions. Their contribution is essential to developing the new design discipline to a level of maturity that has an accessible state of the art and allows it to be learned, taught, and practiced on a larger scale. The work of these people, and of many other members of the HCI community, helps us lift our understanding from the subconscious to the conscious level. It gives us a state of the art to draw upon, so that our process begins with a fast start.

Elements of the Design Process

WE CAN GENERALIZE the interaction design process with these ten elements: constraints, synthesis, framing, ideation, envisioning, uncertainty, selection, visualization, prototyping, and evaluation. They will often be used in the same sequence, and repeated iteratively, but the most productive process is usually out of order; it can sometimes seem almost random. Remember that pinball machine analogy.

The fastest progress toward a successful design will be made when these elements are used quickly and repeated frequently, but usually not in the same order!

Constraints

Understanding the relevant constraints starts the process. The constraints come from everywhere that matters to the project. The "State of the Art," the needs and wants of the users, their preconceptions, mental models and expectations, brand awareness, functional constraints, technology, environment, financial constraints, business constraints, competitive analysis, conversations with relevant people, briefing discussions, brainstorms, and on and on—everything that could be important. The constraints must be absorbed by the subconscious mind of the designer or designers. If the context is complex, a design team is more likely to succeed than an individual, so the "shared mind" of the team will be entrusted to absorb the information.

Synthesis

Synthesis occurs as the subconscious, shared mind of the design team (or the designer if the problem is simple) absorbs all of the relevant issues. The ability of the team members to synthesize ideas is an essential skill of design thinking. The ideas may be about design solutions or other elements in the process, such as a framework or the nature of an experiment or prototype. The tacit

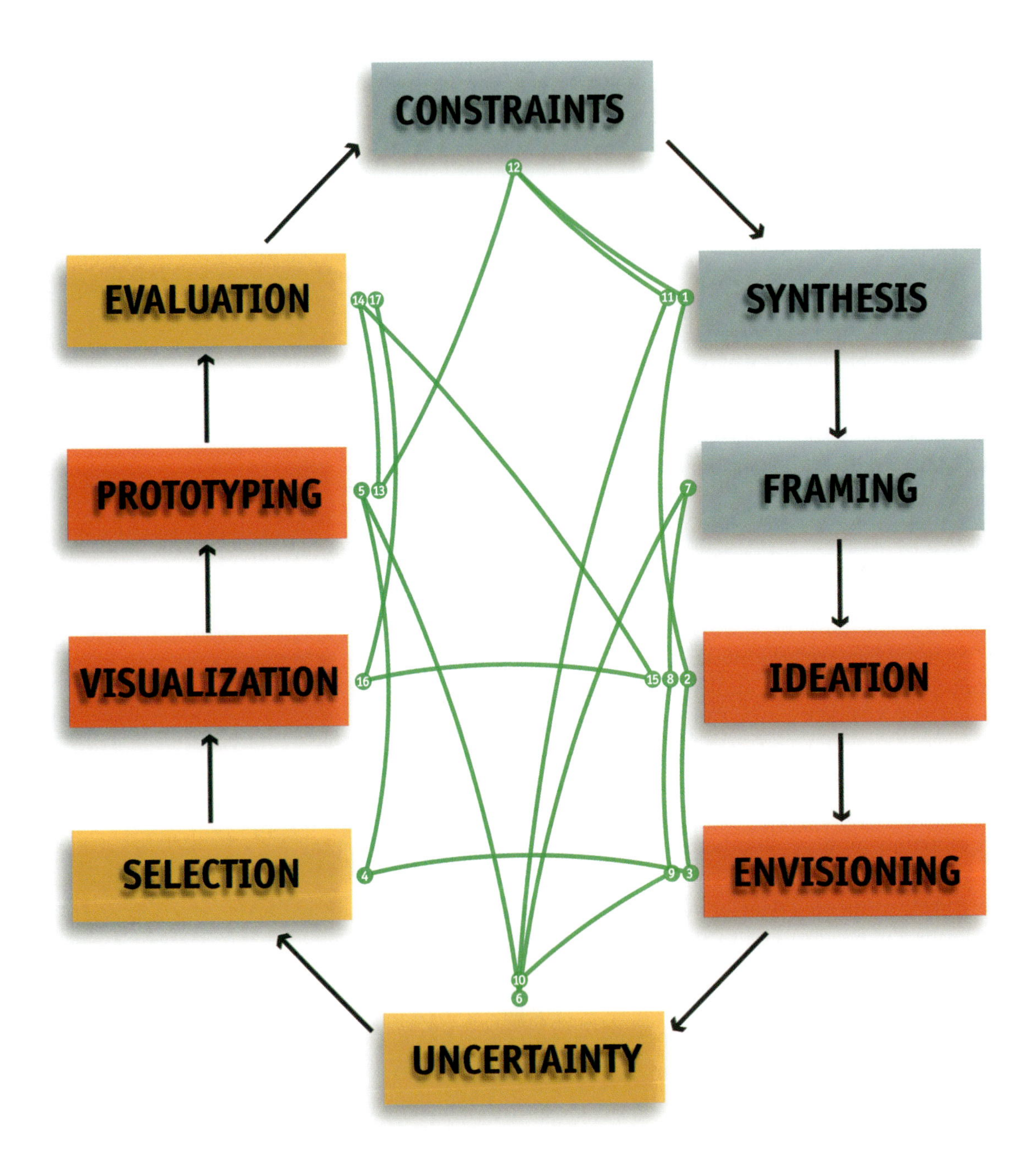

The dark arrows show a general tendency toward a cyclical process, with the color coding of the titles indicating activities of similar types. In real life, as is illustrated by the project shown in the green sequence, the pattern is complex and less orderly than a clockwise cycle.

understanding of the constraints allows the subconscious background processing of information to be happening all the time. This background synthesis explains why people who work in design teams often come up with significant ideas without knowing where they come from. They say, "I had this idea last night," or "I suddenly realized as we were talking . . .". Because it is subconscious, the element of synthesis is not usually mentioned in explicit descriptions of the creative design process. It is vital to success, however, and needs to be appreciated, planned for and enabled. A successful team will feel relaxed enough to synthesize well, but a stressful atmosphere can get in the way.

Framing

Framing articulates the synthesis simply enough for ideas to happen. A framework is in itself a form of synthesis, in that it clarifies the issues by applying insights that create the first level of order from the chaos of all the constraints. It is not a design idea but forms a way of thinking about and evaluating possible design ideas. Coming up with the right framework for a particular project is also a design process, involving many of the other elements described here. One project may be best framed by a journey through the experience, another by a four quadrant analysis of people's attitudes, and another by a nested hierarchy of attributes. The diagram opposite is in itself an attempt to frame the design process, by showing both a generalized likelihood of a cyclical iterative pattern and a specific example of a much more chaotic individual reality.

■ An iterative process that tends to be cyclical but in practice is flexible and pragmatic

Ideation

When the ideas start to arrive, they are not always great ideas, but they seem to the design team (or designer) to have an "Ah ha" quality when they are first thought of. There are multiple levels of design ideas, some of them encompassing the whole context and others about tiny details. If a good framework is in place, it helps to position the pieces, but ideation happens throughout the process, not just between framing and envisioning.

Defer judgment
• OVERLY ADVANCED FEATURES
• SKID ON THE BOTTOM
KIDS
ROLA TUBE
BOLLARDS
contact lens

Brainstorming can give a fast start to ideation and is often most useful early on, as the constraints are being shaken out. A typical brainstorm at IDEO has eight to ten participants, with one or two experienced recorders, dubbed scribes, who record the ideas as they flow from the group. Each session lasts about an hour, and 50 to 100 ideas are recorded. The conference rooms have the rules of brainstorming printed along the top of white boards, to remind everyone to defer judgement, encourage wild ideas, build on the ideas of others, stay focused on the topic, and to keep to one conversation at a time.

Ideas can come at any time, often from unexpected directions. The cycle is often interrupted by a great idea, triggered by an other element in the process. If there is consensus among team members that a new idea has value, it is usually worth stepping back from the process and going back to first principles to help decide what to do next. A good idea can cause a process reset.

Envisioning

■ Brainstorm at IDEO

Photo
Roberto Carra

Ideas are like dreams until they are visualized into some concrete representation. The representation can be any sort of description of the design, whether visual or behavioral, or a combination. You can use shortcuts when you are communicating to team members or peers, but there must be enough clarity in the representation that you know something of what the design is like. The journey from "head in the clouds" to "feet on the earth" can be sudden and traumatic, as it is the envisioning process that helps you immediately see what the idea is really like. Self-delusion is no longer easy.

Uncertainty

Deep uncertainties are likely to follow envisioning, or visualization, or prototyping for that matter, as you analyze the potential of the solution. The design process is good at generating alternatives and making them realistic enough to evaluate in some way. Uncertainty is a necessary factor as a precursor to selection.

The subconscious "shared mind" (or individual mind) is now busy synthesizing unanswered questions about the validity of each of the alternative ideas. Is it simple enough to understand? Is it consistent with what came before? Can it be made to work quickly? There are always plenty of uncertainties that are worth trying out.

Selection

It is time to choose. A manageable number of alternatives must be chosen to take forward to the next step. When a creative team is working well, there are nearly always too many good ideas, and you have to be firm in choosing the most promising group, without feeling too bad about the need to reject the rest. Lively differences of opinion and discussion are normal during this process, unless a clear leader is entrusted by the organization to take the decisions.

Visualization

The visualization element is closely related to both envisioning and prototyping. It may be a small step from the representation envisioned earlier, or it may be taken a lot further. The difference is that envisioning implies a glimpse into the nature of an idea, but visualization is more complete as a representation; it should be convincing as a communication of the potential reality of the concept. visualization implies a representation that is perceived by the viewer as realistic but may at the same time be dysfunctional. This is in contrast to a prototype, which always looks to test some aspect of functionality. For screen-based experiences, sketches are often useful. For behaviors, some kind of script will be wanted. I use the word "visualization" broadly, implying more possibilities than the merely visual.

Prototyping

Prototyping is about testing any aspect of the way a design is expected to work. You can create a prototype that represents an idea that has been selected and visualized. Alternatively, you can test any uncertainty and come up with the simplest and quickest form of prototype that will allow you to examine it, to decide whether to move forward with that aspect of the idea, or to drop it and try another approach. As the iterative cycle of development progresses, prototypes tend to get more holistic and inclusive. In the early stages you are looking for the roughest possible prototype to help you clarify an uncertainty, but as you approach the final result, the prototype looks more and more like the intended design. The final prototype before release for implementation is likely to include realistic interactions, both for behavior and appearance, which can be tested for evaluation and approval.

Evaluation

In practice, evaluation is needed many times during the development process. In the early iterations, the choices can be made quickly by the team members themselves, or the captive "clients" who are assigned to the process. As the design matures, more complete prototypes are likely to be relevant, like the experience prototypes or the live prototypes that we have talked about, in which case a more thorough and structured user evaluation will be worthwhile. The results of the evaluation can form a new state of the art for the next attempt to create a good design, so the addition of the results to the package of constraints can trigger a new cycle of design development. When you are getting close to a good design, the evaluation process is more likely to yield minor adjustments. By this time it is too late to go back to first principles, but evaluation still helps the design team avoid the pitfalls of narcissism. A good motto for designing interactions is to evaluate early, often, and as late as possible.

Notes

For direct links to Web sites, please visit

www.designinginteractions.com

Foreword

1 See www.interaction-ivrea.it.

2 See excerpts from this interview on the DVD.

3 See the interview with David Liddle in chapter 4, "Adopting Technology," and on the DVD.

4 Mitchell Kapor, "The Software Design Manifesto" (1990), www.kapor.com/writing/index.html.

5 See the interview with Bill Atkinson, the designer of HyperCard, in chapter 2, "My PC," and on the DVD.

6 See the interview with Bill Gaver, the designer of the SonicFinder, in chapter 8, "Multisensory and Multimedia," and on the DVD.

Introduction

1 ". . . the term 'laptop' refers to a device which is easily carried while traveling, has its own source of power, a means of storing suitable amounts of data, a full alphanumeric keyboard for input of text, and a screen suitable for displaying a reasonable amount of text and graphics, at a size which is capable of being supported comfortably and easily on a seated person's lap. By this definition, the 'Compass' computer, designed in 1980, and manufactured by GRiD Computer Systems Corp. was indeed the first true laptop." Paul Atkinson, "Man in a Briefcase," *Journal of Design History* 18, no. 2 (2005), doi:10.1093/jdh/epi024.

2 See the interview with John Ellenby in chapter 3, "From the Desk to the Palm," and on the DVD.

3 See chapter 3, "From the Desk to the Palm," for a description of Alan Kay's thinking.

4 The Texas Instruments Tymshare 100, also known as the Silent 700, used an acoustic coupler modem connected to an ordinary telephone

and a thermal printer as a display combined with output. It was not much larger than a briefcase, but too heavy for comfort.

5 See the interview with Bill Verplank in chapter 2, "My PC," and on the DVD.

1 The Mouse and the Desktop

Interview dates: Doug Engelbart, September 2003; Stu Card, March 2002; Tim Mott, September 2003; Larry Tesler, October 2003.

1 See the interview with Doug Engelbart later in this chapter, and on the DVD.

2 See the interview with Stu Card later in this chapter, and on the DVD.

3 See the interview with Tim Mott later in this chapter, and on the DVD.

4 See the interview with Larry Tesler later in this chapter, and on the DVD.

5 See the interview with Bill Atkinson in chapter 2, "My PC," and on the DVD.

6 See the interviews with Stu Card later in this chapter, and Paul Bradley in chapter 2, "My PC," and on the DVD.

7 See www.acypher.com/wwid/Chapters/01Pygmalion.html.

8 Michael Hiltzik, *Dealers of Lightning* (New York: HarperCollins, 1999).

9 Vannevar Bush, "As We May Think," *Atlantic Monthly*, July 1945, www.theatlantic.com/unbound/flashbks/computer/bushf.htm.

10 Douglas C. Engelbart, "A Conceptual Framework for the Augmentation of Man's Intellect," in *Vistas of Information Handling*, vol. 1, ed. Paul William Howerton and David Weeks (Washington: Spartan Books, 1963).

11 Fitts's law discovered that the time to acquire a target is a function of the distance to and size of the target. Mathematically, it is stated as follows:

$$MT = a + b\log_2(2A/W)$$

where

MT = movement time

a, b = regression coefficients

A = distance of movement from start to target center

W = width of the target

12 ID TWO was the U.S. branch of the design firm founded by the author, later joined with David Kelley Design and Matrix Product Design to form IDEO.

13 Bravo was written by Butler Lampson, Tom Malloy, and Charles Simonyi, who went on to become the architect of Microsoft Word.

14 D. C. Smith, "Pygmalion: A Computer Program to Model and Stimulate Creative Thought" (PhD thesis, Stanford University Computer Science Department, 1975).

15 Details of the PARC history can be found in Hiltzik, *Dealers of Lightning*.

2 My PC

Interview dates: Bill Atkinson, September 2003; Paul Bradley, September 2003; Bill Verplank, February 2001; Cordell Ratzlaff, February 2004.

1 Gordon Moore, founder of Intel, made his famous observation in 1965, just four years after the first planar integrated circuit was discovered. The press called it "Moore's Law" and the name has stuck. In his original paper, Moore observed an exponential growth in the number of transistors per integrated circuit and predicted that this trend would continue.

2 Mitchell Waldrop, *The Dream Machine* (New York: Viking, 2001); Michael Hiltzik, *Dealers of Lightning* (New York: HarperCollins, 1999).

3 See the interviews with Larry Tesler in chapter 1 and Bill Atkinson in this chapter, and on the DVD.

4 Bill Atkinson and Diane Ackerman, *Within the Stone* (San Francisco: Browntrout Publishers, 2004).

5 Jef Raskin, *The Humane Interface* (Reading, MA: Addison-Wesley, 2000).

6 The twenty-four Polaroids shown here are less than a quarter of the full collection. Andy Hertzfeld has published the full set on folklore.org/StoryView.py?story=Busy_Being_Born.txt, as part of the story of the original Macintosh. The Polaroids are also published in *Revolution in the Valley* by Andy Hertzfeld (Sebastopol, CA: O'Reilly Media, 2005).

7 Susan Kare was the graphic designer on the Mac team who designed the icons.

8 Bill Lapson, "Lore of the Mouse," retrospective essay written 8 July 1982, from library.stanford.edu/mac/primary/docs/index.html.

9 Hovey-Kelley Design later became David Kelley Design and then IDEO.

10 Deane Hovey memo to Tom Whitney, 4 June 1980, library.stanford.edu/mac/primary/docs/index.html.

11 Under the direction of Dean Hovey, and with Apple represented by Bill Lapson, the four principal designers at Hovey-Kelley Design (three of whom are still working together at IDEO) were Jim Sacks, who originated a lot of the technical concepts, Doug Dayton, who was responsible for the form, Jim Yurchenco, who came up with the integrated chassis that was dubbed the "ribcage," and Rickson Sun, who worked on the electrical design and reliability testing.

12 Rickson Sun memo to Bill Lapson re: "Testing the Mouse," 16 October 1980, library.stanford.edu/mac/primary/docs/index.html.

13 See the interview with Bill Verplank that follows, and on the DVD.

14 See the interview with Cordell Ratzlaff that follows, and on the DVD.

15 See the interview with Bill Gaver in chapter 8, and on the DVD. Bill Gaver designed the SonicFinder for Apple in 1986, but it was never implemented.

16 See www.earwaxproductions.com.

17 Cordell Ratzlaff, Don Lindsay, and Bas Ording.

18 See the interview with Larry Page and Sergey Brin, the founders of Google, in chapter 7, and on the DVD.

19 Knowledge Navigator was the video made at Apple to envisage the future, commissioned by John Sculley and produced by Hugh Dubberly.

3 From the Desk to the Palm

Interview dates: John Ellenby, August 2003; Jeff Hawkins, November 2004; Bert Keeley, October 2004; Rob Haitani, December 2001; Dennis Boyle, September 2003.

1 Taken from a paper by Susan B. Barnes, Fordham University, "Alan Kay: Transforming the Computer into a Communication Medium," www.ieee.org/organitations/history_center/cht_papers/Barnes.pdf. Her notes refer to Alan Kay, "The Early History of Smalltalk," in *Programming Languages*, ed. T. J. Bergin and R. G. Gibson (New York: ACM Press, 1996), 551.

2 Alan Kay, "User Interface: A Personal View," in *The Art of Human Computer Interface Design*, ed. Brenda Laurel (Reading, MA: Addison-Wesley, 1990), 192.

3 Marshall McLuhan, *Understanding Media: The Extensions of Man* (Cambridge: MIT Press, 1994).

4 See discussion of metaphors in the interview with Bill Verplank in chapter 2, "My PC," and on the DVD.

5 Kay, "User Interface: A Personal View," 193.

6 The first laptop, the GRiD Compass computer, sold for $8,150 in 1982.

7 Jerome S. Bruner, *Toward a Theory of Instruction* (New York: W. W. Norton, 1966).

8 Kay, "User Interface: A Personal View," 195.

9 The Hyperion was designed by David Kelley Design, now IDEO.

10 See the interview with John Ellenby on the DVD.

11 "Futures Day" is well documented in Michael Hiltzik, *Dealers of Lightning* (New York: HarperCollins, 1999).

12 Jeff Hawkins, with Sandra Blakeslee, *On Intelligence* (New York: Times Books, Henry Holt, 2004).

13 The industrial design for the Workslate computer was by Mike Nuttall when he was working with the author at ID TWO.

14 The industrial design for the Go computer was by Mike Nuttall and Paul Bradley of Matrix Product Design, working with David Kelley Design for the mechanical engineering of the enclosure.

15 S. Jerrold Kaplan, *Startup: A Silicon Valley Adventure Story* (Boston: Houghton Mifflin, 1994).

16 This command structure was called the "Command Compass" for Momenta, and was designed by Bill Verplank at ID TWO (see his interview in chapter 5, and on the DVD). Bill Buxton had also done a lot of work on a similar concept, which he called "Marking Menus."

17 The industrial design of the GRiD Convertible was by IDEO.

18 When John Ellenby left GRiD, he went on to found Agilis.

19 The "Knowledge Navigator" concept video projected the personal computer of 2010; it was instigated by John Sculley at Apple and produced by Hugh Dubberly and Doris Mitsch.

20 David Goldberg and Cate Richardson (of Xerox PARC), "Touch-Typing with a Stylus," paper presented at the SIGCHI Conference on Human Factors in Computing Systems in Amsterdam, 1993.

21 *Information Appliances and Beyond*, ed. Eric Bergman (San Francisco: Morgan Kaufmann, 2000), 82.

22 See the interview with Rob Haitani on the DVD.

23 See the interview with Larry Tesler in chapter 1, and on the DVD.

24 The design team at IDEO was Dennis Boyle, Greg Twiss, Elisha Tal, Amy Han, and Trae Niest.

25 See "Beyond Techno Gadget," *@issue* volume 6, no. 2.

26 Designed by Palo Alto Design Group in collaboration with Palm, owned by US Robotics at that time.

4 Adopting Technology

Interview dates: David Liddle, October 2003; Mat Hunter, March 2003; Rikako Sakai, January 2002; David Kelley, September 2003; Paul Mercer, November 2004.

1 See the interview with David Liddle later in this chapter, and on the DVD.

2 Gillian Crampton Smith refers to these three phases of adoption of technology in the foreword.

3 Burroughs Corporation and Sperry Rand merged to become Unisys.

4 For more about Purple Moon, see the interview with Brenda Laurel in chapter 6, "Play."

5 Quote from Gavin Green's "Top of the Class," British Airways *Business Life* magazine, February 2004; about BMW designer Chris Bangle.

6 See www.ideo.com/case_studies/social_mobiles/index.html for more about "Social Mobiles."

7 See the interview with Mat Hunter on the DVD.

8 See www.ceiva.com.

9 Jane Fulton Suri leads the human factors disciplines at IDEO. She was collaborating with her counterpart at Kodak, Doug Beaudet, manager of the Human Factors Lab.

10 See www.interaction-ivrea.it.

11 Arnold Wasserman was head of Industrial Design and Human Factors at Xerox, and he commissioned this Design Strategy work from the consulting firm Richardson Smith, in collaboration with internal design teams at Xerox and Xerox PARC.

12 Naoto Fukasawa started his design career at Seiko Epson, designing watches and small electronic consumer products. In 1989 he joined the author's design group in San Francisco, designing a series of award-winning products. After seven years he returned to Tokyo to lead the IDEO office there and earned a reputation as a design influencer, helping the designers inside Japanese companies to think about design in new ways. In 2002 he formed his own practice, Naoto Fukasawa Design.

13 Sam Hecht and Kim Colin formed a design practice called Industrial Facility in London, 2002.

14 See the account of developing mice for Apple in chapter 2, "My PC."

15 Terry Winograd is computer science professor at Stanford. See the interview with him in chapter 7, "The Internet," and on the DVD.

16 See the interview with Paul Mercer on the DVD.

5 Play

Interview dates: Bing Gordon, September 2003; Brendan Boyle, March 2004; Brenda Laurel, November 2001; Will Wright, February 2002.

1 See the interview with Brenda Laurel later in this chapter, and on the DVD.

2 See the interview with David Liddle in chapter 4, and on the DVD.

3 Trip Hawkins was director of strategy and marketing at Apple and responsible for the decision to use a single button for the Apple mouse (see chapter 2, "My PC"). After Electronic Arts, he went on to found the now defunct 3DO.

4 See the interview with Tim Mott in chapter 1, "The Mouse and the Desktop," and on the DVD.

5 The original logo for Electronic Arts was designed by Barry Deutsch, of the San Francisco–based design firm Steinhilber, Deutsch and Gard.

6 See the interview with Will Wright later in this chapter, and on the DVD.

7 See the interview with Dennis Boyle in chapter 3, "From the Desk to the Palm," and on the DVD.

8 "Aerobie Footballs" can be found at www.aerobie.com.

9 "Finger Blasters" can be found at www.recfx.com.

10 "Fib Finder" can be found at www.pressmantoy.com.

11 Brenda Laurel, *Computers as Theatre*, rev. ed (Reading, MA: Addison-Wesley, 1993).

12 *The Art of Human-Computer Interface Design*, ed. Brenda Laurel (Reading, MA: Addison-Wesley, 1990).

13 *Design Research: Methods and Perspectives*, ed. Brenda Laurel (Cambridge: MIT Press, 2004).

14 Brenda Laurel, *Utopian Entrepreneur* (Cambridge: MIT Press, 2001).

15 Christopher Ireland is a principal and the CEO of the consulting and strategic market research firm Cheskin, www.cheskin.com.

16 Jay Forrester, *Urban Dynamics* (Cambridge: MIT Press, 1969).

17 J. E. Lovelock, *Healing Gaia* (New York: Harmony Books, 1991).

18 Bert Hölldobler and Edward O. Wilson, *The Ants* (Cambridge: Harvard University Press, 1990).

19 Kevin Kelly, "Will Wright: The Mayor of SimCity," *Wired* 2:01.

20 Christopher Alexander, Sara Ishikawa, and Murray Silverstein, *A Pattern Language: Towns, Buildings, Construction (Center for Environmental Structure)* (New York: Oxford University Press, 1977).

6 Services

Interview dates: Live | Work, March 2003; Fran Samalionis, March 2003; Takeshi Natsuno, April 2002.

1 See www.livework.co.uk.

2 See the interview with Takeshi Natsuno later in this chapter, and on the DVD.

3 See the interviews with Jeff Hawkins, Rob Haitani and Dennis Boyle in chapter 3, "From the Desk to the Palm," and on the DVD.

4 Mari Matsunaga, *i-mode, The Birth of i-mode, An Analogue Account of the Mobile Internet*, published in English translation by Chuang Yi Publishing Pte. Ltd., Singapore.

5 See the foreword by Gillian Crampton Smith, and the DVD.

6 See the interview with the Live | Work principals on the DVD.

7 Paul Hawken, Amory Lovins and Hunter Lovins, *Natural Capitalism* (Snowmass, CO: Rocky Mountain Institute, 2003).

8 See the interview with Fran Samalionis on the DVD.

9 Dorothy Leonard is William J. Abernathy Professor of Business Administration at Harvard Business School.

10 Amtrak Acela is a high-speed rail service running from Boston to Washington, for which IDEO designed the rolling stock and defined the steps in the customer journey.

11 BankOne is a division of JPMorgan Chase Bank, N.A.

12 Juniper was later purchased by the Canadian bank CIBC and was developed to offer credit card services rather than online banking.

7 The Internet

Interview dates: Terry Winograd, September 2003; Larry Page and Sergey Brin, April 2002; Steve Rogers, May 2003; Mark Podlaseck, June 2003.

1 See the interview with Stu Card in chapter 1, "The Mouse and the Desktop," and on the DVD.

2 *Bringing Design to Software*, ed. Terry Winograd (Reading, MA: Addison-Wesley, 1996).

3 For an overview of Mark Weiser's PARCtab experiment, see seattleWeb.intel-research.net/people/schilit/parctab-pcs-jan96.pdf.

4 See the interview with Jeff Hawkins in chapter 3, "From the Desk to the Palm," and on the DVD.

5 See the interview with Bert Keely in chapter 3, "From the Desk to the Palm," and on the DVD.

6 See the interview with Jun Rekimoto in chapter 9, "Futures and Alternative Nows," and on the DVD.

7 See www.wunderground.com.

8 See investor.google.com, page 27 of registration statement.

9 See current version at www.bbc.co.uk.

10 *The Glass Wall: The Homepage Redesign 2002*, project book, published in a limited edition by the BBC.

11 Mark Podlaseck, Robert Hoch, and Edith Schoenberg, "This Is Not a Catalog: Philip Glass's Works Online," *IEEE MultiMedia*, October/December 2003.

8 Multisensory and Multimedia

Interview dates: Hiroshi Ishii, February 2002; Durrell Bishop, January 2002; Joy Mountford, September 2003; Bill Gaver, May 2003.

1 The Japan Festival 1991 celebrated the 100th anniversary of the Japan Society in London and included a major exhibition at the Victoria and Albert museum.

2 This cross-disciplinary project is staffed by faculty and students from the Interactivity Lab, Software Infrastructures Group, and Graphics Lab. They have built an experimental research facility called the iRoom, located in the Gates Information Sciences Building at Stanford.

3 Steelcase is a thought leader in the design of spaces for multidisciplinary teams, and after making an ownership investment in IDEO in 1991, they have collaborated on the research and development of design solutions for collaborative space.

4 See tangible.media.mit.edu.

5 PingPongPlus is a digitally enhanced version of the classic ping-pong game. It is played with ordinary, untethered paddles and balls and features a "reactive table" that incorporates sensing, sound, and projection technologies.

6 In late 1998, Ishii and Rich Fletcher developed the musicBottles project. They used sensor technology developed by Dr. Joe Paradiso and collaborated with different designers, engineers, and artists to create a custom table and bottles with special electromagnetic tags.

7 Urp, an urban-planning workbench, based on the "I/O bulb" concept originally developed by Dr. John Underkoffler in 1998: the I/O bulb creates high-resolution, bidirectional light flows.

8 The "Illuminating Clay" interface allows users to explore and analyze free-form spatial models to explore landscape design. It was developed by Ben Piper, Dr. Carlo Ratti, Yao Wang, Bo Zhu, Saro Getzoyan, and Hiroshi Ishii.

9 See the interview with Terry Winograd in chapter 8, and on the DVD.

10 The wall and sliding mechanism were built with help from Michael Field and Jerry Friedlander.

11 See the interview with Jeff Hawkins in chapter 3, and on the DVD. Jeff Hawkins, with Sandra Blakeslee, *On Intelligence* (New York: Times Books, Henry Holt, 2004).

12 See www.siggraph.org.

13 At time of writing, Michael Mills was director of design and adjunct professor at Stanford Center for Innovations in Learning (SCIL), www.stanford.edu/~mmills. In August 2005 he joined Yahoo! as director of user experiences for Digital Home Services.

14 Michael Mills led a QuickTime team at Apple consisting of Michael Errant, Jonathan Cohen, and Ying Wang.

15 The additional team members were Chen, Small, and O'Sullivan.

16 John Sculley was the CEO of Apple Computer at that time.

17 Computerized Axial Tomography scanner.

18 This design team was Mills, O'Sullivan, and Yawitz.

19 The Empress Maria Feodorovna was the widow of Alexander III and mother of Nicholas II of Russia.

20 Team members were Arent, Chen, Cohen, Mander, O'Sullivan, Small, and Yawitz.

21 See the interview with Brendan Boyle in chapter 6, and on the DVD.

22 Among his other books, Donald A. Norman is author of *The Invisible Computer* (Cambridge: MIT Press, 1998); *The Design of Everyday Things* (New York: Basic Books, 2002); and *Emotional Design* (New York: Basic Books, 2004).

23 See interview with Cordell Ratzlaff in chapter 1, and on the DVD.

24 J. J. Gibson, *The Ecological Approach to Visual Perception* (Boston: Houghton Mifflin, 1979).

9 Futures and Alternative Nows

Interview dates: Tony Dunne and Fiona Raby, March 2003; John Maeda, July 2003; Jun Rekimoto, May 2003.

1 See the interview with Tony Dunne and Fiona Raby to follow, and on the DVD.

2 This community was part of i3, the European Network for Intelligent Information Interfaces, www.i3net.org, which supported three research programs from 1997 to 2003, bringing together about 450 researchers. The programs were: Connected Community, Inhabited Information Spaces, and Experimental School Environments.

3 See the interview with David Liddle in chapter 4, "Adopting Technology," and on the DVD.

4 See the interview with John Maeda later in this chapter, and on the DVD.

5 See more about William Morris at www.morrissociety.org.

6 See the interview with Jun Rekimoto later in this chapter, and on the DVD.

7 Mark Weiser, who was at Xerox PARC, developed a notion he called "ubiquitous computing."

8 See more about the Dunne and Raby studio at www.dunneandraby.co.uk.

9 An example of "technology as media" is Anthony Dunne and Fiona Raby, *Design Noir: The Secret Life of Electronic Objects* (New York: Princeton Architectural Press, 2001).

10 An example of "technology as product" is "Placebo," a collection of electronic objects that explore mental well-being in relation to domestic electromagnetic fields (2000–2001).

11 An example of "technology as critique" is "Prescription Products: Designs for Fragile Personalities in Anxious Times" (2002), which

draws our attention to an emotionally vulnerable society obsessed with "therapy culture."

12 William McDonough and Michael Braungart, *Cradle to Cradle: Remaking the Way We Make Things* (New York: North Point Press, 2002).

13 Jeremy Rifkin, *The Hydrogen Economy: The Creation of the Worldwide Energy Web and the Redistribution of Power on Earth* (New York: Jeremy P. Tarcher, 2002).

14 John Maeda, *Maeda@Media* (New York: Rizzoli/Thames and Hudson, 2000).

15 See www.nytimes.com/2004/05/20/technology/circuits/20simp.html?ex=1085630.

16 The "Treehouse Studio," acg.media.mit.edu/projects/treehouse.

17 John Maeda's blog: weblogs.media.mit.edu/SIMPLICITY/archives/cat_laws.html.

18 Alan Kay, "Microelectronics and the Personal Computer," *Scientific American* 237, no. 3 (September 1977).

19 See www.csl.sony.co.jp/person/rekimoto.html.

20 ActiveInk computational ink, developed by Hiroaki Tobita.

21 BlockJam interactive music cubes, developed by Henry Newton-Dunn.

22 TouchEngine tactile feedback for touch panels, developed by Ivan Poupyrev.

23 Steven V. Brull, "A Little Sensor with a Big Future," *Business Week*, June 23, 1997; www.businessweek.com/1997/25/b353217.htm.

10 People and Prototypes

1 Current in January 2005, www.design-council.org.uk.

2 The questions asked by Madame L. Amic and answered by Charles Eames were the conceptual basis for an exhibition in Paris at the Musée des Arts Décoratifs in 1969 called "What Is Design?" and for the 1972 film "Design Q & A." See details in *Eames Design* by John Neuhart, Marilyn Neuhart, and Ray Eames (New York: Harry N. Abrams, 1989).

3 The "core skills of design" listed here are taken from an informal talk by Chris Conley, the head of curricula development, IIT Institute of Design faculty, in 2002.

4 In his book *Blink* (New York: Little, Brown, 2005), Malcolm Gladwell describes the sophistication of the subconscious mind in terms of rapid decision making, another advantage of relying on intuition rather than conscious decisions.

5 Henry Dreyfuss Associates, *The Measure of Man and Woman: Human Factors in Design* (New York: John Wiley and Sons, 2002).

6 *Humanscale*, by Niels Diffrient, Alvin Tilley, and Joan C. Bardagjy. The first volume was originally published by MIT Press in 1974, and the other two volumes in 1982; they were kept in print until 2002.

7 William McDonough and Michael Braungart, *Cradle to Cradle: Remaking the Way We Make Things* (New York: North Point Press, 2002).

8 Mitchell Kapor designed Lotus 1-2-3 in the early 1980s. The story is told, and his manifesto reprinted, in *Bringing Design to Software*, ed. Terry Winograd (Reading, MA: Addison-Wesley, 1996).

9 Definition of design: *The American Heritage Dictionary*, 3rd ed. (Boston: Houghton Mifflin, 1993).

10 Nicholas Negroponte, "Beyond Digital," *Wired*, December 1998, col. 6.12. Negroponte is a founder of MIT's Media Lab.

11 "Everything that can be digital will be digital," a tag line coined (or at least adopted) by Razorfish.

12 Jane Fulton Suri is discipline lead for human factors at IDEO. She joined the author in San Francisco in 1987 at ID TWO, one of the ancestors of IDEO.

13 The IDEO methods cards are available from William Stout Architectural Books in San Francisco, or online via the IDEO Web site www.IDEO.com/methodcards.

IDEO is not the only publisher of this kind of user research techniques. In 1999 the Methods Lab at the Helen Hamlyn Research Center at the Royal College of Art in London published a booklet about user research for design. This contains sixteen examples of methods and a finder that forms an index of the sixteen in the context of another thirty-six. The finder groups the methods by type, lists the outputs, and indicates the resources needed.

A paper on this topic called "The Methods Lab: A User Research Methods Typology for an Inclusive Design Process," by Alistair S. Macdonald and Cherie S. Lebbon, was presented at the International Conference on Engineering Design in Glasgow Scotland, August 2001.

14 Daniel H. Pink, in *Fast Company* 75 (October 2003), 104.

15 Morton Grosser, *Gossamer Odyssey: The Triumph of Human-Powered Flight* (Boston: Houghton Mifflin, 1981).

16 See chapter 2, "My PC," Bill Atkinson segment, "Pull Down Menus."

17 *American Heritage Dictionary*, 3rd ed. (Boston: Houghton Mifflin, 1993).

18 M. Buchenau and J. Fulton Suri, "Experience Prototyping," In *Proceedings of Designing Interactive Systems* (New York: ACM Press, 2000), 424–433.

19 C. Burns, E. Dishman, B. Johnson, and B. Verplank, "'Informance': Min(d)ing Future Contexts for Scenariobased Interaction Design," presented at BayCHI (Palo Alto, August 1995). Abstract available at www.baychi.org/meetings/archive/0895.html.

20 S. Houde and C. Hill, "What Do Prototypes Prototype?" *Handbook of*

Human-Computer Interaction, 2nd ed., ed. M. Helander, T. Ê. Landauer, and P. Prabhu (Amsterdam: Elsevier Science, 1997).

21 Y. Y. Wong, "Rough and Ready Prototypes: Lessons from Graphic Design," CHI '92 *Posters and Short Talks* (New York: ACM Press, May 1992), 83-84.

22 T. Erikson, "Notes on Design Practice: Stories and Prototypes as Catalysts for Communication," in *Envisioning Technology: The Scenario as a Framework for the System Development Lifecycle*, ed. J. Carroll (Reading, MA: Addison-Wesley, 1995).

23 P. Ehn and M. Kyng, "Cardboard Computers: Mocking-It-Up or Hands-On the Future," in *Design at Work: Cooperative Design of Computer Systems*, ed. J. Greenbaum and M. Kyng (Hillsdale, NJ: Lawrence Erlbaum, 1991), 169-195.

24 M. Schrage, Serious *Play: How the World's Best Companies Simulate to Innovate* (Boston: Harvard Business School Press, 1999).

25 Maypole Project Overview, available at www.maypole.org.

26 V. Giller, M. Tscheligi, R. Sefelin, A. Makela, A. Puskala, and K. Karvonen, "Maypole Highlights: Image Makers," *Interactions* (New York: ACM Press, November/December 1999), 12-15.

27 *Microserfs*, by Douglas Coupland, has a nice description in the opening chapter of the importance of closed doors to nerds (New York: HarperCollins, 1995).

28 See www.asktog.com/tog.html, a Webzine called "AskTOG," published by Bruce Tognazzini.

29 See www.nngroup.com.

30 Bruce Tognazzini, *Tog on Interface and Tog on Software Design* (Reading, MA: Addison-Wesley, 1992 and 1995).

31 Donald A. Norman, *The Psychology of Everyday Things* (New York: Basic Books, 1988).

32 Donald A. Norman, *Emotional Design* (New York: Basic Books, 2004).

Index

Boldface type indicates the primary interviews.